PROMOTION MANAGEMENT AND MARKETING COMMUNICATIONS

SECOND EDITION

PROMOTION MANAGEMENT AND MARKETING COMMUNICATIONS

SECOND EDITION

TERENCE A. SHIMP
University of South Carolina

The Dryden Press
Harcourt Brace Jovanovich College Publishers
Fort Worth   Philadelphia   San Diego
New York   Orlando   Austin   San Antonio
Toronto   Montreal   London   Sydney   Tokyo

Acquisitions Editor: Robin J. Zwettler
Developmental Editor: Judy Sarwark
Project Editor: Susan Jansen
Design Manager: Jeanne Calabrese
Production Manager: Barb Bahnsen
Permissions Editor: Cindy Lombardo
Director of Editing, Design, and Production: Jane Perkins

Text and Cover Designer: Nancy Johnson
Copy Editor: Karen Vertovec
Compositor: The Clarinda Company
Text Type: 10/12 Palatino

Library of Congress Cataloging-in-Publication Data

Shimp, Terence A.
    Promotion management and marketing communications/
Terence A. Shimp.—2nd ed.
        p. cm.
    Includes bibliographical references and index.
    ISBN 0–03–026643–2
    1. Communication in marketing.   2. Sales promotion.
    3. Advertising.   4. Direct marketing.   I. Title.
HF5415.123.S54   1989
    658.8′2—dc20   89–7758
                                                                    CIP

Printed in the United States of America
234-016-987654

Address orders:
The Dryden Press
Orlando, FL 32887

Harcourt Brace Jovanovich, Inc.
The Dryden Press
Saunders College Publishing

Cover source: (c) 1984 Edward Young.

In memory of my father and to Judy, John, Julie, Susan, my mother, and brothers.

The Dryden Press Series in Marketing

Preface

Promotion Management and Marketing Communications is intended for use in undergraduate or graduate courses that are variously titled promotion management, promotion strategy, or marketing communications. The text integrates marketing-communications theory, concepts, and research with in-depth treatment of all elements of the promotion mix—advertising, sales promotions, personal selling, public relations, and point-of-purchase communications.

Organization

The text is organized to cover first the fundamentals of marketing communications and then to treat in detail the various promotion-mix elements. Chapter 2 reviews the communication-theory fundamentals that apply to all forms of marketing communications and promotion management. Chapter 3 examines the nonpromotional elements of the marketing mix from a communications perspective.

Part 2 covers the behavioral foundations of marketing communications and promotion management. Chapter 4 overviews buyer-behavior theory and research that are pertinent to marketing communications and promotion management. Subsequent chapters discuss the role of attitudes and persuasion in marketing communications (Chapter 5), review message and source factors (Chapter 6), and examine the role of marketing communications in facilitating product adoption and diffusion (Chapter 7).

Part 3 begins the treatment of promotion management. Chapter 8 introduces the promotion-management process; Chapter 9 examines environmental influences on promotion management; and Chapter 10 presents two detailed case histories that show how organizations develop creative marketing-communications solutions to achieve organizational objectives. These cases present students with a moving picture of the forest (an integrated marketing communications and promotion program) prior to studying individual trees (such as advertising, sales promotion, and personal selling).

Part 4 focuses solely on mass-media advertising. Chapter 11 overviews the advertising process and then describes the activities of objective setting and budgeting. Chapter 12 reviews the message-development and creative-strategy aspects of advertising. Media selection is the topic of Chapter 13, while Chapter 14 describes the objectives and methods used for measuring advertising effectiveness.

Part 5 covers three topics that are of growing importance in today's promotion-management and marketing-communications programs: direct-marketing communications (Chapter 15), point-of-purchase communications (Chapter 16), and public relations and sponsorship marketing (Chapter 17).

Sales promotion is the focus of Part 6. Chapter 18 overviews sales promotion, while Chapters 19 and 20, respectively, examine trade-oriented and consumer-oriented sales-promotion topics.

Part 7 contains two chapters that examine personal selling (Chapter 21) and sales management (Chapter 22).

Special Features

Several features serve to distinguish this second edition from the prior edition.

Balance. *Promotion Management and Marketing Communications* attempts to incorporate fully the most positive aspects of the philosophy that "nothing is better than a good theory." At the same time, the approach reflects the equally strong belief that "nothing is better than a good example." A conscientious attempt has been made to bridge the gap between academe and practice. For every academic article referenced, at least two or more relevant citations are presented from practical publications such as *Advertising Age*, *Marketing Communications*, and *Sales and Marketing Management*.

Timeliness. Another noteworthy feature of this second edition is the timeliness of coverage. Theories and concepts are "state of the art," and practical examples are drawn from the most current applications.

Examples, Examples. The text is replete with practical examples drawn from marketing-communications applications. Real-world examples are used to enhance students' understanding of key promotional and marketing-communications concepts. In addition, practical examples drawn from magazine advertisements and other materials are used throughout the text to illustrate concepts and to heighten reading interest and comprehension.

Opening Vignettes and *Focus on Promotion* Sections. To further enhance student interest, each chapter opens with a vignette that sets the stage for the subsequent coverage. A *Focus on Promotion* box is included in each chapter to highlight specific issues relevant to the topical coverage.

Full-Color Insert. Advertisements presented in an eight-page, full-color insert provide students with a number of award-winning examples that tie theory to common practice.

Transparencies. A set of color acetate transparencies is available to instructors who adopt the text. The *Instructor's Manual* contains an additional set of transparency masters that are coordinated with the lecture outlines.

Instructor's Manual. The *Instructor's Manual* for the second edition of *Promotion Management and Marketing Communications* is a dramatic improvement over the original manual. The manual contains an entirely new set of multiple-choice and true-false test questions and includes the following additional items: lecture notes and outlines (including suggestions for use of the transparencies mentioned above), answers to end-of-chapter questions, cases with solutions, and a promotion management project.

Changes in the Second Edition

The second edition of *Promotion Management and Marketing Communications* is substantially different from the first edition. The changes reflect a slight shift in philosophy. For example, this edition places greater emphasis on the managerial aspects of promotion and marketing communications and devotes less attention to consumer behavior. Remaining changes are due largely to the dynamic nature of the topical area. This edition includes the following specific changes:

Chapter 1. The major changes in this chapter are the many new examples and the addition of relevant issues at the beginning of the chapter that highlight the scope of marketing communications and promotion management.

Chapter 2. The chapter deletes some of the more abstract aspects of communications theory that were treated in the first edition and replaces this material with a new section on the semiotics of marketing communications.

Chapter 3.   This chapter combines Chapters 21 and 22 from the previous edition and applies a marketing-communications perspective to the nonpromotional aspects of the marketing mix. The coverage is more focused than that found in the first edition. Examples and relevant research are updated.

Chapter 4.   Replacing Chapter 3 in the first edition, this new chapter examines the behavioral foundations of marketing communications. The coverage has been shortened and made more accessible for students.

Chapter 5.   Corresponding to Chapter 4 in the first edition, this current treatment of attitudes and persuasion strategies is updated with more recent examples and literature citations.

Chapter 6.   The separate treatment of message factors (Chapter 5) and source factors (Chapter 6) from the first edition are combined in a single, shortened chapter. In addition to many new examples and literature updates, the chapter has deleted discussions of several tangential topics (e.g., the congruity model) from the first edition.

Chapter 7.   This chapter is a substantial revision of material on adoption and diffusion processes that previously appeared in Chapter 8.

Chapter 8.   This new chapter introduces the 12-M model as a mnemonic device that integrates the variety of elements involved in the promotion-management process. The chapter discusses issues such as the trend toward regionalized promotion management and the moral issues surrounding promotion decision making.

Chapter 9.   Like its predecessor in the first edition, this chapter looks at the various environmental influences on promotion management. There is expanded coverage of the mature market, minority-population developments, the child and teenager markets, and the increased role of states in regulating promotion.

Chapter 10.   This new chapter presents two case histories that illustrate fully integrated promotion programs. The purpose of these cases is to present students with a moving picture of the forest prior to studying specific trees in subsequent chapters that are devoted to each separate promotion-mix element.

Chapter 11.   This overview of advertising corresponds to Chapter 12 in the first edition. The most notable changes are the expanded and updated presentations of objective setting and budgeting. The chapter also introduces students to the concept of "vaguely right versus precisely wrong" decision making, which is referred to frequently throughout the remainder of the text.

Chapter 12. The treatment of advertising messages and creative strategy in this chapter adds several topics not covered in the previous edition, deletes the coverage of humor, sex, and subliminal advertising (these now appear in Chapter 6), and updates examples and relevant literature.

Chapter 13. This chapter's discussion of media selection in advertising is revised substantially from the corresponding treatment in the first edition. The explanations of reach, frequency, and rating points are improved, and a formal media model is introduced. Descriptions of each medium's strengths, weaknesses, and special characteristics are updated and improved.

Chapter 14. Measuring advertising effectiveness, the subject of this chapter, is presented in a readily comprehensible fashion and illustrated with many examples of current measurement techniques such as people meters.

Chapter 15. The treatment of direct-marketing communications in this chapter updates and expands on the coverage in the first edition.

Chapter 16. New examples of point-of-purchase communications are included in this revised chapter. A section on electronic retailing has been added.

Chapter 17. Public relations and sponsorship marketing are the topics of this substantially revised chapter. The coverage of public relations is vastly improved over the first edition. The role and practice of cause- and event-oriented promotions are additions to the chapter. A section on commercial rumors has also been added.

Chapter 18. This introductory chapter on sales promotion is a complete rework of Chapter 17 in the first edition. A major new section has been added that describes the conditions when sales promotions are and are not profitable.

Chapter 19. This is a new chapter devoted to trade-oriented sales promotions. Some of the topics covered include slotting allowances, forward buying, diverting, and vendor support programs.

Chapter 20. The topic of this chapter, consumer-oriented sales promotions, is updated with current examples concening objectives, methods, and trends.

Chapters 21 and 22. The treatment of personal selling and sales management in these chapters corresponds to their coverage in Chapters 10 and 11 of the first edition. The changes and updates in these new chapters provide students with a much better understanding of the nature and importance of personal selling and sales management.

Acknowledgments

I am grateful to a number of people for their assistance in this project. I sincerely appreciate the thoughtful and constructive comments provided by the following reviewers:

C. Anthony di Benedetto
University of Kentucky
Marian Friestad
University of Oregon
Karen Froelich
North Dakota State University
Donald Glover
University of Denver
Stephen Grove
Clemson University
Esther Headley
Wichita State University
Ronald Hill
American University
William Kilbourne
Sam Houston State University
Michael Luthy
University of Illinois, Champaign
Dennis Martin
Brigham Young University

Darrel Muehling
Washington State University
Edward Riordan
Wayne State University
Alan Sawyer
University of Florida
Stanley Scott
Boise State University
Joseph Sirgy
Virginia Polytechnic Institute
Douglas Stayman
University of Texas at Austin
Mary Ann Stutts
Southwest Texas State University
Linda Swayne
University of North Carolina, Charlotte
Russell Wahlers
Ball State University

Also appreciated are the suggestions made by reviewers of the first edition: Robert Dyer, George Washington University; Denise Essman, Drake University; Robert Harmon, Portland State University; Geoffrey Lantos, Bentley College; John McDonald, Market Opinion Research; John Mowen, Oklahoma State University; and Kent Nakamoto, University of California, Los Angeles.

Several other individuals deserve special thanks. Craig Andrews (Marquette University), Paula Bone (West Virginia University), and Elnora Stuart (Winthrop College) are former Ph.D. students who have shared with me their experiences in using the text and have provided useful suggestions for change. Angie Davis and Ann Marie Hunter (University of South Carolina masters students) were extraordinarily helpful in assisting in the preparation of the *Instructor's Manual*. Sally Passauer, another former student, offered many helpful suggestions for improvement. Thanks go to Robert Dyer (George Washington University), Stephen Calcich (Norfolk State University), Daniel Sherrell (Louisiana State University), and S. Bruce Beuchler (Richtex Corporation) who contributed cases for the *Instructor's Manual* and to Michael Luthy (University of Illinois, Champaign) who prepared the Promotion Management Consulting Project. Andrew Ballentine (retired from Du Pont) and Gary Johnston (Du Pont) deserve a special thank you for their assistance with the Stainmaster^{cm} case in Chapter 10.

I am especially thankful to Don Frederick, my program director, who has provided a congenial and supportive work atmosphere that has made my task more pleasant than it might otherwise have been. I am grateful also to Dean Jim Kane and Associate Deans Jim Hilton and Bill Putnam for granting me a one-semester sabbatical to complete much of the work.

Finally, my great appreciation goes out to Rob Zwettler, Judy Sarwark, Susan Jansen, and Karen Vertovec at The Dryden Press for their understanding, cooperation, and expertise throughout this project.

Terence A. Shimp
University of South Carolina
August 1989

ABOUT THE AUTHOR

Terence A. Shimp, D.B.A. (University of Maryland), is Professor of Marketing and Distinguished Foundation Fellow in the College of Business Administration, University of South Carolina, Columbia. Professor Shimp teaches undergraduate and graduate courses in promotion management, consumer behavior, and research philosophy and methods. He has published widely in the areas of marketing, consumer behavior, and advertising. His articles have appeared in the *Journal of Consumer Research, Journal of Marketing Research, Journal of Marketing, Journal of Advertising Research, Journal of Advertising,* and elsewhere.

Professor Shimp is on the editorial boards of several journals and holds official positions in the Association of Consumer Research and the American Marketing Association.

C O N T E N T S

CHAPTER TWO
Marketing Communications and Meaning Transfer 31

CHAPTER THREE
The Nonpromotional Elements of Marketing Communications 57

PART 2
Behavioral Foundations of Marketing Communications
and Promotion Management 87

CHAPTER FOUR
Behavioral Foundations of Marketing Communications 89

CHAPTER FIVE
Attitudes and Persuasion in Marketing Communications 119

C H A P T E R   T E N
Promotion-Management Practices: Two Case Histories 267

P A R T   4
Media Advertising 289

C H A P T E R   E L E V E N
Advertising Management Overview 291

C H A P T E R   T W E L V E
Advertising Messages and Creative Strategy 329

C H A P T E R   T H I R T E E N
Media Strategy 363

PROMOTION MANAGEMENT AND MARKETING COMMUNICATIONS

SECOND EDITION

PART 1
Introduction

Part 1 introduces the student to the fundamentals of marketing communications and promotion management. **Chapter 1** overviews the nature of marketing communications and promotion management and discusses their importance in modern marketing. The three modes of marketing are presented as a conceptual framework for understanding the various forms of marketing communications and the interrelationships among them. Chapter 1 also discusses the *promotion management process*. Both of these frameworks should be studied thoroughly because they provide an overview for the entire text.

    Chapter 2 helps the student understand the fundamental and underlying concepts of communications. The chapter discusses the basic elements of the *communications process*, explains the definition and dimensions of *meaning*, describes how meaning is learned, and presents a *semiotics* perspective on marketing communications. Each of these topics is related to marketing communications and promotion through illustrations and examples.

Chapter 3 uses a marketing communications perspective in examining the *nonpromotional elements* of the marketing mix. Specifically examined in this chapter are product, package, and brand symbolism as well as price and place communications. These traditional elements of the marketing mix perform significant communications roles in addition to accomplishing more conventional marketing functions.

Overview of Marketing Communications and Promotion Management

IT USED TO BE "FLIP YOUR BIC"; NOW IT'S "SPRITZ YOUR BIC"

arly in 1989, the Bic Corporation introduced pocket-sized perfume spritzers to the United States. The product was heralded by Bic officials as the first inexpensive, quality French perfume. The spritzers, which come in four scents (such as Parfum Bic Jour and Parfum Bic Sport), are packaged in the same shape as Bic's lighters.

An initial $22 million promotional campaign was split between $15 million on advertising and $7 million on sales promotions. The theme of the advertising and sales promotion campaign was: "Four crazy little pocket perfumes. From Paris straight to you." Advertisements carrying this theme appeared in 20 major magazines; television advertisements were run on all three networks and on major cable stations. Advertisements in both media took a playful look at Paris and some of that city's symbols (such as the Eiffel Tower) that are well-known to American consumers. Sales promotions backed up the advertising by offering a $35 French scarf for only $5 with any Bic perfume purchase. Ten million scent strips were made available in stores so that consumers could sample the product.

Public-relations efforts generated further promotion for Bic's pocket-sized perfumes. Video news releases were made available to 150 television stations in the United States and Canada. These news releases generated influential air time at no cost to the Bic Corporation, except for the expense of developing the videos. Special-event marketing also took place by promoting the product in shopping malls and at fashion shows.

Company officials projected first-year sales of $15 million and sales between $50 to $100 million over the long term. A potential stumbling block is the possibility that consumers will be skeptical about a perfume that is promoted as a quality French perfume but costs only $5.[1]■

This vignette for Bic perfume spritzers illustrates many of the topics that are covered throughout the text: advertising, sales promotion, public relations, event marketing, package design, and branding. Marketing communications and promotion management, the subjects of this text, are key determinants of whether a brand achieves corporate objectives. Effective communication and promotion do not ensure success, but they certainly increase the odds.

Coverage in this text includes all major marketing practices that communicate with customers and promote a firm's offering. Illustrative topics and issues include the following:

■ Why do companies such as Pepsi-Cola pay celebrities like singer Michael Jackson millions of dollars to endorse their products?[2]
■ How effective is humor in advertising? For example, what effect does comedian "Joe Isuzu" have on sales of Isuzu automobiles?
■ What are the characteristics of effective salespeople? Are attractive salespeople more successful?
■ What are the best ways to reward and motivate salespeople?
■ What kind of consumer redeems coupons? Why do companies use coupons rather than simply lowering prices?
■ What makes for a good brand name? How important is the choice of brand name to a new product's success?
■ Why is direct marketing (i.e., nonstore retailing) growing so rapidly in the United States and elsewhere?
■ What point-of-purchase techniques are especially effective in encouraging consumers to choose particular brands?
■ What percentage of consumer purchase decisions are made at the point of purchase?
■ What is the role of background music in advertising?
■ How much do companies invest in advertising? How do they determine how much to spend?

---

1. Adapted from Pat Sloan, "$22M Campaign Urges: Spritz Your Bic," *Advertising Age*, February 20, 1989, pp. 3, 69.
2. It is estimated that over 192 million cans of Pepsi-Cola would have to be sold merely to recoup the cost of paying Michael Jackson for endorsing that brand. Source: *Parade*, January 3, 1988, p. 10.

- What factors influence the speed with which new products are adopted?
- What is the Federal Trade Commission's role in regulating advertising?
- How should a company handle accusations that one of its products represents a health or safety problem? For example, should the makers of all-terrain vehicles (ATVs) vigorously deny claims that these vehicles are unsafe, merely disregard the criticisms, or make every effort to understand the criticisms and take corrective action? Should the makers of the Samurai jeep discontinue advertising after being accused of marketing an unsafe vehicle, or should they increase advertising expenditures and deny the claims?

The Increasing Importance and Role of Marketing Communications and Promotion Management

Along with marketing in general, marketing communications and promotion management have increased dramatically in importance in recent years.[3] Indeed, their effective performance is critical to the successful functioning of any organization, business or otherwise.

A major factor contributing to the increased stature and importance of marketing communications and promotion management is the fact that they are practiced against a backdrop of ever-changing social, economic, and competitive developments. Consider, for example, the following major developments and the implications they hold for marketing communications and promotion management practices:

- **Widespread governmental deregulation of many industries.** Deregulation in the airline industry, for example, has led to numerous mergers and, thus, fewer competitors. These developments have influenced marketing and promotion practices through changes such as increased advertising expenditures and a multitude of special promotions such as frequent-flyer programs.

    Deregulation in the financial industry has encouraged banks and other financial institutions to undertake aggressive advertising practices and to use many forms of special events and giveaways to attract and hold customers.
- **Intensified international competition.** Companies have altered their marketing and promotional programs as markets and competitors have begun

---

3. The following articles are just a few of the many publications that have chronicled marketing's growing importance: "Marketing: The New Priority," *Business Week*, November 21, 1983, pp. 96–106; "To Market, To Market," *Newsweek*, January 9, 1984, pp. 70–72; "A New Survival Course for CEO's, "*Marketing Communications*, September 1985, pp. 21–26, 94; "Marketing's New Look," *Business Week*, January 26, 1987, pp. 64–69.

to span the globe.[4] Advertising goals and budgets are formulated with world markets in mind; media are selected from around the world rather than restricted to domestic markets; advertising messages are often formulated to appeal to consumers in different cultures; and sales forces, which once were located only domestically, are now scattered across various world markets.

- **Increased concern for physical fitness and health.** Rising interest in personal fitness and well-being has resulted in the rapid growth of a fitness industry (including health clubs and aerobic centers), changes in eating habits (e.g., eating more poultry and seafood and less red meat), and increases in the marketing of products that promise consumers better health and physical appearance (e.g., weight-loss products). Consumers have changed how they eat, how they play, when they recreate, and what they expect from life and from products. All told, dramatic societal changes have created many challenges and opportunities for responsive and creative marketing and marketing communications practices.

  Hospitals, which used to sit back and wait for patients to show up, now actively promote their services. The Ochsner Hospital in New Orleans, for example, developed a promotional program aimed directly at men. (They decided to direct their program at men because men are more likely than women to neglect their health care.) Ochsner's two-pronged marketing communications program consisted of aggressive television advertising that encouraged men to seek medical checkups and carefully trained telephone personnel that received advertising-prompted inquiries and arranged for appointments with appropriate physicians.[5]

- **Intensified time pressures.** With well over 50 percent of married American women now in the work force and with the rapid growth of two-income households, both women and men have less time available for traditional shopping and consumption behavior. The result has been a trend toward seeking greater *time control*. Consumers now are more determined than ever to tailor daily schedules to their needs rather than having schedules imposed on them.[6] The tremendous popularity of the videocassette recorder and the widespread use of automatic teller machines for conducting banking activities reflect this trend. In both instances, the consumer engages in behavior *when* she or he wants to rather than having a television network or bank impose the hours. There are a multitude of other manifestations of time control, all of which have created further challenges and opportunities for promotion managers and marketing communicators.

4. For an interesting discussion of competition in the United States from Asian competitors, see "The 'Four Tigers' Start Clawing At Upscale Markets," *Business Week,* July 22, 1985, pp. 136, 138, 142. (Note: The "four tigers" are competitors from Korea, Taiwan, Hong Kong, and Singapore.)
5. "Marketing Medicine to Men," Cable News Network's "Healthwatch," January 16, 1988.
6. "31 Major Trends Shaping the Future of American Business," *The Public Pulse* (a publication of the Roper Organization), vol. 2, no. 1, 1986, p. 1.

An Overview of Marketing Communications and Promotion Management

Business enterprises, ranging from the smallest retailers to the largest manufacturers as well as not-for-profit organizations (such as churches, museums, and symphony orchestras), continuously promote themselves to their customers and clients in an effort to accomplish a variety of purposes: (1) *informing* prospective customers about their products, services, and terms of sale, (2) *persuading* people to prefer particular products and brands, shop in certain stores, attend particular entertainment events, and perform a variety of other behaviors, and (3) *inducing action* from customers such that buying behavior is directed toward the marketer's offering and is undertaken immediately rather than delayed. These and other objectives are achieved by using advertisements, salespeople, store signs, point-of-purchase displays, product packages, direct-mail literature, free samples, coupons, publicity releases, and other communications and promotional devices.

Collectively, the preceding activities are called *marketing communications and promotion management.* **Promotion management** tends to be the preferred term among marketing educators, whereas marketing practitioners typically refer more generally to **marketing communications.** Your text employs both terms in its title, *Promotion Management and Marketing Communications,* but it is important that we properly distinguish their fundamental differences before moving on to more specific issues. It will be helpful first to review briefly the concept of marketing mix.

The **marketing mix** consists of four sets of decision spheres: (1) *product decisions* (e.g., the choice of product design, shape, color, package, and brand symbolism), (2) *pricing decisions* (e.g., price level and discount structure), (3) *distribution decisions* (e.g., choice of channel length and dealer network), and (4) *promotion decisions* (e.g., advertising and personal selling). Note that the last marketing-mix element, **promotion,** is the aspect of general marketing that promotion management deals with explicitly. In comparison, marketing communications is a more encompassing term that includes communications via any and all of the marketing mix elements.

Marketing Communications

Marketing communications can be understood best by examining the nature of its two constituent elements, communications and marketing. **Communications** is the process whereby commonness of thought is established and meaning is shared between individuals or between organizations and individuals. **Marketing** is the set of activities whereby businesses and other organizations create transfers of value (i.e., exchanges) between themselves and their customers. Of course, marketing is more general than marketing communications per se, but much of marketing does involve communications activities. Taken together, *marketing communications* represents the collection of all elements in an organization's marketing mix that facilitate exchanges by establishing shared meaning with the organization's customers or clients.

Central to the definition of marketing communications is the notion that *all marketing mix variables,* and not just the promotional variable alone, communicate with customers. The definition permits the possibility that marketing communications can be either intentional, as in the case of advertising or personal selling, or unintentional (though impactual nonetheless), as when a product feature, package cue, or price symbolizes something to customers that the marketing communicator may not have intended.

The definition further recognizes that a marketing organization is both a sender and a receiver of messages. In its role as sender, a marketing communicator attempts to inform, persuade, and induce the marketplace to take a course of action that is compatible with the communicator's interests. As receiver, the marketing communicator attunes itself to the marketplace in order to align its messages to its present market targets, adapt messages to changing market conditions, and spot new communication opportunities.

Sophisticated companies realize the importance of effective marketing communications to corporate success. For example, DuPont, the giant chemical company, describes two-way communications (collecting information *from* the market and distributing information *to* the market) as the essence of marketing. DuPont's marketing communications department operates under the philosophy that marketing communications, when treated as a strategic force and not just as a tactical tool, represents a critical corporate resource for building market share and profits.[7]

Promotion Management

In its broadest sense, promotion means "to move forward."[8] In business, promotion has a similar meaning, namely, to motivate (or move, in a sense) customers to action. Promotion management employs a variety of tools for this purpose: advertising, personal selling, sales promotion, publicity, and point-of-purchase communication. Some brief definitions will clarify the distinctions among these promotional elements. It is important to understand the specific sense in which each of these terms is used so as to avoid later confusion.

Advertising involves either mass communication via newspapers, magazines, radio, television, and other media (e.g., billboards) or direct-to-con-

---

7. Unlike tactics, which deal with short-term, day-to-day activities, strategy involves long-range planning. DuPont's marketing communications department is suggesting that marketing communications must be treated as a strategic resource by being planned and integrated with other critical corporate decisions and not just as something that is done to accomplish current needs. Source: "Communications As a Strategic Marketing Resource," Marketing Communications Department, DuPont, October 1984.
8. *Promotion* is derived from the Latin word *promovere; pro* meaning "forward" and *movere* meaning "to move."

sumer communication via direct mail. Both forms of advertising are paid for by an identified sponsor, the advertiser, but are considered to be nonpersonal because the sponsoring firm is simultaneously communicating with multiple receivers, perhaps millions, rather than talking with a specific person or small group.

Personal selling is person-to-person communication in which a seller attempts to persuade prospective buyers to purchase the company's product or service. Historically, personal selling involved primarily face-to-face interactions but, increasingly, telephone sales and other forms of electronic communication are being used.

Sales promotion consists of all marketing activities that attempt to stimulate quick buyer action, or, in other words, attempt to promote immediate sales of a product (thereby giving us the name "sales promotion"). In comparison, advertising and publicity are designed to accomplish other objectives such as creating brand awareness and influencing customer attitudes. Sales promotions are directed both at the trade (wholesalers and retailers) and at consumers. Trade-oriented sales promotion includes the use of various types of display allowances, quantity discounts, and merchandise assistance. Consumer-oriented sales promotion includes the use of coupons, premiums, free samples, contests/sweepstakes, and rebates.

Publicity, like advertising, is nonpersonal communication to a mass audience, but unlike advertising, publicity is *not* paid for by the company. Publicity usually comes in the form of news items or editorial comments about a company's products or services. These items or comments receive free print space or broadcast time because media representatives consider the information pertinent and newsworthy for their reading or listening audiences. It is in this sense that publicity is "not paid for" by the company receiving the benefits of the publicity.

Point-of-purchase communications include displays, posters, signs, and a variety of other materials that are designed to influence buying decisions at the point of purchase.

The blend of the promotional elements just described its referred to as the **promotional mix.** *Promotional management* is, then, the practice of coordinating the various promotional-mix elements, setting objectives for what the elements are intended to accomplish, establishing budgets that are sufficient to support the objectives, designing specific programs (e.g., advertising campaigns) to accomplish objectives, evaluating performance, and taking corrective action when results are not in accordance with objectives.

Thus, marketing communications and promotion management both contain the notion of communicating with customers. However, marketing communications is a general concept that encompasses communications *via all of the marketing mix variables;* promotion management is restricted to communications undertaken by the subset of mechanisms (such as advertising and personal selling) that are cataloged under the promotion variable in the marketing mix.

Integrated Promotion and Marketing Communications

Some companies erroneously view the promotional mix as the sole communications link with customers. This view often leads to *suboptimization* of an organization's total communications effort. If viewed in isolation, the various promotional elements and other nonpromotional marketing-mix elements may actually work against one another. Successful marketing requires careful integration of all promotional and nonpromotional elements. That is, advertising, sales promotion, personal selling, and publicity must be coordinated with all other company actions that communicate to customers something about a company—activities such as product design, price level, choice of dealers, and so on.[9]

A *product itself* communicates much to customers via its size, shape, brand name, package design, package color, and other features. These product cues provide the customer with subtle ideas about the total product offering. Consider, for example, the advertisement for Crown Royal Canadian whiskey (Figure 1.1). The complex of brand name (suggesting royalty), bottle configuration (somewhat crownlike), packaging graphics (which include a crown set on top of a purple velvet pillow), and carrying pouch (the same royal color as the pillow) are cues designed to portray this brand as special, high in quality, and, indeed, fit for royalty.

Products communicate important information to consumers, often of a symbolic nature, merely by virtue of their configuration, their size, or how portable they are. Consider, for example, the advertisement for Smith Corona's PWP 80 word processor (Figure 1.2). This product appears to be marketed to consumers such as students and salespeople who require an easily transportable word processor. The advertisement features portability by showing a man carrying the product and claiming that the PWP 6 weighs less than 20 pounds and can go "wherever you go. . . .From home to school to office." It is clear that this product's size and portability are as important to its commercial success as is the primary function it performs.

Price is another important communication mechanism. The price level can suggest savings, a deal, or indicate quality, luxury, and prestige. The following experience of a jewelry store merchant in Arizona illustrates price's communication role. During the peak of tourist season, a merchant was having difficulty selling turquoise jewelry. She tried a variety of merchandising and selling techniques with no success. Finally, while preparing to depart for an out-of-town buying trip, she scribbled the following note to one of her salesclerks: "Everything in this display case, price $\times$ ½." Upon returning several days later, she was delighted to find that every turquoise item in the shop had sold. Her delight turned to amazement when she learned that the salesclerk had misread

---

9. A good discussion of the importance of integrated communications is provided by the president and CEO of Ketchum Advertising in Pittsburgh. See John Fitzgerald, "Integrated Communications," *Advertising Age*, February 15, 1988, p. 18.

Use of Packaging to Communicate Prestige

FIGURE 1.1

Source: Reprinted with permission of Joseph E. Seagram & Sons, Inc.

FIGURE 1.2   **Use of Product Design to Communicate Convenience and Portability**

Word processing anybody can pick up.

Who says word processing is a heavy subject?

The Smith Corona PWP 80 portable word processor is not only light in weight, it can make light work of the most complicated projects.

You don't need a PhD in computer science

Our screen adjusts to you, so you don't have to adjust to it.

to understand it.

You don't have to keep one eye on the instruction manual to use it.

In fact, PWP 80 is so simple to operate, you may not even believe you're actually using a state-of-the-art, fully featured word processor.

All you have to do is unfold it and begin.

You type just as you would on a typewriter. Your text appears on the backlit, supertwist 16 line by 80 character liquid crystal display.

Block moves are a cinch, inserts a snap, deletions a breeze.

When you're ready to print, just insert a sheet of paper, select Print and presto, letter-quality printing.

And that's it.

If you're only writing something

With PWP 80, everything is at your fingertips.

short, like a note or recipe, PWP 80 can also function as a con-

ventional, state-of-the-art typewriter.

Of course, there's nothing conventional about PWP 80's features.

Inside, there's 50,000 characters of internal editable memory. (That's about 25 pages.) There's also a built-in disk drive, which makes storage capacity virtually unlimited.

With our amazing Grammar-Right System,™ you'll never write a wrong again. It includes a 75,000 word Spell-Right™ dictionary that alerts you to misspelled words, an Electronic Thesaurus that gives you alternatives to overused words, and Phrase Alert,™ which points out inappropriate phrases—before anyone else does.

DataDisks give you unlimited storage capacity.

And for those of you who are unfamiliar with word processors, we've even included a special Tutorial DataDisk, so you can learn how to use PWP 80 in practically no time.

Best of all, this giant among word processors weighs under 20 pounds. Which means PWP 80 can go wherever you go. From home to school to office.

And that might just be its best feature of all. Because when you consider how remarkable PWP 80 is, it's a wonder you'll want to go anywhere without it.

SMITH CORONA
TOMORROW'S TECHNOLOGY
AT YOUR TOUCH

For more information on this product, write to Smith Corona Corporation, 65 Locust Avenue, New Canaan, CT 06840 or Smith Corona (Canada Ltd.), 440 Tapscott Road, Scarborough, Ontario, Canada M1B 1Y4.

Source: Courtesy Smith Corona Corporation.

the note and *doubled* the price of each item rather than cutting each price in half. It appears that when the turquoise was merchandised at double its original price, tourists perceived it as more valuable and therefore more worthy as a gift or for personal ownership.[10]

Retail stores also have significant communications value for consumers. Stores, like people, possess personalities that consumers perceive readily and tend to associate with the merchandise located in the stores. Two stores selling similar products can project entirely different product images to prospective customers. A brand of clothing sold exclusively through "high-class" specialty shops would project a higher-quality image than if it were sold in a discount department store. This is precisely what happened to the Izod brand of casual sportswear. Until around the late 1970s, Izod was considered the *creme de la creme* in sportswear; then the company began marketing the product in virtually every available retail outlet. The market became saturated and the brand's high-status, high-quality image was destroyed. Izod is now managing a comeback: the company hopes to reestablish its status image by being more selective in the choice of stores that are allowed to merchandise the brand.

The Three Modes of Marketing

To this point, the chapter has presented a general introduction to the nature of marketing communications and promotion management. It is now appropriate to tie the concepts discussed previously into a more thorough framework called the **three modes of marketing.**[11]

According to this perspective, the overall marketing function consists of three overlapping sets of activities, or modes, whereby marketers seek to manage the demand for their offerings. The three modes are the basic offer (Mode 1), persuasive communications (Mode 2), and promotional inducements (Mode 3).

Figure 1.3 illustrates the relations among the three modes and presents a connection between the traditional "marketing concept" and the "promotion concept." The **marketing concept** embodies the notion that the marketer adapts the company's offering to the customer's needs and wants. The basic offer is the mode that is primarily responsible for fulfilling the marketing concept. By comparison, the **promotion concept** attempts to adapt the customer to the marketer's needs and wants. This is accomplished by the other two modes, persuasive communications, and promotional inducements.

There must be a meaningful coordination of efforts to satisfy both the marketing and promotion concepts. Excessive emphasis on customer fulfill-

10. This illustration is presented in Robert B. Cialdini, *Influence: How and Why People Agree to Things* (New York: William Morrow and Company, 1984), pp. 15, 16.
11. Eugene R. Beem and H. Jay Shaffer, *Triggers to Customer Action—Some Elements in a Theory of Promotional Inducement* (Cambridge, MA: Marketing Science Institute, December 1981, Report No. 81–106).

FIGURE 1.3   **The Three Modes of Marketing**

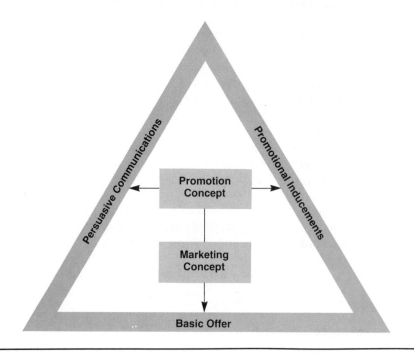

Source: Adapted from Eugene R. Beem and H. Jay Shaffer, *Triggers to Customer Action—Some Elements in a Theory of Promotional Inducement.* (Cambridge, MA: Marketing Science Institute, December 1981), p. 8. Reprinted with permission.

ment (the marketing concept) may lead to unnecessary expenditures and lost profits. Similarly, excessive emphasis on marketer fulfillment (the promotion concept) can lead to disgruntled customers and lost business.

Mode 1: The Basic Offer

The **basic offer** is "the regular or standard substantive benefits which the marketer offers to his targets as a possible solution to some problem."[12] The basic offer has two components: (1) the *product itself* and (2) associated *terms of sale*—price, credit terms, warranties, and availability and delivery promises. The role of the basic offer is to satisfy customers' needs and to move customers to action by offering superior value in comparison to substitute offerings. In general, superior value results from providing customers with more wanted gains or fewer unwanted costs.

12. Ibid., p. 4.

Consider the case of the new mini-sized watermelons. In years past, watermelons fit nicely into Americans' summertime lifestyles. American families tended to be large, and people spent much of their time during the summer outdoors. A watermelon, which typically weighed 20 pounds or more, was sliced and split among family members and friends, who then spit the watermelon seeds on the ground as they ate their slice.

American society has changed dramatically over the past two decades, and watermelon sales have plummeted. The culprits are twofold: (1) today's families are smaller and have no need for an average-sized melon weighing 22 to 25 pounds; and (2) people today, who tend to spend less time outdoors, find eating watermelon indoors messy because of the seeds.

The watermelon industry is fighting back. Florida researchers have produced mini-sized seedless melons (called "Mickylee" and "Minilee"), and growers are considering a major advertising program to improve the watermelon's image. Advertisements will emphasize watermelon's high vitamin-C content, low calories, and good taste. The industry hopes that the new mini-sized and seedless watermelons will bring the fruit indoors, possibly making it a year-round item rather than a product that is consumed once a year at the annual family picnic.[13]

Mode 2: Persuasive Communications

Mode 2, **persuasive communications,** consists of various forms of marketing communications messages designed to enhance customers' impressions of the basic offer.[14] Persuasive communications consist of impersonal verbal messages (advertising and publicity), personal verbal messages (personal selling and word-of-mouth support), and nonverbal messages (such as packaging cues and retailer imagery).

Whereas the basic offer is designed to meet customer needs, persuasive communications are intended to stimulate wants by encouraging customers to imagine the benefits of the basic offer. Marketers attempt to stimulate wants by supplying facts or by appealing to the customer's fancy (i.e., imagination.).[15]

An advertisement for Interplak's Home Plaque Removal Instrument illustrates an appeal to fact in persuasive communications (see Figure 1.4). The advertising copy presents one reason after another for purchasing this product.

13. Adapted from Hannah Miller, "Seedless Watermelons Sprout," *Advertising Age*, May 16, 1988, p. 66S.
14. Ibid., p. 6.
15. Beem and Shaffer, *Triggers to Customer Action*, p. 9, use the fact versus fancy terminology. Similar distinctions in marketing literature are factual versus evaluative and objective versus subjective. For more discussion, see Ivan L. Preston, "Contrasting Types of Advertising Content—A Case of Terminology Gone Wild," in *Proceedings of the 1987 Conference of the American Academy of Advertising*, ed. Florence Feasley (Columbia, SC: American Academy of Advertising, 1987), pp. R25–R30.

FIGURE 1.4   **Use of Fact to Persuade**

High technology has finally conquered the space between your teeth.

You're looking at one of the most important advances in home dental care since the invention of the toothbrush.

The Interplak® Home Plaque Removal Instrument.

After using it just once, your mouth will feel fresher and cleaner than it ever did with ordinary brushing.

The Interplak instrument cleans teeth nearly plaque-free.

It's a scientific fact that if the plaque on your teeth isn't removed daily, it can lead to early gum disease and tooth decay. Clinical studies show that manual brushing removes only some of the plaque build-up. But those same studies prove that the Interplak instrument cleans teeth nearly plaque-free, and reduces gingivitis to improve the health of your gums.

Light years beyond the ordinary toothbrush.

Manual and electric toothbrushes only clean up and down. Or back and forth. But the Interplak instrument cleans circles

Interplak tufts clean plaque from between teeth and under the gums.

around them both, with a patented design that's a stroke of genius.

Ten tufts of bristles rotate 4200 times a minute, reversing their direction 46 times a second to literally scour away plaque and stimulate your gums.

When the tufts reverse direction,

the bristles extend fully, to clean deep between teeth and under your gumline, with a cleaning action that's unsurpassed. And because the bristles are four times softer than the softest toothbrush, they're no more abrasive than manual brushing with toothpaste.

New wisdom in caring for your teeth.

Dental professionals across the country have endorsed the benefits of the Interplak instrument. And they've recommended it to their patients.

It's easy to use, cordless, and it recharges itself every time you place it back in its stand. You can also buy interchangeable brush heads for the whole family.

The Interplak Home Plaque Removal Instrument. The high tech answer to a down to earth need.

INTERPLAK®
HOME PLAQUE REMOVAL INSTRUMENT

Interplak is Acceptable as an effective cleaning device for use as part of a program for good oral hygiene to supplement the regular professional care required for good oral health.
Council on Dental Materials, Instruments and Equipment, American Dental Association.

ADA ACCEPTABLE American Dental Association

Interplak® is the registered trademark of the Dental Research Corporation
© Dental Research Corporation, 1988.

By comparison, Figure 1.5 illustrates the use of pure fancy in associating the catalog retailer, Patagonia, with the daring behavior of John Sherman, who is scaling a sheer cliff while drinking beer and wearing sandals. The implication is that buying from Patagonia is an experience filled with similar excitement, individualism, and distinctiveness.

Mode 3: Promotional Inducements

Promotional inducements comprise "extra substantive benefits, beyond the benefits of the basic offer, intended to motivate particular customer actions."[16] Promotional inducements is a descriptive way of referring to what is more commonly called sales promotion. Marketing practitioners use three forms of promotional inducements: those representing the *character of the basic offer* (e.g., free samples, trial usage, and extra goods at the same price), *price-related inducements* (e.g., discounts, money-off coupons, and trade allowances for dealers), and *inducements that are external to the basic offer* (e.g., premiums, contests, and trading stamps).

The role of promotional inducements is to induce retailers and consumers to adopt the marketer's plan of action. In the case of retailers, this means stocking more of the marketer's product, providing better display space, and promoting the marketer's product more aggressively. In the case of consumers, this means buying more of the marketer's product, buying it sooner than originally planned, and buying it more frequently. Marketers induce these actions by providing retailers and consumers with some form of reward (e.g., price savings and free merchandise).

Figures 1.6 and 1.7 illustrate the use of promotional inducements. A standard price inducement is reflected in the advertisement for Orville Redenbacher's® popcorn products shown in Figure 1.6. Included are a $0.35 manufacturer's coupon offer and a mail-in certificate entitling the consumer to receive a free jar or free carton of microwave popping corn with the submission of three UPC proofs-of-purchase from three jars or cartons of popping corn.

The advertisement for General Mills, the U.S. makers of Yoplait yogurt, includes two forms of promotional inducement, as shown in the the ad in Figure 1.7. First, price inducements provide the customer with a $0.25 savings and a $0.60 savings on the purchase of various Yoplait yogurts. In addition, an inducement external to the basic offer includes a "flip and win" contest in which the customer has a chance to win prizes identified inside Yoplait container lids.

Table 1.1 summarizes the three modes of marketing and the specific components of each mode.

---

16. Beem and Shaffer, *Triggers to Customer Action*, p. 7.

FIGURE 1.5   **Use of Pure Fancy to Persuade**

Source: © 1988 John Sherman; Client, Patagonia, Inc. Reprinted with permission.

A Price-Related Inducement

FIGURE 1.6

Source: Reprinted by permission of Beatrice/Hunt–Wesson, Inc.

FIGURE 1.7   **An Inducement External to the Basic Offer**

Examples of the Three Modes of Marketing   TABLE 1.1

Basic Offer	Persuasive Communications	Promotional Inducements

• Product Itself
• Terms of Sale
   Availability and delivery
   Price
   Credit terms
   Guarantees or warranties
	• Impersonal Verbal Messages
	   Publicity
	   Measured advertising—radio,
	      TV, newspaper, magazine
	   Unmeasured advertising—direct
	      mail, catalog, trade shows,
	      point of purchase
	• Personal Verbal Messages
	   Personal selling messages
	   Word-of-mouth support
	• Nonverbal Messages
	   Packaging of product
	   Inherent in delivery of verbal
	      message
	   Symbolism derived from
	      resellers, customers,
	      pricing, etc.
		• Character of Basic Offer
		   Free sample
		   Free trial use
		   Extra goods at same price
		   Special terms of sale (other than
		      price)
		• Price Related
		   Introductory discounts
		   Money-off coupons
		   Price specials
		   Buy-back allowances to dealers
		• External to Basic Offer
		   Premium promotions—trading
		      stamps, contests,
		      sweepstakes, games, free
		      gift in pack, continuity
		      coupons
		   "Free" offers to customers
		   "Right to buy" other products—
		      "self-liquidator,"
		      "commodity continuities"
		   Cash awards—sales contests,
		      "spiffs" to dealers

Source: Eugene R. Beem and H. Jay Shaffer, *Triggers to Customer Action—Some Elements in a Theory of Promotional Inducement* (Cambridge, MA: Marketing Science Institute, December 1981), p. 5. Reprinted with permission.

Each Mode Reinforces the Other Modes

It now should be apparent that the three modes of marketing overlap and reinforce each other.[17] The basic offer provides the distinctiveness that persuasive communications can feature. For example, the advertisement for the Interplak Home Plaque Removal Instrument (Figure 1.4) is possible in this form only because the product itself possesses some unique features and competitive advantages.

The basic offer also provides the foundation for effective promotional inducements. However, inducements alone cannot create product acceptance. The promotional inducement for Orville Redenbacher's popcorn products (Figure 1.6) is designed to encourage consumers to purchase this brand repeatedly, but this will not happen on a large scale unless consumers are satisfied with the taste, price, size, and freshness of Orville Redenbacher's popcorn products.

17. Ibid., p. 14.

Persuasive communications and promotional inducements both reinforce the basic offer. By associating the product with a luxury symbol (royalty), the advertisement for Royal Crown (Figure 1.1) may serve to enhance the basic offer by giving consumers the impression that Royal Crown is luxurious and of high quality. Promotional inducements reinforce the basic offer by adding substantive customer gains or subtracting costs, as in the case of the Yoplait offer (Figure 1.7).

Finally, promotional inducements and persuasive communications are mutually reinforcing. When placed strategically in an advertisement, a promotional inducement (such as an exciting contest or sweepstakes offer) can draw attention to other aspects of the persuasive communications. (Figure 1.7 illustrates this point.)

The Promotion Management Process

Previous discussion has pointed out that the promotion management component of the total marketing communications mix consists of six major tools: personal selling, mass-media advertising, direct-mail advertising, sales promotion, point-of-purchase communications, and public relations/publicity. These tools operate in concert with one another to help accomplish various marketing objectives.

The overall promotion management process consists of a logical sequence of decisions that must be made in order to implement effective promotional programs and achieve marketing objectives. Figure 1.8 illustrates the promotion management process in terms of six major steps: situation analysis, marketing objectives, promotion budget, integration and coordination, promotion management program, and evaluation and control.[18]

Step 1: Performing a Situation Analysis

The initial step in the promotion management process is to perform a thorough analysis of the situation confronting the particular product, brand, or service that is under consideration. Two types of analyses are needed. First, an *internal analysis* must be made of an organization's strengths and weaknesses. Financial considerations and personnel matters are the primary issues in an internal analysis. A company with strong financial reserves and a talented team of promotion specialists has numerous opportunities for developing creative and per-

18. The promotion management process as conceptualized here is an adaptation of two related works: Michael L. Ray, "A Decision Sequence Analysis of Developments in Marketing Communication," *Journal of Marketing*, vol. 37 (January 1973), pp. 29–38; and James F. Engel, Martin R. Warshaw, and Thomas C. Kinnear, *Promotional Strategy: Managing the Marketing Communications Process*, 5th ed. (Homewood, IL: Richard D. Irwin, 1983), p. 34.

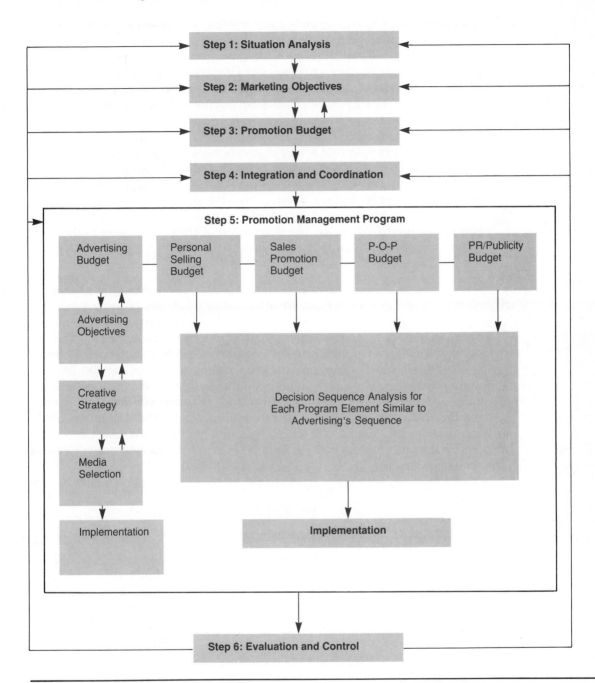

Source: Adapted from Michael L. Ray, "A Decision Sequence Analysis of Developments in Marketing Communication," *Journal of Marketing,* Vol. 37, January 1973, p. 31; and James F. Engel, Martin R. Warshaw, and Thomas C. Kinnear, *Promotional Strategy,* Fifth Edition, (Homewood, IL: Richard D. Irwin, 1983), p. 34.

haps expensive promotional programs, whereas an impoverished firm is limited in what it can hope to accomplish.

An *external analysis* is the second component of a situation analysis. This analysis involves a thorough review of environmental factors that are likely to influence promotional effectiveness and product success. The economic situation, competitive activity, sociocultural developments, legal climate, and channel of distribution considerations are typical factors involved in an external situation analysis.

An earlier discussion of Mickylee and Minilee watermelons indicated that watermelon sales have declined due to societal changes toward smaller families, less outdoor activities, greater desire for product convenience, and so on. These developments suggest a need for changes in the basic offer (e.g., smaller, seedless melons) and increased persuasive communication efforts to enhance the product's image. The description of Dutch Boy paint in the *Focus on Promotion* points out another situation analysis and the implications it holds for the marketing of this product.

Step 2: Establishing Marketing Objectives

Establishing meaningful and realistic marketing objectives is the step that follows the situation analysis. (Note that this discussion is about general marketing objectives and not marketing communications objectives per se.) **Marketing objectives** involve such matters as (1) overall sales levels, (2) marketing cost considerations, and (3) sales performance with respect to specific market segments and geographical locales or in terms of time schedules. Sherwin Williams undoubtedly established specific market share objectives for Dutch Boy, perhaps hoping to attain as high as a 30 to 40 percent share among young, upscale purchasers.

Step 3: Setting the Promotion Budget

The promotion budget establishes the overall amount of funds that can be allocated to the various promotion-mix elements. As shown in Figure 1.8 (by the two-way arrows), marketing objectives and the promotion budget are interactive decisions. That is, the initial statement of marketing objectives provides the basis for determining the size of the promotion budget; however, objectives often have to be revised due to insufficient funds.

Step 4: Integrating and Coordinating Promotion Elements

The promotion elements must work together if overall marketing objectives are to be accomplished. To achieve optimal effectiveness, advertising campaigns, sales promotion deals, point-of-purchase programs, and publicity releases

FOCUS ON PROMOTION

Repositioning an Old Brand

Dutch Boy is a brand of paint that has been marketed in the United States for over 80 years. The brand, historically marketed to a mass audience rather than being positioned to appeal to one particular segment, was not doing well in sales until its recent purchase by the much larger, financially secure Sherwin Williams company. Research by Sherwin Williams revealed that younger, more fashion-oriented consumers account for the largest portion of paint buyers—nearly 38 percent of all paint purchases are made by consumers in the 18 to 34 age group. With this in mind, Sherwin Williams repositioned Dutch Boy to appeal to these younger, fashion-oriented consumers.

As part of the effort to reposition Dutch Boy, Sherwin Williams redesigned the packaging, reverting to the original 1907 illustration of a Dutch boy. This change was based on research showing that consumers feel the portrait conveys a feeling of quality. Advertising expenditures were increased greatly and a series of ads that were more like music videos than commercials were designed. The commercials were set to fast-paced music and emphasized consumers' personal lifestyles by showing users painting with Dutch Boy and then enjoying the fruits of their labor—fashionable high-sheen results emulating the European decorating style that has become increasingly popular in the United States.[19]■

must be integrated with one another and coordinated with personal selling efforts. Many promotional programs have been unsuccessful due to coordination failures such as the following:

- An industrial sales force was unable to obtain sufficient trade support for a new product because the anticipated advertising campaign to presell the product was two months behind schedule.
- New point-of-purchase displays for a supermarket product were less effective than marketers had anticipated because the displays were not coordinated with the advertising theme used to stimulate consumer buying interest.

19. This illustration is adapted from Cyndee Miller, "Dutch Boy Repositions Itself to Reach Upscale, Fashion-Oriented Consumers," *Marketing News*, vol. 22, July 4, 1988, p. 1.

- Retailers had insufficient inventories to cover consumer demand for a heavily couponed brand because the sales force was unaware of the coupon campaign and did not encourage retailers to stock up.

The preceding examples illustrate problems that occur when the promotion-mix elements operate independently rather than working in concert. Coordination is not something that occurs automatically; it has to be planned and managed. To overcome these types of problems, many companies have created organizational positions in which one individual is responsible for ensuring that proper coordination is achieved. Organization titles differ, but in some companies the label for this position is Marketing Communications Director. Coordination is handled in other campaigns by having individual vice-presidents of the promotion elements (e.g., V.P. of Sales, V.P. of Advertising and Sales Promotions) report directly to the chief marketing executive.

Step 5: Implementing the Promotion Management Program

The fifth step in Figure 1.8 presents a decision-sequence analysis only for the advertising component of the promotion mix. It is important to realize that similar sequences apply to the other promotional elements (e.g., sales promotion); however, it would be duplicative to discuss every sequence. It also is important to recognize that every stage in the decision sequence is interrelated with every other stage. This is indicated in Figure 1.8 by including two-way arrows between a particular stage (e.g., advertising budget) and its subsequent stage (e.g., advertising objectives). Actually, were it not so cumbersome, a more realistic representation would show arrows between all of the stages (e.g., from the advertising budget to media selection) because, in reality, decisions with respect to any one stage are influenced by decisions made for every other stage.

Advertising Budget. The decision sequence for advertising, as well as for every other promotional element, begins by setting an initial budget, which, as in the case of the overall promotion budget (Step 3), is subject to revision in light of proposed advertising objectives. In the case of Dutch Boy, for example, the 1988 budget tripled the advertising expenditures over any previous levels spent in the history of the brand. Budgets for advertising are often set as a fixed percentage of the anticipated sales during the next fiscal period. The budget may have to be revised upward if the advertising objectives are particularly ambitious or revised downward in view of financial exigencies.

Advertising Objectives. As described previously, marketing objectives (Step 2) are typically stated in terms of sales or cost considerations. In comparison, advertising objectives are more often stated in terms of communication goals. The following are illustrative goals: (1) increase customer's brand awareness; (2) facilitate customer understanding of the product, its attributes, benefits, and advantages; (3) enhance customer's attitude toward the marketer's offering; and (4) generate trial purchase behavior.

The other promotion-mix elements have their own specific objectives. For example, personal selling objectives are frequently stated in terms of sales volume levels or numbers of new accounts. Sales promotion objectives include generating trial-purchase behavior, increasing the level of repeat purchasing, and getting more and better display space from retailers. Point-of-purchase objectives are directed at achieving superior display space and generating greater levels of in-store decision making.

Regardless of the specific nature of the objectives, it is critical that clearly defined, realistic, measurable, and consistent objectives be set for each promotional mix element. Such objectives direct the remainder of the promotional program (e.g., establishing advertising creative strategy and formulating media selection) as well as provide a quantitative basis for assessing program effectiveness and taking corrective action when necessary.

Creative Strategy. Creative advertising strategy, which deals with message content and presentation, follows from the statement of objectives. For example, if the objective is to facilitate prospective customers' understanding of product attributes and benefits, then a message format such as the one for Interplak's Home Plaque Removal Instrument (Figure 1.4) is appropriate. If, however, the objective is merely to attract attention or to appeal to the consumer's imagination, then a different creative strategy is called for, such as in the case of the advertisement for Patagonia (Figure 1.5).

Media Selection. The choice of advertising media (television magazines, direct mail, etc.) is influenced by all of the preceding considerations: the available budget, objectives, and creative strategy. Many packaged-goods companies (e.g., Procter & Gamble) depend heavily on television advertising because of that medium's ability to reach mass audiences and to demonstrate product features or the kind of people who use the product. Television is an ideal medium for Dutch Boy's efforts aimed at fashion-conscious and upscale consumers. Other media (newspapers, radio, magazines, etc.) serve a variety of other functions, as is discussed in detail in Chapter 13.

Implementation. Implementation involves putting promotional programs into action. In the case of advertising, this means producing commercials and advertisements, selecting media and specific vehicles within media, buying broadcast time and print space, and ultimately printing or airing advertisements.

Step 6: Evaluating and Controlling Promotional Programs

The promotion management process does not end with implementation of advertising campaigns, sales promotion programs, or other promotional efforts. Rather, sophisticated promotion management requires that all programs be measured for effectiveness and that corrective action be taken where necessary. Effectiveness is evaluated by comparing actual performance against objectives. For example, if a sales force has as its objective to increase the number of accounts by 10 percent and accomplishes only a three percent growth, the reason for the deficit must be evaluated and corrective action taken. This does not necessarily mean that the sales force is responsible for the failure. The objective may have been set too high, or unforeseen developments may have prevented the accomplishment of the objective. Formal evaluation is necessary to cull out which reason (or reasons) is most plausible.

The value of a formal evaluation program is that it suggests possible revisions in the promotion management program for subsequent planning periods. This is shown in Figure 1.8 by the feedback flows from Step 6 to all five preceding steps. An evaluation may reveal that (1) the situation analysis was incomplete and needs to be expanded, (2) the marketing objectives are unreasonable and need to be revised, (3) the promotion budget is insufficient to accomplish desired objectives, or (4) the various program elements are not being coordinated sufficiently.

In sum, actual decision making does not proceed in the orderly fashion suggested by the straightforward presentation and the simplified model portrayed in Figure 1.8. The various steps, however, do capture the fundamentals of sophisticated promotion management programs and provide a set of working terminology that will be referred to throughout the text.

Summary

This chapter introduces the fundamentals of marketing communications and promotion management. *Marketing communications* represents the collection of all elements in an organization's marketing mix that facilitate exchanges by bringing about shared meaning with the organization's customers or clients. This description emphasizes that all marketing-mix variables, and not just the promotional variable alone, communicate with customers. Product features, package cues, store image, and price are just some of the nonpromotional variables that perform important marketing communications functions.

Promotion, in its broadest sense, means "to move forward." However, its general meaning in marketing is confined to those communications activities that include advertising, personal selling, sales promotion, publicity, and point-of-purchase communications. The blend of these promotional activities is referred to as the *promotional mix. Promotion management* is the practice of coordinating the various promotion-mix elements, setting objectives, establishing budgets, designing specific programs to accomplish objectives, and taking corrective actions when results are not in accordance with objectives.

The *Three Modes of Marketing* serve as a useful conceptual framework to tie together the various marketing communications and promotion-mix elements. According to this framework, there are three overlapping sets of activities or modes whereby marketers seek to manage the demand for their offerings: (1) the basic offer, which is the product itself and its associated terms of sale; (2) persuasive communications, which consist of personal and impersonal messages that are designed to enhance customers' impressions of the basic offer; and (3) promotional inducements, which are extra substantive benefits (e.g., free samples, coupons, bonus packs) that are used to motivate particular customer actions. All three modes overlap and reinforce each other.

The overall promotion management process is also reviewed in this introductory chapter. Promotion management consists of a sequence of decisions that must be made in order to implement effective promotional programs and achieve marketing objectives. The six major steps of this process include: (1) performing a situation analysis, (2) establishing marketing objectives, (3) setting the promotion budget, (4) integrating and coordinating promotion elements, (5) implementing the promotion management program, and (6) evaluating and controlling promotional programs.

Discussion Questions

1. Discuss the following statement: "Promotion management is to marketing communications what personal selling is to marketing."

2. Marketing communications elements may communicate with customers in either an intentional or unintentional fashion. Explain what this means, and use several examples to back up your response.

3. In what sense does a retail outlet represent a communication vehicle for a manufacturer's product?

4. Compare and contrast the marketing concept and the promotion concept. What "modes" of marketing are used to actualize each of these concepts?

5. Finding a proper balance between the marketing and promotion concepts is essential for effective marketing. How can this be accomplished?

6. A manufacturer of sporting goods introduced a new line of fishing equipment (rods, reels, etc.). The items are sold at a premium price, but product quality is only average for the industry. The manufacturer's strategy is to advertise the merchandise very heavily and offer various inducements (e.g., price rebates) to move merchandise through retail outlets. Use Figure 1.3 to explain the manufacturer's strategy in terms of the three modes and the marketing and promotion concepts.

7. What is the "basic offer" that your college or university offers students? What "persuasive communications" does it use to recruit students? Does it use any "promotional inducements"?

8. What is the difference between an "internal" and "external" situation analysis?

9. Figure 1.8 portrays a number of feedback flows from Step 6, evaluating and controlling promotional programs, to the preceding steps. Explain the underlying dynamic, or process, that each feedback flow is attempting to capture.

10. With reference to the watermelon example given earlier in the chapter, describe the proposed program in "three-modes-of-marketing" terms. Also, offer your opinion on whether or not American consumers can be encouraged to consume watermelons as an indoor fruit throughout the year.

Exercises

1. Select a specific product and, using illustrations, provide a detailed description of the important marketing communications and promotion-mix elements used by two companies that are competing for sales of this product.

2. Select two brands from a product category different than the one used in the first exercise and perform a detailed analysis of their similarities and differences from a "three-modes-of-marketing" perspective.

3. Identify three or four illustrations of product features that, in your opinion, are probably used by manufacturers to perform marketing communications functions in addition to their more basic product performance roles.

Marketing Communications and Meaning Transfer

THERE'S NO GOLD IN "7UP GOLD"

or many years, the Seven-Up Company marketed a single soft-drink brand, regular 7Up. Like many other companies in the 1970s and 1980s, it decided to extend the "parent" brand name to offspring brands—and Diet 7Up and Cherry 7Up were born. Buoyed by the success of these brand extensions, it seemed natural to follow-up with another extension: 7Up Gold.

Seven-Up executives had high hopes that 7Up Gold would capture around 1 percent of the estimated $26.6 billion annual U.S. soft-drink market. Anticipated revenues of $266 million, or more, would have made the product a big success. Unfortunately, after Seven-Up invested as much as $10 million in advertising and promoting 7Up Gold, the brand had gained only one-tenth of 1 percent of the market. How could such ambitious projections by a major company turn out to be so overblown? A variety of factors no doubt contributed to the product's failure. Some possible reasons follow.

By way of backdrop, it is interesting to note that 7Up Gold was actually invented at the Dr Pepper Company before it merged with the Seven-Up Company in 1986. Dr Pepper's invention became 7Up Gold—a caffeinated drink with a ginger-ale taste, a cinammon-apple overtone, and a reddish caramel hue. This new brand was not a cola or a lemon-lime drink, but like Dr Pepper itself, 7Up Gold fit no established soft-drink category.

7Up Gold's disappointing performance is partially explained by the extremely competitive nature of the soft-drink market. Every new soft drink must spend heavily in order to gain shelf space and a position in the consumer's mind. Perhaps the biggest problem confronting 7Up Gold was the confusion created by a cola-like, brownish-hued, caffeinated 7Up product. It took years and great resources for the company to create a unique niche for its original 7Up brand—a clear, crisp, decaffeinated product that is the virtual antithesis of cola. 7Up Gold simply failed to fit consumers' image of what 7Up stands for. By the fall of 1988, after 7Up Gold had been on the market for less than one year, the Seven-Up Company decided to discontinue heavy advertising and promotional support for 7Up Gold.[1]■

The preceding vignette describes an unfortunate outcome for an otherwise successful company. It points out that success does not come easily in the highly competitive environments that characterize so much of today's business activity. The vignette also serves to show that product performance depends on a company's ability to effectively communicate meaning to a target market.

The topics covered in this text—advertising, personal selling, sales promotion, public relations, package design, point-of purchase promotion, and so on—all involve *communicating* with a company's prospective or current customers to convey desired *meanings*. Therefore, an understanding of the communication process and the nature of meaning and how meaning is transferred are basic to an appreciation of promotion management and marketing communications.

The chapter begins with a discussion of communication objectives and brand-concept management, turns next to a formal description of the communication process, and then discusses the nature of meaning and the semiotics of marketing communications.

Communication Objectives and Brand-Concept Management

Communication Objectives

Promotion management methods and marketing communications variables are designed to achieve desired communication effects. All marketing communications efforts are directed at accomplishing any one or more of the following five objectives:[2]

1. Adapted from Douglas C. McGill, "7Up Gold: The Failure of a Can't Lose Plan," *The New York Times*, February 11, 1989, p. 17.
2. These objectives were delineated by John R. Rossiter and Larry Percy, *Advertising & Promotion Management* (New York: McGraw-Hill, 1987), p. 131.

1. Building product category wants.
2. Creating brand awareness.
3. Enhancing brand attitude.
4. Influencing brand purchase intention.
5. Facilitating purchase.

Objective #1: Building Category Wants.   Every marketing organization is interested ultimately in having people select its specific offering, or
brand, rather than choosing a competitive offering. However, consumers have
to want the general product category before they buy a specific brand in that
category. This is what marketers mean by building category wants, which is
also called creating *primary demand*.

Examples of marketers' attempts to build category wants are extensive.
For example, as mentioned in Chapter 1, consumers are becoming increasingly
concerned with their health and physical well-being. As a result of this societal
trend, marketers have successfully created various health-related category
wants. Several examples follow. (1) Sales of poultry products and seafood have
skyrocketed, while consumption of beef and pork has declined rather dramatically. (2) Products containing bran and other natural fibers, promoted as can-
cer preventatives, are widespread on grocery shelves. (3) Products containing
calcium are consumed in increasing quantities due largely to fears of osteopo-
rosis as one ages. (Do you recall seeing the television commercial showing a
badly stooped-shouldered older woman stepping off a train?) (4) Consumers
now also "need" a variety of athletic shoes to accommodate the special requirements demanded by each specialized sport. Whereas weekend athletes used to
be able to get by with a single pair of "sneakers," consumers are now convinced that they need a different pair of shoes for each activity—jogging, tennis, cycling, aerobics, walking, and hiking, to name a few. Beyond performing
a specific function, each shoe type is rich in *symbolic meaning*, a topic for a later
section in this chapter.[3]

**Objectives #2, 3, and 4: Creating Brand Awareness, Enhancing Attitude,
and Influencing Purchase Intention.**   Once category wants are created, marketers
compete against one another for shares of total customer expenditures, each
attempting to establish *secondary demand* for its particular brand. Each marketer
must direct its efforts at creating awareness for its brand and favorably influencing attitudes and intentions.

Awareness involves familiarizing consumers with the company's brand,
informing people about its special features and benefits, and showing how it
is different and hopefully superior to competitive brands. These objectives are

---

3. For an interesting discussion of the meaning and social significance of all types of shoes, see
   Susan B. Kaiser, Howard G. Schutz, and Joan L. Chandler, "Cultural Codes and Sex-Role Ide-
   ology: A Study of Shoes," *The American Journal of Semiotics*, vol. 5, no. 1 (1987), pp. 13–34.

accomplished through advertising, sales promotion, and other marketing communications methods. If the marketer is successful in creating consumer awareness, consumers may form favorable *attitudes* toward the company's brand and possibly develop an *intention* to purchase that brand the next time a product want arises.

Objective #5: Facilitating Purchase. Whether consumers ultimately purchase the marketer's brand depends on whether the promotion and marketing communications variables *facilitate* purchasing. That is, advertising may generate consumer awareness and build favorable attitudes, but if at the point of purchase consumers evaluate the product as, say, over-priced compared to competitive brands, then the likelihood of that brand being purchased is reduced. But if a company's marketing communications efforts are really effective, consumers will understand why the brand is higher priced and perhaps will find it more desirable *because* of its premium price. Thus, effective advertising, packaging, and other marketing communications variables serve to facilitate purchasing and overcome impediments created by the nonpromotional marketing mix variables (product, price, and place/distribution).

Brand-Concept Management

Achieving the latter four communication objectives—from creating brand awareness to facilitating purchase—requires successful brand-concept management throughout a brand's life cycle. **Brand-concept management** is "the planning, implementation, and control of a brand concept throughout the life of the brand."[4] A *brand concept* is the specific *meaning* that marketing managers create for a brand and then communicate to the target market. A brand concept, or brand meaning, is accomplished by promoting a brand as appealing to any of three categories of basic consumer needs: functional needs, symbolic needs, and experiential needs.[5]

Consumers' **functional needs** are those involving current consumption-related problems, potential problems, or conflicts. Brand-concept management directed at functional needs attempts to provide solutions by communicating that the brand possesses specific attributes or benefits that will solve consumers' problems. Domino's Pizza's guarantee that its pizza will be delivered "hot and fresh" is an appeal to consumers' desire for fresh rather than warmed-over pizza. Verbatim's "DataHold" solution for static electricity problems is aimed at preventing data loss when working with floppy disks (see Figure 2.1). Numerous other illustrations of appeals to functional needs are prevalent in advertising. In industrial selling, salespeople typically appeal to their custom-

---

4. C. Whan Park, Bernard J. Jaworski, and Deborah J. MacInnis, "Strategic Brand Concept-Image Management," *Journal of Marketing*, vol. 50 (October 1986), p. 136.
5. This discussion is based on Park et al., ibid.

An Appeal to Functional Needs   FIGURE 2.1

Problem: Mysterious Data Loss
Solution: New Verbatim DataHold
Protects when Static Strikes.

Static danger is everywhere. Your customer's data is vulnerable to loss from an unseen enemy—static electricity!

Just walking across a carpeted floor builds up a static charge of up to 1500 volts—enough to ZAP data.

Strike higher profits with Verbatim. Now you can give your customers the best possible protection for their

data. DataLife now features DataHold, Verbatim's ingenious diskette liner that disperses damaging static charges instantly.

Your sales should surge when customers compare DataLife to other popular brands which retain static charges up to four minutes.

So, profit from protection. DataHold, available exclusively from Verbatim DataLife.

Verbatim.
A Kodak Company

Verbatim • 1200 W.T. Harris Blvd. • Charlotte, N.C. 28213 • 800-538-1793

Source: Courtesy Verbatim Corporation, Charlotte, North Carolina.

ers' functional needs—that is, needs for higher-quality products, quicker delivery time, better service, and so forth.

Symbolic needs are those involving *internal* consumer needs such as the desire for self-enhancement, role position, or group membership. Brand-concept management directed at symbolic needs attempts to establish meaning by associating a brand with people, places, or other symbolically rich objects. Marketers of personal beauty products, alcoholic beverages, and cigarettes are frequent users of appeals to symbolic needs. For years, Winston ads have promoted meaning by claiming Winston to be the cigarette for "real people," apparently implying that only nonphony (i.e., "real") people smoke Winston.[6] The Marlboro cigarette ad (see Figure 2.2) portrays a person rich in symbolism. The famous cowboy character symbolizes that brand as matching the self-image of individuals who wish to be viewed as masculine and individualistic.[7] Paradoxically, both cigarette advertisements say nothing of a functional nature, yet they still communicate a message to the consumer. That is, each brand becomes whatever each consumer wishes to read into the advertising that symbolizes the brand.

Consumers' **experiential needs** are those representing desires for products that provide sensory pleasure, variety, stimulation, and so on. A product such as Levi's 501 jeans satisfies many consumers' experiential needs; the jeans are extraordinarily rich in symbolic significance.[8] Brand-concept management directed at these experiential needs promotes brands as being high in *sensory value* (tasting good, feeling wonderful, smelling great, etc.), different from other brands, out of the ordinary, and so on.

In summary, this section has overviewed the various communication objectives that promotion management and marketing communications activities attempt to accomplish. Also described are the various consumer needs that companies direct their efforts at in managing brand concepts and accomplishing communication objectives. It now will be instructive to review the fundamental process involved in all forms of marketing communications.

6. A number of advertising campaigns during the mid-to-late 1980s used the "real people" theme. For example, beef was promoted as "real food for real people." These campaigns probably represent a backlash against societal trends toward better, safer, and more health-conscious lifestyles leading to reduced consumption of products such as red meats and cigarettes. The "real people" claims are an oblique way of implying that it is personally and socially acceptable to consume these products because only the "phonys" ("nonreal" people) have reduced or discontinued their consumption of these products.

7. This long-standing advertising campaign has been incredibly successful. In fact, in 1986 alone, the Marlboro brand earned Philip Morris a profit of approximately $2 billion on sales of $7 billion. In an industry with over 250 brands, Marlboro sells nearly 25 percent of all the cigarettes sold in the United States. Source: "Here's One Tough Cowboy," *Forbes*, February 9, 1987, p. 108.

8. See Michael R. Solomon, "Deep-Seated Materialism: The Case of Levi's 501 Jeans," in *Advances in Consumer Research*, vol. 13, ed. Richard J. Lutz (Provo, UT: Association for Consumer Research, 1986), pp. 619–622.

An Appeal to Symbolic Needs FIGURE 2.2

Source: Reprinted by permission of Philip Morris Incorporated.

The Communications Process

What Is Communications?

The word **communications** is derived from the Latin word *communis,* which translated means "common." Communications then can be thought of as the *process of establishing a commonness or oneness of thought between a sender and a receiver.*[9] This definition sets forth two important ideas. First, communications is a process and, as such, has elements and interrelationships that can be modeled and examined in a structured manner. Second, there must be a commonness of thought developed between sender and receiver if communication is to occur. Commonness of thought implies that a *sharing* relationship must exist between sender (an advertiser, for instance) and receiver (a consumer, for example).

Consider a situation in which a salesperson is delivering a sales presentation to a purchasing agent who appears to be listening to what the salesperson is saying but who actually is thinking about a personal problem. From an observer's point of view, it would appear that communication is taking place; however, communication is *not* occurring because thought is not being shared. The reason for the lack of communication in this instance is, of course, the inattentiveness of the intended receiver. Though sound waves are bouncing against his eardrums, he is not actively receiving and thinking about what the salesperson is saying.

An analogy can be drawn between a human receiver and a television set. A television set is continuously bombarded by electromagnetic waves from several or many different stations; yet it will only receive the station to which the channel selector is tuned. Human receivers are also bombarded with stimuli from many sources, and like the television set, people are selective in what information they choose to process.

Both sender and receiver must be active participants in the same communicative relationship in order for thought to be shared. Communications is something one does *with* another person, not something one does *to* another person. A British advertising researcher conveys the same idea when she reminds us that the question for advertisers is *not* "What does advertising *do* to people?" but rather "What do people do *with* advertising? What do people use advertising for?"[10]

9. Wilbur Schramm, *The Process and Effects of Mass Communications* (Urbana, IL: University of Illinois Press, 1955), p. 3.
10. Judie Lannon, "New Techniques for Understanding Consumer Reactions to Advertising," *Journal of Advertising Research*, vol. 26 (August/September 1986), pp. RC6–RC9.

Elements in the Communications Process

All communication activities involve the following eight elements:

1. a source
2. encoding
3. a message
4. a channel
5. a receiver
6. decoding
7. feedback potential
8. the possibility of noise

As shown in the model in Figure 2.3, the **source** (or sender) is a person or group of people (such as a business firm) who has thoughts (ideas, sales points, etc.) to share with some other person or group of people. The source

Elements in the Communications Process   FIGURE 2.3

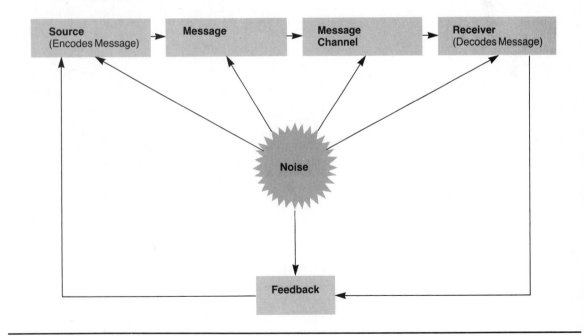

encodes a message to accomplish the communication objectives described previously. **Encoding** is the process of putting thought into symbolic form. The source selects specific *signs* from a nearly infinite variety of words, sentence structures, symbols, and nonverbal elements to encode a message that will communicate effectively with the target audience. The **message** itself is a symbolic expression of a sender's thoughts. It is the manifestation of the encoding process and is the instrument used in sharing thought with a receiver. The message takes the form of an advertisement, a sales pitch, or other marketing communications applications.

The **message channel** is the path through which the message moves from source to receiver. Companies use broadcast (radio and television) and print media (newspapers and magazines) to channel advertising messages to current and potential customers. Messages also are transmitted to customers via salespeople, direct-mail brochures, and point-of-purchase displays.

The **receiver** is the person or group of people with whom the sender attempts to share thoughts. In marketing communications, receivers are the prospective and present customers of an organization's product or service. **Decoding** involves activities undertaken by receivers to interpret marketing messages, that is, to take meaning away from the messages. Because the meaning formation process plays such a crucial role in all marketing communications, the last major section in this chapter discusses in detail the nature of meaning.

A message moving through a channel is subject to the influence of extraneous and distracting stimuli. These stimuli interfere with reception of the message in its pure and original form. Such interference and distortion is called **noise.** Noise may occur at any stage in the communication process (see Figure 2.3). For example, at the point of message encoding, the sender may be unclear about what the message is intended to accomplish. A likely result is a poorly focused and perhaps even contradictory message rather than a message that is clear-cut and integrated. Noise also occurs in the message channel—a fuzzy television signal, a crowded magazine page on which an advertisement is surrounded by competitive clutter, and a personal sales interaction that is interrupted repeatedly by telephone calls are examples of channel noise. Noise can also be present at the receiver/decoding stage of the process. An infant might cry during a television commercial and block out critical points in the sales message; passengers in an automobile might talk and not listen to a radio commercial; or the receiver simply may not possess the knowledge base needed to fully understand the promotional message.

The final element, **feedback,** affords the source a way of monitoring how accurately the intended message is being received. Feedback enables the source to determine whether the original message hit the target accurately or whether it needs to be altered to evoke a clearer picture in the receiver's mind. Thus, the feedback mechanism offers the source some measure of control in the communications process. Advertisers frequently discover that their target markets do not interpret campaign themes exactly as intended. Using research-based feedback from their markets, management can reexamine and often correct in-effective or misdirected advertising messages.

Semiotics of Marketing Communications

The process described in the preceding section focused on promotion manage-ment and marketing communications in general terms of how marketers com-municate with their customers. Fundamental to the communications process is the concept of meaning. Marketers attempt to convey meaning and consumers "receive" meaning, which may or may not be the same as the meaning in-tended by the marketing communicator. This section discusses the nature of meaning in marketing communications using a semiotics perspective. **Semiot-ics,** broadly speaking, is the study of meaning and the analysis of meaning-producing events.[11] The fundamental concept in semiotics is the sign.

The Nature of Signs

Marketing communications in all of its various forms uses signs to convey meanings. A **sign** is something physical and perceivable by our senses that represents, or signifies, something (the referent) to somebody (the interpreter) in some context.[12] Consider, for example, the word sign "pickup truck." The primary and explicit, or *denotative,* meaning of the word "pickup truck" is straightforward; that is, a vehicle with a cab compartment for passengers and space in the rear for hauling people and objects. The secondary and implicit, or *connotative,* meaning of pickup truck is considerably more diverse. What comes to mind when *you* think of pickup truck? Perhaps you conjure up an image of a farmer hauling animals, crops, or farm equipment. Possibly you think of unshaven men riding three abreast and drinking beer in a vehicle that has a gun rack in the back window. Or maybe you think of a "suburban aris-tocrat" who uses the truck primarily for driving to work Monday through Fri-day and for hauling plants, rubbish, kids, and golf clubs on the weekend.

The same sign, "pickup truck," means different things to different people and different things at different times. The image of pickup truck has changed dramatically in recent years. While historically pickups were owned almost ex-clusively by rural people and craftsmen (such as plumbers) and were used

11. For an in-depth treatment of semiotics in marketing communications and consumer behavior, see David Glen Mick, "Consumer Research and Semiotics: Exploring the Morphology of Signs, Symbols, and Significance," *Journal of Consumer Research*, vol. 13 (September 1986), pp. 196–213. For an interesting application of a semiotic analysis, see Morris B. Holbrook and Mark W. Grayson, "The Semiology of Cinematic Consumption: Symbolic Consumer Behavior in *Out of Africa*," *Journal of Consumer Research*, vol. 13 (December 1986), pp. 374–381.
12. This definition is based on John Fiske, *Introduction to Communication Studies* (New York: Me-thuen, Inc., 1982), p. 44, and Mick, p. 198.

FIGURE 2.4   **Overlapping Fields of Experience**

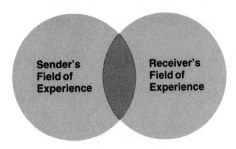

Source: M. Wayne DeLozier, *The Marketing Communications Process* (New York: McGraw-Hill, 1976), p. 6.

primarily for work and secondarily for pleasure, in more recent times (due largely to effective marketing efforts by Japanese manufacturers) the pickup truck has taken on meaning as a dual-purpose vehicle, used first for pleasure and only secondarily for work.

Effective communication takes place when signs are common to both the sender's and the receiver's fields of experience. Figure 2.4 illustrates this point. A *field of experience*, also called the perceptual field, is the sum total of all experiences a person has had during his or her lifetime. Signs contained in the perceptual field are numerous. The larger the *overlap* or *commonness* in their perceptual fields, the greater the likelihood that signs used by the sender will be decoded by the receiver in the manner intended by the sender.

Advertisers, salespersons, and other marketing communicators sometimes employ signs that are not part of their target audience's perceptual field. Effective communication is severely compromised when, for example, marketing communicators use words that customers do not understand.

The Meaning of Meaning

Although we use signs to share meaning with others, the two terms (signs and meanings) should not be construed as synonymous.[13] Signs are simply stimuli, that are used to evoke an intended meaning within another person's head. The words we use do not have meanings; instead, *people have meanings for words*. Meanings are internal responses people hold for external stimuli. Many times people have different meanings for the same words. There is simple proof of this. Ask five of your friends who have never taken a marketing course to

13. Much of the subsequent discussion is based on David K. Berlo, *The Process of Communication* (San Francisco: Holt, Rinehart & Winston, 1960), pp. 168–216.

FOCUS ON PROMOTION

What Is the Meaning of "Necktie"?

What comes to mind when you hear the word "necktie"? An initial thought, no doubt, is that a necktie is simply a piece of material that is wrapped around a person's neck and is shaped into a knot. Most people, at least in the Western world, would share this same denotative meaning for necktie.

But there's much more below the surface. Despite the fact that ties serve absolutely no function, the average tie wearer has a collection of 25 to 30 ties.[14] Ties come in a wide-variety of colors, designs (stripe, paisley, foulard), materials (silk, wool, cotton, polyester), shapes (wide, narrow, straight bottom, pointed bottom, bow), and prices. What do ties say about their wearers? What do they mean?

The exact meaning conveyed depends on a combination of factors: the tie's design, its color and material, the context in which it is worn (at the office or after work), and the clothes it is worn with (a suit, a blazer, or simply with a shirt). The necktie sign may connote "power" (a silk, yellow, foulard tie worn with a charcoal grey suit), "preppiness" (a silk, striped tie worn with a navy blue blazer), "daringness" (a brightly colored Italian tie worn with a double-breasted suit), or conformity, conservatism, and a variety of other meanings.

The diversity of meanings people have for neckties is what makes the study of marketing communications so fascinating. A product as physically simple as the necktie—a virtually useless strip of material—is incredibly rich in meaning. ■

define what "marketing" means to them. You will probably receive five decidedly different responses. The discussion of neckties in the *Focus on Promotion* section above offers further insight into the difference between signs and meaning.

If signs have no meaning, it follows that meaning cannot be transmitted. "Only messages are transmittable, and meanings are not in the message, they are in the message-users."[15] Good communicators are people who select verbal and nonverbal signs that they feel will elicit the intended meaning. Marketing communicators must be especially careful to use signs that will evoke the intended meaning in prospective buyers. All too often companies communicate

14. Lucy Kaylin, "The Semiotics of the Tie," *Gentleman's Quarterly,* July, 1987, p. 112.
15. Berlo, *The Process of Communication,* p. 175.

their product offerings in terms familiar to themselves but not in terms familiar to their potential customers.

To this point we have referred to meaning in the abstract. Now a definition is in order. **Meaning** can be thought of *as the set of internal responses and resulting predispositions evoked within a person when presented with a sign or stimulus object.*[16] It should be clear at this point that meaning is *internal*, rather than external, to an individual. Meaning, in other words, is psychological in that it represents a person's "subjective perception and affective reaction to stimuli."[17]

Imagine, for example, two consumers seated in front of a television set watching a commercial for cat food. For one of the consumers, the commercial represents a display of adorable animals consuming a product that this consumer now will consider buying for her own pet cat. For the other consumer, who is not a pet lover, the commercial represents a disgusting portrayal of unappealing animals and an unappetizing product. It is clear: the identical message has decidedly different meanings for these two consumers.

Meaning Transfer: From Culture, to Object, to Consumer

The culture and social systems in which marketing communications takes place are loaded with meaning. Through socialization, people learn cultural values, beliefs, and become familiar with the artifacts that are associated with these values and beliefs. The artifacts of culture (e.g., the Lincoln monument and Ellis Island are signs of freedom; Norman Rockwell paintings symbolize small-town America and family values; Wall Street symbolizes opulence and perhaps avarice) are charged with meaning, and this meaning is transferred from generation to generation.

Marketing communicators attempt to *draw meaning from the culturally constituted world* (i.e., the everyday world filled with artifacts such as the preceding examples) and transfer that meaning to consumer goods. Advertising is an especially important instrument of meaning transfer. The role of advertising in transferring meaning has been described in this fashion:

> Advertising works as a potential method of meaning transfer by bringing the consumer good and a representation of the culturally constituted world together within the frame of a particular advertisement. . . . The known properties of the culturally constituted world thus come to reside in the unknown properties of the consumer good and the transfer of meaning from world to good is accomplished.[18]

When exposed to advertising, the consumer is not merely drawing information

16. Ibid., p. 184.
17. Roberto Friedmann and Mary R. Zimmer, "The Role of Psychological Meaning in Advertising," *Journal of Advertising,* vol. 17, no. 1 (1988), p. 31.
18. Grant McGracken, "Culture and Consumption: A Theoretical Account of the Structure and Movement of the Cultural Meaning of Consumer Goods," *Journal of Consumer Research,* vol. 13 (June 1986), p. 74.

from the ad but is actively involved in assigning meaning to the advertised product.[19]

In illustration of the preceding points, consider the advertisement for Red Devil paints and stains (see Figure 2.5). The ad makes no functional claims about the product other than saying that Red Devil makes "The best little paints and stains in the world." However, the ad is loaded with symbolism. The advertiser's clear intent is to have consumers "think luxury" when they think of Red Devil. Thus, Red Devil is shown embedded in the context of seven culturally rich, symbolic products that are owned and consumed by the "rich and famous" (items such as a Lamborghini automobile, Concorde jetliner, pearl earrings, silver tea set, and champagne).

The makers of Red Devil no doubt hope to achieve several objectives with this campaign: create consumer awareness of Red Devil, enhance consumer attitudes toward this brand, and facilitate purchase by conveying the belief that Red Devil is worth its price. Of course, not all consumers will take the same meaning away from reading this ad. It is reasonable to assume, however, that the primary market for this brand is the same upscale group of consumers that Dutch Boy brand is aiming at (see *Focus on Promotion* in Chapter 1). As such, these consumers are familiar with the symbols contained in the Red Devil advertisement and are likely to assign the meaning "high quality" to Red Devil by virtue of associating the brand with the luxury symbols contained in the ad.

Japlish: Meaning Transfer in Japanese Commerce. The process of meaning transfer is universal; however, the specific signs that are used to transfer meaning are highly variable. Take the practice of using foreign language or foreign-sounding language for domestic marketing purposes. In the United States, foreign languages other than French are rarely used in packaging and advertising, and even French is used sparingly. By comparison, much package labelling and brand naming in Japan uses English names or combines English and Japanese language; this combination of languages is called "Japlish".[20] Japanese products are marketed by Japanese companies in Japan with names like "deodoranto" (deodorant), "appuru pai" (apple pie), and "Pocari Sweat" (a branded ion-supply drink). Japanese automobiles are marketed with English-sounding names such as "Fairlady," Bongo Wagon," and "Cherry Vanette."

The use of English names or English transmutations symbolizes Japanese people's desire for modernization and cosmopolitanism. The use of English in Japanese promotional efforts involves consumers with a product by investing that product with connotations that the native Japanese language is less able

19. For further discussion, see Grant McCracken, "Advertising: Meaning or Information," in *Advances in Consumer Research*, vol. 14, eds. Melanie Wallendorf and Paul F. Anderson (Provo, UT: Association for Consumer Research, 1987), pp. 121–124.
20. This section is based on John F. Sherry, Jr. and Eduardo G. Camargo, " 'May Your Life Be Marvelous:' English Language Labelling and the Semiotics of Japanese Promotion," *Journal of Consumer Research*, vol. 14 (September 1987), pp. 174–188.

FIGURE 2.5   **Use of Symbolic Association to Convey Meaning**

to achieve.[21] In other words, English-sounding words and phrases connote something positive (such as modernity); Japanese marketers hope that this positive connotation transfers to the consumer goods that they label.

Japanese marketing communicators' use of English sometimes approaches the bizarre. In beverage advertising, for example, cans are frequently adorned with poetic statements in English. The following examples are illustrative:[22]

> Give Cheers to
> Asahi Draft Beer! and
> May your life be Marvelous.
> Natural taste is alive
> Asahi Draft Beer.
> (From the label of "Live" beer)

> Imagine gives you fine taste and fashionable feeling. If it's a good time for you, serve well chilled and appreciate taste.
> ("Imagine" soft drink)

> Welcome to heaven
> As Time brings
> softness
> found in this can.
> ("Mild" coffee)

> Pokka White Sour is refreshing and white like Alpine snow. Its sour taste of yogurt will extend on your tongue softly and be a sweetheart.
> ("Pokka White Sour" yogurt)

Signals, Signs, and Symbols

As noted earlier, the concept of sign is basic to semiotics and the study of meaning. The term "sign" itself is a bit too general, however. This section presents a more fine-tuned treatment of signs by distinguishing among "signals," "signs," and "symbols."[23] Note first, though it may seem a bit confusing, that all three concepts are forms of signs; that is, sign is the general concept that encompasses the three more finely delineated forms.

Signal Relations. A product or specific brand in a product category is a **signal** of something if it is *causally related* to it. The signaling relation can go either way: the product *causes* something, or the product is the *result* of something; in other words, the product can be either cause or effect. For example, eating excessive quantities of ice cream signals getting fat (product is

---

21. Ibid., p. 176.
22. Ibid., pp. 180, 181.
23. These distinctions and the following discussion are based on Jeffrey F. Durgee, "Richer Findings from Qualitative Research," *Journal of Advertising Research*, vol. 26 (August/September 1986), pp. 36–44.

cause); serving guests Häagen-Dazs ice cream signals that one has good taste (the product is effect). For other examples of signalling relations, see Table 2.1.

Sign Relations.   The term "sign" is used here in a more specific sense than previously. A product or brand is a sign of something if both product/brand and referent belong to the same cultural context. A sign gets its meaning from other items in its context and vice versa. For example, the "Polo" logo (see Figure 2.6) signifies a sense of high status, financial well-being and even royalty, because the sport of polo is associated with the British royalty. Ralph Lauren was obviously well aware of this when he selected the word "Polo" to signify his company's products. When buying a sign, one is *buying the whole sign context*, which brings some degree of truth to the aphorism: "you are what you own."

The distinction between signal and sign is not always perfectly clear. Each situation has to be analyzed independently. Consider, for example, the "Night belongs to Michelob" campaign that has been heavily advertised on television for several years. Is Michelob a signal or sign in this campaign? Michelob (the brand) and night (the referent) are *not* causally related; Michelob does not cause the night to occur or vice versa. The campaign is not, therefore, a "signal" relationship. Michelob does, however, "signify" the night; Anheuser-Busch, the maker of Michelob, wants beer drinkers to automatically consider Michelob and night-time recreation as belonging in the same cultural context— "up-town people," excitement, entertainment, action, bars, and so on. Interestingly, this same company advertises its "Natural Light" brand to *signify* food; the brand is always advertised in the context of food—"Natural Light

---

TABLE 2.1   **Examples of Signal, Sign, and Symbol Relations**

Signal: (Result or Cause of)
Chevy station wagon—large family (result of)
Suzuki Samurai—excitement, accidents (cause of)
Jaguar XJ-S—wealth, status, luxury driving (result and cause)
Ford pickup truck—country or suburban living (result of)

Sign: (Part of Context of)
Chevy station wagon—middle class, children, suburbs
Suzuki Samurai—sun, fun, freedom
Jaguar XJ-S—"yuppies," success
Ford pickup truck—hunting, fishing

Symbol: (Associated with)
Chevy station wagon—apple pie, hot dogs, patriotism
Suzuki Samurai—Japanese warriors
Jaguar XJ-S—jungle cat
Ford pickup truck—blue-collar workers

and food go together." Other beer advertisers, as well as advertisers of many other product categories, promote their brands as signs of something desirable. What do the makers of "Old Milwaukee" beer want that brand to signify?

Symbol Relations. A product, or brand, is a symbol of something (a referent) when the product and referent *have no prior intrinsic relationship but rather are put together arbitrarily or metaphorically*. Examples of symbolic usage abound. Prudential Insurance advertises itself as "The Rock" and portrays itself in the context of the Rock of Gibraltar. The rock metaphor symbolizes strength and security. Merrill-Lynch features a bull in its advertising, undoubtedly because in financial circles the bull is a symbol of growth and prosperity. Athletic teams often become known by their symbols; fans can then show their support by wearing the symbols of their favorite teams.

Figurative, nonliteral language is widely used by marketing communicators when establishing symbolic relations. Various forms of figurative language used in advertising include simile, metaphor, and allegory.[24]

24. The following discussion is based on three articles by Barbara B. Stern: "Figurative Language in Services Advertising: The Nature and Uses of Imagery," in *Advances in Consumer Research*, vol. 15, ed. Michael J. Houston (Provo, UT: Association for Consumer Research, 1987), pp. 185–190; "How Does an Ad Mean? Language in Services Advertising," *Journal of Advertising*, vol. 17, no. 2 (1988), pp. 3–14; and "Medieval Allegory: Roots of Advertising Strategy for the Mass Market," *Journal of Marketing*, vol. 52 (July 1988), pp. 84–94.

Simile uses a comparative term such as "like" or "as" to join items from different classes of experience. "Love is *like* a rose" personifies the use of simile.[25] For many years, viewers of the soap opera "Days of Our Lives" have listened to the program open with the intonation of the simile: "Like sands through an hourglass, so are the days of our lives." The "hanimals" advertising campaign for Citizen Noblia watches is a delightful illustration of the use of simile in advertising. In the magazine ads, Noblia watches are displayed on human hands painted to look like animals (including the peacock, giraffe, whale, swan, zebra, seal, alligator and owl), and the advertising captions employ simile with phrases such as "beautiful as a peacock" (see Figure 2.7 for an example). Sales of Citizen Noblia watches have increased by 300 percent between 1986 and 1988, in great part due to this campaign.[26]

Metaphor differs from simile in that the comparative term (as, like) is omitted ("Love is a rose"; "She has a heart of gold"; "He has stone hands"). Metaphor applies a word or a phrase to a concept or object that it does not literally denote in order to suggest a comparison. For example, Jaguar XJ-S is claimed to be "the stuff of legends"; Wheaties is the "cereal of champions"; Budweiser is the "king of beers"; and Chevrolet is "the heartbeat of America." The advertiser in using metaphor hopes that by repeatedly associating its brand with a well-known and symbolically meaningful referent, the meaning contained in the referent will eventually carry-over (rub off, so to speak) from the referent to the brand. Kids who identify with sports stars eat Wheaties in hopes that they too can become champions.

Allegory represents a form of *extended metaphor*.[27] Allegorical presentation equates the objects in a particular narrative (such as the advertised brand in a television commercial) with meanings lying outside the narrative itself.[28] In addition to the use of metaphor, two other determining characteristics of allegorical presentation are personification and moral conflict.[29]

Through *personification*, the abstract qualities in a narrative are treated as person-like. For example, the character "Mr. Clean" personifies heavy-duty cleaning ability; "Mr. Goodwrench" exemplifies professional, efficient car service; and "Betty Goodeal" (Figure 2.8) embodies Toyota's effort to make the ever-growing segment of women automobile purchasers feel more comfortable when visiting a Toyota showroom.

Along with metaphor and personification, *moral conflict* is a necessary characteristic of allegory. "Allegory occurs only when the personified abstractions as terms in the metaphor act out inner conflicts."[30] Moral conflict is a

---

25. Stern, "Figurative Language in Services Advertising."
26. The sales-increase statistic was presented on CBS's "West 57th" program that aired on July 23, 1988.
27. For a fascinating discussion of historical and modern usage of allegory, see Stern, "Medieval Allegory: Roots of Advertising Strategy for the Mass Market."
28. Stern, "How Does an Ad Mean? Language in Services Advertising," p. 186.
29. Stern, "Medieval Allegory: Roots of Advertising Strategy for the Mass Market," p. 86.
30. Ibid.

Illustration of Simile in Advertising   FIGURE 2.7

FIGURE 2.8   **Use of Personification**

Source: Courtesy Southeast Toyota Distributors, Inc.; Agency: Tinsley Advertising.

facet of everyday life. Some consumers are torn between purchasing a domestically made automobile, which may not offer the best deal, or buying an imported car and hurting fellow citizens whose jobs in the automobile industry are threatened. Another conflict, perhaps more personal than moral, exists for all of us when we are confronted with hedonistic desires to receive immediate pleasure (e.g., ordering a large pizza at 10 p.m.) and offsetting feelings of guilt (doing this would not be good for my waistline). General Motors' Mr. Goodwrench campaign illustrates just such a conflict and indicates how marketing communicators use allegory to their advantage.

> Mr. Goodwrench . . . represents the abstract quality of "good car care service," appealing to the consumer's desire to avoid accident or death. The ad's conflict situation has two levels, the first of which is a battle between duty (take care of your car) and inclination (laziness). In terms of the consumer caretaking role, Mr. Goodwrench has two enemies. The more obvious one is the careless consumer, inclined to risk damage to his or her car by not changing the oil regularly. In the war against inertia, a modern equivalent of sloth, Mr. Goodwrench is a surrogate for the "better" quality of disciplined car care, who counsels action as opposed to indolence: "Mr. Goodwrench recommends regular oil changes with GM Goodwrench Motor Oil: The Life Preserver."[31]

Section Wrap-Up

This section has provided a detailed discussion of the nature of meaning in marketing communications and the elements involved in meaning transfer. Perhaps the most important lesson to learn is that marketers utilize a variety of different signs, nonverbal as well as verbal, in their efforts to accomplish various communication objectives. In the final analysis, marketing communicators hope to manage brand concepts by creating desired meanings for their brands. *Meaning* is the fundamental concept in all of marketing communications. The following chapter expands this discussion on meaning by examining nonpromotional elements in the marketing mix (e.g., package design, color choice, and store displays) and the roles they perform in creating meaning for the brands they promote.

Summary

The promotional arm of marketing is geared toward achieving various communication objectives. These include building product category need, creating brand awareness, enhancing brand attitudes, influencing purchase intentions, and facilitating purchase. These objectives are realized by managing brands throughout their life cycles. Brand concepts are managed by appealing to customers' functional, symbolic, and experiential needs through effective communications.

31. Ibid., p. 88

Communications is the process of establishing a commonness, or oneness, of thought between a sender and a receiver. The process consists of the following elements: a source who encodes a message; a channel that transmits the message; a receiver who decodes the message; noise, which interferes with or disrupts effective communications at any of the previous stages; and a feedback mechanism that affords the source a way of monitoring how accurately the intended message is being received.

The concept of *signs* is introduced to explain how thought is shared between senders and receivers and how meaning is created. The larger the overlap, or commonness, in their perceptual fields, the greater the likelihood that signs used by the sender will be decoded by the receiver in the manner intended by the sender.

Signs are used to share meaning, but signs and meaning are not synonymous. *Meanings* are internal responses people hold for signs. Meaning is found within an individual's perceptual field. No two people have exactly the same meaning for the same sign; each sign elicits a meaning peculiar to each individual's field of experience.

Meaning is acquired through a process whereby stimuli (i.e., signs in the form of words, symbols, etc.) become associated with physical objects and evoke within individuals responses that are similar to those evoked by the physical objects themselves. Marketing communicators use a variety of techniques to make their brands stand for something, to embellish their value, or, in short, to give them meaning. This is accomplished by (1) relating the brand to a referent in a cause-effect relation (signal), (2) relating the brand to a desirable referent in some context (sign), or (3) relating the brand to a symbolic referent that has no prior intrinsic relation to the brand (symbol). Simile, metaphor, and allegory are forms of figurative language that perform symbolic roles in marketing communications.

Discussion Questions

1. Discuss the nature and importance of feedback. In what ways do marketing communicators get feedback from present and prospective customers?

2. Contrast verbal and nonverbal communications. How do marketers employ nonverbal communications in communicating with prospective buyers?

3. Why does the same sign evoke different meanings within different people?

4. How can a marketing communicator (such as an advertiser or salesperson) reduce noise when communicating a product message to a customer?

5. The famous California Raisins commercial humanized raisins by using claymatic characterizations. Raisins dressed in sunglasses and sneakers were shown dancing to "I Heard It through the Grapevine." Explain how this ad illustrates allegorical presentation in advertising.

6. The *Focus on Promotion* discussion of neckties explained that millions of men wear this product even though it performs no functional purpose. What is the meaning of the necktie in the United States? What does this sign stand for?

7. The opening vignette for 7Up Gold indicated that this brand was a failure, at least initially. Using concepts presented in this chapter, offer your explanation of why 7Up Gold failed.

Exercises

1. Some magazine advertisements show a picture of a product, mention the brand name, but have virtually no verbal content except, perhaps, a single statement about the brand. Locate two or three ads of this type and explain what meaning you think the advertiser is attempting to convey in each instance. Ask two friends to offer their interpretations of the same ads and then compare their responses to determine the differences in meaning that these ads have for you and your friends.

2. Arrange an interview with a salesperson, preferably one who calls on business accounts rather than a retail clerk. Ask this individual to explain how he or she acquires feedback during the course of a sales presentation. Also, ask him or her to explain the various forms of noise that occur most often during sales presentations and how he or she deals with the noise.

3. Provide several examples of advertisers' use of appeals to functional, symbolic, and experiential needs in managing brand concepts.

4. Give three examples each of the use of signals, signs, and symbols in marketing communications.

5. Provide two examples each of the use of simile, metaphor, and allegory in marketing communications.

The Nonpromotional Elements of Marketing Communications

A CREATIVE RESPONSE TO A SERIOUS HEALTH PROBLEM

Rubber Ducky condoms premiered on Florida and Texas beaches during the spring break of 1988. The marketers of the product selected the name "Rubber Ducky" to lighten up a subject that has become serious because of the fear surrounding the AIDS epidemic. Aimed at teens, Rubber Ducky condoms feature on the package an animated duck character dressed in a Miami Vice-type outfit. The condoms themselves are available in such colors as "hundred-dollar green" and "hot pink." Advertising support is based on a "Protection is cool" theme. Rubber Ducky condoms are sold in gas stations, surf shops, record stores, and other outlets typically frequented by teens. This brand may be no different in a physical sense than competitive brands, but the creative marketing-communications techniques have great attention value and may serve to convey effectively the message that "protection *is* cool."[1]■

1. Based on Shannon Thurmond, "Ducky Bills Condoms As 'After-Party Animal.'," *Advertising Age*, May 2, 1988, p. 96.

This chapter examines the nonpromotional elements of the marketing mix and extends the theme from Chapter 2, emphasizing that all marketing and promotion elements communicate with consumers by using *symbols to create meaning*. Marketing scholars and practitioners have become increasingly aware that product, price, and place variables perform valuable communications roles in addition to their other marketing functions. The "Rubber Ducky" illustration personifies the creative use of brand name, package, and color symbolism.

The chapter first examines product characteristics, with special emphasis on packaging and brand-name symbolism. These product features communicate a variety of messages, such as quality, value, status, and strength. The communications roles of price and place variables are discussed later in the chapter. A product's price does more than merely inform the customer how much it will cost to acquire the product. In addition, the price can communicate snob appeal, quality, prestige, and a variety of other meanings that influence consumer choice behavior. In similar fashion, various characteristics of a retail store—architecture, store signs, and interior layout—evoke specific meanings and influence consumers' decisions to shop in a store and their behavior while in the store.

Product, Package, and Brand Symbolism

In a communications sense, products can be viewed as *symbols* that communicate meaning and help consumers to express their lifestyles.[2] Consumers do not purchase a physical product per se; they purchase psychological satisfaction and functional benefits. For example, consumers do not purchase cosmetics; rather, they purchase the promise of beauty; instead of buying drill bits, they purchase holes.

The remainder of this section examines how people respond to various product, package, and brand-name cues. Though the discussion centers on individual elements in the product message, bear in mind that the true test of a product's communications effectiveness is how consumers respond to the total product.

The Package

The package is the most important component of the product as a communication device. The growth of supermarkets and other self-service retail outlets has necessitated that the package assume marketing functions beyond the traditional role of merely containing and protecting the product. One of packaging's most important jobs is establishing perceptual cues "to drive associations

---

2. Joseph W. Newman, "New Insights, New Progress, for Marketing," *Harvard Business Review*, vol. 35 (November-December 1957), p. 100.

established in advertising into the customer's mind."[3] H. J. Heinz, wanting to give its wine vinegar a more upscale image, chose a wine bottle look-alike and inscribed the black label and neck band with bright aristocratic-type graphics. The new design hit the shelves in 1984, and sales increased by 12 percent in only a year.[4] Consumers obviously associated this new package design with prestige and quality.

The package serves further as the final vehicle to (1) close the sale, (2) break through competitive clutter at the point of purchase, and (3) justify price/value to the consumer.[5] Clearly, the package is a vital element in the marketing communications mix. It is often referred to in terms such as: "Packaging is the least expensive form of advertising"; "Every package is a five-second commercial"; and "The package *is* the product."[6]

Known as the "silent salesman," the package can often make or break a brand in today's consumer goods market. Even products that require personal selling must be packaged in a way to reinforce the salesperson's claims and to continue to resell itself once the consumer has the product in the home.

The importance of packaging can best be illustrated with examples. Research has shown on numerous occasions that the package influences brand preference and choice. After new packaging was introduced, the cleaning solution Fantastik experienced a 40 percent sales increase, moving from number two in sales to become the industry leader.[7] Research by Campbell Soup Company found that young professionals were not buying V-8 juice in the same quantities as other groups. The apparent reason was that these consumers rarely bought canned goods. When Campbell introduced V-8 in aseptic cartons, sales to upscale consumers increased immediately.[8]

In general, when a product is homogenous or unexciting, packaging becomes a useful way to differentiate the product from available substitutes. Packaging accomplishes this by serving as a "continuous communicator." That is, "it works uninterruptedly in store and home to present the product: to say what it is, how it is used, and what it can do to benefit the user."[9]

In the case of new or untried brands, the consumer often is looking, consciously or unconsciously, for a cue that tells him or her what the brand is all about. The tendency to equate the brand with an information cue, such as the package, is called **sensation transference.** Consumers impute information from

3. "Packaging Remains an Underdeveloped Element in Pushing Consumer Buttons," *Marketing News*, October 14, 1983, p. 3.
4. Nancy L. Croft, "Wrapping Up Sales," *Nation's Business*, October 1985, pp. 41–42.
5. "Packaging Research Probes Stopping Power, Label Reading, and Consumer Attitude among the Targeted Audience," *Marketing News*, July 22, 1983, p. 8.
6. Michael Gershman, "Packaging: Positioning Tool of the 1980s," *Management Review*, August 1987, pp. 33–41.
7. "Texize Says New Package Boosted Fantastik to Lead," *Advertising Age*, November 17, 1975, p. 141.
8. Gershman, "Packaging: Positioning Tool of the 1980s."
9. John Deighton, "A White Paper on the Packaging Industry," Dennison Technical Papers, December 1983, p. 5.

the package to the product itself. Hence, the marketing communicator's task is to transmit desired meaning by designing, coloring, and shaping packages that are compatible with what the consumer is looking for in the product. It is important to note, however, that although the package is capable of communicating quality, economy, prestige, and other desirable attributes, repeat purchases will occur only if the product delivers what the package promises.

Symbolic Packaging Components. Packaging's symbolic components include color, design, shape, size, physical materials, and product information labeling. All of these components must interact harmoniously to evoke within buyers the set of meanings intended by the company. The notion underlying good packaging is *gestalt*. That is, people react to the whole, not to the individual parts of a situation. The whole is greater than the sum of its parts when the parts interact synergistically. Sometimes, however, inconsistent package elements negate each other and produce poor package communication. The following package components are discussed individually to facilitate analysis. Throughout the discussion, however, bear in mind that the consumer perceives these components within their total context.

In general, marketing communicators should use symbols that are familiar to consumers rather than expecting consumers to learn the connotations of new symbols. The Coca-Cola company, for example, finally settled on a new package (after 150 attempts) for its line extension Diet Coke. The chosen package is very similar to that used for regular Coke; the primary difference is simply that the red and white colors are reversed. This assured consumer association with the well-known and easily recognized Coke symbol.[10]

The Use of Color in Packaging. Colors have the ability to communicate many things to prospective buyers, including quality, smell, taste, and the product's ability to satisfy the consumer's psychological needs. Many research studies have documented the important role that color plays in affecting our senses. In one study, marketing researchers tested color's cueing role using *vanilla pudding* as the experimental product. The researchers altered the color of vanilla pudding by adding food colors to create three "flavors": dark brown, medium brown, and light brown. The pudding, which actually was vanilla, was perceived as tasting like chocolate pudding. The *dark brown* pudding was considered to have the best chocolate flavor and to be the thickest. The *light brown* pudding was perceived to be the creamiest, possibly because cream is white in color.[11]

Colors affect people emotionally. The so-called high-wavelength colors of red, orange, and yellow possess strong excitation value and induce elated

10. "After 150 Tries Comes a Winning Design," *Advertising Age*, October 18, 1982, pp. M4–M5.
11. Gail Tom, Teresa Barnett, William Lew, and Jodean Selmants, "Cueing the Consumer: The Role of Salient Cues in Consumer Perception," *The Journal of Consumer Marketing*, vol. 4 (Spring 1987), pp. 23–27.

A Package Redesign Decision

FIGURE 3.1

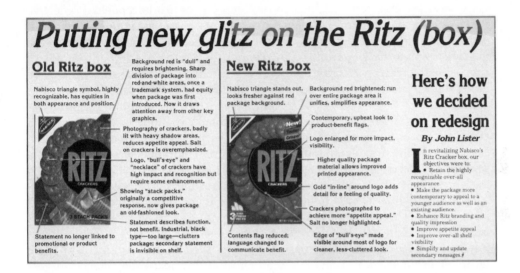

Source: John Lister, "Here's How We Decided to Redesign." Reprinted with permission from the May 12, 1956 issue of *Advertising Age*, p. 52. Copyright 1956 Crain Communications, Inc.

mood states.[12] *Red* is often described in terms such as active, stimulating, energetic, and vital. Some well-known brands that emphasize red in their packaging include Sunmaid raisins, Close-up toothpaste, and Ritz crackers. Using Ritz crackers as an example, Figure 3.1 offers an insightful look into the reasoning that was behind the package redesign decision for this product.

Orange is an appetizing color that is often associated with food. Popular food brands using orange packaging include Wheaties, Uncle Ben's rice, Sanka coffee, and Stouffer's frozen entrees. *Yellow,* a good attention getter, is a warm color that has a cheerful effect on consumers. Cheerios, Kodak, and Pennzoil are just a few of the many brands that use yellow packages. *Green* connotes abundance, health, calmness, and serenity. Green packaging is sometimes used for beverages (e.g., Heineken beer, Seven-Up), often for vegetables (e.g., Green Giant), and most always in packaging for mentholated products (e.g., Salem cigarettes). *Blue* suggests coolness, refreshingness, and water. Blue is often associated with laundry and cleaning products, including brands such as Windex and Downey fabric softener. Finally, *white* signifies purity, cleanliness,

12. This comment and parts of the following discussion are based on statements appearing in Joseph A. Bellizzi, Ayn E. Crowley, and Ronald W. Hasty, "The Effects of Color in Store Design," *Journal of Retailing*, vol. 59 (Spring 1983), pp. 21–45. Many of the brand-name examples in this section were suggested in "Color Is Prime 'Silent Communicator'," *Marketing News*, April 25, 1986, p. 15.

mildness, and in recent years, generic brands. Gold Medal flour, Grape-Nuts, and Lean Cuisine are a few food brands that feature white packages.

In addition to the emotional impact that color brings to a package, elegance and prestige can be added to products by the use of polished reflective surfaces and color schemes using whites and blacks or silvers and golds.[13] An example of the effective use of a white and black color scheme is found in the elegantly simple package utilized by Chanel #5 perfume. Another example of prestige-enhancing packaging is that for LeSueur peas, which for years have stood out on grocery shelves because of their metallic silver labels.

Design and Shape Cues in Packaging.   Variations in the design and shape of a package communicate differences in the product to consumers. *Design* refers to the organization of the elements on a package. An effective package design is one that permits good eye flow and provides the consumer with a point of focus. Package designers bring various elements together in a package to help define a brand's image. These elements include shape, size, and label design. The package design for many products can establish brand personality and help cut through the clutter of product offerings at the point of purchase.[14] The design can be used to convey a feeling of modernity, to "play upon nostalgia and a yearning for the more simple and forthright days of yesteryear,"[15] to suggest that the producer is serious and technical minded,[16] or to convey a variety of other feelings to consumers.

One way of evoking different connotations and reactions is through the choice of slope, length, and thickness of lines on a package. *Horizontal lines* suggest restfulness and quiet, evoking feelings of tranquility. There appears to be a physiological reason for this reaction—it is easier for people to move their eyes horizontally than vertically. Vertical movement is less natural and produces greater strain on eye muscles than horizontal movement. *Vertical lines* evoke feelings of strength, confidence, and even pride. Various baseball teams convey these feelings by wearing "packages" (i.e., uniforms) with vertical lines (e.g., the New York Yankees and Minnesota Twins). In basketball the new NBA entry, the Charlotte Hornets, selected vertical stripes for their uniforms, which, interestingly use the atypical uniform colors of pink and teal. *Slanted lines* suggest upward movement to most people. This is because people in the Western world read from left to right and thus view sloped lines as ascending rather than descending. Diet Coke's packaging illustrates the use of upward-slanting lines (see Figure 3.2). Perhaps the intent is to represent symbolically the product as fitting into the ambitious and upwardly mobile lifestyles of the

13. Dennis J. Moran, "Packaging Can Lend Prestige to Products," *Advertising Age*, January 7, 1980, pp. 59–60.
14. Kate Bertrand, "Shaping Packaging for Impact," *Advertising Age*, July 26, 1984, pp. 43–44.
15. Moran, "Packaging Can Lend Prestige," p. 60.
16. B. V. Yovovich, "Designers Make Their Mark on the Shelves," *Advertising Age*, October 10, 1983, p. M-37.

The Use of Upward-Slanting Lines in Packaging to Convey Upward Mobility   FIGURE 3.2

Source: Courtesy of The Coca-Cola Company.

many young professionals who are a prime market for Diet Coke and other weight-conscious products.

Shapes, too, arouse certain emotions and have specific connotations. In general, round, curving lines connote femininity, whereas sharp, angular lines suggest masculinity. The oval shape of the famous L'eggs pantyhose package is an example of true femininity. The egg-shaped L'eggs package elicits perceptions of a fragile yet protected product and connotes fashion and perhaps even sex appeal.[17]

17. "Packaging Remains an Underdeveloped Element in Pushing Consumer Buttons."

The shape of a package also affects the apparent volume of the container. In general, if two packages have the same volume but a different shape, the taller of the two will appear to hold a greater volume inasmuch as height is usually associated with volume.

Physical Materials in Packaging. An important consideration in packaging is the materials that make up a package. Some marketers are inclined to emphasize cost over all other considerations. The selection of package materials based solely, or primarily, on cost considerations may be the result of a misguided engineer or accountant; the most important consideration should be the marketing communications implications of the materials chosen. Increased sales and profits often result when upgraded packaging materials are used to design more attractive and effective packages. Admittedly, sometimes a high cost for packaging materials will not be offset by increased sales; thus, profits will be reduced. In any event, cost should *not* be the sole criterion for material selection; instead, it should be viewed in its relationship to sales. Here the economic concept of *marginal analysis* is applicable.[18]

From a behavioral viewpoint, materials used to construct a package can arouse consumer emotions, usually subconsciously. Packages constructed of *metal* evoke feelings of strength, durability, and coldness; *plastics* connote newness, lightness, cleanliness, and perhaps cheapness.[19] Materials that are *soft*, such as velvet and fur, are associated with femininity. *Foil* has a high-quality image and can evoke feelings of prestige.[20] *Wood* arouses feelings of masculinity. The men's cologne "English Leather," for example, has enjoyed much success using a wooden box and a bottle with a large wooden knob as a cap. English Leather's name and rectangular package present an overall image of masculinity by blending design, shape, brand name, and materials in a consistent fashion.

Product Information on Packages. Product information can come in several forms. In a sense, all of the previous package components (such as color and design) inform consumers (i.e., convey meaning) about what is inside the package. However, when used in the more restricted sense (as it is used here) *product information* refers to key words on the package, information on the back panel, ingredients, warnings, pictures, and illustrations. An example of the effectiveness of information included on packages comes from a field experiment that measured weekly sales of bread. When the "Made with

---

18. The logic underlying the principle of economic analysis is that additional investment is justified so long as the additional revenue generated by that investment exceeds the additional cost; that is, the marginal revenue must be greater than the marginal cost.
19. Burleigh B. Gardner, "The Package as Communication," in *Marketing for Tomorrow . . . Today,* eds. M. S. Moyer and R. E. Vosburgh (Chicago: American Marketing Association, 1967), pp. 117–118.
20. Kevin Higgins, "Foil's Glitter Attracts Manufacturers Who Want Upscale Buyers," *Marketing News,* February 3, 1984, p. 1.

100% Natural Ingredients: No Artificial Additives" statement was affixed to the package, both market penetration and buying frequency increased. When the message was removed, sales returned to their prior level.[21]

The words "new," "improved," and "free" frequently appear on packages. These words stimulate immediate trial purchases or restore a brand purchase pattern for consumers who have previously tried but have since switched to other brands. Furthermore, these key words presumably offer consumers what they want—something new, improved, or free.

There is some question whether the key words just cited have been overworked in the marketplace. One study suggests that the "new" and "improved" claims on packages do *not* significantly affect consumer evaluations of certain household and personal care products.[22] However, more research is necessary to support this point. Perhaps there is a need to find new motivating words. Some examples may be the use of numerals, as in Gleem II (toothpaste) and Clorox 2 (laundry bleach). These names inform consumers that there is a new and improved version of an old brand without directly using hackneyed words such as new and improved.

One of the most effective means of providing consumers with information about a brand, as well as projecting the appropriate image, is the use of *pictures and illustrations*. Printing techniques have improved to the point that realistic pictures and illustrations of a product can be imprinted on the package with high fidelity. Pictures are far more effective than words in projecting the desired image for a brand.

In some instances, putting a short, memorable slogan on a package is a good marketing tactic. These slogans are best used when a strong association has been built between the brand and the slogan through extensive and effective advertising. The slogan on the package, by virtue of being a concrete reminder of the brand's advertising, can facilitate the consumer's retrieval of advertising content and thereby enhance the chances of a trial purchase. Not only is the package a critical communication device in the store, it also provides a focus for much advertising effort in television commercials. A recent study revealed that television commercials feature the package about 40 percent of the time.[23]

Evaluating the Package: The VIEW Model.   A number of individual factors have been discussed in regard to what a package communicates to buyers. The most important concern, however, is whether the overall package is an effective marketing communications vehicle. Four considerations can be used to evaluate a package and its communications value: visibility, informa-

21. William H. Motes and Arch G. Woodside, "Field Test of Package Advertising Effects on Brand Choice Behavior," *Journal of Advertising Research*, vol. 24 (February-March 1984), pp. 39–45.
22. Edward H. Asam and Louis P. Bucklin, "Nutrition Labeling for Canned Goods: A Study of Consumer Response," *Journal of Marketing*, vol. 37 (April 1973), pp. 36–37.
23. "Packaging Plays Starring Role in TV Commercials," *Marketing News*, January 30, 1987, p. 6.

tion, emotional appeal, and workability. The acronym VIEW provides a useful device for remembering these criteria.[24]

Visibility signifies the ability of a package to attract attention at the point of purchase. Visibility is determined by a variety of factors. For example, brightly colored packages are more visible than dull packages. Novel packaging graphics, sizes, and shapes also may enhance a package's visibility. The objective is to have a package stand out on the shelf yet not be so garish that it detracts from a brand's image.

The second consideration, *information,* deals with product usage instructions, claimed benefits, slogans, and supplementary information (e.g., cooking recipes and sales promotion offers) that are presented on or in a package. Package information is useful for (1) stimulating trial purchases, (2) encouraging repeat purchase behavior, and (3) providing correct product-usage instructions. The objective is to provide the right type and quantity of information without cluttering the package with excessive information, which could interfere with the primary information or cheapen the look of the package.

Emotional appeal, the third component, is concerned with the ability of a package to evoke a desired feeling or mood. Emotional appeals for product packaging represent the connotative meaning conveyed by a package, compared with the denotative meaning conveyed by the previous component, information. In many situations, the role of packaging is to evoke positive feelings and associations in the prospective buyer's mind. For example, a soap package may convey a feeling of softness and femininity, a record-album jacket (which is itself a package) may suggest sensuousness, and a jewelry container may transmit a feeling of elegance. Package designers attempt to evoke specific feelings and moods through the use of color, shape, packaging materials, and so on.

The final component of the VIEW model is *workability,* which involves how a package "works" or functions rather than how it communicates. Several considerations are involved: (1) Does the package protect the product contents? (2) Does it facilitate easy storage on the part of both retailers and consumers? (3) Does it simplify the consumer's task in getting to and using the product? Several recent innovations in packaging workability include pourable-spout containers for motor oil and other products, microwavable containers for many food items, aseptic cartons, and the now widely used zip-lock packaging. Sargento introduced zip-lock packaging for its shredded cheese and increased sales by 15 percent. Post cereals (e.g., Raisin Bran) and Oscar Mayer hot dogs also experienced sales increases when they switched to zip-lock packaging.[25]

Workability is, of course, a relative matter. The objective is to design a package that is as workable as possible yet is economical for the producer and

24. Dik Warren Twedt, "How Much Value Can Be Added Through Packaging," *Journal of Marketing,* vol. 32 (January 1968), pp. 61–65.
25. Julie Liesse Erickson, "Food Marketers Find Good Things Come in New Packaging," *Advertising Age,* May 2, 1988, pp. 3, 101.

consumer. For example, consumers prefer food packages that completely prevent food from getting stale or spoiling, but the manufacturer's ability to provide this degree of workability is limited by cost. At the other extreme, some marketers skimp in their package design and use inexpensive packages that are unsuitable because they are difficult to use and frustrate consumers.

Most packages do not perform well on all of the VIEW criteria, but packages need not always be exemplary on all four VIEW components because the relative importance of each criterion varies greatly from one product category to another. Emotional appeal dominates for some products (e.g., perfume), information is most important for others (e.g., directions for using a new digital audio-tape machine), while visibility and workability are generally important for all products (especially frequently purchased self-service items). In the final analysis, the relative importance of packaging requirements depends, as always, on the particular market and the product's competition. Marketing communicators hope that their packages appeal to target audiences and will yield an advantage over competitors.

Brand Name

Creating a strong brand name and a strong reputation is invaluable for several reasons: (1) a strong brand generates consistent sales volume and revenue year after year; (2) a strong brand commands a higher price and larger gross margin; (3) a strong brand provides a platform for introducing new brands; (4) a strong brand provides the manufacturer with leverage when dealing with distributors and retailers; and (5) without a strong brand, the marketer is forced to compete on the basis of price, to be a low-cost producer.[26]

According to a recent survey, the most recognized and esteemed brand names in America are Coca-Cola, McDonald's, American Express, Kellogg's, IBM, Levi's, and Sears. Key factors that make brand images strong include: (1) product quality where products do what they do very well (e.g., Windex); (2) consistent advertising and other marketing communications in which brands tell their story often and well (e.g., McDonald's); and (3) brand personality, where the brand stands for something (e.g., Disney and Marlboro).[27]

The brand name is, perhaps, the single most important element found on the package. It identifies the product and differentiates it from others on the market. The brand name and package graphics work together to communicate and position the brand's image. A good brand name can evoke a feeling of trust, confidence, security, strength, durability, speed, status, and many other desirable associations.

---

26. Graham Phillips, "The Role of Advertising—Or, the Importance of a Strong Brand Franchise," from a talk in 1986 to senior U.S. marketing executives under the auspices of The Conference Board.
27. James Lowry, "Survey Finds Most Powerful Brands," *Advertising Age*, July 11, 1988, p. 31.

Through brand names, a company can create excitement, elegance, exclusiveness, and various sensory perceptions. Ninety-nine percent of the customers of Polo brand clothing have never seen nor will ever play a match of polo, yet Ralph Lauren was able to "establish a feeling of moneyed elegance and adventure in one word."[28]

Several fundamental requirements guide brand name selection. A brand name should (1) *distinguish* the product from competitive items, (2) *describe* the product or its benefits, (3) *motivate* the consumer to want to purchase the product, (4) be *compatible* with the product, (5) help *create and support a brand image* (see the *Focus on Promotion* section on the role of animal names), (6) be *brief, readable, memorable, and easy to pronounce*, (7) *connote the appropriate meaning when said aloud* (e.g., when pronounced aloud, the detergent name "BOLD" sounds strong and powerful), and (8) *tell the consumer what to expect inside the product or what to expect from its use* (e.g., the coffee "DECAF" tells the consumer that he or she is buying a decaffeinated coffee).[29]

Perhaps the key question the marketer must ask when selecting a brand name is, "Does the name fit the product?"[30] A recent survey reveals that consumers hate the trend in corporate naming whereby companies rename their corporations with names that say nothing about the company or the products it markets. Names that are especially disliked include Allegis, Unisys, Navistar, Primerica, Nynex, and USX.[31]

Physical Characteristics of the Product

The product itself has characteristics that communicate with buyers. The product's color, shape, and size are among the physical features that consumers perceive as important in making their buying decisions. One of the best examples of a product whose physical characteristics communicate with buyers is the Contac cold capsule. Recognizing the value of product communications, the company designed a package with a small, circular window that reveals one of the cold capsules. The capsule itself has a clear plastic end that allows the consumer to see the "tiny little time pills" of red, yellow, and white. When Contac first appeared on the market, it was the only 12-hour cold capsule; all others were 4-hour tablets. The advertising message told consumers that Contac has "tiny little time pills" that release their medicinal powers periodically over a 12-hour period. The company evidently intended for the consumer to imagine one of the pill colors, say red, taking immediate effect for the first four

28. Moran, "Packaging Can Lend Prestige," p. 59.
29. Items 1 to 3 are from Walter P. Margulies, "Animal Names on Products May be Corny, but Boost Consumer Appeal," *Advertising Age*, October 23, 1972, p. 78. The other items represent a summary of views from a variety of other sources.
30. Dennis J. Moran, "How a Name Can Label Your Product," *Advertising Age*, November 10, 1980, p. 53.
31. Paul Farhi, "To Some Corporations, What's in a Name Can Be Plenty," *The State*, Columbia, SC, July 10, 1988, p. 4G.

FOCUS ON PROMOTION

Creating an Image with Animal Names

An interesting application of branding by American marketers is the widespread use of animal names. Over the years, automobile companies have used animal names such as Mustang, Thunderbird, Bronco, Cougar, Lynx, Skyhawk, Skylark, Firebird, Jaguar, and Ram. Because animal names are among the earliest words we learn as children, their meaning and associations are strongly engrained within us. We learn, for example, that a jaguar is sleek and has speed, strength, stamina, and power—all attributes that the makers of Jaguar automobiles hope consumers will associate with their product. We were taught that tigers are sure-footed animals; Uniroyal chose to name its tires "Tiger Paw" because the name implies that the tires are able to grip the road.

In addition to being memorable, animal names can also conjure up vivid images. This is very important to the marketing communicator because, as discussed in the following chapter, concrete and vivid images facilitate consumer information processing. Consider, for example, the following brand names and their associated imagery. Dove soap suggests softness, grace, gentleness, and purity. Billy Goat vacuum cleaners and Eagle Claw fishhooks elicit sharp, indelible pictures in the minds of consumers and suggest distinct brand benefits. In addition, animal names and their associated imagery have been used successfully with children's products. Tiger Bread, Bunny Bread, Giraffe Cookies, and Pink Panther Flakes are but a few of the many animal names that have been used in the children's market.[32] ∎

hours, followed by, say, the yellow ones and then the white ones. The multicolored pills apparently served to reinforce the advertising-induced belief that Contac capsules work for 12 full hours.

Product color plays an important communications role. For example, the color of bathroom soap reinforces the brand name (e.g., Irish Spring soap is green) and also provides the consumer with a choice of colors to match the bathroom decor. The red color in Close-Up toothpaste is emblematic of love, which supports the sex appeal theme used in advertising that brand. Bristol-Myers Company's Nuprin analgesic effectively differentiated itself from competitive ibuprofen brands by simply coloring the product bright yellow. An executive for Nuprin's advertising agency said: "That Nuprin is yellow is su-

32. Margulies, "Animal Names," p. 78.

FIGURE 3.3a   **Illustration of Product Shape**

perficial to the product superiority, yet it opens peoples' minds that this product is different."[33]

   Shape is often used in products to communicate desired meanings. Animal and cartoon characters are used in children's vitamin pills and cereals, for example. A recent marketing fascination has been the use of dinosaur characters. Examples include Chef Boyardee's pasta in dinosaur shapes (see Figure 3.3a) and Converse's line of "Conasaur" high-top canvas shoes (see Figure 3.3b). The latter product has dinosaur character "molds" on the shoe soles that

33. Patricia Winters, "Color Nuprin's Success Yellow," *Advertising Age,* October 31, 1988, p. 28.

Source: Courtesy of Converse Inc.

imprint dinosaur characters in the dirt when children walk. There is little doubt that millions of parents purchased, or were pestered to purchase, these shoes solely (no pun intended) to satisfy their children's desire to turn their neighborhoods into primordial landscapes blanketed with dinosaur tracks.

The *taste, touch,* and *smell* of products also possess communications value. The Listerine "taste bad" advertising reinforces the belief that a medicinal product must taste bad in order to be effective—a learning experience that many people have retained from childhood. A similar example relates to *tactile* communications. For many years, antiseptics used in treating cuts produced a sting when applied to an open wound. One company succeeded in producing an antiseptic solution that did not sting, but the product failed because consumers did not believe it was an effective germ killer. The physical characteristic of *olfaction* (the sense of smell) plays a huge role in influencing consumer feelings and behavior but is virtually unstudied in the academic marketing literature. The fact that virtually every household cleaning product is now lemon-scented, a nonfunctional product attribute, demonstrates marketers' knowledge that "smell sells."

There are hundreds of examples of how a product's physical characteristics communicate various messages to consumers; further discussion would take us beyond the scope of the present chapter. The purpose here has been to illustrate the importance of recognizing this form of communications when formulating and designing products. You should think about other examples that are memorable to you personally.

Price and Place Communications

This section examines the roles price and place play in marketing communications, how each of these variables evokes meanings within consumers, and how price and place contribute to the image of the firm's total product offering.

The Role of Price in Marketing Communications

Traditionally price has been viewed in rate-of-exchange terms. That is, price is the amount of money a seller asks for a product and a buyer is willing to give up to acquire the product. For an exchange to take place, the buyer and seller must agree upon a set rate. This interaction between buyer and seller is summarized by economists in their law of demand, which states that as the price of a commodity rises, the quantity demanded by consumers declines, and vice versa. This inverse relationship defines the traditional, negatively sloped demand curve.

Although the law of demand is applicable to many products and services, particularly for undifferentiated products such as agricultural commodities, the traditional economic viewpoint fails to consider the impact that marketing practices have on consumer demand. Firms know that price can be used as a communications cue to differentiate product offerings and to satisfy consumers' psychological needs.

Consumers often use price as an indicator of quality.[34] Under such circumstances, the demand curve for a product may indicate a positive relationship between price and quantity demanded over some portion of the price range. That is, a higher price is related to higher demand for the product. This phenomenon, referred to as *backward-bending demand*, is often observed for luxury items such as expensive perfume, jewelry, and prestige automobiles. For example, Mercedes-Benz executives correctly predicted that increasing prices would not hurt product sales but, to the contrary, would benefit sales because customers would perceive the higher-priced cars as more prestigious. Similarly, Rolls Royce had a two-year waiting list after its prices doubled.[35]

Under what circumstances is price used as a cue to quality? The following section addresses this question by looking at two general categories of factors—product and consumer characteristics—that are favorable to the use of price as an indicator of quality.

Characteristics of the Product.   Research has shown that whether consumers will use price as a cue to indicate quality, prestige, or other ascriptions depends on the following product characteristics.

Perceived Variance in Product Quality.   When consumers perceive a high *brand-to-brand variance* in quality within a product category, they are likely to use price to cue quality.[36] For example, most consumers perceive table salt as having little or no quality variation across brands; one brand of salt is perceived to be the same in quality as another brand. In this case, price would not serve as an indicator of quality, and consumers would be unlikely to pay a premium price for any one brand.

On the other hand, consumers perceive cosmetics as having wide brand-to-brand quality variations. A consumer who is concerned about skin care is more likely than an unconcerned consumer to select a higher-priced brand of cleansing cream or lotion; this is because the consumer believes that the higher price reflects hidden qualities. It is for similar reasons that consumers may be resistant to purchase Bic perfume spritzers (refer to opening vignette in Chapter 1) because they may consider a $5 French perfume to be drastically inferior to more expensive perfumes.

---

34. Early research that detected this role for price include Harold J. Leavitt, "A Note on Some Experimental Findings about the Meaning of Price," *The Journal of Business*, vol. 22 (July 1954), pp. 205–210; and Donald S. Tull, R. A. Boring, and M. H. Gonsior, "A Note on the Relationship of Price and Imputed Quality," *The Journal of Business*, vol. 37 (April 1964), pp. 186–191.
35. Mary Louise Hatten, "Don't Get Caught with Your Prices Down: Pricing in Inflationary Times," *Business Horizons*, vol. 25 (March-April 1982), pp. 23–28.
36. Benson Shapiro, "The Psychology of Pricing," *Harvard Business Review*, vol. 46 (July-August 1968), p. 25.

The Product as a Component.   When the consumer views a product as an important component of a larger product or when a product's use contributes significantly to the quality of the final product, the consumer will be inclined to use price to indicate product quality. This is the case when one product is used as an additive, ingredient, or component of another product. For example, an experienced cook who is preparing a gourmet meal is undoubtedly aware that the spices will affect the quality of the finished food. In fact, the cook may perceive the contribution made by the spices to be much higher than their cost, and thus will pay a higher price for quality spices to decrease the risk of a poor-tasting dinner (without significantly increasing the cost).[37] Similarly, a person buying an expensive sports car will not be too concerned about paying more for one brand of AM-FM stereo cassette deck when a less expensive brand is perceived as lower in quality.

The Product as a Gift.   Some products are purchased as gifts more frequently than others. For these products, a high price serves to reduce the purchaser's risk of embarrassment in giving a poor-quality gift or to enhance the purchaser's sense of self-worth. A man who gives his fiancée a bottle of perfume for her birthday will be inclined to use price as an indicator of quality in making his brand selection. Of course, the price of the perfume is only one cue among several, including fragrance, brand name, and packaging. But price becomes an important informational cue in the selection of a gift because a higher price gives the giver greater assurance that he or she will gain the desired approval of the recipient.

Consumers often purchase more expensive products and brands when making gift selections for holidays, social gatherings, and other special occasions. The advertisement for Cross pens (see Figure 3.4) plays on people's desire to give a quality gift that will be remembered ("When you give Cross writing instruments, your feelings of love and friendship are remembered for a lifetime"). Unlike most advertisements, which fail to mention price, this ad unabashedly indicates that Cross pens range in price from $11.50 to $1,250.00. This implicates Cross' motive in wanting consumers to think higher prices mean higher quality, ensuring a more prestigious gift.

Brand-Name Familiarity.   Another variable that affects the importance of the price cue is the familiarity and strength of the brand name. When brands in a product category are physically homogeneous and brand names are unfamiliar to consumers, price becomes a powerful cue in evaluating the quality of a brand.[38] In fact, a familiar brand name is often as important or more important than the price cue in communicating product or service quality.[39] In cases of low brand familiarity or in the absence of a brand name, price

37. This example is adapted from Shapiro, ibid.

38. J. Douglas McConnell, "An Experimental Examination of the Price-Quality Relationship," *The Journal of Business*, vol. 41 (October 1968), p. 442.

39. Kent B. Monroe, "Buyers' Subjective Perceptions of Price," *Journal of Marketing Research*, vol. 10 (February 1973), p. 73.

Gift Giving and Product Quality   FIGURE 3.4

Source: Courtesy of A. T. Cross Company.

cues provide useful information that is unavailable through the brand-name cue.[40] Basically, then, price becomes a strong communications cue in the absence of other product cues such as brand name.

New Products. A new product offers the marketer a good opportunity to use price to communicate product quality. Quite often marketers use a *skimming* pricing strategy in the introductory stage of a product's life cycle. Skimming refers to the strategy of setting a high price to catch the relatively price-inelastic segment of the market. If the strategy is successful, the firm can gain a quick return on its initial investment. Furthermore, if consumers perceive the high price as an indicator of product quality, the firm can continue to use this strategy to reinforce consumers' beliefs about its quality.

40. Jerry C. Olson, "Price as an Informational Cue: Effects on Product Evaluations," in *Consumer and Industrial Buying Behavior*, eds. A. G. Woodside, J. N. Sheth, and P. D. Bennett (New York: Elsevier North-Holland, 1977), p. 278.

If the market rejects the product because of its high price, the firm is still in a position to lower its price and stress the value of its product offering.

At the other end of the continuum is *penetration* pricing. In penetration pricing, the firm elects to introduce the product at a low price because management believes that demand is fairly elastic. The communications value of price in this case is quite low except to tell the consumer that the product is either a popularly priced brand or a value brand.

Durable versus Nondurable Products.   There appears to be a relatively strong positive relationship between consumers' price-quality perceptions of durable goods and the sales of durable goods. However, for nondurable goods, the price-quality relationship is weak.[41] One study found that the price-quality relationship is poorest for convenience foods, especially frozen foods. Correlations between price and quality for packaged food products was near zero.[42]

One possible explanation for these findings is that higher-income consumers are much less affected by shifts in economic conditions than are lower-income consumers. Higher-income consumers can continue to make purchase decisions using price as a cue to variables such as quality, status, and snob appeal, whereas consumers with lower incomes are generally hit hardest by recession and inflation and therefore begin to substitute lower-priced nondurables or forestall purchasing. Another explanation for the strong price-quality relation for durable goods, but not nondurables, is that consumers lack specific product knowledge for infrequently purchased durable goods and therefore rely on price as a surrogate of quality.

Characteristics of the Consumer.   As with product characteristics, several generalizations that are important in price communications can be made regarding consumer characteristics.

Product Experience.   For consumers who lack experience and information about a product, price takes on added importance as an informational cue. For example, carpeting is a product with which most people have relatively little buying experience because it is purchased on an infrequent basis. Price should therefore represent an important cue in consumers' quality perceptions. Research supports this expectation.[43]

41. Peter C. Riesz, "Price Versus Quality in the Marketplace, 1961–1975," *Journal of Retailing,* vol. 54 (Winter 1978), pp. 15–28. A similar finding was reported more recently by Eitan Gerstner, "Do Higher Prices Signal Higher Quality?" *Journal of Marketing Research,* vol. 22 (May 1985), pp. 209–215.
42. Peter C. Riesz, "Price-Quality Correlations of Packaged Food Products," *The Journal of Consumer Affairs,* vol. 13 (Winter 1979), pp. 236–247.
43. John J. Wheatley and John S. Y. Chiu, "The Effects of Price, Store Image, and Product Respondent Characteristics on Perceptions of Quality," *Journal of Marketing Research,* vol. 14 (May 1977), pp. 181–186.

A mother who wants to buy her son golf clubs for his birthday may not know what makes one set of clubs better than another. Price is likely to be important to her in evaluating quality differences for different sets of clubs. Likewise, a father who is attempting to protect his family from intruders may decide to buy dead-bolt locks for the home. Most likely he will not be aware of brand names, and price becomes an important cue to the sturdiness and dependability of different brands.

Products that are affected by rapid changes in technology or products that are subject to changes in style and fashion confront consumers with new situations. Major changes in product features, functions, or style place consumers in less-informed positions than they were before encountering the product. These changes make consumers more sensitive to price cues when judging product quality.

Snob Appeal. Some consumers use the price of a product as a means of expressing status or prestige. The price appeals to the snobbishness in the purchaser. "A person may know that the more expensive model is no better than the cheaper one and yet prefer it for the mere fact that it is more expensive. He may want his friends and neighbors to know that he can afford spending all that money, or he may feel that his prestige and social position require that he should always buy the most expensive of everything."[44] Products that are visible to others and reflect one's taste, social position, or group standing are more likely to be purchased for their snob appeal.

Although a high price may enhance a brand's image, it may also price the brand out of the market for substantial groups of consumers.[45] Therefore, the costs of lost consumer groups must be weighed against the potential benefits of greater exclusivity, and thus, higher status and snob appeal.

Confidence in One's Judgment. A consumer who has little confidence in his or her ability to make a good product choice will rely on price and other cues to a greater extent than will a more confident person. In purchasing a component stereo system, the confident consumer is less likely to rely on price to indicate quality, whereas the consumer who is unsure of him- or herself will tend to rely on price in making his or her quality evaluation.

The Role of Place in Marketing Communications

The distribution component, or *place* variable, in marketing deals with such matters as channels of distribution, middlemen, and the types of retail outlets that carry products and services. The following discussion focuses exclusively

44. Tibor Scitovsky, "Some Consequences of the Habit of Judging Quality by Price," *Review of Economic Studies*, vol. 12, no. 2 (1944–1945), p. 103.
45. K. V. Ventataraman, "The Price-Quality Relationship in an Experimental Setting," *Journal of Advertising Research*, vol. 21 (August 1983), p. 51.

on the retailing component of place. Retail outlets perform important marketing communications roles by affecting consumers' perceptions of the merchandise carried in stores as well as their overall perception, or image, of the store itself.

Dimensions of Store Image. A store's *image* is composed of many dimensions, each interacting with the others to influence the overall image the store holds for each consumer group. Among the more important dimensions of a store's image are its architecture and exterior design, interior design, personnel, lines of merchandise, signs and logos, location, displays, and name.

Architecture and Exterior Design. Several aspects of a store's architecture and exterior design tell the consumer what to expect inside the store. In a sense, the store exterior is like the package on a product. Among the components making up the architecture and exterior design of a store are the shape, store front, and building materials used.

A store's *shape* can communicate subtle meanings to consumers. Transamerica constructed its 853-feet-tall structure in the shape of a pyramid. The purpose of the building's shape was to create a suitable image for a previously "obscure" company and to make it more widely known.[46] This structure, hovering over San Francisco, communicates that Transamerica is progressive and perhaps even ahead of its time (see Figure 3.5). It also has provided Transamerica with the basis for its creative "Power of the Pyramid" advertising campaign that appears both on television and in magazine ads. You may recall the television commercial showing King Kong scaling the Transamerica building only to be rebuked by a Fay Wray look-a-like. Eye-catching magazine ads actually used three-dimensional representations of the Transamerica building.

A store's *front* is usually the first part of the store that consumers come in contact with. The store front serves, in a sense, as the store's permanent advertisement. It provides information to consumers and conveys an impression about the store. For example, the store front for Harrods, the famous London department store, evokes a feeling of grandeur and stateliness (see Figure 3.6).

A store's *exterior appearance* is determined to a large extent by the building materials used in constructing the store. The Royal Bank in Toronto communicates financial strength and banking security by the building it occupies—each pane in the Royal Bank's glass exterior has been dipped in actual gold dust. The communications value is obvious (see Figure 3.7).

Interior Design. The store's interior must communicate an image that is consistent with that of the store's exterior. Some of the components of the store's interior design are color scheme, fixtures, lighting, and aisles.

A store's *color scheme* is one of the prime factors affecting buyer moods. As mentioned earlier in the chapter, colors have different emotional qualities,

46. Lloyd Shearer, "San Francisco's New Landmark—A Corporate Pyramid," *Parade*, January 14, 1973, p. 10.

Transamerica Building in San Francisco: Illustration of How a Building's Physical Size and Shape Communicate with Consumers   FIGURE 3.5

Source: Courtesy of Transamerica Corporation.

FIGURE 3.6   **Harrods in London: Illustration of the Communication Role of a Store's Exterior**

Source: Courtesy of the British Tourist Authority, 40 West 57th Street, New York, New York 10019.

**The Royal Bank in Toronto: Illustration of the Communication
Role of Building Materials**

FIGURE 3.7

and these emotional qualities must be appropriate for the kind of clientele served as well as for the class of merchandise being sold.

"Hot" colors such as red, orange, and peach affect the autonomic nervous system, increasing blood circulation, heart rate, muscular activity, and even sociability. These colors can also stimulate appetite and thirst. For this reason, many fast-food restaurants use these colors. Nightclubs frequently use the more relaxing colors of blue and associated hues to calm their customers and induce them to stay. Bright orange and yellow colors are suggested for retailers who sell bland-colored products, such as items often found in hardware stores.[47]

Colors can modify physical characteristics in a store. Light, cool tones in the blue family can be used to make a small store appear larger, while deep, warm tones (such as brown) on a narrow, distant wall and light, cool tones on long side walls can be used to make a long, narrow store appear shorter and wider.[48]

In-store *fixtures and lighting* can communicate elegance, traditionalism, conservatism, and a host of other feelings. For example, Banana Republic's jungle-outpost motif makes excellent use of fixtures. These fixtures cost between $75 and $100 per square foot, but daily sales per square foot range between $300 and $500 in most stores and are as high as $1,000 in New York City.[49] The following example further illustrates the importance of fixtures and lighting in contributing to a store's personality.

> A leading Southern department store originally possessed a distinctive image emphasizing the traditionalist values of its city. The lighting and fixtures were old-fashioned, and the total store atmosphere was congruent with the city-wide interest in antiques, old families, old homes, old restaurants, and historical monuments. Then the women's apparel merchandiser modernized his department. He introduced new fixtures and lighting, more high-fashion styling, and a promotional flavor similar to any aggressive store in this field. The fortunes of the store declined in a definite progression—first women's apparel, then children's, then men's, and finally all hard-line departments. A management consultant determined that the store had dissipated the strongest component in its image, the key to which lay in the women's apparel department. It had become indistinguishable from any other store. On his advice, the store set about restoring its traditionalist, distinctively period personality. The old-fashioned lights and fixtures and ultra-conservative styling were brought back. As management reformulated the symbolic meaning which had given the store distinction and character, its fortunes changed sharply for the better in the same progression as they had declined—first women's apparel and ultimately the hard-lines.[50]

All store features are important inasmuch as they contribute to producing a relaxed and pleasurable shopping experience. For example, Nordstrom's Inc., a Seattle-based apparel, shoe, and softgoods retailer that has a legendary rep-

47. Nory Miller, "Spaces for Selling," *American Institute of Architects Journal*, vol. 67 (July 1978), p. 38.
48. Louis Cheskin, *Color for Profit* (New York: Liveright Publishing Corporation, 1951), pp. 65–66.
49. "The Age of McFashion," *Newsweek*, September 28, 1987, pp. 66–68.
50. Pierre Martineau, "The Personality of the Retail Store," *Harvard Business Review*, vol. 36 (January-February 1958), pp. 50–51.

utation for its outstanding customer service, epitomizes the value of creating a pleasant store atmosphere. Nordstrom's atmosphere is slow and easygoing, almost like a small boutique. Many of the stores in the Nordstrom chain have piano players that play throughout the day.[51]

One study summarizes this section well. Marketing researchers found that consumers view *store atmosphere* (composed of a combination of such variables as lighting, layout, color, and music) as relatively important compared with shopping hours, parking access, travel time, product assortment, price, and service. They also found that degree of arousal and perceived pleasantness of the store atmosphere influenced (1) enjoyment of shopping, (2) time spent browsing, (3) willingness to talk to sales personnel, (4) tendency to spend more money than originally planned, and (5) likelihood of returning to the store.[52]

Merchandise.   The kind of merchandise a store carries reflects upon its image. Today, image is everything in retail merchandising. Outstanding stores that have established clear images through their merchandise selection include Esprit, The Gap, Aca Joe, Benetton, The Limited, and Banana Republic. These stores are geared to respond quickly to changing trends in consumer tastes. For example, at Benetton's, all sweaters are woven in gray wool and then dyed to match the colors that prove to be in demand each season.

Signs and Logos.   Many retailers realize that the signs they put up in front of their establishments perform an important function beyond merely catching the consumer's attention and identifying their store. A store's sign and its logo tell customers something about a store's personality. "A sign can say 'discount' or 'high fashion' with color and design as well as with words. More and more signs are geared to do just that."[53] For example, the Holiday Inn sign introduced in the mid-1980s projects a rather sophisticated, modern look in comparison to the garish and somewhat carnival-like sign used for years by this motel chain.

Summary

This chapter has described how a host of marketing mix variables communicate meaning to consumers.

The package, perhaps the most important component of the product as a communications device, reinforces associations established in advertising, breaks through competitive clutter at the point of purchase, and justifies price/value to the consumer. Package design relies upon the use of symbolism to

51. "Why Rivals Are Quaking As Nordstrom Heads East," *Business Week,* June 15, 1987, pp. 99–100.
52. Robert J. Donovan and John R. Rossiter, "Store Atmosphere: An Environmental Psychology Approach," *Journal of Retailing,* vol. 58 (Spring 1982), pp. 34–57.
53. "Chains Sign Up for Proper Image," *Chain Store Age,* December 1972, p. 37.

support a brand's image and to convey desired information to consumers. A number of package cues are used for this purpose, including color, design, shape, brand name, physical materials, and product information labeling. These cues must interact harmoniously to evoke within buyers the set of meanings intended by the marketing communicator. Sometimes, however, inconsistent package elements negate each other and produce poor package communication.

The brand name is perhaps the single most important element found on a package. The brand name works with package graphics and other product features to communicate and position the brand's image. The brand name identifies the product and differentiates it from others on the market. A good brand name can evoke a feeling of trust, confidence, security, strength, durability, speed, status, and many other desirable associations. A good brand name must satisfy a variety of fundamental requirements: It must describe the product and its benefits, help create and support a brand image, be brief, be memorable, be easy to pronounce, and so on.

Aside from the package and brand name, the product itself has physical characteristics that also perform significant communications functions. The product has color, shape, size, and other features that consumers perceive as important in their buying decisions.

The chapter also examined the marketing communications roles of two nonpromotional mix variables—price and place—by describing how these variables evoke meanings within consumers and how they interact with other marketing communications variables.

The marketing communications role of price stems from consumers' tendency to use price as an indicator of product quality. This tendency is most pronounced when (1) consumers perceive high brand-to-brand variance in quality within a product category; (2) the product is viewed by the consumer as an important additive, ingredient, or component of a larger product or its use contributes significantly to the quality of the final product; (3) the product is purchased as a gift; (4) brands of a product are physically homogeneous and brand names are unfamiliar to consumers; (5) the product is new to a market; (6) consumers lack experience and information about a product; (7) consumers wish to express status or prestige in using a product; and (8) consumers lack confidence in their ability to make a good product-choice decision.

Turning to the place variable, focus is placed on how retail stores project personalities and the factors that determine a store's image. Among the more important dimensions of a store's image are the architecture and exterior design, interior design, lines of merchandise, and signs and logos.

Discussion Questions

1. One of packaging's jobs is to "drive associations established in advertising into the consumer's mind." Give a specific explanation of what this means and use several marketplace illustrations to support your explanation.

2. What is "sensation transference"? Provide two specific examples to support your answer.

3. The notion underlying good packaging is "gestalt." Explain what this means and provide one example of an actual package that embodies this packaging ideal.

4. In your opinion, why do so many marketers use the words "new" and "improved" on their product packages?

5. Why do consumers rely on price as an indicator of product quality?

6. How may advertising desensitize consumers to a high price? Give several examples to support your answer.

7. How may a price that consumers perceive to be too low suppress sales? Provide actual examples to support your response.

8. Do you feel the consumer is getting "cheated" when he or she purchases a brand that is "status-priced"? Why or why not?

9. Consider the following products: (a) an automobile, (b) a pair of running shoes, (c) a new navy blue suit for job interviewing, (d) a set of automobile tires, (e) a bag of nachos, (f) an electric pencil sharpener, (g) a videocassette recorder, and (h) a diamond ring. Which of these products lend themselves to "quality pricing"? For those that do, what noneconomic factors may be present to permit such a pricing strategy?

10. A variety of factors influence the tendency for consumers to impute product quality from price cues. Which of the factors discussed in the text would also apply to industrial buyers? For example, would industrial buyers tend to rely on price as an indicator of quality when there is brand-to-brand variance in quality within a product category?

11. Select a store in your college/university community and describe the factors that contribute to your image of that store.

12. In what ways can a retailer project a quality-store image? A value-store image? A discount-store image?

Exercises

1. Pick two competitive brands in any product category and describe the meaning that the physical features (not the packages or brand names) of each brand communicates. Be specific with reference to color, shape, or other pertinent characteristics.

2. Select a different product category than used in Exercise 1 and apply the VIEW model to three competitive brands within that category. Do the following: (a) Discuss all four components of the model (i.e., define each component and how it applies to your selected product). (b) Weigh each component in the model in terms of your perception of its relative packaging importance in your chosen product category; do this by distributing ten points among the four components, with more points meaning more importance and the sum of the allocated points totaling exactly 10. (Note: this weighting procedure involves what marketing researchers refer to as a constant sum scale.) (c) Next, evaluate each brand in terms of your perception of its performance on each packaging component by assigning

a score from 10 ("performs extremely well") to 1 ("does not perform well"). (d) Combine the scores for each brand by multiplying the brand's performance on each component by the weight of that component and then summing the products of these four weighted scores. The summed score for each of your three chosen brands will reflect your perception of how good that brand's packaging is in terms of the VIEW model—the higher the score, the better the packaging in your opinion. Summarize the scores for the three brands in terms of an overall assessment of how good each brand's packaging is.

3. Select yet another product category and analyze the brand names for three competitive brands in that category. Analyze each brand name in terms of the fundamental requirements that were described in the text. Order the three brands in terms of which has the best, next best, and worst brand name. Support your ranking with specific reasons.

4. Identify five brand names (other than the ones used in the text) that, in your opinion, are especially notable in terms of their concreteness and the vividness of the imagery that the names evoke.

5. Architectural and exterior-design features play important roles in communicating meaning to consumers. For each of the following features, provide two illustrations of retail establishments in your university/college community and explain what the feature communicates to you: (a) physical size, (b) shape, (c) store facade, (d) outside lighting, (e) building materials, and (f) signs and logos. (Note: You should use different retail establishments to illustrate each feature.)

6. Identify five product categories in which there is one brand that charges premium prices in comparison with other brands in that category. For each product category, provide a detailed explanation of how the "premium pricer" is able to charge higher prices than competitors. Be sure to relate your explanations to the chapter's discussion of specific product and consumer characteristics that influence the likelihood that consumers will impute quality from price.

7. Offer your analysis of the Rubber Ducky condom campaign presented in the opening vignette. Using concepts from this and the previous chapter, explain the meaning conveyed to you by Rubber Ducky's package and brand name.

PART 2

Behavioral Foundations of Marketing Communications and Promotion Management

Part 2 builds a foundation for better understanding the nature and functioning of marketing communications and promotion management by examining four important topics: theory and research dealing with buyer behavior, attitude and persuasion theory, source and message factors in marketing communications, and adoption and diffusion processes.

Chapter 4 examines two sides of consumer behavior: the logical, thinking person and the pleasure-seeking, feeling person. **Chapter 5** continues the overview of buyer behavior by discussing the central concepts of attitudes and persuasion. These topics are important because marketing communications and promotion represent organized efforts to influence and persuade customers to make choices that are compatible with the marketing communicator's interests while simultaneously satisfying the customer's needs.

Chapter 6 describes source and message factors in marketing communications. One- versus two-sided messages, comparative advertising, humorous messages, subliminal advertising, source credibility, and endorser effectiveness are some of the topics covered. **Chapter 7** looks at the adoption and diffusion processes and the role of promotion management in facilitating these processes and achieving acceptance for new products.

Behavioral Foundations of Marketing Communications

TWO CONTRASTING AUTOMOBILE PURCHASES

he success of marketing communications strategy and action depends on an understanding of consumer behavior. However, this understanding is complicated by the fact that at times consumers differ rather dramatically in how and why they make purchase choices. The automobile purchase decisions of Jack and Doug, two businessmen aged "thirty something," illustrate this point.

Jack, who has always owned American-made automobiles, became extremely dissatisfied with his last purchase. Eventually, his dissatisfaction reached the point where he had to "take action." He began actively searching for another automobile by reviewing articles in *Consumer Reports*, visiting dealerships, paying close attention to automobile advertisements, and talking with friends and acquaintances. He knew exactly what he wanted in a new car—durability, good gas mileage, suitable passenger and luggage space, good resale value, and an automatic transmission that shifted smoothly. Jack narrowed the choice to three possibilities: a Toyota Camry, a Ford Taurus, and a Honda Accord. After test driving all three cars and engaging in intense negotiations with the three respective dealers, Jack selected the Ford Taurus. We see from this brief description that Jack was deliberate, logical, and systematic in his purchase.

Consider, by comparison, the automobile choice made by Doug, who has been generally satisfied with his 1987 Caprice; in fact, he was recently overheard saying "I'll hang onto the 'Old Chevy' for at least another year or two." To the surprise of his associates, Doug arrived at work one morning in a new, red Acura Legend Coupe. With virtually no prior thought about buying a new car (certainly not one with a $27,000 price tag), Doug, on a whim, stopped at an Acura dealership on his way home from work, fell in love with the red Acura Legend Coupe, and decided on the spot to purchase it. Though Doug had voiced some minor complaints about his Caprice, his friends suspected he had been fantasizing about owning a car more compatible with his "swinging" self-image.∎

Marketing communicators and promotion managers direct their efforts toward influencing *consumer choice behavior*. To accomplish this goal, appropriate advertising messages, packaging cues, brand names, sales presentations, and other communications activities are designed to stimulate the intended market to action. Because a fundamental understanding of consumer behavior is essential to a full appreciation of the intricacies of marketing communications and promotion management, the ideas presented in this chapter lay an important foundation to subsequent topical chapters.

This chapter looks at factors that determine consumers' responses to marketing communications stimuli and examines two alternative accounts of how consumers process and respond to these stimuli.

The first perspective examined is a **consumer information processing model (CIP).** From a CIP perspective, consumers such as Jack in the opening vignette are seen as logical, highly cognitive, and systematic decision makers. An alternative perspective is the **hedonic, experiential model (HEM),** which views consumers such as Doug as driven not by rational and purely logical considerations but, rather, by emotions in pursuit of "fun, fantasies, and feelings."[1]

The CIP Perspective and Information-Processing Stages

Successful marketing practitioners understand what makes consumers behave as they do. Marketing practitioners use this understanding to construct communication stimuli that consumers will attend to, understand, remember, and ultimately use in making consumption choices. The information-processing situation faced by consumers and the corresponding communications imperatives for marketing communicators have been described in the following terms:

1. Elizabeth C. Hirschman and Morris B. Holbrook, "Hedonic Consumption: Emerging Concepts, Methods, and Propositions," *Journal of Marketing*, vol. 46 (Summer 1982), pp. 92–101; Morris B. Holbrook and Elizabeth C. Hirschman, "The Experiential Aspects of Consumption: Consumer Fantasies, Feelings, and Fun," *Journal of Consumer Research*, vol. 9 (September 1982), pp. 132–140.

The consumer is constantly being bombarded with information which is potentially relevant for making choices. The consumer's reactions to that information, how that information is interpreted, and how it is combined or integrated with other information may have crucial impacts on choice. Hence, [marketing communicators'] decisions on what information to provide to consumers, how much to provide, and how to provide that information require knowledge of how consumers process, interpret, and integrate that information in making choices.[2]

The following sections discuss consumer information processing in terms of eight interrelated stages:[3]

1. *Exposure* to information.

2. *Selective attention*.

3. *Comprehension* of attended information.

4. *Degree of agreement* with comprehended information.

5. *Retention in memory* of accepted information.

6. *Ability to retrieve* information from memory.

7. *Consumer decision making* from available options.

8. *Action* taken on the basis of the decision.

Exposure to Information

The marketing communicator's fundamental task is to get information to consumers, who, it is hoped, will process the information and be persuaded to undertake the course of action advocated by the marketer. By definition, **exposure** means simply that consumers come in contact with the marketer's message (i.e., they see a magazine ad, hear a radio commercial, etc.). Exposure does not ensure that a message will have any impact; it is, however, an essential preliminary step to subsequent stages of information processing.

Selective Attention

Attention means to focus on and think about a message that one has been exposed to. Consumers attend to only a small fraction of marketing communications stimuli because demands placed on attention are great; therefore, attention must be highly *selective*. Selectivity is necessary because information-processing capacity is limited, and effective utilization of this capacity requires the consumer to allocate mental energy (i.e., processing capacity) to only information that is *relevant and of interest to current goals*.[4] For example, once their

---

2. James B. Bettman, *An Information Processing Theory of Consumer Choice* (Reading, MA: Addison-Wesley, 1979), p. 1.

3. William J. McGuire, "Some Internal Psychological Factors Influencing Consumer Choice," *Journal of Consumer Research*, vol. 4 (March 1976), pp. 302–319.

4. Bettman, *An Information Processing Theory of Consumer Choice*, p. 77.

initial curiosity is satisfied, most nonsmokers will pay relatively little attention to smokeless cigarette advertisements, because the product is less relevant to them than it is to smokers.[5]

There are three kinds of attention: involuntary, nonvoluntary, and voluntary. **Involuntary attention** requires little or no effort on the part of a receiver. A stimulus intrudes upon a person's consciousness even though he or she does not want it to. In this case, attention is gained on the basis of the intensity of the stimulus—examples include a loud sound and a bright light. **Nonvoluntary attention,** sometimes called spontaneous attention, occurs when a person is attracted to a stimulus and continues to pay attention because it holds interest for him or her. A person in this situation neither resists nor willfully attends to the stimulus initially. However, once the individual's attention is attracted, he or she continues to give attention because the stimulus has some benefit or relevance. Generally, advertisers create messages to gain the nonvoluntary attention of an audience, since in most situations consumers do not willfully search out advertising messages. Therefore, advertisements must attract and maintain attention by being interesting and, often, entertaining. Finally, **voluntary attention** occurs when a person *willfully* notices a stimulus. Consumers who are considering the purchase of, say, a new automobile will consciously direct their attention to automobile advertising. Also, people who have recently made important purchase decisions will voluntarily attend to messages to reassure themselves of the correctness of their decision.

As this discussion indicates, attention is highly selective. The following discussion reviews six sets of factors that explain selectivity; the first two factors represent message characteristics and the remaining four reflect consumer characteristics. In other words, attention selectivity is determined both by properties of the marketing stimulus itself and by factors that rest in the consumer's background and psychological makeup.

Stimulus Intensity.   Intense stimuli (those that are louder, more colorful, bigger, etc.) are more likely than less intense stimuli to attract attention. This is because it is difficult for consumers to avoid intense stimuli, thus leading to involuntary or nonvoluntary attention. One need only walk through a shopping mall, department store, or supermarket and observe the various packages, displays, and signs to appreciate the special efforts marketing communicators take to attract consumers' attention.

Advertisements, too, utilize *intensity* to attract attention. The advertisement for BASF computer diskettes, (see Figure 4.1), catches the reader's attention with its use of lightning and bright colors. Another example of stimulus intensity, which you may recall having seen on television several years ago, was Jacko (the Australian football player turned television actor) endorsing Energizer batteries. Jacko, dressed in a shirt resembling the graphics on the En-

---

5. For further discussion on smokeless cigarettes, see "RJR Sends 'Smokeless' Signals," *Advertising Age*, September 21, 1987, p. 87.

Use of Intensity to Attract Attention

FIGURE 4.1

Source: Advertisement (c) 1989; courtesy of BASF Corporation Information Systems.

ergizer battery, shouted frenetically, "What's the longest lasting battery you can buy? I'm gonna surprise ya. New Energizer." The fast pace of the commercial *demanded* the consumer's attention (and in so doing, probably offended a sizable number of viewers).

Stimulus Novelty.   Novel marketing communications using unusual, distinctive, or unpredictable stimuli are effective attention-attracting devices. Unusual stimuli tend to produce greater attention than those that are familiar to a receiver. This phenomenon is based on the behavioral concept of *human adaptation*. People tend to adapt to the conditions around them. As a stimulus becomes more familiar, people become desensitized to it. For example, if you drive past a billboard on the way to school or work each day, you probably notice it less on each occasion. If the billboard were removed, you probably would notice it was no longer there. In other words, we *notice by exception*.

The advertisement for *Woman's World* magazine (see Figure 4.2) shows a novel, eye-catching caricature of a periscope-headed man (Mr. Tunnel Vision). In reading this ad, you learn that it is aimed at media buyers who are not presently placing advertisements in this publication.

Past Reinforcement.   The first of four consumer characteristics that affect selective attention, *past reinforcement* represents the idea that people are more likely to attend those stimuli that have become associated with *rewards*. For example, attractive members of the opposite sex, babies, idyllic locations, appetizing food items, and gala events are some of the commonly used stimuli in advertisements. These symbols are inherently appealing to most people because they are firmly associated in our memories with past good times and enjoyment. Pepsi-Cola's most successful commercial ever showed an adorable little boy rollicking on the ground with puppies who were licking his face. Viewers could not help but pay attention to this commercial; its gaiety reminded people of their own children or perhaps of their own childhood.

Need States.   Consumers are most likely to attend those stimuli that are congruent with current goals and needs. A student who wants to move out of a dormitory and into an apartment, for example, will be constantly on the lookout for information pertaining to apartments. Classified ads and overheard conversations about apartments will be attended even when the apartment seeker is not actively looking for information.

In similar fashion, advertisements for food products are especially likely to be attended when people are hungry. For this reason, many restaurant and fast-food marketers advertise on radio during "drive time" when people are leaving work. Fast-food advertisers also promote their products on late-night television. You may recall the late-night television commercials for Burger King restaurants that asked rhetorically, "Aren't You Hungry?" and then proceeded to announce the expanded, late-night operating hours of many Burger King

Use of Novelty to Attract Attention

FIGURE 4.2

**SECOND IN A SERIES OF REVEALING
PORTRAITS OF MEDIA PEOPLE WHO
HAVEN'T CONSIDERED WOMAN'S WORLD.**

Mr. Tunnel Vision

Now there's a familiar face. His point of view is so narrow he misses a lot of what's going on in the world. Especially Woman's World.

There's never been anything like it. It's the bright light at the end of the tunnel for advertisers trying to reach women.

Too bad Mr. Tunnel Vision is blind to the fact that Woman's World is the plucky cinderella magazine enjoyed by over 5,000,000 loyal readers* week after week after week.

It's so chock-full of fast, fun, informative features on health and beauty, food and fashion, home decorating and needlecrafts, it's an advertiser's showcase.

When it comes to ad page visibility, there's no competition. Hardworking Woman's World pushes the Seven Sisters right out of the picture.

Unfortunately, Mr. Tunnel Vision has a blind spot when it comes to Woman's World. He chooses to close his eye to our product, our audience, our numbers.

Hopefully, you see the bigger media picture and will give us a call at (212) 953-3344.

Woman's World THE WOMAN'S WEEKLY

Sources: 1987 SMRB and MRI Fall 1987

Smart media people are exploring it.

Source: Courtesy Bauer Publishing.

outlets. McDonald's followed with a campaign featuring a moon-headed caricature of a man ("Mac Tonight") seated at a piano crooning a rendition of Bobby Darin's classic song "Mack the Knife." Both campaigns were attempts to increase late-night consumption of fast food. Whether they succeeded in substantially increasing evening sales is unknown; however, there is no doubt that these commercials grabbed the viewer's attention.

Persisting Values.   People are most likely to notice stimuli that relate to those aspects of life that they value highly. Advertisers and salespeople frequently use references to family, love, belongingness, caring, sharing, charity, and other persisting values to attract attention and influence consumer attitudes. When I was an MBA student with a wife and two small children, I was approached by an insurance agent who wanted to sell me a better policy than the one I owned. I vividly recall being told that if I were to die without life insurance, my wife might be forced to pursue a life of prostitution. This inane sales point certainly grabbed my attention. (The insensitive salesman also received a quick invitation to leave.)

Expectations.   Attention is guided by present expectations. We tend to notice what our mind-set has prepared us to look for. As a child you may have stared at a sky filled with cumulus clouds and attempted to locate certain figures and formations such as animals or people's faces. The sought-after figure was invariably found, provided you were sufficiently patient. In similar fashion, a consumer who is interested in purchasing clothing will notice ads for new styles and fashions when perusing a magazine yet will avoid ads for other products.

In sum, attention involves allocating limited processing capacity in a selective fashion. Effective marketing communications demands that stimuli be designed to activate consumer interest. This is no easy task: marketing communications environments (e.g., stores, advertising media, and noisy offices during sales presentations) are inherently cluttered with competitive stimuli and messages that also vie for the prospective customer's attention. Research shows that *clutter* in television advertising reduces the effectiveness of individual commercials. Commercials appearing later in a stream of multiple commercials and those for low-involvement products are particularly susceptible to clutter effects.[6]

Comprehension of What Is Attended

To comprehend is to understand and to make meaning out of complex stimuli and symbols. The term *comprehension* often is used interchangeably with *perception*; both terms refer to *interpretation*. Because people respond to their percep-

---

6. Peter H. Webb, "Consumer Initial Processing in a Difficult Media Environment," *Journal of Consumer Research*, vol. 6 (December 1979), pp. 225–236; Peter H. Webb and Michael L. Ray, "Effects of TV Clutter," *Journal of Advertising Research*, vol. 19 (June 1979), pp. 7–12.

tions of the world and not to the world as it actually is, the topic of comprehension or perception is one of the most important subjects in marketing communications.

The perceptual process of interpreting stimuli is called **perceptual encoding.** Two main stages are involved.[7] **Feature analysis** is the initial stage whereby a receiver examines the basic features of a stimulus (size, shape, color, angles, etc.) and from this makes a preliminary classification. For example, a consumer is able to distinguish a motorcycle from a bicycle by examining such features as size, presence of an engine, number of controls, and so on.

The second stage of perceptual encoding, **active-synthesis,** goes beyond merely examining physical features—it involves a more refined perception. The *context* or situation in which information is received plays a major role in determining what is perceived and interpreted. In other words, stored in consumers' memories are expectations of which stimuli (products, brands, people, and so on) are likely to be associated with certain contexts. Interpretation results from combining, or synthesizing, stimulus features with expectations of what should be present in the context in which a stimulus is perceived. For example, a simulated fur coat placed in the window of a discount clothing store (the context) is likely to be perceived as a cheap imitation; however, the same coat, when attractively merchandised in an expensive boutique (a different context), might now be looked upon as a high-quality, stylish garment.

The important point in the preceding discussion is that consumers' comprehension of marketing stimuli is determined by stimulus features and by characteristics of the consumers themselves. While expectations play a particularly important role, needs, moods, attitudes, and personality traits also influence consumer perceptions. A classic study demonstrates the relationship between a physiological need, hunger, and perception. A group of hungry sailors at a submarine base were asked to identify "barely perceptible" objects on a screen. Though the screen actually was blank, the hungry sailors reported seeing eating utensils.[8] Figure 4.3 provides a humorous, albeit revealing, illustration of selective perception.

An individual's *mood* also can influence his or her perception of stimulus objects. Recent research has found that when people are in a good mood they are more likely to retrieve from memory positive rather than negative material; are more likely to perceive the positive side of things; and, in turn, are more likely to respond positively to a variety of stimuli.[9] These findings have potentially important implications for both advertising strategy and personal selling activity. Both forms of marketing communications are potentially capable of

7. Bettman, *An Information Processing Theory of Consumer Choice*, p. 79.
8. David C. McClelland and J. W. Atkinson, "The Projective Expression of Needs: I. The Effect of Different Intensities of the Hunger Drive on Perception," *Journal of Psychology*, vol. 25 (April 14, 1948), pp. 205–222.
9. Alice M. Isen, Margaret Clark, Thomas E. Shalker, and Lynn Karp, "Affect, Accessibility of Material in Memory, and Behavior: A Cognitive Loop," *Journal of Personality and Social Psychology*, vol. 36 (January 1978), pp. 1–12; Meryl Paula Gardner, "Mood States and Consumer Behavior: A Critical Review," *Journal of Consumer Research*, vol. 12 (December 1985), pp. 281–300.

FIGURE 4.3   **Humorous Illustration of Selective Perception**

Source: Courtesy of John Jonik in *Psychology Today.*

placing consumers in positive moods and may enhance consumer perceptions and attitudes toward marketers' offerings.

People do indeed choose messages and parts of messages that best fit into their cognitive structures. Often this means that people *misinterpret* or *miscomprehend* messages so as to make them more consistent with their existing beliefs, opinions, or other cognitive-structure elements. This typically is done without our conscious awareness; nonetheless, distorted perception and message miscomprehension are facts of life.

A tragic case that points out the prevalence of selective perception and misinterpretation occurred in August 1988 when the crew of the USS *Vincennes* shot down an Iranian commercial airliner in the Persian Gulf, killing 290 people. The crew, under stress, had been warned that Iranian F-14 warplanes were in the area; therefore, they expected to see an F-I4 warplane attacking their ship. They "saw" a warplane (actually a commercial airliner) and shot it down—a tragic case of human error.[10]

An example of selective perception in a marketing context can be seen in a study that examined viewer miscomprehension of three forms of televised communication: programming content, commercials, and public-service announcements (PSAs). Nearly 3,000 people from test sites throughout the United States were exposed to two communication units from a pool of 60 units (i.e., 25 commercials, 13 PSAs, and 22 program excerpts). Respondents answered six true-false questions immediately after viewing the communication units. Two of the six statements were always true, and the remainder were always false; half related to objective facts, and half were inferences. A high rate of miscomprehension was uncovered across all three forms of communications, with an average miscomprehension of nearly 30 percent. Surprisingly, advertisements were not miscomprehended any more than the other communication forms.[11]

Agreement with What Is Comprehended

A fourth information-processing stage involves the manner by which individuals *yield to,* that is, agree with, what they have comprehended in a message. Comprehension by itself does not ensure that a persuasive message will change consumers' attitudes or influence their behavior. The quality of message arguments and the credibility of the source delivering a message are im-

10. "A Case of Human Error," *Newsweek*, August 15, 1988, pp. 18–19.
11. Jacob Jacoby and Wayne D. Hoyer, "Viewer Miscomprehension of Televised Communication: Selected Findings," *Journal of Marketing*, vol. 46 (Fall 1982), pp. 12–26. It is relevant to note that the Jacoby and Hoyer research has stimulated considerable controversy. See Gary T. Ford and Richard Yalch, "Viewer Miscomprehension of Televised Communications—A Comment," *Journal of Marketing*, vol. 46 (Fall 1982), pp. 27–31; Richard W. Mizerski, "Viewer Miscomprehension Findings Are Measurement Bound," *Journal of Marketing*, vol. 46 (Fall 1982), pp. 32–34; and Jacob Jacoby and Wayne D. Hoyer, "On Miscomprehending Televised Communication—A Rejoinder," *Journal of Marketing*, vol. 46 (Fall 1982), pp. 35–43.

portant determinants of whether consumers accept persuasive arguments. These topics are treated in detail in Chapter 6.

Retention of What Is Accepted and Search and Retrieval of Stored Information

Retention and search/retrieval are discussed together because both involve *memory* factors relevant to consumer choice. The subject of memory is a complex topic that has been studied extensively. Theories abound and research findings are often contradictory. Research problems need not greatly concern us here, however, because our interest in the subject is considerably less technical and more practical.[12]

From a practical perspective, memory involves the related issues of what consumers remember (i.e., recognize and recall) about marketing stimuli and how they access and retrieve information when making consumption choices. The subject of memory is inseparable from the process of learning, so the following paragraphs first discuss the basics of memory, then examine learning fundamentals, and, finally, place special emphasis on the practical application of memory and learning principles of marketing communications.

Memory consists of long-term memory (LTM), short-term, or working, memory (STM), and a set of sensory stores (SS). Information is received by one or more sensory receptors (sign, smell, touch, and so on) and passed to an appropriate SS, where it is rapidly lost (within fractions of a second) unless attention is allocated to the stimulus. Attended information is then transferred to STM, which serves as the center for current processing activity by bringing together information from the sense organs and from LTM. *Limited processing capacity* is the most outstanding characteristic of STM; individuals can process only a limited amount of information at any one time. An excessive amount of information will result in reduced recognition and recallability. Furthermore, information in STM that is not elaborated upon (i.e., thought about or rehearsed) will be lost from STM in about 30 seconds or less.[13] (This is what happens when you get a phone number from a telephone directory but then are distracted before you have an opportunity to dial the number. You must refer to the directory a second time and then repeat the number to yourself, i.e., rehearse it, so that you will not forget it again.) Telephone companies have

12. Several valuable sources for technical treatments of memory operations are available in the marketing literature. See Bettman, *An Information Processing Theory of Consumer Choice*, chap. 6; James B. Bettman, "Memory Factors in Consumer Choice: A Review," *Journal of Marketing*, vol. 43 (Spring 1979), pp. 37–53; Andrew A. Mitchell, "Cognitive Processes Initiated by Advertising," in *Information Processing Research in Advertising*, ed. R. J. Harris (Hillsdale, NJ: Lawrence Erlbaum Associates, 1983), pp. 13–42; Jerry C. Olson, "Theories of Information Encoding and Storage: Implications for Consumer Research," in *The Effect of Information on Consumer and Market Behavior*, ed. A. A. Mitchell (Chicago: American Marketing Association, 1978), pp. 49–60.
13. Richard M. Shiffrin and R. C. Atkinson, "Storage and Retrieval Processes in Long-Term Memory," *Psychological Review*, vol. 76 (March 23, 1969), pp. 179–193.

recognized this problem and have placed a redial feature on many new telephone models.

Information is transferred from STM to LTM, which cognitive psychologists consider to be a virtual storehouse of unlimited information. Information in LTM is organized into coherent and associated cognitive units, which are called *schemata, frames, scripts,* and *memory organization packets*. Though differing conceptually, all of these terms reflect the idea that LTM consists of *associative links* among related information, knowledge, and beliefs.[14] Figure 4.4 presents Doug's (the consumer described earlier in the chapter) *knowledge structure* for the Acura Legend Coupe.

The marketing practitioner's job is to provide positively valued information that consumers will store in long-term memory and that will increase the odds consumers will ultimately choose the marketer's offering over competitive options. Stated differently, the marketing communicator's task is to facilitate consumer learning. Learning represents changes in the content or organization of information in consumers' long-term memories.[15] Marketing communicators continuously attempt to alter consumers' long-term memories by facilitating learning of information that is compatible with the marketer's interest. For example, the advertisement for Claussen pickles (Figure 4.5) is an ingenious attempt to have consumers learn two points: that this brand of pickles is available only in refrigerated cases, and that Claussen pickles are fresher and tastier than competing, nonrefrigerated brands that are "parked on a grocer's warm shelf."

Three types of learning are relevant to marketing communications activity.[16] One type is the *strengthening of linkages among specific memory concepts*. The Ford Motor Company has invested heavily in promoting the theme "At Ford, Quality is Job 1." The purpose is to affix in consumer's memories a strong linkage between these two concepts, Ford cars and quality. Marketing communicators strengthen linkages by *repeating* claims, presenting them in more *concrete* fashion (a topic treated in some detail shortly), and finding creative ways to convey the point that the marketer's product has some desirable feature.

A second form of learning is to *facilitate the formation of entirely new linkages*. Consider, by way of illustration, what happens when scientists or government researchers report that a product has certain beneficial effects not heretofore known about. Companies quickly capitalize on these scientific findings by aggressively advertising the new product benefits. For example, in the late-1980s researchers reported that aspirin taken daily in small quantities reduces the likelihood of heart attacks. With this information, advertisers began actively promoting their brands as "heart-attack fighters." This was done in a semi-subtle fashion, but the point was clear: aspirin advertisers wanted consumers to learn that this product has benefits other than relieving headaches.

14. See Mitchell, "Cognitive Processes Initiated by Advertising."
15. Ibid.
16. Ibid.

FIGURE 4.4   **A Consumer's Knowledge Structure for an Acura Legend Coupe**

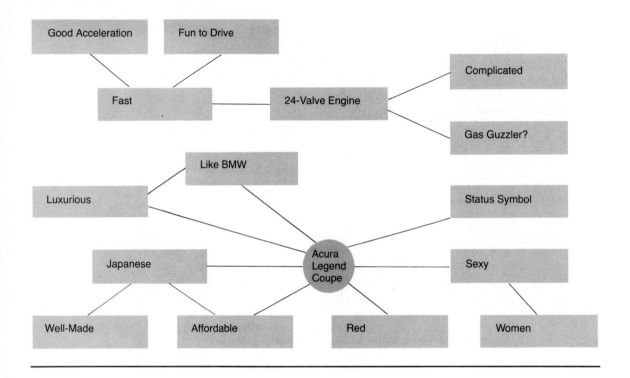

A new anti-heart-disease link was created for aspirin in the minds of many consumers. At about the same time, the makers of oat bran began promoting this product as a means of reducing cholesterol. Grocery stores could not keep the product in stock, because consumers had formed a new link between oat bran and good health.

A third form of learning, one which is more a result of consumer experience than of marketer influence, occurs *when new ideas or beliefs are formed when the consumer generalizes from previous experience.* On a humorous note, consider the cartoon in Figure 4.6 from Gary Larson's "The Far Side." (Look at it now before reading on.) Some people immediately pick up on the levity in the cartoon, while others see no humor at all. Understanding the cartoon's humor requires that one *generalize* to the situation in the cartoon from what happens in a basketball game. Specifically, when a player fires up a shot that completely misses the basket, fans spontaneously hoot in unison: "Airrrr ball . . . airrrr ball." Gary Larson has generalized to the plight of the Neanderthal man who is ridiculed ("Airrrr spearrrr . . . airrrrr spearrrr! . . .") when his spear falls short of the mammoth.

Facilitating Consumer Learning

FIGURE 4.5

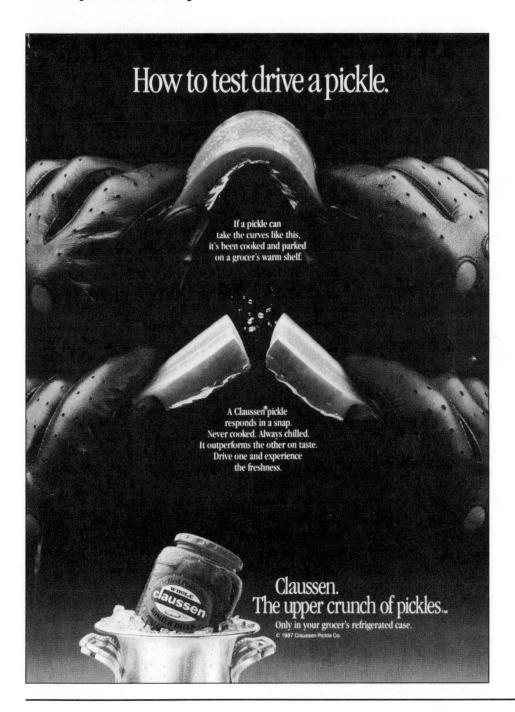

FIGURE 4.6   **Humorous Illustration of Generalization**

F O C U S   O N   P R O M O T I O N

The Use of Color to Identify
a Distinct Product Benefit

Marketing personnel at Procter & Gamble Co. faced a major challenge when they replaced unisex Luvs Deluxe diapers with diapers designed differently for boys and girls. P&G hoped that consumers would regard the specially designed diapers as superior to competitors' brands of unisex diapers. But how could they get that point across? The answer was simple: just take advantage of the widely recognized cue that blue signifies boy and pink stands for girl. P&G gave new Luvs diapers two different colors and packaged them in pink and blue boxes, thereby successfully conveying the point that their diapers for boys and girls are truly distinct.■

In similar fashion, many consumers develop generalizations such as "you only get what you pay for," "airline food is miserable," "store brands are good values," "Reebok shoes are made well," and so forth. Generalizations vary in their degree of generality and range from nonspecific generalizations (e.g., "you only get what you pay for") and product-specific generalizations (e.g., "American beers are bland in comparison with European beers") to brand-specific generalizations (e.g., "Campbell soups are good"). All levels of generalization influence consumer choice behavior, but the third level is probably of greatest relevance to marketers. It is important to point out that many brand-specific generalizations are a function of a company's product-quality and customer-service decisions rather than merely a result of advertising and other promotional activities.

Information that is learned and stored in memory has an impact on consumer choice behavior only when it is *searched and retrieved*. Precisely how retrieval occurs is beyond the scope of this chapter.[17] Suffice it to say that retrieval is facilitated when a new piece of information is linked, or associated, with another concept that is itself well known and easily accessed. Procter & Gamble used a simple but creative strategy to make it easy for consumers to remember that new Luvs diapers come in separate designs for boys and girls (see *Focus on Promotion*).

The Use of Concretizing and Imagery.   Concretizing and imagery are used extensively in marketing communications to facilitate both consumer learning and retrieval of product and brand informaton. *Concretizing* is based on the straightforward idea that it is easier for people to remember and retrieve

17. A good discussion is provided by Darlene V. Howard, *Cognitive Psychology* (New York: Macmillan, 1983), chap. 6.

concrete rather than abstract information. Examples of concretizing abound. Here are a few illustrations:

1. A discus thrower was the focal point in a television commercial for Delta Airlines designed to highlight the rather abstract theme that Delta uses teamwork. This was concretized by intermingling shots of the discus thrower in the process of releasing a discus with shots of Delta employees in action on their jobs. At the point of discus release, a Delta aircraft is shown lifting off. The discus thrower is embraced and congratulated by teammates as the commercial closes—a graphic juxtaposition of Delta's theme, "it takes teamwork to get an airline in flight."

2. To demonstrate the argument that Tums E-X is "twice as strong as Rolaids," the commercial shows a sledge hammer behind Tums and a regular-sized hammer behind Rolaids. The commercial cuts from product shots to shots of the sledge hammer driving in a nail twice as quickly as the regular hammer. This nail-driving comparison is a clear concretization of Tums' claim that it is twice as strong as Rolaids.

3. A television commercial for Kraft's Singles cheese shows two children dressed in identical animal-like costumes at a school play. The announcer states that just because things look the same, it does not mean they really are the same. The commercial then shows the children removing their animal heads to reveal the difference—one child is a brown-haired boy and the other is a red-haired girl. Continuing with this concrete illustration of how apparently equal-looking things are actually different, the commercial goes on to claim that only Kraft Singles, unlike "imitation" cheeses, contain the equivalent of five ounces of milk per slice.

4. The makers of Fab-1-Shot detergent needed to convey the selling point that their brand contains detergent and softener all in one convenient and easy-to-use package. They accomplished this by showing people in laundry rooms accompanied by music from "Sweet Georgia Brown" (the theme song of the Harlem Globetrotters and symbolic of basketball in general) shooting packets of Fab-1-Shot into washing machines. This commercial enables consumers to *imagine* themselves also using this convenient and labor-saving laundry product.

The preceding advertising examples highlight the important role of concretization in advertising. Underlying some of the illustrations, especially the last one, is the use of imagery. *Imagery*, by definition, represents a mental event involving visualization of a concept or relationship.[18] To better under-

18. Kathy A. Lutz and Richard J. Lutz, "Imagery-Eliciting Strategies: Review and Implications of Research," in *Advances in Consumer Research*, vol. 5, ed. H. Keith Hunt (Ann Arbor, MI: Association for Consumer Research, 1978), pp. 611–620. For a more recent in-depth treatment of imagery see Deborah J. MacInnis and Linda L. Price, "The Role of Imagery in Information Processing: Review and Extensions," *Journal of Consumer Research*, vol. 13 (March 1987), pp. 473–491.

stand the notion of imagery, think of the following words: pencil, tennis racket, dancing, duck-billed platypus, satisfaction, and standard deviation. The first two, pencil and tennis racket, no doubt evoke distinct images in your mind; dancing also probably elicits a visualization, and some of you might even possess a visual concept for platypus. It is doubtful, however, that you have an image for satisfaction or standard deviation, both of which are inherently abstract concepts.

Mental imagery plays an important role in various aspects of consumer information processing (comprehension, recall, retrieval). For practical purposes, the issue is this: What can marketing communicators do to elicit imagery? Three different strategies are possible: (1) use visual or pictorial stimuli, (2) present concrete verbal stimuli, and (3) provide imagery instructions.[19] Only the first two of these will be discussed, as the third is not used extensively in marketing communications, although advertisers occasionally instruct listeners or readers to imagine themselves engaged in some behavior. The advertisement for Club Med shown in Figure 4.7 illustrates this form of imaging instructions ("Imagine, for a moment, nothing . . .").

Pictures and visuals are best remembered (compared with abstract or concrete verbalizations) because pictures are best able to elicit imagery. A more formal explanation is provided by the **dual-coding theory,** which holds that pictures are represented in memory in verbal as well as visual form, whereas words are less likely to have visual representations.[20] It would be expected, therefore, that visual imagery would play an important role in advertising, point-of-purchase stimuli, and other marketing communications.

Consumer researchers have found that people remember significantly greater numbers of company names when the names are paired with meaningful pictorials. The name "Jack's Camera Shop," for example, is better remembered when the store name is presented along with a playing-card jack shown holding a movie camera to its eye.[21] Many marketing communicators use similar pictorials, as can be proven by a perusal of the Yellow Pages of any city telephone directory.

Visual imagery also reinforces the verbal content of an advertisement to create a favorable brand attitude and a desire to buy. The verbal message may stimulate short-run sales with price-off statements, but the nonverbal message sets the stage for long-term brand attitudes and sales.[22] Thus, a retailer may use more highly verbalized messages for immediate sales, whereas the manu-

---

19. Lutz and Lutz, "Imagery-Eliciting Strategies," pp. 611–620.
20. Allan Paivio, "Mental Imagery in Associative Learning and Memory," *Psychological Review,* vol. 76 (May 1969), pp. 241–263; John R. Rossiter and Larry Percy, "Visual Imaging Ability as a Mediator of Advertising Response," in *Advances in Consumer Research,* vol. 5, ed. H. Keith Hunt (Ann Arbor, MI: Association for Consumer Research, 1978), pp. 621–629.
21. Kathy A. Lutz and Richard J. Lutz, "The Effects of Interactive Imagery on Learning: Application to Advertising," *Journal of Applied Psychology,* vol. 62 (August 1977), pp. 493–498.
22. John R. Rossiter and Larry Percy, "Visual Imaging Ability as a Mediator of Advertising Response," pp. 621–629.

FIGURE 4.7   **Illustration of Imaging Instructions**

A CLUB MED VACATION BEGINS WHERE CIVILIZATION ENDS.

Imagine, for a moment, nothing.

No clocks. No ringing phones. No traffic jams. No radios. No newspapers. No crowds.

Now imagine this. An island village where aqua seas brush dazzling white shores. Where lush green palms line wandering pathways. Where crystal blue skies change magically to golden sunsets.

Where you can indulge in everything from windsurfing, snorkeling and tennis, to afternoon classes in water aerobics or painting, to secluded moments on miles of sun-drenched beach.

Imagine not just three meals, but three gourmet banquets every single day. With freshly baked breads and pastries and free-flowing wine.

Where evenings are always filled with entertainment, dancing and a special atmosphere that turns new faces into old friends in moments.

If all this captures your imagination, drop by and see your travel agent or call 1-800-CLUB MED. It just may be the beginning of the end of civilization as you know it.

CLUB MED
The antidote for civilization.™

Activities vary by village. © 1988 Club Med Sales, Inc., 40 West 57th Street, New York, NY 10019.

CIRCLE NO. 106 FOR READER SERVICE

facturer would be more likely to opt for the visual imagery (nonverbal), long-term sales approach.[23]

Finally, effective visual imagery in advertising can place the audience member in a number of imagined or fantasy-like situations that are conducive to sales of the marketer's product. For example, the advertisement may place the consumer behind the wheel of a powerful sports car cruising down a beautiful country road; in a pair of new basketball shoes leaping high off the floor over an opponent to make an acrobatic, Jordanesque dunk shot; in a fur coat attending an important social event; basking in the sun on an ocean liner cruising toward the Caribbean; rushing toward an important meeting carrying a new leather briefcase; or delivering packages of food and toys to needy people on Christmas Eve.

There is no doubt that imagery and concretization have numerous potential applications for advertising, point-of-purchase displays, personal selling, and other marketing communications practices.[24] Much of what we feel and visualize internally is what we see. Perhaps as much as 70 to 80 percent of what we learn is visual.[25]

Deciding among Alternatives

The six preceding stages have examined how consumers receive, encode, and store information that is pertinent to making consumption choices. Stored in consumers' memories are numerous information packets for different consumption alternatives. This information is in the form of bits and pieces of *knowledge* (e.g., Nike is a brand of tennis shoes), *specific beliefs* (e.g., "the Hyundai Excel is made in Korea"), and *evaluations of purchase consequences* (e.g., manufacturer reputability is more important than price when buying sophisticated electronic equipment).

The issue for present discussion is this: When making a purchase decision, how do consumers integrate and weigh information to decide whether to make a purchase, which product to purchase, which brand to choose, and at which retail outlet to actualize their choice?

Because *information processing capacity is limited*, consumers use simplifying strategies, or *heuristics* (rules), to make consumption choices. However, before describing specific heuristics, it should be instructive to review a decision that all of us have made and which, in many respects, is one of the most important decisions we will ever make—namely, the choice of which college or university to attend. For some of you, there really was no choice—you went to a school you had always planned on attending, or perhaps your parents

23. Ibid.
24. For an extensive list of visual imagery "principles," see John R. Rossiter, "Visual Imagery: Applications to Advertising," in *Advances in Consumer Research*, vol. 9, ed. A. A. Mitchell (Ann Arbor, MI: The Association for Consumer Research, 1982), pp. 101–106.
25. Roger N. Shepard, "The Mental Image," *American Psychologist*, vol. 33, February 1978, pp. 125–137.

insisted on a particular institution. Others, especially those of you who work full- or part-time, may have selected a school purely as a matter of convenience or affordability; in other words, you really did not seriously consider other institutions. But some of you actively evaluated several or many colleges and universities before making a final choice. The process was probably done in somewhat the following manner: you *received information* from a variety of schools and *formed preliminary impressions* of these institutions; you *established criteria* for evaluating schools (academic reputation, distance from home, cost, curricula, availability of financial assistance, quality of athletic programs, etc.); you *formed weights* regarding the relative importance of these various criteria; and you eventually *integrated this information* to arrive at the all-important choice of which college to attend. Now, let's use this example to better understand the different types of heuristics and the terminology that follows.

What heuristics do consumers use and what are the implications for marketing communications? Perhaps the simplest of all heuristics is **affect referral.**[26] With this strategy the individual simply calls from memory his or her attitude, or affect, toward relevant alternatives and picks that alternative for which the affect is most positive. In the college decision, for example, you may decide that you like a school simply because your friends attend it. There is no need to go through a rigorous decision-making process. In general, this type of choice strategy would be expected for frequently purchased items where risk is minimal. Such items are typically considered to be *low-involvement* purchases.

By comparison, consider the situation in which a decision involves considerable financial, product performance, or psychological risk. A **compensatory heuristic** is likely to be used when making a choice under such risky, or *high-involvement*, circumstances. To understand how and why compensation operates, it is important to realize that rarely is a particular consumption alternative completely superior or dominant over other relevant alternatives. Although one brand may be preferable to others with respect to one, two, or several benefits, it is unlikely that it is superior in terms of all attributes or benefits that consumers are seeking. In making choices under such circumstances, consumers must give something up in order to get something else. High-involvement decision making requires that trade-offs be made. If you want more of a particular benefit, you typically have to pay a higher price; if you want to pay less, you often give something up in terms of performance, dependability, or durability. Returning to the university choice decision, a frequent trade-off is between the quality of academic and athletic programs.

The compensatory heuristic requires that the consumer (1) establish importance weightings for each salient choice criterion, (2) form perceptions (beliefs) of how well each alternative satisfies each criterion, (3) integrate this information somehow, and (4) arrive at a total "score" for each relevant alternative. Theoretically, then, choice is made by selecting the alternative with

26. Peter L. Wright, "Consumer Choice Strategies: Simplifying vs. Optimizing," *Journal of Marketing Research*, vol. 11 (February 1975), pp. 60–67.

the highest overall score. The chosen alternative probably is not the best in terms of all criteria, but its superiority on some criteria offsets, or compensates for, its lesser performance on other criteria.[27]

In addition to compensatory choice behavior, consumers use a variety of so-called **noncompensatory heuristics.** Three in particular are the conjunctive, disjunctive, and lexicographic heuristics. According to the *conjunctive heuristic,* which is derived from the word "conjoin," the consumer establishes cutoffs, or minima, on all pertinent choice criteria; an alternative is retained for further consideration only if it meets or exceeds *all* minima. As seen in the hypothetical university choice, for example, a particular consumer may establish these cutoffs: a viable school must have a major in architecture, be no farther than 500 miles from home, and cost no more than $5,000 per year. All schools meeting these criteria receive further consideration, perhaps involving the application of a compensatory heuristic to arrive at a choice from the remaining options.

The *disjunctive heuristic,* derived from the word "disjoin," is a second noncompensatory heuristic. Whereas the conjunctive heuristic requires that an acceptable alternative meet or exceed the minimum on choice criterion 1 *and* choice criterion 2 *and* choice criterion n, the disjunctive heuristic accepts an alternative if it meets *any* of the minimum standards. That is, an alternative is acceptable if it meets or exceeds choice criterion 1 *or* choice criterion 2 *or* choice criterion n. It should be apparent that a disjunctive heuristic is basically one of "nearly anything is acceptable," which would represent the choice behavior of only the most indiscriminate of consumers under the rarest of circumstances.

A third noncompensatory heuristic, the *lexicographic heuristic,* operates in a fashion analogous to the way in which a lexicon (dictionary) is compiled and the way in which users search to locate a word. To find a word, for example, *communicate,* one searches for words beginning with c, then *co, com,* and so on until the desired word, *communicate,* is located. In other words, there is a strict alphabetical ordering of words in a dictionary. The lexicographic heuristic embodies the same notion, namely, for a particular purchase decision, consumers' choice criteria are ranked according to relative importance. Choice alternatives are then evaluated on each criterion, starting with the most important one. An alternative is selected if it is judged superior on the most important criterion. If, however, as often is the case, two or more alternatives are judged as equal on the most important criterion, then the consumer examines these alternatives on the next most important criterion, then on the next most important, and so on until the tie is broken.

The foregoing discussion should not be misinterpreted to mean that consumers invariably use one and only one choice heuristic. On the contrary, a

---

27. The best known illustration of compensation in consumer behavior is the Fishbein attitude model, which states that one's attitude toward performing an act is the sum of one's beliefs regarding the consequences of the act weighed by one's evaluations of these consequences. Further discussion of this model will be delayed until Chapter 5, which describes attitude formation and change in the context of the general topic of persuasion.

more likely possibility, especially in high-involvement decisions, is that **phased strategies** are used, that is, consumers use a combination of heuristics in sequence or in phase with one another.[28] Consider a personal computer purchase decision that Susan Allender, a self-employed person who operates a home-based direct-mail company, plans to make. Susan needs a computer to maintain a mailing list, control inventory, and use for accounting and word-processing purposes. After considerable search and research, she concludes she needs a computer that has a hard disk, 640K of RAM, a laser printer, and a total price not exceeding $4,000.

Susan's initial phase (using a conjunctive heuristic) is to eliminate all models that fail to satisfy all of her minimal requirements. Two remaining options, an IBM model and a Zenith, are then evaluated attribute by attribute using a compensatory heuristic. Susan regards these models as best for her needs but is undecided about which is better. After considerable additional deliberation, she reorders the relative weighting of choice criteria such that manufacturer reputability takes on added significance. Her choice, ultimately, is the IBM, because she would rather pay a higher price to ensure that her new acquisition will be backed by the best-known firm in the computer industry.

Acting on the Basis of the Decision

It might seem that consumer choice behavior operates in a simple, lock step fashion. This, however, is not necessarily the case. People do not always behave in a manner consistent with their preferences.[29] A major reason is the presence of events that disrupt, inhibit, or otherwise prevent a person from following through on his or her intentions.[30] Take the case of the hypothetical computer purchaser described previously. Although Susan decided to purchase an IBM, when she goes to a preferred retail outlet to make the purchase, she might find that it is out of stock, that it is higher priced than she had originally thought, or that the salespersons are not as knowledgeable as she had hoped. Any of these factors could result in her purchasing the alternative Zenith computer, her second choice, or even some other computer.

Situational factors are even more prevalent in the case of low-involvement consumer behavior. Stock-outs, price-offs, in-store promotions, and shopping at a store other than where one regularly shops are just some of the factors that lead to the purchase of brands that are not necessarily the most preferred and which would not be the predicted choice based on some heuristic, such as affect referral.

What all this means for marketing communications and promotion management is that the three modes of marketing (as discussed in Chapter 1) must

---

28. Bettman, *Information Processing Theory*, p. 184.
29. Martin Fishbein and Icek Ajzen, *Beliefs, Attitude, Intention, and Behavior: An Introduction to Theory and Research* (Reading, MA: Addison-Wesley, 1975).
30. For further reading on the role of situational variables, see Russell W. Belk, "Situational Variables and Consumer Behavior," *Journal of Consumer Research*, vol. 2 (December 1975), pp. 157–164.

be coordinated and integrated to achieve the desired objectives. That is, marketers must design a *basic offer* that is congruent with consumer wants, employ *persuasive communications* that consumers will process and that will be persuasive, and devise *promotional inducements* that will influence consumers to choose the marketer's offering at the point of purchase.

A CIP Wrap-Up

A detailed account of consumer information processing has been presented to this point. As noted in the introduction, the CIP perspective provides an appropriate description of consumer behavior when the behavior is deliberate, thoughtful, or, in short, *highly cognitive.* Much consumer behavior, as well as the behavior of industrial and organizational buyers, is of this nature. On the other hand, much behavior is motivated more by emotional, hedonic, and experiential considerations. Therefore, we need to consider the HEM perpective and the implications it holds for promotion managers and marketing communicators.

The HEM Perspective

The hedonic, experiential model (HEM) is an alternative view to the CIP framework, though the two are not necessarily mutually exclusive. Products viewed from an HEM perspective are more than mere objective entities (perfume, cars, sofas, etc.) and are, instead, subjective symbols representing love, pride, status, achievement, pleasure, and so forth. **Hedonic consumption** is the consumer's multisensory images, fantasies, and emotional arousal elicited when purchasing and using products.[31]

People often consume services and products in the pursuit of fun, amusement, fantasy, arousal, sensory stimulation, or just sheer enjoyment.[32] Products most compatible with the hedonic perspective include the performing arts (opera, modern dance), the so-called plastic arts (photography, crafts), popular forms of entertainment (movies, rock concerts), fashion apparel, sporting events, leisure activities, and recreational pursuits (wind surfing, hang gliding, golf, tennis).[33]

From a marketing communications viewpoint, how do the HEM and CIP perspectives differ? Whereas the communication of CIP-relevant products tends to emphasize verbal stimuli and is designed to affect consumers' product knowledge and beliefs, the communication of hedonic-relevant products emphasizes nonverbal content and is intended to generate images, fantasies, and positive emotions and feelings. Thus, product consumption from the hedonic

---

31. Hirschman and Holbrook, "Hedonic Consumption," and Holbrook and Hirschman, "Experiential Aspects of Consumption."
32. Hirschman and Holbrook, "Hedonic Consumption."
33. Ibid., p. 91.

perspective results from the *anticipation* of having fun, fulfilling fantasies, receiving enjoyment, or having pleasurable feelings. Comparatively, product choice behavior from the CIP perspective is based on the *thoughtful evaluation* that the chosen alternative will be more functional and provide better results than will other alternatives.

A vivid contrast between the CIP and HEM orientations is illustrated in the differences in the advertisements for Miracle Whip (Figure 4.8) and Chantilly (Figure 4.9). The former ad uses verbal content in describing objective product benefits, with the intent of convincing consumers that Miracle Whip is better for them because it is lower in fat, contains fewer calories and less cholesterol, and tastes tangier than mayonnaise. The ad exemplifies the CIP approach in that it attempts to move the consumer through all the CIP stages discussed previously. That is, Kraft, Inc., which markets Miracle Whip, expects the consumer to *attend* the specific message arguments (e.g., 36 percent less fat), *agree* with them, *retain* them in memory, use this information to *form* a more favorable attitude toward Miracle Whip and a less favorable evaluation of mayonnaise, and, ultimately, *choose* Miracle Whip over mayonnaise the next time the consumer has a need for this general product category.

Comparatively, the Chantilly advertisement (see Figure 4.9) offers absolutely no explicit information about specific product features. Rather, the ad appeals to the consumer's *feelings* (for those readers who have experienced a similar state of intense romance) or perhaps *fantasies* (for those wishing for such a relationship). In any event, the apparent communications objective is to encourage men to purchase Chantilly perfume for their lovers or for women to purchase it for themselves in anticipation of romantic encounters.

The prior discussion and examples have emphasized advertising, but it should be apparent that the differences between CIP and HEM perspectives of consumer behavior apply as well to other forms of marketing communications, especially to personal selling. A salesperson may emphasize product features and tangible benefits in attempting to sell a product, or he or she may also attempt to convey the fun, fantasies, and pleasures that prospective customers can enjoy with product ownership. Successful salespersons employ both approaches and orient the dominant approach to the consumer's specific "hot buttons." That is, successful salespersons know how to adapt their presentations to different customers.

Finally, no one marketing-communications approach, whether CIP or HEM, is effective in all instances. What works best depends on the specific character and needs of the targeted market segment and on the form of communication and marketing effort competitors undertake.

FIGURE 4.9   **The HEM Approach to Advertising**

Source: Courtesy Houbigant Inc.

Summary

This chapter describes the fundamentals of consumer choice behavior. Two relatively distinct perspectives of choice behavior are the consumer information processing (CIP) perspective and the hedonic, experiential model (HEM). The CIP approach views the consumer as an analytical, systematic, and logical decision maker. According to this perspective, consumers are motivated to achieve desired goal states. The CIP process involves attending, encoding, retaining, retrieving, and integrating information so that a person can achieve a suitable choice among consumption alternatives.

The HEM perspective is an alternative to the CIP view. Supporters of this approach believe that consumer choice for many products results from the mere pursuit of fun, fantasy, and feeling. Therefore, some consumer behavior (such as in the consumption of the arts, popular forms of entertainment, and leisure activities) is based on emotional considerations rather than on objective, functional, and economic factors.

The distinction between the CIP and HEM views of consumer choice is an important one for marketing communications and promotion management. The techniques and creative strategies for affecting consumer choice behavior clearly are a function of the prevailing consumer orientation. Specific implications and appropriate strategies are emphasized throughout the chapter.

Discussion Questions

1. Describe the eight information-processing stages.
2. Distinguish among involuntary, nonvoluntary, and voluntary attention.
3. Attention is said to be highly selective. What does this mean?
4. Describe four or five general factors that account for the selectivity of attention.
5. In what sense are marketing communications environments cluttered? Give an example.
6. Explain each of the following related concepts: perceptual encoding, feature analysis, and active-synthesis.
7. Why do consumers selectively perceive, distort, and miscomprehend messages? Present an example of misperception based on your personal experience that parallels the USS *Vincennes* example given in the text.
8. What is meant by "concretizing"? Provide two examples.
9. What is "imagery"? Provide two examples of imagery-eliciting advertisements.
10. What is a heuristic? Distinguish between compensatory and noncompensatory heuristics.
11. Distinguish between conjunctive and disjunctive choice heuristics using the choice of a new compact disc player as your example.
12. In what sense would the consumption of a Saturday afternoon college football game represent an hedonic- or experiential-based behavior.

Exercises

1. Review advertisements and provide two examples each of ads that attempt to attract consumer attention via the use of intense and novel stimuli.

2. Provide specific illustrations of advertisements that attempt to facilitate consumer learning by establishing linkages between specific memory concepts or by attempting to establish entirely new linkages.

3. Interview a small sample of consumers and attempt to discover some of the generalizations that people have about McDonald's, Burger King, and other fast food chains.

4. Identify two examples of advertisements that attempt to promote mental imagery.

5. Provide two examples each of concrete and abstract visual advertisements.

6. Provide two examples of how package designers use concrete visuals.

7. Describe a purchase decision you have made within the past year and characterize it in terms of the decision heuristics you might have used.

8. Provide examples of advertisements that appear to be directed at CIP consumers and examples of ads directed at HEM consumers.

Attitudes and Persuasion in Marketing Communications

AMERICANS' SHIFTING ATTITUDES TOWARD AND PREFERENCES FOR BEVERAGES

American drinking habits have changed greatly during the last third of the twentieth century. Historically, most Americans became coffee drinkers upon reaching adulthood, yet today the majority of consumers of all ages prefer soft drinks and rarely, if ever, drink coffee. Coffee and tea were traditionally consumed during pre-noon hours, but today many Americans instead choose caffeinated soft drinks as their morning picker-upper. In fact, over 10 percent of all soft drinks sold are consumed during the morning hours. In 1988, Coca-Cola experimented in select markets with an advertising campaign promoting Coke for breakfast.

Alcohol drinking preferences have also changed. Fewer Americans are drinking dark liquors (e.g., whiskey and scotch), while sales of light liquors (e.g., vodka and gin) have increased. Overall, Americans have reduced their consumption of hard liquors and have turned more to beer and wine.

Preferences for beer and wine have also shifted in recent decades. Until the 1980s, beer consumed in the United States was almost entirely popular-priced domestic brands; sales of premium-priced imported brands have increased greatly in recent years. Wine drinking has also changed: Americans are consuming more expensive wines as well as a greater proportion of domestically produced brands. Discriminating American consumers traditionally showed a strong preference for foreign wines, especially French and Italian brands. Today more Americans are consuming premium American wines, such as Cabernets and Chardonnays priced at $4 or $5 a bottle. Some have referred to this trend as the "new California Gold rush" because marketing premium Californian wines has become very profitable.[1]■

With reference to the opening vignette, why do people form favorable attitudes toward certain types of beverages? How long lasting are these attitudes? What can marketing communicators do to change consumers' attitudes? This chapter addresses these and related topics by examining two specific subjects that are fundamental to understanding the workings of marketing communications: attitudes and persuasion.

Attitudes and persuasion are closely related topics. To understand one requires an understanding of the other. **Attitude** is a mental property of the consumer, whereas **persuasion** is an effort by a marketing communicator to *influence* the consumer's attitude and behavior in some manner.

The analogy of an automobile race should clarify the distinction between attitude and persuasion and their mutual interdependence. An automobile race consists of a driver with a vehicle and the objective of beating competitive drivers to the finish line. So it is in promotion management and marketing communications. The driver (marketing communicator) has a vehicle at his disposal (the markets' thoughts about and opinions of—i.e., attitude toward—his brand). He is trying to accelerate the vehicle (persuade the market) toward the finish line before fellow drivers (the competition) get there. Thus attitude is the object and persuasion the objective of the marketing communications "race."

For example, the opening vignette indicated that American's drinking preferences have changed greatly in the last few decades. Many consumers hold neutral or unfavorable attitudes toward coffee; coffee marketers would like to persuade consumers to have more favorable attitudes and purchase greater quantities of coffee. On the other hand, most consumers hold favorable attitudes toward soft drinks. Marketing communicators for these products hope to beat competitive drivers to the finish line (the race for market share, Pepsi versus Coke, and so on).

The Nature and Role of Attitudes

Attitude is one of the most extensively examined topics in all of marketing. The reason is simple: Understanding how people feel toward different objects (such as brands within a product category) makes it possible to predict

1. Discussion on the new "gold rush" is based on Tony Clifton, "A Rush for Liquid 'Gold'," *Time*, July 11, 1988, pp. 48–49.

and influence behavior so that it is compatible with the communicator's interests.

What Is an Attitude?

Attitudes are *hypothetical constructs;* they cannot be seen, touched, heard, or smelled. Because attitudes cannot be observed, a variety of perspectives have developed over the years in attempting to describe what they are.[2] Fortunately, there is now widespread agreement that the term attitude should be used to refer to a general and enduring positive or negative feeling about some person, object, or issue.[3] "I like Diet Pepsi," "Hearing people say 'Let's do lunch' nauseates me," and "I love the Boston Celtics" are examples of consumer attitudes that express feelings toward different objects with varying degrees of intensity.

The preceding description of attitude focuses on feelings and evaluations, or what is commonly referred to as the **affective** component of an attitude. The affective component is what is generally being referred to when people use the word "attitude." However, attitude theorists recognize two additional components, cognitive and conative.[4] The **cognitive** component refers to a person's *beliefs* (i.e., knowledge and thoughts, which sometimes are erroneous) about an object or issue (e.g., "Reebok shoes are more stylish than Nike"; "Nike Air Jordans are high-quality basketball shoes"). The **conative** component represents one's behavioral tendency toward an object. In consumer-behavior terms, the conative component represents a consumer's *intention* to purchase a specific item. Gordon W. Allport integrated these two components when formulating his classic definition: "Attitudes are learned predispositions to respond to an object or class of objects in a consistently favorable or unfavorable way."[5]

A clear progression is implied: from initial cognition, to affection, to conation. An individual becomes aware of an object, such as a new product, then acquires information and forms beliefs about the product's ability to satisfy consumption needs (cognitive component). Beliefs are integrated and evaluated, and feelings toward the product are developed (affective component). On the basis of these feelings, an intention is formed to purchase or not to purchase the new product (conative component). An attitude, then, is character-

2. A number of major theories of attitudes and attitude-change processes have developed over the last half century. Seven particularly significant theories are reviewed in Richard E. Petty and John T. Cacioppo, *Attitudes and Persuasion: Classic and Contemporary Approaches* (Dubuque, IA: Wm. C. Brown Company, 1981).

3. Ibid., p. 7.

4. See, for example, Richard P. Bagozzi, Alice M. Tybout, C. Samuel Craig, and Brian Sternthal, "The Construct Validity of the Tripartite Classification of Attitudes," *Journal of Marketing Research,* vol. 16 (February 1979), pp. 88–95; Richard J. Lutz, "An Experimental Investigation of Causal Relations among Cognitions, Affect, and Behavioral Intention," *Journal of Consumer Research,* vol. 3 (March 1977), pp. 197–208.

5. Gordon W. Allport, "Attitudes," in *A Handbook of Social Psychology,* ed. C. A. Murchinson (Worcester, MA: Clark University Press, 1935), pp. 798–844.

ized by progressing from "thinking" (cognitive), to "feeling" (affective), to "behaving" (conative).[6]

An illustration will help clarify the notion of attitude progression. Consider the description in the previous chapter of Jack's purchase of a Ford Taurus. Jack knew precisely what he wanted in a new automobile: economy, reasonable passenger and luggage space, good resale value, and a smooth-shifting automatic transmission. He acquired a variety of information about the Ford Taurus and other models from friends and acquaintances, advertisements, and his own shopping experiences. He formed beliefs about product features and specific automobile models as a result of this information search and processing activity. These beliefs (representing the cognitive-attitude component) led Jack to form specific feelings (affective component) about various automobile models. He liked the Toyota Camry but considered it a bit too expensive for his budget. He also liked the Honda Accord, except for what he considered to be a rather jerky-shifting automatic transmission. Overall, his most positive affect was toward the Ford Taurus, and his intention to purchase this model (conative component) finally materialized when he drove the new automobile from the Ford dealership.

Why Have Attitudes?

Why do people form attitudes? What role or function do attitudes serve?[7] Attitudes are generally considered to perform any of four functions: utilitarian, value-expressive, ego-defensive, and knowledge functions.[8]

Utilitarian Function.   An attitude has utility for consumers by facilitating and simplifying decision making. Jack's belief that the Honda Accord does not shift smoothly enabled him to eliminate this model from further serious consideration and thus saved him the time, and perhaps mental turmoil, of having to choose between the Ford Taurus and the Honda Accord.

Marketing communicators appeal to the utilitarian function when they attempt to capitalize on, or sometimes exploit, consumer beliefs. For example, many consumers now know that saturated fats are bad and that excessive in-

6. The view that this strict progression applies to all behavior and that cognition must necessarily precede affect is not uncontested. Various alternative "hierarchies of effect" have been postulated. For further discussion, see Michael L. Ray, "Marketing Communication and the Hierarchy of Effects," in *New Models for Mass Communication Research*, ed. P. Clarke (Beverly Hills, CA: Sage Publications, 1973), pp. 147–175. For a thorough recent review see Thomas E. Barry, "The Development of the Hierarchy of Effects," in *Current Issues and Research in Advertising*, eds. James H. Leigh and Claude R. Martin, Jr. (Ann Arbor, MI: Division of Research, Graduate School of Business, University of Michigan, 1987), pp. 251–296.
7. Parts of the following discussion extend from similar treatments by Petty and Cacioppo, *Attitudes and Persuasion*, pp. 7–8, and by Henry Assael, *Consumer Behavior and Marketing Action* (Boston, MA: Kent Publishing Company, 1984), pp. 170–172.
8. Daniel Katz, "The Functional Approach to the Study of Attitudes," *Public Opinion Quarterly*, vol. 24 (Summer 1960), pp. 163–204.

take of food high in saturated fats can lead to dangerous levels of the "bad" variety of cholesterol (low-density lipoprotein, or LDP). Holding the attitude that saturated fat is bad thus serves a utilitarian function for consumers by steering them away from food items high in saturated-fat content.

Value-Expressive Function.

When holding a certain attitude allows a person to express an important value to others, the value-expressive function is served. For example, expressing one's pleasure from attending symphonies and operas tells others that one has sophistication. Telling friends that you support Mothers Against Drunk Driving (MADD) might label you as a concerned and responsible person. Similarly, in a consumer context, expressing a favorable opinion toward a certain clothing store may serve to identify you as a discriminating dresser.

Appeals to the value-expressive function are common in marketing communications. Salespeople routinely appeal to value expressiveness by emphasizing virtues, such as prestige and status, that the customer will enjoy by buying a certain brand. Many advertisements during the 1980s portrayed young professional types using or consuming products such as Mexican beers, sushi, pasta makers, and coffee-bean grinders. These products became emblematic of the "yuppie" crowd, and for a consumer to express a favorable attitude toward, say, eating sushi, served a value-expressive function by saying "I'm hip."

Ego-Defensive Function.

Attitudes that are held because they help protect people from unflattering truths about themselves serve the ego-defensive function. Students who spend too much time partying and having fun can defend their egos by saying "I'm in college to have a good time; I don't care about grades." The heavy drinker protects himself by holding the view that "I'm just a social drinker." The smoker who can't break the habit may take comfort in thinking "I could quit if I really wanted to."

Advertisers of self-help and personal-care products are especially likely to appeal to ego defense. For example, one advertiser probably had this in mind when introducing the catchy theme "You're not getting older, you're getting better." Alcohol and drug rehabilitation centers attempt to impress upon the abuser (or the abuser's family) that he or she *does* have a problem and that the first step toward solution is to admit it. Admitting the problem is virtually equivalent to discarding one's ego-defensive attitude.

Knowledge Function.

A final function that attitudes perform is assisting people in organizing knowledge and in better understanding the events and people around them. For example, those people who hold the attitude that investment bankers and other financial types are "shady characters" probably had little difficulty understanding, in their minds, why insider trading scandals rocked Wall Street in the mid-1980s and why on October 19, 1988 ("Black Monday"), a massive fall in stock prices occurred. People who dislike

Republicans readily "understand" how the Reagan Administration could have become involved in the Iran-Contra affair. Consumers who retain World War II animosities toward Japan find it easy to omit Japanese automobiles from consideration when in the market for a new car.

It should be understood that none of the preceding views are necessarily endorsed here. They do, however, demonstrate how attitudes, held rightly or wrongly, serve knowledge functions for people, including consumers, in all walks of life.

In summary, attitudes perform various useful functions for consumers. Attitudes are also helpful to marketing communicators, who by diagnosing attitudes can understand why consumers behave as they do and can predict how consumers might behave in the future.

How Well Do Attitudes Predict Behavior?

Marketing communicators research consumers' attitudes with expectations of being able to accurately predict which brands consumers will purchase, in which stores they will shop, and so on. Whether attitudes do, in fact, predict behavior accurately has been controversial in the study of consumer behavior as well as in the more general study of psychology.

A major review of the psychology literature on attitude-behavior consistency concluded that it is *unlikely* that attitudes are closely related to overt behavior.[9] Researchers in a marketing context examined the relationship between consumers' attitudes toward brands of major appliances and their actual brand choices and found that attitudes were not strongly predictive of which brands consumers chose.[10]

Do these findings mean that attitudes do not predict behavior? The answer is, emphatically, "No!" Attitudes can and do provide reasonably accurate predictions of behavior under the right conditions. The real issue is determining *when* attitudes predict behavior.[11] Accurate prediction depends on two major factors: appropriate measurement and the choice of the proper behavior to study.

Measurement Considerations. A fundamental problem in much attitude research has been invalid data resulting from the measurement of attitudes and behavior *at different levels of specificity*. Four important components of any overt behavior must be considered in order to obtain accurate measures: a

9. A. W. Wicker, "Attitudes Versus Actions: The Relationship of Verbal and Overt Behavioral Responses to Attitude Objects," *Journal of Social Issues*, vol. 25 (Autumn 1969), pp. 41–78.

10. George S. Day and Terry Deutscher, "Attitudinal Predictions of Choices of Major Appliance Brands," *Journal of Marketing Research*, vol. 19 (May 1982), pp. 192–198.

11. D. T. Regan and R. H. Fazio, "On the Consistency between Attitudes and Behavior: Look to the Method of Attitude Formation," *Journal of Experimental Psychology*, vol. 13 (1977), pp. 28–45; see also Deborah L. Roedder, Brian Sternthal, and Bobby J. Calder, "Attitude-Behavior Consistency in Children's Responses to Television Advertising," *Journal of Marketing Research*, vol. 20 (November 1983), pp. 337–349.

target, an action, a context, and a time.[12] For example, when a college senior buys a conservative, navy blue suit for the purpose of job interviewing, "buying" is the *action* (rather than borrowing, stealing, etc.); the *target* is "a navy blue suit"; the *context* is "for the purpose of job interviewing"; and the *time* is "during the senior year in college."

Attitude will not predict behavior unless both are measured at the same level of specificity. If, at the beginning of the semester, someone asked, "What is your opinion of navy blue suits?" your response might have been, "I don't like suits very much, and navy blue suits are particularly boring." If, then, at a later date you actually purchased a navy blue suit, your behavior would be inconsistent with your previously announced attitude toward navy blue suits. This inconsistency would result because the measure of your attitude was too general and lacked specificity. Your expressed attitude would probably have been considerably different if the question had been, "What is your opinion of buying a navy blue suit for job interviewing this semester?" Because this question is specific with regard to the purpose and timing of purchasing a navy blue suit, your response would probably reflect a somewhat favorable attitude (because you know that navy blue suits are generally regarded as appropriate attire for job interviewing). This response would then be consistent with your subsequent act of purchasing a navy blue suit.

Thus, in order to predict a specific behavior accurately, the attitude measurement must also be specific with regard to action, target, context, and time. The strength of the attitude-behavior relationship is strengthened appreciably when these requirements are satisfied. (To fully understand the material just covered, it would be beneficial for you to construct a personal example that illustrates a situation involving an action, target, context, and time.)

Type of Behavior.   Another determinant of attitude-behavior consistency is the type of behavior to be predicted. Type of behavior refers to whether the behavior is based on direct or indirect experience with the attitude object. *Direct experience* is gained by the consumer when he or she has actually tried or used the attitude object, whereas *indirect experience* refers to any product knowledge or experience short of actual use.

A series of psychological experiments demonstrated that attitudes based on direct experience predict behavior better than attitudes based on indirect experience.[13] The researchers in one study tried to predict the proportion of time people would play with different puzzles based on their attitudes toward the puzzles. One group of subjects (the direct-experience group) played with sample puzzles *prior* to indicating their attitudes toward the puzzles. Another

12. Martin Fishbein and Icek Ajzen, *Belief, Attitude, Intention, and Behavior: An Introduction to Theory and Research* (Reading, MA: Addison-Wesley, 1975).

13. R. H. Fazio, M. P. Zanna, and J. Cooper, "Direct Experience and Attitude-Behavior Consistency: An Information Processing Analysis," *Personality and Social Psychology Bulletin*, vol. 4 (Winter 1978), pp. 48–52; R. H. Fazio and M. P. Zanna, "On the Predictive Validity of Attitudes: The Roles of Direct Experience and Confidence," *Journal of Personality*, vol. 46 (June 1977), pp. 228–243.

group (the indirect-experience group) received verbal descriptions of the various puzzles but did not actually play with them prior to revealing their attitudes. Both groups, after indicating their attitudes, then played with the various puzzles. The researchers recorded subjects' puzzle-playing behavior in terms of the proportion of time they devoted to each puzzle. The correlation between attitudes and behavior was predictably higher for the direct-experience group (r = .53) than for the indirect-experience group (r = .21).[14]

In a more realistic marketing study, researchers performed an experiment with undergraduate business students using a new cheese-filled pretzel product as the experimental topic. The researchers divided students into two groups: A direct-experience group, which actually sampled the pretzels, and an indirect-experience group, which read an advertisement about the pretzels but did not sample them. The results indicated considerably higher levels of attitude-behavior consistency for the direct-experience subjects than for the indirect-experience subjects.[15]

In sum, the most notable conclusion from the research findings cited and from the prior discussion on measurement issues is that attitudes can and do predict behavior reasonably accurately *under the appropriate conditions:* Measurements of attitudes must be as specific as the behavior being predicted, and consumers must have direct rather than indirect behavior experience with the attitude object.

Persuasion in Marketing Communications

The foregoing discussion of attitudes, the *object*, provides us with useful concepts as we turn now to the strategic issue of how marketing communicators influence customers' attitudes and behaviors through persuasive efforts, the *objective*. Persuasion is the essence of marketing communications. Salespeople attempt to convince customers to purchase one product rather than another; advertisers appeal to consumers' fantasies and feelings and attempt to create desired images for their brands in hopes that consumers will someday purchase their brands; manufacturers use coupons, samples, rebates, and other devices to induce consumers to try their products and to purchase now rather than later.

The Ethics of Persuasion

It is worth mentioning at this point that the word *persuasion* may suggest to you something manipulative, exploitative, or unethical. At times, marketing communicators' persuasion efforts are all of these. Shrewd operators bamboo-

14. Regan and Fazio, "On the Consistency between Attitudes and Behavior."
15. Robert E. Smith and William R. Swinyard, "Attitude-Behavior Consistency: The Impact of Product Trial Versus Advertising," *Journal of Marketing Research*, vol. 20 (August 1983), pp. 257–267.

zle the unsuspecting and credulous into buying products or services that are never delivered. Elderly consumers, for example, are occasionally hustled into making advance payments for household repairs (e.g., roof repairs) that are never performed. Shyster realtors sell swamp land in Florida. Yes, persuasion by some marketing communicators *is* unethical. Of course, so sometimes are persuasive efforts by government officials, clergymen, teachers, your friends, and even you. Persuasion is a part of daily life in all its facets. The practice of persuasion can be noble or deplorable. There is nothing wrong with persuasion per se; it is the practitioners of persuasion who sometimes are at fault. To paraphrase an old adage: Don't throw the persuasion baby out with the bath water; just make sure the water is clean.

Multitude of Persuasion Possibilities

It would be erroneous to think that persuasion is a single method, practice, or technique. Rather, there theoretically are as many persuasion methods as there are persuasion practitioners. This is a bit of an exaggeration, but it serves to emphasize that persuasion practices are highly diverse. This diversity makes persuasion an incredibly fascinating and complex topic to study.

Another important point is that the topic of persuasion can be looked at from two different perspectives. One perspective involves examining the specific persuasive techniques used by practitioners. This is a fascinating topic, but it is beyond the objective of the present chapter. Later chapters on advertising, personal selling, direct marketing, and other promotional practices will touch on persuasive practices used by the practitioners in these various areas.[16] The other perspective treats persuasion from the perspective of the "persuadee"; that is, what determines whether the recipient of a persuasive effort will in fact be persuaded and what are the characteristics of a persuasive message that make it more or less persuasive. This perspective fits into the purpose of the present chapter.

To motivate the following discussion, it will be useful to consider examples of persuasive efforts by three different companies: Jenn-Air, Lands' End, and American Express. An advertisement for Jenn-Air (see Figure 5.1) consists of a mouth-watering illustration of shish kebab, a catchy headline, body copy containing several message arguments (e.g., "Its built-in ventilation system eliminates smoke and cooking odors"), and an illustration of the product in use. The Jenn-Air ad is attempting to persuade people to think favorably of this product and to consider purchasing it because of its many advantages.

Figure 5.2 contains an advertisement for Lands' End—a catalog company that markets high-quality, moderately priced clothing. This advertisement says nothing about Lands' End per se. It assumes the reader is already familiar with

---

16. An extremely readable, entertaining, and insightful treatment of persuasion techniques (and procedures for countering these techniques) is provided by Robert B. Cialdini, *Influence: How and Why People Agree to Things* (New York: William Morrow and Company, 1984).

FIGURE 5.1   **Persuasive Advertisement for Jenn-Air**

the company and its products. What the ad does is to point out a usually forgotten benefit associated with mail-order shopping—the excitement a child feels when he receives something just for him in the mail. This is flagged for particular attention to grandparents who can participate in the grandchild's life even from a long distance.

A final illustration of persuasive techniques is the ad for American Express, shown in Figure 5.3. Though shown here on a single page, this ad ran on two pages when it appeared in magazines. The interesting thing about the ad is that it says virtually nothing about the advertised service. Rather, the ad simply portrays two well-known sports personalities, Wilt Chamberlain (of basketball fame; he once scored 100 points in a single game) and Willie Shoemaker (of race horsing fame; he has ridden hundreds of horses to victory, many after passing the age when most jockeys have followed their horses to pasture). The verbal content in the ad simply notes how long each athlete has held "membership" in the American Express "club." This particular execution is just one in a series of ads run by American Express, each portraying a different celebrity.

The diversity of persuasive postures in the preceding examples serves to highlight the fact that there are many ways to "skin the persuasion cat." The following section identifies five sets of factors that are fundamental in the persuasion process. Three sets of factors (message arguments, peripheral cues, and communication modality) deal with persuasion vehicles under the marketing communicator's control. The other two factors (receiver involvement and receiver's initial position) deal with characteristics of the targets of persuasion.

Message Arguments.   The *strength or quality of message arguments* (e.g., the stated advantages of owning a Jenn-Air range) is often the major determinant of whether and to what extent persuasion occurs. Consumers are much more likely to be persuaded by convincing and believable messages than by weak arguments. It may seem strange, then, that much advertising fails to present substantive information or compelling arguments. The reason is that the majority of advertising, particularly television commercials, is for product categories (e.g., soft drinks, detergents) in which interbrand differences are modest or virtually nonexistent.[17] There is not a whole lot American Express can say to encourage people to use their bank card. The ingenious idea of card "membership," however, serves to give consumers a sense of selectivity and status by implying that the user will possess something that celebrities use.

Peripheral Cues.   A second major determinant of persuasion is the presence of cues that are peripheral to the primary message arguments. These include such elements as the message source (e.g., celebrity endorsers such as "The Stilt" and "The Shoe" in the American Express ad), background

17. L. Bogart, "Is All This Advertising Necessary?" *Journal of Advertising Research,* vol. 18 (October 1978), pp. 17–26.

Persuasive Advertisement for American Express

FIGURE 5.3

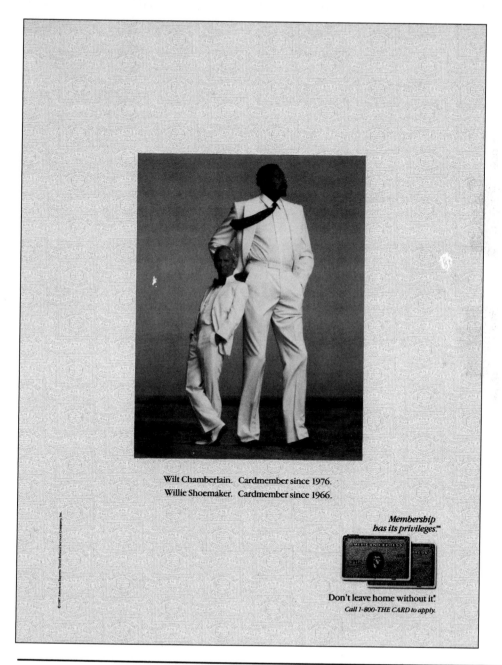

Wilt Chamberlain. Cardmember since 1976.
Willie Shoemaker. Cardmember since 1966.

*Membership
has its privileges.*

Don't leave home without it.
Call 1-800-THE CARD to apply.

Source: Courtesy American Express PRS Company.

FOCUS ON PROMOTION

Measuring Consumer Involvement

The concept of involvement, which has been mentioned several times to this point in the text, is fundamental to all consumer behavior and marketing communications. You may be wondering "How is involvement measured?" One measure, called the **Personal Involvement Inventory,** consists of the following 20 items.[18] Involvement is measured with regard to a specific product that is placed at the top of the 20 semantic differential scales. A consumer's responses to all 20 scales are summed to form a total involvement score. Items on the left are scored (1) low involvement to (7) high involvement on the right. Totaling the 20 items gives a score from a low of 20 to a high of 140.

(insert name of object to be judged)

important	unimportant[a]
of no concern	of concern to me
irrelevant	relevant
means a lot to me	means nothing to me[a]
useless	useful
valuable	worthless[a]
trivial	fundamental
beneficial	not beneficial[a]
matters to me	doesn't matter[a]
uninterested	interested
significant	insignificant[a]
vital	superfluous[a]
boring	interesting
unexciting	exciting
appealing	unappealing[a]
mundane	fascinating
essential	nonessential[a]
undesirable	desirable
wanted	unwanted[a]
not needed	needed

[a]Indicates item is reverse scored.

18. See Judith Lynne Zaichkowsky, "Measuring the Involvement Construct," *Journal of Consumer Research*, vol. 12 (December 1985), pp. 341–352.

music, scenery, and graphics. As will be explained in a later section, under certain conditions these cues may play a more important role than message arguments in determining the outcome of a persuasive effort.

Communication Modality.

A third important mediator of persuasion is the mode of communication, whether television, radio, or magazines. Experiments have shown that a likable communicator is more persuasive when presenting a message via broadcast media, whereas an unlikable source is more persuasive when the communication is written.[19] The reason for this phenomenon is that people pay closer attention to the quality of message arguments when processing written rather than broadcast messages.

Receiver Involvement.

The personal relevance that a communication has for a receiver is a critical determinant of the extent and form of persuasion. Highly involved consumers (e.g., people who are in the market for an expensive, risky product) are motivated to process message arguments when exposed to marketing communications, whereas uninvolved consumers are likely to exert minimal attention to message arguments and to focus instead on peripheral cues. The upshot is that *involved and uninvolved consumers have to be persuaded in different ways*. This will be detailed fully in a following section titled "Elaboration Likelihood Model."

Receiver's Initial Position.

Scholars now agree that persuasion results not from external communication per se but from the self-generated thoughts, or **cognitive responses,** that consumers produce in response to persuasive efforts. Persuasion, in other words, is self-persuasion, or, stated poetically, "thinking makes it so."[20]

What are cognitive responses and why do they occur? In response to persuasive attempts, people will (if involved in the communication issue) think about and evaluate message claims and react mentally. Three general forms of reaction (cognitive responses) are supportive arguments, counter arguments, and source derogations.[21] **Supportive arguments** occur when a receiver agrees with a message's arguments. **Counter arguments** and **source derogations** occur when the receiver challenges message claims (i.e., counter argues) and when the receiver disputes the source's ability to make such claims (i.e., derogates the source).

19. Shelly Chaiken and Alice H. Eagly, "Communication Modality as a Determinant of Persuasion: The Role of Communicator Salience," *Journal of Personality and Social Psychology,* vol. 45 (August 1983), pp. 241–256.
20. Richard M. Perloff and Timothy C. Brock, " 'And Thinking Makes It So': Cognitive Responses to Persuasion," in *Persuasion: New Directions in Theory and Research,* eds. M. E. Rioloff and G. R. Miller (Beverly Hills, CA: Sage Publications, 1980), pp. 67–99.
21. Peter L. Wright, "The Cognitive Processes Mediating the Acceptance of Advertising," *Journal of Marketing Research,* vol. 10 (February 1973), pp. 53–62. Also see Amitava Chattopadhyay and Joseph W. Alba, "The Situational Importance of Recall and Inference in Consumer Decision Making," *Journal of Consumer Research,* vol. 15 (June 1988), pp. 1–12.

Whether a persuasive communication accomplishes its objectives depends on the balance of cognitive responses. If the combination of counter arguments and source derogations exceeds supportive arguments, it is unlikely that many consumers will be convinced to undertake the course of action advocated. Marketing communications, however, may effectively persuade consumers if more supportive than negative arguments are registered.

The preceding point, though stated in terminology different from that used previously in this text, should not come as any great surprise. You may recall that in Chapter 2 a similar point was made concerning the communications process, namely that communications (persuasion) is *not* something you do to people; it is something done with people.

The Elaboration Likelihood Model

The various factors that play a role in the persuasion process can be combined into a coordinated explanation, or theory, of persuasion. The **Elaboration Likelihood Model (ELM)** postulates two different mechanisms by which persuasion occurs. These are the "central" and "peripheral" routes to persuasion.[22] Figure 5.4 displays the ELM and the two persuasion routes.

Understanding this theory requires that you first understand what is meant by *elaboration likelihood.* The concept of *elaboration* deals with mental activity in response to a persuasive message. To elaborate on a message is to *think diligently about what the message is saying,* to carefully evaluate the arguments in the message, to agree with some, disagree with others, and so on. Whether and to what extent a person engages in elaboration depends on that person's interest in and ability to understand the message. Consider a message about personal computers that presents one technical detail after another. Readers who are familiar with and interested in computers will pay close attention to this message. Their *elaboration likelihood* is high. Readers who are uninterested and unknowledgable about computers will have low elaboration likelihoods. In general, the strength of one's elaboration likelihood (high or low) will determine the type of persuasion process, central or peripheral, by which an individual might be persuaded.

The **central route,** the left side of Figure 5.4, postulates that when a receiver is involved in a message topic and considers it to be personally relevant, he or she will be *motivated* to attend to and comprehend message arguments (see the *Motivation to Process* box in Fig. 5.4). If the receiver is then *able* to process the arguments (see the *Ability to Process* box)—that is, he or she has the intellectual capacity or is not distracted—*cognitive response activity* will occur. The nature of the cognitive processing—whether predominantly favorable (support arguments), predominantly unfavorable (counter arguments and source derogations), or neutral—will lead to *cognitive structure changes,* which

---

22. This theory was developed by Petty and Cacioppo, *Attitudes and Persuasion.*

The Elaboration Likelihood Model of Persuasion

FIGURE 5.4

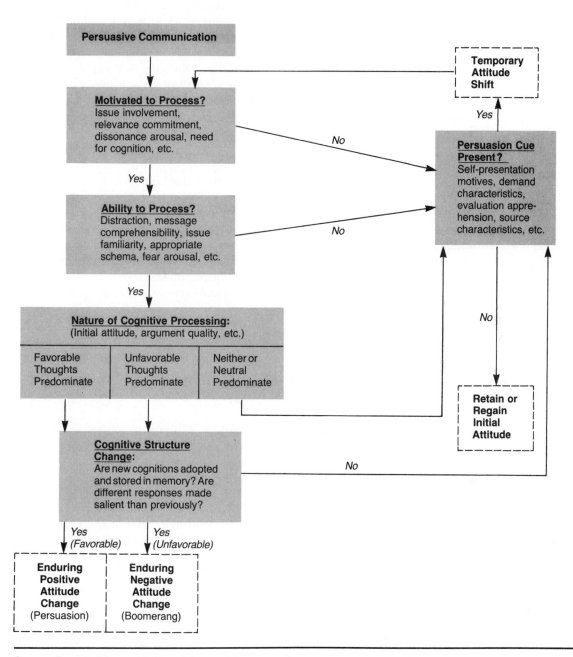

Source: Reprinted by permission of the publisher, from Richard E. Petty and John T. Cacioppo, "Central and Peripheral Routes to Persuasion: Application to Advertising," in Larry Percy and Arch G. Woodside (eds), *Advertising and Consumer Psychology,* (Lexington, Mass.: Lexington Books, copyright 1983, D. C. Heath and Company) pp. 3–24.

take the form of enduring positive or negative *attitude change.* In the former case, the message accomplishes what the communicator intends, that is, *persuasion,* whereas in the latter case, it *boomerangs.*

In the event that some or all of the foregoing antecedents fail to occur (the receiver is unmotivated or unable to process information, does not engage in cognitive processing, etc.), the ELM provides for an alternative, **peripheral route** to persuasion, which is shown on the right side of Figure 5.4. In the peripheral route, persuasion occurs not as a result of a consumer's processing salient message arguments but by virtue of his or her attending to relevant (though peripheral to the main message argument) persuasion cues. However, according to the ELM theory, people experience only *temporary attitude change* when persuaded via the peripheral route in comparison to the *enduring change* experienced under the central route.

Thus, in circumstances in which receivers think about and process message arguments (i.e., when the elaboration likelihood is high), persuasion may occur (if the message does not boomerang) and, if so, attitudes that are formed will be relatively enduring and somewhat resistant to change. Comparatively, when the elaboration likelihood is low (because the communication topic is not particularly relevant to the message recipient), attitude change may nevertheless occur (by virtue of receivers' processing peripheral cues) but will only be temporary unless consumers are exposed continuously to the peripheral cues.

Empirical Support

The ELM theory makes intuitive sense, but a theory is only as good as the empirical evidence that supports it. In fact, considerable empirical evidence has been marshalled in support of this two-route ELM theory of persuasion. One illustrative study will be described.[23]

Researchers performed an experiment by influencing college students either to want to process message arguments (high-involvement subjects) or not to want to (low-involvement subjects). Four different advertisements were created for "Edge," a fictitious brand of disposable razor, by varying advertising messages in terms of argument quality (strong or weak) and type of endorsement (message endorsed either by celebrity athletes—golfer Jack Nicklaus and tennis player Tracy Austin—or by ordinary citizens). Two of the four experimental ads for Edge razor are presented in Figure 5.5. Note that the ad on the left side is endorsed by the two "celebrity endorsers," though their pictures are not shown in the figure, and that the message arguments are "strong," that is, meaningful and believable (e.g., "New advanced honing method creates unsurpassed sharpness"). The ad on the right side is endorsed by ordi-

23. Richard E. Petty, John T. Cacioppo, and David Schumann, "Central and Peripheral Routes to Advertising Effectiveness: The Moderating Role of Involvement," *Journal of Consumer Research,* vol. 10 (September 1983), pp. 135–146.

Advertisements from the Edge Razor Experiment   FIGURE 5.5

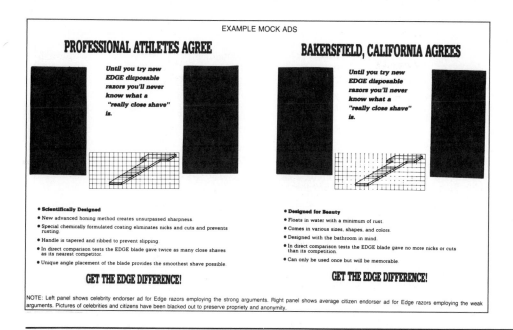

NOTE: Left panel shows celebrity endorser ad for Edge razors employing the strong arguments. Right panel shows average citizen endorser ad for Edge razors employing the weak arguments. Pictures of celebrities and citizens have been blacked out to preserve propriety and anonymity.

Source: Richard E. Petty, John T. Cacioppo, and David Schumann, "Central and Peripheral Routes to Advertising Effectiveness: The Moderating Role of Involvement," *Journal of Consumer Research*, Vol. 10, September 1983, p. 140. Reprinted by permission.

nary "citizen endorsers" and the arguments are "weak" (e.g., "Floats in water with a minimum of rust"). The remaining two experimental ads, not shown in Figure 5.5, mixed strong arguments with citizen endorsers or weak arguments with celebrity endorsers.

According to the ELM theory's prediction, under the *central route*, the *high involvement* subjects should be motivated to process message arguments about Edge razor and be persuaded by the strength of message arguments. That is, positive attitude change would be expected in the group presented with strong, believable arguments, and negative attitude change would be expected in the group exposed to weak, specious arguments. *Low involvement* subjects, by comparison, would be expected to "travel" the *peripheral route*, concentrate on the message source, and be more persuaded by the celebrity than by the noncelebrity endorsers. (Before reading on, think about how the results of the experiment should have turned out.)

Experimental results (summarized in Table 5.1) were generally in accordance with the ELM predictions. Specifically, the nature of the endorser had a

TABLE 5.1   **Summary of Results for Edge Razor Experiment: Means and Standard Deviations for Each Experimental Cell on the Attitude Index**

	Low Involvement		High Involvement	
	Weak Arguments	Strong Arguments	Weak Arguments	Strong Arguments
Citizen Endorser	−.12	.98	-1.10	1.98
	(1.81)	(1.52)	(1.66)	(1.25)
Celebrity Endorser	1.21	1.85	-1.36	1.80
	(2.28)	(1.59)	(1.65)	(1.07)

Note: Attitude scores represent the average rating of the product on three nine-point semantic differential scales anchored at -4 and +4 (bad–good, unsatisfactory–satisfactory, and unfavorable–favorable). Standard deviations are in parentheses.

Source: R. E. Petty, J. T. Cacioppo, and D. Schumann, "Central and Peripheral Routes to Advertising Effectiveness: The Moderating Role of Involvement," *Journal of Consumer Research,* Vol. 10, September 1983, p. 141.

significant impact on product attitudes only under low-involvement information-processing conditions. Argument quality had an impact on product attitudes under both low and high involvement, but the impact on attitudes was significantly greater under high than low involvement. Thus, this study and others support the proposition that different features of a marketing communications effort may be more or less effective, depending on receivers' information-processing involvement.[24]

Practical Implications of the ELM

In recognizing two alternative paths to persuasion, the ELM points out that the form of persuasion will depend both on the characteristics of the market and the strengths of the marketing communicator's relative market position.[25] If consumers are interested in learning about a product, and a company's brand has clear advantages over competitive brands, then the persuasion tact to be taken is crystal clear: Put together a message telling people explicitly why your brand is superior. The result should be equally clear: Consumers will be

24. See Petty, Cacioppo, and Schumann, "Central and Peripheral Routes," for discussion of other studies.
25. It is worth noting that the central and peripheral paths represent endpoints on a continuum of persuasion strategies and are not intended to imply that persuasion is an either-or proposition. In other words, in many cases there is a combination of central and peripheral processes operating simultaneously.

swayed by your arguments, which will lead to enduring attitude change and a strong chance that they will select your brand over competitors' brands.

However, the fact of the marketplace is that consumers are generally not overly enthused about a product that is not much different than what the competitors have to offer. Thus, the marketing communicator, faced with the "double whammy" (only slightly-involved consumers and a "me-too" product), has to find ways to create interest, excitement, and sometimes trivial reasons for differentiating his brand from competitors' offerings. Here, peripheral cues take on added significance. It matters not only what a salesperson has to say but also how professionally she appears and whether she has style. It is not just what a television commercial says but how it is said, what props are used, what music is played in the background, how attractive the models are, and so on.

In practice, then, persuasive marketing communications efforts include a combination of message arguments and peripheral cues. The winners in the persuasion race typically have either a better *basic offer* (back to Mode 1 in Chapter 1), employ better *persuasive communications* (Mode 2), use more enticing *promotional inducements* (Mode 3), or have some superior combination of all of these.

The Theory of Reasoned Action

The Elaboration Likelihood Model is a general persuasion theory. However, to help you understand communication efforts by marketers, it will be profitable to review one additional theory. Some of you will have been exposed to this theory either in a psychology or consumer behavior course. A refresher won't hurt.

The **theory of reasoned action** proposes that much human behavior is planned, systematic, reasoned, and under conscious control.[26] The theory proposes that all actions, including consumer choice behavior, are based on two primary determinants: *attitudes* and *normative influence*. You are now familiar with the concept of attitude. Some discussion of normative influence is needed.

Normative influence represents the influence that important others, sometimes called *referent groups*, have on us. What we think, what we want in life, and what we actually do are all influenced by the people we love, like, respect, or identify with. We internalize the influence of others into our own thought processes and this influence, along with our personal attitudes, determines how we behave. Products are symbolic objects, and much consumer behavior is influenced more by a product's social meaning than by its functional utility. Because products have symbolic significance, people look to oth-

26. Fishbein and Ajzen, *Belief, Attitude, Intention, and Behavior.*

ers for information and approval when making product, store, and brand choice decisions.[27]

The theory of reasoned action is based on the idea that the best predictor of one's behavior is one's behavioral intentions. That is, we typically behave in a manner consistent with our intentions. Intentions, in turn, are postulated to be determined by our personal attitudes (what is labeled "Aact" in the theory) and our subjective norms (SN). Subjective norms are named as such because they represent each individual's personal, subjective interpretation of normative influences. Aact and SN both have their own set of determinants. The following three equations capture the essence of the theory:

$$B \sim B1 = \text{Aact} + \text{SN} \tag{5.1}$$

$$\text{Aact} = \sum_{i=1}^{n} b_i e_i \tag{5.2}$$

$$\text{SN} = \sum_{j=1}^{k} NB_j MC_j \tag{5.3}$$

where:

B = overt behavior
BI = behavioral intention
Aact = attitude toward performing a specific behavior
SN = subjective norm (i.e., internalization of what others think one should do)
b_i = the expectation or belief that the performance of behavior B will lead to desired outcome i
e_i = the positive or negative evaluation of the ith outcome
NB_j = the expectation that performance of behavior B is desired or expected by an important person or referent group j
MC_j = the motivation to comply with the jth person or group
n,k = the number of salient outcomes and groups, respectively

An illustration should help in understanding the preceding equations and their constituent elements. Consider the decision facing Julie, a senior psychology major, who is in the process of deciding where to attend graduate

27. For discussions of reference groups and the symbolic significance of products, see William O. Bearden and Michael J. Etzel, "Reference Group Influence on Product and Brand Purchase Decisions," *Journal of Consumer Research*, vol. 9 (September 1982), pp. 183–194; V. Parker Lessig and C. Whan Park, "Promotional Perspectives of Reference Group Influence: Advertising Implications," *Journal of Advertising*, vol. 7 (1978), pp. 41–47; C. Whan Park and V. Parker Lessig, "Students and Housewives: Differences in Susceptibility to Reference Group Influence," *Journal of Consumer Research*, vol. 4 (September 1977), pp. 102–110; and Michael R. Solomon, "The Role of Products as Social Stimuli: A Symbolic Interactionism Perspective," *Journal of Consumer Research*, vol. 10 (December 1983), pp. 319–329.

school for her MBA degree. She has narrowed the choice to two universities: the major university in her home state and a prestigious private university located nearly 1,000 miles from her home. Thus, the behavior in question, B, is the choice between two universities.

To predict her choice, it is first necessary to know what she considers to be the salient outcomes or consequences of her decision as well as which people's opinions she considers important. Table 5.2 presents a hypothetical set of outcomes and referents along with Julie's personal belief (b_i) and evaluations (e_i) pertaining to the n outcomes, and her normative beliefs (NB_j) and motivations to comply (MC_j) with the k salient referents.

Application of the Theory of Reasoned Action: Hypothetical   TABLE 5.2
University Choice Process

Salient Choice Outcomes	Evaluation (e_i)[a]	Beliefs (b_i)[b]	
		State U.	Private U.
High quality of education	+5	+1	+3
Favorable job opportunities	+5	0	+3
Low cost	+3	+2	-2
Close to home	+2	+3	-2
Ample recreational/cultural opportunities	+2	+1	+3
$\sum_{i=1}^{n} b_i e_i =$		+19	+26

Salient Choice Referents	Motivations to Comply (MC_j)[c]	Normative Beliefs (NB_j)[d]	
		State U.	Private U.
Parents	+4	+3	-1
Potential employers	+5	0	+3
Friends	+3	+2	+1
$\sum_{j=1}^{k} NB_j MC_j =$		+18	+14
$\sum_{i=1}^{n} b_i e_i + \sum_{j=1}^{k} NB_j MC_j =$		+37	+40

---

[a]Higher scores indicate more favorable evaluations. For example, quality of education (+5) is more important to Julie in choosing a university than is distance from home (+2).

[b]Positive scores indicate Julie's belief that a university will deliver a salient outcome, whereas negative scores indicate her belief that a university is undesirable with respect to some outcome. For example, Julie perceives Private U. to be more costly.

[c]Higher scores indicate stronger motivations to comply with a referent. Julie is, for example, more strongly motivated to comply with her parents' beliefs than with those of her friends.

[d]Positive scores indicate Julie's normative belief that a referent thinks she should attend a particular university, whereas negative scores evidence her belief that a referent opposes her attending a university.

As shown in Table 5.2, the outcomes that Julie considers most salient in choosing an MBA program are, in descending order of importance, quality of education, job opportunities upon completion of her degree, cost, distance from home, and recreational/cultural opportunities during the period of her education. Her expectations and evaluations of each of these are shown in Table 5.2, along with her normative beliefs and motivations to comply with three salient referents: parents, potential employers, and friends.

Julie's total scores for Aact, SN, and their sum are displayed at the bottom of Table 5.2. By making the simplifying assumption that Aact and SN are equally important, it can be surmised from the data that Julie will choose to attend the prestigious private university rather than her state institution. Although she had solid reasons for wanting to stay closer to home (parental pressure, friendships, and cost considerations), the overriding importance of educational quality and true job opportunities dictated that she travel away from home and attend the private university.

Attitude Change Strategies

The theory of reasoned action offers marketing communicators various suggestions for influencing and persuading consumers. There are three major strategies for changing the attitude component.[28]

Change an Existing Belief.   Marketing communicators continually attempt to alter consumer perceptions about their brands on one or more product attributes. In terms of the model elements in the theory of reasoned action, this amounts to changing consumers' beliefs. As an example, consider the chapter's opening vignette describing American's drinking preferences. Coffee makers would like more consumers to think (believe) that coffee is a more refreshing beverage than soft drinks. Several advertising campaigns in recent years have emphasized the theme that coffee is a drink for "with it" young adults, typified by Maxwell House's campaign featuring Bronson Pinchot and other celebrities (e.g., Mariel Hemingway) in various executions of the same theme. California wineries have been successful in changing the belief that good premium wines are available only from Europe. Many wine consumers now know that high-quality wines are available from California as well as elsewhere in the United States.

Change an Existing Evaluation.   This strategy attempts to influence consumers to reassess the value of a particular attribute and to alter their *evaluations* of the attribute's value. Marketers of cereal and other food products have been able to convince consumers that bran and other fibers are more important ingredients than consumers previously thought. Consumers used to emphasize primarily taste when buying products like cereal, but now, due to

28. Richard J. Lutz, "Changing Brand Attitudes through Modification of Cognitive Structure," *Journal of Consumer Research*, vol. 1 (March 1975), pp. 49–59.

health concerns and marketing efforts, people have elevated the importance of bran content and other health considerations when making choice decisions.

Add a New Attribute.   A third strategy marketing communicators use to change the attitude component is attempting to get consumers to add an entirely new product attribute into their cognitive structures. This attribute, of course, would be one on which the marketer's product fares especially well. Consumers never thought about fluoride in toothpaste until marketers began promoting that fact. Now it would be unthinkable to purchase toothpaste without fluoride. Likewise, the current prevalence of low-calorie ("lite") products was a major marketplace development in the 1970s.

Normative Influence Strategies

In addition to influencing consumer behavior by strategies directed at changing consumers' attitudes, marketing communicators also appeal to normative influences, the other major determinant of behavior. Changes in consumers' normative structure elements (i.e., normative beliefs and motivations to comply) may lead to changes in their behavior. Marketers have limited ability, in most instances, to influence consumers' subjective norms, but this does not discourage communicators from attempting to do so. Advertising campaigns for products that affect bystanders (e.g., smoking) often appeal to an individual's sense of concern for what impact his or her behavior may have on others.

Advertisers also make frequent attempts to show how their products will enhance the consumer's status in the eyes of important referents or prevent embarrassment. The ad for Sunlight dishwashing detergent in Figure 5.6 shows one brand's recognition of the role that social influence plays in making choice decisions.

Summary

Marketing communications in its various forms (advertising, personal selling, and so on) involves efforts to persuade consumers by influencing their attitudes and ultimately their behavior. This chapter describes the role and nature of attitudes, the functions they serve, and the ways they can be changed.

The nature of persuasion is discussed with particular emphasis on the Elaboration Likelihood Model (ELM). Two alternative persuasion mechanisms are described: A *central route,* which explains persuasion under conditions where the receiver is involved in the communication topic, and a *peripheral route,* which accounts for persuasion when receivers are not highly involved.

The *theory of reasoned action* is discussed in terms of its two primary components: attitudes (Aact) and subjective norms (SN). Strategies for changing attitudes and influencing subjective norms are described.

FIGURE 5.6   **An Appeal to Normative Influence**

Discussion Questions

1. Distinguish among the cognitive, affective, and conative components of an attitude and provide examples of each using your attitude toward the idea of personally pursuing a career in selling and sales management.

2. Explain how your attitude toward a personal career in selling and sales management might serve utilitarian, value-expressive, ego-defensive, and knowledge functions.

3. Explain the roles of measurement considerations and type of behavior as determinants of the degree of attitude-behavior consistency.

4. Accurate attitude measurement requires specificity with regard to action, target, context, and time. Using a campus blood drive as the illustration, explain how each of these criteria applies.

5. Distinguish between message arguments and peripheral cues as fundamental determinants of persuasion. Provide several examples of each from actual television commercials.

6. Receiver involvement is the fundamental determinant of whether people may be persuaded via a central route or via a peripheral route. Explain.

7. There are three general strategies for changing attitudes. Explain each using a hotel chain as your illustration.

8. The ad for Sunlight dishwashing detergent (Figure 5.6) might be viewed, on the one hand, as insulting to modern women and men by virtue of its stereotypic casting of women in the role of "good housewife." A less serious interpretation would hold that the ad actually is poking fun at this form of stereotyping. What is your interpretation of what the ad is conveying?

Exercises

1. Identify five magazine advertisements and using concepts from the ELM explain how each attempts to persuade consumers.

2. Construct a series of questions for measuring attitudes toward a product of your choosing that satisfy the "specificity" requirements described in the text.

3. Using Table 5.2 as prototype, construct a similar table showing your salient choice outcomes and referents and your ratings for two models of automobiles you might consider purchasing upon graduation.

4. Identify two examples each of the attitude-change strategies described in the chapter. Be specific in your descriptions.

Message and Source Factors in Marketing Communications

MICHAEL JACKSON SINGS "I'M BAD," BUT PEPSI EXECUTIVES KNOW HE'S GOOD FOR SALES IN JAPAN

uppose you are the advertising manager for Pepsi Cola and your job is to find a way to increase sales of Pepsi in Japan. Pepsi's market share in Japan fell from a high of nearly 25 percent in the early 1970s to about 5 percent by 1987, while Coca-Cola's share held strong at 40 to 45 percent. What would you do to elevate Pepsi Cola's position in Japan?

Pepsi's solution was to hire Michael Jackson and sponsor his worldwide tour of Japan, Australia, New Zealand, and elsewhere. Jackson proved to be a hit: Ticket sales for his concerts in Japan exceeded 350,000, with reports of scalpers getting as much as $1,000 per ticket.

Pepsi's sponsorship of Jackson's tour reportedly cost the company more than $10 million. Yet it was expected that having him endorse Pepsi Cola would increase the company's Japanese market share to around 10 percent within a year of sponsoring the tour. Every share point amounts to millions of dollars in sales volume.[1] ■

1. Adapted from "Michael 'Pepsi' Jackson," *Advertising Age*, September 28, 1987, p. 80.

Companies frequently use celebrities such as Michael Jackson in their efforts to persuade consumers to purchase their products. The previous chapter explained that all forms of marketing communications and promotion ultimately are directed at *persuading* consumers to undertake some behavior that benefits the marketer. It should be clear, however, that persuasion is no easy task. Every marketer is competing against competitors who are attempting to persuade consumers in an opposite direction—for example, toward drinking Coca-Cola rather than Pepsi Cola. A further complication is the fact that consumers are inundated daily with persuasive appeals, including advertisements, public service announcements, telephone pitches, and retail sales presentations. Moreover, consumers are uninterested in much of what marketing communicators have to say, often bored, and frequently skeptical if not downright cynical of marketers' claims. For these reasons, consumers learn to fend off persuasive marketing efforts through selective nonattention and selective perception; in other words, they "hear what they want to hear."

The result is that marketing communicators must be "persuasive" in order to persuade. But what does it mean to be persuasive? No simple answer is possible. The saying "You can skin a cat in many ways" applies equally well to marketing communications: There are many ways to influence and persuade consumers.[2] In this chapter we will discuss a variety of message appeals and source characteristics that marketing communicators use in attempting to persuade by favorably influencing consumers' attitudes and actions.

The term **message** refers to the verbal and nonverbal persuasive techniques that are used in all forms of marketing communications—advertisements, sales presentations, publicity releases, sales promotions, package information, and so on. The term **source** refers to the person, people, or even object who delivers the message. An extensive variety of message techniques and source characteristics are employed by marketing practitioners to persuade consumers.

Message Factors

Salespeople, advertisers, and other marketing communicators deal regularly with questions such as: "How do I get my point across?" "How should I present my arguments to have the most impact?" "Should I save my best argument for last or use it to start the presentation?" "Would humor be effective?"

This section examines two broad categories of message factors that play important roles in achieving marketing communications objectives: **Message structure** involves the framework, or skeleton, of marketing messages and includes considerations such as the use of one- versus two-sided arguments,

2. It should be clear that consumers are not puppets and are not easily persuaded. The thrust of the preceding comment is to suggest that marketers use a variety of persuasive attempts. Generally these efforts are moral and legal. Sometimes they are immoral, stupid, illegal, or all of the above.

comparative versus noncomparative messages, and the order in which the most important arguments are presented. **Message content** fleshes out the skeleton and deals with the types of appeals used. Topics discussed under this category include the use of humor, fear appeals, the role of music, sex appeals, and subliminal advertising.

Where possible, an attempt is made to identify some *generalizations* about messages. It is important to realize, however, that generalizations are not the same as scientific laws or principles. These "higher" forms of scientific truth (such as Einstein's general theory of relativity and Newton's law of gravitation) have not yet been established in the realm of marketing communications. Two reasons explain why. First, the buyer behavior that marketing communications is designed to influence is complex and dynamic; consequently, it is difficult to arrive at straightforward explanations of how communication elements operate in all situations and across all types of market segments. Second, because the scientific knowledge of marketing communications is based on research that necessarily has been conducted under somewhat artificial conditions (e.g., laboratory experiments with college students), it is impossible to draw clear-cut inferences to applied marketing settings. Thus, the generalizations presented should be considered suggestive rather than definitive. It is well we heed the philosopher's advice: "Seek simplicity and distrust it."[3]

Message Structure

Three structural issues are discussed in this section: one- versus two-sided messages; comparative versus noncomparative messages; and climax, anticlimax, and pyramidal orders of argument presentation.

Message-Sidedness.   All persuasive messages can be viewed in terms of whether message arguments are presented in a one- or two-sided fashion. In a **one-sided message,** the entire orientation is toward the communicator's position. Advertisements typically use one-sided messages. The weaknesses in the communicator's position or the strengths of opposing views are never mentioned. The following claim for "Pensive," a fictional brand of ballpoint pen, illustrates a one-sided advertising appeal: "Pensive's quality of construction is surpassed by none, and the styling reflects a timeless simplicity of line."[4]

A **two-sided message** attempts to establish credibility for the marketing communicator without deterring purchase. This is done by presenting the product in a positive fashion on the basis of attributes that are important to

3. Abraham Kaplan, *The Conduct of Inquiry: Methodology for Behavioral Science* (New York: Intext Educational Publishers, Chandler Publishing Co., 1964).
4. Michael A. Kamins and Henry Assael, "Two-Sided Versus One-Sided Appeals: A Cognitive Perspective on Argumentation, Source Derogation, and the Effect of Disconfirming Trial on Belief Change," *Journal of Marketing Research,* vol. 24 (February 1987), pp. 29–39.

brand choice, but disclaiming or limiting product or brand performance claims on product attributes that are of relatively minor significance to the consumer.[5] Two-sided appeals can be either *refutational* or *nonrefutational*.[6] In the former, a product's weaknesses or limitations are refuted within the specific marketing communication. For example, in comparison to the one-sided claim for Pensive pen, a two-sided refutational statement in an advertisement might claim: "Pensive's barrel is made of plastic and not metal, but its styling is unique." This statement acknowledges a weakness but then refutes it by implying that the limitation of having a plastic barrel is not really a weakness at all, because the pen has a unique styling. In a nonrefutational two-sided message, the weakness is presented without any refutation. For example, "Pensive's barrel is plastic and not metal."[7]

Is a message more persuasive when it presents one side or both sides of an issue? As always, there is no simple answer. However, it generally would be expected that a two-sided message would be more effective than a one-sided message because two-sided messages are perceived as *more credible*. Also, two-sided messages are considered *more informative* because they are used less regularly and are less expected than one-sided versions.[8] In the final analysis, which approach is more effective depends on at least three characteristics of the audience that receives the message: (1) initial opinion on the issue, (2) educational level, and (3) exposure to subsequent arguments by competitive firms.

Initial Opinion.   A one-sided argument is generally preferable if an audience already *agrees* with the marketing communicator's position. A one-sided argument serves to strengthen or reinforce the prior beliefs of consumers who already agree with the communicator's position; a two-sided message may place some doubts in their minds.

If, however, the audience initially *disagrees* with the communicator's viewpoint, a two-sided argument will generally be more effective. For consumers who initially disagree with the communicator, a two-sided message is more effective because it serves to enhance the communicator's credibility; that is, the communicator is perceived to be more objective and honest. The one-sided approach is more likely to be disregarded by the audience because it runs counter to what they already believe.

5. Michael A. Kamins and Lawrence J. Marks, "Advertising Puffery: The Impact of Using Two-Sided Claims on Product Attitude and Purchase," *Journal of Advertising*, vol. 16, no. 4 (1987), p. 7.
6. Ibid.
7. These examples are shorter versions of the actual experimental manipulations used by Kamins and Assael, "Two-Sided Versus One-Sided Appeals."
8. For further discussion on this point and review of other pertinent issues, see Linda L. Golden and Mark I. Alpert, "Comparative Analysis of the Relative Effectiveness of One- and Two-Sided Communication for Contrasting Products," *Journal of Advertising*, vol. 16, no. 1 (1987), pp. 18–25.

Educational Level.   Research by social psychologists has shown that two-sided arguments are more effective in changing opinions of better-educated people, whereas one-sided arguments are more effective for less-educated people. One explanation for this generalization is that better-educated individuals are capable of seeing both sides of an argument. By admitting to some weaknesses in an argument or by recognizing some of the strengths in the competing side, a communicator is perceived by the educated audience as more objective and reliable. Lesser-educated people, on the other hand, are more likely to accept what they are told and fail to see another side of an issue.

Exposure to Subsequent Counter Arguments.   If a communicator knows (or anticipates) that the audience will be exposed to subsequent counterclaims (i.e., persuasive arguments running counter to the communicator's position), a two-sided message is generally preferable. By presenting a two-sided argument and then refuting the opposing arguments, a communicator can prepare receivers to discount subsequent counter arguments when they are made by competing communicators.

A two-sided refutational message makes it possible, in other words, for a marketing communicator to *inoculate* an audience against a competitor's subsequent counterclaims. "Inoculate" is used in this sense as a metaphor to describe a situation analogous to what occurs in human immunology. That is, just like a cholera vaccine given in a small dosage enables a person's immune system to ward off the real effects of cholera when traveling in India or another less-developed country, two-sided messages can serve to inoculate the firm's brand from a subsequent attack from a competitor.

Various studies support the inoculation role of two-sided refutational messages in a marketing context.[9] Researchers in one study tested inoculation theory by examining the issue of installing inflatable air bags in new cars.[10] Would consumers' beliefs about the advantages of air bags (e.g., safety considerations) be more resistant to change when a one-sided message was followed by an *attack advertisement* challenging the belief or when a two-sided message was followed by the same attack advertisement?

The one-sided ad stated that the belief in question (safety) was obviously valid and then presented three arguments to support the belief. The two-sided refutational ad also stated that the belief in question was valid but also mentioned three counter arguments opponents might use to attack air bags. The two-sided advertisement then proceeded to refute the validity of these counter arguments. In support of the inoculation role for two-sided messages, this

---

9. For example, Kamins and Assael, "Two-Sided Versus One-Sided Appeals"; George J. Szybillo and Richard Heslin, "Resistance to Persuasion: Inoculation Theory in a Marketing Context," *Journal of Marketing Research,* vol. 10 (November 1973), pp. 396–403; and Alan G. Sawyer, "The Effects of Repetition of Refutational and Supportive Advertising Appeals," *Journal of Marketing Research,* vol. 10 (February 1973), pp. 23–33.

10. Szybillo and Heslin, "Resistance to Persuasion: Inoculation Theory in a Marketing Context."

study revealed that beliefs of subjects exposed to the two-sided message were more resistant to change from the attack advertisement than were the beliefs of subjects who received only one-sided arguments.

Given the evidence on the conditions favoring either one- or two-sided messages, several practical suggestions can be offered. First, where it is possible to segment consumers into loyal and nonloyal categories, a good strategy may be to direct one-sided ads toward the loyal group (those whose initial opinion is already favorable toward the advertised product) and two-sided ads toward the nonloyal group. Although mass advertising makes it virtually impossible to target only loyal or nonloyal customers, this problem might be overcome by designing separate direct-mail versions of the sales message to each segment.

For new product introductions, the product innovator should consider using two-sided advertisements. The innovator's arguments favoring its brand will eventually undergo retaliation from competitors who will argue that their brands are superior. A two-sided campaign could thus serve to inoculate consumers against such counter advertising. In a similar vein, sales representatives can also use the inoculation effects of a two-sided sales presentation by admitting to any minor weaknesses in their products.

Though there are legitimate reasons for using two-sided messages under certain marketing communications conditions, advertising agencies and their clients generally are reluctant to do so. There seems to be an inherent fear in admitting to product weaknesses or competitor's strengths.

Comparative Messages.   The practice in which marketing communicators *directly compare* their products against competitive offerings, typically claiming that the promoted item is superior in one or several important purchase considerations, is referred to as **comparative messages.** Personal salespeople have always used comparative messages in arguing the advantages of their products over competitors' products. Likewise, print advertisers (newspapers, magazines) have used comparative claims for decades. It was not until the early 1970s, however, that television commercials began making direct-comparison claims. Since then all media have experienced notable increases in the use of comparative advertising.

An example of comparative advertising is the ad for Visa Gold Card in Figure 6.1. Visa describes various products and services it believes are superior to American Express' offerings.

Advertisers face a number of difficult questions when deciding whether to use comparative advertising. The following quotation is a useful summary of the issues:

> Is comparative advertising more effective than noncomparative advertising? How do comparative and noncomparative advertisements compare in terms of differential impact on awareness, believability, credibility, comprehension and advertiser identification? Do they differ with regard to effects on purchase intentions, brand preferences, purchase behavior? What are the effects of copy claim variation and substantiation on the performance of competitive advertisements? Is ef-

Illustration of a Comparative Advertisement   FIGURE 6.1

Why Is The American Express Card Green?

Envy.

The fact is, with an impressive array of products and services like this, Visa® could make anyone a bit envious.

**Visa Gold Card.
Outdelivering American Express.**

Visa Gold provides full value auto rental insurance,* emergency travel and medical assistance, and at least $150,000 in automatic travel accident insurance—$50,000 more than American Express. Plus Purchase Security and Extended Protection* which covers most of your purchases against theft, fire, loss, or breakage. And Visa Gold will bring both emergency cash and a replacement card right to you anywhere in the world. Something American Express just can't deliver.

**Visa Travelers Cheques.
Better To Travel With.**

Visa can promptly refund lost or stolen cheques at over 248,000

locations around the world—twice as many as American Express. Which gives you twice as much reason to travel with Visa Travelers Cheques.

**Visa Business Card.
Better For Business.**

Visa's Business Card offers deferred payment plans, emergency travel assistance services, convenient cash access, and specifically tailored expenditure reporting services. And it is accepted at more than six million merchants—that's almost three times more than the American Express Corporate Card.

**Visa Cash Access.
Easier Access Worldwide.**

If you need cash from just your Visa card, you're covered with over 248,000 banking branches around the world. In addition, with your Personal Identification Number provided by your issuing bank and

your Visa card you can get cash at over 32,000 cash machines around the world. Combined, this is more than ten times as many places as American Express.

**Visa Classic Card.
The Accepted Leader.**

Visa Classic is the accepted leader because it's honored at nearly three times as many places as American Express. And six times as many Visa cards are used throughout the world.

So next time you have to choose, remember which card is green.
And why.

**It's Everywhere
You Want To Be.®**

*Excess reimbursement insurance, certain conditions and exclusions apply.

©Visa U.S.A. Inc. 1989

fectiveness influenced by factors such as prior brand loyalty or competitive position? Should companies use comparative advertisements and, if so, under what conditions?[11]

Researchers have performed a number of comparative-advertising studies since the mid-1970s. Findings are inconclusive and even contradictory at times. Lack of definitive results is to be expected, however, because advertising is a complex phenomenon that varies greatly from situation to situation in terms of executional elements, audience characteristics, media characteristics, and other factors. To repeat a theme presented at the beginning of this chapter, simple answers should not be expected, and in fact, they are rarely found. The research does, however, permit the following general observations:[12]

1. *Situational factors* (i.e., characteristics of audience, media, message, company, and product) play an important role in determining whether comparative advertising is more effective than noncomparative advertising. For example, one study found that product superiority claims in a comparative advertisement were evaluated significantly less favorably by subjects who had a prior preference for the comparison brand (i.e., the brand that the advertised brand was compared against) than for subjects who did not have a prior preference for the comparison brand.[13]

2. Comparative advertising may be more suitable for *low-involvement products* (e.g., convenience goods) than for durable goods, certain services, and other high-involvement products. This observation is speculative because the research support is limited, but it is not without logical support. Specifically, advertisements for low-involvement products have difficulty attracting the consumer's attention; therefore, comparative advertisements may be more effective for these products because the relative novelty of comparative advertising provides a means of attracting viewer attention. High-involvement products, on the other hand, are more concerned with conveying information and influencing purchase intentions than with merely attracting attention.

3. Comparative advertising may be particularly effective for promoting *new brands that possess distinct advantages relative to competitive brands.* One study found that comparative advertising is more effective for a new market entrant, whereas noncomparative advertising appears to be more effective for established brands.[14] When a new brand has a distinct advantage

11. Stephen B. Ash and Chow-Hou Wee, "Comparative Advertising: A Review with Implications for Further Research," in *Advances in Consumer Research*, vol. 10, eds. R. P. Bagozzi and A. M. Tybout (Ann Arbor, MI: Association for Consumer Research, 1983), p. 374.
12. The following comments are adapted from Ash and Wee, "Comparative Advertising," primarily p. 374.
13. V. Kanti Prasad, "Communications Effectiveness of Comparative Advertising: A Laboratory Analysis," *Journal of Marketing Research*, vol. 13 (May 1976), pp. 128–137.
14. Terence A. Shimp and David C. Dyer, "The Effects of Comparative Advertising Mediated by Market Position of Sponsoring Brand," *Journal of Advertising*, vol. 7, no. 3 (1978), pp. 13–19.

over competitive brands, comparative advertising provides a powerful method to convey this advantage. As compared to noncomparative advertising, comparative advertising has also been shown to increase the perceived similarity between a challenger brand in a product category and the category leader.[15]

4.   The effectiveness of comparative advertising increases when comparative claims are made to appear more *credible*. There are various ways to accomplish this: (1) have an independent research organization support the superiority claims, (2) present impressive test results to back up the claims, (3) use a credible source as spokesperson, and (4) use a two-sided message presentation.

5.   Because comparative advertising is generally perceived by consumers to be more *interesting* than noncomparative advertising, comparative advertising may also be appropriate for established brands that have experienced static sales using noncomparative advertising.

6.   *Print media* appear to be better vehicles than broadcast media for comparative advertisements. Print lends itself to more thorough comparisons, and consumers have control over the time needed to process the large amount of information that is usually found in comparative ads.

Order of Presentation.   The fundamental issue with the order-of-presentation element of message structure is this: When presenting a one-sided message, should the marketing communicator present the *most important points* at the beginning, in the middle, or at the end of the message? To address this question, it is necessary to establish the working vocabulary for various order structures. A **climax** order is used when a communicator presents the strongest arguments *at the end* of the message. An **anticlimax** order exists when the most important points are presented *at the beginning*. In a **pyramidal** order, the most important materials appear *in the middle*.

No one order of presentation stands out as best for every situation. Useful generalizations do emerge, however, when the level of audience interest in the communication topic is taken into account.

When an audience has a *low level of interest* in the material being presented, the *anticlimax order* of presentation tends to be the most effective. The anticlimax order is superior when audience interest is low due to the attention-gaining potential of presenting the stronger, more interesting material first. However, the communicator runs the risk of audience letdown by finishing with weak points.

When an audience has a *high level of interest* in the material being presented, the *climax order* tends to be most effective. Under conditions of high audience involvement, the message's emphasis can be directed at affecting at-

15. Gerald J. Gorn and Charles B. Weinberg, "The Impact of Comparative Advertising on Perception and Attitude: Some Positive Findings," *Journal of Consumer Research*, vol. 11 (September 1984), pp. 719–727.

titudes rather than merely gaining attention. The climax order is therefore favored because the later points exceed expectations created by points presented initially, and the audience is likely to be left with a favorable opinion toward both the communicator and the communications topic.

The *pyramidal order* is the least effective order of presentation, regardless of the level of audience interest.

From the marketing communicator's perspective, for *low-involvement* products (i.e., those products that involve little purchase risk and are typically inexpensive), the strongest message arguments should typically be presented early in the message. For *high-involvement* products, the strongest arguments should be delayed until later in the message. It is unwise in any case to place strong arguments in the middle (pyramidal order) of a message. Material in the middle is attended to least, is the least well learned, and is the least persuasive.

Message Content

Message content deals with what is said in a message and how it is said. The following discussion is limited to five content topics that have great relevance for marketing practitioners: (1) fear appeals, (2) the use of humor, (3) the role of music, (4) sex appeals, and (5) subliminal messages. Advertisers, salespersons, public relations spokespeople, and other marketing communicators use all of these message styles to varying degrees in hopes of gaining attention, achieving impact, and ultimately producing sales.

Fear Appeals.   Companies sometimes use fear appeals in attempting to motivate customers to action. The underlying logic when using fear appeals is that fear will stimulate audience involvement with a message and thereby promote acceptance of message arguments. The appeals may take the form of social disapproval or physical danger. For example, mouthwashes, deodorants, toothpastes, and other products make us aware of the *social disapproval* we may suffer if our breath is not fresh, if our underarms are not dry, or if our teeth are not white. Smoke detectors, automobile tires, unsafe sex, and driving under the influence of alcohol and other drugs are products and themes that communicators use to induce fear of *physical danger* in consumers.

Aside from the basic ethical issue of whether fear should be used at all, the fundamental issue for marketing communicators is determining how intense the fear presentation should be. Numerous fear-appeal studies have been performed by psychologists and marketing researchers, but the fact remains that there still is no consensus on the "optimum" level of fear. Some studies have reported that a "low" level of fear is most effective[16], whereas other re-

16. The classic demonstration is a study on dental hygiene practices. See I. Janis and S. Feshbach, "Effects of Fear-Arousing Communications," *Journal of Abnormal and Social Psychology*, vol. 48 (January 1953), pp. 78–92.

searchers contend that a "moderate" level of fear is more effective than levels of fear that are either too low or too high.[17]

In an attempt to reconcile the apparently contradictory findings, two marketing researchers arrived at the conclusion that differences in research findings are probably attributable to the different definitions of high, moderate, and low fear appeals employed in different studies. These researchers summarized the early fear-appeal literature by concluding:

> Neither extremely strong nor very weak fear appeals are maximally effective. It seems that appeals at a somewhat moderate level of fear are best. A simple explanation for this might be that if an appeal is too weak, it just does not attract enough attention. If it is too strong, on the other hand, it may lead people to avoid the message or ignore the message's recommendations as being inadequate to the task of eliminating the feared event.[18]

This conclusion, which has been termed the *inverted-U explanation*, has not stood up under scrutiny.[19] The only reasonable generalization worth offering at this point is that the optimum level of fear appeal probably depends on the *degree of relevance* a topic has for an audience—the greater the relevance, the lower the optimal level of fear. In other words, people who are highly involved in a topic can be motivated by a relatively small amount of fear, whereas a more intense level of fear is required to motivate uninvolved people.[20]

The long-standing series of television ads by Michelin Tires illustrates this point. The commericals show adorable babies sitting on tires and in various scenarios surrounded by tires (e.g., wearing yellow rain suits). These commercials are subtle reminders (low levels of fear) for parents to consider buying Michelin tires to ensure their children's safety.

When using fear appeals, advertisers stand a greater chance of converting nonusers of a product to its use than of convincing consumers to switch brands.[21] Thus, for instance, fear appeals should be more useful in converting blade users to electric shavers than in changing a consumer's brand preference from Norelco to Remington.

Humor.   Politicians, actors and actresses, after-dinner speakers, professors, and indeed all of us at one time or another use humor to create a desired reaction. Salespeople and advertisers also turn to humor in the hopes of achieving various communication objectives. Whether humor is effective

---

17. Michael L. Ray and William L. Wilkie, "Fear: The Potential of an Appeal Neglected by Marketing," *Journal of Marketing*, vol. 34 (January 1970), pp. 54–62.
18. Ibid., p. 55.
19. For further discussion, see Herbert J. Rotfeld, "Fear Appeals and Persuasion: Assumptions and Errors in Advertising Research," forthcoming in *Current Issues and Research in Advertising*, vol. 11 (1988).
20. Peter Wright, "Concrete Action Plans in TV Messages to Increase Reading of Drug Warnings," *Journal of Consumer Research*, vol. 6 (December 1979), pp. 256–269.
21. John J. Wheatley, "Marketing and the Use of Fear-Anxiety Appeals," *Journal of Marketing*, vol. 35 (April 1971), pp. 62–64.

and what kinds of humor are most successful are matters of some debate among marketing communications practitioners and scholars.[22]

Humor, when used correctly and in the right circumstances, can be an extremely effective advertising technique. The famous "Where's the beef?" campaign for Wendy's hamburgers transformed its spokesperson, Clara Peller, into a celebrity; it also led to a phenomenal 15 percent increase in sales shortly after the ad was aired.[23] Other famous humorous ads include the long-standing campaign for Miller Lite beer (with Rodney Dangerfield and a cast of oddball characters) and the successful Joe Isuzu ads that lampoon consumers' negative impressions about automobile salespeople and dealer advertising.

Despite the frequent use of humor in advertising, relatively little is known in a definitive scientific sense about its effects on customer behavior. Researchers, however, have deduced the following tentative generalizations:[24]

1.   Humorous messages *attract attention*.

2.   Humor can *inhibit consumers' understanding* of the intended meaning of a message.

3.   Because humor is a pleasant form of distraction, it can produce an *increase in persuasion* by effectively "disarming" receivers' natural selective perception and reducing their tendencies toward counter arguing with persuasive selling claims.

4.   Humor tends to *enhance source credibility*, thereby improving the persuasive impact of an ad message.

5.   A humorous context may *increase liking* for the source and *create a positive mood*, thereby enhancing the persuasive effect of the message.

6.   To the extent that a humorous context functions as a *positive reinforcer*, a persuasive communication placed in such a context may be more effective.

7.   The effects of humor can *differ due to differences in audience characteristics*. Advertisers must use humor carefully since consumers display a variety of tastes in what is humorous and what is not. For example, what is funny in New York might not be funny in Minneapolis.

Because humorous appeals seem to inhibit comprehension but enhance message attention and acceptance, it has been suggested that humor in advertising should be used only in situations in which the *audience is familiar* with

---

22. A thorough review of the issues and controversy is provided by Thomas J. Madden, University of South Carolina working paper, College of Business Administration, Columbia, SC, August 1988.
23. "Prime Ribbing," *Time*, March 26, 1984, p. 54.
24. Brian Sternthal and C. Samuel Craig, "Humor in Advertising," *Journal of Marketing*, vol. 37 (October 1973), pp. 12–18.

the product—not in situations where the product is substantially new or when there are a large number of facts for consumers to understand.[25]

Humorous appeals are not equally effective for all consumers. Using data on magazine readership patterns from the Starch magazine readership database (see Chapter 14 for details about Starch data), researchers determined that men had higher attention scores than women for humorous ads and that magazines with predominantly white audiences had higher attention scores for humorous ads than did those with predominantly black readers.[26]

Whatever the effects marketing communicators are trying to achieve, they should proceed cautiously because: (1) the effects of humor can differ due to differences in audience characteristics, (2) the definition of what is funny in one country or region of a country is not necessarily the same in another country or region, and (3) a humorous message may be so distracting to an audience that receivers ignore the message content. Advertisers should carefully research their intended market segments before venturing into humorous advertising. Likewise, salespeople should use caution because of the danger of possibly insulting customers or of coming off like a buffoon when using inappropriate or excessive amounts of humor.

Music.   Michael Jackson, Lionel Richie, Bruce Springsteen, the Pointer Sisters, Elvis Presley, Linda Ronstadt, and the Beatles are just some of the musicians whose music is used to "move merchandise." In addition to these well-known celebrities, nonvocal musical accompaniment and unknown vocalists are used extensively in promoting everything from fabric softeners to automobiles.[27]

Many marketing communications practitioners and scholars think that music performs useful communication functions such as attracting attention, putting consumers in a positive mood, and making them more receptive to message arguments.

Although music's role in marketing is an incredibly understudied subject, a few recent studies have begun to demonstrate the roles that music performs. In one study music was used as an *unconditioned stimulus* in an effort to influence experimental subjects' preference for a ballpoint pen, the *conditioned stimulus*.[28] Unconditioned and conditioned stimuli are terms used in classical conditioning research. An unconditioned stimulus (UCS) is one that evokes

25. Brian Sternthal and C. Samuel Craig, *Consumer Behavior: An Information Processing Perspective* (Englewood Cliffs, NJ: Prentice-Hall, 1982), p. 272.
26. Thomas J. Madden and Marc G. Weinberger, "The Effects of Humor on Attention in Magazine Advertising," *Journal of Advertising*, vol. 11, no. 3 (1982), pp. 4–14.
27. Julie Candler, "Music Takes a Front Seat in Auto Campaigns," *Advertising Age*, May 5, 1986, p. S32; Christine Demkowych, "Music on the Upswing in Advertising," *Advertising Age*, March 31, 1986, p. S5; Merle Kingman, "Music Is the Magic for Most of the Best," *Advertising Age*, March 14, 1988, p. 26.
28. Gerald J. Gorn, "The Effects of Music in Advertising on Choice Behavior: A Classical Conditioning Approach," *Journal of Marketing*, vol. 46 (Winter 1982), pp. 94–101.

pleasant feelings or thoughts in people. A conditioned stimulus (CS) is one that is emotionally or cognitively "neutral" prior to the onset of a conditioning experiment. In simple terms, classical conditioning is achieved when the pairing of UCS and CS results in a transfer of feeling from the UCS (music in the present case) to the CS (the ballpoint pen).

Experimental subjects in this research were informed that an advertising agency was trying to select music for use in a commercial for a ballpoint pen. Subjects then listened to music while they viewed slides of the pen. The positive UCS for half the subjects was music from the movie *Grease*, and the negative UCS for the remaining subjects was classical eastern Indian music. The simple association between music and the pen influenced product preference—nearly 80 percent of the subjects exposed to the *Grease* music chose the advertised pen, whereas only 30 percent of the subjects exposed to the Indian music chose the advertised pen.

Another application of music in marketing communications is as background in retail settings. Two recent experiments have shown how effective background music can be in stimulating customer purchasing.

The first experiment examined the effects of background music in a *supermarket setting*. A single supermarket was studied over a nine-week period by comparing sales volume during those days when slow-tempo background music was played (72 beats per minute or slower) versus days when fast-tempo music was in the background (94 beats per minute or more). The dramatic finding obtained was that daily sales volume averaged approximately $16,740 on days when slow-tempo music was played but only about $12,113 when fast-tempo music was played—for an average increase of $4,627 per day, or a 38.2 percent increase! The slow-tempo music apparently lowered the pace at which customers moved through the store and increased their total expenditures since they had a longer opportunity to purchase more.[29]

In a second field experiment, the same researcher examined the effects of background music on *restaurant customers'* purchase behavior. A restaurant alternated playing slow- and fast-tempo music on Friday and Saturday nights over a one-month period. Slow music increased the amount of time customers remained seated at their tables—an average of 56 minutes per customer group during slow-music nights compared to an average of 45 minutes during fast-music nights. Also, customers during slow-music nights spent significantly larger amounts on alcoholic beverages (an average of $30.47 per customer group) compared to fast-music nights ($21.62 per customer group).[30]

In addition to background music, many stores are experimenting with *foreground music*. This type of music is, as the name suggests, "out front" and intended to be heard as soon as the customer enters the store. The music is chosen to be compatible with the listening interests of the store's clientele.

29. Ronald E. Milliman, "Using Background Music to Affect the Behavior of Supermarket Shoppers," *Journal of Marketing*, vol. 46 (Summer 1982), pp. 86–91.
30. Ronald E. Milliman, "The Influence of Background Music on the Behavior of Restaurant Patrons," *Journal of Consumer Research*, vol. 13 (September 1986), pp. 286–289.

Thus, a store catering to teenagers may use loud rock music, whereas a store appealing to middle-aged professionals would perhaps select a repertoire of classical music.

In the final analysis, music appears to be effective in creating customer moods, affecting sales, and stimulating buying preferences and choices. Of course, considerably more research is needed to fully understand the scientific role of music in accomplishing various marketing communications functions. Marketplace wisdom, as manifested by marketing communicators' nearly universal use of music in advertisements and in retail settings, clearly suggests that music is an effective form of nonverbal communication.

Sex Appeals. Sex appeals in advertising are often explicit. Consider the following commerical.

> The scene: a bedroom. The action: a young woman pulls on silky bikini panties and a bra. While the camera slides seductively over the blonde's bare body, the woman coos that her underwear "brings out the best in me." No, this isn't an X-rated scene from "Love Kittens" but a new cable commercial for Berlei USA lingerie that [was] broadcast on independent network television.[31]

Whereas the use of such explicit sex was unthinkable just a few years ago, it now represents part of a new trend toward more sexually explicit advertising.[32] The trend is not restricted to the United States; indeed, sexual explicitness is more prevalent and more overt elsewhere, for example, in Brazil and Western Europe.

Whether such advertising is effective and under what conditions it may be effective remain largely unexplored issues.[33] Complicating the matter is the fact that sex in advertising actually takes two forms: *nudity* and *suggestiveness*. It is uncertain which form is more effective.[34]

What role does sex play in advertising? Actually, there are several potential roles. First, sexual material in advertising acts as an initial *attentional lure* and also holds attention for a longer period, given that the models are attractive or the scene is pleasant.[35] This is called the "stopping power" role of sex.[36]

31. "Goodbye, Mr. Whipple," *Newsweek*, March 26, 1984, p. 62.
32. A content analysis of magazine advertising for the years 1964 and 1984 indicates that the percentage of ads with sexual content has *not* changed. What has changed, however, is that sexual illustrations have become more overt. Female models are more likely than male models to be portrayed in nude, partially nude, or suggestive poses. See Lawrence Soley and Gary Kurzbard, "Sex in Advertising: A Comparison of 1964 and 1984 Magazine Advertisements," *Journal of Advertising*, vol. 15, no. 3 (1986), pp. 46–55.
33. For a review of the scientific issues involved in studying sex in advertising, see Robert S. Baron, "Sexual Content and Advertising Effectiveness: Comments on Belch et al. (1981) and Caccavale et al. (1981)" in *Advances in Consumer Research*, vol. 9, ed. Andrew Mitchell (Ann Arbor, MI: Association for Consumer Research, 1982), pp. 428–430.
34. Michael A. Belch, Barbro E. Holgerson, George E. Belch, and Jerry Koppman, "Psychophysiological and Cognitive Responses to Sex in Advertising," in *Advances in Consumer Research*, vol. 9, ed. Andrew Mitchell (Ann Arbor, MI: Association for Consumer Research, 1982), pp. 424–427.
35. Baron, "Sexual Content and Advertising Effectiveness," p. 428.
36. B. G. Yovovich, "Sex in Advertising—The Power and the Perils," *Advertising Age*, May 2, 1983, p. M-4.

A second potential role is to *enhance recall*. The available evidence suggests that sexual content or symbolism will enhance recall only if it is appropriate to the product category and the creative advertising execution.[37] Sexual appeals produce significantly better recall only if the advertising execution has an *appropriate relationship* with the advertised product.[38] A sexual advertising theme for a product such as "Musk by English Leather" (see Figure 6.2) probably reflects an effective sex appeal in view of the nature of both the product and target market. Comparatively, the use of sex in ads for industrial equipment, a frequent practice in past years, would likely be inappropriate and result in diminished recall of copy points.

A third role performed by sexual content in advertising is to evoke *emotional responses* such as feelings of attraction or even lust. These reactions can increase an ad's persuasive impact, with the opposite occurring if the ad elicits negative feelings such as disgust, embarrassment, or uneasiness.[39]

Whether sexual content elicits a positive reaction or a negative one depends on the *appropriateness or relevance* of the sexual content to the advertised subject matter. An interesting marketing experiment tested this by varying magazine ads for two products, a ratchet wrench set (a product for which a sexual appeal is irrelevant) and a body oil (a relevant sex-appeal product). The study also manipulated three versions of dress for the female model who appeared in the ads: in the "demure model" version, she was shown fully clothed in a blouse and slacks; in the "seductive model" version, she wore the same clothing as in the demure version, but the blouse was completely unbuttoned and knotted at the bottom, exposing some midriff and cleavage; in the "nude model" version, she was completely undressed. Study findings revealed that the seductive model/body oil combination was perceived most favorably by all respondents, whereas the nude model/body oil combination was perceived as the least appealing advertisement. Females regarded the nude model/ratchet set as least appealing.[40]

Similar results were obtained from focus-group research involving television commercials for Underalls pantyhose. One commercial focused on the derrieres of two women: one had a "terrific looking rump" (according to the research report) and the other had panty lines that looked awful. The woman with the panty lines tells viewers that "Underalls make you look like I wish I looked." Focus-group tests on this commercial revealed that respondents liked the commercial and did not find it offensive. Reactions were very unfavorable, however, to a second version of this commercial that differed from the first by using the tagline "Underalls make me look like I'm not wearing nothing." This

37. Larry Percy, "A Review of the Effect of Specific Advertising Elements upon Overall Communication Response," in *Current Issues and Research in Advertising*, vol. 2, eds. J. H. Leigh and C. R. Martin, Jr. (Ann Arbor, MI: Graduate School of Business Administration, 1983), p. 95.
38. David Richmond and Timothy P. Hartman, "Sex Appeal in Advertising," *Journal of Advertising Research*, vol. 22 (October-November 1982), pp. 53–61.
39. Baron, "Sexual Content and Advertising Effectiveness," p. 428.
40. Robert A. Peterson and Roger A. Kerin, "The Female Role in Advertisements: Some Experimental Evidence," *Journal of Marketing*, vol. 41 (October 1977), pp. 59–63.

Use of Sex Appeal in Advertising FIGURE 6.2

ad was viewed as offensive because looking like one is wearing "nothing" is not regarded as a primary product benefit.[41]

The implication to be drawn from the previously cited research is that sexual content stands little chance of being effective unless it is directly relevant to an advertisement's primary selling point. When used appropriately, sexual content is capable of eliciting attention, enhancing recall, and creating a favorable association with the advertised product.

Subliminal Messages and Symbolic Embeds.   The word *subliminal* refers to the presentation of stimuli at a rate or level that is below the conscious threshold of awareness. An example would be playing self-help messages on audiotapes (e.g., to help one quit smoking) at a decibel level indecipherable to the naked ear. Stimuli that cannot be perceived by the conscious senses may nonetheless be perceived *subconsciously*. This possibility has generated considerable concern from advertising critics and has fostered much speculation from researchers.

Original outcry occurred in response to research by James Vicary in 1957, who claimed to have increased sales of Coca-Cola and popcorn in a New Jersey movie theatre by using subliminal messages. At five-second intervals during the movie *Picnic*, subliminal messages saying "Drink Coca-Cola" and "Eat Popcorn" appeared on the screen for a mere 1/3,000th of a second. Although the naked eye could not possibly have seen these messages, Vicary claimed that sales of Coca-Cola and popcorn increased 58 and 18 percent respectively.[42] Though Vicary's research is *scientifically meaningless* because he failed to use proper experimental procedures, the study nonetheless raised public concerns about subliminal advertising and led to Congressional hearings.[43] Federal legislation was never enacted, but since then subliminal advertising has been the subject of criticism by advertising critics, a matter of embarrassment for advertising practitioners, and an issue of theoretical curiosity to marketing communications scholars.

The fires of controversy were fueled again in the early 1970s with the publication of three provocatively titled books: *Subliminal Seduction, Media Sexploitation,* and *The Clam Plate Orgy*.[44] The author of these books, Wilson Key, claimed subliminal advertising techniques are used extensively and have the power to influence consumers' choice behaviors.

---

41. This research was performed by the research department of the Needham, Harper, and Steers advertising agency and is described in B. G. Yovovich, "Sex in Advertising," p. M-5.
42. This description is adapted from Martin P. Block and Bruce G. Vanden Gergh, "Can You Sell Subliminal Messages to Consumers?" *Journal of Advertising*, vol. 14, no. 3 (1985), p. 59.
43. Vicary himself acknowledged that the study that initiated the original furor over subliminal advertising was based on too small an amount of data to be meaningful. See Fred Danzig, "Subliminal Advertising - Today It's Just Historic Flashback for Researcher Vicary," *Advertising Age*, September 17, 1962, pp. 42, 74.
44. Wilson B. Key, *Subliminal Seduction: Ad Media's Manipulation of a Not So Innocent America* (Englewood Cliffs, NJ: Prentice-Hall, 1972); *Media Sexploitation* (Englewood Cliffs, NJ: Prentice-Hall, 1976); *The Clam Plate Orgy: And Other Subliminal Techniques for Manipulating Your Behavior* (Englewood Cliffs, NJ: Prentice-Hall, 1980).

Many advertising practitioners and marketing communications scholars discount Key's arguments and vehemently disagree with his conclusions. Part of the difficulty in arriving at clear answers as to "who's right and who's wrong" stems from the fact that commentators differ in what they mean by "subliminal advertising." In fact, there are three distinct forms of subliminal stimulation: A first form presents *visual stimuli* at a very rapid rate by means of a device called a tachistoscope (say, at 1/3,000th of a second such as in Vicary's research). A second form uses *accelerated speech in auditory messages*. The third form involves the *embedding of hidden symbols* (such as a sexual images or words) in print advertisements.

This last form, *embedding*, is what Key has written about and is the form that advertising researchers have studied. However, it is important to remember that embeds (for example, the word SEX airbrushed into an advertisement) are *not* truly subliminal since they are visible to the naked eye. Nonetheless, the remaining discussion of "subliminal" messages is restricted to the practice of embedding.

To better appreciate embedding, look at the advertisement for Edge shaving cream presented in Figure 6.3. One need not be a Freudian psychologist to realize that the ad contains considerable sexual innuendo. Aside from the symbolism associated with the water tunnel and the look of ecstasy on the man's face, note also that the volcanic-looking mountain below the man's lips is not really a mountain at all; rather, it is a nude woman resting on her back with her knees in a raised position. Notice also that above the man's upper lip are three nude figures that have been airbrushed into the lather (a male with extended arms on the right side of the man's face, a female directly below his nose, and another female to the left of his nose).

Is there proof that embedded symbols in advertisements do in fact influence consumers' product and brand choices? To answer this we first need to examine the process that would have to operate in order for embedding to influence consumer choice behavior. The Edge shaving cream advertisement provides a useful vehicle for motivating this discussion. The first step in the process is that the consumer would have to consciously or subconsciously process the embedded symbol (e.g., see the nude woman in the Edge magazine ad). Second, as the result of processing the cue, the consumer would have to develop a greater desire for Edge shaving cream than he had before seeing the ad. Third, because advertising is done at the brand level and because advertisers are interested in selling their brands and not just any brand in the product category, effective symbolic embedding would require that consumers develop a desire for the specific brand, Edge in this case, rather than just any brand in the category. Finally, the consumer would need to transfer the desire for the advertised brand into actual purchase behavior.

Is there evidence to support this chain of events? Empirical work is just beginning to accumulate. Three recent advertising studies have attempted to tackle the issue. Only one study will be described here, however, because the other two, though interesting in their own right, are too far removed

FIGURE 6.3   **Illustration of Embedding**

Subliminally Embedded and Non-Embedded Ads for Chivas Regal   FIGURE 6.4

from actual advertising practice to have much relevance for the present discussion.[45]

Researchers in the third study located actual advertisements containing symbolic embeds. An ad for Marlboro Lights cigarettes was described as follows: "This ad pictures two men on horseback riding through a rocky terrain. Embedded in the rocks to the right of the riders is a representation of male genitals." An ad for Chivas Regal Scotch whiskey received this description: "This ad is a picture of a large bottle of whiskey. The bottle has a handle on the left through which is passed a chain. On the right side of the bottle below the neck is embedded the image of a nude female seen from the back [i.e., her backside, not the back of the bottle]. The image appears as a reflection on the bottle."[46]

The researchers tested these two embedded ads and created two corresponding ads that were identical except that the embedded symbols were re-

45. The other studies are Ronnie Cuperfain and T. K. Clarke, "A New Perspective of Subliminal Perception," *Journal of Advertising*, vol. 14, no. 1 (1985), pp. 36–41; and Myron Gable, Henry T. Wilkens, Lynn Harris, and Richard Feinberg, "An Evaluation of Subliminally Embedded Sexual Stimuli in Graphics," *Journal of Advertising*, vol. 16, no. 1 (1987), pp. 26–31.
46. William E. Kilbourne, Scott Painton, and Danny Ridley, "The Effect of Sexual Embedding on Responses to Magazine Advertisements," *Journal of Advertising*, vol. 14, no. 2 (1985), pp. 48–56.

moved. Figure 6.4 presents the embedded and non-embedded Chivas Regal ads.[47] (Which ad, left or right panel, contains the nude?) Over 400 college students participated in the experiment. Each subject was exposed either to the Marlboro and Chivas ads with the embeds or the two ads without the embeds. Post-exposure measures of subjects' attitudes toward each brand indicated that subjects exposed to the embedded version of the Chivas Regal ad had *significantly more favorable attitudes* toward that brand than did subjects exposed to the non-embedded ad. There were no differences in attitudes toward Marlboro Lights regardless of whether subjects viewed the embedded or non-embedded version.

This experiment offers partial support that sexual embeds in magazine advertisements may increase consumers' attitudes toward advertised products.[48] Whether these results generalize to other products is unknown. The fact that the sexual embed enhanced attitudes only for the liquor product but not the tobacco product goes along with the earlier discussion about the role of *relevance* for effective non-subliminal sexual appeals. Liquor is arguably a more sexually oriented product than cigarettes and is therefore probably a more appropriate product for sexual embeds.

Despite this limited evidence that sexual embeds *may* influence consumers' attitudes, there are a variety of practical problems that probably prevent embedding from being effective in a realistic marketing context. Perhaps the major reason why advertising embeds likely have little effect is because they have to be concealed to preclude detection by consumers. Many consumers would resent such "tricky" advertising efforts if they knew they existed. Thus, precluding detection from consumers means that embeds are relatively weak in comparison to more vivid advertising representations. (Have you spotted the nude yet in the Chivas Regal bottle?) Because the majority of consumers devote relatively little time and effort to processing advertisements, a weak stimulus means that most consumers could not possibly be influenced.[49]

Even if consumers did attend and encode sexual embeds under natural advertising conditions, there remains serious doubt that this information would have sufficient impact to affect product or brand choice behavior. Standard (superliminal) advertising information itself has a difficult time influencing consumers. There is no theoretical reason to expect that subliminal information is any more effective. For example, do you really think that men would run out to buy Edge shaving cream just because they consciously or subconsciously spot a nude woman in the advertisement for that product?

---

47. These ads were not presented in the article by Kilbourne et al. but were reproduced in Jo Anna Natale, "Are You Open to Suggestion?" *Psychology Today*, September 1988, p. 28.
48. This article has been criticized on technical grounds that need not concern us here. For an excellent review of the literature and for a discussion of a view opposing subliminal advertising, see Joel Saegert, "Why Marketing Should Quit Giving Subliminal Advertising the Benefit of the Doubt," *Psychology & Marketing*, vol. 4 (Summer 1987), pp. 107–120.
49. For further discussion of the practical difficulties associated with implementing subliminal advertising, see Timothy E. Moore, "Subliminal Advertising: What You See Is What You Get," *Journal of Marketing*, vol. 46 (Spring 1982), p. 41.

In sum, the topic of subliminal advertising (particularly the Wilson Key variety of symbolic embeds) makes for interesting speculation and discussion, but scientific evidence in support of its practical effectiveness is virtually non-existent. The following quotation sums up the issue clearly:

> A century of psychological research substantiates the general principle that more intense stimuli have a greater influence on people's behavior than weaker ones. While subliminal perception is a bona fide phenomenon, the effects obtained are subtle and obtaining them typically requires a carefully structured context. Subliminal stimuli are usually so weak that the recipient is not just unaware of the stimulus but is also oblivious to the fact that he/she is being stimulated. As a result, the potential effects of subliminal stimuli are easily nullified by other ongoing stimulation in the same sensory channel or by attention being focused on another modality. These factors pose serious difficulties for any possible marketing application.[50]

Source Factors

A *marketing message* (an ad, sales presentation, publicity release, etc.) was defined previously as "what" is said and "how" it is said. By comparison, the source represents "who" says it. Actually, the term *source* will be used very broadly to include the person, group, or organization that presents a message or is identified in some way with the message. In marketing communications, consumers might view any one or a combination of the following as communications sources: (1) a celebrity endorser (such as Bill Cosby), (2) a company sales representative, (3) a "typical person" endorser (e.g., a "man-in-the-street" endorsement for a new movie), (4) a media vehicle (such as the *Wall Street Journal*), (5) a trade association (such as the American Dairy Association), and (6) a reference group (such as fellow college students). Clearly, the notion of source is a multifaceted concept.

The source as a component in the communications process often has tremendous persuasive influence on consumers' attitudes and behavior. Some communicators are more persuasive than others. Two people can deliver the same massage to an audience, yet one communicator may be considerably more persuasive.

What are some of the characteristics that make one communicator more persuasive than another? This section attempts to answer that question after first describing the various types of sources found in marketing communications.

Marketing Communications Sources

The most notable marketing-communications sources are (1) sales representatives, (2) the media, (3) celebrity endorsers, and (4) typical-person endorsers. Each of these is discussed in the next few pages.

---

50. Ibid,. p. 46.

Sales Representatives.   Sales representatives represent a critically important source of information, especially in business-to-business marketing. Company image and the salesperson's competence often complement one another. For example, a company's overall image will exert considerable influence on the effectiveness of sales representatives in their day-to-day contact with customers. In an industrial selling experiment, customers were exposed to a ten-minute filmed sales presentation on a new chemical ingredient used in making paint. One group saw a "good" presentation by a salesman representing a high-credibility company (Monsanto); another group observed a "poor" presentation by the same well-known firm. Two other groups saw "good" and "poor" sales presentations by sales representatives representing a relatively low-credibility firm. Customers were more likely to favor the products of a poor sales representative from a well-known company than the products of a good sales representative from an unknown company.[51]

The effect demonstrated by this research is that sales representatives from well-known companies have an advantage in the short run, even though customers may perceive the sales representatives to be low in competence and trustworthiness. Reputable companies may be more able to get by with less-competent salespeople (at least in the short run), whereas less well-known companies must carefully select and train their salespeople in order to compete with the more reputable firms. More will be said in Chapter 21 about how sales representatives can become more effective communicators.

The Media.   Consumers sometimes view the media as sources of information. For example, *Good Housekeeping* and *Parents Magazine* have established themselves in many consumers' minds as credible sources. Both have set standards that advertisers must meet in order to advertise in their magazines. Furthermore, they use seals of approval to endorse certain consumer products. Companies seek the approval of these media to gain a measure of prestige that is associated with these seals.

Celebrity Endorsers.   Television stars, movie actors, and famous athletes are widely used in magazine ads and television commercials to endorse products. Celebrities are in great demand as product spokespersons. In fact, it is estimated that one-third of all television commercials use endorsements, most often involving athletic or entertainment celebrities.[52] Some especially effective celebrity endorsers from past years are shown in the *Focus on Promotion* section.

Advertisers and their agencies are willing to pay huge salaries to those celebrities who are liked and respected by target audiences and who will, it is

51. Theodore Levitt, "Communications and Industrial Selling," *Journal of Marketing,* vol. 31 (April 1967), pp. 15–21.
52. H. M. Spielman, "Pick Product Presenter Prudently," *Marketing News,* September 8, 1987, p. 5.

FOCUS ON PROMOTION

Effective Celebrity Endorsers from Past Years

The trade magazine *Advertising Age* annually selects one celebrity as the most effective star presenter. Michael J. Fox was selected in 1987 for his role in the Diet Pepsi commercial in which a beautiful new neighbor knocks unexpectedly on his apartment door and asks if she could possibly borrow a Diet Pepsi. You may recall this commercial and Fox's heroic efforts to satisfy his new neighbor's request. He crawls down a fire escape, braves the rain, traffic, and a street gang, and finally has to contend with a locked kitchen window before delivering the Diet Pepsi.[53]

Other celebrities who have received *Advertising Age's* Star Presenter award are:

1988	Wilford Brimley
1987	Michael J. Fox
1986	Paul Hogan
1985	William ("The Refrigerator") Perry
1984	Cliff Robertson
1983	John Cleese
1982	Rodney Dangerfield
1981	John Houseman
1980	Brooke Shields
1979	Robert Morley
1978	James Garner and Mariette Hartley
1977	Bill Cosby
1976	O. J. Simpson
1975	Karl Malden ∎

hoped, favorably influence consumers' attitudes and behavior toward the endorsed products. This is probably justified in view of research, which shows that consumers' attitudes and perceptions of quality are enhanced when celebrities endorse products.[54] The vignette at the beginning of this chapter shows that a celebrity such as Michael Jackson can have a tremendous influence on product sales.

---

53. "Only One Spot, But Fox Delivers," *Advertising Age*, May 2, 1988, p. 48.
54. See, for example, R. B. Fireworker and H. H. Friedman, "The Effects of Endorsements on Product Evaluation," *Decision Sciences*, vol. 8 (July 1977), pp. 576–583; and H. H. Friedman, Salvatore Termini, and R. Washington, "The Effectiveness of Advertisements Utilizing Four Types of Endorsers," *Journal of Advertising*, vol. 5 (Summer 1976), pp. 22–24.

Top celebrities receive enormous payments for their endorsement services. Some top celebrity fees average $2 million to $3 million a year for the endorsement of a single product.[55] For example, Bruce Willis, of the television show "Moonlighting," was paid $2 million for promoting Seagram Golden wine coolers.[56] Heavyweight boxer Mike Tyson received an estimated $3.5 million from Pepsi-Cola for endorsing Diet Pepsi (see Figure 6.5). It is estimated that Tyson could earn as much as $7 million a year in product endorsements if he were to remain heavyweight champion (and keep his personal life in order).[57]

Many celebrities endorse multiple products. For example, West German tennis star Boris Becker receives $560,000 a year from Coca-Cola, $70,000 from Ford, $630,000 from Puma, and $560,000 from Fila, among others.[58] American tennis star Chris Evert gets $500,000 a year for wearing Ellesse tennis clothes, $100,000 for wearing Rolex watches, and $200,000 for doing Lipton tea commercials.[59]

What makes a celebrity an effective endorser for a particular product? Basically, there has to be a *meaningful relationship, a relevant link between the star and the product.* Wilford Brimley, star of the television series "Our House," is a perfect endorser for Quaker Oatmeal cereal, a wholesome product endorsed by a man associated with healthy, happy people. Victoria Principal, of beautiful-flowing-hair fame, is ideal for promoting Jhirmack's Lite shampoo. Dom Deluise the portly gourmand/gourmet and actor, is an excellent choice to endorse Ziploc plastic food bags. Dr. J (Julius Erving), of basketball fame, is a great individual to promote Dr. Scholl's Tritin foot spray. Was Jacko, the Australian football player turned actor, an appropriate spokesman for Eveready Battery's Energizer brand? Apparently not; Energizer's market share lead over rival Duracell fell dramatically by seven percentage points during the ten-month period when Jacko endorsed the brand.[60] The only thing Jacko energized was his wallet!

Typical-Person Endorsers.   A frequent advertising approach is to show regular people using or endorsing products. Figure 6.6 shows a magazine ad focusing on the inspirational case of Bill Demby, a veteran who lost both legs in Vietnam but is still able to lead an active life (he even plays basketball!) thanks to the artificial limbs made possible by DuPont's advanced plastic technology.

Testimonial advertising is widespread. For example, physicians are shown dressed in lab coats to promote one cold capsule over other brands. Audi of America, following negative publicity about problems with automatic transmis-

55. "Star Turns That Can Turn Star-Crossed," *U.S. News & World Report*, December 7, 1987, p. 57.
56. Patricia Winters, "Wine Coolers Press Agencies to Ignite Sales," *Advertising Age*, January 20, 1988, pp. 1, 92.
57. Patrick McGeehan, "Endorsement KO?" *Advertising Age*, July 4, 1988, p. 3.
58. "In the Money," *Parade Magazine*, August 14, 1988, p. 17.
59. Tim Harper, "Evert's Grand Slam," *Advertising Age*, June 27, 1988, p. 90.
60. Julie Liesse Erickson, "Eveready Loses Power in Market," *Advertising Age*, July 11, 1988, p. 4.

A Wealthy Celebrity Endorser

FIGURE 6.5

FIGURE 6.6   **Product User as Endorser**

For Bill Demby, the difference means getting another shot.

When Bill Demby was in Vietnam, he used to dream of coming home and playing a little basketball with the guys.

A dream that all but died when he lost both his legs to a Viet Cong rocket.

But then, a group of researchers discovered that a remarkable Du Pont plastic could help make artificial limbs that were more resilient, more flexible, more like life itself.

Thanks to these efforts, Bill Demby is back. And some say, he hasn't lost a step.

At Du Pont, we make the things that make a difference.

Better things for better living.

REG. US. PAT & TM. OFF.

Source: Courtesy Du Pont Company Photo.

sions in its model 5000 sedans, used dozens of owner testimonials (as well as celebrity endorsements) in an attempt to stop falling sales.

Many advertisements that portray typical-person users often include multiple people rather than a single individual. There is a theoretical reason why multiple sources should be more effective than a single source. Specifically, portraying multiple people increases the likelihood of generating higher levels of *message involvement* and correspondingly greater message *elaboration* (recall the discussion on involvement and elaboration in the context of the Elaboration Likelihood Model in Chapter 4). In turn, greater elaboration increases the odds that strong message arguments will favorably influence attitudes.

This line of reasoning was tested in an experiment that manipulated (1) one versus four person-in-the-street endorsers for a new pizza chain advertisement, and (2) strong versus weak arguments favoring eating this chain's pizza. As theorized, the four-person advertisement was found to be more effective (as measured by cognitive responses and attitude measures) than the single source when message arguments were strong. On the other hand, the single source was superior when weak arguments were used. The practical implication for marketing communicators is that increasing the number of endorsers will not necessarily increase persuasive impact; the message arguments must themselves be impactual.[61]

Other Marketing Communication Sources.　Industries, trade associations, and organizations can also serve as sources of information. For example, the food industry, the United Auto Workers union, the federal government, and United Way may be perceived as potential sources of information. Still another approach is to gain the endorsement of a well-respected association, such as the Council for Dental Therapeutics of the American Dental Association. This group has been used for years by Proctor & Gamble to promote Crest toothpaste. Here the advertiser relies upon the perceived prestige and expertise of this respected council to promote its brand.

Source Attributes

Now that you have some understanding of the types of marketing communications sources, further explanation is needed regarding what makes a source effective and the different source attributes that facilitate effectiveness. Three basic source attributes contribute to a source's effectiveness: (1) *power*, (2) *attractiveness*, and (3) *credibility*. Each involves a different mechanism by which the source affects consumer attitudes and behavior. As described in Table 6.1, power operates through a compliance mechanism, attractiveness through identification, and credibility via internalization.[62]

61. David J. Moore and Richard Reardon, "Source Magnification: The Role of Multiple Sources in the Processing of Advertising Appeals," *Journal of Marketing Research*, vol. 24 (November 1987), pp. 412–417.

62. This classification scheme is generally identified with the work of Herbert C. Kelman, "Processes of Opinion Change," *Public Opinion Quarterly*, vol. 25 (Spring 1961), pp. 57–78.

TABLE 6.1   **Source Attributes and Receiver Processing Modes**

Source Attributes	Receiver Processing Modes	Result
Credibility ———————→ Internalization ↘		Attitude Change
Attractiveness ———————→ Identification		
Power ———————→ Compliance ↗		

The following sections elaborate on these source attributes and the associated processes through which each operates. Although these attributes are conceptually different, all three or any combination of two are frequently combined in a single source. Thus, a source may be perceived as both attractive and credible, powerful and credible but not attractive, and so on.

Power: The Process of Compliance. **Compliance** results through a power relationship between the participants in the communications process. That is, a receiver complies with the persuasive efforts of the source because the source has the power, legitimate or otherwise, to administer rewards or punishments. General illustrations of compliance are parent-child and employer-employee relations. For the most part, this form of persuasive influence is *not* prevalent in marketing communications.

Because the powerful source controls rewards and punishments, he or she can often induce compliance to his or her advocated position. However, compliance is relatively superficial in the sense that a compliant individual does what he or she is "forced" to do and does not necessarily adopt the complied-to position as a matter of personal desire or preference.

Sales representatives sometimes possess a degree of power over buyers, especially in a *seller's market* where demand exceeds supply and buyers are dependent on their vendors for supplies of raw materials, parts, or merchandise. Purchasing personnel may feel that if they do not comply with a sales representative's requests, their orders may be delayed (in favor of competitors' requests) or cut off completely.

Attractiveness: The Process of Identification. Source attractiveness consists of three related ideas: *similarity, familiarity,* and *liking*.[63] That is, a source is considered attractive to receivers if they share a sense of similarity or familiarity with the source or if they simply like the source regardless of whether the two are similar in any respect. (For example, I like Michael Jordan a lot, but we are very different. He is a young, wealthy, incredibly talented,

63. H. C. Triandis, *Attitudes and Attitude Change* (New York: John Wiley & Sons, 1971).

basketball player. I am over 40, not very wealthy, and have lost what little basketball talent I used to have.)

Persuasion occurs via an *identification process* when receivers find something in the source that they consider attractive. This does not mean simply physical attractiveness but includes any number of virtuous characteristics that receivers may perceive in a source: intellectual skills, personality properties, lifestyle characteristics, athletic prowess, and so on. When receivers perceive a source to be attractive, they are very likely to adopt the attitudes, behaviors, interests, or preferences of the source. This is what is meant by **identification.**

Marketing communicators recognize that people have a natural tendency to seek relationships with other people whom they like and with whom they feel a sense of similarity and familiarity. An audience can perceive a communicator as similar to themselves in a number of ways: in personality, race, religion, political philosophy, interests, self-image, or group affiliation. The fact that people tend to be more influenced by others similar to themselves is, in part, due to the tendency for people to like others similar to themselves. People also assume that others who are similar to themselves probably form their opinions and make their judgments using the same criteria that they would use.

Sales managers capitalize on this principle and select salespersons who are reasonably matched (intellectually, socially, educationally) with their customers. A sales representative who can establish common interests increases the chances that his or her customers will view him or her positively. A good sales representative learns early what the interests, opinions, and background of a prospective customer are. Once the representative discovers a commonality, he or she attempts to develop the relationship around their similar interests. Likewise, advertisers employ spokespersons who are liked, and perhaps even admired, by advertising audiences.

Communication researchers have not studied attractiveness extensively, and the research that has been conducted has focused on only one dimension of attractiveness—physical attractiveness. Most research has found that a physically attractive source increases attitude change.[64] Specific findings include the following:[65]

1. Attractive models increase a communicator's effectiveness in a limited way.

2. Attractive models produce more favorable evaluations of ads and advertised products than do less attractive models.

3. Physically attractive communicators are more liked than unattractive communicators.

64. Lynn R. Kahle and Pamela M. Homer, "Physical Attractiveness of the Celebrity Endorser: A Social Adaptation Perspective," *Journal of Consumer Research*, vol. 11 (March 1985), pp. 954–961.
65. W. Benoy Joseph, "The Credibility of Physically Attractive Communicators: A Review," *Journal of Advertising*, vol. 11, no. 3 (1982), pp. 15–24.

4.   Although attractive communicators are perceived by receivers as more
      dynamic than unattractive communicators, the attractive communicators
      are not generally considered to be more credible.

Credibility: The Process of Internalization.   In its most basic sense,
credibility refers to the tendency to believe or trust someone. When an information source is perceived as credible, the source can change attitudes through
a psychological process called **internalization.** Internalization occurs when the
receiver accepts the source's position as his or her own attitude. An internalized attitude tends to be maintained even if the source of the message is forgotten or if the source switches to a different position.[66] The most important
properties of source credibility are expertise and trustworthiness.

Expertise refers to the knowledge, experience, or skills possessed by a
source as they relate to the communications topic. Expertise is a perceived
rather than absolute phenomenon. Whether a communications source is indeed an expert is unimportant; all that matters is how he or she is perceived
by the target audience. A source whom an audience perceives as an expert on
a given subject is more persuasive in changing audience opinions pertaining to
his or her area of expertise than is a source whom an audience does not perceive as possessing the same characteristic.

Marketing communicators use a variety of techniques in attempting to
convey source expertise. Salespersons often receive extensive training so that
they are very knowledgeable of their company's products. Companies that sell
high-technology products frequently recruit sales representatives from university programs in engineering, computer science, and other scientific fields.

Efforts to achieve source credibility are widespread in advertising. Advertisements sometimes employ words and phrases to imply that the advertised
product is technologically sophisticated. Advertisers frequently show products
being used in situations that imply something positive about product quality
and performance. Motor oil and automobile tires, for example, are advertised
in racetrack settings, and sporting goods are displayed on or alongside the
playing arena. Another technique that advertisers use to enhance credibility is
the strategic selection of various props (such as lab coats and scientific para-
phernalia) that, when worn or used by a source, give the impression of credibility. Moreover, athletic professionals are often used as brand spokespersons—Chris Evert, Mike Tyson, Jack Nicklaus, Dr. J, John Elway, Michael
Jordan, Larry Bird, and Carl Lewis are just a few well-known endorsers.

Trustworthiness refers to the honesty, integrity, and believability of a
source. While expertise and trustworthiness are not mutually exclusive, often
a particular source is perceived as highly trustworthy but not particularly high
in expertise. The degree of honesty or trustworthiness of a source depends
primarily on the audience's perception of the source's *intent.* If the audience

---

66. Richard E. Petty, Thomas M. Ostrom, and Timothy C. Brock, eds., *Cognitive Responses in Per-
    suasion* (Hillsdale, NJ: Lawrence Erlbaum Associates, 1981), p. 143.

believes that the source has underlying motives, especially ones that will personally benefit the source, he or she will be less persuasive than someone the
audience perceives as having nothing to gain or as completely objective.

Television advertisements attempt to increase trustworthiness by using
"candid" interviews with homemakers. In these commercials, the homemaker is
often asked to explain why she purchases the company's brand or is asked if
she would be willing to trade one box of her detergent, say, for two boxes of
another leading detergent. This approach has also been used by asking homemakers to compare their brand of product with another, both in disguised
form. The homemaker acts surprised when she learns that the sponsor's brand
performs better than her regular brand. In all of these cases, the advertiser is
attempting to show a degree of objectivity and, thereby, to establish greater
trustworthiness for the message.

Advertisers also use the *overheard conversation* technique to enhance credibility. A television advertisement might show a middle-aged person overhearing one man explain to another why his brand of arthritis pain-relief medicine
is the best on the market. In this case, the commercial attempts to have audience members place themselves in the position of the person overhearing the
conversation. The investment firm E. F. Hutton perfected this technique in a
continuing series of ads with the tag line, "When E. F. Hutton talks, everyone
listens."

An experiment tested whether a hidden-camera spokesperson (i.e., one
who is presumably extolling the virtues of a product without being aware of
it) is more persuasive than a typical-person spokesperson (i.e., one who is
aware of his or her spokesperson role). The researchers hypothesized that the
hidden-camera spokesperson should be considered more trustworthy because
he or she makes favorable product claims but does not come across as having
ulterior motives. The hidden-camera spokesperson was, in fact, shown to be
less biased and more credible.[67]

In general, communicators must establish that they are not attempting to
manipulate the audience, that they have nothing to gain by their persuasive
attempts, and that they are objective in their presentations. By doing so, they
establish themselves as trustworthy and, therefore, credible.

Summary

This chapter discusses both message and source factors in marketing communications. The section on message factors looks at both message-structure and
message-content factors. Message structure refers to the organization of elements in marketing communications messages. Three structural issues that
have particular relevance to marketing communicators are message-sidedness

67. James M. Hunt, Theresa J. Domzal, and Jerome B. Kernan, "Causal Attributions and Persuasion: The Case of Disconfirmed Expectancies," in *Advances in Consumer Research*, vol. 9, ed. A.
Mitchell (Pittsburgh: Association for Consumer Research, 1982), pp. 287–292.

(one-sided versus two-sided messages), comparative versus noncomparative messages, and order of presentation (climax order, anticlimax order, and pyramidal order).

Message content deals with what is said in a message. Content elements that are widely used by marketing communicators and which are discussed in this chapter include fear appeals, humor, music, sex appeals, and subliminal messages.

The chapter also reviews source factors in marketing communications. Marketing communications sources influence receivers by processing one or more of three necessary attributes: power, attractiveness, and credibility. Source power influences receivers via a compliance mechanism; attractiveness operates through identification; and credibility functions via the process of internalization.

Discussion Questions

1. A company markets a line of household laundry products and cleaning items. The channel of distribution is direct to consumers. Consumers of the company's products are highly heterogeneous in terms of socioeconomic and demographic characteristics, but most of them are highly brand-loyal. This company is in the process of developing a national advertising campaign to generate greater product usage from its existing consumer base. Comment on the advisability of developing a two-sided message.

2. Develop a list of products for which you feel fear appeals might be a viable approach to persuading consumer acceptance of a brand. What kinds of products do not lend themselves to fear appeals? Explain why you feel these products are not appropriate for fear appeals.

3. Television commercials for inexpensive, low-risk consumer packaged goods (low-involvement products) are often received by consumers in an unenthusiastic and passive information-processing mode. In view of this, comment on the relative merits of climax versus anticlimax orders of presentation.

4. Consumers occasionally find television commercials to be humorous and enjoyable. Some advertising pundits claim that such commercials may capture attention but are frequently ineffective in selling products. Do you agree with this position? Justify your position.

5. Advertisers and agencies seem reluctant to use two-sided messages. From their perspective, present an argument that looks at both sides of the issue.

6. The advertising agency for an automobile-tire manufacturer is considering using a fear-appeal message to promote its client's tires. What would you suggest to promote its client's tires? What would you suggest to the advertising agency in terms of fear-appeal strength?

7. An internationally known manufacturer of high-quality stereo equipment has learned from a pretest of several advertisements that its top-of-the-line stereo receiver was evaluated more highly when the message admitted to a weakness in the receiver. It is well known throughout the industry and among avid audi-

ophiles that the receiver's amplifiers burn out much sooner than comparable competitors' models. However, the receiver is far superior to its rivals in terms of total harmonic distortion, channel separation, intermodulation distortion, and other specifications. Should the firm use a two-sided message in its advertising? Why or why not?

8. Industrial advertisers sometimes use magazine advertisements with "decorative models"—that is, scantily clad females who are there to adorn the ad but who serve no function in terms of the sales message. Why do you think industrial advertisers use decorative models? Present arguments explaining why you think such advertising is effective or ineffective.

9. Explain why a marketing communicator would prefer to change consumer attitudes through an internalization process rather than through compliance or identification.

10. Distinguish between an attractive and a credible source. Provide two or three examples of well-known product spokespersons who, in your opinion, are high in both attractiveness and credibility. Justify why you consider these individuals to possess both attributes.

11. What are the requirements for a trustworthy source? Provide several examples of well-known product spokespersons who, in your opinion, are particularly trustworthy. In what sense are these individuals trustworthy?

Exercises

1. Provide two or three examples of music in advertisements that you think are particularly effective. For each example, explain why you think the music is effective.

2. Clip several examples of comparative advertisements from magazines. Analyze each ad in terms of why you think the advertiser used a comparative-advertising format and whether you think the advertisement is effective. Justify your position.

3. Identify three or four television commercials that you regard as humorous. Interview five people and ask their opinions of these commercials. Summarize the responses for each commercial.

4. Collect advertisements from magazines and locate two or three illustrations of each of the following: credible sources, attractive sources, and trustworthy sources. Explain why you chose each example to illustrate a particular source characteristic.

5. Interview five students who are not presently taking or have not previously taken this course. Ask them to describe what characteristics they think a successful sales representative for a computer manufacturer must possess. Then ask them the same question for an automobile salesperson. (Reverse the order of the salesperson's job status from interview to interview.) Summarize the responses separately for each type of salesperson in terms of attractiveness, credibility, trustworthiness, and any other characteristics that your respondents have used to describe these successful salespeople.

Adoption and Diffusion Processes: The Role of Marketing Communications and Promotion Management

ROGAINE: A "HAIR-RAISING" PRODUCT

he Upjohn Co., a drug manufacturer, began marketing *Loniten* for the treatment of high blood pressure (hypertension) in the early 1980s. *Loniten* is Upjohn's brand name for the drug *minoxidil*.

Within one year after Upjohn began marketing *Loniten,* a serendipitous discovery was made: People taking *Loniten* to control high blood pressure discovered a surprising side effect—80 percent of the users experienced hair growth on some part of the body, often on the upper cheek or forehead! Marketing officials at Upjohn quickly realized that minoxidil might have a much more attractive future as a hair restorer than as a hypertension drug.

The Food and Drug Administration (FDA) prevented Upjohn from marketing minoxidil as a hair restorer until further testing was conducted. However, parties falling outside of the FDA's regulatory umbrella, namely dermatologists and many physicians, immediately began prescribing minoxidil to their balding patients upon learning of Upjohn's discovery. As many as 30 percent of minoxidil users experienced hair growth after rubbing minoxidil on their scalps twice daily. Younger men and those with small areas of baldness seemed to respond best to minoxidil treatment.

Minoxidil users have been willing to pay $100 or more a month to prevent further hair loss. It takes between eight months and one year before any hair growth appears. To maintain that growth, minoxidil must be applied twice a day for the rest of the user's life. When users discontinue daily minoxidil applications, all of the new hair falls out within three to four months.

After several years of testing, the FDA concluded (as of August 1988) that minoxidil is safe and effective for spurring hair restoration. Shortly thereafter, Upjohn Co. began nationwide marketing of its brand of hair restorer, *Rogaine*. With the marketing of *Rogaine*, the price of minoxidil treatments is expected to drop to about $50 a month. Competitive brands will undoubtedly battle *Rogaine* for market share, and the price should drop even more.[1]■

New Products and Innovativeness

Marketers introduce new products such as *Rogaine* on a continuous basis. For most industries and companies, introducing a stream of new products is absolutely essential for success and long-term growth. Likewise, the continued viability of many nonbusiness organizations (such as charitable groups, trade associations, religious organizations, and political parties) depends on their ability to develop and introduce new ideas to their constituencies.

Despite the huge investments and concerted efforts to introduce new products and ideas, many are never successful. It is impossible to pinpoint the percentage of new ideas and products that eventually fail because organizations vary in how they define a "success"; estimates range from as high as 90 percent to as low as a 33 percent failure rate among new product introductions.[2]

This chapter describes the processes involved in the acceptance of product innovations. Discussion focuses on the characteristics of people who are more and less likely to be innovative, the role of personal influence in facilitating new product acceptance, and the role of promotion management in ensuring that new products are successful.

The Degree of Innovativeness

An **innovation** is an idea, practice, product, or service that an individual perceives to be new. How people view an object determines whether it is an innovation. People who believe something is an innovation behave differently toward the object than people who do not perceive the object as new.

The degree of newness is an important dimension of innovation. Innovations can be classified along a continuum according to their degree of impact on established consumption patterns. Table 7.1 presents an innovativeness

---

1. Facts for this description are from various newspaper articles and from "Baldness: Is There Hope?" *Consumer Reports*, September 1988, pp. 543–547.
2. "Survey Finds Sixty-Seven Percent of New Products Succeed," *Marketing News*, February 8, 1980, p. 1.

The Innovation Continuum

TABLE 7.1

Continuous Innovations			Discontinuous Innovations
Line Extensions (For example, new flavors, sizes, packages)	Minor Product Modifications (For example, annual new models in cars or new fashions)	Major Product Modifications (For example, compact cars when first introduced or color television vs. black & white)	New Technologies (For example, the invention of the computer or jet aircraft)

Source: Thomas S. Robertson, Joan Zielinski, and Scott Ward, *Consumer Behavior* (Glenview, IL: Scott, Foresman and Company, 1984), p. 369.

continuum, labels the end points "continuous" and "discontinuous," and provides examples of different degrees of innovativeness along the continuum.[3] It is important to realize that there are many gradations along this continuum. The categories described next are merely convenient end- and mid-points along the continuum.

A **continuous innovation** is one that generally represents a *minor change* from existing products and which has limited impact on customers' consumption patterns. That is, the consumer can buy and use the new product in much the same way that he or she has used another product to satisfy the same need. Table 7.1 shows that new flavors, sizes, and packages represent typical continuous innovations. Companies routinely introduce new flavors of food products (e.g., regular potato chips, then barbecue flavored, then Cajun spiced, etc.), new scents for cleaning products (e.g., lemon scented), new package designs (e.g., the zip-lock bags for cereal discussed in Chapter 3), and many other slight product modifications. All of these are continuous innovations.

In comparison, a **discontinuous innovation,** which anchors the other extreme of the innovation continuum (see Table 7.1), requires *substantial relearning* and fundamental alterations in basic consumption patterns. The automobile, computer, birth-control products, and television are probably the most significant mass-marketed discontinuous innovations of the twentieth century.

Most new products are continuous innovations or **dynamically continuous innovations.** This latter term represents innovations that require *some disruption in established behavioral patterns* rather than fundamental alterations. Compact disc (CD) players, digital audiotape (DAT) players, disposable cameras, disposable contact lenses, and cellular phones are some of the more notable dynamically continuous innovations that have appeared in recent years.

---

3. The innovation continuum notion is attributable to Thomas S. Robertson, *Innovation Behavior and Communication* (New York: Holt, Rinehart, , and Winston, 1971), p. 7.

FIGURE 7.1   **Model of New-Product Adoption Process**

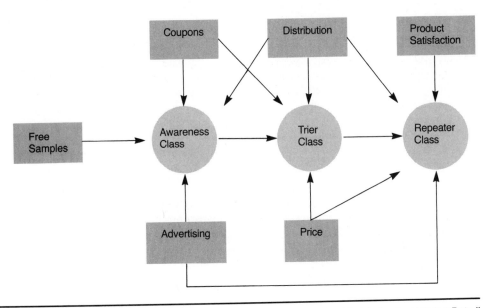

Source: Chakravarthi Narasimhan and Subrata K. Sen, "New Product Models for Test Market Data," *Journal of Marketing,* Vol. 47, Winter 1983, p. 13. Reprinted with permission from *Journal of Marketing,* published by the American Marketing Association.

The Role of Marketing Communications and Promotion Management

Regardless of a product's degree of innovativeness, an organization's marketing-communications specialists and promotion-management team have major roles to play in ensuring new product success. Perhaps this can best be appreciated by showing a relatively simple model of the new-product adoption process.[4] This model, shown in Figure 7.1, indicates with circles the three main stages through which an individual becomes a new-brand consumer: awareness class, trier class, and repeater class. The variables in blocks surrounding the circles are marketing mix and promotion elements that are responsible for "moving" consumers through the three classes and ultimately creating new product users.

The first step in adoption is to make the consumer aware of a new product's existence. Figure 7.1 shows that four marketing-mix variables influence the **awareness class:** free samples, coupons, advertising, and distribution. The

4. The following discussion is adapted from Chakravarthi Narasimhan and Subrata K. Sen, "New Product Models for Test Market Data," *Journal of Marketing,* vol. 47 (Winter 1983), pp. 13, 14.

first three variables are distinctly promotion-mix variables, and the fourth, distribution, is closely allied with promotion in that the sales force is responsible for gaining distribution, providing reseller support, and making point-of-purchase materials available to the trade.

Once a consumer becomes aware of a new product or brand, there is an increased probability that the consumer will actually try the new offering. Coupons, distribution, and price are the variables that affect the **trier class.** Only the first of these, coupons, is a promotion element, but as mentioned in Chapter 1 and elaborated upon in Chapter 3, price and distribution variables perform important communications functions in addition to their more basic economic roles.

Repeat purchasing, the **repeater class,** is a function of four primary forces: advertising, price, distribution, and product satisfaction. That is, consumers are more likely to continue to purchase a particular brand if advertising reminds them about the brand, if the price is considered reasonable, if the brand is accessible, and if product quality is considered satisfactory.

It is evident from this discussion that promotion management is essential to new product success. The following sections explain in greater detail the processes by which innovations are adopted by individual consumers and diffused throughout the marketplace.

The Adoption Process

The **adoption process** consists of the mental stages an individual goes through in accepting and becoming a repeat purchaser of an innovation. Marketing communicators play a role in accelerating the rate of new-product adoption and thereby increasing the probability of product success. As firms have become more sophisticated marketers, the rate of adoption in consumer markets has increased.[5]

Although consumers are accepting new products more readily than ever, there is still a high percentage of failure in the introduction of new products. Understanding the factors that facilitate or impede successful adoption is crucial to a full appreciation of the role of marketing communications and promotion management in modern marketing.

The adoption process consists of five stages: (1) knowledge, (2) persuasion, (3) decision, (4) implementation, and (5) confirmation.[6] As Figure 7.2 indicates, each stage is a necessary precondition to a subsequent stage. The figure also shows various conditions and characteristics that act to increase or

5. Richard W. Olshavsky, "Time and Rate of Adoption of Innovations," *Journal of Consumer Research*, vol. 6 (March 1980), pp. 425–428; William Qualls, Richard W. Olshavsky, and Ronald E. Michaels, "Shortening of the PLC—An Empirical Test," *Journal of Marketing*, vol. 45 (Fall 1981), pp. 76–80.
6. Everett M. Rogers, *Diffusion of Innovations*, 3d ed. (New York: The Free Press, 1983), p. 7.

FIGURE 7.2   **Model of the Innovation-Decision Process**

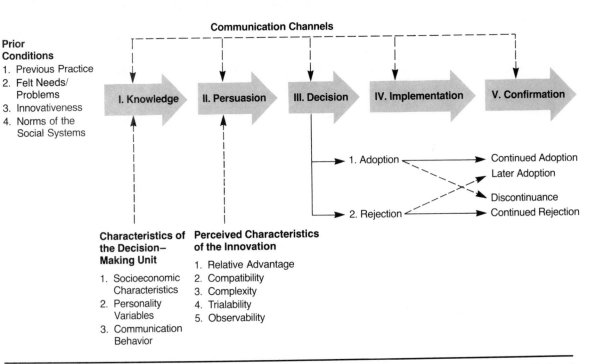

retard the innovation-decision process. Among the broad groups of variables that influence the various stages are *prior conditions* (e.g., the consumer's previous consumption practices), *characteristics of the decision-making unit* (e.g., socioeconomic characteristics), and *perceived characteristics of the innovation* (e.g., relative advantages).

Knowledge Stage

In the knowledge stage, which is similar to the "awareness class" mentioned previously, the individual becomes aware of an innovation and learns something about how the innovation functions. For example, an individual learns that digital audiotape players cost anywhere from $500 to $2,000, that they play tape cartridges that are smaller than the tapes used in conventional tape players, and that they combine the features of conventional audiotape with the advantages of compact disc players.

Distinct differences exist between those who know about an innovation early and those who are late in recognizing it. On average, those who recognize an innovation early have a higher level of education, a higher social status, a greater exposure to mass media and interpersonal channels of communications, and greater social participation; they are also more cosmopolitan than those who are aware of an innovation later.[7] VCR owners in the United States, for example, are better educated and better-off financially than most Americans.[8]

Advertising plays a crucial role in making consumers aware of and knowledgeable about new products. Sometimes advertising is terribly redundant, but without it product adoption would be much slower. Salespersons also perform an important role in making customers knowledgeable about new products. In the pharmaceutical industry, for example, salespersons (called *detailmen*) inform physicians about new drug products and provide details about product features, benefits, side effects, and so on.

Persuasion Stage

The mental activity at the knowledge stage was mainly cognitive (or thinking), but at the persuasion stage it is mainly affective (or feeling). Though an individual may be aware of an innovation for a long period of time and may know how to use it, he or she may not have developed any feeling or affect (i.e., attitude) toward the innovation. The persuasion stage begins when the individual develops an *attitude* toward the innovation.

In forming an attitude, a consumer often goes through a *vicarious trial* of the product. This helps the consumer to reduce the uncertainty of using the new product or service. The advertisement back in Chapter 4 (see Figure 4.5) for Claussen pickles illustrates an effort to create a vicarious trial experience. Take a moment to review the ad on page 103. The catchy headline, "How to test drive a pickle," and picture of hands in driving gloves bending a pickle place the magazine reader in a position of trying this product vicariously and "feeling" that this brand is indeed fresher than other pickles.

Promotion management plays a major role in ensuring that consumers form positive attitudes toward innovative products and services. This is done by influencing five innovation-related characteristics that undergird consumers' attitudes toward new products and services: relative advantage, compatibility, complexity, trialability, and observability.

Relative Advantage.   The degree to which an innovation is perceived as better than an existing idea or product is termed **relative advantage.**

7. Ibid., pp. 168–169.
8. "VCRs: Coming on Strong," *Time*, December 24, 1984, p. 45. By the end of 1984, there were 17 million VCRs in use in the United States—one for every five homes with a television.

Relative advantage is a function of whether a person perceives the new product to be better than competitive offerings, not a function of whether the product is objectively better. Relative advantage is positively correlated with an innovation's adoption rate; that is, the greater an innovation's relative advantages vis-a-vis existing offerings, the more rapid the rate of adoption to be expected.

In general, relative advantages exist to the extent that a new product offers (1) *increases in comfort,* (2) *savings in time and effort,* and (3) *immediacy of reward.* For example, microwave ovens have the relative advantage of being faster than conventional ovens; pain killers that give quick relief are superior to those that take longer to work; "Fab 1 Shot" offers the advantage of ease of use by combining detergent with fabric softener; Max Factor's "No Color" mascara, the first clear lash definer, is relatively advantageous compared to traditional mascaras because it eliminates embarrassing smudges, smears, and running.

Relative advantages depend on the inherent characteristics of the product itself but can also be influenced by persuasive communications. For example, overnight package delivery (such as provided by Federal Express) offers the real relative advantage of quicker delivery in comparison to conventional mailing; however, advertising must accentuate this real advantage in order for potential users to fully appreciate the advantages of using overnight delivery. Advertising also serves to negate the relative advantages claimed by marketers of new competitive products. For example, Federal Express's market for document delivery (e.g., legal documents) will be eliminated unless it can offset the inroads made by fax mail services.

Compatibility.   The degree to which an innovation is perceived to fit into a person's way of doing things is termed **compatibility.** In general, the more compatible an innovation is with a person's needs, personal values, beliefs, and past experiences, the more rapid its rate of adoption. Innovations that are compatible with a person's existing situation are less risky, more meaningful, and require less effort to incorporate into one's consumption lifestyle. The adoption of acupuncture by American physicians has been slow because the procedure does *not* fit into their accustomed methods of anesthetizing patients.

Establishing compatibility is partially a function of product design. Beyond this, marketing communicators are largely responsible for ensuring compatibility in the minds of customers by selecting the right combination of packaging, brand, price, and other symbols that will convey compatibility with the target market's beliefs, past experiences, and so on.

A case in point is the purchase of handguns in the United States. Many consumers think they need a handgun to protect themselves and their families from thieves, rapists, and other criminals. Historically, handguns were purchased only by men. Now it is estimated that upwards of 40 percent or more of all handguns are sold to women.[9] Societal changes and the efforts of handgun marketers have combined to make this product more *compatible* with the lifestyles of female consumers.

Complexity. The degree of perceived difficulty of an innovation is termed **complexity.** The more difficult an innovation is to understand or use, the slower the rate of adoption. Home computers have been adopted slowly because many homeowners perceive computers as too difficult to understand and use. Advertisers have confronted this by creating subtle (and not-so-subtle) television commercials to convey the idea that anyone can easily learn to use a computer, even little kids. Companies have also redesigned their products and introduced new computers that are easier to use.

Trialability. The extent to which an innovation can be used on a limited basis is referred to as **trialability.** In general, products that lend themselves to trialability are adopted at a more rapid rate. Trialability is tied closely to the concept of *perceived risk.* Test drives of new automobiles, free samples of food products at local supermarkets, and small packages of new detergents all permit the consumer to try a new product on an experimental basis. The trial experience serves to reduce the risk of a consumer's being dissatisfied with a product after having permanently committed to it through an outright purchase.

The Macintosh advertisement (see Figure 7.3) was a novel effort by Apple Computer, Inc., to give people the opportunity to try the computer in the comfort of their homes for one full day. The "Test Drive a Macintosh" promotion was indeed a success. Approximately 200,000 Macintoshes were "test driven" during the promotional period, and dealers attributed 40 percent of their sales volume during this period to the promotion.[10]

Observability. The degree to which other people can observe one's ownership and use of a new product is referred to as **observability,** or *visibility.* The more a consumption behavior can be sensed by other people (i.e., seen, smelled, etc.), the more visible it is said to be. Thus, driving an automobile with a new type of engine is less visible than driving an automobile with a unique body design; wearing a new perfume fragrance is less visible than adopting a hairstyle that is avant-garde. In general, innovations that are high in visibility lend themselves to rapid adoption if they also possess relative advantages, are compatible with consumption lifestyles, and so on. Products whose benefits lack observability are generally slower in adoptability.

The important role of product observability is illustrated by Nike Shoe Co.'s use of "Air Pockets" in its athletic shoes. These highly visible inserts in

9. This statistic is based on a report aired on ABC's "20/20" program on August 19, 1988.
10. William A. Robinson and Kevin Brown, "Best Promotions of 1984: Back to Basics," *Advertising Age,* March 11, 1985, p. 42.

FIGURE 7.3   **Novel Effort to Promote Product Trialability**

Source: Reprinted by permission of Apple Computer, Inc. Apple and the Apple logo are registered trademarks of Apple Computer, Inc. Macintosh is a trademark licensed to Apple Computer, Inc.

the heel section of Nike shoes clearly convey the product benefit of comfort by showing that running and jumping in Nike shoes is like landing on a protective mattress. Nike could have designed their shoes so that the air pocket was concealed from observation; instead, they decided to make the feature conspicuous and in so doing provided themselves with the easily communicable point that Nike shoes are more comfortable than competitive brands. At the time of this writing, Reebok is said to be developing its own visible feature for conveying the benefit of product comfort.

In sum, the persuasion stage represents an important area of concern for marketing communicators. In this stage, the potential adopter is making up his or her mind about the innovation. Many times an individual will mentally or vicariously "try" the innovation to see how it applies to his or her present situation. Advertisers facilitate this vicarious trial by showing the new product being used by people with whom the target audience identifies positively. Sales representatives do the same by informing prospective customers of other desirable individuals who have already purchased the product. Through the right choice of symbols and appeals, marketing communicators can assist product designers in expediting the rate of product adoption and in increasing the chances of product success.

Decision and Implementation Stages

The **decision stage** (return to Figure 7.2) represents the period during which a person *mentally chooses* either to adopt or reject an innovation. For example, a long-time wearer of contact lenses decides to discard her old, permanent contacts in favor of new, disposable contacts. Another consumer rejects the idea of disposable contacts on the grounds that they are too expensive and that it would be extravagant for her to buy this new product when her old contacts are still in good condition.

The **implementation stage** occurs when a person puts the new product or idea to use. In the previous stage (decision), the individual simply makes a mental commitment either to use the product or sample it on a trial basis. However, no full-scale commitment is made. In the implementation stage, the individual wants answers to questions such as, "How do I use this product?" and "How do I solve these operational problems?" Salespersons and professionals (e.g., optometrists) perform important functions in such instances by providing technical assistance and by giving the customer helpful suggestions for using the product.

Confirmation Stage

People often seek additional information after making an important adoption decision in an attempt to confirm the wisdom or appropriateness of their decision. The **confirmation stage** represents the time period in which postdecisional dissonance, regret, and dissonance reduction occur. People seek out friends in hopes of being told how wise their choice was and are responsive to impersonal sources of information (e.g., magazine ads) that buttress their decision. If a person cannot be adequately assured of the correctness of an adoption decision, he or she may discontinue the adoption. Sales representatives have a special role in this stage. An axiom in personal selling is, "You must continue to sell after the sale."

The Diffusion Process

In comparison to the adoption process, which focuses on the individual consumer (a micro viewpoint), the diffusion process is concerned with the broader issue of how an innovation is communicated and adopted *throughout the marketplace* (a macro viewpoint). In simple terms, **diffusion** is the process of "spreading out." In a marketing communications sense, this means that a product or idea is adopted by more and more customers as time passes. By analogy, consider a situation where gas is released into a small room. The fumes eventually spread throughout the entire room. Similarly, product innovations spread ideally to all parts of a potential market. The word *ideally* is used because, unlike the physical analogy, the communication of an innovation in the marketplace is often impeded by factors such as unsuitable communication channels, competitive maneuverings, and other imperfect conditions.

This section deals with the *aggregate behavior* of groups of customers in comparison to the individual mental stages used to describe the adoption process. Specifically, it examines the characteristics that are typical of each group in the diffusion process.[11]

Adopter Categories

As a product spreads through the marketplace over time, different types of consumers adopt the product. The diffusion literature identifies five general groups of adopters: (1) innovators, (2) early adopters, (3) early majority, (4) late majority, and (5) laggards. As a matter of convention, these five categories are presumed to follow a normal statistical distribution with respect to each group's mean time of adoption following the introduction of an innovation (see Figure 7.4). That is, in accordance with the properties of a normal distribution, 68 percent of all people who ultimately adopt an innovation fall within plus ("late majority") or minus ("early majority") one standard deviation of the

11. For further discussion, see Hubert Gatignon and Thomas S. Robertson, "A Propositional Inventory for New Diffusion Research," *Journal of Consumer Research*, vol. 11 (March 1985), pp. 849–867.

Classification of Adopter Groups

FIGURE 7.4

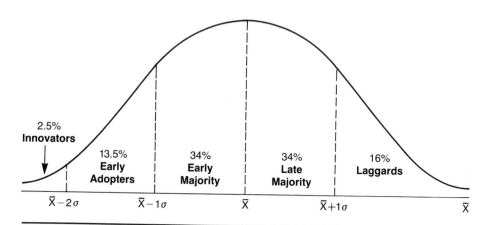

Source: Reprinted with permission of The Free Press, a Division of Macmillan, Inc., from *Diffusion of Innovations,* Third Edition, by Everett M. Rogers, p. 165. Copyright © 1962, 1971, 1983 by The Free Press.

mean time of adoption. The other adopter categories are interpreted in a similar manner. Though the categorization is arbitrary, it has been found meaningful in the study of the diffusion process.

Innovators. The small group of innovators are the first people to accept a new idea or product. Innovators exhibit a high level of *venturesomeness.* They also are more willing to *take risks,* because innovation requires risk taking. For example, with reference to the opening vignette, when dermatologists and physicians initially started offering minoxidil treatments, most balding people were unwilling to invest $100 or more per month for 8 to 12 months before they knew if minoxidil would work for them. Only a relatively few, the innovators, were willing initially to invest in minoxidil. Of course, the success that some of the innovators experienced with minoxidil justified the expenditure from later adopters.

Another characteristic of innovators is that they are willing to seek social relationships outside of their local peer group; that is, they are *cosmopolites.* Innovators also tend to be *younger, higher in social status,* and *better educated* than later adopter groups.

Innovators interact mostly with other innovators and rely heavily on *impersonal* informational sources, rather than on other people, to satisfy their information needs. For example, the early users of minoxidil were probably more likely than most consumers to have read technical or semi-technical articles about the drug and its role in hair restoration. Innovators generally have been found to display a *broader range of interests* than noninnovators.[12]

Early Adopters.   Early adopters are the second group to adopt an innovation. The size of this group is defined statistically as 13.5 percent of all potential adopters.[13] Early adopters are *localites*, in contrast to innovators, who were described as cosmopolites. The early adopter is well integrated within his or her community and is *respected* by his or her friends.[14] Because of this respect, the early adopter is often sought for advice and information about new products and services. The respect he or she commands among peers makes the early adopter a very important determinant of the success or failure of an innovation. *Opinion leaders* come primarily from the early-adopter group. Their characteristics and role in the diffusion process are discussed later in the chapter.

Early Majority.   Approximately 34 percent of all potential adopters of an innovation fall into the early-majority group. As shown in Figure 7.4, the early majority adopt the product prior to the mean time of adoption. Members of this group are *deliberate* and *cautious* in their adoption of innovations.[15] They spend more time in the innovation-decision process than the two earlier groups. Though the group displays some opinion leadership, it is well below that shown by early adopters. This group is slightly above average in education and social status but below the levels of the early-adopter group.

Late Majority.   As shown in Figure 7.4, the late majority is depicted as 34 percent of potential adopters just below the average time of adoption. The key word that characterizes the late majority is *skepticism*.[16] By the time they adopt an innovation, the majority of the market has already done so. Peers are the primary source of new ideas for the late majority, who make little use of mass media. Demographically, they are below average in education, income, and social status.

Laggards.   The final group to adopt an innovation is referred to as laggards; they represent the bottom 16 percent of potential adopters. These people are *bound in tradition*.[17] As a group, laggards focus on the past as their frame of reference. Their collective attitude may be summarized as, "If it was

12. Thomas S. Robertson and James N. Kennedy, "Prediction of Consumer Innovators: Application of Discriminant Analysis," *Journal of Marketing Research*, vol. 5 (February 1968), pp. 64–69, citing *America's Tastemakers*, Research Reports Nos. 1 and 2 (Princeton, NJ: Opinion Research Corporation, 1959).
13. That is, the area under the normal curve between one and two standard deviations from the mean.
14. Rogers, *Diffusion of Innovations*, pp. 248–249.
15. Ibid.
16. Ibid.
17. Ibid., p. 250.

good enough for my parents, it's good enough for me." Laggards are tied closely to other laggards and to their local community and have limited contact with the mass media. This group, as might be expected, has the lowest social status and income of all adopter groups. If and when laggards adopt an innovation, it usually occurs after one or more innovations have replaced the earlier innovation.

Managing the Diffusion Process[18]

The actual course of diffusion for a new product is partly determined by a company's marketing actions (product quality, sales-force efforts, advertising level, price strategy, etc.) and partly by external forces that are largely beyond a firm's control (competitive actions, shifts in consumers' buying moods and desires, the state of the economy, etc.). However, to the extent possible, firms hope to manage the diffusion process so that the new product or service accomplishes the following objectives:

1. Secures initial sales as quickly as possible (i.e., achieves a *rapid takeoff*).
2. Achieves cumulative sales in a steep curve (i.e., achieves *rapid acceleration*).
3. Secures the highest-possible sales potential in the targeted market segment (i.e., achieves *maximum penetration*).
4. Maintains sales for as long as possible (i.e., achieves a *long-run franchise*).

Figure 7.5 displays the desired diffusion pattern that satisfies the preceding conditions and compares it with the typical diffusion pattern. The typical pattern following a product's introduction involves a relatively slow takeoff, a slow rate of sales growth, maximum penetration below the full market potential, and a sales decline sooner than what would be desired.

What can promotion management do to make the typical pattern more like the desired pattern? First, *rapid takeoff* can be facilitated by having a promotion budget that is sufficiently large to permit (1) aggressive sales force efforts that are needed to secure trade support for new products, (2) intensive advertising to create high product-awareness levels among the target market, and (3) sufficient sales promotion activity to generate desired levels of trial-purchase behavior. Second, *rapid acceleration* may be accomplished (1) by ensuring that product quality is suitable and will promote positive word-of-mouth communication, (2) by continuing to advertise heavily to reach later adopter groups, (3) by ensuring that the sales force provides reseller support, and (4) by using sales promotion creatively so that incentives are provided for repeat-purchase behavior. Third, *maximum penetration* can be approached (1) by

---

18. This section is adapted from Thomas S. Robertson, Joan Zielinski, and Scott Ward, *Consumer Behavior* (Glenview, IL: Scott, Foresman and Company, 1984), pp. 380–382.

FIGURE 7.5   **"Desired" and "Typical" Diffusion Patterns**

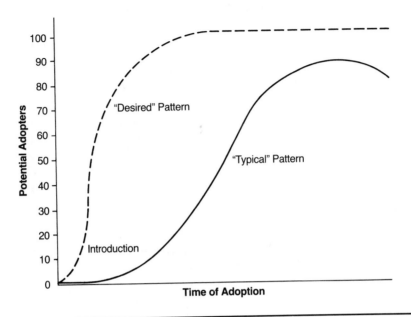

Source: Thomas S. Robertson, Joan Zielinski and Scott Ward, *Consumer Behavior* (Glenview, IL: Scott, Foresman and Company, 1984), p. 381.

continuing the same strategies that stimulated rapid acceleration and (2) by revising product design and advertising strategies in such a fashion that the product or service appeals to the needs of the later adopters. Finally, a *long-run franchise* can be maintained by ensuring (1) that the "old" product continues to meet the market's needs, (2) that distribution is suitable to reach the market, and (3) that advertising continues to remind the market about the product.

Sometimes all of the marketing effort in the world cannot salvage a product that lacks relative advantages and is more complex to use than competitive offerings. The IBM PCjr illustration in the *Focus on Promotion* section shows how the best-intentioned efforts may not succeed.

Stimulating Word-of-Mouth Influence

People in all buying capacities—consumers buying automobiles, industrial purchasing agents buying new equipment, physicians ordering drug products, hospitals ordering supplies, athletic teams purchasing equipment, and so on—rely on two major sources of information to assist them in making decisions:

F O C U S   O N   P R O M O T I O N

Failure to Achieve a Long-Run Franchise:
The Case of IBM's PCjr

IBM introduced the PCjr in November 1983. Despite a marketing budget estimated at $40 million, the initial sales were sluggish (i.e., the PCjr experienced a very *slow takeoff*). IBM undertook a number of efforts to rescue the PCjr. A first step was to help dealers by allowing them to delay payments six months longer than normal. Second, a number of new features and options were added to the PCjr. IBM then combined dramatic price cuts with blitzkrieg advertising in a number of media, even direct mail. Next, dealers were offered a $250 rebate and encouraged to pass on the savings to consumers by selling the PCjr with heavily discounted software and peripheral equipment. Sales increased from a few units in July 1984 to over 90,000 units in November of the same year. Thus, IBM, through its aggressive actions, was able to transform a "dog" into a product with a relatively *rapid acceleration*.[19]

Unfortunately for IBM, these heroic actions were unable to achieve a *long-term franchise* for the PCjr. By the mid-1980s Apple Computer, Inc. had introduced the successful Macintosh, a much more user-friendly product than the PCjr, and low-priced IBM clones from the Far East were reaching the United States in large numbers. The PCjr was removed from the market shortly thereafter.■

---

impersonal and personal sources. *Impersonal* sources include information received from television, magazines, and other mass-media sources. *Personal* sources, the subject of this section, include word-of-mouth influence from so-called opinion leaders and other peers. Research has shown that the more favorable information a potential new-product adopter has received from peers, the more likely that individual is to adopt the new product or service.[20]

Opinion Leaders

An **opinion leader** is a person who frequently influences other individuals' attitudes or overt behavior.[21] Opinion leaders perform several important func-

---

19. These comments are based on "A Flop Becomes a Hit," *Time,* December 24, 1984, p. 60.

20. Johan Arndt, "Role of Product-Related Conversation in the Diffusion of a New Product," *Journal of Marketing Research,* vol. 4 (August 1967), pp. 291–295; Dorothy Leonard-Barton, "Experts as Negative Opinion Leaders in the Diffusion of a Technological Innovation," *Journal of Consumer Research,* vol. 11 (March 1985), pp. 914–926.

21. Rogers, *Diffusion of Innovations,* p. 271.

tions: they inform other people (followers) about new products and ideas, they provide advice and reduce the follower's perceived risk in purchasing a new product, and they provide positive feedback to support or confirm decisions that followers have already made. Thus, an opinion leader is an *informer, persuader,* and *confirmer*.

Opinion leadership influence is typically restricted to one or several consumption topics rather than applying universally across many consumption domains. That is, a person who is an opinion leader with respect to issues and products in one consumption area (say, motorcycling or skiing or cooking) is not generally influential in other unrelated areas. It would be very unlikely, for example, that one person would be respected for his or her knowledge and opinions concerning all three of the listed consumption topics. Moreover, opinion leaders are found in every social class. In most instances, opinion-leadership influence moves horizontally through a social class instead of vertically from one class to another.

Opinion leaders have profiles that are distinctly different than non-opinion-leaders' profiles. In general, opinion leaders (1) are more *cosmopolitan* and have greater contact with the mass media than do followers, (2) are usually *more gregarious* than the general population and have more social contacts and thus more opportunity for discussing and passing information than followers, (3) tend to have slightly *higher socioeconomic status* than followers, and (4) are generally *more innovative* than followers.

What motivates opinion leaders to give information? It seems that opinion leaders are willing to participate in word-of-mouth (WOM) communications with others because they *derive satisfaction* from telling others what their opinions are and what they know about new products and services. In order to share what they know about innovations and thus gain satisfaction from telling others, the opinion leaders continually strive to keep themselves informed (often feeling an obligation to do so).

Prestige is at the heart of WOM. "We like being the bearers of news. Being able to recommend gives us a feeling of prestige. It makes us instant experts."[22] Being an expert in marketplace matters does bring prestige. Researchers have recently referred to the marketplace expert as a **market maven.**[23] Market mavens are "individuals who have information about many kinds of products, places to shop, and other facets of markets, and initiate discussions with consumers and respond to requests from consumers for market information."[24] In other words, the market maven is looked upon as an important source of information and receives prestige and satisfaction from supplying information to friends and others.

---

22. This quote is from the famous motivational researcher, Ernest Dichter, in Eileen Prescott "Word-of-Mouth: Playing on the Prestige Factor," *The Wall Street Journal,* February 7, 1984, p. 1.
23. A "maven" (or mavin) is one who is an expert in everyday matters.
24. Lawrence F. Feick and Linda L. Price, "The Market Maven: A Diffuser of Marketplace Information," *Journal of Marketing,* vol. 51 (January 1987), pp. 83–97.

A vice-president of marketing for Paramount Pictures suggests that the key to generating good WOM is by finding "cheerleaders," that is, consumers who will "get the talk started." Usually this is a carefully selected target group that is most likely to love a new movie.[25] In the book industry, cheerleading is stimulated by giving free copies of a new book to a select group of opinion leaders. For example, in the case of *Megatrends*, a leading seller by John Naisbitt, the book publisher sent more than 1,000 copies to chief executive officers of major corporations. Within one month of publication, it became a "must read" book by literally thousands of businesspeople.[26]

Thus, positive word-of-mouth communication is a critical element in a new product's or service's success. Unfavorable WOM can have devastating effects on adoption, because consumers seem to place more weight on negative information in making evaluations than on positive information.[27]

Marketing communicators can do several things to minimize the level of negative word-of-mouth:[28] (1) At the minimum, companies need to show customers that they are responsive to legitimate complaints; (2) manufacturers can do this by providing detailed warranty and complaint-procedure information on labels or in package inserts; (3) retailers can demonstrate their responsiveness to customer complaints through employees with positive attitudes, store signs, and inserts in monthly billings to customers; (4) companies can offer toll-free numbers to provide customers with an easy, free way to voice their complaints and suggestions. By being responsive to customer complaints, companies can avert negative WOM and perhaps even create positive WOM.[29]

Summary

The continual introduction of new products and services is critical to the success of most business organizations. The likelihood of success depends in part on the degree of innovativeness. Innovations are classified along a continuum ranging from slightly new at one end (*continuous innovations*) to dramatically different at the other end (*discontinuous innovations*).

The concepts of adoption and diffusion explain the processes by which new products and services are accepted by more and more customers as time passes. The *adoption process* views the mental stages an individual goes through in accepting and becoming a repeat purchaser of an innovation. The process consists of five stages: knowledge, persuasion, decision, implementation, and

25. Prescott, "Word-of-Mouth."
26. Ibid.
27. Richard J. Lutz, "Changing Brand Attitudes through Modification of Cognitive Structure," *Journal of Consumer Research*, vol. 1 (March 1975), pp. 49–59; Peter Wright, "The Harassed Decision Maker: Time Pressures, Distractions, and the Use of Evidence," *Journal of Applied Psychology*, vol. 59 (October 1974), pp. 555–561.
28. Marsha L. Richins, "Negative Word-of-Mouth by Dissatisfied Consumers: A Pilot Study," *Journal of Marketing*, vol. 47 (Winter 1983), p. 76.
29. Ibid.

confirmation. Each of these stages is affected by a wide array of variables, which act to expedite or retard the rate of product adoption.

The *diffusion process* is concerned with the broader issue of how an innovation is communicated and adopted throughout the marketplace. *Diffusion*, in simple terms, is the process of "spreading out." Diffusion scholars have identified five relatively distinct groups of adopters. These groups, moving from the first to adopt an innovation to the last, are *innovators, early adopters, early majority, late majority,* and *laggards.* Research has shown that these groups differ considerably in terms of such variables as socioeconomic status, risk-taking tendencies, and peer relations.

Opinion leadership and word-of-mouth influence are important elements in facilitating more rapid product adoption and diffusion. *Opinion leaders* are individuals who are respected for their product knowledge and opinions. Opinion leaders inform other people (followers) about new products and services, provide advice and reduce the follower's perceived risk in purchasing a new product, and confirm decisions that followers have already made. In comparison to followers, opinion leaders are more cosmopolitan, more gregarious, have higher socioeconomic status, and are more innovative. Positive word-of-mouth influence is often critical to new-product success. It appears that people talk about new products and services because they gain a feeling of prestige from being the bearer of news. Marketing communicators can take advantage of this prestige factor by stimulating cheerleaders, who will talk favorably about a new product or service.

Discussion Questions

1. Classify the following products and services as continuous, dynamically continuous, or discontinuous innovations: light beer, biogenetic engineering, liquid yogurt, low-salt foods, the Jarvik artificial heart, three-wheel "dirt" bikes (i.e., machines resembling motorcycles with three balloon wheels), satellite dishes for homeowner use, skin-care products for men, metal golf clubs ("Pittsburgh persimmon") used as a substitute for wood golf clubs.

2. Using facial skin-care products for men as the illustration, explain the process by which marketing variables can influence men to become part of the awareness, trier and repeater classes (refer to Figure 7.1).

3. The Double Dog is the brand name for a distinctive hotdog bun that has two cuts and allows two weiners to be eaten at once. Based on what you now know about the adoption process, what is the likelihood that this product will receive wide consumer acceptance?

4. What determines whether a new product or service has relative advantages over competitive offerings? What are the relative advantages of disposable cameras produced by Kodak and other companies?

5. What is meant when we say that a potential adopter of a product or service "vicariously tries" the product before adopting it? What can marketing communicators do to promote vicarious trial?

Exercises

1. Pick a new product or service and describe in detail how this product or service satisfies the following success requirements: relative advantages, compatibility, communicability, trialability, and observability.

2. Interview three people who have recently attended a particular movie. Determine how they learned about this movie and why they decided to see it. Probe for detailed responses rather than superficial replies. Integrate their responses into a coherent explanation of movie-attendance behavior.

3. Suppose you are the manager of a new restaurant located in your college or university community. Your fledgling restaurant cannot yet afford media advertising, so the promotional burden rests upon stimulating positive word-of-mouth communication. Develop a strategy of how you would go about doing this.

4. The researchers who conceived the concept of "market maven" (see footnote 24) devised the following six-item scale to measure the concept.

    (1) I like introducing new brands and products to my friends.

    (2) I like helping people in providing them with information about many kinds of products.

    (3) People ask me for information about products, places to shop, or sales.

    (4) If someone asked where to get the best buy on several types of products, I could tell him or her where to shop.

    (5) My friends think of me as a good source of information when it comes to new products or sales.

    (6) Think about a person who has information about a variety of products and likes to share this information with others. This person knows about new products, sales, stores, and so on, but does not necessarily feel he or she is an expert on one particular product. How well would you say that this description fits you?

Each item is responded to on a seven-point scale, ranging from strongly disagree (= 1) to strongly agree (= 7). Scores range from a low of 6 (strongly disagrees to all six items) to 42 (strongly agrees to all six items).

Administer the scale to two friends whom you regard as "market mavens" and to two friends who are not market mavens. See if the mavens receive predictably higher scores than the nonmavens. Also, comment on whether you think these six items do a good job of measuring market mavenness. What additions or deletions, if any, would you make?

PART 3

Promotion-Management Strategy, Planning, and Execution

The purpose of the three chapters in Part 3 is to provide a bridge between the general marketing-communications topics covered in Parts 1 and 2 and the specific promotion practices (such as advertising, sales promotion, and personal selling) that are covered in the remaining chapters.

Chapter 8 overviews the promotion management process by structuring promotion in terms of an integrative and memory-facilitating device called the 12-M Model. The model contains 12 elements, each beginning with the letter "M," that collectively describe promotion management.

Chapter 9 looks at three general categories of environmental factors that affect promotion decision making: technological, demographic, and regulatory forces. Coverage includes such topics as new forms of technology affecting advertising practices, demographic developments, and regulatory practices by the Federal Trade Commission, the National Association of Attorneys General, and the National Advertising Review Board.

Chapter 10 presents two detailed illustrations of integrated marketing communications and promotion management programs. The Du Pont Stainmaster[cm] case shows how a manufacturer of carpeting profited from borrowing advertising programs and other promotional practices more typically observed in the marketing of consumer packaged goods. The second case involves a program undertaken by the United States Agency for International Development. This program used creative marketing-communications practices to teach mothers in undeveloped countries how to deliver oral rehydration therapy (ORT) to save the lives of their dehydrated children. This case provides a socially meaningful application of marketing communications programs in a nontraditional situation.

Promotion-Management Process

THE ROLE OF PROMOTION IN THE SNEAKER WARS

T he athletic-shoe industry (which includes tennis shoes, running shoes, aerobic shoes, etc.) is a virtual amateur to sophisticated marketing and promotion management. However, beginning in the 1970s and accelerating through the eighties, athletic-shoe companies such as Reebok, Nike, and L.A. Gear became aggressive and sophisticated marketers. These companies and others are fighting a veritable war for market share. With industry sales in 1988 of over $3 billion, Reebok was the clear market leader with 32.3 percent share. Nike, with an 18.6 percent share, was the closest follower, while newly aggressive L.A. Gear lagged far behind with only a 2.3 percent market share. Effective promotion management is essential to these "sneaker-war" opponents in their efforts to maintain or increase market shares.

These companies must continuously introduce exciting new lines and styles in an effort to satisfy American consumers' insatiable desire for new athletic shoes. Aggressive personal selling is critical in the attempt to get retailers to carry one manufacturer's brand over competitive brands. Heavy advertising expenditures are essential for creating attractive brand images. For example, Reebok spends more than $40 million annually on campaigns such as "Reeboks let U.B.U.," featuring zany characters and a funky style. Nike invests over $35 million a year on associating its product with Michael Jordan, Bo Jackson, and other famous athletes. The much smaller L.A. Gear spends a much larger percentage of its revenue on advertising in order to compete with the competitive giants. In fact, it spent approximately $25 million in 1989 on advertising, much of which was devoted to its first effort at television advertising. You may recall viewing the interesting television commercial that intercut scenes of a young man competing in a championship basketball game with scenes of him playing a one-on-one match with a beautiful young woman on a beachside court.[1]■

In Chapter 1, promotion was described in its broadest sense as meaning "to move forward," to motivate, to move customers to action. Discussion pointed out that the promotion-management component of the total marketing-communications mix consists of six major tools: personal selling, mass-media advertising, direct-mail advertising, sales promotion, point-of-purchase communications, and public relations/publicity. These tools were described as operating in concert with one another to help accomplish various marketing objectives.

The overall promotion-management process was characterized in terms of a logical sequence of six major steps: situation analysis, marketing objectives, promotion budget, integration and coordination, promotion-management program, and evaluation and control. It would be worthwhile at this time for you to return to Chapter 1 and briefly review Figure 1.8 and the surrounding discussion on pages 22–28.

The 12-M Model

To more fully appreciate the nature and functioning of promotion management beyond the decision-sequence overview given in Chapter 1, this chapter structures promotion in terms of an integrative and memory-facilitating device, or mnemonic, called the **12-M Model.** Subsequent discussion concerning this model provides detailed descriptions of the elements and processes involved in promotional activities.

Figure 8.1 lays out the elements and relations of promotion management. Each of the 12 elements has a label beginning with the letter "M."[2] The model contains four general components, which are designated by Roman numerals: (I) Marketing Structure, (II) Managing the Environment, (III) Market Satisfac-

1. Statistics are based on Marcy Magiera and Pat Sloan, "Sneaker Attack," *Advertising Age,* June 20, 1988, pp. 3, 104, and Marcy Magiera, "L.A. Gear Takes Off," *Advertising Age,* August 8, 1988, p. 44.
2. Other marketing authors have used combinations of M-words to form their own unique M-models. For example, one text has an "Eight-M Formula" for describing an advertising campaign—J. Paul Peter and James H. Donnelly, Jr., *A Preface to Marketing Management,* 4th. ed. (Plana, TX: Business Publications, Inc., 1988), p. 141. The present 12-M model has very little relation to Peter and Donnelly's Eight-M Formula.

The 12-M Model of Promotion Management

FIGURE 8.1

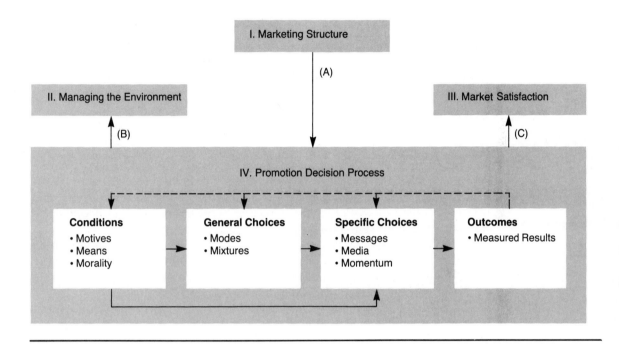

tion, and (IV) Promotion Decision Process. This last element, the decision process, consists of a set of promotion-management *conditions* (**m**otives, **m**eans, and **m**orality), *general choices* (**m**odes and **m**ixture), *specific choices* (**m**essages, media, and **m**omentum), and *outcomes* (**m**easured results).

An Overview

The *Promotion Decision Process (PDP)* is the cornerstone of the 12-M model and represents the bulk of this chapter's discussion. Initially, however, it will be helpful to overview the general relations portrayed in Figure 8.1. Note first that the PDP is shown to be influenced by *Marketing Structure* (relation (A) in Figure 8.1). As will be described in detail, marketing structure represents the organizational arrangement employed by a firm for performing its marketing and promotional functions. Thus, the way a company is organized has great influence on how it makes promotional decisions and how these decisions are implemented.

The PDP ultimately is directed at accomplishing two fundamental goals: *Managing the Environment* and achieving *Market Satisfaction* (relations (B) and (C) in Figure 8.1). The promotional component of the marketing mix is not, of course, the sole means of achieving these goals, but it does perform an instrumental role. Personal selling, for example, is absolutely crucial in determining whether customer complaints are being responded to properly and whether customers remain satisfied. Public-relations efforts play a critical role during times of crisis and determine whether customers remain satisfied with a firm's products that are being scrutinized or attacked by critics. Advertising effectiveness is instrumental in offsetting competitors' efforts, in overcoming sales declines during periods of short-term economic slides, and in a variety of other attempts at managing environmental forces.

Marketing Structure

Marketing structure is the *organizational arrangement* employed in a company to achieve its overall marketing and promotional objectives. The structure used is instrumental in determining how well a company is able to manage its environment, satisfy its markets, and implement effective promotion decisions. In recent years many well-known companies (e.g., Procter & Gamble Co., Campbell Soup Co., Coca-Cola Co., Pepsi-Cola Co., and IBM Corp.) have revamped their marketing structures in order to (1) better serve their immediate *customers* (i.e., wholesalers, brokers, and retailers), (2) do a better job in satisfying their ultimate *consumers'* needs, and (3) outperform *competitors.*

All three Cs (customers, consumers, and competitors) have placed pressure on companies to reorganize.[3] Retailers have become more sophisticated and better informed—largely due to the advent of optical-scanning devices and the near-instantaneous information that they provide—and, as a result, expect more service and support from their manufacturer suppliers than in past years. Greater choices than ever before are available to consumers, thereby forcing each company to do a better job in order to win the consumer's loyalty and beat competitors.

Pepsi-Cola Co. used to organize its marketing of soft drinks by channel of distribution—retail (e.g., grocery stores), vending machines, and fountain sales. Three separate organizations marketed Pepsi-Cola nationally to customers within each channel. Now Pepsi-Cola has reorganized its marketing department into four large regions. The staff in each region is responsible for marketing to all customers (retail, vending, and fountain) within the region. The advantage of such *regionalized marketing* structures is that they enable marketing staffs to be more responsive to customer needs and competitive actions.[4]

Along similar lines, Campbell Soup Co. has reorganized its marketing department into more than 20 regional units. Each unit contains a combined marketing and sales force and has its own promotional budget, media-buying power, and discretion over marketing and promotional strategies. In the past

3. Laurie Freeman, "Why Marketers Change," *Advertising Age*, February 22, 1988, p. 24.
4. "The Marketing Revolution at Procter & Gamble," *Business Week*, July 25, 1988, pp. 72–76.

these decisions were made at Campbell Soup by a centralized national office.[5] In addition, Frito-Lay, the well-known marketer of snack foods, has carved its market into seven regions. As with other regional marketing efforts, this has permitted Frito-Lay to target its programs more finely than ever before and to better accommodate regional differences in taste preferences.[6]

The most dramatic marketing restructuring in many years occurred recently at Procter & Gamble. This marketing superstar of packaged goods (detergents, soaps, snacks, cookies, paper products, etc.) has altered (not abolished) the traditional brand-management system that it innovated in 1931 and has established a *product category* management structure. Under this new system, each of P&G's 39 product categories (detergents, paper products, etc.) is run by a *category manager*. Advertising, sales, manufacturing, research, engineering, and other staffs report directly to the category manager, who has direct profit responsibility.[7]

The reorganization promises to reduce internal bickering for resources among brand managers and to curtail the tendency toward excessive short-term orientation that the brand-management system fostered. All brand managers (for example, the managers of Tide and Cheer) within a particular product category report directly to a category manager (detergent in this example), who has responsibility for allocating resources among brand managers and seeing that long-term objectives and overall corporate welfare are paramount over short-term expediencies and individual brand performance.

In sum, an organization's marketing structure is its direct link with the environment, plays an instrumental role in determining market satisfaction, and has great influence on the specific promotion decision-making process.

Managing the Environment

Every business as well as not-for-profit organization operates in a dynamic relation with its environment. From your introductory marketing course, you will recall that a variety of external forces constitute the environment for marketing decisions. These include economic, competitive, technological, social/cultural, and regulatory influences.

The relationship between promotion management and the environment is illustrated in Figure 8.2. The figure shows, via double-headed arrows, that all marketing-mix decisions (product, distribution, etc.) are subject to various environmental influences. Specific decisions with respect to the six components of the promotional mix also must be adjusted so as to be compatible with environmental conditions and must be formulated in a way that enables a firm to *manage* environmental forces rather than merely react to these forces.

5. "Marketing's New Look," *Business Week*, January 26, 1987, pp. 64–69.
6. Jennifer Lawrence, "Frito Makes Regional Advances," *Advertising Age*, July 4, 1988, p. 21. For further reading on the trend toward regional marketing, see Thomas W. Osborn, "Opportunity Marketing," *Marketing Communications*, September 1987, pp. 49–63.
7. "The Marketing Revolution at Procter & Gamble," p. 73.

FIGURE 8.2   **Managing Environmental Influences**

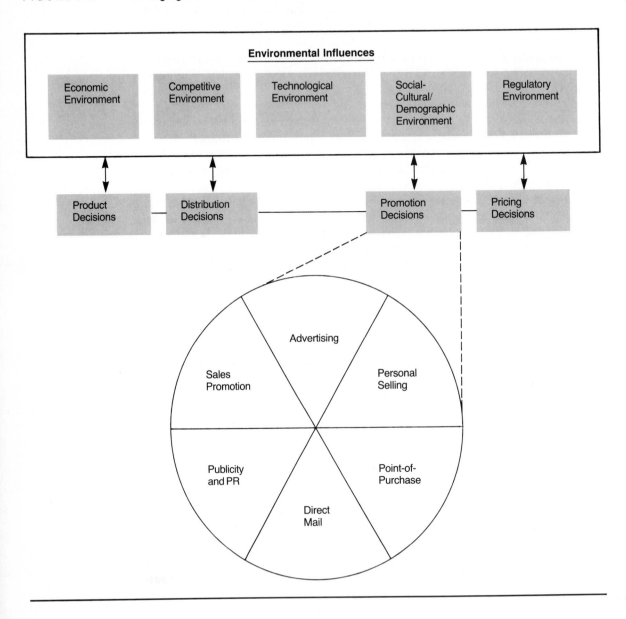

Environmental management captures the idea that through its promotional efforts and other marketing activities a firm can attempt to *modify* existing environmental conditions.[8] In other words, managers in specific areas of promotion (advertising, sales promotion, sales, and so on) must attempt to influence and alter environmental circumstances so that the organization's interests are best served. Organizations are not able to completely manage their environments. It is critical, nevertheless, that they monitor their environments and are prepared to alter policies, strategies, and tactics to be compatible with environmental circumstances and developments. Successful companies anticipate environmental developments and are prepared in advance, rather than simply reacting to significant changes after they have occurred.

The athletic-shoe companies featured in the chapter's opening vignette have been remarkably effective in managing their environments. Changes in the cultural and social environment (e.g., the increased emphasis in the United States on health and fitness) provided opportunities for new types of athletic shoes that are customized to meet the demands of specific sports (e.g., aerobic shoes). Nike's initial success was largely attributed to its being in the vanguard of the running trend, while Reebok's early success was due in large part to its spotting the need for special aerobic shoes. These companies have also effectively withstood the competitive inroads of many domestic and foreign competitors by building prestigious and quality brand images through a combination of effective advertising and good product performance.

The operative theme in the foregoing discussion is that organizations must be *proactive* in dealing with their various environments and not simply reactive. Effective environmental management requires anticipation of forthcoming changes and anticipatory action rather than belated reaction after competitors have already responded to the changes. Many declining industries in the United States (e.g., women's dress shoes and steel manufacturing) were notoriously slow in responding to environmental changes.

Market Satisfaction

The touchstone of all marketing and promotional activities is ultimately the degree of market satisfaction. Satisfying customers depends, of course, on the suitability of all marketing-mix elements, not just the promotional components. Nevertheless, the promotional components play an important role by informing customers about new products and brands and their relative advantages and by avoiding the tendency to over-inflate expectations. The cost of not satisfying customers can be great. For example, because of persistent complaints that they make poor-quality cars, General Motors found it necessary to intro-

---

8. Carl P. Zeithaml and Valarie A. Zeithaml, "Environmental Management: Revising the Marketing Perspective," *Journal of Marketing*, vol. 48 (Spring 1984), pp. 46–53; "Kotler: Rethink the Marketing Concept," *Marketing News*, September 14, 1984, pp. 1ff.

duce a new "Bumper to Bumper" warranty on most 1989 models. The warranty covers virtually the entire car for three years or 50,000 miles and is estimated to cost GM up to $500 million per year.[9]

Companies that have a true commitment to marketing and long-term customer satisfaction realize that marketing efforts must go beyond merely making a sale. These companies emphasize doing things that build *long-term relationships* with customers. They realize that "You do not manage a company by focusing on R&D (an input), production (an output), or finance (a scoreboard), but rather by a thorough driving orientation toward the market and the customer."[10]

Delivering greater market satisfaction can be accomplished in a number of ways. In general, it involves listening to the customer and focusing on *retaining* existing customers and building *relations* rather than always going after more and more new customers.[11] The sales force has a critical role to perform in ensuring customer satisfaction and retention. Directing advertising and other promotional efforts at well-defined market segments is another way to enhance customer satisfaction. This requires concentrating on clearly defined target markets and developing real or imagined advantages over competitive offerings.

The Promotion Decision Process

Having now overviewed the general factors that give rise, influence, or constrain promotion-management activities in all of their various forms, we now turn to the specific elements of the decision process. The following discussion is keyed to Figure 8.1. It will be helpful to briefly overview the PDP before proceeding with discussions of specific features. The model shows that *conditions* (motives, means, and morality) influence *general choices* (modes and mixture) and also *specific choices* (messages, media, and momentum). *Outcomes* in the form of measured results follow from the general and specific choices made. These outcomes, in turn, feed back (dashed lines in Figure 8.1) to the conditions and to the general and specific choices. Corrective actions (e.g., increased sales-promotion expenditures, new advertising campaigns) are called for when measured results indicate that performance has fallen below expectations.

9. "The High Cost of Selling Quality," *Fortune*, August 29, 1988, p. 11.
10. "A New Survival Course for CEO's," *Marketing Communications*, September 1985, pp. 21–26, 94.
11. For further discussion of retention marketing, see Laura A. Liswood, "Once You've Got 'Em, Never Let 'Em Go," *Sales and Marketing Management*, November 1987, pp. 73–77. For a theoretical yet highly readable account of relational marketing, see F. Robert Dwyer, Paul H. Schurr, and Sejo Oh, "Developing Buyer-Seller Relationships," *Journal of Marketing*, vol. 51 (April 1987), pp. 11–27.

Conditions

Promotion management involves making general and specific choices in the context of an existing state of circumstances, or conditions. These conditions are termed motives, means, and morality in the 12-M model.

Motives. Promotion managers' general and specific choices are grounded in underlying goals or objectives, which we term **motives.**[12] It is important to recognize that *motives* is used here with reference to organizational goals and not personal incentive, though the two are not completely inseparable. This is the situation especially in smaller organizations where owners and managers are often one and the same people.

Promotion managers base their decisions on specific motives they hope to accomplish. Of course, the content of the motives varies within specific areas of the promotion mix because the components of the mix have different capabilities. For example, whereas mass-media advertising is ideally suited for creating consumer awareness of a new or improved brand, point-of-purchase communications are perfect for influencing in-store brand selection, and personal selling is unparalled when it comes to informing buyers about product improvements.

Specific chapters later in the text will detail the motives that each component of the promotion mix is designed to accomplish; for present purposes it will suffice to merely list various motives (objectives) that promotion managers hope to accomplish:

- Facilitate the successful introduction of new products.
- Build sales of existing products by increasing frequency of use, variety of uses, or the quantity purchased.
- Inform the trade and consumers about product improvements.
- Build the company's image.
- Generate sales leads.
- Persuade middlemen (dealers, distributors, etc.) to handle the company's product.
- Stimulate point-of-purchase sales.
- Develop brand awareness, acceptance, and insistence.
- Increase customer loyalty.
- Let consumers know where to buy the product.
- Improve corporate relations with special-interest groups.
- Offset bad publicity about a company's products.

12. The term "objectives" is generally used when describing promotion management goals. For example, Step 2 in the overview of the promotion management process presented in Chapter 1 referred to marketing objectives. The present usage of motives in lieu of objectives is justified on the grounds that the mnemonic value of another m-word exceeds any loss created by deviating from convention.

- Generate good publicity.
- Counter competitors' marketing and promotional efforts.
- Provide customers with reasons for buying now rather than delaying a purchase choice.

Means.   An organization's wherewithal or resources represent its **means** for accomplishing the motives it has established for its various promotional tools. *Budget* is the term more typically used when describing promotion resources, but means and budget will be used interchangeably here. Means represents the amount of financial and nonfinancial resources (e.g., the availability of products to barter for advertising services) that a promotion manager has available during a given period, typically the fiscal year in most corporations. For example, as mentioned in the opening vignette, advertising managers at Reebok, Nike, and L.A. Gear had approximately $40, $35, and $25 million, respectively, for advertising their athletic shoes in 1989.

The amount of resources allocated to specific promotion managers is typically the result of an involved process in most sophisticated corporations. Companies use different budgeting processes in allocating funds to promotion managers and other organizational units. At one extreme is *top-down budgeting* (TD), in which senior management decides how much each subunit receives. At the other extreme is *bottom-up budgeting* (BU), in which managers of subunits (e.g., brand managers and category managers) determine how much they need to achieve their motives; these amounts are then combined to establish the total marketing budget.

Most budgeting practices involve a combination of top-down and bottom-up budgeting. For example, in the *bottom-up/top-down process* (BUTD), subunit managers submit budget requests to a chief marketing officer (say, a vice-president of marketing), who coordinates the various requests and then submits an overall budget to top management for approval. This is the form of budgeting used at Procter & Gamble with its 39 new category managers. Within each product category, brand managers submit budgets to the category manager, who in turn coordinates an overall category budget. The 39 category budgets are coordinated by a vice-president of marketing and submitted to top management for approval. The *top-down/bottom-up process* (TDBU) reverses the flow of influence by having top managers first establish the total size of the budget and then divide it among the various subunits.

Recent research in Great Britain has shown that combination budgeting methods (BUTD and TDBU) are used more often than the extreme methods (TD or BU).[13] The BUTD process is by far the most frequently used, especially in more sophisticated firms where marketing-department influence is high compared to finance-department influence.[14]

---

13. Nigel F. Piercy, "The Marketing Budgeting Process: Marketing Management Implications," *Journal of Marketing*, vol. 51 (October 1987), pp. 45–59.
14. Ibid. See Figure 2, p. 55.

Morality.   Another condition that influences general decisions and specific promotion-management practices is the set of principles and standards, or **morals,** that individual managers bring to the job and that the corporate culture encourages. Business is like every other societal institution in that most business practitioners are honest, upright, and ethical. Yet, just as there are unethical politicians, crooked cops, and licentious television evangelists, there also are a relatively small number of businesspeople who are immoral on the job. Salespeople sometimes tell falsehoods and stretch the truth, advertisers at times engage in outright deception, and so on. For example, in light of the health-consciousness trend of the 1980s, some advertisers have exploited consumers' concerns and fears by stretching what their products are capable of doing. Advertisers of margarine and vegetable products promote their individual brands as if they are unique in having no cholesterol, despite the fact that *no* vegetable products contain cholesterol. As one critic observed, that is like saying: "Always use Mobil gas because there's no cholesterol in it."[15] The tendency for advertisers to misrepresent the health virtues of their products has prompted a widely respected national publication to comment: "If advertisers aren't willing to tell the truth, the whole truth, and nothing but the truth when it comes to health, they should leave the subject alone."[16]

A free-market economy demands the highest moral standards from its participants. In the absence of such standards from salespeople, advertisers, public relations people, and other representatives, the free market can deteriorate into "an economy of greed."[17] The three keys to a successful business career are to "make money, have fun, be ethical," not necessarily in that order of importance.[18]

General Choices

As shown in Figure 8.1, promotion managers have two general choices: which modes to use and how to mix, or integrate, the modes.

Modes.   The term *modes* is used here in the same sense as it was used in Chapter 1, which described the "Three Modes of Marketing." As you will recall, the three modes are: Mode 1, the *basic offer* (the product itself and terms of sale); Mode 2, *persuasive communications* (verbal and nonverbal messages); and Mode 3, *promotional inducements* (extra substantive benefits beyond the benefits of the basic offer).

Although the three modes overlap and reinforce each other, only Modes 2 and 3 are discussed further because Mode 1, the basic offer, is a determination of general marketing management and not promotion management

---

15. Zachary Schiller and Reginald Rhein, Jr., "Marketing Commentary," *Newsweek,* August 10, 1987, p. 47.
16. Ibid.
17. Don Peppers, "A Practical Guide to Playing Fair," *The New York Times,* Sunday, July 24, 1988.
18. Ibid.

per se. Mode 2, *persuasive communications*, consists of messages directed to target customers (via a combination of personal selling, advertising, publicity, and point-of-purchase devices) that are intended to enhance the impression of the basic offer and to stimulate wants for it. Mode 3, *promotional inducements* (i.e., sales promotion), are used to induce customers and consumers to adopt the marketer's plan of action. This is accomplished by using free samples, trial usage, coupons, discounts, rebates, allowances, and other promotional inducements.

Mixture.   A fundamental issue confronted by all companies is deciding exactly how to allocate resources between the two general modes, persuasive communications and promotional inducements. Industrial-goods companies typically emphasize *personal selling;* trade advertising, technical literature, and trade shows are additional important elements in their promotional mixes.[19]

For consumer-goods companies, the mix issue is in many respects more complicated and controversial because greater options are available. Personal selling is important in a consumer-good company's *push* efforts, but the real difficulty and controversy arises when deciding how best to *pull* a product through the channel.[20] The issue boils down to a decision of how much to spend on advertising vis-a-vis sales promotion.

Over the past decade, the trend has been in the direction of greater expenditures on sales promotion. Sales-promotion expenditures have increased at an average rate of 13 percent (from approximately $33 billion in 1977 to $110 billion in 1987), while advertising expenditures have grown annually by only 10 percent (from $23.4 billion in 1977 to $60.3 billion in 1987).[21] Between 1977 and 1987, sales promotion's share of the advertising/sales-promotion split has grown from 58 percent in 1977 to 65 percent in 1987.[22]

What is the optimum mixture of expenditures between advertising and sales promotion? Unfortunately, no specific answer is possible because the promotion-mix decision is an *ill-structured problem*.[23] In other words, there is no way of knowing for a given level of expenditure what the optimum allocation

19. Donald W. Jackson, Jr., Janet E. Keith, and Richard K. Burdick, "The Relative Importance of Various Promotional Elements in Different Industrial Purchase Situations," *Journal of Advertising*, vol. 16, no. 4 (1987), pp. 25–33.

20. The terms *push* and *pull* are metaphors, as you probably recall from your introductory marketing course, that characterize the nature of the promotional thrust through the channel of distribution. The *push* metaphor suggests a forward thrust from manufacturer to the trade (wholesalers or retailers) on to the consumer. Personal selling to the trade is the primary push technique. *Pull* means that a manufacturer promotes directly to consumers with intentions they will bring pressures to bear on retailers to stock the promoted product. In actuality, manufacturers use a combination of pull and push techniques. These techniques complement one another and are not perfectly substitutable.

21. Nathaniel Frey, "Ninth Annual Advertising and Sales Promotion Report," *Marketing Communications*, August 1988, pp. 9–19.

22. Ibid.

23. Thomas A. Petit and Martha R. McEnally, "Putting Strategy into Promotion Mix Decisions," *The Journal of Consumer Marketing*, vol. 2 (Winter 1985), pp. 41–47.

between advertising and sales promotion should be. At least four factors account for this inability to determine a mathematically optimum mix:[24]

1.   Advertising and sales promotion are somewhat *interchangeable* in that both tools can accomplish some of the same promotional motives. Because of this, it is impossible to know exactly which tool or combination of tools is better in every situation.

2.   The fact that the combined effect of these two promotional tools is greater that what they would achieve individually (a *synergistic effect*) makes it difficult to determine the exact effects that different combinations of advertising and sales promotion might generate.

3.   Advertising and sales promotion not only operate synergistically with each other, they also *interact with other elements of the marketing mix*. Thus, the effectiveness of these tools is impossible to evaluate without considering the overall marketing mix.

4.   The optimum advertising and sales-promotion mix is affected by various *market forces*—the nature of the buying process, characteristics of the market, the extent of competition, and so on.

The result is that there simply is no way to take all of the preceding factors into account to determine which combination of advertising and sales promotion is the best among the many possibilities.[25] Thus, rather than seeking an optimum mixture, it is more reasonable to develop a workable, *satisfactory* mixture. The following *key issues* need to be addressed to accomplish a satisfactory mix of advertising and sales promotion:[26]

1.   A careful *cost-value analysis* of each proposed mix has to be performed to determine whether distribution, sales, and profit objectives can be achieved in view of the intended expenditure.

2.   An evaluation must be made of how well the proposed levels of advertising and sales promotion *fit with each other and complement one another*.

3.   *Strategic considerations* in determining the differing purposes of advertising and sales promotion must be studied carefully. A key strategic consideration is whether short-term or long-term considerations are more important given a brand's life-cycle stage. An appropriate mixture for mature brands is likely to be much different than the mixture for brands recently

24. This discussion is based on Petit and McEnally, p. 43.
25. Ibid.
26. The following key issues are adapted from Joseph W. Ostrow, "The Advertising/Promotion Mix: A Blend or a Tangle," *AAAA Newsletter*, August 1988, pp. 6–7. Parenthetically, note this article title refers to advertising versus promotion. Mr. Ostrow, like other marketing practitioners, drops the leading word "sales" when referring to sales promotion. Whereas in the academic marketing community we refer to promotion in a general sense to include all forms of promotional tools (advertising, personal selling, sales promotion, etc.), practitioners use the word "promotion" in reference to sales promotion per se.

introduced. The latter probably require a proportionately much larger investment in sales promotion (e.g., couponing and sampling) in order to generate trial purchases, whereas mature brands require proportionately greater advertising investment to maintain or enhance the brand's image.

4. *Brand equity* represents a final consideration in evaluating a satisfactory combination of advertising and sales promotion. Brand equity represents the goodwill (equity) that an established brand has built up over the period of its existence. Poorly planned or excessive sales promotions can seriously damage a brand's equity position by cheapening its image. If a brand is frequently on sale or regularly offers some form of promotional inducement, consumers will delay purchasing it until they can get a deal. The effect is that the brand becomes a price object purchased more for its price discount or promotional inducement than for its basic-offer value.

The matter of mixing advertising and sales promotion has been summed up aptly in the following fashion:

> As one views the opportunities inherent in ascertaining the proper balance between advertising and [sales] promotion, it should be quite clear that both should be used as one would play a pipe organ, pulling out certain stops and pushing others, as situations and circumstances change. Rigid rules, or continuing application of inflexible advertising-to-promotion percentages, serve no real purpose and can be quite counterproductive in today's dynamic and ever-changing marketing environment. A short-term solution that creates a long-term problem is no solution at all.[27]

The short-term "solution" alluded to is spending excessive amounts on sales promotion to create quick sales while failing to invest sufficiently in advertising to build a brand's long-term image. That is, excessive sales promotion can rob a brand's future. An appropriate mixture involves spending enough on sales promotion to ensure sufficient sales volume in the short term while simultaneously spending enough on advertising to ensure the growth or preservation of a brand's equity position. The *Focus on Promotion* section offers useful suggestions for balancing sales promotion and advertising.

Specific Choices

The general choice and mixture of promotional modes is just the beginning. Within each mode there are many choices to be made regarding the types of *messages* to use, what *media,* and what *momentum* (see Figure 8.1).

Messages. As established in previous chapters on communication fundamentals (Chapter 2) and message factors (Chapter 6), the message is a critical component of marketing communications effectiveness. Managers of

27. Ibid., p. 7.

FOCUS ON PROMOTION

Creative Solutions for Sales Promotion

Herb Baum, president of Campbell, USA, the makers of Campbell's soup and other products, contends that many managers are not very creative or sophisticated when making sales-promotion decisions. He offers three useful suggestions for increasing the sophistication and creativity of sales promotion so that it is balanced effectively with advertising.[28]

First and foremost, know your product. This should go without saying, but it doesn't. All too often, people who work on promotions go too far with too little information about product positioning, competitive stance, target audience . . . etc. How else can you explain the preponderance of [sales] promotions that have little or nothing to do with concurrent advertising?

I suspect this is a simple communications problem. Product managers not keeping promotion managers informed . . . promotion managers not keeping suppliers informed . . . suppliers not pressing for the information they need. . . . Sooner or later we're all guilty of assuming that everybody else knows our business as well as we do. At Campbell Soup Company we have an effective way of dealing with this. At our promotion staff meetings, each promotion manager is assigned the task of presenting any new product advertising or new product introductions to the entire department. This forces the promotion managers to get to know their products, and product strategies better, and the entire department learns more about our company's products. Furthermore, promotion managers are always prepared to present their product profiles to whomever may need the information. This helps us all communicate more consistently and efficiently—both internally and with outside agencies and suppliers.

My second suggestion is to plan your time. Too often, mediocre promotions are defended as "the best we could do in the time available." Shorter lead times mean fewer options. It's that simple. And when you're trying to be creative you want all of your options open.

How much time is enough? The key here is strategic promotion planning. I've found it's a good rule of thumb to start thinking about next year's promotion while this year's program is still running. That's when you're most in touch with the circumstances of the promotion period you'll be planning for. It's a great time to use your golden hindsight to good advantage.

My third piece of advice would be to test the waters. I've seen millions spent on advertising research and little or nothing for the study of promotion. In fact, most of us have access to a

Continued

---

28. Adapted from Herb Baum, "Creative Promotion: An Indispensible (sic) Marketing Tool," *Marketing Communications*, April 1988, p. 82. Reprinted with permission.

Continued
wealth of raw data that goes largely untapped. How much do you know about what your promotions have done in the past? When was the last time you saw an in-depth analysis of previous promotions?

I can tell you that [sales] promotion deserves much more attention and respect than it has received in the past. From *this* president's perspective, good creative promotion is an indispensable marketing tool.■

every promotional element have choices to make regarding how best to present their persuasive arguments to achieve established motives. Consider the following examples:

Sales managers decide on the form and content of sales presentations. One important consideration is whether the presentation should follow a fixed script (a "canned" presentation) or be allowed to vary from prospect-to-prospect. *Public-relations directors,* when faced with adverse publicity, choose how best to defend their company's products without appearing excessively contrite or defensive. The public relations person walks a fine line between being an apologist and a dogmatist. Effective public relations people are able to come across sincerely but forcefully in support of their company's products that are under attack. *Advertising creative directors* have numerous message choices. What image to create, how to position the brand, and what specific types of appeals to use (e.g., sex, humor, fear) are just some of the many choices. As described in the chapter's opening vignette, Reebok chose in its 1988–1989 campaign to position its shoes as a brand that encourages individualism—"Reeboks lets U.B.U." L.A. Gear's advertising message in 1988–1989 used sex appeal and a hero theme by intercutting scenes of a high-school basketball player in a championship game with scenes of him playing a one-on-one match with a young woman on a beachside court.

Subsequent chapters will deal with specific message issues as they relate to each promotional element. For example, Chapter 12 covers advertising messages and creative strategy; Chapter 15 discusses message issues in direct-marketing applications; and Chapter 21 touches on sales-presentation strategies as well as on many other topics related to personal selling.

Media.   All marketing communications messages require an agency or instrument (a medium) for transmission. Though the term *media* is typically thought of with respect to advertising media (television, magazines, radio, etc.), the concept of media is relevant to *all* promotional tools. For example, personal sales messages can be delivered via face-to-face communications or by telemarketing; these different media have different costs and different levels of relative effectiveness. Point-of-purchase materials are delivered in a variety of ways—via in-store signs, electronically, musically, and otherwise. Each of these represents a different medium.[29]

Detailed discussions of media are reserved for specific chapters. For example, Chapter 13 discusses advertising media in detail, and Chapter 16 describes various point-of-purchase media.

Momentum. In a dictionary sense, the word *momentum* refers to *impetus*, the *force or speed* of movement. The concept of momentum is used here metaphorically to convey these same ideas. Simply developing an advertising message, personal sales presentation, or publicity release is insufficient. The effectiveness of each of these message forms depends on their timing (speed, so to speak) and force (amount of effort). Insufficient momentum, that is, poorly timed messages and insufficient investment, is ineffective at best and a waste of money at worst.

As is the case with almost every decision faced by promotion managers, momentum is a relative matter: There is no level of momentum equally appropriate for all situations. For example, the amount of investment appropriate for one advertiser may be woefully inadequate for another. L.A. Gear, as pointed out in the opening vignette, is spending a much larger portion of its sales on advertising (approximately $25 million) than either of its much larger competitors, Nike and Reebok. This is because L.A. Gear is a relatively new and unestablished brand, therefore requiring a very strong commitment to advertising in order to build its brand name and create a desired image.

Critical to the concept of momentum is the need to *sustain an effort* rather than starting and stopping—that is, advertising for a while, then discontinuing the effort for a longer while, and so on. In other words, some companies never create nor sustain momentum because their marketplace presence is inadequate. "Out of sight, out of mind" is probably a more relevant saying in reference to brands in the marketplace than to people. We generally do not forget our friends and family, but today's product "friend" is tomorrow's "stranger" unless it is kept before our consciousness.

Outcomes

Communication motives (objectives) are set, modes are selected and mixed, messages and media are chosen, programs are implemented and possibly sustained, and results occur. But what specifically are the results? For a local advertiser, say a sporting-goods store that is running an advertised special on athletic shoes for a two-day period in May, the results are the number of Nike,

---

29. You no doubt have noted the switch in this paragraph between "media" and "medium." The former is plural, the latter singular. Thus, "medium" is the appropriate descriptor when referring only to, say, television; however, "media" is the correct usage when referring to television, magazines, and radio as a collection of advertising vehicles.

Reebok, L.A. Gear, and other brands sold. When you try to sell an old automobile through the classified pages, the results are the number of phone inquiries you receive and whether you ultimately sell the car. For a national manufacturer of a branded product, results typically are not so quick to occur. Rather, a company invests in point-of-purchase communications, sales promotions, and advertising, and then waits, often for many months, to see whether these programs deliver the desired sales volume.

Regardless of situation, it is critical to **measure results.** The preceding discussion suggests that results are measured solely in terms of *sales volume.* In actuality, results of promotional programs more typically are measured in terms of *communication outcomes* rather than sales. This is because sales volume is determined by *all* of the elements of the marketing mix, not just the promotional elements, as well as by various environmental forces. Consequently, increases in sales volume cannot be attributed solely to sales promotion, advertising, or other promotional elements. Communication outcomes provide a more precise measure of promotional effectiveness.

Detailed discussions of communication measures are postponed until appropriate chapters (e.g., Chapter 14 on measuring advertising effectiveness), but a few comments are in order at this time. A *communication measure* is one that deals with a nonsales target: brand awareness, message comprehension, attitude toward the brand, purchase intentions, and so forth. All of these are communication (rather than sales) objectives in the sense that, for example, an advertiser has attempted to convey (communicate) a certain message argument or overall impression. Thus, the goal for L.A. Gear athletic shoes may be to increase brand awareness in the target market by 20 percent within six months of starting a new advertising campaign. This motive (a 20 percent increase in awareness) would be based on knowledge of the awareness level prior to the campaign's debut. Post-campaign measurement would then reveal whether the target level was achieved.

It is essential to measure results of all promotional programs. Failure to achieve targeted results prompts corrective action (see dashed lines, or feedback loops, in Figure 8.1). Corrective action might call for greater investment, a different combination of modes, revised creative strategy, different media allocations, or a host of other possibilities. Only by systematically setting targets (motives) and measuring results is it possible to know whether promotional programs are working as well as they should.

Summary

This chapter introduces the 12-M model of promotion management as a useful integrative and mnemonic device for understanding the overall promotion process. The model (Figure 8.1) contains four general components: marketing structure, managing the environment, market satisfaction, and the promotion-decision process.

The *marketing structure,* which involves the organizational arrangement for accomplishing a firm's marketing task, plays an instrumental role in determining how important promotion is in the overall marketing mix and how promotion decisions are made and implemented. The "guts" of promotion management is the *promotion-decision process.* The process is aimed at two fundamental objectives: *managing the environment* and *market satisfaction.* The latter objective is the embodiment of the marketing concept covered in Chapter 1. The former objective involves making efforts to anticipate and alter environmental forces (especially competitive maneuvers) rather than merely reacting belatedly to changes in the marketplace—changes that might disrupt or seriously impede a company's success.

The *promotion-decision process* consists of a set of conditions, general choices, specific choices, and outcomes. The conditions include *motives* (objectives), *means* (budgets), and *morality.* General choices include *modes* (persuasive communications and promotional inducements) and *mixtures* of modes. Specific choices entail decisions about *messages, media,* and *momentum.* Outcomes of these decisions represent *measured results.*

Discussion Questions

1. Discuss the difference between the brand-management and category-management organizational structures at Procter & Gamble. Describe what implications the change from brand to category management will have for decisions at Procter & Gamble regarding "conditions" and "general choices" in Figure 8.1.

2. Changes in the so-called "three Cs of marketing" (customers, consumers, and competitors) have imposed pressures on companies to alter their marketing organizational structures. Explain.

3. Explain the concept of "environmental management." Compare this idea with the notion presented in many introductory marketing texts that the environment is "uncontrollable."

4. Motives and means, as initial conditions in the promotion-decision process, are necessarily interdependent. Explain how these two conditions are interdependent and provide a supportive example to illustrate your point.

5. What is the distinction between top-down (TD) and bottom-up (BU) budgeting? Why is BUTD budgeting used in companies that are more marketing oriented, whereas TDBU budgeting is found more frequently in finance-driven companies?

6. Distinguish between Mode 2 (persuasive communications) and Mode 3 (promotional inducements). Provide examples of each.

7. Promotion management has been described as an "ill-structured problem." Explain what this means.

8. Describe why you think the "balance of power" has moved from advertising toward sales promotion in many companies' promotional budgets.

9. Achieving a balance between advertising and sales promotion involves taking various factors into consideration. Two of the most important are "strategic" and

"brand equity" considerations. Explain precisely how these considerations are relevant to the decision about the relative influence placed on advertising and sales promotion. Select a specific brand of a well-known grocery product as a basis for motivating your discussion.

10. Explain the concept of "momentum." Using the same brand that you selected for answering the previous question, describe your understanding of how this brand accomplishes a suitable level of momentum.

Exercises

1. Assume you are the fund-raising chairperson for an organization on your campus, say a student chapter of the American Marketing Association. It is your job to identify a suitable project *and* to manage the project's promotion. For the purpose of this exercise, identify a fund-raising project idea and apply the 12-M model to show how you might go about promoting this project. Be sure to address all 12 Ms in your discussion, but place special focus on the 9 Ms in the Promotion-Decision Process component of the model.

2. Select a well-known brand from a packaged-good product sold in grocery stores, drug stores, or other mass-merchandise outlets. Analyze this brand's promotional activities at the general- and specific-choice levels (i.e., modes, mixture, messages, etc.). Describe the specific promotional choices and programs this brand has employed in the past year or so. You cannot be expected to know exactly how the brand is promoted, but your casual observations should provide some idea. Moreover, by reviewing the *Business Periodical Index* in your library, you should be able to identify various articles in business periodicals that describe your chosen brand's promotional activities (e.g., articles published in *Advertising Age, Business Week, Drug Store Age, Fortune, Forbes, Grocery World,* and *The Wall Street Journal*).

Environmental Influences on Promotion Management

THE DECADE OF THE MATURE MARKET

he 1980s was the decade of the baby boomers, of yuppies, of physical fitness, and lean bodies. With the aging of the U.S. population, however, the 1990s will be the decade of the mature market. More and more marketing efforts will be directed at consumers who are middle-aged and older and greater emphasis will be placed on health and health-promoting products.

Indicative of this trend is ConAgra's new line of "Healthy Choice" frozen foods developed specifically for the over-50 market. Each of the ten dinners in the line is prepared with lean meats and light sauces, contains less than 325 calories, and satisfies the U.S. Food and Drug Administration's guidelines on acceptable levels of sodium, cholesterol, and fat intake.

This new product line and segmentation strategy has strong success potential for several reasons. First, the market for low-calorie frozen dinners has experienced a high growth rate throughout the 1980s, enjoying a 13 percent growth in 1987 alone. Second, the total market size of over-50 consumers in the United States is vast; more than 65 million consumers occupied this age category in 1990. Third, older consumers, as with the rest of society, are increasingly concerned with good health and proper eating habits. Finally, many (though certainly not all) older Americans have tremendous discretionary incomes. These consumers are more able to afford Healthy Choice's premium price (about $3.19 per dinner) than are younger consumers, who may be strapped with mortgages and other fixed-debt payments, expenses that older consumers are out from under.[1]■

The opening vignette illustrates how one company has responded to a major marketplace development, the aging of the U.S. population. In general, promotion decisions are subject to persistent environmental pressures. The task of promotion management is to adapt and respond appropriately to these pressures and, where possible, to manage (i.e., influence and alter) environmental circumstances so that the organization's interests are best served.[2]

Of course, organizations are not always able to manage their environments. It is critical, nevertheless, that they monitor their environments and are prepared to alter policies, strategies, and tactics to be compatible with environmental circumstances and developments. Successful companies anticipate environmental developments and are prepared in advance, rather than simply reacting to major changes after they have occurred.

Environmental influences consist of five major elements: economic, competitive, technological, socio-cultural/demographic, and regulatory. All of the environmental forces play major roles in promotion management. However, this chapter will focus on only three major forces: the technological, demographic, and regulatory environments. Detailed discussions of the economic and competitive environments are beyond the primary scope of the text and would, in fact, be redundant with comparable presentations found in basic marketing texts. Likewise, discussions of the socio-cultural environment are found in any consumer behavior text.

The Technological Environment

Technological advances during the past several decades have been incredible, leading one marketing scholar to observe that technology is the "most dramatic force shaping people's destiny."[3] Technological developments affect all aspects of our lives and, of course, also influence the behavior of promotion managers and other marketing communicators. This influence is felt both indirectly and directly.

1. Adapted from Julie Liesse Erickson, "ConAgra Dishes Up Health Line," *Advertising Age*, January 16, 1989, pp. 3, 54.
2. This discussion is alluding to the concept of "environmental management" described in the previous chapter. See also Carl P. Zeithaml and Valarie A. Zeithaml, "Environmental Management: Revising the Marketing Perspective," *Journal of Marketing*, vol. 48 (Spring 1984), pp. 46–53.
3. Philip Kotler, *Marketing Management: Analysis, Management, and Control*, 5th ed. (Englewood Cliffs, NJ: Prentice-Hall, 1984), p. 99.

Indirect influence refers to technological developments that do not affect marketing communications technology itself but which influence other aspects of social/economic and marketing behavior. For example, technological advances spur the development of new products, thereby presenting challenges and opportunities for advertisers, salespeople, and other marketing communicators. Other technological developments affect society in general, consumers more specifically, and thus marketing communicators as well. The advent of birth-control pills, for example, had profound effects on family size, women's rights, and household incomes (as more wives began to work); consequently, birth-control pills influenced various aspects of consumer behavior and marketing communications indirectly.

Various technological developments which have had *direct effects* on promotion and marketing communications will now be discussed.

Advances Related to Personal Selling

Personal selling has been influenced by several major technological advances, most of which involve computer technology and improvements in communication transmission made possible by satellite transmission and glass optical fibers that transmit light pulses instead of electric signals.

Teleconferencing is one major development. Satellite teleconferences permit individuals (such as sales managers) at one location to engage in audiovisual interaction with individuals in other geographical sites. Sales managers can use teleconferences to update their sales forces on new product and marketing programs. For example, General Motors of Canada introduced a new line of cars and trucks to dealers with a television-type teleconference that reached more than 6,000 people.[4]

The *videocassette recorder (VCR)* is not just a favorite household entertainment device; it also has found its way into use by sales departments. For example, Avon purchased 20,000 VCRs for its sales force and provided each salesperson with a monthly cassette showing the company's new products and sales presentations.[5]

Perhaps the greatest technological innovation to influence personal selling is the *laptop, or portable, computer*. More and more companies are providing their sales representatives with laptop computers for order entry and other forms of information inputs. Electronic order entry involves the transmission of sales orders from remote sites (i.e., locations where salespersons work and live) directly to mainframe computers at sales branches and corporate headquarters. In the past, several days were required for orders to be transmitted via the mail. Now, salespeople can electronically transmit daily orders and

4. Laurel Leff, "When Meetings Go on Camera," *Marketing Communications*, January 1983, pp. 25–27.
5. "VCRs: Coming on Strong," *Time*, December 24, 1984, p. 47.

thereby expedite order processing and fulfillment. This information is transmitted to the sales office via telephone modems. The availability of portable computers in the field with telephone transmission to sales offices has improved selling efficiency, enhanced the quality of information sent from the field to sales managers, and reduced the time to prepare sales reports.[6] Hewlett-Packard, which claims to have the largest automated sales force in the world, increased the amount of time salespeople actually spend selling by 27 percent when it provided its salespeople with portable computers.[7]

Other technological advances affecting personal selling include facsimile (fax) machines, cellular telephones, and videocassette monitors. *Fax machines* permit salespeople to transmit urgent sales reports, letters, and other documents to their sales office's fax machine. Stand-alone pay facsimile stations are now proliferating in office buildings, airports, hotels, and other sites frequented by salespeople.[8]

Cellular telephones are freestanding units that do not require electronic cables and other hardware called for by conventional telephones. Rather, cellular telephones make transmissions via satellite linkages. The advantage of the cellular telephone is that it permits telephone contact from a salesperson's or manager's automobile or any other site where a conventional phone is unavailable.

Visual aids enhance the quality of sales presentations, increase impact, and reduce the amount of time it takes to deliver a sales presentation.[9] For these reasons, a variety of presentation aids have come on the market to improve sales effectiveness and efficiency.

Advances Related to Advertising

Technological developments have affected advertising in three related ways: (1) how messages are transmitted, (2) how messages are produced, and (3) how messages are received by consumers (or perhaps, how messages are avoided).

Cable television is probably the major technological development related to advertising. Cable television has altered people's viewing habits and increased the media outlets available to advertisers. The "cabling of America" has created vast viewing opportunities for consumers but has complicated the advertiser's job. Audiences are now fragmented, compared with pre-cable audiences, who were limited to the three major networks. (More discussion is devoted to this topic in Chapter 13).

6. Thayer C. Taylor, "Seagram Looks to Laptops for Help," *Sales and Marketing Management*, January 1988, p. 67.
7. Jef Graham, "Information Support Systems Catapult Sales to New Levels," *Marketing Communications*, February 1988, pp. 19–23.
8. "The Fax of Selling," *Sales and Marketing Management*, January 1989, p. 20.
9. Melissa Campanelli, "Hi-Tech Imagery Creates Better Sales Presentations," *Sales and Marketing Management*, January 1989, p. 83.

Videocassette recorders have affected advertising as well as personal selling. Advertising has been affected by VCRs in at least two ways. First, people are exposed to fewer television advertisements because they spend some of their time viewing movies and other nontelevision content. Second, when viewing prerecorded television programs, people are "zapping" commercials with the fast-scan button. Advertising technicians are trying to develop new types of commercials that will enable commercial messages to get across even when played at fast-scan speeds.

Methods of producing television commercials have changed as a result of computer developments and other technological advances. Computer-generated commercials represent one form of innovative technology in television production. One particularly intriguing commercial is from a firm named TRW. The commercial was designed to dramatize the copy claim: "Just when you think you've seen the whole picture, the picture changes." A bird/fish interlocking pattern was generated by computer to provide a graphic juxtaposition of the verbal claim.

> The commercial opens with a closeup of a bird's eye, which winks at the camera. As the camera pulls away from the bird, which is carrying a cherry in its beak, the screen displays more and more computer graphic birds, fully animated and flying in unison. Eventually, the birds are seen to be part of an interlocking pattern. When they finally lock together, a positive-negative illusion is created. Within the negative spaces of the birds, the cherries turn into the eyes of fish. As the birds begin to disappear, the computer graphic fish begin to swim in unison. The camera continues to pull away until the birds and fish become merely the dots in a half-tone pattern of a man's face. At this moment, the man winks.[10]

Scenes from this fascinating and ingenious commercial are shown in Figure 9.1.

Other technological developments in advertising include improvements in printing processes that have led to vast improvements in the quality of advertising reproductions in print media, particularly newspapers. For example, the *quality of color reproduction in newspaper ads* has improved considerably in recent years (e.g., in *USA Today*). Another advancement in print media is the ability to reproduce chemically and *encapsulate the smell* of cosmetics, soaps, and other items and imprint these on magazine advertisements. These scratch-and-sniff ads provide advertisers with the opportunity to reach consumers through the sense of smell in addition to the visual sense. Advertisers also are using *pop-ups* in magazine ads and even *three-dimensional (3-D) representations* of products. For example, Toyota ran a magazine ad containing a 3-D shot of one of its automobiles seen through a viewmaster. Coca-Cola received tremendously favorable response to its 3-D commercial carried at halftime during the 23rd Superbowl between the Cincinnati Bengals and the San Francisco 49ers. Millions of pairs of 3-D glasses were provided free to consumers prior to the game

10. Hooper White, "Computers & Commercials: The Production Revolution," *Advertising Age Yearbook 1984* (Chicago: Crain Communications, 1984), p. 24.

FIGURE 9.1   **Scenes from TRW's Computer-Generated Commercial**

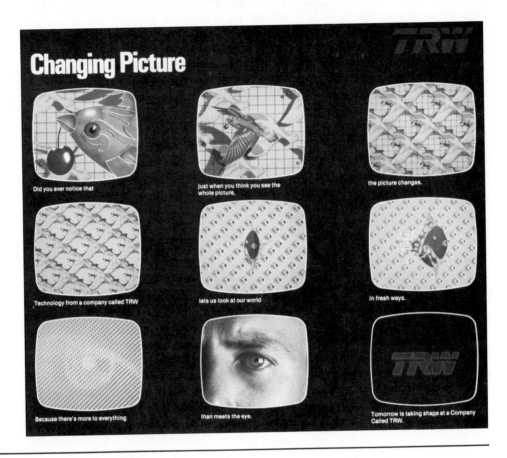

Source: Courtesy of TRW Inc.

to hype interest in viewing Coca-Cola's ad. Consumer involvement in this one advertisement is possibly unparalleled in the history of advertising.

Advances Related to Direct Mail

As discussed later in Chapter 15, direct-mail marketing has experienced a phenomenal increase in recent years. Part of this increase is due to fundamental developments in American society (e.g., the increase in the number of working women), but technological factors are also instrumental. Three factors in particular stand out.[11] First, the *computer* has revolutionized direct-mail marketing

11. Robert F. DeLay, "Direct Marketing: Healthy & Growing," *Advertising Age Yearbook 1984* (Chicago: Crain Communications, 1984), pp. 13, 14.

and has, in certain respects, made direct mail feasible on the scale that it is practiced today. Storage and retrieval of huge mailing lists depends on electronic processing. Moreover, the power of computers to search through huge data files and generate tailor-made lists has facilitated sophisticated market segmentation in the direct-mail industry. The computer also facilitates analyzing and evaluating the effectiveness of direct-mail.

Simple as it may seem, a second technological factor responsible for the rapid growth of direct mail is the emergence and widespread adoption of *credit cards*. Credit cards facilitate consumer ordering and expedite credit checking by direct marketers.

A third development underlying direct marketing's growth is the availability of toll-free *WATS numbers*. The ability to place a purchase order by phone immediately after reading a direct-mail advertisement or viewing a direct-marketing television commercial increases the chances that consumers and industrial buyers will order an advertised item.

Advances Related to Point-of-Purchase Communications

Point-of-purchase displays have become much more aesthetically appealing, more functional, and more effective as a result of technological advances. It is now economically feasible to construct displays out of building materials (e.g., wood veneer) that are economical as well as attractive. The design of large, integrated or component displays (e.g., one display devoted entirely to hair-care products) has made it possible for manufacturers and retailers to increase sales, for retailers to conserve floor space, and for consumers to simplify their shopping.

A major innovation in point-of-purchase merchandising is the electronic *interactive display unit*. These units perform informational and sometimes transactional functions. They often combine still and motion photography, computer graphics, stereo sound, and an interactive touchscreen to enable consumers to acquire product information and transact orders. For example, to facilitate furniture purchasing, the Furniture Industry Council devised an interactive display that enables shoppers to decorate their homes electronically. Shoppers enter their room dimensions into a computer and then select chairs, sofas, and room accessories that are stored in the computer's memory bank. Shoppers electronically "move" the furniture around the room and change the colors of the walls, floor, and upholstery. In addition, through a special "chromakey" process, the shopper is projected into the room so she can envision herself in the just-decorated room. A color photo of the electronically decorated room is printed out so the shopper has visual evidence to take back home.[12] Chapter 16 further describes advances in interactive displays.

Another exciting development is the *computerized shopping cart*, the "VideOcart," which presents product and sales information to shoppers as

---

12. Cyndee Miller, "Furniture Industry Woos Baby Boomers with a Little 'Magic'," *Marketing News*, January 16, 1989, p. 14.

they move their carts down supermarket aisles. These carts are described further in Chapter 16.

The Demographic Environment

Demographic variables are measurable characteristics of populations, including characteristics such as age distribution, household living patterns, income distribution, minority population patterns, and regional population statistics. By monitoring demographic shifts, marketers are better able to (1) identify and select market segments, (2) forecast product sales, and (3) select media for reaching target customers.[13]

The demographic structure of the United States is experiencing dramatic and profound changes. The following statement emphasizes to marketers the importance of staying attuned to demographic trends.

> You cannot understand the consumer marketplace today without an appreciation of demographic trends. . . . Demographic characteristics help shape preferences, determine attitudes, and mold values. So when these characteristics change rapidly, as they have in recent years, the marketplace changes too.[14]

Some of the major trends include the following:

1. *A maturing society.* There now are more people over age 65 than there are teenagers living in the United States.

2. *Lure of the Sunbelt.* Between 1984 and 1990 the populations of the ten Sunbelt states increased by at least 20 percent compared to a *total* population increase of approximately 5 percent during this period.[15]

3. *Women on the move.* In the early 1960s approximately 30 percent of married women worked outside the home. Now the percentage exceeds 60 percent.

4. *Rise of minorities.* The combined population of Hispanics, Blacks, and Asian Americans is growing at a disproportionately faster rate than the remainder of the population. Together, these minorities will constitute about 17 percent of the total U.S. population by the year 2000 in comparison with their 14.4 percent representation in 1983.[16]

The following sections will focus on six major demographic topics that are important to promotion managers and marketing communicators: (1) population growth and regional geographic developments, (2) the changing age

13. Thomas S. Robertson, Joan Zielinski, and Scott Ward, *Consumer Behavior* (Glenview, IL: Scott, Foresman and Company, 1984), p. 340.
14. "The Year 2000: A Demographic Profile of the Consumer Market," *Marketing News*, May 25, 1984, p. 8.
15. Alex Kucherov, "10 Forces Reshaping America," *U.S. News and World Report*, March 19, 1984, pp. 40–52.
16. "Prediction: Sunny Side Up," *Time*, September 19, 1983, p. 28.

structure, (3) the changing American household, (4) the changing roles of women, (5) income dynamics, and (6) minority population developments.

Population Growth and Regional Geographic Developments

The world population is experiencing an incredible and alarming increase. In 1960 the population was barely over 3 billion people, in 1984 it approached 5 billion, and by the year 2025 it is projected to exceed 8 billion.[17] In contrast to much of the rest of the world, the United States is slow in population growth. Approximately 23 million people were added to the U.S. population in the 1970s, and a like amount were added in the 1980s. However, only 18 million additional people are expected to be added to the U.S. population in the 1990s.[18]

In 1987, the U.S. population was approximately 242 million. It is expected to grow to approximately 260 million by 1995 and to approximately 268 million by 2000. Table 9.1 presents these population figures along with the distribution by age group and, at the bottom, median-age data. Figure 9.2 presents population-growth statistics between 1980 and 1987 for the ten most populated states.

What makes the U.S. population most interesting is not its size or growth per se but rather the *shifts that are taking place in its geographical distribution.* Historically, the population was concentrated in the industrial Northeast and Midwest, but by the year 2000 a solid majority of Americans will be southerners or Pacific coasters. In fact, as can be seen in Table 9.2, which ranks the 100 top U.S. markets based on their 1987 populations, approximately 50 percent of these markets are southern or Pacific-coast cities. This table contains additional information pertaining to these metropolitan areas' incomes, retail sales, and Buying Power Indexes. For example, it is noted in Table 9.2 that the 1987 Buying Power Index (BPI) for the largest U.S. market, Los Angeles-Long Beach, was 3.83; the BPI for the fiftieth largest market, Louisville, was 0.38. These statistics mean that the Los Angeles-Long Beach market represents approximately 4 percent of the total retail buying influence in the United States, whereas the Louisville market accounts for approximately 0.4 percent of the buying influence. You should find it interesting to peruse these statistics for some of your favorite markets. Further details are provided at the bottom of the table.

The Changing Age Structure

One of the most dramatic features of the American population is its relentless aging; the median age of Americans was 28 in 1970 and 30 in 1980; it will rise

---

17. "People, People, People," *Time*, August 6, 1984, pp. 24, 25.
18. William Lazer, *Handbook of Demographics for Marketing and Advertising* (Lexington, MA: Lexington Books, 1987), p. 6.

TABLE 9.1   **Projections of the Population of the United States by Age: 1983–2000**

Age	Population (numbers in thousands)				
	1983	**1985**	**1990**	**1995**	**2000**
Under 5	17,846	18,453	19,198	18,615	17,626
5–9	15,960	16,611	18,591	19,337	18,758
10–14	17,766	16,797	16,793	18,772	19,519
15–19	19,180	18,416	16,968	16,968	18,943
20–24	21,871	21,301	18,580	17,142	17,145
25–29	21,170	21,838	21,522	18,822	17,396
30–34	19,070	19,950	22,007	21,698	19,019
35–39	16,278	17,894	20,001	22,052	21,753
40–44	13,171	14,110	17,846	19,945	21,990
45–49	11,175	11,647	13,980	17,678	19,763
50–54	11,144	10,817	11,422	13,719	17,356
55–59	11,463	11,245	10,433	11,040	13,280
60–64	10,734	10,943	10,618	9,883	10,487
65–69	9,005	9,214	9,996	9,736	9,096
70–74	7,352	7,641	8,039	8,767	8,581
75–79	5,263	5,556	6,260	6,640	7,295
80–84	3,284	3,501	4,089	4,671	5,023
85 and over	2,512	2,697	3,313	4,074	4,926
Total	234,223	238,631	249,657	259,559	267,955
Median Age	30.8	31.4	33.2	34.7	36.3

Source: U.S. Bureau of the Census (1984), "Projections of the Population of the United States by Age, Sex and Race: 1983–2080." *Current Population Reports* Series P-25 (No. 952), Table 6, Washington, D.C.: U.S. Government Printing Office.

to 33 by 1990 and 36 by the year 2000.[19] In 1990 there are more than 30 million Americans over the age of 65; by comparison, slightly more than 19 million are under the age of five (refer to Table 9.1).

The Baby-Boom Generation.   The changing age structure is attributable in large part to what demographers term the **baby boom**—the 74 million Americans born between 1947 and 1964.[20] The effects of the baby boom (and subsequent bust) can be seen in Figure 9.3 which portrays three major developments:

1. By 1995 there will be 5.2 million more Americans aged 2 to 13 than in 1985; the original baby boomers are creating a mini baby boom as they reach childbearing age.

19. "The Year 2000."
20. Bryant Robey and Cheryl Russell, "The Year of the Baby Boom," *American Demographics*, May 1984, p. 19.

Growth of the Ten Most Populated States   FIGURE 9.2

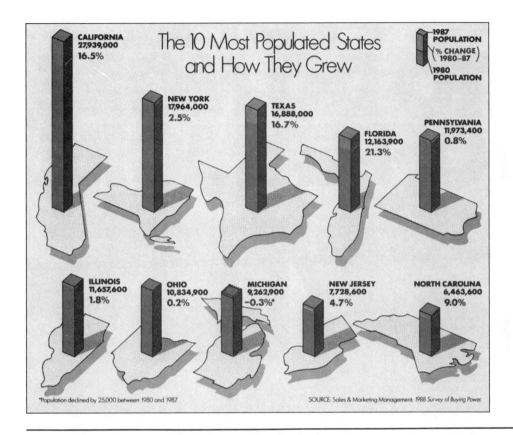

*Population declined by 25,000 between 1980 and 1987   SOURCE: Sales & Marketing Management, 1988 Survey of Buying Power

Source: Sales & Marketing Management, October 1988, p. 14. Copyright 1988 Survey of Buying
Power. Reprinted by permission of Sales & Marketing Management.

2. The number of teenagers and young adults is declining. By 1995 there
    will be 8.8 million *fewer* Americans aged 14 to 30 than in 1985. This is due
    to the low birth rate during the 1960s and 1970s, which resulted in rela-
    tively few people (the "baby busters") to move through those age groups.

3. As the baby-boom generation ages, the number of people aged 31 to 56
    will grow by 20.9 million between 1985 and 1995.

The preceding developments hold considerable promise for many marketers but may cause problems for others. First we will consider the possibility
of problems. Marketers who appealed to the teenage and young-adult markets
during the 1970s have suffered as the size of these markets declined. The blue-
jeans industry is a case in point. Blue-jeans sales reached a tremendous peak

TABLE 9.2   The Top 100 U.S. Markets

Rank Metro Market	POPULATION 1987	1992	% Change 1987-92	Black	Hispanic	INCOME Avg. Household EBI 1987	1992	RETAIL SALES Total Retail Sales ($000) 1987	1992	% Change 1987-92	BUYING POWER INDEX BPI (U.S.=100,000) 1987	1992	ECONOMIC ACTIVITY 1987*	PER DIEM Meals & Lodging
1. Los Angeles-Long Beach	8,544.0	9,233.9	8.1%	1,071.6	2,741.4	$41,980	$58,005	$56,746,834	$86,778,659	52.9%	3.8273	3.8682	$224,260.5	$138.90
2. New York	8,528.2	8,698.5	2.0	2,227.9	1,713.8	38,269	52,122	47,732,464	70,011,678	46.7	3.6612	3.5212	419,970.7	175.80
3. Chicago	6,177.3	6,209.5	0.5	1,473.1	612.8	41,235	59,385	40,744,473	60,728,332	49.0	2.7573	2.7194	220,982.4	157.10
4. Philadelphia	4,855.0	4,937.9	1.7	942.2	132.5	39,611	56,517	32,943,827	49,317,973	49.7	2.1427	2.1220	124,157.5	130.45
5. Detroit	4,358.9	4,393.2	0.8	914.8	80.0	37,701	53,219	29,363,285	43,308,930	47.5	1.8671	1.8228	135,043.7	107.20
6. Boston-Lawrence-Salem-Lowell-Brockton	3,718.1	3,746.5	0.8	203.4	96.1	45,241	63,460	30,766,529	45,315,815	47.3	1.8835	1.8295	130,113.4	141.15
7. Washington, DC	3,624.9	3,858.2	6.4	939.7	113.6	49,606	69,970	29,294,343	45,346,104	55.3	1.9123	1.9606	82,090.2	153.20
8. Houston	3,233.0	3,405.8	5.3	632.1	597.6	36,812	50,777	22,796,309	31,325,570	37.4	1.3850	1.3395	93,155.2	105.28
9. Atlanta	2,662.8	2,965.2	11.4	629.1	31.9	37,625	52,625	20,794,968	33,022,028	58.8	1.2013	1.2786	56,953.2	148.90
10. Nassau-Suffolk, NY	2,661.7	2,698.6	1.4	186.8	122.3	58,310	81,507	21,824,947	32,262,990	47.8	1.4313	1.3940	58,642.4	104.35
11. St. Louis	2,463.7	2,513.7	2.0	425.5	25.4	37,588	53,103	16,439,385	24,176,173	47.1	1.0480	1.0270	70,335.7	101.10
12. Dallas	2,430.2	2,647.6	8.9	405.0	273.4	38,609	57,399	17,907,833	26,959,993	50.5	1.0952	1.1598	76,180.5	105.00
13. Minneapolis-St. Paul	2,336.4	2,457.3	5.2	56.1	25.1	42,603	61,942	17,640,652	27,307,743	54.8	1.1219	1.1591	80,158.7	108.90
14. Baltimore	2,333.6	2,409.7	3.3	581.1	23.8	36,583	49,962	15,247,372	22,452,611	47.3	.9731	.9463	50,215.4	104.00
15. San Diego	2,313.9	2,591.7	12.0	130.6	400.5	42,506	59,065	15,293,123	24,612,452	60.9	1.0429	1.1065	33,745.1	114.40
16. Anaheim-Santa Ana	2,230.3	2,417.3	8.4	28.8	390.2	47,961	65,759	17,071,107	26,109,455	52.9	1.1072	1.1156	54,345.2	105.60
17. Riverside-San Bernardino	2,171.5	2,530.5	16.5	109.6	465.7	36,885	50,256	12,096,998	19,410,541	60.5	.8598	.9303	20,735.7	81.45
18. Pittsburgh	2,119.1	2,072.4	-2.2	174.9	11.8	33,120	45,109	12,322,375	16,483,802	33.8	.8415	.7661	44,265.7	114.55
19. Phoenix	1,986.1	2,306.9	16.2	63.0	292.6	35,019	48,612	13,076,432	20,863,544	59.6	.8397	.9203	38,857.0	95.60
20. Tampa-St. Petersburg Clearwater	1,979.3	2,210.7	11.7	194.1	111.6	30,640	43,158	13,442,895	21,794,931	62.1	.8236	.8857	30,056.2	109.20
21. Oakland	1,978.4	2,107.9	6.5	292.9	246.4	45,004	62,534	13,828,009	21,151,652	53.0	.9668	.9752	32,200.0	112.40
22. Newark	1,902.4	1,918.1	0.8	430.8	155.6	47,395	66,218	12,329,603	17,989,393	45.9	.9046	.8745	69,687.3	129.75
23. Cleveland	1,842.7	1,813.2	-1.6	345.7	26.3	35,438	50,617	12,736,299	18,378,247	44.3	.7914	.7587	52,693.3	99.00
24. Miami-Hialeah	1,818.2	1,944.5	6.9	344.1	772.3	33,973	47,352	14,751,212	22,786,423	54.5	.8034	.8197	41,744.7	124.95
25. Seattle	1,796.8	1,913.8	6.5	65.6	337.1	41,459	60,135	13,063,631	20,115,011	54.0	.8685	.9053	95,622.9	111.10
26. Denver	1,675.8	1,823.9	8.8	87.9	184.9	37,450	54,469	11,751,410	17,643,910	50.1	.7564	.7924	39,295.9	121.45
27. San Francisco	1,595.8	1,663.2	4.2	132.0	210.8	47,264	65,909	14,886,534	22,274,975	49.6	.9138	.9017	66,917.2	167.05
28. Kansas City, MO-KS	1,542.7	1,605.6	4.1	194.9	38.0	38,297	54,533	11,016,106	16,570,423	50.4	.6894	.6919	45,731.2	105.10
29. Cincinnati	1,423.6	1,428.2	0.3	180.8	8.4	35,945	53,083	9,513,583	14,381,290	51.2	.6012	.6020	44,650.3	90.10
30. San Jose	1,422.8	1,500.0	5.4	45.9	292.6	51,972	72,739	10,772,138	16,166,083	50.1	.7331	.7274	43,188.7	120.45
31. Milwaukee	1,390.9	1,383.7	-0.5	153.1	36.6	37,290	53,891	8,469,597	12,046,824	42.2	.5856	.5663	42,532.5	90.15
32. Sacramento	1,354.6	1,516.8	12.0	76.4	152.1	38,173	52,236	9,145,316	14,536,598	59.0	.6012	.6316	18,011.0	89.75
33. Norfolk-Virginia Beach-Newport News, VA	1,337.5	1,435.2	7.3	384.5	23.1	36,368	51,242	8,642,148	13,444,875	55.6	.5344	.5519	19,109.9	91.85
34. New Orleans	1,337.4	1,374.3	2.8	436.2	53.1	29,879	44,202	8,852,525	13,305,104	50.3	.5101	.5176	28,175.3	134.00
35. Columbus, OH	1,314.2	1,350.3	2.7	151.6	9.1	33,848	49,331	8,959,190	13,632,789	52.2	.5474	.5550	31,918.0	92.15
36. Bergen-Passaic, NJ	1,302.8	1,310.9	0.6	99.4	111.2	50,596	70,732	11,216,841	16,482,438	46.9	.7058	.6834	34,985.7	94.55
37. San Antonio	1,271.5	1,363.1	7.2	93.9	660.7	31,677	46,935	7,172,213	10,520,639	46.7	.4554	.4731	19,775.4	96.15
38. Fort Worth-Arlington	1,256.4	1,419.4	13.0	140.1	110.9	36,855	54,841	8,407,246	12,953,868	54.1	.5318	.5825	29,497.2	90.00
39. Indianapolis	1,229.0	1,260.1	2.5	179.1	9.8	36,007	53,609	8,869,296	13,631,985	53.7	.5290	.5428	29,910.8	92.40
40. Fort Lauderdale-Hollywood-Pompano Beach	1,190.3	1,304.0	9.6	144.3	52.3	36,435	51,349	10,067,896	16,117,748	60.1	.5849	.6185	18,102.6	110.65
41. Portland, OR	1,169.4	1,202.4	2.8	33.3	27.3	32,701	51,124	8,132,744	12,602,938	55.0	.4901	.5169	26,751.6	100.85
42. Hartford-New Britain-Middletown-Bristol	1,104.3	1,134.7	2.8	82.8	50.2	45,400	62,613	8,679,548	12,945,822	49.2	.5487	.5381	51,136.8	109.45
43. Charlotte-Gastonia-Rock Hill, NC-SC	1,088.1	1,161.8	6.8	236.2	9.2	32,976	47,088	7,354,092	11,599,685	57.7	.4411	.4613	28,891.1	95.80
44. Salt Lake City-Ogden	1,056.4	1,131.8	7.1	9.1	54.0	32,991	49,360	5,513,568	8,219,275	49.1	.3686	.3836	17,630.8	91.45
45. Rochester, NY	996.1	1,007.8	1.2	89.6	22.4	39,655	52,665	6,299,533	8,951,892	42.1	.4308	.4033	24,955.5	91.65
46. Oklahoma City	989.1	1,059.2	7.1	89.4	23.6	31,207	45,473	7,380,929	10,734,024	45.4	.4086	.4164	24,747.0	89.10
47. Monmouth-Ocean, NJ	970.5	1,048.4	8.0	62.7	29.4	45,287	63,591	7,014,500	11,099,316	58.2	.4749	.4950	12,213.9	N.A.
48. Buffalo	970.3	946.3	-2.5	110.7	15.5	34,492	45,431	5,762,669	7,952,430	38.0	.3844	.3463	23,533.3	98.25
49. Memphis	968.5	995.6	2.8	403.8	9.8	30,455	44,103	6,728,896	10,246,901	52.3	.3752	.3797	26,112.3	77.10
50. Louisville	966.1	963.8	-0.2	127.9	6.1	33,035	49,783	6,392,975	9,564,549	49.6	.3877	.3890	30,939.1	81.60
51. Middlesex-Somerset-Hunterdon, NJ	962.4	1,012.0	5.2	52.3	51.0	51,991	72,592	7,537,696	11,554,442	53.3	.5007	.5060	31,761.8	N.A.
52. Nashville	960.9	1,031.0	7.3	159.6	7.6	34,359	50,550	6,167,214	9,590,056	55.5	.3914	.4138	23,829.5	90.75
53. Orlando	959.0	1,117.3	16.5	129.0	38.6	33,347	46,576	7,210,402	12,040,284	67.0	.4085	.4553	16,673.5	107.85
54. Dayton-Springfield, OH	935.0	922.4	-1.3	123.2	6.8	34,062	49,350	5,904,252	8,586,885	45.4	.3823	.3705	20,439.8	73.15
55. Birmingham	928.7	951.2	2.4	267.6	6.2	28,898	41,280	4,871,001	7,048,916	44.7	.3288	.3245	24,188.9	97.95
56. Greensboro-Winston-Salem-High Point, NC	914.9	953.4	4.2	186.7	6.6	32,030	45,441	6,007,669	9,191,955	53.0	.3667	.3718	29,336.4	90.70

*Manufacturing & Service Shipments/Receipts ($MiL.)

Rank	Metro Market	POPULATION 1987	1992	% Change 1987-92	Black	Hispanic	INCOME Avg. Household EBI 1987	1992	RETAIL SALES Total Retail Sales ($000) 1987	1992	% Change 1987-92	BUYING POWER INDEX BPI (U.S.=100,000) 1987	1992	ECONOMIC ACTIVITY 1987*	PER DIEM Meals & Lodging
57.	Providence-Pawtucket-Woonsocket, RI	903.7	925.9	2.5%	29.9	21.1	$36,206	$51,489	$6,053,472	$9,106,035	50.4%	.3790	.3766	$31,607.5	$100.55
58.	Jacksonville, FL	890.1	987.4	10.9	198.1	18.0	32,590	45,636	5,505,484	8,385,439	52.3	.3518	.3687	19,454.5	88.65
59.	Albany-Schenectady-Troy	853.8	865.3	1.3	34.4	10.1	37,838	51,150	5,678,644	8,209,593	44.6	.3701	.3514	15,925.8	96.10
60.	Honolulu	836.2	873.6	4.5	16.8	62.0	44,796	63,408	5,567,310	8,490,973	52.6	.3595	.3647	14,620.5	124.95
61.	Bridgeport-Stamford-Norwalk-Danbury, CT	834.9	849.9	1.8	74.2	50.9	59,874	84,406	8,149,446	12,180,060	49.5	.5062	.4992	23,054.1	106.50
62.	Richmond-Petersburg, VA	829.4	872.6	5.2	244.3	7.8	37,233	52,305	6,056,580	9,248,329	52.7	.3600	.3628	32,995.5	N.A.
63.	West Palm Beach-Boca Raton-Delray Beach	804.0	938.9	16.8	116.7	44.7	39,317	56,155	6,593,307	11,331,548	71.9	.4058	.4622	13,419.8	103.45
64.	New Haven-Waterbury-Meriden, CT	784.6	796.0	1.5	75.0	30.7	44,121	61,693	5,953,486	8,841,803	48.5	.3796	.3712	17,401.7	98.75
65.	Tulsa, OK	749.2	800.2	6.8	57.9	11.7	30,250	41,990	4,442,152	6,054,048	36.3	.2836	.2780	20,147.8	88.20
66.	Austin	745.1	849.1	14.0	75.0	154.8	34,435	51,439	4,833,318	7,478,393	54.7	.3077	.3409	13,935.1	103.85
67.	Scranton-Wilkes-Barre, PA	732.2	733.1	0.1	5.0	3.4	30,162	42,762	4,318,954	6,281,914	45.4	.2751	.2666	14,527.5	N.A.
68.	Worcester-Fitchburg-Leominster, MA	670.2	683.9	2.0	10.5	15.7	39,119	54,036	4,215,725	6,258,601	48.5	.2863	.2792	16,815.1	102.80
69.	Raleigh-Durham, NC	667.9	736.4	10.3	185.1	6.0	36,992	53,815	4,291,034	6,906,424	61.0	.2854	.3099	17,589.9	N.A.
70.	Allentown-Bethlehem, PA	664.8	682.1	2.6	10.2	17.7	35,513	49,021	4,302,427	6,343,611	47.4	.2790	.2727	17,143.0	N.A.
71.	Grand Rapids, MI	654.9	683.7	4.4	39.1	17.1	36,827	55,084	4,400,314	6,926,608	57.4	.2749	.2891	17,209.3	90.30
72.	Syracuse, NY	651.0	653.7	0.4	34.1	6.4	38,041	51,346	3,979,453	5,665,341	42.4	.2703	.2536	14,956.5	94.40
73.	Akron	648.5	637.3	-1.7	61.9	3.6	34,179	48,659	3,994,632	5,771,249	44.5	.2604	.2489	11,160.0	85.55
74.	Tucson	640.6	708.6	10.6	17.4	149.7	28,998	38,921	3,634,277	5,438,511	49.6	.2374	.2426	10,522.7	101.65
75.	Oxnard-Ventura, CA	632.3	696.3	10.1	12.2	161.1	48,034	67,257	3,736,796	5,876,565	57.3	.2805	.2921	8,598.8	90.75
76.	Gary-Hammond	629.0	619.8	-1.5	135.8	47.5	32,213	41,730	3,801,019	5,232,651	37.7	.2344	.2117	13,357.1	N.A.
77.	Omaha	621.0	636.1	2.4	49.2	13.4	39,611	59,397	4,105,663	6,226,790	51.7	.2728	.2795	18,979.3	76.45
78.	Greenville-Spartanburg, SC	619.1	647.7	4.6	115.4	5.0	28,003	39,164	3,881,381	5,901,008	52.0	.2273	.2291	14,399.2	N.A.
79.	Toledo	615.6	610.1	-0.9	67.3	17.5	35,290	51,959	4,732,575	7,015,161	48.2	.2698	.2664	18,616.4	88.50
80.	Las Vegas	610.9	708.2	15.9	66.5	48.2	31,817	45,575	4,656,184	7,502,891	61.1	.2635	.2924	9,431.7	92.65
81.	Knoxville, TN	601.8	621.7	3.3	38.5	4.3	29,309	42,196	4,555,236	6,971,162	53.0	.2444	.2484	11,567.5	N.A.
82.	Fresno, CA	600.8	653.8	8.8	28.2	206.0	35,874	48,846	3,361,246	4,865,333	44.7	.2342	.2350	7,438.5	84.60
83.	Springfield, MA	591.4	596.0	0.8	36.3	26.2	35,780	48,675	4,304,932	6,239,662	44.9	.2531	.2413	14,934.7	89.15
84.	Harrisburg-Lebanon-Carlisle, PA	584.5	601.0	2.8	38.2	7.0	36,312	51,380	4,456,142	6,711,613	50.6	.2615	.2603	12,705.3	100.60
85.	El Paso	570.0	605.7	6.3	23.6	394.6	28,527	40,857	2,630,277	3,712,130	41.1	.1732	.1732	9,457.8	N.A.
86.	Wilmington, DE	557.1	577.1	3.6	84.5	10.4	40,235	56,895	3,779,816	5,661,045	49.8	.2445	.2441	17,420.4	119.50
87.	Baton Rouge	553.7	584.1	5.5	160.4	9.5	31,687	46,686	3,288,374	4,806,915	46.2	.2037	.2081	13,638.2	N.A.
88.	Jersey City, NJ	552.5	548.6	-0.7	73.5	172.1	32,176	43,901	2,957,284	4,246,280	43.6	.2099	.1975	12,860.0	94.55
89.	Tacoma, WA	546.9	581.9	6.4	34.1	15.1	29,081	37,639	3,116,479	4,610,229	47.9	.1998	.1945	9,208.6	N.A.
90.	Little Rock-North Little Rock	515.3	537.3	4.3	102.7	4.6	34,154	49,358	3,219,687	4,871,132	51.3	.2053	.2083	14,160.4	79.15
91.	Youngstown-Warren, OH	512.0	499.4	-2.5	56.6	6.9	32,470	45,260	2,925,554	4,080,198	39.5	.1954	.1818	12,243.7	N.A.
92.	Bakersfield, CA	511.0	578.0	13.1	25.9	129.2	35,377	47,856	2,946,526	4,439,768	50.7	.1983	.2056	5,874.2	N.A.
93.	Charleston, SC	498.9	533.5	6.9	162.5	7.9	28,719	39,959	2,883,843	4,346,841	50.7	.1729	.1758	7,436.2	N.A.
94.	New Bedford-Fall River-Attleboro, MA	495.7	508.8	2.6	8.7	11.6	33,725	45,978	3,893,673	5,775,088	48.3	.2117	.2065	8,935.0	91.15
95.	Albuquerque	486.5	527.1	8.3	10.6	195.2	29,735	41,383	3,040,143	4,478,185	47.3	.1854	.1886	7,739.4	91.75
96.	Lake County, IL	486.0	510.7	5.1	34.1	27.3	52,096	74,694	3,444,723	5,380,367	56.2	.2375	.2453	11,444.5	N.A.
97.	Mobile, AL	477.6	495.4	3.7	151.6	5.1	29,320	43,322	2,791,425	4,297,878	54.0	.1726	.1777	7,535.2	N.A.
98.	Stockton, CA	454.2	526.0	15.8	23.2	103.1	34,531	46,734	2,373,867	3,683,837	55.2	.1666	.1740	6,549.6	N.A.
99.	Johnson City-Kingsport-Bristol, TN-VA	451.6	460.6	2.0	10.0	2.4	28,020	40,538	2,513,090	3,787,031	50.7	.1596	.1594	8,501.4	N.A.
100.	Columbia, SC	450.2	476.5	5.8	132.8	6.0	34,348	50,907	2,716,027	4,301,727	58.4	.1766	.1869	9,635.6	N.A.

*Manufacturing & Service Shipments/Receipts ($Mil.)

Notes: All **Population** figures are shown in thousands. **Income** data show average household Effective Buying Income (EBI), a figure roughly equivalent to disposable (after-tax) income developed exclusively by Sales & Marketing Management. **Retail Sales** figures are also listed in thousands ($000), with projections shown in current dollars. The **Buying Power Index (BPI)** combines local-to-national ratios of population, EBI, and retail sales, weighting them according to their relative importance. The resulting figure indicates the share of total U.S. buying power accounted for by a given market. **Economic Activity** data (shown in millions) reflect the combined totals of all manufacturing shipments and service receipts produced by a particular metro market during 1987. The **Per-Diem** meals and lodging figure combines the average cost of three meals and a single night's lodging, providing an indicator of basic daily operating expenses in these markets.
SOURCE: Sales & Marketing Management; 1988 Survey of Selling Costs, 1988 Survey of Industrial & Commercial Buying Power, and 1988 Survey of Buying Power (Parts I and II).

FIGURE 9.3   **The Legacy of the Baby Boom and Bust (U.S. Population by Age: 1985 and 1995, in Millions)**

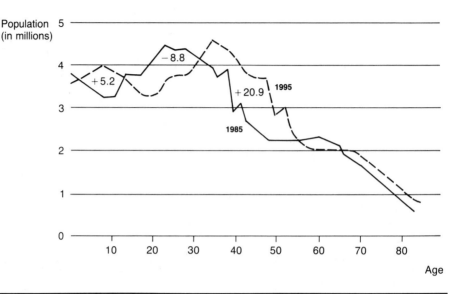

Source: U.S. Census Bureau. Reprinted in Bryant Robey and Cheryl Russell, "The Year of the Baby Boom," *American Demographics*, May 1984, p. 20.

in 1981, when an estimated 600 million pairs were sold in the United States alone.[21] Since then, sales have declined, due in large part to the baby-boom generation's changing tastes and preferences as they have matured and turned to other types of clothing.

On the positive side, the baby-boom generation offers tremendous potential for many marketers. Research shows that baby boomers are an attractive market for high-tech products, branded merchandise, quality durable goods, and investments such as securities, insurance, and real estate.[22]

The Mature Market. Throughout the 1980s baby boomers have been lavished with attention from marketers. However, the 1990s is being heralded as the decade of the mature market. What precisely is the **mature market?** Actually, there is disagreement about the age brackets that constitute this market.[23] Sometimes a "65 and over" classification is used, since age 65 nor-

21. Beyond the Blue Horizon," *Time*, August 20, 1984, p. 106.
22. For a discussion of the psychology underlying baby boomers' purchasing behavior, see Robert B. Settle and Pamela L. Alreck, "The Psychology of Expectations," *Marketing Communications*, March 1988, pp. 19–27.
23. William Lazer, "Dimensions of the Mature Market," *The Journal of Consumer Marketing*, vol. 3 (Summer 1986), p. 24.

mally marks retirement. In this text we will use the U.S. Bureau of the Census's designation, which classifies mature people as those who are *55 and older*.

Nearly 53 million Americans are 55 or older in 1990, representing approximately 21 percent of the total U.S. population (refer again to Table 9.1). It is worth noting in Table 9.1 that the number of middle-aged households (those 35 and older) is increasing dramatically as members of the baby-boom generation grow older. By 1995 there will be in excess of 73 million Americans between the ages of 35 and 54. In terms of specific age groups, the 35 to 44 age group will increase by nearly one-third during the ten-year period between 1985 and 1995, a period when the total U.S. population will grow barely nine percent. The 45 to 64 age group is another substantial group. The numbers are rather astounding, in fact. Compared to the total population of Canada, there are twice as many people in the United States who are 45 to 64 years old. This age group is bigger than the combined populations of Denmark, Finland, Sweden, Norway, Austria, and Belgium.[24] The 45 to 64 market accounts for about 40 percent of all spending power in the United States.[25]

Historically, many marketers have ignored the mature market, but the aging of the American population would urge against this in the future.[26] Not only are mature consumers numerous, they also are wealthier and more willing to spend than ever before. People over age 50 control about $7 trillion of wealth, which is nearly 70 percent of the net worth of all U.S. households.[27] Mature consumers are less likely to shop by price alone and are more concerned with product quality and store service. In addition, they are more likely to purchase expensive items.[28]

A variety of implications accompany marketing communications efforts that are directed at the mature market. In advertising directed at this group, it would be advisable to portray them as active, vital, busy, forward looking, and concerned with looking attractive and being romantic.[29] Advertisers are beginning to appeal to the mature market in a flattering fashion as typified by the use of attractive, middle-aged models to represent clothing, cosmetics, and other products that had been the exclusive advertising domain of youthful models.

In closing this section, it is important to point out that just because mature consumers share a single commonality (i.e., they are age 55 or older), they by no means represent a homogeneous market segment. Indeed, the Bureau of the Census divides the 55 and over people into four distinct age segments: 55 to 64 ("olders"); 65 to 74 ("elders"); 75 to 84 ("the very old"); and 85 and

24. Stephen O. Frankfurt, "Middle Age: A Forgotten Market," *Advertising Age*, January 21, 1980, p. 56.
25. Ibid.
26. Randall Rothenberg, "Ad Industry Faulted on Over-50's," *The New York Times*, May 11, 1988, p. 42.
27. Peter Petre, "Marketers Mine for Gold in the Old," *Fortune*, March 31, 1986, p. 70.
28. " 'Fifty-Ups'—The Next Wave?" *Marketing Communications*, January 1988, p. 11.
29. "Market Profile: The Graying of America's Consumer," *POPAI News*, vol. 7, no. 1 (1983), p. 5.

FOCUS ON PROMOTION

From "Healthy Indulgers" to "Frail Recluses"

A national mail survey of 1,000 people aged 55 and older was completed in 1988. Respondents were classified into four groups based on how they answered the survey questions: Healthy Hermits, 38 percent; Ailing Outgoers, 34 percent; Frail Recluses, 15 percent; and Healthy Indulgers, 13 percent. These categories are unrelated to age per se, because people vary greatly in terms of how fast they age physically as well as their self-image related to age.

Healthy Hermits, though in good health, are psychologically withdrawn from society. They represent a good market for various services such as tax and legal advice, financial services, home entertainment, and do-it-yourself products. Direct mail and print media are the best media for reaching this group.

Continued

over.[30] On the basis of age alone, consumers in each of these groups differ, sometimes dramatically, in terms of lifestyles, interest in the marketplace, reasons for buying, and spending ability. Moreover, it is important to realize that age alone is not the best indicator of how an individual lives or what role consumption plays in that lifestyle. The *Focus on Promotion* above elaborates on this point and describes four groups of mature consumers based on a combination of health and self-image characteristics.

Children and Teenagers.   At the other end of the age spectrum are children and teenagers. The group of young Americans aged 19 and younger has fallen dramatically from 40 percent of the population in 1965 (during the baby-boom heyday) to approximately 29 percent of the population in 1990. Yet, this is a substantial group with over 70 million occupants. (See Table 9.1 for specific breakouts by age group, that is, under 5, 5 to 9, 10 to 14, and 15 to 19.)

Elementary-school-age children, aged 6 to 11, are influential consumers. These children have direct influence on product purchases and indirect influence on what their parents buy.[31] Figure 9.4 presents data on what products children aged 6 to 11 buy with their own money and what purchases they influence.

30. Lazer, "Dimensions of the Mature Market," p. 24.
31. See Horst H. Stipp, "Children As Consumers," *American Demographics*, February 1988, pp. 27–32; Ellen Graham, "As Kids Gain Power of Purse, Marketing Takes Aim at Them," *The Wall Street Journal*, January 19, 1988, p. 1.

Ailing Outgoers are diametrically the opposite of "Healthy Hermits." Though in poor health, they are socially active, health conscious, and interested in learning to do new things. Home health care, dietary products, planned retirement communities, and entertainment services are some of the products and services most desired by this group. They can be reached via sales promotions and through select mass media tailored to their positive self-image and active, social lifestyle.

Frail Recluses are withdrawn socially and are in poor health. Various health and medical products and services, home entertainment, and domestic-assistance services (e.g., lawn care) can be successfully marketed to this group. They can be reached by mass media and special-assistance services.

Healthy Indulgers are in good health, are relatively wealthy, and are socially active. They are independent and want the most out of life. They are a good market for financial services, leisure/travel/entertainment, clothes, luxury goods, and high-tech products and services. They are accessible via in-store promotions, direct mail, and specialized print media.[32] ∎

For example, nearly 60 percent of all children buy candy and gum, and approximately 30 percent buy toys, soft drinks, and presents. Over 80 percent of children aged 6 to 11 influence their parents' choice of clothing and toys. Approximately 30 percent influence the brand choice of products such as toothpaste. This may explain why, for example, Colgate-Palmolive Company has come out with a toothpaste, Colgate Junior, marketed specifically to children (see Figure 9.5).

Teenagers, including 12-year-olds as well as conventional teens between the ages of 13 and 19, are estimated to have spent $78 billion for personal and household purchases in 1988, up from $65 billion in 1985.[33] With nearly two-thirds of all mothers in the work force, teenagers now have purchasing influence and power far greater than ever before. Teenagers are noted for several outstanding characteristics: they are highly conformist, narcissistic, and fickle consumers.[34] These characteristics pose great opportunities and challenges for marketers and promotion managers. An accepted product can become a huge success when the teenage bandwagon selects a brand as a personal mark of the "in crowd." However, today's accepted product or brand can easily become tomorrow's passé item.

32. The research was performed by George P. Moschis and is reported in "Survey: Age Is Not Good Indicator of Consumer Need," *Marketing Communications*, November 21, 1988, p. 6.
33. Graham, "As Kids Gain Power of Purse, Marketing Takes Aim at Them."
34. Ibid. Also, Selina S. Guber, "The Teenage Mind," *American Demographics*, August 1987, pp. 42–44.

FIGURE 9.4 **Children's Purchases and Purchase Influences**

What Children Buy

Children don't just buy candy and gum with their own money. More than one-fourth frequently buy toys, soft drinks, and presents.

(Percent of children aged 6 to 11 who have spent their own money on specific products in the past two to three weeks, 1987)

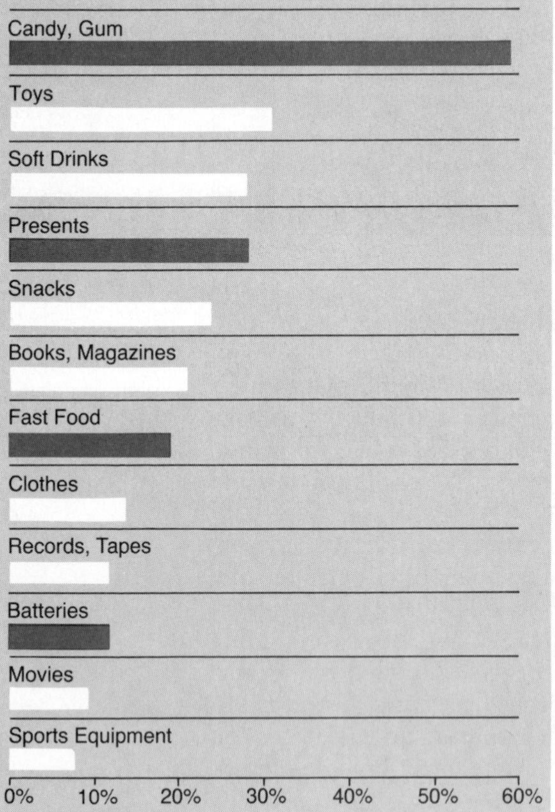

Candy, Gum

Toys

Soft Drinks

Presents

Snacks

Books, Magazines

Fast Food

Clothes

Records, Tapes

Batteries

Movies

Sports Equipment

0%   10%   20%   30%   40%   50%   60%

Children's Influence

Most children say they help their parents select their own clothes, toys, cereal, ice cream, and soft drinks.

(Percent of children aged 6 to 11 who say they influence their parents' purchases of specific products, 1987)

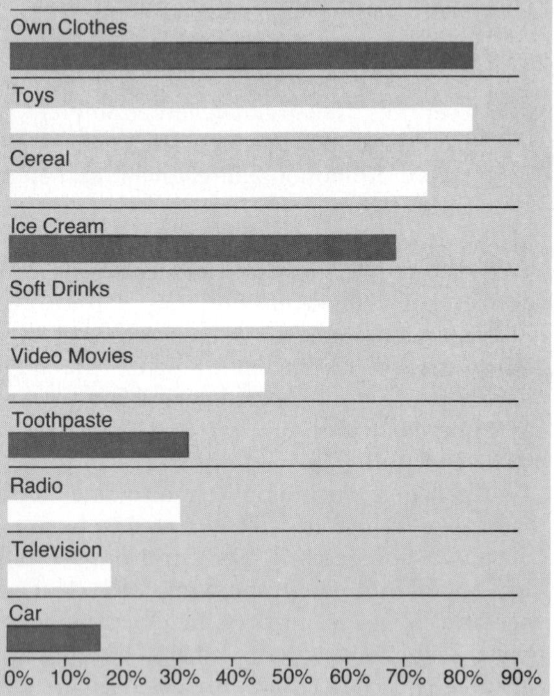

Own Clothes

Toys

Cereal

Ice Cream

Soft Drinks

Video Movies

Toothpaste

Radio

Television

Car

0%   10%   20%   30%   40%   50%   60%   70%   80%   90%

Source: Youth Monitor, Winter 1987, Yankelovich, Skelly and White/Clancy, Shulman, Inc.

A Product Marketed Specifically to Children

FIGURE 9.5

Source: Courtesy of Colgate-Palmolive Company.

The Changing American Household

The traditional American household, as portrayed stereotypically in television and other mass media, is a family consisting of mother, father, and two or three children. Millions of such households do, in fact, exist in the United States, but the composition of households is changing dramatically. In 1950, families (i.e., a married couple with or without children) constituted 90 percent of all households; this percentage fell to 72.3 percent in 1985 and is projected to fall to 68.2 percent by 2000.[35] Nonfamily households, that is, a person living alone or with an unrelated other person(s), will experience a huge increase, jumping from approximately 24 million of such households in 1985 to nearly 34 million nonfamily households by the year 2000.[36]

American households have been altered forever by the combined effects of changes in marriage patterns, widespread birth control, working women, and rising divorce rates.[37] Households are growing in number, shrinking in size, and changing in character. The number of new households has grown twice as fast as the population, while household size has declined rapidly in all 50 states.[38] In 1970 there were 3.14 persons per household in the United States; this number is expected to fall to 2.48 by 2000.[39]

The changing composition of the American household has tremendous implications for marketing communicators, especially advertisers. Advertising will have to reflect the widening range of living situations that exist. This is particularly true in the case of the "singles market."[40] Singles represent a large and ever-growing group. There are, for example, over 9 million men in the United States who live without female partners and do their own shopping, cooking, and household chores.[41] The total singles market (not just men) accounts for roughly one-eighth of all consumer spending in the United States.[42]

The growth of the singles market is changing the way in which advertising is done. Many advertisers make special appeals to the buying interests and needs of singles, appealing in food ads, for example, to such needs as ease of preparation, maintenance simplicity, small serving sizes, etc. Reaching singles requires special media-selection efforts because (1) singles tend not to be big prime-time television viewers but are skewed instead toward the late-fringe

35. Richard Kern, "USA 2000," *Sales and Marketing Management*, October 27, 1986, pp. 8–30.
36. Ibid.
37. Peter Francese, "Baby Boom's Echo Keeps Economy Moving," *Advertising Age*, July 19, 1984, p. 12.
38. Ibid.
39. Kern, "USA 2000," pp. 8–30.
40. The "singles" label is certainly too crude to constitute a true market segment because a variety of different groups are included in the general category (people who have never been married, divorced people, widowed people, etc.).
41. "Marketers Slighting Many Male 'Settlers'," *Advertising Age*, July 25, 1983, p. 47.
42. Gay Jervey, "Y & R Study: New Life to Singles," *Advertising Age*, October 4, 1982, p. 14.

hours (i.e., after 11 p.m.); (2) singles are disproportionately more likely than the rest of the population to view cable television; and (3) singles are heavy magazine readers.[43]

It is important to recognize the great heterogeneity that actually exists in the so-called singles market. For example, the never-married segment of the singles market tends to prefer upbeat radio programming but does not read the newspaper as much as other groups. In comparison, divorced singles are heavier users of various mass media such as cable television.[44]

The Changing Roles of Women

Historically, marketing communicators portrayed women in stereotypical roles as wife, mother, homemaker, and hostess or as single girls preparing for these roles.[45] However, major changes over the past two decades in the roles of women have forced marketing communicators to develop a wider range of appeals that reflect women's changing needs and status.

Some of the most notable changes in women's roles are the following: (1) the number of women in the nation's work force increased from under 25 million in 1960 to nearly 50 million today; fully 70 percent of the women between the ages of 25 and 54 are in the labor force;[46] (2) today, women head almost one-third of all households compared with one in seven in 1950;[47] and (3) a larger share of women are remaining single into their thirties; this trend results from more educational and occupational opportunities, as well as disenchantment with marriage because of the divorce rate.[48]

Although marketing communicators have made strides in reflecting women's changing roles, it is probably fair to conclude that women are still being portrayed in a limited range of roles that do not fully reflect the actual working position and status of women in today's society.[49] Fortunately, this is changing, albeit slowly, as advertisers begin to recognize the importance of women as major decision makers. The following passage characterizes the modern woman that advertisers must appeal to in the future.

43. Ibid.
44. Alan J. Bush and John J. Burnett, "Assessing the Homogeneity of Single Females in Respect to Advertising, Media, and Technology," *Journal of Advertising*, vol. 16, no. 3 (1987), pp. 31–38.
45. Alladi Venkatesh, "Changing Roles of Women—A Lifestyle Analysis," *Journal of Consumer Research*, vol. 7 (November 1980), p. 189.
46. Susan E. Shank, "Women and the Labor Market: The Link Grows Stronger," *Monthly Labor Review*, vol. 111 (March 1988), pp. 3–8.
47. Daphne Spain and Suzanne M. Bianchi, "How Women Have Changed," *American Demographics*, May 1983, pp. 18–25.
48. Ibid.
49. A number of studies have detected stereotypical role portrayal of women. For a review, see Roger A. Kerin, William J. Lundstrom, and Donald Sciglimpaglia, "Women in Advertisements: Retrospect and Prospect," *Journal of Advertising*, vol. 8, no. 3 (1979), pp. 37–42.

Advertising which remains locked into the traditional roles of mother/homemaker will play to a decreasing audience in the future. Although a woman may fulfill these roles in a partial capacity, the desire to shed this image will lead to dual roles, role switching, and role blending. Thus, both women and men can be expected to be portrayed in roles which show a person in more than one capacity; a man doing "woman's" work, and men and women jointly deciding on a purchase decision. In short, the modern woman is not, and will not, accept a thrusting into traditional roles, and expects to be found in an expanding number of positions replacing her male counterpart.[50]

Because of women's involvement in the labor force, the choice of advertising media used to reach women has changed. Traditional media, like daytime television, are ineffective for reaching vast numbers of working women. Outdoor advertising, direct mail, radio, and magazines are increasingly important media for getting advertising messages to working women.

Income Dynamics

American society is characterized by increasing numbers of people at both extremes of the income distribution. At the low end, there are more than 30 million Americans living below the poverty level.[51] The situation is particularly bleak for blacks and Hispanics, whose poverty rates far exceed that for whites.

At the other end of the distribution, a number of American households are enjoying continually rising incomes. Today over 13 percent of all households earn over $50,000. These households earned 36 percent of the country's total household income in 1985, hold 67 percent of all securities, and own 62 percent of all real estate.[52] These impressive figures are due in large part to the increasing numbers of dual-income households.

Automobile companies, financial services, home-construction firms, and many other companies are interested in the affluent consumer because of his or her spending power. Yet despite this emphasis on spending power, there appears to be a subtle shift taking place in many consumers' attitudes toward consumption. There has been a transition from a "disposable psychology" to an "investment psychology." Many affluent and relatively affluent Americans are showing much more enthusiasm for quality merchandise, things that will last, and values that will grow. This shift has been referred to as the "Europeanization of America."[53]

Special marketing communications efforts are required to reach and motivate the affluent market. In terms of advertising claims, appeals to elegance, quality, and durability are especially effective. Media selection is critical be-

50. Ibid., p. 41.
51. "A Portrait of America," *Newsweek*, January 17, 1983, p. 31.
52. "New Boundaries of Affluence," *Marketing Communications*, February 1986, pp. 33–60.
53. "The Rich, the Very Rich, and the Super Rich," *Marketing Communications*, November/December 1982, p. 25.

cause research shows that media-behavior patterns change with increases in income—television viewing and radio listening drop, and magazine readership increases.

Minority-Population Developments

America has always been a melting pot, and it became even more so in the 1980s and especially the 1970s, which is known as the "decade of the immigrant." The numbers of immigrants admitted to the United States in the 1970s surpassed those for any year since 1924.[54] The largest number of immigrants were Asians and Pacific islanders, who together represented an increase of nearly 128 percent in 1980 over their U.S. population base in 1970.

Black Americans. By the year 2000, black people in the United States will total approximately 36 million, or 13.4 percent of the U.S. population—almost 1.5 times the 1985 population of Canada.[55] Black Americans are characterized more by their common heritage than by skin color. This heritage "is conditioned by an American beginning in slavery, a shared history of discrimination and suffering, confined housing opportunities, and denial of participating in many aspects of the majority culture."[56] Although many black Americans share a common culture in that they have similar values, beliefs, and distinguishable behaviors, blacks do not represent a single culture any more than whites do.

Black Americans represent an attractive market for many companies. Several notable reasons account for this: (1) the aggregate income of black consumers exceeds $140 billion; (2) the average age of black Americans is considerably younger than that for whites; (3) blacks are geographically concentrated; approximately two-thirds of all blacks live in the top 15 U.S. markets; (4) black consumption in some product categories is disproportionately greater than general population usage (e.g., blacks purchase over one-third of all hair-conditioning products); and (5) blacks tend to purchase prestige and name-brand products in greater proportion than do whites.[57]

These impressive figures notwithstanding, many companies make no special efforts to communicate with blacks. This is foolish, for research indicates that blacks are responsive to advertisements placed in black-oriented media and to advertisements that make personalized appeals by using black models and advertising contexts with which blacks can identify.[58] However, several

54. "Lands of Our Fathers," *Newsweek*, January 17, 1983, p. 22.
55. Lazer, *Handbook of Demographics for Marketing and Advertising*, p. 92.
56. James F. Engel, Roger D. Blackwell, Paul W. Miniard, *Consumer Behavior*, 5th ed. (Hinsdale, IL: The Dryden Press, 1986), p. 410.
57. David Astor, "Black Spending Power: $140 Billion and Growing," *Marketing Communications*, July 1982, pp. 13–14.
58. Ibid.

major corporations do have effective programs for communicating with black consumers. Anheuser-Busch, for example, advertises in black-oriented media, uses black models and entertainers, and has a number of sales promotions that appeal to black consumers. The Eastman-Kodak Company also recognizes the importance of black consumers and reflects this by advertising on network black radio, on Black Entertainment Television, and in black magazines such as *Ebony* and *Essence*.

In general, greater numbers of companies are realizing the importance of directing special marketing communications efforts to black consumers. The black consumer market is not homogeneous, however. Blacks exhibit different purchasing behaviors according to their lifestyles, values, and demographics. Therefore, companies must use different advertising media, distribution channels, advertising themes, and pricing strategies as they market to the various subsegments of the black subculture.

Hispanic Americans. In 1987 there were nearly 19 million Hispanics living in the United States. The largest percentage are Mexican Americans (63 percent), followed by Puerto Rican Americans (12 percent), Hispanic Americans from Central and South America (11 percent), Cuban Americans (5 percent), and other Hispanic Americans (9 percent).[59] It is projected that Hispanics will make up 11.3 percent of the U.S. population by 2000.[60] Experts predict that by the year 2020 Hispanics will surpass blacks as the largest minority in the United States—there will be nearly 47 million Hispanics and 45 million blacks.[61] About 75 percent of U.S. Hispanics are concentrated in five states: California, Texas, New York, Florida, and Illinois.

According to the U.S. Bureau of the Census, Hispanics in the United States have several outstanding characteristics in comparison with other members of the American population. They are younger, have larger families, tend to live in urban clusters, and are becoming increasingly mobile as they begin to fan out from the five states in which they are concentrated.[62]

Marketing communicators need to be aware of several important points when attempting to reach Hispanic consumers:

1. Over 40 percent of Hispanic Americans speak only Spanish or just enough English to get by; consequently, many Hispanics can be reached only via Spanish-language media.[63]

59. Joe Schwartz, "Hispanics in the Eighties," *American Demographics*, vol. 10 (January 1988), pp. 42–45.
60. Lazer, *Handbook of Demographics for Marketing and Advertising*, p. 92.
61. Renee Blakkan, "Reaching a Growing Market Where It Lives," *Advertising Age*, March 19, 1984, p. M10.
62. Craig Endicott, "Marketing to Hispanics: Making the Most of Media," *Advertising Age*, March 19, 1984, p. M10.
63. "Hispanic Ethnic Market: 27,000,000 by 2000," *POPAI News*, vol. 6, no. 2 (1982), p. 7.

2. A further reason for using Spanish-language media is that over one-half of Hispanics use Spanish media primarily; 70 percent watch, listen to, or read Spanish media every week.[64]

3. Over 70 percent of Hispanics report resenting ads that appear to be little more than perfunctory adaptations of English ads.[65]

4. Advertisers must be very careful in using the Spanish language. A number of snafus have been committed when advertisers translate their English campaigns to Spanish. For example, Frank Perdue, an East coast marketer of chickens, had his famous slogan ("It takes a strong man to make a tender chicken") translated into Spanish so he could read it to Hispanics. Amusingly (probably to everyone other than Frank), the translation was incorrect; the Spanish-version stated, "It takes a sexually excited man to make a tender chicken."[66]

The Spanish-speaking market represents a golden opportunity for many companies. Yet it is estimated that as many as 80 percent of U.S. companies make no special efforts to reach Hispanic consumers.[67] Many companies consider Anglo advertising to be sufficient for reaching Hispanic consumers; however, the fact remains that large numbers of Hispanics are more comfortable with their native language and prefer to read and listen in Spanish.[68]

Asian Americans.   Asian Americans are being heralded as the newest "hot ethnic market."[69] The demographics support this optimistic outlook. Asian Americans on average are better educated, have higher incomes, and occupy more prestigious job positions than any other segment of American society including whites.[70] Presently there are approximately 5 million Asians living in the United States; that number is expected to increase to 10 million by the turn of the century.

Asian Americans have considerable purchasing power, but just as a *single* black or Hispanic market does not exist, nor is there a *single* Asian market. Asian Americans include many nationalities (Chinese, Japanese, Filipino, Vietnamese, Koreans, etc.), and within each nationality there is considerable variation in terms of English-language skills, assimilation into the American culture, and financial well-being.

Some firms have been successful in marketing to specific Asian groups by customizing marketing programs specifically to Oriental values and lifestyles

---

64. Ibid.
65. Ibid.
66. "Snafus Persist in Marketing to Hispanics," *Marketing News*, June 24, 1983, p. 3.
67. Robert E. Mack, "A Golden Growth Opportunity," *Marketing Communications*, March 1988, pp. 54–57.
68. Ibid.
69. John Schwartz, Dorothy Wang, and Nancy Matsumoto, "Tapping into a Blossoming Asian Market," *Newsweek*, September 7, 1987, pp. 47–48.
70. Richard Kern, "The Asian Market: Too Good To Be True?" *Sales and Marketing Management*, May 1988, pp. 39–42.

rather than merely translating Anglo programs. For example, Metropolitan Life, an insurance company, conducted research that determined that Asian parents' top priority was their children's security and education. Metropolitan translated this finding into a successful campaign targeted to Koreans and Chinese. An advertisement portrayed a baby in a man's arms with the heading: "You protect your baby. Who protects you?" This ad along with the attraction of Asians to Metropolitan Life's sales force resulted in a substantial increase in insurance sales to Asians.[71]

The Regulatory Environment

Advertisers, sales managers, and other marketing communicators are faced with a variety of regulations and restrictions that influence their decision-making latitude. Although regulation is inherently antithetical to the philosophical premises of a free-enterprise society, the history of the past century has shown that regulation is necessary. Regulation protects *consumers and competitors* from fraudulent, deceptive, and unfair practices that some businesses choose to perpetrate.

Regulation is needed most *when consumer decisions are based on false or limited information.*[72] Under such circumstances, consumers are likely to make decisions they would not otherwise make and, as a result, incur economic, physical, or psychological injury. Competitors are also harmed because they lose business they might have otherwise enjoyed.

In theory, regulation is justified if the benefits realized exceed the costs. What are the benefits and costs of regulation?[73] Regulation offers three major *benefits:* First, *consumer choice* among alternatives is improved when consumers are better informed in the marketplace. For example, consider the "Alcoholic Beverage Labeling Act of 1988," which requires manufacturers to place the following warning on all containers of alcoholic beverages:

> GOVERNMENT WARNING: (1) According to the Surgeon General, women should not drink alcoholic beverages during pregnancy, due to the risk of birth defects. (2) Consumption of alcoholic beverages impairs your ability to drive a car or operate machinery, and may cause health problems.[74]

This regulation serves to inform consumers that drinking has negative consequences. Pregnant women and their unborn children in particular will benefit if this warning prompts consumers to exercise the alternative not to drink alcoholic beverages.

A second benefit of regulation is that when consumers become better informed, *product quality tends to improve* in response to consumers' changing

71. Schwartz, Wang, and Matsumoto, "Tapping into a Blossoming Asian Market."
72. Michael B. Mazis, Richard Staelin, Howard Beales, and Steven Salop, "A Framework for Evaluating Consumer Information Regulation," *Journal of Marketing*, vol. 45 (Winter 1981), pp. 11–21.
73. The following discussion is adapted from Mazis et al.
74. Senate bill S.2047.

needs and preferences. For example, when consumers began learning about the dangers of fat and cholesterol, manufacturers started marketing healthier food products. When regulators prevented makers of aspirin and analgesic products from making outrageously false and misleading claims, companies were forced to introduce new alternatives (e.g., Tylenol and Advil) as a means of taking market share away from entrenched aspirin brands.[75]

A third regulatory benefit is *reduced prices* resulting from a reduction in a seller's "informational market power." For example, prices of used cars undoubtedly would fall if dealers were required to inform prospective purchasers about a car's defects, since consumers would not be willing to pay as much for automobiles with known problems.

Regulation is not costless. One cost incurred by companies is the *cost of complying* with a regulatory remedy. For example, U.S. cigarette manufacturers are now required to rotate over the course of a year four different warning messages for three months each. Obviously, this is more costly than the single message that was required previously. *Enforcement costs* incurred by regulatory agencies and paid for by taxpayers represent a second cost category. A third cost is the costs to buyers and sellers of *unintended side effects* that might result from regulations. A regulation may unintentionally harm sellers if buyers switch to other products or reduce their level of consumption after regulation is imposed. The cost to buyers may increase if sellers pass along, in the form of higher prices, the costs of complying with a regulation.

In sum, regulation is theoretically justified only if the *benefits exceed the costs*. The following sections examine the two forms of regulation that affect promotion decision making: governmental regulation and industry self-regulation.

Governmental Regulation of Promotion

Governmental regulation takes place both at the federal and state levels. All facets of promotion (personal selling, sales promotion, advertising, telemarketing, etc.) are subject to regulation, but advertising is the one area in which regulators have been most active. This is because advertising is the most conspicuous aspect of marketing communications. The Federal Trade Commission is the government agency that has primary responsibility for regulating promotion at the federal level, and the National Association of Attorneys General has become the most active force at the state level.

The **Federal Trade Commission (FTC),** created in 1914, was concerned during its early years with preventing *anticompetitive practices*, that is, protecting businesses rather than consumers. By 1938, Congress realized that the FTC's mandate should be expanded to offer more assistance to consumers as

---

75. For a fascinating history of advertising and regulatory activity in the aspirin/analgesic industry, see Charles C. Mann and Mark L. Plummer, "The Big Headache," *The Atlantic Monthly*, October 1988, pp. 39–57.

well as businesses, especially in the area of false and misleading advertising. The *Wheeler-Lea Amendment of 1938* accomplished this objective by changing a principal section of the original FTC Act of 1914 from "unfair methods of competition" to "unfair methods of competition and unfair or deceptive acts or practices in commerce." This seemingly minor change enhanced the FTC's regulatory powers appreciably and provided a legal mandate for the FTC to protect consumers against fraudulent business practices. The FTC's regulatory authority cuts across three broad areas that directly affect marketing communicators: deceptive advertising, unfair practices, and information regulation.

FTC's Regulation of Deceptive Advertising.   In a general sense, consumers are deceived by an advertising claim or campaign when (1) the impression left by the claim/campaign is *false;* that is, there is a claim-fact discrepancy, and (2) the false claim/campaign is *believed* by consumers. The important point is that a false claim is not necessarily deceptive by itself. "What matters is what consumers believe. A false claim does not harm consumers unless it is believed, and a true claim can generate harm if it generates a false belief."[76]

Although the FTC makes deception rulings case by case, it does employ some general guidelines in deciding whether **deceptive advertising** has occurred in a particular case. Deception policy at the FTC is not inscribed in granite but rather is subject to shifts, depending on the regulatory philosophy of different FTC chairpersons and the prevailing political climate. The FTC's present enforcement policy against deception reflects the conservative political mood and the corresponding opposition to business regulation.

The current deception policy declares that the FTC will find a business practice deceptive "if there is a representation, omission or practice that is likely to mislead the consumer acting reasonably in the circumstances, to the consumer's detriment."[77] The three elements that follow undergird this policy:[78]

1.   *Misleading.* There must be a representation omission, or practice that is likely to mislead the consumer. A *misrepresentation* is defined by the FTC as an express or implied statement contrary to fact, whereas a *misleading omission* is said to occur when qualifying information necessary to prevent a practice, claim, representation, or reasonable expectation or belief from being misleading is not disclosed.

76. J. Edward Russo, Barbara L. Metcalf, and Debra Stephens, "Identifying Misleading Advertising," *Journal of Consumer Research*, vol. 8 (September 1981), p. 120.

77. Public copy of letter dated October 14, 1983, from FTC Chairman James C. Miller III to Senator Bob Packwood, Chairman of Senate Committee on Commerce, Science, and Transportation.

78. For a thorough and insightful discussion of these elements and other matters surrounding FTC deception policy, see Gary T. Ford and John E. Calfee, "Recent Developments in FTC Policy on Deception," *Journal of Marketing*, vol. 50 (July 1986), pp. 82–103.

2. *Reasonable Consumer.* The act or practice must be considered from the per-spective of the reasonable consumer. The FTC's test of reasonableness is *whether the consumer's interpretation or reaction to an advertisement is reason-able.* That is, the commission determines the effect of the advertising prac-tice on a reasonable member of the group to which the advertising is targeted. "For instance, if a company markets a cure to the terminally ill, the practice will be evaluated from the perspective of how it affects the ordinary member of that group. Thus, terminally ill consumers might be particularly susceptible to exaggerated cure claims. By the same token, a practice or representation directed to a well-educated group, such as a prescription drug advertisement to doctors, would be judged in light of the knowledge and sophistication of that group."[79]

3. *Material.* The representation, omission, or practice must be material. A material representation involves *information that is important to consumers and which is likely to influence their choice or conduct regarding a product.* In general, the FTC considers information to be material when it pertains to the central characteristics of a product or service (performance features, size, price, etc.). Hence, if an athletic-shoe company falsely claimed that its brand possesses the best shock-absorption feature on the market, this would be a material misrepresentation to the many runners who make purchase choices based on this factor. On the other hand, for this same company to falsely claim that it has been in business for 25 years—when in fact it has been in business for only 18 years—likely would not be regarded as material, since most consumers would not make a purchase choice based on this reason.

An important case involving the issue of materiality is under litigation at the time of this writing. Kraft, makers of Single American cheese slices, is claiming that its $11 million advertising campaign for this product did not in-fluence consumer purchases.[80] The FTC challenged Kraft on grounds that ad-vertisements for Kraft Singles falsely claimed that each slice contains the same amount of calcium as five ounces of milk. Kraft responded that its ads (1) did not convey the misleading representation claimed by the FTC, but (2) even if this representation had been conveyed, it would not have mattered because calcium is a relatively unimportant factor in consumers' decision to purchase Kraft Singles. (Out of nine factors rated by consumers in a copy test, calcium was rated no higher than seventh.)

Kraft's defense, in other words, is that its calcium claim, whether false or not, is nondeceptive because that product attribute is *immaterial* to consumers. Or, in other words, Kraft's defense amounts to the following: (1) Yes, we (Kraft) may have made claims about the calcium benefits of Kraft Singles, but

79. Chairman Miller's letter to Senator Packwood.
80. The campaign ran in 1984 and 1985, but the FTC did not file a complaint until 1987.

(2) our advertising was ineffective; (3) therefore, the issue of deceptiveness is moot because (4) the product attribute our advertising made claims about (i.e., calcium) is immaterial to consumers.[81]

Regulation of Unfair Practices.   As noted at the beginning of this section, the Wheeler-Lea Amendment of 1938 gave the Federal Trade Commission authority to regulate **unfair,** as well as *deceptive*, acts or practices in commerce. Unfairness is necessarily a somewhat vague concept. For this reason, the unfairness doctrine received limited use by the FTC until 1972, when in a famous judicial decision *(FTC v. Sperry & Hutchinson Co.)* the Supreme Court noted that consumers as well as businesses must be protected from unfair trade practices.[82] Unlike deception, a finding of unfairness to consumers may go beyond questions of fact and relate merely to public values.[83] The criteria used to evaluate whether a business act is unfair involve such considerations as whether the act (1) offends public policy as it has been established by statutes, (2) is immoral, unethical, oppressive, or unscrupulous, and (3) causes substantial injury to consumers, competitors, or other businesses.[84]

The FTC has applied the unfairness doctrine in three major areas: (1) advertising substantiation, (2) promotional practices directed to children, and (3) trade-regulation rules.[85]

Advertising Substantiation.   The ad-substantiation program is based on a simple premise: It is unfair for advertisers to make claims about their products without having a reasonable basis for making the claims. Unfairness results, according to the FTC, from imposing on the consumer the unavoidable economic risk that the product may not perform as advertised if neither the consumer nor the manufacturer has a reasonable basis for belief in the product claim. The ad-substantiation program requires advertisers to have documentation (i.e., test results or other data) indicating that they have a "reasonable basis" for making a claim *prior to the dissemination of advertisements.*[86]

In 1987 the FTC charged Walgreen, a large retail drugstore chain, with making unsubstantiated claims for Advil pain reliever. Walgreen had advertised Advil as a "prescription pain reliever. . ." and "an anti-inflammatory . . . source of comfort for people who experience arthritis pain." The FTC

81. This interpretation is based on Julie Liesse Erickson, "Kraft Takes on FTC, Cites 'Ineffective' Ads," *Advertising Age,* July 4, 1988, p. 39.
82. For further discussion, see Dorothy Cohen, "Unfairness in Advertising Revisited," *Journal of Marketing,* vol. 46 (Winter 1982), p. 74.
83. Dorothy Cohen, "The Concept of Unfairness as It Relates to Advertising Legislation," *Journal of Marketing,* vol. 38 (July 1974), p. 8.
84. Cohen, "Unfairness in Advertising Revisited," p. 8.
85. Ibid., pp. 75–76.
86. For further discussion, see Dorothy Cohen, "The FTC's Advertising Substantiation Program," *Journal of Marketing,* vol. 44 (Winter 1980), pp. 26–35; and Debra L. Scammon and Richard J. Semenik, "The FTC's 'Reasonable Basis' for Substantiation of Advertising: Expanded Standards and Implications," *Journal of Advertising,* vol. 12, no. 1 (1983), pp. 4–11.

ruled that Walgreen did not have a reasonable basis for this claim. The case was dropped when Walgreen consented not to make unsubstantiated claims for Advil or other analgesic drug products.[87]

Unfairness Involving Children.

Because children are more credulous and less well-equipped than adults to protect themselves, public-policy officials are especially concerned with protecting youngsters. When applied to cases involving children, the unfairness doctrine is especially useful because many advertising claims are not deceptive per se but are nonetheless potentially unethical, unscrupulous, or inherently dangerous to children. For example, the FTC considered a company's use of Spider Man vitamin advertising unfair because such advertising was judged capable of inducing children to take excessive and dangerous amounts of vitamins.[88]

Trade-Regulation Rules.

Whereas most Federal Trade Commission actions are taken on a case-by-case basis, the use of trade-regulation rules (TRRs) enables the FTC to issue a regulation that restricts an entire industry from some unfair and objectional practice. For example, the FTC issued a TRR to vocational schools that would have required the schools to disclose enrollment and job placement statistics in their promotional materials. The rule was later rejected by a court of appeals on grounds that the FTC had failed to define the unfair practices that the rule was designed to remedy.[89] During the Reagan Administration, the FTC's use of industry-wide trade-regulation rules stopped completely.

Information Regulation.

Although the primary purpose of advertising regulation is the prohibition of deceptive and unfair practices, regulation also is needed at times to provide consumers with information they might not otherwise receive.[90] Many believe that the corrective advertising program is the most important of the FTC's information provision programs.[91]

Corrective advertising is based on the premise that a firm that misleads consumers should have to use future advertisements to rectify any deceptive impressions it has created in consumers' minds. In other words, the purpose is to prevent a firm from continuing to deceive consumers; the purpose is not to punish the firm. The texts of four early corrective advertisements are shown in Figure 9.6. In parentheses at the bottom of each corrective ad is the FTC's

87. Cited in the "Legal Developments in Marketing" section of the *Journal of Marketing*, vol. 52 (January 1988), p. 131.
88. Cohen, "Unfairness in Advertising Revisited," p. 74.
89. Ibid., p. 75.
90. Ivan L. Preston, "A Review of the Literature on Advertising Regulation," in James H. Leigh and Claude R. Martin, eds., *Current Issues and Research in Advertising 1983* (Ann Arbor, MI: University of Michigan, 1983), p. 14.
91. The following discussion borrows heavily from the excellent review article by William L. Wilkie, Dennis L. McNeill, and Michael B. Mazis, "Marketing's 'Scarlet Letter': The Theory and Practice of Corrective Advertising," *Journal of Marketing*, vol. 48 (Spring 1984), p. 11.

FIGURE 9.6   **Texts of Four Early Corrective Ads**

Profile Bread

"Hi, (celebrity's name) for Profile Bread. Like all mothers, I'm concerned about nutrition and balanced meals. So, I'd like to clear up any misunderstanding you may have about Profile Bread from its advertising or even its name.

"Does Profile have fewer calories than any other breads? No. Profile has about the same per ounce as other breads. To be exact, Profile has seven fewer calories per slice. That's because Profile is sliced thinner. But eating Profile will not cause you to lose weight. A reduction of seven calories is insignificant. It's total calories and balanced nutrition that count. And Profile can help you achieve a balanced meal because it provides protein and B vitamins as well as other nutrients.

"How does my family feel about Profile? Well, my husband likes Profile toast, the children love Profile sandwiches, and I prefer Profile to any other bread. So you see, at our house, delicious taste makes Profile a family affair."

(To be run in 25% of brand's advertising, for one year.)

Amstar

"Do you recall some of our past messages saying that Domino Sugar gives you strength, energy, and stamina? Actually, Domino is not a special or unique source of strength, energy, and stamina. No sugar is, because what you need is a balanced diet and plenty of rest and exercise."

(To be run in one of every four ads for one year.)

Ocean Spray

"If you've wondered what some of our earlier advertising meant when we said Ocean Spray Cranberry Juice Cocktail has more food energy than orange juice or tomato juice, let us make it clear: we didn't mean vitamins and minerals. Food energy means calories. Nothing more.

"Food energy is important at breakfast since many of us may not get enough calories, or food energy, to get off to a good start. Ocean Spray Cranberry Juice Cocktail helps because it contains more food energy than most other breakfast drinks.

"And Ocean Spray Cranberry Juice Cocktail gives you and your family Vitamin C plus a great wake-up taste. It's . . . the other breakfast drink."

(To be run in one of every four ads for one year.)

Sugar Information, Inc.

"Do you recall the messages we brought you in the past about sugar? How something with sugar in it before meals could help you curb your appetite? We hope you didn't get the idea that our little diet tip was any magic formula for losing weight. Because there are no tricks or shortcuts; the whole diet subject is very complicated. Research hasn't established that consuming sugar before meals will contribute to weight reduction or even keep you from gaining weight."

(To be run for one insertion in each of seven magazines.)

Source: William L. Wilkie, Dennis L. McNeill, and Michael B. Mazis, "Marketing's 'Scarlet Letter': The Theory and Practice of Corrective Advertising," *Journal of Marketing*, Vol. 48, Spring 1984, p. 13. Reprinted with permission from *Journal of Marketing*, published by the American Marketing Association.

stipulation for how often the corrective ad was to appear. For example, the stipulation for Profile Bread required the corrective statement to be printed or aired in 25 percent of Profile's ads for one full year.

The most prominent corrective advertising order to date is the case of Warner-Lambert's Listerine mouthwash. According to the FTC, Warner-Lambert had over a number of years misled consumers into thinking that Listerine was able to prevent colds and sore throats or lessen their severity. The FTC required Warner-Lambert to run the following corrective advertisement statement: "Listerine will not help prevent colds or sore throats or lessen their severity." The corrective campaign ran for 16 months (from September 1978 to February 1980) at a cost of $10.3 million, most of which was spent on television commercials.

Several studies evaluated the effectiveness of the Listerine corrective advertising order.[92] The FTC's own study revealed only partial success for the Listerine corrective campaign. On the positive side, there was a 40 percent drop in the amount of mouthwash used for the misconceived purpose of preventing colds and sore throats; on the negative side, 57 percent of Listerine users continued to rate cold and sore throat effectiveness as a key attribute in their purchasing decision (only 15 percent of Scope users reported a similar goal), and 39 percent of Listerine users reported continued use of the mouthwash to relieve or prevent a cold or sore throat.

The FTC walks a fine line when issuing a corrective advertising order and specifying the remedial action a deceptive advertiser must take. The objective is to restore the marketplace to its original position prior to the deceptive advertising so that a firm does not continue to reap the rewards of its past deceptive practices. However, there is always the possibility that the corrective advertising effort may go too far and severely damage the firm and perhaps, unintentionally, hurt other companies in the industry. A national study of a corrective advertising order against STP oil additive determined that corrective advertising action in this case worked as intended: False beliefs were corrected without injuring the product category or consumers' overall perceptions of the STP Corporation.[93]

Regulation of Promotion by the States.   Individual states have their own statutes and regulatory agencies to police the marketplace from fraudulent business practices. Most if not all states have departments of consumer affairs or consumer protection. In recent years, during the sweeping deregulation climate in Washington, states have become more vigorous in their own regulatory activities. The **National Association of Attorneys General (NAAG),** which includes Attorneys General from all 50 states, has played a particularly active

---

92. See ibid. for review.
93. Kenneth L. Bernhardt, Thomas C. Kinnear, and Michael B. Mazis, "A Field Study of Corrective Advertising Effectiveness," *Journal of Public Policy & Marketing,* vol. 5 (1986), pp. 146–162. This article is "must reading" for anyone interested in learning more about corrective advertising.

role in light of the FTC's reduced role. For example, during 1987 NAAG issued guidelines directed at advertising practices in the airline and car-rental industries. In another instance, attorneys general from 22 states filed a complaint against Honda of America, alleging that Honda's three-wheel, all-terrain vehicles are "rolling death traps."[94]

An FTC commissioner recently predicted that states will become even more active in their efforts to regulate advertising deception and other business practices.[95] This poses a potentially significant problem for many national advertisers who might find themselves subject to multiple, and perhaps inconsistent, state regulations. It is somewhat ironic that many national companies would prefer to see a stronger Federal Trade Commission. In other words, these firms are better off with a single regulatory agency that (1) institutes uniform national guidelines/rules, and (2) keeps the marketplace as free as possible from the fly-by-night operators that tarnish the image of all businesses.

Advertising Self-Regulation

Self-regulation, as the name suggests, is undertaken by advertisers themselves rather than by governmental bodies. Advertising self-regulation has flourished in many countries, particularly in developed countries such as Canada, France, and the United Kingdom.[96] In the United States in the 1970s, self-regulation was a response to heightened consumer criticism of advertising and stricter government controls.[97] Four major groups sponsor self-regulation programs: (1) advertising associations (e.g., American Association of Advertising Agencies, Association of National Advertisers), (2) special industry groups (e.g., the Council of Better Business Bureaus), (3) media associations, and (4) trade associations.[98]

The *advertising clearance process* is a form of self-regulation that takes place behind the scenes *before* a commercial or other advertisement reaches consumers.[99] A magazine advertisement or television commercial undergoes a variety of clearance steps prior to appearing in media. Clearance includes (1) advertising agency clearance, (2) approval from the advertiser's legal department and perhaps also from an independent law firm, and (3) media approval (e.g., television networks have guidelines regarding standards of taste).[100] A finished ad

94. Paul Harris, "Will the FTC Finally Wake UP?" *Sales and Marketing Management*, January 1988, pp. 57–59.
95. Andrew J. Strenio, Jr., "The FTC in 1988: Phoenix Or Finis?" *Journal of Public Policy & Marketing*, vol. 7 (1988), pp. 21–39.
96. J. J. Boddewyn, "Advertising Self-Regulation: Private Government and Agent of Public Policy," *Journal of Public Policy & Marketing*, vol. 4 (1985), pp. 129–141.
97. Priscilla A. LaBarbera, "Analyzing and Advancing the State of the Art of Advertising Self-Regulation," *Journal of Advertising*, vol. 9, no. 4 (1980), p. 27.
98. Ibid., p. 28.
99. For a thorough discussion, see Eric J. Zanot, "Unseen But Effective Advertising Regulation: The Clearance Process," *Journal of Advertising*, vol. 14, no. 4 (1985), pp. 44–51, 59.
100. Ibid.

that makes it through the clearance process and appears in advertising media is then subject to the possibility of *post hoc* regulation from the FTC, NAAG, other government bodies (e.g., the Food and Drug Administration), and the National Advertising Review Board.

The National Advertising Review Board. Self-regulation by the Council of Better Business Bureaus' National Advertising Division (NAD) and **National Advertising Review Board (NARB)** has been the most publicized and perhaps most effective form of self-regulation. The NAD and NARB were established with the goal of sustaining "high standards of truth and accuracy in national advertising."[101] NARB is the umbrella-like term applied to the combined NAD/NARB self-regulatory mechanism; however, by strict definition, NARB is a court of appeals consisting of 50 representatives who are formed into five-member panels to hear appeals of NAD cases when one or more of the involved parties is dissatisifed with the initial verdict.[102] NAD is the investigative arm of NARB and is responsible for "receiving or initiating, evaluating, investigating, analyzing and holding initial negotiations with an advertiser on complaints or questions from any source involving truth or accuracy of national advertising."[103]

The NAD/NARB resolves approximately 100 cases each year. In 1988, 103 cases were resolved: Forty-one of the contested advertisements were brought to the NAD by competing advertisers, 37 were initiated by the NAD staff, and the remainder came from local Better Business Bureaus and consumer groups. Food and beverages (24 cases) and child-directed ads (23 cases) were the categories most frequently involved.[104] A review of two recent advertising cases will demonstrate the nature of NAD/NARB activities.

Kellogg's Special K. Kellogg agreed to modify advertising for its Special K brand cereal after the NAD questioned one aspect of Kellogg's claims. Television spots claimed that Special K's "200-calorie breakfast helps you keep the muscle while you lose the fat." Kellogg substantiated its claim that Special K contains the highest protein of all breakfast cereals, but NAD contested the advertising on grounds of whether it was appropriate for Kellogg to direct the claims to quick weight-loss dieters, the intended audience, who may benefit more from supplementary protein "of higher biological value." Kellogg complied by redirecting subsequent advertisements to state that Special K contributes to a nutritionally balanced diet and exercise program.[105]

101. *Statement of Organization and Procedures of the National Advertising Review Board* (Washington, DC: National Advertising Review Board, June 19, 1980).
102. Eric J. Zanot, "A Review of Eight Years of NARB Casework: Guidelines and Parameters of Deceptive Advertising," *Journal of Advertising*, vol. 9, no. 4 (1980), p. 20.
103. *Statement of Organization and Procedures.*
104. "NAD Tackles 103 Cases in '88," *Advertising Age*, January 16, 1989, p. 49.
105. "NAD Slaps Kellogg Over Special K Ads," *Advertising Age*, March 21, 1988, p. 70.

Magic Shaving Powders.   This shaving product is marketed to black men to provide relief from shaving bumps. Originally contested advertising claims were ruled by NAD to be substantiated, but then a competitor took the case to the National Advertising Review Board (i.e., the "court of appeals"). The competitor contested the advertising claim of "no better way than Magic," which, according to the competitor, suggested that a brand-to-brand comparison test had occurred, when it had not. The NARB supported the competitor's challenge. The makers of Magic Shaving Powders agreed to revise the "no better way" claim to prevent possible misinterpretations.[106]

The preceding cases illustrate some of the fundamentals of the NAD/NARB self-regulatory process. This section details the specific activities that are involved from the time a complaint is initiated until it is resolved.[107]

Complaint Screening and Case Selection.   The self-regulatory process begins with the NAD screening complaints against allegedly deceptive or misleading advertising. Complaints originate from four major sources: (1) competitors, (2) consumers and consumer groups, (3) Better Business Bureaus, and (4) NAD's own monitoring activities. The NAD pursues those complaints that it regards as having merit.

Initial NAD Evaluation.   Some cases are administratively closed because they fall outside NAD's jurisdiction, but in most cases NAD contacts the advertiser and opens a dialogue. There are three possible outcomes from this dialogue: (1) the disputed advertisement is found acceptable; (2) the advertisement is considered questionable; or (3) the advertisement is deemed unacceptable because NAD feels it violates a precedent or may be misinterpreted by consumers.

Advertiser's Initial Response.   Advertisers can respond to NAD by providing sufficient substantiation to show that the disputed advertising claim is justified or by discontinuing or modifying the claim.

NAD's Final Evaluation.   All ads that have been discontinued or modified are publicly reported by NAD. For example, the two cases discussed previously were reported in *Advertising Age*, a publication that has wide distribution in the advertising community. Ads for which advertisers have provided substantiation are then reviewed by NAD to assess the adequacy of the evidence provided. In most instances NAD rules that the disputed claims have been adequately substantiated. Claims that NAD considers insufficiently substantiated are subject to appeal to NARB (as was the case with Magic Shaving Powder).

---

106. "Magic Loses at NAD," *Advertising Age*, October 17, 1988, p. 64.
107. The following discussion borrows heavily from the thorough presentation by Gary M. Armstrong and Julie L. Ozanne, "An Evaluation of NAD/NARB Purpose and Performance," *Journal of Advertising*, vol. 12, no. 3 (1983), pp. 19–23.

Advertiser's Final Response.   The NAD's ruling may be upheld, reversed, or dismissed by NARB. However, because NAD/NARB is merely a self-regulatory body *without legal jurisdiction or power*, the ultimate resolution of disputed cases depends on voluntary cooperation between advertisers and NAD/NARB.

In conclusion, self-regulation has a variety of potential benefits to consumers and businesses. It can strenghten effectiveness by "discouraging exaggerated or misleading promises which lower the believability and selling power of advertising."[108] Self-regulation may also reduce the need for government regulation. Furthermore, because advertisers are strongly motivated to point out their competitor's deceptive advertising practices, their efforts to protect themselves help to maintain the general integrity of advertising and, in so doing, to protect consumers. Thus, the evidence seems to indicate that consumers have benefitted substantially from NAD/NARB's self-regulatory efforts.[109]

Summary

This chapter examines the role of environmental influences on promotion management by concentrating on three major environmental forces: the technological, demographic, and regulatory environments. Technological developments influence promotion and marketing communications both indirectly and directly. The discussion focuses primarily on the direct effects that various technological advances have had on personal selling, advertising, direct marketing, and point-of-purchase communications.

Six major demographic developments are reviewed in this chapter: (1) population growth and regional geographic developments, (2) the changing age structure, (3) the changing American household, (4) the changing roles of women, (5) income dynamics, and (6) minority population developments. The presentation covers a variety of topics relevant for promotion managers, such as developments with the "baby-boom" generation and the growth of the "mature market."

The regulatory environment is described with respect to both government regulation and industry self-regulation. The Federal Trade Commission's role is explained in terms of its regulation of deception, unfair practices, and information regulation. Specific topics covered include the advertising substantiation program, trade-regulation rules, and the corrective advertising program. Self-regulation by the Council of Better Business Bureaus' National Advertising Division (NAD) and National Advertising Review Board (NARB) are discussed, with emphasis placed on the process by which the NAD/NARB regulates national advertising.

108. LaBarbera, "Analyzing and Advancing the State of the Art of Advertising Self-Regulation."
109. Armstrong and Ozanne, "An Evaluation of NAD/NARB Purpose and Performance," p. 25.

Discussion Questions

1. The opening vignette described "Healthy Choice" dinners, which ConAgra has marketed to consumers aged 50 and over. Excluding items marketed almost solely to older people (e.g., denture-care products), describe several mass-market products which, in your opinion, could be marketed successfully to the mature market.

2. Technological developments have direct and indirect influence on marketing and marketing communications. Describe several *indirect* technological advances (other than those mentioned in the chapter) and discuss the implications they have for promotion managers and marketing communicators.

3. What is the Buying Power Index? How is it constructed? What implications does it hold for marketing communications and other forms of marketing decision making? (To answer these questions, you may need to review a text in principles of marketing or marketing research or read an issue of *Sales and Marketing Management*, which developed the BPI measure.)

4. Demographers tell us that households in the United States are growing in number, shrinking in size, and changing in character. What implications do these changes hold for marketing communicators?

5. As a percentage of the total population, young Americans aged 19 and younger represent a much smaller percentage of the total population today (approximately 29 percent) than they did a quarter of a century ago (approximately 40 percent in 1965). If you were the marketer of exclusively youth-oriented products, what implications would this development have for your firm?

6. References are often made to the "childrens market," the "singles market," and the "mature market." Are these truly markets in the rigorous sense of market segmentation?

7. Black, Hispanic, and Asian consumers do not represent three homogeneous markets; rather, they represent many markets composed of people who merely share a common race and/or language. Explain.

8. Theoretically, one benefit of business regulation is improvement in product quality. The text cited lower cholesterol and fat content in food products as one illustration of this. Identify two additional instances in which regulation has improved product quality.

9. What is the distinction between a deceptive and an unfair business practice?

10. The text drew a distinction between "disposable" and "investment" psychologies of consumption and also discussed the "Europeanization of America." Describe these developments in detail and explain what implications they hold for marketing and marketing communications.

11. In your opinion, should a firm be required to have substantiating evidence (i.e., test results or other data) for an advertising claim prior to making the claim? Why or why not?

12. Give examples of advertising claims which, if found false, probably would be considered material and claims which probably would be evaluated as immaterial.

13. What is your opinion of the defense Kraft used in claiming that calcium is an immaterial product attribute?

14. In theory, corrective advertising represents a potentially valuable device for regulating deceptive advertising. In practice, however, corrective advertising must perform a very delicate balancing act by being "strong enough without being too strong." Explain the nature of this strong-enough-without-being-too-strong dilemma.

15. Describe the distinction between the self-regulatory roles of the NAD and NARB.

Exercises

1. Identify three or four advertising campaigns that appear to be directed at "nontraditional" households.

2. Identify two or three examples of deceptive or unfair marketing communications practices that you have experienced in the past year or so. Explain precisely why each practice is, in your opinion, deceptive or unfair.

3. Interview two or three salespersons and question them about the roles that portable computers and other technological developments play in their job performance.

Promotion-Management Practices: Two Case Histories

OOPS. . .NAIL POLISH ON THE NEW CARPET

magine that you have recently purchased light-colored carpeting for the living and dining rooms in your home at a cost of $1,250. The carpeting looks great. Your home looks entirely different than it did with the outdated, soiled carpeting that you replaced. Imagine now that a family member decides to paint her fingernails in the living room. Reaching for a soft drink, she knocks over the nail-polish bottle, and polish spills everywhere. Disaster has struck—the carpeting is ruined!

This would have been the outcome several years ago, but now there are carpets that resist stains such as nail polish. One stain-resistant brand is marketed by Du Pont under the name "Stainmaster."[1] Its ability to resist stains has surprised even people who purchased Stainmaster[cm] carpeting mainly for this reason. For example, a Massachusetts woman spilled bright red nail polish on her new wheat-colored Stainmaster[cm] carpet and thought it was ruined, but, using only soap and water, she had the stain out in less than five minutes. A Michigan family installed off-white This carpeting throughout their new house. Around Easter, the mother and her children were coloring eggs when a cup of bright green egg coloring was accidentally spilled. "I was sick," the mother commented. "I was sure it would never come out of the carpet. But I blotted up as much as I

1. "Stainmaster" is Du Pont's registered certification mark.

could, then saturated the stained area several times with warm water. Every bit of the coloring came out without the need of any cleaning agent."[2]■

This stain-resistance feature provided the Du Pont Corporation with a distinct relative advantage over competitors. It also posed a major challenge, for most of Du Pont's past business experience had been restricted to selling its hundreds of technologically advanced products to other companies. Prior to the Stainmaster[cm] introduction, Du Pont had relatively little experience in attempting to create consumer demand for its branded products.[3] The following pages chronicle the evolution of the Stainmaster[cm] marketing communications program and describe the steps taken to accomplish the company's marketing communications objectives.

In general, this chapter's purpose is to acquaint students with the "big picture" of promotion management as a prelude to subsequent chapters' specialized treatment of specific promotion topics. Up to this point in the text, you have been introduced to the general aspects of promotion management and marketing communications and the behavioral foundations that undergird their practical implementation. The chapters that follow provide an in-depth treatment of each of the promotion-mix elements: four chapters are devoted to advertising, three discuss sales promotion, two focus on personal selling, and so on.

There is a danger that the following component-by-component coverage might convey the idea that each element of the promotion mix is self-sustaining and independent of the other elements. Nothing could be further from the truth. In practice, all of the promotion-mix elements must be coordinated to achieve overall marketing communications objectives.

Hence, the reason for this chapter. To minimize the tendency for students to study the trees but lose sight of the forest, this chapter will show what the forest—that is, an integrated marketing communications program—looks like before individual trees (advertising, sales promotion, etc.) are examined. Two practical case histories accomplish this purpose. The first examines Du Pont's highly successful introduction of Stainmaster[cm] carpeting.[4] The second deals with a fascinating application of marketing communications methods in the public sector by the United States Agency for International Development.

2. Based on "What Are They Saying about 'Stainmaster'[cm]?" *Du Pont Magazine*, March/April 1988, pp. 24–25.
3. Edward E. Messikomer, "Du Pont's 'Marketing Community'," *Business Marketing*, October 1987, p. 90.
4. I am extremely grateful to Mr. Gary A. Johnston, Marketing Communications Group Manager, Du Pont's External Affairs Department, for providing many of the materials for this case-history discussion.

Du Pont's Marketing of "Stainmaster"^{cm} Carpeting

As you may recall from your reading back in Chapter 1, the promotion management process comprises six major steps: situation analysis, marketing objectives, promotion budget, integration and coordination, promotion management program, and evaluation and control. (It would be useful to review this material and the integrative framework shown in Figure 1.8.) The most important of these steps as they apply to Du Pont's program for Stainmaster^{cm} carpet are discussed in the following pages.

Situation Analysis

Until a short time ago, Du Pont's business perspective could be summarized in terms of three fundamental factors.[5] First, the company was dominated by *technologically driven* decision making. In other words, new product and other major decisions typically had their genesis in Du Pont's chemical laboratories rather than originating from the marketplace. Second, Du Pont's marketing orientation was almost exclusively *business to business.* That is, very few of Du Pont's 2,500 or so products were marketed to final consumers; rather, most were marketed to other companies. Although business-to-business marketing is undergoing dramatic changes throughout industry, historically it has been far less sophisticated than consumer marketing.

A final factor characterizing Du Pont's past business perspective was its *premier economic and technological position around the world.* Until the 1970s, Du Pont, like many other U.S. industrial firms, had distinct technological and economic advantages over its international competition. This enabled Du Pont to achieve financial success without having to concentrate on sophisticated marketing methods. However, as international competition has intensified during the past two decades, Du Pont has been forced to elevate the quality and sophistication of its marketing efforts. Du Pont remains a very profitable and successful enterprise, but its recent gains are attributable largely to the fact that it has evolved into a truly marketing-oriented organization. This corporate-mindset change set the stage for the development and introduction of Stainmaster^{cm} carpet.

To understand how Stainmaster^{cm} came about, it is necessary first to understand Du Pont's role in the carpet business.[6] Du Pont is not a carpet manufacturer per se. Rather, it manufactures carpet *fiber*. It markets fiber to carpet

---

5. This discussion is adapted from Messikomer, "Du Pont's Marketing Community."
6. The following comments are based partially on an outline of a lecture delivered by Andrew Ballentine, a retired Du Pont marketing communications executive, to the University of South Carolina chapter of the American Marketing Association. I am deeply grateful to Mr. Ballentine for bringing this material to my attention and for mentoring me in the area of business-to-business marketing.

mills who spin the fiber into yarn, tuft and dye it, and produce finished carpet. These mills (companies such as Bigelow, J. P. Stevens, Milliken, and West Point Pepperell) market finished carpeting to architects and decorators, wholesalers, and directly to larger retailers.

Synthetic carpeting had experienced sustained growth for nearly four decades following World War II, but sales reached a plateau in 1979. The product was in the late maturity stage of its life cycle. On top of this, carpet had become basically a *commodity product* (i.e., an undifferentiated good).[7] The result was that consumers typically went to a discount carpet store with a color and style in mind and bought on the basis of price. Brand name had relatively little influence on the buying decision. To break out of this commodity trap, Du Pont's Strategic Business Team was charged in 1982 with developing a greatly improved carpet that would provide Du Pont with distinct competitive advantages.

Before the marketing revolution at Du Pont, the team would have sent company chemists back to the lab to "come up with something." Under the new marketing mindset, they decided to ask consumers what was important to them when purchasing carpet. A major marketing research study was designed. The research revealed that consumers regard stain and soil resistance as important as color, styling, and price.

This marketplace-based information gave Du Pont's chemists something specific to work on. By 1985 they had a solution. The new product ultimately became "Stainmaster,[cm]" which essentially is a stain-blocking chemical that is applied to the fiber at the carpet mill during the dyeing process. Carpet manufactured with the Stainmaster[cm] process has superior stain resistance compared to any carpet on the market. Most household stains—including fruit drinks, blueberry pie, and tomato juice—can be removed completely from Stainmaster[cm] with water and mild detergent. Stainmaster[cm] is not universally stain resistant, however; it can be permanently stained by substances such as bleach, shoe polish, and India ink.[8]

In light of this situation, it was concluded that substantial profits could be made by being the first fiber producer to offer a revolutionary new anti-stain fiber system for carpet. It was also concluded that the only way Stainmaster[cm] would be successful was by differentiating the product at the consumer level.

Marketing Objectives

The stain-resistance feature provided Du Pont with a means to escape the commodity trap. Product introduction took place in the fall of 1986. Overriding marketing objectives were to gain widespread distribution for Stainmaster,[cm]

7. "Branding Builds Business for Stainmaster[cm] Carpets," *Marketing Communications*, February 1988, p. 42.
8. "A Sheltered Investment," *Du Pont Magazine*, January/February 1987, p. 20.

to promote it as a premium product, and to ensure that the product performed exactly as claimed. Toward this end, agreements were reached with a select group of 21 carpet mills who were licensed to manufacture carpet with the Stainmaster^{cm} process. A licensing and certification program ensured that these mills would produce Stainmaster^{cm} carpet exactly as specified by Du Pont.

Promotion Budget

To accomplish the marketing objectives, Du Pont invested nearly $50 million in the introductory promotional effort for Stainmaster.^{cm} The budget was allocated accordingly:

Budget Category	Percent of Budget
Consumer advertising	48
Cooperative advertising	27
Point-of-purchase materials	20
Publicity	3
Trade advertising	2

Promotion Management Program

The marketing communications challenge was to come up with a way to promote the stain-resistance advantage and convince homeowners to ask for a Du Pont certified Stainmaster^{cm} carpet. To an unprecedented degree, Du Pont sought to encourage final consumers to demand carpet made with Stainmaster,^{cm} thereby *pulling* the product through the distribution channel. This required familiarizing consumers with the distinct stain-resistance feature of Stainmaster^{cm} and convincing them that stain resistance made Stainmaster^{cm} an excellent investment. Another readily promotable benefit was the fact that consumers no longer needed to avoid purchasing carpet in light colors, since the ability to resist stains made such colors safer than ever.

Specific communications objectives were designed for retailers and consumers. At the retail level, Du Pont's primary objectives were to convince dealers of the volume and profit benefits associated with stocking and selling Stainmaster^{cm} carpet. For consumers, the primary objective was to create strong consumer awareness of the Stainmaster^{cm} name and its stain-resistance feature. Awareness was expected to reach 50 percent of all target customers (i.e., women between the ages of 25-54 with annual household incomes of at least $30,000) within 60 days after product launch and 70 percent in one year. The promotional program utilized television advertising, point-of-purchase displays, direct mail, and dealer programs.

Television Advertising.   Du Pont spent $50 million in its introductory marketing communications campaign.[9] Much of the effort focused on national television advertising. Advertisements recreated common household disasters, all with a humorous twist. An initial Clio-Award-winning commercial (the "Academy Award" for television commercials) showed a red-haired boy throwing his tray of food onto the floor. His mother is shown easily removing the peas, carrots, and cherries from the carpet without a trace of stain. (See the storyboard for this commercial in Figure 10.1)

Another in the series of Stainmaster[cm] commercials shows a party scene in which a piece of chocolate cake is falling toward the carpet. An elegantly dressed woman races through the crowd and leaps to intercept the cake just before it hits the carpet. In a subsequent repeat performance, she is unsuccessful in her attempt to prevent a wine glass from reaching the carpet. While this action is taking place on the screen, an announcer's voice-over suggests that sooner or later every household will need Stainmaster[cm] carpet to prevent the inevitable stain-producing accidents. (See the storyboard for this commercial in Figure 10.2.)

Point-of-Purchase Displays.   In addition to television advertising, which served to invigorate consumer interest in carpet and prompt visits to carpet outlets, Du Pont used effective point-of-purchase displays to demonstrate the stain-resistant properties of Stainmaster[cm] to consumers. Displays were placed in 10,000 retail outlets throughout the United States. The display consists of one beaker filled with a red fruit drink, another filled with water, and a supply of swizzle sticks. Affixed to each stick are separate patches of Stainmaster[cm] carpet and a competitive brand. Consumers are instructed to dip a swizzle stick in the fruit juice and then to swish the stick in the clear water. Stainmaster[cm] emerges stain free, whereas the competitive carpet remains covered with fruit juice. This dramatic demonstration is a perfect extension of television advertising for Stainmaster[cm] and provides consumers with concrete reinforcement of the advertising claims.

Direct Mail.   Du Pont further appealed to consumers with direct-mail letters. Figure 10.3 contains a letter that I received. The letter invites the consumer to visit any of several retail outlets in the local market (specific stores were named on a second page, but are not shown in the figure). The primary attraction for encouraging the consumer to visit a Stainmaster[cm] dealer is the promise of a free *Carpet Decorating Ideas* book. Needless to say, this form of personalized approach is appealing to many consumers.

Dealer Programs.   Beyond reaching final consumers and encouraging them to visit stores, it was imperative that Du Pont also provide retail dealers with sufficient incentive to actively promote Stainmaster[cm] carpet. Du

9. "Branding Builds Business for Stainmaster[cm] Carpets," p. 42.

Du Pont's "Landing" Commercial for "Stainmaster^{cm}" Carpet

FIGURE 10.1

E-86847

BBDO
Batten, Barton, Durstine & Osborn, Inc.

Client: DU PONT CARPET FIBERS

Product: STAINMASTER

Title: "LANDING"

Time: 30 SECONDS

Comml. No.: DDTC 6023

CONTROL TOWER: Flight 124 fly runway heading to

3,000. Right turn to two-seven-zero. You are cleared for take-off.

AVO: Introducing Du Pont

certified Stainmaster carpet.

Stainmaster gives you

a revolutionary new level of protection

against stains and spills

that's better than any other carpet you can buy today.

Because you never know . . .

STARTER: Gentlemen, start your engines.

AVO: New Stainmaster.

AVO: From Du Pont Carpet Fibers.

Source: Courtesy Du Pont Flooring Systems.

FIGURE 10.2   **Du Pont's "Great Saves" Commercial for "Stainmaster^{cm}" Carpet**

Source: Courtesy Du Pont Flooring Systems.

Direct Mail Letter for Du Pont's "Stainmaster^cm" Carpet   FIGURE 10.3

E. I. du Pont de Nemours & Company
INCORPORATED
WILMINGTON, DELAWARE 19898

TEXTILE FIBERS DEPARTMENT

Terence Shimp
101 Smith Mrkt Ct
Columbia, SC 29210

You have been selected by the DuPont Company to participate in the biggest promotional event in our history. It's called "Decorating Days" and it features DuPont Certified STAINMASTER^cn Carpet, America's first choice in stain resistant carpet.

We invite you to visit one of the retail stores on the enclosed list, right now during "Decorating Days," and take full advantage of the special opportunities prepared for you.

There's a FREE Carpet Decorating Ideas Book Waiting for You!

It's packed with advice on what to look for in carpet, and how to buy it. And it's loaded with exciting pictures and information to help you use new carpet colors and textures in your home in fresh, exciting ways...thanks to today's easy-to-care-for DuPont STAINMASTER^cn carpet.

You Can Choose from Great New Colors and Styles!

Your retailer has DuPont STAINMASTER^cn carpet in many fabulous new colors and styles. So your decorating choices are practically unlimited.

You'll Get Great Values!

There's never been a better time to buy DuPont STAINMASTER^cn Carpet, or a better place than at one of the participating retailers on the enclosed list. Visit one today. Insist on decorating with DuPont Certified STAINMASTER^cn Carpet. And make sure you pick up your FREE copy of the Carpet Decorating Ideas Book.

Sincerely,

Christine Roberts

Christine Roberts
Customer Service Representative

P.S. Hurry! "Decorating Days" end May 30.

Source: Courtesy Du Pont Flooring Systems.

Pont's biggest promotion of all time, called "Decorating Days," was designed with this purpose in mind. Participating dealers received 100 free copies of the *Carpet Decorating Ideas* book along with the swizzle stick point-of-purchase display. Throughout the six-week "Decorating Days" promotion, Du Pont ran commercials on the three major television networks and on cable television. Print ads appeared in 19 consumer magazines and hundreds of Sunday newspapers; all of the ads included a toll-free number for dealer information.

Du Pont provided dealers with "Retail Promotion" kits that included newspaper advertising copy and radio scripts. Figure 10.4 shows two of six radio scripts made available to retailers; one is a 60-second ad and the other is 30 seconds long. The retailer's advertising was partially paid for by Du Pont through its cooperative advertising program.[10] In addition to supporting dealers' advertising, Du Pont awarded retail salespeople for their sales of Stainmaster^{cm} carpet during the "Decorating Days" promotion.

Program Evaluation

The marketing communications program that introduced Stainmaster^{cm} carpet was an overwhelming success. Consumer awareness registered 29 percent just 90 days after product launch, an impressive level for a product category that only a short time ago had been a commodity item. After 18 months, consumer awareness was 78 percent. Retailer awareness was 100 percent, and Stainmaster^{cm} was stocked in virtually all carpet stores. Shipments of Stainmaster^{cm} were nearly three times larger than the company's optimistic forecast. Large retailers pressured carpet mills to buy into the Stainmaster^{cm} program. Ultimately, Du Pont was able to significantly differentiate itself from competitors and create consumer name recognition and preference for Du Pont Stainmaster^{cm} carpet; in so doing, Du Pont realized a substantial increase in its market share and was able to command a premium price.

Returning to the product-adoption concepts covered in Chapter 7, it can be seen that much of Du Pont's early success was due to the unique *relative advantage* (stain resistance) of Stainmaster.^{cm} However, that technological feature alone would not have facilitated a successful introduction. It was necessary to make the advantage *observable* (i.e., visible and concrete rather than abstract). This was accomplished through a combination of attention-getting creative advertising and the swizzle stick point-of-purchase display. Successful introduction also required that Stainmaster^{cm} be promoted as a product that is *compatible* with consumers' needs and past experiences. This was accomplished through creative television advertising showing carpet-staining circumstances that most all consumers could readily imagine happening in their own lives. All in all, Du Pont's marketing communications efforts were creative, well targeted, carefully integrated, and undoubtedly well worth the $50 million introductory investment.

¶ 10. Cooperative advertising is described in detail in Chapter 19.

Radio Scripts for "Stainmaster^{cm}" Carpet

FIGURE 10.4

Script #1—Decorating:60

ANNCR: During Du Pont STAINMASTER Carpet Decorating Dollar Days at Joe's Carpets, you get so much more for your decorating dollars—the possibilities are endless.

WOMAN: Honey, we could save enough on Du Pont STAINMASTER Carpet to re-upholster the couch, or decorate the spare room...

MAN: Or decorate my golf bag with some new irons!

WOMAN: And with the savings on Du Pont STAINMASTER, we could have a ball with accessories! Throw pillows, vases and lamps...

MAN: I could have a ball. A bowling ball!

ANNCR: This gives you some idea of what you could do with the money you'll save on Du Pont STAINMASTER Carpet during Du Pont Decorating Dollar Days. (Add your 15 second special offer here)

WOMAN: We could knock out a wall! Even screen-in the porch!

MAN: Screen! Yeah, screen! A big screen TV!

ANNCR: Look for the Du Pont Decorating Dollar Days display at Joe's Carpet World on Main Street in Westport. Hurry in.

Script #2—Decorating:30

ANNCR: During Du Pont STAINMASTER Carpet Decorating Dollar Days, you get so much more for your decorating dollars the possibilities are endless.

WOMAN: Honey, we could save enough on Du Pont STAINMASTER Carpet to decorate the spare room!

MAN: Or decorate my golf bag with some new irons!

ANNCR: For great savings on Du Pont STAINMASTER Carpet look for the Du Pont Decorating Dollar Days display at Joe's Carpet World on Main Street in Westport.

WOMAN: We could screen-in the porch!

MAN: Screen! Yeah, screen! A big screen TV!

ANNCR: Hurry to Joe's Carpet World. Hurry in.

Source: Courtesy Du Pont Flooring Systems.

Combatting Dehydration in Underdeveloped Countries

This section presents a detailed case history of an extraordinarily effective communications program designed by the United States Agency for International Development. The program was implemented in Honduras and Gambia to combat diarrheal dehydration. This case extends the Stainmaster presentation by showing how *all* facets of promotion management can and should be integrated. It also illustrates the application of conventional marketing communications methods in a nonbusiness situation. This is an important lesson, for societal problems (such as drug abuse, AIDS, and environmental protection) increasingly are being combatted with marketing communications techniques that generally are identified with the marketing of for-profit goods and services.

As surprising as it may seem to those of us living in an advanced industrialized society, diarrhea is one of the world's leading killers. Every year, millions of children under the age of five die due to diarrheal dehydration.[11] Children in developing countries typically have diarrhea several times a year. Local practice often leads mothers to purge their children and to withhold food or stop breastfeeding when they realize that the diarrhea bout is more severe than usual. The mother does not realize that dehydration, caused by the diarrhea, is the problem. Dehydration advances rapidly, and the child loses his or her appetite and the capacity to absorb vital liquids. Death can follow within hours.

Working with the Ministries of Health in Honduras and Gambia, the U.S. Agency for International Development and its contractors (experts in health, communications, anthropology, evaluation and behavioral psychology) developed a public health education program to deliver *oral rehydration therapy (ORT)* to large numbers of rural and isolated people threatened by diarrheal dehydration. Using mass media, simple printed materials, and health-worker training, rural women were taught what ORT is, how to use it in the home, and how to monitor their child's progress during the diarrheal episode.[12]

Situation Analysis

Oral rehydration therapy (ORT) is an established medical treatment for combatting an infant's loss of body fluid and electrolytes during a diarrheal episode. The therapy involves having mothers administer an oral rehydration solution that is prepackaged or can be made at home by mixing appropriate portions of sugar, salt, and water. The solution is administered to a dehydrated child at the rate of approximately one liter per day.

11. Anthony J. Meyer, Clifford H. Block, and Donald C. E. Ferguson, "Teaching Mothers Oral Rehydration," *Horizons*, vol. 2 (April 1983), pp. 14–20. The remaining discussion borrows liberally from this source.
12. *After Twelve Months of Broadcasting: A Status Report on the Project in Honduras and The Gambia* (Washington, DC: Academy for Educational Development, Inc., January 1984), p. 1.

The key to effective ORT is the correct preparation and administration of the oral rehydration solution (ORS). Mothers must know how to mix the ingredients in exact proportions to avoid ineffective or potentially dangerous concentrations of sodium. They must also know how to give the solution correctly, that is slowly and continuously over a 24-hour period even if a child vomits or refuses the liquid.

The challenge confronting the Agency for International Development was to design a communications and promotion program that would teach mothers a new form of behavior. The task was to increase the likelihood that rural people would mix and administer ORS. Such behavior, although fully within the mothers' capacities, was not being performed. Hence, the Agency's imperative was to *alter behavior*. Changing attitudes, even those that may contribute to what people do, was of secondary importance.[13]

A number of important questions had to be answered: (1) Who in the total population should be selected as the principal target audience? (2) What communication channels are most appropriate? (3) What behaviors should be advocated? (4) What resources are needed to conduct the program?

Preprogram research was conducted in both Honduras and Gambia to assist planners in thoroughly understanding the problem that the subsequent communication and promotion programs would address.[14] Focus-group interviews, surveys, and product-preference trials were conducted to provide answers to the preceding questions. Among the many findings, the research uncovered some traditional health beliefs with which the communication programs would have to deal. Rural Gambian mothers most often attributed diarrhea to some natural cause, such as dirt or wind, or to some supernatural cause. In Honduras, there was widespread belief that diarrhea is caused by "la bolsa," a sack believed to exist in everyone and to contain worms that leave the sack after becoming agitated.

An important research question involved the proper method for delivering the ORS solution: as a new medicine, a traditional tea, or a new local remedy. Prior to the research, it was assumed that mothers would prefer a product that was similar to their existing method for treating diarrhea, namely, a herbal tea solution. The research evidence indicated that this assumption was incorrect—mothers seemed to prefer a modern medicine rather than the herbal tea.

Contrary to preresearch doubts, the research further revealed that mothers were able to mix the ORS solution in the correct proportions. They learned the mixing instructions very quickly, after only one or two explanations, even when the instructions were delivered via a tape recorder.

Overall, the preprogram research resulted in a detailed communications program consisting of (1) behavioral objectives, (2) target-audience selection,

13. Ibid., p. 7.
14. The following description of the preprogram research is from Elizabeth M. Booth and Mark Rasmuson, "Traditional and Empirical Inputs in Program Design: The Role of Formative Evaluation in the Mass Media and Health Practice Project," Washington, DC: Academy for Educational Development, Inc., May 1984.

(3) specific instructional messages, (4) culturally appropriate message formats, (5) plans for media use and integration, and (6) a complete plan of action.

Objectives

Several local practices and beliefs that contribute to dehydration were singled out for modification. These included the practice of mothers purging and withholding food from infants and the belief that breast milk causes diarrhea. Most important of all was the goal to get mothers to administer the proper oral rehydration solution and thereby reduce the number of infant deaths caused by diarrhea.

In the final analysis, the success of the program depended on providing a large number of people with information they would find important and practical. To be successful, the program had to "make an impact on the consciousness of the intended audience by rising above the everyday clutter of advice and suggestions to become an important new priority in their lives. It must change what people do as well as what they think and believe. . . .It requires: a sensitive understanding of how people are affected by specific health problems, articulate crafting of useful and practical educational messages, and a coordinated distribution network that reaches each individual through various channels simultaneously."[15]

The Budget

As will be seen shortly, the communications programs in Honduras and Gambia were remarkably successful. Yet the results were accomplished with very small budgets. Figure 10.5 illustrates the total costs and specific cost categories for each country. Costs exclude technical assistance from the U.S. Agency for International Development but include local salaries, benefits, travel, transportation, research, printing, production, and broadcast. Costs were significantly lower in Gambia because (1) air time was provided free, (2) commercial printing costs were much lower, and (3) preprogram research costs were lower because the prior experience in Honduras permitted significant savings.[16]

The first-year expenditures in Honduras amounted to $135,000, of which $18,000 (approximately 13 percent) involved the combination of expenses for preprogram research and ongoing monitoring. The remaining $117,000 was spent on various communication media that were used to educate Honduran mothers about oral rehydration therapy. There were, for example, 29,000 radio broadcasts aired at a cost of $33,000 during the first year in Honduras.

Total first-year expenditures in Gambia amounted to $41,000. Approximately 20 percent ($8,000) was invested in preprogram research and ongoing monitoring, and the remaining $33,000 was spent on educational activities.

15. *After Twelve Months of Broadcasting,* p. 8.
16. Ibid., p. 25.

First-Year Budgets for Honduras and The Gambia

FIGURE 10.5

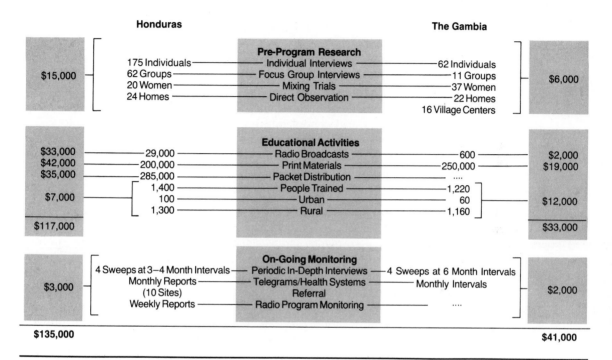

Source: After Twelve Months of Broadcasting: A Status Report on the Project in Honduras and The Gambia, (Washington, DC: Academy for Education Development, January 1984).

Integration and Coordination

Successful marketing communications programs require that the various promotion-mix elements work together to accomplish overall marketing objectives. To achieve optimal effectiveness, advertising campaigns, sales promotions, and publicity releases must be integrated with one another and coordinated with personal selling efforts.

Success in Honduras and Gambia depended on the combination of three communication media: radio broadcasts, print materials, and person-to-person communications using health workers and community volunteers. The careful integration of broadcast, print, and face-to-face support was essential. Radio alerted hundreds of thousands of Hondurans and Gambians about ORT. In Honduras, radio taught mothers how to measure a liter using local bottles. In Gambia, radio taught mothers to understand the printed mixing instructions. Printed materials and graphics (posters and flags) helped mothers recall what to do at the actual time of using ORT. Health workers, who contacted mothers individually or in small groups, provided the needed credibility for key messages delivered by radio and in print.

Program Implementation in Honduras[17]

The communications program in Honduras was aimed at two target groups: (1) a primary audience of rural mothers/grandmothers with children under the age of five and community volunteer health-care workers called guardians and (2) a secondary audience of physicians, nurses, fathers of children under five, rural schoolteachers and schoolchildren, and regional health promoters. The program was designed to teach the primary audience the proper preparation and administration of a prepackaged oral rehydration solution (Litrosol) and to teach the secondary audience to support the primary audience by encouraging the use of ORT. The *Focus on Promotion* section describes the creative program used to promote Litrosol.

Program Implementation in Gambia

The primary audience for the program in Gambia was rural mothers, grandmothers, and older female siblings of children under five. The secondary market consisted of various health-care workers (such as health inspectors and nurses). The communication program was designed (1) to teach the primary audience to mix a simple sugar and salt (S/S) rehydration solution properly and to administer the solution along with breast milk and soft foods during episodes of diarrhea and (2) to teach the secondary audience to mix and administer the S/S solution properly and to take care of moderate and severe diarrhea in the health centers.

Accomplishing these objectives required some creative thinking, because most people in Gambia are unfamiliar with print materials of any kind. The solution involved a national contest, which began with the distribution of 200,000 copies of a color-coded flyer that provided instructions for the correct mixing and administering of the S/S solution. In conjunction with the flyers, radio announcements literally led listeners through each panel of the color-coded flyer. Mothers were repeatedly told how to mix the formula, how to administer it, what to do in the case of vomiting, and how to tell if the child was improving. Radio announcers also told them about other mothers with "happy baby" flags flying over their homes. These flags served as a symbol to people of the village that the "happy baby" home was a source of information on the diarrhea medicine.

---

17. The following discussion summarizes the presentation found in two sources: *After Twelve Months of Broadcasting*, pp. 10–32, and Meyer, Block, and Ferguson, "Teaching Mothers Oral Rehydration," pp. 16–20.

FOCUS ON PROMOTION

The Use of a Visible Symbol to Promote Litrosol

Litrosol, the prepackaged oral rehydration formula, was widely publicized through posters, pamphlets, and radio programs. A central campaign theme was developed around the concept of a loving image—a red heart was chosen as the central visual symbol to signify the love that mothers have for their children. Thousands of spot radio broadcasts and dozens of weekly programs were broadcast on carefully selected local stations. The programs built on the loving theme that was used in print materials. Local health workers and health professionals were trained to use and promote Litrosol. A simple flag with the red heart symbol was given to each trained health worker. Radio programs announced that Litrosol was available at houses that displayed the red heart flag.

The integration of radio, graphics, and health workers proved to be a powerful combination.[18] Several dramatic results occurred within a year: (1) nearly half of the entire sample of mothers had tried Litrosol at least once; (2) recognition of Litrosol as a diarrheal remedy went from 0 percent to 93 percent; (3) knowledge levels concerning the procedure for mixing Litrosol received over 90 percent correct responses; (4) nearly 90 percent of mothers knew to continue breastfeeding during diarrheal bouts; and (5) a 40 percent decrease in the percentage of deaths involving diarrhea was achieved.■

Another element in the program was a prize giveaway contest. Any mother could win a prize—a plastic liter container or a bar of soap wrapped in a label with the "happy baby" symbol printed on it—by demonstrating to a health-care worker that she could mix the S/S solution correctly. Winning mothers' names were included in a drawing for 15 radios. Follow-up radio programs used the testimonials of "happy baby" winners to continually reinforce the value and importance of the sugar, salt, and water solution. There was also a community prize each week for the village in which the most mothers participated in the contest. The contest was concluded with a one-hour radio broadcast in which the Gambian president's wife announced the names of grand-prize winners.

18. Summative evaluation was conducted under an Agency for International Development contract to Stanford University Institute for Communication Research. These data are from their extensive evaluation activities, not from the AEP formative research.

The integrated communications program in Gambia yielded some dramatic results, just as it had in Honduras. After eight months of the program, 66 percent of mothers knew the correct home mix solution, and 47 percent reported having used the solution to treat their children's diarrhea.

Evaluation and Control

Sophisticated promotion management requires that all programs be measured for effectiveness and that corrective action be taken when necessary. At six-month intervals, evaluation research was conducted to determine the amount of learning to date among target audiences and to identify strengths and weaknesses in the promotional campaign. Program monitoring in Honduras, for example, detected that mothers did not understand the concept of dehydration nor did they associate it with diarrhea and Litrosol. Therefore, subsequent promotional activity deemphasized the abstract concept of dehydration and focused instead on the physical manifestations of dehydration. This change in emphasis resulted in an increase from 20 percent to 77 percent of mothers who understood the signs of dehydration.[19]

A Wrap-up

The ORT programs in Honduras and Gambia illustrate the use of some very sophisticated communications efforts. There are, in fact, four features of the oral rehydration program that could serve as models for any marketing communications endeavor.

Communications Grounded in Research.   Marketing communicators sometimes jump immediately to the tasks of creating messages and selecting media before they have a thorough understanding of the marketplace. Such an approach stands a good chance of failing unless the marketing communicator has had extensive prior experience with the intended audience. Many communication programs are doomed to fail because companies have not done their homework in adequately understanding the marketplace in terms of its culture, values, beliefs, stereotypes, and behavioral habits.

The project directors for the ORT program did not commit such a mistake. They conducted extensive preprogram research in both Honduras and Gambia prior to designing communication programs for these countries. The information acquired from this research enabled the project directors to develop communication programs that were compatible with the beliefs, attitudes, and health-care practices of both mothers and health-care workers.

19. Booth and Rasmuson, "Traditional and Empirical Inputs."

Use of Unifying Creative Message Themes.   Another mistake committed by many marketing communicators is the failure to design communication programs around a central creative theme. In the absence of a unifying theme, programs tend to flounder because they lack direction and meaning.

Such a mistake was not made in Honduras or Gambia. The loving theme with the red heart symbol in Honduras and the happy baby theme in Gambia provided unifying forces for the communication programs in these countries. By directing communication efforts around these themes, the chances were increased substantially that mothers would gain awareness of the ORT programs and become sufficiently motivated to learn how to mix the oral rehydration solution properly and administer it when necessary.

Coordination of Communications Efforts.   Three communication channels—radio, print, and interpersonal—were carefully coordinated to accomplish communication objectives. Mothers learned about the oral rehydration solution through radio, pamphlets and flyers provided instructions for its proper mixing and administration, and the availability of trained health-care workers—with red heart and happy baby flags flying over their homes—enhanced the credibility of the ORT program and provided another source of information for mothers who required additional assistance.

Monitoring Program Performance.   Another mistake marketing communicators sometimes commit is failing to monitor communication programs to determine whether they are working as originally intended. Project directors in Honduras and Gambia avoided this mistake by performing ongoing research to ensure that the programs were accomplishing their objectives. This periodic monitoring identified several problems that were quickly corrected. The ultimate results were, as a result of the midcourse corrections, much more effective than they otherwise would have been.

Summary

This chapter provides an aerial view of the "forest" as a prelude to subsequent chapters' in-depth, ground-level analysis of specific "trees"—that is, components of the promotion mix. Two case histories, one from the private sector and the other from the public sector, are presented to show how organizations plan and integrate various marketing communications techniques and promotion management tools to achieve marketing objectives.

The example of Du Pont's Stainmaster^{cm} carpeting illustrates how a historically business-to-business oriented company was able to break out of the commodity trap it confronted in the early 1980s by introducing an innovative new carpeting. Du Pont's creative use of television advertising, point-of-purchase displays, and direct mail created consumer pull for Stainmaster^{cm}, while its use of attractive dealer incentives accomplished the necessary trade push. All in all, this integrated marketing communications program resulted in unprecedented levels of consumer brand awareness in this product category and in a substantial increase in Du Pont's market share.

The remainder of the chapter describes a program developed by the U.S. Agency for International Development to combat diarrheal dehydration in Honduras and Gambia. This program is an outstanding example of how conventional marketing practices can be applied to not-for-profit situations. The presentation centers on the six major steps of the promotion management process as they apply to this major world problem: situation analysis, marketing objectives, promotion budget, integration and coordination of program elements, promotion management program, and evaluation and control.

Discussion Questions

1. Why does the situation analysis represent a critical first step in the process of developing a marketing communications program?

2. Analyze the two television commercials that were used in introducing Stainmaster^{cm} carpeting (see Figures 10.1 and 10.2). Specifically, explain what each ad attempts to convey and why each ad is or is not effective. Use concepts from Chapter 4 (e.g., stages of the CIP process) and Chapter 5 (e.g., ELM and theory of reasoned action) as formal grounding for your response.

3. In your own words, describe what a commodity product is. From the marketer's perspective, explain why it is undesirable to be involved in marketing a commodity product.

4. Analyze Du Pont's swizzle-stick promotion. Using concepts from Chapter 4, explain why this promotion probably was effective. Also, comment on the following statement by someone who is critical of point-of-purchase displays: "The 'Stainmaster^{cm}' display was a waste; it simply duplicated what consumers already learned from Du Pont's television advertising."

5. What objectives would the direct-mail piece shown in Figure 10.3 accomplish that television advertising and point-of-purchase displays could not?

6. What was the importance of using the "red heart" theme in Honduras and the "happy baby" theme in Gambia as symbols of the ORT programs?

7. The Academy for Educational Development, the chief consultant to the U.S. Agency for International Development in the ORT program, characterized their task as one of changing mothers' behavior rather than attitudes. On the other hand, marketers of conventional products frequently place their promotional emphasis on creating favorable images for their brands. How can you account for this apparent contrast in communication objectives?

8. It could be argued that the communications task in, say, Gambia was simpler than the promotional task faced by marketers of conventional products such as shampoo and personal computers. Take a position on this point and thoroughly support your position.

9. The communications program in Gambia included a giveaway contest in which mothers could receive a prize by demonstrating an ability to mix the salt, sugar, and water solution correctly. Winners then became eligible to win a bigger prize in a drawing. Moreover, there was a community prize each week for the village that turned out the most mothers for the contest. With reference to material presented in Part 2 of the text, what are the social-psychological principles that would justify the use of these promotional techniques?

Exercises

1. Analyze current Stainmaster^cm advertising and visit a Stainmaster^cm dealer to determine the more recent marketing communications efforts that are being used to promote this brand. Analyze their effectiveness.

2. Evaluate competitive brands of stain-resistant carpeting and compare their marketing communications programs with the Stainmaster^cm program.

3. Choose any not-for-profit issue or program that interests you and analyze the marketing communications program that is being used to market (or perhaps de-market) greater (or less) consumption of the behavior in question.

PART 4

Media Advertising

Part 4 contains four chapters on media advertising. **Chapter 11** first provides an overview of advertising and its economic and social aspects. Discussion then turns to managerial aspects of advertising. After describing the overall advertising-management process, detailed discussions are devoted to the first two aspects of advertising management: objective setting and budgeting.

Chapter 12 provides in-depth treatment of the creative-strategy aspect of the advertising-management process. Topics covered include requirements for effective advertising messages, advertising planning, means-end chains and MECCAS models, creative message strategies, and corporate image/issue advertising.

Media strategy is the focus of **Chapter 13.** The chapter provides thorough discussions of the four major activities involved in media strategy: target-audience selection, objective specification, media and vehicle selection, and media-buying activities. The chapter also provides analyses of five major advertising media: television, radio, magazines, newspapers, and outdoor.

The last chapter in Part 4, **Chapter 14,** deals with measuring advertising effectiveness. The chapter describes four general categories of advertising-research methods: measures of advertising exposure, awareness, persuasion, and action. Research methods that are widely used by advertising practitioners are explained in this chapter.

Advertising Management Overview

ADVERTISING SPENDING AT GENERAL MOTORS CORPORATION

or nearly 50 years General Motors Corporation (GMC) was the dominant automaker in the world. It held over 50 percent of the market share in the United States and made vast profits year after year. Then along came the energy crisis in the early 1970s that was followed by a shift in American preferences toward smaller cars and a dramatic increase in the sales of imported automobiles from Japan. Unable or unwilling to compete on the basis of price and quality, GMC watched its market share erode and profits decline. While still holding the largest market share in the United States, GMC has been forced to become a more efficient manufacturer and a more sophisticated marketer.

In an attempt to revive the images of its cars, GMC made the biggest advertising investment in its history by spending over $90 million to launch three new cars in 1988. The Oldsmobile division spent approximately $50 million to introduce its new Cutlass Supreme; Pontiac's spending for the Grand Prix topped $30 million; and Buick invested over $10 million to advertise the sporty Reatta.

The advertising campaign for the Cutlass Supreme emphasized styling and performance. Pontiac used the "Car of the Year" award from *Motor Trend* magazine as the cornerstone for its Grand Prix campaign. The advertising stressed road performance in an effort to attract young, educated consumers who often prefer imported cars over domestic models. Buick's Reatta, targeted for older consumers who want both sporti-ness and comfort in an automobile, used the advertising theme: "Go ahead. You de-serve it."

At the time of this writing, it is too early to predict how successful these advertis-ing campaigns will be. One thing is certain, however: Lack of success will not be due to lack of trying. GMC may never again be the dominant automaker it once was, but it knows now more than ever how important advertising is for bolstering a sagging cor-porate image.[1]■

Advertising is a complex social and economic phenomenon and a stra-tegically important sphere of managerial decision making. The opening vi-gnette suggests that advertising will play an important role in GMC's future success. While other business decisions, such as making a commitment to product quality, will be even more important to GMC's performance, adver-tising will play a major role in enhancing the company's image and encour-aging consumers to once again perceive GMC as a maker of high-quality, exciting automobiles.

In this first of four advertising chapters, initial discussion focuses on the *social and economic dimensions* of advertising. This introductory material is im-portant to a full understanding of the role of advertising in society. It also prepares one to intelligently evaluate much of the criticism that advertising often receives. As will be pointed out, advertising certainly is not without fault, yet much of the criticism leveled against advertising is without merit.

The remaining discussion concentrates on *managerial considerations* related to advertising. The bulk of the presentation focuses on two advertising man-agement tasks: specifying the motives and means for advertising (i.e., estab-lishing advertising objectives and setting budgets).

Economic and Social Aspects of Advertising

Because we are surrounded by advertising, nearly everyone has definite impressions and feelings about how advertising works and how it may or may not serve the economy and society. Before discussing the economic and social implications of advertising, it will be useful to specify clearly what advertising is and examine the functions it performs.

Advertising is "paid, nonpersonal communication through various media by business firms, nonprofit organizations, and individuals who are in some

---

1. Information and statistics are based on Raymond Serafin and Patricia Strnad, "In High Gear," *Advertising Age,* January 25, 1988, p. 12.

way identified in the advertising message and who hope to inform or persuade members of a particular audience."[2]

Advertising has four relatively distinct characteristics in comparison with the other tools of promotion management:[3]

1. *Public presentation.* Advertising is massive and public in nature; it is out where everyone can see it.

2. *Pervasiveness.* Advertising is nearly omnipresent; it seems to be everywhere all the time.

3. *Amplified expressiveness.* Through its utilization of music, dramatic visualizations, and creative expressiveness, advertising dramatizes and sometimes exaggerates product offerings.

4. *Impersonality.* Advertising is a relatively impersonal form of communication because it is transmitted via mass media and not person to person.

Advertising Expenditures and Functions

In its most basic sense, advertising is an economic investment, an investment regarded very favorably by numerous businesses and not-for-profit organizations. Advertising expenditures in the United States approached $110 billion in 1987.[4] U.S. companies are fully committed to heavy advertising; indeed, in 1986 U.S. companies spent more on advertising than did 66 other nations combined. The biggest spenders following the United States were Japan ($18.3 billion), the United Kingdom ($8.2 billion), West Germany ($8.1 billion), Canada ($4.8 billion), and France ($4.5 billion). The United States averaged $424.07 in per-capita advertising spending compared to an average for all countries of $51.43, which is less than 15 percent of the U.S. average.[5]

In fact, the top 100 U.S. advertisers spent more on advertising ($28.4 billion) than did all the advertisers in any other country.[6] Table 11.1 presents these top 100 advertisers, their individual rankings, and total advertising expenditures. Note that Philip Morris Companies is ranked number one with advertising expenditures in 1987 exceeding $1.5 billion! Procter & Gamble is number two, having spent nearly $1.4 billion on advertising in 1987. Interestingly, this is the first time in 24 years that P&G was not the number one advertising spender. Even the U.S. government had advertising expenditures ex-

2. S. Watson Dunn and Arnold M. Barban, *Advertising: Its Role in Modern Marketing,* 6th ed. (Hinsdale, IL: The Dryden Press, 1978), p. 7.
3. Sidney J. Levy, *Promotional Behavior* (Glenview, IL: Scott, Foresman and Company, 1971), pp. 64, 65.
4. "Ad Spending Rises 7.4%," *Advertising Age,* June 13, 1988, p. 64.
5. Lena Vanier, "U.S. Ad Spending Double All Other Nations Combined," *Advertising Age,* May 16, 1988, p. 36.
6. R. Craig Endicott, "Philip Morris Unseats P&G as Top Advertising Spender," *Advertising Age,* September 28, 1988, p. 1.

TABLE 11.1

The 100 Leading U.S. Advertisers, 1987 (dollars in thousands)

100 Leading National Advertisers

Rank	Advertiser	Ad spending	Rank	Advertiser	Ad spending	Rank	Advertiser	Ad spending
1	Philip Morris Cos.	$1,557.8	35	Schering-Plough Corp.	$250.2	69	Hershey Foods Corp.	$122.8
2	Procter & Gamble Co.	1,386.7	36	Walt Disney Co.	249.8	70	Seagram Co.	122.3
3	General Motors Corp.	1,024.9	37	Honda Motor Co.	245.4	71	Cosmair Inc.	117.2
4	Sears, Roebuck & Co.	886.5	38	H.J. Heinz Co.	245.3	72	CPC International	115.3
5	RJR Nabisco	839.6	39	IBM Corp.	240.8	73	Kroger Co.	115.3
6	PepsiCo Inc.	704.0	40	Grand Metropolitan PLC	231.6	74	Loews Corp.	115.2
7	Eastman Kodak Co.	658.2	41	Campbell Soup Co.	230.7	75	Dr Pepper/Seven-Up	114.1
8	McDonald's Corp.	649.5	42	Tandy Corp.	225.1	76	Subaru of America	113.2
9	Ford Motor Co.	639.5	43	BCI Holdings Corp.	223.2	77	Wm. Wrigley Jr. Co.	112.5
10	Anheuser-Busch Cos.	635.1	44	American Express Co.	212.5	78	Prudential Insurance Co.	111.3
11	K mart Corp.	631.8	45	Time Inc.	196.6	79	Warner Communications	110.4
12	Unilever NV/PLC	580.7	46	Pfizer Inc.	182.1	80	Delta Air Lines	108.6
13	General Mills	572.2	47	Nissan Motor Co.	181.4	81	Wendy's International	107.6
14	Chrysler Corp.	568.7	48	IC Industries	169.3	82	Philips NV	107.2
15	Warner-Lambert Co.	558.1	49	Volkswagen AG	167.3	83	B.A.T. Industries PLC	105.3
16	AT&T	531.0	50	Mobil Corp.	166.3	84	Daimler-Benz AG	105.0
17	Kellogg Co.	524.9	51	Revlon Group	165.2	85	Gillette Co.	103.8
18	J.C. Penney Co.	513.5	52	Hyundai Group	164.3	86	Stroh Brewery Co.	102.9
19	Pillsbury Co.	473.9	53	U. S. Dairy Associations	161.4	87	Clorox Co.	102.1
20	Johnson & Johnson	459.3	54	Beecham Group PLC	153.3	88	BMW AG	99.5
21	Ralston Purina Co.	436.6	55	AMR Corp.	152.6	89	S.C. Johnson & Son	96.4
22	Kraft Inc.	400.7	56	Mazda Motor Corp.	151.9	90	Goodyear Tire & Rubber Co.	95.0
23	American Home Products	390.4	57	American Brands	151.4	91	Hallmark Cards	93.9
24	Mars Inc.	378.6	58	ITT Corp.	151.3	92	E&J Gallo Winery	93.6
25	Coca-Cola Co.	364.7	59	Du Pont Co.	149.7	93	MCA Inc.	91.4
26	Bristol-Myers Co.	358.9	60	Bayer AG	145.4	94	Marriott Corp.	88.5
27	Quaker Oats Co.	344.4	61	Adolph Coors Co.	144.7	95	Franklin Mint	86.6
28	Nestle SA	340.8	62	Nynex Corp.	142.8	96	Southland Corp.	86.1
29	U.S. Government	311.3	63	Bell Atlantic Corp.	138.6	97	United Biscuits (Holdings)	84.8
30	Colgate-Palmolive Co.	279.8	64	UAL Corp.	137.8	98	Borden Inc.	84.7
31	Sara Lee Corp.	278.1	65	Dow Chemical Co.	135.7	99	Monsanto Co.	84.7
32	General Electric Co.	272.6	66	Noxell Corp.	134.9	100	Ameritech	83.4
33	Toyota Motor Corp.	257.7	67	Hasbro Inc.	134.3			
34	American Cyanamid	250.4	68	Texas Air Corp.	124.3		**Note:** Dollars are in millions.	

Source: Reprinted with permission from the September 28, 1988 issue of *Advertising Age*, p. 1. Copyright 1988 by Crain Communications, Inc.

ceeding $300 million, making it the twenty-ninth leading advertiser in 1987. Nearly two-thirds of the U.S. government's advertising effort goes to military recruiting, while the remainder is allocated among the Postal Service, Amtrak rail services, the U.S. Mint (e.g., commemorative coins), AIDS awareness, and so forth.

Businesses would not make the massive investments shown in Table 11.1 unless advertising performed useful functions. Consider the incredible results advertising has generated for a product like Marlboro cigarettes. At a time when American consumers are reducing their consumption of cigarettes, with annual sales declining at a rate of 1.5 to 2 percent annually, Marlboro sales have grown more than 3 percent per year since 1980. This one product accounts for 28 percent of Philip Morris' $25 billion in revenues and earns $2 billion operating profit on sales of $7 billion. Approximately one out of every four packs of cigarettes consumed in the United States is Marlboro; the brand is also experiencing great growth outside the United States.[7] It goes without saying that Marlboro's cowboy advertising campaign is largely responsible for its success.[8]

In general, advertising is recognized as performing the following five *functions:* (1) informing, (2) persuading, (3) reminding, (4) adding value, and (5) assisting other company efforts.[9]

Informing. Advertising makes consumers aware of new products, informs them about specific brands, and educates them about particular product features and benefits. Because advertising is an *efficient form of communication* (i.e., it is capable of reaching mass audiences at a relatively low cost per contact), it facilitates the introduction of new products and increases demand for existing products.

Persuading. Effective advertising persuades customers to try advertised products. Sometimes the persuasion takes the form of influencing *primary demand,* that is, creating demand for an entire product category. More frequently, advertising attempts to build *secondary demand,* that is, demand for a specific company's brand.

Reminding. Advertising also keeps a company's brand fresh in the consumer's memory. When a need arises that is related to the advertised product, past advertising impact makes it possible that the advertiser's brand will come to the consumer's mind as a purchase candidate.

7. Jeffrey A. Trachtenberg, "Here's One Tough Cowboy," *Forbes,* February 9, 1987, p. 108.
8. For an informative and sobering report on the magnitude and strategic direction of cigarette advertising, see Ronald M. Davis, "Current Trends in Cigarette Advertising and Marketing," *The New England Journal of Medicine,* vol. 316 (March 19, 1987), pp. 725–732.
9. These functions are similar to those identified by the noted advertising pioneer James Webb Young. See, for example, "What Is Advertising, What Does It Do," *Advertising Age,* November 21, 1973, p. 12.

Adding Value.   Advertising adds value to products and specific brands by influencing consumers' perceptions. Effective advertising causes brands to be viewed as more elegant, more stylish, more prestigious, and perhaps superior to competitive offerings.

Advertisers use a variety of procedures to add value to their brands. One interesting application is **vicarious modeling,** which attempts to influence consumers' perceptions and behaviors by having them observe the actions of others (e.g., models in advertisements) and the consequences of the models' behavior.[10] For example, in a magazine-advertising effort to increase long-distance phone calls to other countries, AT&T portrayed a series of touching personal situations in which people were reunited by phone. Figure 11.1 shows one of the ads in this campaign—"Whisper in her ear again. Call France." Other vicariously modeled situations include an American soccer coach talking with a young German boy that he coached; a Japanese man calling his mother in Japan to share his appreciation for her wisdom and advice; and an elderly British gentleman calling his childhood sweetheart in London. Of course, AT&T's campaign is intended to encourage the consumer to call an old friend or relative who lives abroad in order to rekindle the closeness and friendship.

Assisting Other Company Efforts.   Advertising is just one member of the promotion team. The advertising player is at times a "scorer" who accomplishes goals by itself. At other times advertising's primary role is that of an "assister" who facilitates other company efforts in the marketing communications process. For example, advertising may be used as *a vehicle for delivering sales promotions.* That is, advertisements are the physical vehicles for delivering coupons and sweepstakes and attracting attention to these sales promotion tools.

Another crucial role of advertising is to *assist sales representatives.* Advertising presells a company's products and provides salespeople with valuable introductions prior to their personal contact with prospective customers. Sales effort, time, and costs are reduced because less time is required to inform prospects about product features and benefits. Moreover, advertising legitimizes or makes more credible the sales representative's claims.[11]

Advertising also *enhances the results of other marketing communications.* For example, consumers can identify product packages in the store and recognize the value of a product more easily after having seen it advertised on television or in a magazine.

10. For further discussion of the procedures and principles underlying vicarious modeling, see Walter R. Nord and J. Paul Peter, "A Behavior Modification Perspective on Marketing," *Journal of Marketing,* vol. 44 (Spring 1980), pp. 36–47.
11. The synergism between advertising and personal selling is not always a one-way flow from advertising to personal selling. In fact, one study has demonstrated a reverse situation, in which personal sales calls sometimes pave the way for advertising. See William R. Swinyard and Michael L. Ray, "Advertising-Selling Interactions: An Attribution Theory Experiment," *Journal of Marketing Research,* vol. 14 (November 1977), pp. 509–516.

Illustration of Vicarious Modeling   FIGURE 11.1

Source: Courtesy AT&T.

TABLE 11.2   Two Schools of Thought on Advertising's Role in the Economy

	Advertising = Market Power	Advertising = Information
Advertising	Advertising affects consumer preferences and tastes, changes product attributes, and differentiates the product from competitive offerings.	Advertising informs consumers about product attributes and does not change the way they value those attributes.
Consumer-Buying Behavior	Consumers become brand loyal, less price sensitive, and perceive fewer substitutes for advertised brands.	Consumers become more price sensitive and buy best "value." Only the relationship between price and quality affects elasticity for a given product.
Barriers to Entry	Potential entrants must overcome established brand loyalty and spend relatively more on advertising.	Advertising makes entry possible for new brands because it can communicate product attributes to consumers.
Industry Structure and Market Power	Firms are insulated from market competition and potential rivals; concentration increases, leaving firms with more discretionary power.	Consumers can compare competitive offerings easily and competitive rivalry is increased. Efficient firms remain, and as the inefficient leave, new entrants appear; the effect on concentration is ambiguous.
Market Conduct	Firms can charge higher prices and are not as likely to compete on quality or price dimensions. Innovation may be reduced.	More-informed consumers put pressures on firms to lower prices and improve quality. Innovation is facilitated via new entrants.
Market Performance	High prices and excessive profits accrue to advertisers and give them even more incentive to advertise their products. Output is restricted compared to conditions of perfect competition.	Industry prices are decreased. The effect on profits due to increased competition and increased efficiency is ambiguous.

Source: Paul W. Farris and Mark S. Albion, "The Impact of Advertising on the Price of Consumer Products," *Journal of Marketing,* vol. 44, Summer 1980, p. 18.

Advertising's Economic Role

There are two divergent schools of thought on advertising's economic role: *advertising = market power* versus *advertising = information*. Table 11.2 summarizes these two perspectives.[12] You should study this table prior to reading the detailed comments that follow describing each school of thought.

Advertising = Market Power. The view that advertising yields market power is based on the major premise that advertising is able to *differentiate physically homogeneous products*. It follows from this assumption that ad-

---

12. The following discussion follows closely the excellent review in Paul W. Farris and Mark S. Albion, "The Impact of Advertising on the Price of Consumer Products," *Journal of Marketing,* vol. 44 (Summer 1980), pp. 17–35.

vertising will foster brand loyalty, thereby encouraging customers to be less price sensitive than they would be in the absence of advertising. In turn, entry barriers are increased; in order to enter an industry, new firms must spend relatively more (than established firms) on advertising to overcome existing brand-loyalty patterns. It follows that established firms are relatively insulated from potential rivals and have discretionary power to increase prices and influence the market in other ways. According to the advertising = market power position, the result is that firms charge higher prices than they would in the absence of advertising and are able to earn excessive profits.

Advertising = Information.　The advertising-equals-information perspective provides an antithesis to the market-power viewpoint. The information school purports that by informing consumers about product attributes and benefits, advertising increases consumers' price sensitivity and their ability to obtain the best value. Barriers to entry for prospective new firms are reduced because advertising enables these new firms to communicate product attributes and advantages to consumers.

According to the information perspective, advertising allows consumers to easily compare competitive offerings, which leads to increased competitive rivalry. Product innovation is facilitated via new entrants, and quality is improved. Furthermore, prices are forced downward because consumers, informed by advertising, put pressure on firms to lower prices.

A Synthesis.　The world is never as simple and straightforward as these two antithetical views of advertising would lead us to believe. Neither view is entirely correct or adequate by itself. Critics of the advertising = market power view contend that a number of factors other than advertising (e.g., superior product quality, better packaging, and better distribution) also account for brand loyalty and price insensitivity.[13] Advertising is not the sole marketing force responsible for a firm's market power.

Similarly, advertising does not possess all the virtues that advocates of the advertising = information school would lead us to believe. Critics of this view contend that advertising goes beyond merely providing consumers with information; in fact, it influences consumers' relative preferences for different products attributes. It follows from this contention that advertising may create the same undesirable consequences (i.e., market concentration, price insensitivity, entry barriers, etc.) claimed by the advertising = market power proponents.[14]

In sum, advertising's macroeconomic role is neither all good nor all bad. The exact role varies from situation to situation, and generalities are meaningless. On balance, advertising has negative economic effects (as claimed by the market-power school) to the extent that only one or a few advertisers in a given

13. For more discussion, see ibid., p. 19.
14. For more discussion, see ibid., p. 20.

product-market situation possess differential advantages over competitors in terms of advertising spending ability or effectiveness. However, when any one competitor's advertising efforts can be countervailed by other advertising, the positive economic effects of advertising (as claimed by the information school) outweigh the negative.[15]

Advertising's Social Role

The role of advertising in society has been debated for centuries. Advertising is claimed by its practitioners to be largely responsible for much of what is good in life and is criticized by its opponents as being responsible for the bad. Following is a succinct yet elegant account of why advertising is so fiercely criticized:

> As the voice of technology, [advertising] is associated with many dissatisfactions of the industrial state. As the voice of mass culture it invites intellectual attack. And as the most visible form of capitalism it has served as nothing less than a lightning-rod for social criticism.[16]

A variety of specific criticisms have been leveled against advertising. Because the issues are complex, it is impossible in this chapter to treat each criticism in great detail. The purpose of this discussion is merely to introduce the basic issues. [17] The following criticisms are illustrative rather than exhaustive.

Advertising Is Deceptive.   As discussed in Chapter 9, deception is said to occur when an advertisement falsely represents a product and consumers believe the false representation. Is advertising deceptive according to this general definition? Some advertising *is* deceptive—the existence of governmental regulation and industry self-regulation attests to this fact. It would be very naive, however, to assume that all or most of advertising is deceptive. The advertising industry is not much different from other institutions in a pluralistic society. Lying, cheating, and outright fraud are universal, occurring at the highest levels of government (e.g., Watergate) and in the most basic human relationships (e.g., husbands and wives). Advertising is not without sin, but neither does it hold a monopoly on sin.

15. Kent M. Lancaster and Gordon E. Miracle, "How Advertising Can Have Largely Anticompetitive Effects in One Sector But Largely Procompetitive Effects in Another," University of Illinois Working Paper No. 7, Urbana, IL, November 1979.
16. Ronald Berman, "Advertising and Social Change," *Advertising Age*, April 30, 1980, p. 24.
17. The interested reader is encouraged to review the following three articles for an extremely thorough, insightful, and provocative debate over the social role of advertising in American society. Richard W. Pollay, "The Distorted Mirror: Reflections on the Unintended Consequences of Advertising," *Journal of Marketing*, vol. 50 (April 1986), pp. 18–36; Morris B. Holbrook, "Mirror, Mirror, on the Wall, What's Unfair in the Reflections of Advertising?" *Journal of Marketing*, vol. 51 (July 1987), pp. 95–103; Richard W. Pollay, "On the Value of Reflections on the Values in 'The Distorted Mirror'," *Journal of Marketing*, vol. 51 (July 1987), pp. 104–109. Professors Pollay and Holbrook present alternative views of whether advertising is a "mirror" that merely reflects societal attitudes and values or a "distorted mirror" that is responsible for unintended and undesirable social consequences.

Advertising Is Manipulative.   The criticism of manipulation asserts that advertising has the power to influence people to behave in certain ways that they would not otherwise were it not for advertising. Taken to the extreme, this suggests that advertising is capable of moving people against their own free wills. What psychological principles would account for such power to manipulate? As you will recall from Chapter 6, the evidence certainly does not support subliminal advertising, which has provided advertising critics with the most provocative explanation underlying the claim of manipulation.

In general, the contention that advertising manipulates is without substance. Undeniably, advertising does attempt to persuade consumers to purchase particular products and brands. But persuasion and manipulation are not the same thing. Persuasion is a legitimate form of human interaction that all individuals and institutions in society perform.

Advertising Is Offensive and in Bad Taste.   Advertising critics contend that much advertising is insulting to human intelligence, is vulgar, and is generally offensive to the tastes of many consumers. Several grounds exist for this criticism: (1) inane commercials of the "ring around the collar" genre, (2) sexual explicitness or innuendo in all forms of advertisements, (3) television commercials that advertise unpleasant products (hemorrhoid treatments, feminine-hygiene products, etc.), and (4) repetitious usage of the same advertisements *ad infinitum, ad nauseam.*

Undeniably, much advertising *is* disgusting and offensive. Yet, the same can be said for all forms of mass media presentations. For example, many network television programs verge on the idiotic, and theater movies are often filled with inordinate amounts of sex and violence.

This certainly is not to excuse advertising for its excesses. Recently, for example, criticism has been leveled against advertising for the increased use of male eroticism. Men are now portrayed as passive sex objects in the same fashion that women have been treated (e.g., in Calvin Klein ads).[18] While this trend is disturbing to some, in advertising's defense it is likely that many consumers are not at all offended but rather enjoy this new form of advertising.[19]

Advertising Creates and Perpetuates Stereotypes.   The contention at the root of this criticism is that advertising tends to portray certain groups in very narrow and predictable fashion: Blacks and other minorities are portrayed disproportionately often in working-class roles rather than in the full range of positions they actually occupy; women are too often stereotyped as housewives or as sex objects; and senior citizens are frequently characterized as feeble and forgetful people.

Advertising *is guilty* of perpetuating stereotypes. However, it would be unfair to blame advertising for *creating* these stereotypes, which, in fact, are

18. Andrew Sullivan, "Flogging Underwear," *The New Republic,* January 18, 1988, pp. 20–24.
19. Ibid., p. 24.

FOCUS ON PROMOTION

College Students' Opinions of Advertising

Most everyone has a definite opinion about advertising, and views can vary widely. Some see advertising as a valuable social and economic force, while others view it in a much less positive light. What do college marketing students think about advertising?

This question was put to the test recently. An opinion survey was distributed to over 1,500 marketing students in colleges and universities around the country. Respondents rated seven statements on a seven-point scale ranging from "strongly agree to "strongly disagree." The survey included three statements about advertising's social implications and four statements about its economic effects:

Statements about Advertising's Social Implications

1. Most advertising insults the intelligence of the average consumer.
2. Advertising often persuades people to buy things they shouldn't buy.
3. In general, advertisements present a true picture of the product being advertised.

Statements about Advertising's Economic Effects

4. Advertising is essential.
5. In general, advertising results in lower prices.
6. Advertising helps raise our standard of living.
7. Advertising results in better products for the public.

Continued

perpetuated by all elements in society. Spreading the blame does not make advertising any better, but it does show that advertising is probably not any worse than the rest of society.

People Buy Things They Do Not Really Need.   A frequently cited criticism suggests that advertising causes people to buy items or services that they do not need. This criticism is a value-laden judgment. Do you need a new blouse or shirt? Do you need a college education? Who is to say what you or anyone else needs? Although advertising most assuredly influences consumer tastes and encourages people to undertake purchases they may not otherwise make, it is difficult to determine what consumers need or do not need.

Here is what the survey revealed about marketing students' opinions toward advertising:

Statement	Agree	Neither Agree or Disagree	Disagree
1	42.6%	16.6%	40.8%
2	61.5	14.1	24.4
3	31.0	14.9	54.1
4	94.8	2.4	2.8
5	19.8	20.6	59.6
6	40.6	38.0	21.4
7	53.9	24.1	22.0

Regarding the social implications of advertising, (statements 1 through 3), marketing students are about evenly mixed on the matter of whether advertising insults their intelligence. Most (61.5 percent) agree that advertising is persuasive, while the majority (54.1 percent) do not think that advertising presents a true picture about advertised products. In terms of advertising's economic effects (statements 4 through 7), marketing students around the country overwhelmingly agree (94.8 percent) that advertising is essential. Yet nearly 60 percent do not believe that advertising lowers prices. A majority (53.9 percent) agree that advertising leads to better products, but only about 41 percent think that advertising raises the standard of living.

These results reveal that even a fairly homogeneous group like marketing students holds a diversity of opinions about the negative and positive consequences of advertising. It is little wonder that society at large is even more divided.[20] ∎

Advertising Plays upon People's Fears and Insecurities. Some advertisements appeal to the negative consequences of not buying a product—rejection by members of the opposite sex, bad breath, failure to have provided for the family if one should die without proper insurance coverage, etc. Some advertisers must certainly plead guilty to this charge. However, once again, advertising possesses no monopoly on this transgression.

---

20. This study was performed by J. Craig Andrews, "Dimensionality of Beliefs about Advertising," *Journal of Advertising*, vol. 18, no. 1 (1989), pp. 26–35.

In Sum. The institution of advertising is certainly not free of criticism. What should be clear, however, is that advertising reflects the rest of society, and any indictment of advertising probably applies to society at large. Responsible advertising practitioners, knowing that their practice is particularly susceptible to criticism, have a vested interest in producing legitimate advertisements. Advertising, when done honestly and ethically, can serve society well.

The Advertising-Management Process

A completed advertisement, such as a television commercial or magazine ad, often results from the efforts of various research, production, creative, media, and other services. Most national and regional advertisements and some local advertisements reflect the collective work of various advertising services and institutions.

Four major groups are involved in the total advertising process: (1) companies and other organizations that advertise (e.g., General Motors Corporation, the U.S. Government), (2) advertising agencies (e.g., Ogilvy and Mather, J. Walter Thompson, and Tokyo-based Dentsu), (3) advertising production companies (i.e., independent businesses that photograph, film, and otherwise produce advertisements), and (4) advertising media (newspapers, television, etc.).

Although the advertising industry involves a number of collective efforts, the following discussion is restricted to the first group, the advertisers themselves.

The discussion of the advertising-management process is based on the framework in Figure 11.2. The figure shows that advertising strategy extends from a company's overall *corporate and marketing strategies. Advertising strategy* consists of objective setting (motives), budgeting (means), message strategy, and media strategy. *Strategy implementation* represents the execution of advertising messages in specific media. *Control activities* are undertaken to determine whether advertising results have met preestablished objectives and to determine whether corrective action is necessary.

Corporate and Marketing Strategies

Corporate strategy is set by top management and represents the long-range (typically three to five years) objectives, plans, and budgets for all corporate units and departments. Corporate strategy (1) is formulated in view of the enterprise's inherent *strengths* and *weaknesses* and (2) is based on analyses of economic, competitive, social, and other pertinent factors that represent *opportunities* and *threats* for a business enterprise.

For example, in the chapter's opening vignette regarding GMC's advertising campaigns for three 1988 automobiles, corporate leaders apparently consid-

ered GMC's biggest weakness to be a bad corporate image. The company's major strength—tremendous financial wherewithal—permitted it to invest over $90 million in advertising the Cutlass Supreme, Grand Prix, and Reatta. The major opportunity facing GMC in 1988 was the chance to greatly enhance the company's sagging image and to establish its products as competitive with imported automobiles. Japanese, European, and domestic competition represent the most significant threat confronting GMC.

Marketing strategy, an extension of corporate strategy, involves the plans, budgets, and controls needed to direct a firm's product, promotion, distribution, and pricing activities. The purpose of the marketing strategy is to coordinate the various marketing-mix elements and to ensure that marketing efforts are in line with corporate strategy. The Buick Reatta, for example, is targeted to older baby-boomers and the upscale end of the mature market. It combines sportiness with comfort and roominess and is priced around $25,000.

Advertising Strategy

Advertising strategy is guided by corporate and marketing strategies. These more general strategies determine how much can be invested in advertising, at what markets advertising efforts need to be directed, how advertising must be coordinated with other marketing elements, and to some degree, how advertising is to be executed.

An advertising campaign that was introduced by Pepsi-Cola in 1984 and continues today illustrates these strategic relations.[21] Corporate officers at Pepsi-Cola dedicated the company to tapping the youth market in a fashion unprecedented in the soft-drink industry. In keeping with this marketing reorientation, Pepsi-Cola moved away from its use over the past half-century of jingles and image-oriented campaigns ("Join the Pepsi generation," "Have a Pepsi day") to a new campaign ("Pepsi, the choice of a new generation") that conveyed a young, contemporary theme. In line with this theme, Pepsi-Cola invested millions of dollars to identify itself with Michael Jackson. Pepsi has invested well over $100 million in advertising since this campaign began.

Advertising strategy involves four major activities (see Figure 11.2). The first two, *objective setting* and *budgeting*, are described later in this chapter. Pepsi-Cola's objective, for example, was to create a contemporary image that appealed to youth. The company has budgeted millions of dollars to achieve this general objective. General Motors invested over $90 million in advertising the Cutlass Supreme, Grand Prix, and Reatta. A major motivation underlying GMC's ad campaigns was to present the corporation to consumers as a company capable of manufacturing sporty, high-performance automobiles.

A third aspect of advertising strategy is *message strategy*. The strategy underlying GMC's 1988 advertising campaign for the Pontiac Grand Prix was to take advantage of *Motor Trend's* "Car of the Year" award by presenting the Grand Prix as a sporty, high-performance automobile. Message strategy is treated fully in the following chapter.

Media strategy, a final aspect of advertising strategy, involves the selection of media categories and specific vehicles to deliver advertising messages. GMC's campaigns for the Cutlass Supreme, Grand Prix, and Reatta all involved heavy advertising on television, radio, and in magazines. Chapter 13 covers media strategy in detail.

Strategy Implementation

Strategy implementation deals with the tactical, day-to-day activities that must be performed to carry out an advertising campaign. For example, whereas the decision to emphasize television over other media is a strategic choice, the selection of specific types of programs and times at which to air a commercial is a tactical, strategy-implementation matter. Chapter 12 (which deals with message strategy) and Chapter 13 (which discusses media strategy) touch on implementation issues.

21. The following discussion is based on various sources but borrows most heavily from Fred Danzig, "Pepsi-Cola Gambles on the Young," *Advertising Age,* March 5, 1984, pp. 3, 62.

Control Activities

Control activities are a critical aspect of advertising management for they ensure that objectives and plans are being accomplished. Control activities involve comparing actual results with intended or projected results. This often requires that baseline measures be taken before an advertising campaign begins (to determine, for example, what percentage of the target audience is aware of the brand name) and then afterwards to determine whether the objective was achieved. Because research is fundamental to advertising control, Chapter 14 is devoted exclusively to evaluating advertising effectiveness.

Setting Advertising Objectives

Advertising objectives are motives or goals that advertising efforts attempt to achieve. Setting objectives is advertising management's first task in formulating advertising strategy. Setting advertising objectives is possibly the most difficult task of advertising management, yet setting objectives provides the foundation for all remaining advertising decisions.[22]

There are three major reasons for setting advertising objectives:[23]

1. Advertising objectives are an *expression of management consensus*. The process of setting objectives literally forces top marketing and advertising management to agree upon the course advertising is to take for the following planning period as well as the tasks it is to accomplish for a product category or specific brand.

2. Objective setting *guides* the budgeting, message strategy, and media strategy aspects of advertising strategy (see Figure 11.2). The objectives determine how much money should be spent and provide guidelines for the kinds of message strategy and media choice needed to accomplish the objectives.

3. Advertising objectives provide *standards* against which results can be measured. As will be described in detail later, good objectives set precise, quantitative yardsticks of what advertising hopes to accomplish. Subsequent results can then be compared with these standards to determine whether the advertising accomplished what it was intended to do.

Types of Advertising Objectives

There are several categories of advertising objectives that guide subsequent advertising strategy. A convenient way of looking at these categories is in

22. Charles H. Patti and Charles F. Frazer, *Advertising: A Decision-Making Approach* (Hinsdale, IL: The Dryden Press, 1988), p. 236.
23. Ibid., pp. 237–239.

terms of the following journalistic-type questions: Who, What, Where, When, and How Often.[24]

Who? The most basic consideration underlying advertising-strategy formulation is the *choice of a target market*. Objectives related to the *who* question specify the target market in terms of demographics, lifestyle, or other characteristics that influence choice behavior. For example, GMC's Buick Reatta is aimed at older, upscale consumers who want both sportiness and comfort in an automobile.

What? The *what* question involves two categories of consideration: (1) *what emphasis* and (2) *what goals*. The *emphasis* issue relates to what product features or benefits need to be emphasized or what emotions need to be evoked when advertising a brand. The *goals* issue deals with what specific communication or sales goals need to be accomplished at the present stage in a brand's life cycle.

Advertising may be designed to accomplish several goals: (1) to make the target market aware of a new brand, (2) to facilitate consumer understanding of a brand's attributes and its benefits compared to competitive brands, (3) to enhance attitudes, (4) to influence purchase intentions, and (5) to encourage product trial. We will return to these *what-goal* issues shortly for more detailed discussion.

Where? When? How Often? Which geographic markets need to be emphasized, what months or seasons are best, and how often should the product be advertised are additional issues that need to be addressed when setting advertising objectives.

Although advertising practitioners must take all of the preceding categories into consideration when setting objectives, subsequent attention focuses exclusively on the *what-goal* category. The reason is that the other considerations are all situation specific, but the goal issue is relevant to all situations and brands.

In order to fully understand why and when certain goals are appropriate as advertising objectives, it is first necessary to examine how consumers respond to advertising.

Hierarchy-of-Effects Models

Advertising scholars have traditionally explained how advertising influences consumers and how consumers respond to advertising in terms of **hierarchy-of-effects models**. The hierarchy metaphor implies that for advertising to be

---

24. This formulation has its origins in a broadly similar scheme constructed by John R. Rossiter and Larry Percy, "Advertising Communication Models," Working Paper, N.S.W. Institute of Technology, Sydney, Australia, September 22, 1983.

successful it must move consumers from one level to the next, much in the same way that one climbs a ladder—one step and then the next until the ultimate goal point on the ladder is reached.

Although there are numerous hierarchy-of-effects models,[25] all are predicated on the idea that advertising moves people from an initial state of *unawareness* about a product/brand to a final stage of *purchasing* that product/brand. Intermediate stages in the hierarchy represent progressively closer steps to purchase. Consider the following hierarchy:

We can best understand exactly what each of these stages means by examining an actual advertisement. Consider the new ScorchGuard® iron depicted in Figure 11.3. When this product was first introduced to the market, consumers were initially *unaware* of its existence (some no doubt remain unaware to this day). The initial advertising imperative, therefore, was to make people *aware* of the ScorchGuard® brand name. However, mere awareness would not have been enough to get people to buy the ScorchGuard®. Advertising had to persuade consumers that the ScorchGuard® is somehow different and better than competitive brands of irons. The ad attempts to accomplish this by informing consumers that the ScorchGuard® beeps in eight seconds and then shuts off automatically to prevent scorching (*beliefs/knowledge*). These distinctive advantages are designed to create favorable *attitudes* toward the ScorchGuard® with the expectation that many consumers will be sufficiently impressed to want to buy this brand the next time they need a new iron (*pur-*

---

25. For thorough discussions see Thomas E. Barry, "The Development of the Hierarchy of Effects: An Historical Perspective," *Current Issues and Research in Advertising*, vol. 10, eds. James H. Leigh and Claude R. Martin, Jr. (1987), pp. 251–296 (Ann Arbor, MI, Division of Research, Graduate School of Business Administration, University of Michigan); Ivan L. Preston, "The Association Model of the Advertising Communication Process," *Journal of Advertising*, vol. 11, no. 2 (1982), pp. 3–15; and Ivan L. Preston and Esther Thorson, "Challenges to the Use of Hierarchy Models in Predicting Advertising Effectiveness," in *Proceedings of the 1983 Convention of the American Academy of Advertising*, ed. Donald W. Jugenheimer (Lawrence, KS: American Academy of Advertising, 1983).

FIGURE 11.3 **Illustration of the Role of Advertising in Moving Consumers through the Hierarchy-of-Effects Stages**

chase intention). This intention may eventually develop into an actual *purchase* of a ScorchGuard® iron.

Another, more economical way of describing the hierarchy of effects is accomplished with the use of three summary terms: cognition, affect, and conation. Although you have been introduced to these terms in Chapter 5, it may be helpful to review their meaning. *Cognition* refers to the consumer's knowledge and facts about a particular product or brand that are stored in memory. Cognition encompasses the stages of awareness and beliefs/knowledge in the preceding hierarchy. *Affect,* when used as a noun and not a verb, refers to feelings, or attitude in the hierarchy. *Conation* refers to striving for a product or brand. Purchase intentions and the actual purchase are elements of conation.

The Integrated Information-Response Model

The preceding traditional view of how advertising works has been widely criticized because it suggests there is a single response pattern that describes how advertising works. However, the pattern in the traditional hierarchy applies only in instances of *high-involvement behavior,* in which the purchase decision is important to the consumer and has significant risks associated with it. A more comprehensive model is needed to capture fully the diversity of consumer behavior in response to advertising.

The **integrated information-response model** (see Figure 11.4) provides the comprehensiveness that is needed.[26] The model takes its name from the idea that consumers integrate information from two sources—advertising and direct product-usage experience—in forming attitudes and purchase intentions toward products and brands.

It will be useful first to overview the model's general characteristics. Note that the model has five column headings: information source, information acceptance, cognitions, affect, and conation. Two *information sources* are available to the consumer: advertising and one's own direct experience in using a particular product/brand. *Information acceptance* (due to factors such as source credibility as discussed in Chapter 6) ranges between low and high levels. Extending from information acceptance are *cognitions,* which are shown in Figure 11.4 as either lower- or higher-order beliefs. Lower-order beliefs, which result from processing advertisements, represent the consumer's mere awareness or recognition that an advertiser has claimed that its brand possesses some feature or benefit. For example, having read the advertisement for the ScorchGuard® iron, you now know that it beeps in eight seconds and shuts off automatically. This knowledge is a lower- rather than higher-order belief because merely registering what an advertiser has said a product will do is not the same as ac-

26. Robert E. Smith and William R. Swinyard, "Information Response Models: An Integrated Approach," *Journal of Marketing,* vol. 46 (Winter 1982), pp. 81–93.

FIGURE 11.4   **Integrated Information-Response Model**

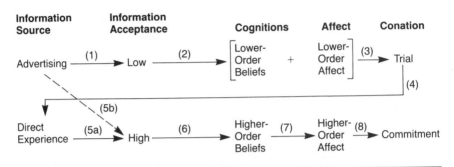

Detailed Sequence

Source: Adapted from Robert E. Smith and William R. Swinyard, "Information Response Models: An Integrated Approach," *Journal of Marketing*, Vol. 46, Winter 1982, p. 85. Adopted with permission from *Journal of Marketing*, published by the American Marketing Association.

tually experiencing the product doing what the advertisement said it will do.

Higher-order beliefs, which result from direct product-usage experience, represent the consumer's acceptance that a brand does in fact do (or fail to do) what the advertiser has claimed it will do. (If you used the ScorchGuard® and it performed exactly as Hamilton Beach, its maker, claimed, you then would *really believe* the product advantages—this is what is meant by higher-order belief.) *Affect* is also shown to be lower- or higher-order. Lower-order affect is little more than a favorable (or unfavorable) disposition toward a brand after having learned about it from, say, a magazine advertisement. For example, one consumer's response to learning about the ScorchGuard® iron might be "That's a great idea. With all the confusion in my house, I need a safe iron so I don't scorch good clothes or burn the house down." Higher-order affect, on the other hand, represents the consumer's actual feelings about a product after using it ("The ScorchGuard® is a fantastic iron. It's the easiest-to-use iron I've ever tried, and it's safe!"). Finally, *conation* ranges from a one-time trial purchase (as with an inexpensive packaged good) all the way to a commitment to regularly incorporate a product or brand into one's consumption lifestyle.

Having laid out the terminology of the integrated information-response model, we can now discuss the three patterns of consumer response to advertising that are implied by the model.

Pattern 1: Cognition → Affect → Commitment.   The pattern of cognition to affect to commitment is the traditional hierarchy-of-effects model described previously. This is shown in Figure 11.4 by the dashed arrow from advertising to high information acceptance (path 5b) and on, in turn, to higher-order beliefs (path 6), to higher-order affect (path 7), and ultimately to commitment (path 8).

This pattern is applicable when consumers fully accept advertising-message claims, form attitudes toward the advertised brand, and become firmly committed to purchasing the advertised product. Because advertising has limited ability to form higher-order beliefs, this response pattern, though a theoretical possibility, is the exception rather than the rule.

Pattern 2: Cognition → Trial → Affect → Commitment. The sequence from cognition to trial to affect to commitment is captured in Figure 11.4 by the flow of solid arrows from advertising to low information acceptance (path 1), on through lower-order beliefs and lower-order affect (path 2), then to trial (path 3), and ultimately to commitment as a function of direct experience and the higher-order beliefs and affect that result (paths 5a through 8).

This response pattern typifies *low-involvement learning.* When consumers are passive rather than active learners of product and brand information, higher-order affect most likely results only *after* the consumer has had direct experience using a product —it is not based on advertising information alone.

Pattern 3: Cognition → Trial → Trial → Trial. . . . . The pattern from cognition to multiple trials is implicit in Figure 11.4 and suggests that in the case of relatively homogenous product categories there may be no such thing as higher-order affect either before or after direct-usage experience. In such instances consumers may consistently switch brands and never form a strong preference for any one brand. The consumer, in other words, learns about several brands in a product category but never develops strong affect or preference for any one brand. Rather, the consumer continuously shifts his or her allegiance from one brand to the next, constantly trying, trying, and trying but never developing a strong commitment or preference for any particular brand.

Alternative Advertising Objectives

The alternative response patterns in the integrated information-response model point out that advertising objectives must be set in accordance with the response pattern that characterizes the advertiser's particular product and market situation. For example, because the information response pattern for consumers who are in the market for a new automobile is different than the pattern for consumers choosing a brand of toothpaste, advertising objectives must also differ.

To more fully understand the implications that the alternative response pattern hold for objective settings, let us continue the discussion of advertising *goals* alluded to previously. As noted, advertising accomplishes goals such as (1) making consumers *aware* of a new brand, (2) facilitating their *understanding* of the brand's attributes and benefits, (3) enhancing their *attitudes* toward the brand, (4) influencing *purchase intentions,* and (5) encouraging them to *try* a brand.

The first goal, awareness, is essential for all three response patterns. That is, creating high levels of awareness is an important prerequisite to swaying consumer choice toward the marketer's brand. Though important under all circumstances, the awareness goal is relatively more important for patterns 2 and 3 than pattern 1. In other words, consumers may be willing to try a new brand of an inexpensive packaged good merely because they have seen it advertised on television, but few consumers would ever purchase a new automobile model simply because they learned of its existence.

Other goals are more critical for achieving success under high- than low-involvement situations. Accomplishing the second goal, understanding, is essential for advertising success when consumers are highly involved in product choice. In this situation, advertising must persuade highly involved consumers that the advertised product possesses features and benefits that make it superior to competitive offerings or a better value for the price. Consumer acceptance of the advertiser's claims leads to "higher-order beliefs" (refer again to Figure 11.4), then on to "higher-order affect," and perhaps finally to a preference for and "commitment" to purchase the advertised brand.

Requirements for Setting Advertising Objectives

Advertising objectives direct advertising activity by (1) identifying specific target audiences, (2) specifying the message arguments needed to move the audience to action, and (3) selecting media that will reach the intended market. Advertising objectives are *statements* of what advertising must accomplish to overcome problems or realize opportunities facing a brand.

However, not all statements represent good advertising objectives. Consider the following examples:

> Example A: The advertising objective for Brand A this year is to increase sales.
> Example B: The advertising objective for Brand B is to increase the target audience's brand awareness from 60 percent to 90 percent by July 31st.

These extreme examples differ in two important respects. First, Example B is obviously more specific. Second, whereas Example A deals with a sales objective, Example B involves a nonsales goal. The sections that follow describe the specific criteria that good advertising objectives must satisfy. [27]

---

27. The following discussion is influenced by the classic work on advertising planning and goal setting by Russell Colley. His writing, which came to be known as the DAGMAR approach, set a standard for advertising objective setting. See Russell H. Colley, *Defining Advertising Goals for Measured Advertising Results* (New York: Association of National Advertisers, 1961).

Objectives Must Include a Precise Statement of Who, What, and When. Objectives must be *stated in precise terms*. At a minimum, objectives should specify the target audience (who), indicate the specific goal to be accomplished (what; e.g., awareness level), and indicate the relevant time frame (when) in which to achieve the objective.

For example, the advertising campaign for the Buick Reatta might include objectives such as these: "Within six months from the beginning of the campaign, research should show that 90 percent of older baby-boomers and affluent mature consumers are familiar with the Reatta name and that at least 75 percent know that it is a two-seat automobile that features a combination of sportiness and comfort."

Advertising objectives provide valuable agendas for communication between advertising and marketing decision makers and offer benchmarks against which to compare actual performance. These functions are satisfied, however, only if objectives are stated precisely.

Example B represents the desired degree of specificity and, as such, would give executives something meaningful to direct their efforts toward as well as a clear-cut benchmark for assessing whether the advertising campaign has accomplished its objectives. Example A, by comparison, is much too general. Suppose sales have actually increased by 2 percent during the course of the ad campaign. Does this mean the campaign was successful since sales have in fact increased? If not, how much increase is necessary for the campaign to be regarded as a success?

Objectives Must Be Quantitative and Measurable. This requirement implies that ad objectives should be stated in quantitative terms, as are the hypothetical objectives given for the Reatta in the preceding example. A nonmeasureable objective for the Reatta would be a vague statement such as "Advertising should increase consumer knowledge." This objective lacks measurability because it fails to specify the product features for which consumers are to possess knowledge.

Objectives Must Specify the Amount of Change. In addition to being quantitative and measurable, objectives must specify the amount of change they are intended to accomplish. Example A ("to increase sales") fails to meet this requirement. Example B ("to increase awareness from 60 to 90 percent") is satisfactory because it clearly specifies that anything less than a 30 percent awareness increase would be considered unsuitable performance.

Objectives Must Be Realistic. Unrealistic objectives are as useless as having no objectives at all. An unrealistic objective is one that cannot be accomplished in the time allotted to the proposed advertising investment. For example, a brand that has achieved only 15 percent consumer awareness during its first two years on the market could not realistically expect a small advertising budget to increase the awareness level to, say, 65 percent.

Objectives Must Be Internally Consistent. Advertising objectives must be compatible (internally consistent) with objectives set for other components of the promotional mix. It would be incompatible for a manufacturer of packaged goods to proclaim a 25 percent reduction in sales force size while simultaneously stating that advertising's objective is to increase retail distribution by 20 percent. Without adequate sales force effort, it is doubtful that the retail trade would give a brand more shelf space.

Objectives Must Be Clear and in Writing. For objectives to accomplish their purposes of fostering communication and permitting evaluation, they must be stated clearly and in writing so that they can be disseminated among their users and among those who will be held responsible for seeing that the objectives are accomplished.

Using Direct versus Indirect Advertising Objectives

Direct objectives are those that seek an *overt behavioral response* from the audience. **Indirect objectives** are aimed at *communication tasks* that need to be accomplished before overt behavioral responses can be achieved.[28] We will see in the following discussion that direct objectives are appropriate and realistic under certain advertising circumstances, while indirect (communication) objectives must be used in other instances.

Direct objectives are appropriate when the purpose of the advertising is to accomplish a specific *action-forcing activity*. There are four primary instances of this form of advertising:[29]

1. *Advertising by retailers.* Sometimes retail advertising merely informs prospective customers about a new store or attempts to elevate a store's image. This type of advertising would be regarded as "indirect" in that the purpose is not to generate immediate buyer action. On the other hand, much of the advertising undertaken by supermarkets, mass merchandisers (e.g., K-Mart), and other retailers promotes new or sale items and is designed to bring customers to the store. This type of advertising has a direct objective—to sell merchandise immediately or in the very near future. With such a short time frame in mind and with knowledge of product sales volume when the merchandise is not on special, it is reasonable for the retail advertiser to state the ad objective in terms of a direct measure such as *sales volume*.

    For example, a specialty electronics store has accurate information from past records regarding the number of VCRs it sells on a typical Friday-through-Sunday weekend, say 300 units. Suppose the store chooses

---

28. Patti and Frazer, *Advertising: A Decision-Making Approach,* p. 241.
29. Ibid.

to run a 25 percent-off price special on all VCRs for next weekend only. Newspaper ads will be run Monday through Friday announcing the special. The purpose of the sale is to increase store traffic and triple the number of VCRs sold compared to a typical weekend. In this case, the direct advertising objective, to sell 900 VCRs next weekend, represents a precise, quantitative (i.e., measurable), and possibly realistic advertising objective.

2. *Direct-response advertising.* Much advertising via the mail or in mass media (e.g, television or newspapers) is designed to generate immediate action. When " Junk Apparel Company" runs an ad in the *Parade* supplement to the Sunday newspaper announcing the availability of three pairs of 100 percent polyester slacks for a total price of $19.95, the purpose is plain and simple: to sell tons of slacks. The purpose is not to create brand awareness or to enhance the company's image; rather, the objective is for thousands of consumers to place an order within the next week or so.

In general, direct-response advertising is designed to generate immediate sales volume. Therefore, it is reasonable to set a planned volume level as the advertising objective.

Similarly, when "World Vision," a charitable organization, runs newspaper advertisements throughout the United States informing the public that 28 million people in Bangladesh are homeless following devastating floods, the purpose is to generate donations for the Bangladesh Flood Relief. World Vision's advertising objective is to generate an immediate overt response—financial donations.

3. *Sales-promotion advertising.* Sales promotions in the form of coupons, contests, premium offers, and other techniques are delivered via advertisements in media such as newspapers and magazines. This form of advertising is expected to generate quick buyer action as indicated by the number of coupons redeemed or the number of people who enter a contest. In such instances, it is appropriate for the advertiser/sales promoter to establish a direct objective such as "obtain a 5 percent coupon redemption level" or "encourage 100,000 people to enter a contest."

4. *Business-to-business advertising.* Businesses that market their products to other businesses rather than to final consumers often use advertising as a means of generating prospects for their salespeople. Thus, the effectiveness of the advertising can be gauged by the number of telephone or mail inquiries received from prospective customers.

Consider the case of a manufacturer of medical equipment that announces its most recent product innovation in a trade publication read by the manufacturer's primary prospects. The advertisement requests interested parties to call 1-800-555-1111 for further information. The number of expected inquiries represents an appropriate advertising objective, and the number actually received within, say, the next two months indicates how successful the advertisement is.

Indirect (communication) objectives are appropriate, indeed necessary, in all advertising situations other than the four just described. This is especially the case for *national advertisers*, in contrast to local advertisers such as the neighborhood supermarket, whose reason for advertising typically is indirect rather than direct. For example, the local McDonald's franchise near your campus advertises to generate immediate store traffic, but McDonald's corporate advertising at the national level is typically designed to accomplish various indirect objectives: (1) to announce new menu items; (2) to convey the idea that McDonald's is a good corporate citizen via practices such as hiring older people (you may recall the touching ad showing an elderly gentleman's first day working at McDonald's); or (3) to convey the impression that McDonald's is a fun place to take your family.

Direct objectives such as sales volume or profit goals are typically unsuitable goals for advertising efforts by national advertisers because these outcomes are the *consequence of a host of factors* in addition to advertising. A brand's sales and profits in a given period result from the prevailing economic climate, competitive activity, and all marketing-mix variables—price level, product quality, distribution efficiencies, personal-selling activity, and so forth. It is virtually impossible to determine precisely what role advertising has had in influencing sales and profits in a given period, because advertising is just one of many possible determinants of sales and profit performance. The following analogy makes the point vividly.

> Some argue that evaluating advertising only by its impact on sales is like attributing all the success (or failure) of a football team to the quarterback. The fact is that many other elements can affect the team's record—other players, the competition, and the bounce of the ball. The implication is that the effect of the quarterback's performance should be measured by the things he alone can influence, such as how he throws the ball, how he calls the plays, and how he hands off. If, in a real-world situation, all factors remained constant except for advertising (for example, if competitive activity were static), then it would be feasible to rely exclusively on sales to measure advertising effectiveness. Since such a situation is, in reality, infeasible, we must start dealing with response variables that are associated more directly with the advertising stimulus.[30]

A second reason that sales response is an unsuitable objective for advertising effort is that the effect of advertising on sales is typically *delayed or lagged*. That is to say, advertising during any given period influences sales during later periods. GMC's advertising of the three models discussed in the chapter's opening vignette may have an immediate impact on consumers' attitudes toward the Cutlass Supreme, Grand Prix, and Reatta, but may not influence purchases until a later date when consumers are actively in the market for a new car. Thus, advertising may have a decided impact on consumers' brand awareness, product knowledge, attitudes, and, ultimately, purchase behavior, but this influence may not be evident during the period when advertising's effect is measured.

30. David A. Aaker and John G. Myers, *Advertising Management*, 2d ed. (Englewood Cliffs, NJ: Prentice-Hall, 1982), pp. 93–94.

Direct objectives (sales and profits) are therefore not suitable measures of advertising effectiveness when the purpose of the advertising is to generate product awareness, influence attitudes, enhance the corporate image, or accomplish other indirect (communication) objectives.

In sum, if an overt behavioral response can be attributed with reasonable certainty to a particular advertising placement or to an overall campaign, then the objective should be stated in terms of sales volume or some other direct indicator of advertising effectiveness. If, on the other hand, the advertising's objective is to increase awareness levels, favorably influence attitudes, or perform other indirect functions, then sales volume *may not be* an appropriate objective.

Vaguely Right versus Precisely Wrong.   The previous sentence intentionally ended on a somewhat noncommittal note concerning the matter of when it is appropriate to use sales as the advertising objective. The preceding discussion has presented the "traditional view" of the appropriateness of using direct versus indirect advertising objectives.

However, some advertising specialists contend that advertisers should *always* state objectives in terms of sales volume and that failure to do so is a "cop-out." The logic of this "nontraditional view" is that advertising's purpose is not to create awareness, or to enhance attitudes, or to influence purchase intentions, but rather to generate sales. Thus, according to this position, it is always possible to measure, if only vaguely and imprecisely, whether advertising has contributed to increased sales. Indirect objectives and corresponding measures (e.g., awareness levels) are claimed to be "precisely wrong" in contrast to sales measures that are "vaguely right."[31]

There is no simple resolution to the matter of whether direct (sales) or indirect (communication) objectives are more appropriate. However, one thing is certain: Every advertising effort should carry with it a clear statement of what it is intended to accomplish. This statement should be specific, measurable, realistic, and in writing.

Budgeting for Advertising

The advertising budgeting decision is, in many respects, the most important decision advertisers make. If too little money is spent on advertising, sales volume will not be as high as it could be, and profits will be lost. If too much money is spent, expenses will be higher than they need to be, and profits will be reduced.

The budgeting decision is also one of the most difficult advertising decisions. The difficulty arises because it is hard to determine precisely how effec-

31. Leonard M. Lodish, *The Advertising and Promotion Challenge: Vaguely Right or Precisely Wrong?* (New York: Oxford University Press, 1986), Chapter 5.

tive advertising has been or might be in the future. The predicament is that the sales-response function to advertising is influenced by a multitude of factors (quality of advertising execution, intensity of competitive advertising efforts, customer taste, and other considerations), thereby making it difficult if not impossible to know with any certainty what amount of sales advertising will generate.

Another reason that advertising budgeting is a complicated process is the fact that advertising budgets are largely the result of *organizational political processes.*[32] Separate organizational units view the advertising budget differently. "For the accounting department, it's an expense, usually the largest after rent and payroll. For the marketing team, it's the big push that make the phones ring and it's never big enough. For top management, it's an investment, a speculation formulated to bring in the most revenue for the least amount of cash."[33] Research has shown that the size of the advertising budget is positively influenced by the political power of the marketing department.[34]

Advertising Budgeting in Theory

In theory, advertising budgeting is a simple process, provided one accepts the premise that the best (optimal) level of any investment is the level that maximizes profits. This assumption leads to a simple rule for establishing advertising budgets: *continue to invest in advertising as long as the marginal revenue from that investment exceeds the marginal cost.* Profits are maximized at the point where marginal revenue is equal to marginal cost.

The reader will recall from basic economics that marginal revenue (MR) and marginal cost (MC) are the change in total revenue and total cost, respectively, that result from producing and selling an additional item. The "profit-maximization rule" is then a matter of simple economic logic: Profit maximization can occur only at the point where MR = MC. At any point below this (i.e., where MR > MC), profits are not maximized because at a higher level of output more profit can be earned. Similarly, at any point above this (i.e., where MC > MR), there is a marginal loss.

In practical terms, this means that advertisers should continue advertising as long as it is profitable to do so. For example, suppose a company is currently spending $1 million on advertising and is considering the investment of another $200,000. Should the investment be made? The answer is simple: only if the additional advertising generates more than $200,000 revenue. Now say the same company is contemplating an additional advertising expenditure of $300,000. Again, the company should go ahead with the advertising if it can be certain that the investment will yield more than $300,000 in additional revenue.

32. Nigel Piercy, "Advertising Budgeting: Process and Structure as Explanatory Variables, "*Journal of Advertising,* vol. 16, no. 2 (1987), pp. 34–40.
33. Kathleen Weeks, "How to Plan Your Ad Budget," *Sales and Marketing Management,* September 1987, p. 113.
34. Nigel Piercy, "Advertising Budgeting: Process and Structure as Explanatory Variables."

It is evident from this simple exercise that advertising budget setting is a matter of answering a series of "if-then" questions— "if $X are invested in advertising, then what amount of revenue will be generated?" Because budgets are set before the fact, this requires that the "if-then" questions have advance answers. In order to employ the profit-maximization rule for budget setting, the advertising decision maker must know the advertising-sales response function for every brand for which a budgeting decision will be made. Because such knowledge is rarely available, theoretical (profit maximization) budget setting is an ideal that is generally nonoperational in the real world of advertising decision making.

Budgeting Considerations in Practice

Advertising decision makers must consider several different factors when establishing advertising budgets. The most important consideration should be the *objectives* that advertising is designed to accomplish. That is, the level of the budget should follow from the specific objectives established for advertising; more ambitious objectives require larger advertising budgets. If advertising is intended to increase a brand's market share, then a larger budget is needed than would be required if the task were simply to maintain consumer awareness of the brand name.

Competitive advertising activity is another important consideration in setting ad budgets. In highly competitive markets, more must be invested in advertising in order to increase or at least maintain market position. A case in point was the massive advertising budget General Motors Corporation invested in the three models described in the opening vignette. Faced with stiff domestic competition from Ford and Chrysler and intense competition from Japanese and European automakers, it was necessary for GMC to invest heavily in these models to cut through the competitive clutter and have the desired impact.

A third major consideration is the *amount of funds available.* In the final analysis, advertising budget setting is determined in large part by decision makers' perceptions of how much they can afford to spend on advertising. Because top management often views advertising budgets with suspicion and considers them to be inflated, advertising managers face the challenge of convincing these management officials that proposed budgets are indeed affordable. Because this is no easy task, especially when hard data on advertising effectiveness is unavailable, advertising budget setters have tended to use simple decision rules (heuristics) for making budgeting decisions.

Budgeting Methods

In view of the difficulty of accurately predicting sales response to advertising, companies ordinarily set budgets by using judgment, applying experience with analogous situations, and using simple rules-of-thumb as guides to setting budgets.[35] The two most pervasive heuristics used by both industrial advertisers and consumer-goods advertisers are the percentage-of-sales and objective-and-task methods.[36]

Percentage-of-Sales Budgeting. In using the **percentage-of-sales method,** a company sets its advertising budget for a particular brand by simply establishing the budget as a fixed percentage of *past* or *anticipated* sales volume. Assume, for example, that a company allocates three percent of anticipated sales to advertising and that the company projects next year's sales to be $10,000,000. Its advertising budget would be set at $300,000.

A recent survey of the top 100 consumer-goods advertisers in the United States found that 53 percent employ the percentage-of-anticipated sales method and 20 percent use the percentage-of-past-sales method.[37] This is to be expected, since budget setting should logically be set in accordance with what a company expects to do in the future rather than based on what it accomplished in the past.

What percentage of sales revenue do most companies devote to advertising? Actually, the percentage is highly variable. Toiletry and cosmetic companies spend an especially large percentage of sales on advertising. For example, Noxell Corporation—makers of Cover Girl, Noxema, and other products—spent approximately 32.6 percent of its 1987 U.S. sales on advertising. Manufacturers of durable goods, by comparison, invest a relatively small proportion. In 1987 Ford Motor Company allocated slightly over 1 percent of sales to advertising. Goodyear Tire & Rubber Company invested approximately 1.6 percent of sales in advertising.[38]

The percentage-of-sales method is frequently criticized as being illogical. Criticism is based on the argument that the method *reverses the logical relationship between sales and advertising.* That is, the true ordering between advertising and sales is that advertising causes sales; stated alternatively, sales are a function of advertising: *Sales = f (Advertising).* Contrary to this logical relation, implementing the percentage-of-sales method amounts to reversing the causal order by setting advertising as a function of sales: *Advertising = f (Sales).* That is, when sales are anticipated to increase, the advertising budget also increases; when sales are expected to decline, the budget is reduced.

The illogic of the percentage-of-sales method is demonstrated by the fact that this method could lead to potentially erroneous budgeting decisions such

35. Gary L. Lilien, Alvin J. Silk, Jean-Marie Choffray, and Murlidhar Rao, "Industrial Advertising Effects and Budgeting Practices," *Journal of Marketing,* vol. 40 (January 1976), p. 21.
36. The extensive use of the percentage-of-sales and objective-and-task methods in an industrial context has been documented by Lilien et al., ibid., while support in a consumer context is provided by Kent M. Lancaster and Judith A. Stern, "Computer-based Advertising Budgeting Practices of Leading U.S. Consumer Advertisers," *Journal of Advertising,* vol. 12, no. 4 (1983), p. 6.
37. Lancaster and Stern, ibid.
38. These statistics are based on company reports in *Advertising Age's* special issue of "100 Leading National Advertisers, Part 1," September 28, 1988, at various pages.

as cutting the advertising budget when a brand's sales are expected to decline. Rather than decreasing the amount of advertising, it may be wiser to increase advertising in order to prevent further sales erosion. When used blindly, the percent-of-sales method is little more than an arbitrary and simplistic rule of thumb for what needs to be a sound business judgment. Used without justification, this budgeting method is another application of "precisely wrong" (versus "vaguely right") decision making.[39]

In practice, most sophisticated marketers do *not* use percentage of sales as the sole budgeting method. Instead, they employ the method as an initial pass, or first cut, for determining the budget and then alter the budget forecast depending on the objectives and tasks that need to be accomplished.

The Objective-and-Task Method. The **objective-and-task method** is generally regarded as the most sensible and defendable advertising budgeting method. In using this method, advertising decision makers must clearly specify the role they expect advertising to play and then set budgets accordingly. The role is typically identified in terms of a *communication objective* (e.g., increase brand awareness by 20 percent) but could be stated in terms of sales volume or market-share expectations (e.g., increase market share from 15 percent to 25 percent).

The objective-and-task method is the advertising budget procedure used most frequently by both consumer and industrial companies. Surveys in the 1980s have shown that over 60 percent of consumer-goods companies and 70 percent of industrial-goods companies use this budgeting method.[40] These percentages represent a dramatic increase in comparison with the 12 percent of respondents in a 1974 survey who indicated using the objective-and-task method.[41]

The following steps are involved when applying the objective-and-task method:[42]

1. The first step is to establish specific *marketing objectives* that need to be accomplished, such as sales volume, market share, and profit contribution.

    To illustrate this and the remaining steps, consider the case of Samsung, a Korean electronics company. As of 1988, Samsung marketed approximately 13 percent of the VCRs and 20 percent of the microwave ovens sold in the United States, though most of the VCRs and microwave

---

39. See Lodish, *The Advertising and Promotion Challenge: Vaguely Right or Precisely Wrong?*, Chapter 6.

40. Charles H. Patti and Vincent J. Blasko, "Budgeting Practices of Big Advertisers," *Journal of Advertising Research*, vol. 21 (December 1981), pp. 23–29; Vincent J. Blasko and Charles H. Patti, "The Advertising Budgeting Practices of Industrial Marketers," *Journal of Marketing*, vol. 48 (Fall 1984), pp. 104–110.

41. Andre J. San Augustine and William F. Foley, "How Large Advertisers Set Budgets," *Journal of Advertising Research*, vol. 15 (October 1975), p. 13.

42. Adapted from Lilien et al., "Industrial Advertising and Budgeting," p. 23.

ovens were marketed under private names (e.g., J. C. Penney and Sears brands manufactured by Samsung).[43] Samsung's marketing objective in the United States is to increase its market share substantially, especially sales of products under Samsung's own brand name rather than under private labels. Samsung aspires to be the Korean equivalent of the extremely successful Japanese Panasonic.

2. The second step in implementing the objective-and-task method is to assess the *communication functions* that must be performed to accomplish the overall marketing objectives.

Samsung must accomplish two communication functions in order to realize its overall marketing objective: It must increase U.S. consumer awareness of the Samsung brand name and persuade consumers that Samsung manufactures quality products and not just low-price items.

3. The third step is to determine *advertising's role in the total communication mix* in performing the functions established in step two.

Given the nature of its products and communication objectives, advertising is a crucial component in Samsung's mix.

4. The fourth step is to establish *specific advertising goals in terms of the levels of measurable communication response* required to achieve marketing objectives.

Samsung might establish goals such as (1) increase awareness from the present level of, say, 45 percent of the target market, to 75 percent, and (2) expand the percentage of survey respondents who rate Samsung products as "high quality" from, say, 15 percent to 30 percent.

5. The final step is to *establish the budget* based on estimates of expenditures required to accomplish the advertising goals.

In view of Samsung's challenging objectives, it was decided in 1988 to increase the advertising budget by 50 percent to approximately $10 million. Most of this was spent on television advertisements that ran during the coverage of the 1988 Summer Olympics.[44]

Other Budgeting Heuristics. The *match competitors* (also known as competitive parity) and *affordability* methods are additional heuristics used by industrial and consumer-goods advertisers. The **match-competitors method** sets the ad budget by basically following what competitors are doing. A company may learn that its primary competitor is devoting 10 percent of sales to advertising and then decide next year to spend the same percentage advertising its own brand. In the **affordability method,** the funds that remain after budgeting for everything else go into advertising. Only the most unsophisticated and impoverished firms would be expected to budget in this manner.

---

43. These figures are based on Ira Teinowitz, "Koreans Dial Up Ad Spending," *Advertising Age,* June 13, 1988, p. 12.
44. Ibid.

These techniques are used most frequently by smaller firms, who tend to follow industry leaders. However, affordability and competitive considerations influence the budgeting decisions of all companies. In reality, most advertising budget setters combine a variety of methods rather than depending exclusively on one heuristic. For example, an advertiser may have a fixed percentage-of-sales figure in mind when starting the budgeting process but subsequently adjust this figure in light of anticipated competitive activity, funds availability, and other considerations.

Companies often find it necessary to adjust their budgets during the course of a year in line with sales performance. Many advertisers operate under the belief that they should "shoot when the ducks are flying."[45] In other words, advertisers spend most heavily during periods when products are hot and cut spending when funds are short; however, they should always maintain a decent ad budget even when sales take a downturn.

Budget Allocation

Corporations typically market multiple brands. Advertising budgeting thereby becomes a matter of allocating the total corporate advertising budget among different brands that compete for limited advertising resources. The theoretical objective is to make the allocation decision in such a fashion as to maximize the total corporate contribution rather than to suboptimally maximize the contribution of any one brand or subset of brands.

All too often, however, budgets are set brand-by-brand in an attempt to optimize individual brand contribution rather than considering overall corporate contribution. The result is that the sum of individually optimum budgets is likely to exceed the funds available to the corporation for total advertising. An ideal budgeting method should consider the budgeting requests and contribution potential of all brands simultaneously.

A multi-brand advertising budget allocation model, called **ADSPLIT,** has been developed recently.[46] ADSPLIT uses mathematical optimization procedures to derive near-optimum spending levels for individual brands such that all the budgets combined maximize the overall corporate profit from advertising. ADSPLIT works by (1) imposing a constraint on the overall corporate advertising budget, (2) placing upper and lower budget constraints for each brand, and (3) building in sales-response functions for each brand based only on advertising and price (and not on any other marketing-mix variables).

Further technical details are beyond the scope of this chapter. Nonetheless, the important point to realize is that the ADSPLIT model is an advance over simplistic budgeting procedures because it considers budgets for multiple

45. Kathleen Weeks, "How to Plan Your Ad Budget," *Sales and Marketing Management,* September 1987, p. 114.
46. Amiya K. Basu and Rajeev Batra, "ADSPLIT: A Multi-Brand Advertising Budget Allocation Model," *Journal of Advertising,* vol. 17, no. 1 (1988), pp. 44–51.

brands simultaneously and attempts to maximize overall corporate contribution rather than individual brand performance.

Summary

This chapter offers an introduction to advertising and an overview of the advertising-management process. Advertising is shown to perform five major functions: informing, persuading, reminding, adding value, and assisting other company efforts. Advertising's economic role is examined by comparing two schools of thought: *Advertising = Market Power* versus *Advertising = Information*. The first perspective views advertising negatively and assumes that advertising has the power to influence brand loyalty, which, in turn, is assumed to lead to negative consequences such as price insensitivity, high industry-concentration levels, barriers to entry, price increases, and excessive profits. An alternative perspective, Advertising = Information, presents a positive picture by portraying advertising as a useful purveyor of information, a role that allows consumers to compare competitive offerings, resulting in increased competitive rivalry, reduced prices, and more product innovativeness. Both schools of thought present extreme views on advertising's economic impact. Neither view is sufficient by itself because the actual role of advertising varies greatly from industry to industry.

An overview of the advertising-management process is given, and two aspects, objective setting and budgeting, are described in detail. Objective setting depends on the specific response pattern to advertising. The *integrated information-response model* is presented, and three different response patterns are described. Requirements for developing effective advertising objectives are discussed. A final section describes the problems associated with using sales volume or other financial goals as the advertising objectives.

The chapter concludes with an explanation of the advertising budgeting process. The budgeting decision is one of the most important advertising decisions and also one of the most difficult. The complication arises with the difficulty of determining the sales response to advertising. In theory, budget setting is a simple matter, but the theoretical requirements are generally unattainable in practice. For this reason, advertising practitioners use various rules of thumb (heuristics) to assist them in arriving at satisfactory, if not optimal, budgeting decisions. Percentage-of-sales budgeting and objective-and-task methods are the dominant budgeting heuristics.

Discussion Questions

1. Of the five advertising functions described in the chapter, which is the most important?

2. Explain the differences between the Advertising = Market Power and Advertising = Information views on advertising's economic role.

3. "Advertising strategy should flow from corporate and marketing strategy." Explain.

4. Let us assume that the lawn-fertilizer industry consists of five manufacturers, all producing virtually identical products. However, one firm is far superior to the others in advertising success. This firm has achieved a 45 percent market share and charges prices about 15 percent higher than its competitors. Explain this situation in terms of the Advertising = Market Power versus Advertising = Information views on advertising's economic role.

5. A manufacturer of office furniture has established the following advertising objective for next year: "Increase sales by 20 percent." Comment on this objective's suitability. Provide a better objective.

6. What reasons can you give for certain industries (e.g., food and pharmaceuticals) investing considerably larger proportions of their sales in advertising than other industries, such as automobiles?

7. Why is it so difficult to measure precisely the specific impact that advertising has on sales and profits?

8. Compare the difference between "precisely right" versus "vaguely wrong" advertising objectives. Give an example of each.

9. Some critics contend that the use of the percentage-of-sales budgeting technique is illogical. Explain.

10. Would it be possible for an advertising budget setter to use two or more budgeting heuristics in conjunction with one another? Describe how this could be done.

Exercises

1. Advertising is often accused of various "sins." The social criticisms of advertising that were mentioned in the text include claims that advertising is deceptive, manipulative, and offensive and that it plays on people's insecurities and fears. Find evidence from print advertisements that support any of these claims. Point out specifically how each ad you have clipped is subject to criticism.

2. Interview three or four local businesses and identify their advertising objectives. Investigate whether they set formal ad objectives and, if not, whether they have some rather clear-cut, though implicit, objectives in mind.

3. While interviewing the same businesses from question 2, investigate their advertising budgeting practices. Determine whether they establish formal ad budgets and identify the specific budgeting methods used.

Advertising Messages and Creative Strategy

THE CASE OF PAJAMA MAN: WHAT'S GOING ON?

hilip Morris Inc. began an advertising campaign in the late 1980s for its cigarette brand, Benson & Hedges, to reestablish the brand with a more upscale image. A series of magazine advertisements depicted users—mostly young, classy, affluent women—in settings compatible with the upscale image being projected for the brand. For example, in one execution, several women were shown in a trendy, attractive living room drinking wine, smoking cigarettes, and sharing an apparently frivolous moment. In another ad, an attractive young couple along with an older man were depicted in a kitchen preparing dinner, drinking wine, smoking, and seeming to have a good time. A third execution portrayed two attractive young women in a classy restaurant smoking cigarettes, drinking wine, having fun, and so on. These magazine executions contain virtually no verbal content other than the statement "For people who like to smoke. . .Benson & Hedges, because quality matters."

While all of the preceding ads are fairly straightforward, another ad in the Benson & Hedges campaign, dubbed "Pajama Man" by industry spokespersons, represents a particularly intriguing piece of advertising. As can be seen in Figure 12.1, the ad captures a group of people in a moment of after-dinner merriment; the people are shown smoking cigarettes, drinking wine, and enjoying a laugh. In the midst of all this is an image: a man in pajamas is standing in the doorway being saluted by the older gentleman; later (in the lower scene), the "pajama man" is embracing one of the party guests.

Who is this man supposed to be? Why is he included in the scene? More generally, what is this advertisement attempting to accomplish? Is the ad effective?■

Answering the preceding questions is difficult. Only Philip Morris knows how effective the ad was in accomplishing the specific objectives that were established for the campaign. It goes without question, however, that the ad was a real attention getter and a truly creative piece of advertising.

What makes a good advertising message? What is the process that leads to the creation of advertising messages? What are the different types of creative strategies, and when and why are they used? How does corporate advertising differ from product- or brand-oriented advertising? Why is corporate advertising used?

These questions are addressed in this chapter. While Chapter 6 introduced the subject of messages from a general, marketing communications perspective, this chapter examines only advertising messages. First, the question of what makes good advertising and the related issue of advertising creativity are discussed. Next, the process underlying the formulation of advertising strategy is covered. Third, detailed descriptions of specific creative strategies are provided. Fourth, the concept of mean-end chains is introduced as a mechanism to bridge the advertiser's creative process with the consumer's values related to product consumption. A final section moves the discussion away from product- and brand-oriented advertising to corporate image and issue advertising.

What Makes Good Advertising?

It is easy, in one sense, to define "good" advertising: Advertising is good if it accomplishes the advertiser's objectives. This perspective defines good advertising from the output side, or in terms of what it accomplishes. It is much more difficult to define good advertising from an input perspective, or in terms of the composition of the advertisement itself. This is because students of advertising (practitioners and scholars) have different philosophies about advertising and different experiential bases from which they have drawn their philosophies. For example, a practitioner of direct-mail advertising probably has a different opinion about what constitutes good advertising than does the advertising agency (Wells, Rich, Greene) that developed the pajama-man advertisement for Benson & Hedges.

Thus, simple definitions of what constitutes good advertising are generally little more than misleading attempts to generalize from a base of limited experiences. For example, the following definition offered by one well-known advertising practitioner is meaningless in its generality: "A good advertisement

"Pajama-Man" Advertisement

FIGURE 12.1

Source: Reprinted by permission of Philip Morris Incorporated.

is one which sells the product *without drawing attention to itself.*"[1] This is equivalent to saying that a newscaster is good only if he or she does not attract attention to him or herself, or that a professor is good if no one notices him or her. Of course, this is unrealistic.

Although it is impractical to provide a singular, all-purpose definition of what constitutes good advertising, it *is* meaningful to talk about general characteristics of good advertising.[2] At a minimum, good, or effective, advertising satisfies the following considerations:

1. It must extend from *sound marketing strategy*. Advertising can be effective only if it is compatible with other elements of a well-orchestrated marketing strategy.

2. Effective advertising must take *the consumer's view*. Consumers buy product benefits, not attributes. Therefore, advertising must be stated in a way that relates to the consumer's needs, wants, and values and not strictly in terms of the marketer's needs and wants.[3]

3. Effective advertising is *persuasive*. Persuasion usually occurs when there is a benefit for the consumer and not just for the marketer.

4. Advertising must find a unique way to *break through the clutter*. Advertisers continuously compete with competitors for the consumer's attention. This is no small task considering the massive number of print advertisements, broadcast commercials, and other sources of information available daily to consumers. Indeed, the situation in television advertising has been characterized as "audio-visual wallpaper," implying sarcastically that consumers pay just about as much attention to commercials as they do to the detail in their own wallpaper after it has been on the walls for awhile.[4]

5. Good advertising should *never promise more than it can deliver*. This point speaks for itself, both in terms of morality (recall discussion in Chapter 8) and in terms of good business sense. Consumers learn quickly when they have been deceived, and they resent it.

6. Good advertising *prevents the creative idea from overwhelming the strategy*. The purpose of advertising is to persuade and influence; the purpose is not to be cute for cute's sake or humorous for humor's sake. For example, the famous Miller Light beer advertisements use humor effectively in conveying the dual ideas that this product "tastes great and is less filling."

1. David Ogilvy, *Confessions of an Advertising Man* (New York: Atheneum, 1986), p. 90.
2. The following points are a mixture of the author's views and perspectives presented by A. Jerome Jewler, *Creative Strategy in Advertising* (Belmont, CA: Wadsworth Publishing Company, 1985), pp. 7–8, and Don E. Schultz and Stanley I. Tannenbaum, *Essentials of Advertising Strategy* (Lincolnwood, IL: NTC Business Books, 1988), pp. 9–10.
3. Note the similarity here to the earlier discussion on the "three modes of marketing" in Chapter 1, where we distinguished between the "marketing concept" (the marketer adapting to the customer's needs and wants) and the "promotion concept" (attempting to adapt the customer to the marketer's needs and wants).
4. Stan Freberg, "Irtnog Revisited," *Advertising Age*, August 1, 1988, p. 32.

Comparatively, the ineffective use of humor results in people remembering the humor but forgetting the selling message.

Good advertising, in sum, "is advertising that is created for a specific customer. It is advertising that understands and thinks about the customer's needs. It is advertising that communicates a specific benefit. It is advertising that pinpoints a specific action that the consumer takes. Good advertising understands that people do not buy products—they buy product benefits . . . . Above all, [good advertising] gets noticed and remembered, and gets people to act."[5]

Being Creative

Good, effective advertising is usually *creative*. That is, it effectively differentiates itself from the mass of mediocre advertisements; it is somehow different and out-of-the-ordinary. Advertising that is the same as most other advertising is unable to break through the competitive clutter and grab the consumer's attention.

It is easier to give examples of creative advertising than to define exactly what it is. Consider three examples: (1) The California Raisin Association's advertisement using claymatic raisin characters shuffling to the beat of "I heard it through the grapevine"; (2) Wendy's advertisement with the gruff old lady shouting "Where's the beef?"; and (3) Isuzu's campaign featuring the liar, "Joe Isuzu," who in the role poked fun at used-car salesmen while making sales claims for Isuzu vehicles. Most of you probably remember all three commercials vividly. They got your attention because they gave you solid reasons for wanting to watch them, and they made their selling points in an entertaining fashion.

Jazz musician Charlie Mingus described creativity about as well as it can be described: "Creativity is more than just being different. Anybody can play weird, that's easy. What's hard is to be simple as Bach. Making the simple complicated is commonplace, making the complicated simple, awesomely simple, that's creativity."[6] In view of this perspective on creativity, is the Benson & Hedges pajama-man ad creative?

Making an Impression

Good, effective, creative advertising must make a relatively lasting impact on consumers. This means getting past the clutter from other advertisements, activating attention, and giving consumers something to remember about the advertised product. In other words, advertising must *make an impression*.

---

5. Schultz and Tannenbaum, *Essentials of Advertising Strategy*, p. 75. This quote actually describes what these authors term "creative advertising," but they are using creative in the same sense as the present use of good, effective advertising.
6. Lou Centlivre, "A Peek At the Creative of the '90s," *Advertising Age*, January 18, 1988, p. 62.

There are different kinds of impressions that advertising can have or make on the consumer. Research with television commercials has identified a structured, well-defined hierarchy of impressions that includes five major types of advertising impressions.[7]

Brand name. The most likely aspect of a commercial that viewers retain in memory is the **brand name.** Consumers often remember little else but what brand was advertised.

Generics. The second most typical impression consists of generics. **Generics** represent major *selling claims* that are associated with the advertised brand (e.g., Del Monte is the first national brand of vegetables to introduce a no-salt line; Häagen-Dazs has the finest ice cream in the world) or *outstanding characteristics* of an advertising campaign (e.g., the funky scenes and zany characters in Reeboks' U.B.U. campaign; the fact that every Benson & Hedges ad includes people drinking wine).

Feelings. Next in the impression hierarchy is the generation of **feelings.**[8] Television commercials and other forms of advertisements evoke a variety of positive and negative feelings. Positive feelings include reactions such as pride, excitement, warmth, tenderness, amazement, confidence, and so on. Negative feelings include fear, boredom, sadness, anger, irritation, and disgust.

Commercial Specifics. Retention of **commercial specifics** is the fourth most frequent form of impression. Commercial specifics involve elements in the execution of the advertisement such as the spokesperson or endorser (e.g., Whitney Houston for Coca-Cola, "Joe Isuzu" for Isuzu cars and trucks, Jaclyn Smith for K-Mart, Bill Cosby for Jell-O), the music (e.g., the music accompanying "the night belongs to Michelob" commercials), the overall situation (e.g., an emotional ad for Hallmark greeting cards), and characters (e.g., Rodney Dangerfield, John Madden, and other personalities in the Miller Lite commercials; Alex the dog and Spuds MacKenzie in beer commercials; the cast from "M*A*S*H" in IBM's personal-computer commercials).

Specific Sales Message. The last impression viewers typically retain is the **specific sales message.** However, repeated exposures and persis-

---

7. Dave Vadehra, "Making a Lasting Impression: What Viewers Remember Leads to 'Outstanding' Commercials," *Advertising Age*, April 25, 1983, pp. M-4, M-38.
8. Vadehra refers to this as "attitudinal response," but "feelings" is probably a more apt descriptor in view of recent scholarly attention that has attempted to disentangle the related but different notions of attitudes, emotions, and feelings. See David A. Aaker, Douglas M. Stayman, and Richard Vezina, "Identifying Feelings Elicited by Advertising," *Psychology & Marketing*, vol. 5 (Spring 1988) pp. 1–16.

tence during the course of an advertising campaign can enable a sales message to be retained as a "generic" element.[9] For example, Orson Welles, in his long-standing capacity as spokesman for Paul Masson wines, was probably the most outstanding impression initially, but over time, the sales message ("Paul Masson will not be sold before its time") likely became as well remembered as the commercial's inimitable spokesperson.

In Sum.   To be effective, advertising must make some form of positive impression on receivers. Impressions range from mere brand-name recognition to getting consumers to comprehend and retain the specific sales message.

Advertising-Strategy Formulation

Sophisticated advertising requires that companies develop formal advertising plans and strategies. **Advertising plans** provide the framework for the actual execution of advertising strategies. To appreciate the role of an advertising plan, imagine an analogous situation where a collegiate football team approaches an upcoming game without any idea of how it is going to execute its offense or defense. Without a game plan, the team would have to play in the same spontaneous fashion as do players in a "pick up" game. Under such circumstances there would be numerous missed assignments and overall misexecution. The team very likely would lose unless the game was against a badly mismatched opponent.

So it is with advertising. Companies compete against opponents who generally are well prepared. This means that a firm must enter the advertising "game'" with a clear plan in mind. An advertising plan is developed for a specific action for the upcoming advertising period. The plan basically evaluates where a product or brand's previous advertising has been, proposes where the next period's advertising should head, and justifies the proposed plans.

To put an advertising plan into action requires (1) careful evaluation of consumer behavior related to the product/brand, (2) detailed evaluation of the competition, and (3) a coordinated effort to tie the proposed advertising program into the brand's overall marketing strategy.

Because an advertising plan involves a number of planning steps and details that are beyond the scope of this chapter, attention now turns to the advertising strategy that extends directly from the advertising plan.[10]

9. Vadehra, "Making a Lasting Impression: What Viewers Remember Leads to 'Outstanding' Commercials," p. M–4.
10. For more details on the advertising plan, see Don E. Schultz, Dennis Martin, and William P. Brown, *Strategic Advertising Campaigns* (Lincolnwood, IL: NTC Business Books, 1987), Chapter 4; and Schultz and Tannenbaum, *Essentials of Advertising Strategy*, Chapter 2.

The preceding football analogy is useful in explaining advertising strategy. In football, a coaching staff develops a game *plan* by doing such things as (1) reviewing films from last year's game with the upcoming opponent, (2) assessing why their team won or lost, (3) evaluating the opponent's performances so far this year and assessing the strengths and weaknesses of the opponent's personnel, and (4) determining in the final analysis what will have to be done this year to win.

A game *strategy* extends directly from the plan. For example, the coaching staff decides that the opponent's defensive line is too tough to run against and that their pass coverage is weak, as it has been in the past; therefore, the coaches determine that their team will have to pass frequently to win. A "passing attack" would thus represent the team's game strategy.

We can carry the football analogy through to advertising. **Advertising strategy** is what the advertiser says about the product or brand being advertised. It is the formulation of a sales message that communicates the product or brand's primary benefit or how it can solve the consumer's problem.[11]

A Five-Step Program

Formulating an advertising strategy requires the advertiser to undertake a formal program.[12] The following presentation is built around a five-step program. Each step is illustrated by discussing a $30 million television advertising campaign undertaken in late 1988 by the Beef Industry Council.[13]

In an attempt to enhance the image of beef and revive sales at a time when American eating habits had moved toward greater consumption of poultry and seafood products, this campaign employed the services of a variety of well-known celebrities (actress Julia Louis-Dreyfus, Lauren Bacall, and Madeline Kahn; television star Timothy Busfield; model Kim Alexis; country singer Reba McIntire; and basketball players Larry Bird and Michael Cooper). The 1988–1989 campaign replaced a previous campaign that featured actors Cybill Shepherd and James Garner.

Step 1: Specify the Key Fact.   The *key fact* in an advertising strategy is a single-minded statement from the *consumer's point of view* that identifies why consumers are or are not purchasing the product/service or are not giving the brand proper consideration.

Research performed for the Beef Industry Council in the late 1980s undoubtedly revealed that many American consumers reduced their consumption of beef, or eliminated it entirely from their diets, because they regarded it as

11. Schultz and Tannenbaum, *Essentials of Advertising Strategy*, p. 4.
12. The following discussion is an adaptation from Schultz, Martin, and Brown, *Strategic Advertising Campaigns*, pp. 240–245.
13. General information for this discussion is based on Julie Liesse Erickson, "Star-Studded Cast Flavors New Beef Ads," *Advertising Age*, September 12, 1988, p. 3. Much of the interpretation is conjectural on the author's part, however, and is not based on direct information received from the Beef Industry Council.

high in fat and cholesterol and not an "in" food. The key fact that the Beef Industry Council probably wanted to convey in developing its 1988 advertising strategy was that beef is an "in" food—"Real food for real people."

Step 2: Primary Marketing Problem. Extending from the key fact, this step states the problem from the *marketer's point of view*. The primary marketing problem may be an image problem, a product perception problem, or a competitive problem.

The Beef Industry Council was faced with these problems: beef's image was less than desirable, the perception of beef as a non-nutritional product had to be overcome, and beef had to win back sales from poultry and seafood—its product-category competitors.

Step 3: Communications Objective. This is a straightforward statement about what effect the advertising is intended to have on the target market and how it is intended to persuade consumers.

The use of famous celebrities that represent the mainstream of American culture undoubtedly was designed to communicate an overall impression such as this: "These celebrities are 'in' people; they eat beef and enjoy it greatly; therefore, beef is an 'in' food that I, too, should incorporate more into my diet."

Step 4: Creative Message Strategy. The guts of the overall advertising strategy is the creative message strategy, sometimes also called the *creative platform*.[14] Implementing creative message strategy requires the following:

Define the Target Market. The target market for the advertising strategy and related marketing program is defined in terms of demographics, geographics, psychographics, media-consumption habits, and product/brand usage patterns.

The Beef Industry Council defined its market as "light users" of beef, that is, people who eat beef less than six times in any typical two-week period. The predominant choice of female celebrities suggests that the strategy was aimed slightly more at women than men, since women probably consume less beef and hold less-favorable attitudes toward it. Also, the choice of specific celebrities indicates that the target market consists of people who are likely to be relatively heavy television viewers and who enjoy sporting events.

Identify the Primary Competition. Who are the primary competitors in the segment the brand is attempting to tap? It is necessary to answer this question to know exactly how to position a product against consumers' perceptions of competitive product's advantages and disadvantages.

As noted, poultry and seafood products are the primary competitors for beef sales.

14. For example, Jewler, *Creative Strategy in Advertising.*

Choose the Promise.   The primary benefit or major selling idea that the product/brand promises to offer must be selected. In most cases, the "promise" is a consumer benefit or solution to a problem.

Beef cannot hope to "out-nutrition" poultry and seafood, since most consumers are familiar with research that shows these products to be more nutritious. However, the Beef Industry Council can promise that beef is "good" food—a food that is relatively nutritious and that is irreplaceable when, say, the consumer wants a hamburger and will accept no substitute. The promise, then, is actually a collection of eating concepts (taste, nutrition, convenience, fun, fulfillment) rather than a single product benefit. Consumers are being told that beef fits with their lifestyle and is an "in" food—"Real food for real people."

Reasons Why.   These are the supporting facts to back up the promise. In some instances advertisers can back up advertising claims with factual information that is relevant, informative, and interesting to consumers. In many instances it is impossible to physically prove or support the promise being made, such as when the promise is symbolic or psychological. In instances such as this, advertisers turn to authority figures, experts, or celebrities to support the implicit advertising promise.

This is precisely why the Beef Industry Council chose the cast of well-known and respected celebrities, who represent a variety of backgrounds and lifestyles that consumers find appealing.

Step 5: Corporate/Divisional Requirements.   The final step in formulating an advertising strategy involves the mandatory requirements that must be included in an ad. This aspect of advertising strategy formulation is relatively technical and uncreative. Basically, it reminds the advertiser to include the corporate slogan, a standard tag line (e.g., "Beef is real food for real people"), any regulatory requirements (e.g., in cigarette advertising), and so on.

In sum, advertising strategy lays out the details for the upcoming advertising program. It insists on a disciplined approach to analyzing the product/brand, the consumer, and the competition. A single-minded benefit is the outcome. The strategy becomes a blueprint, road map, or guide to subsequent advertising efforts. Every proposed tactical decision is evaluated in terms of whether it is compatible with the strategy.

Means-End Chains and Advertising Strategy

The consumer is, or at least should be, the foremost determinant of advertising messages. The notion of a means-end chain provides a useful framework for understanding the relationship between consumers and advertising messages. Means-end chaining focuses on the linkages between *attributes* of products (the means), the *consequences* for the consumer provided by the attributes, and the personal *values* (the ends) the consequences reinforce.[15]

Attributes are features or aspects of the to-be-advertised product or brand. For example, attributes of beef include positive features such as taste and ease of preparation and negative features (real or perceived) such as fat content and cholesterol. **Consequences** (desirable or undesirable) are received by consumers when consuming products. Good taste, fun times (e.g., enjoying a hamburger with friends), high calories, and fears of bad health are just some of the consequences that consumers associate with eating beef. **Values** represent important beliefs that people hold about themselves and that determine the relative desirability of consequences. Values related to eating include feelings of self-control. In general, values are *subjective*, *idiosyncratic* to each consumer, relatively *enduring*, *widely held* by consumers in a target market, and serve to *organize the meanings* for products and brands in consumers' memories.[16]

Figure 12.2 diagrams an illustrative means-end chain for beef. It can be seen that this hypothetical chain includes an assemblage of positive (approach) and negative (avoid) aspects of beef attributes and consequences from consuming beef. To the extent that this chain is representative for large numbers of American consumers, it is little wonder that the Beef Industry Council would have great difficulty in its advertising efforts to improve beef's image and increase beef consumption.

Advertising Applications of Means-End Chains

The concept of means-end chains is much more than just a framework for understanding how consumers perceive products and brands. The real value is in developing creative advertising messages. The relationship between advertising strategy and means-end chains has been labeled MECCAS models, an acronym standing for *Means-End Conceptualization of Components for Advertising Strategy*.[17]

---

15. This discussion is based on various writings by Professors Gutman and Reynolds, who along with several colleagues have popularized means-end theory in advertising. For example, see Jonathan Gutman, "A Means-End Chain Model Based on Consumer Categorization Processes," *Journal of Marketing*, vol. 46 (Spring 1982), pp. 60–72; Thomas J. Reynolds and Jonathan Gutman, "Advertising Is Image Management," *Journal of Advertising Research*, vol. 24 (February-March 1984), pp. 27–36; Thomas J. Reynolds and Jonathan Gutman, "Laddering Theory, Method, Analysis, and Interpretation," *Journal of Advertising Research*, vol. 28 (February/March 1988), pp. 11–31; Thomas J. Reynolds and Alyce Byrd Craddock, "The Application of MECCAS Model to the Development and Assessment of Advertising Strategy: A Case Study," *Journal of Advertising Research*, vol. 28 (April/May 1988), pp. 43–59.

16. J. Paul Peter and Jerry C. Olson, *Consumer Behavior: Marketing Strategy Perspectives* (Homewood, IL: Irwin, 1987), p. 117.

17. Jerry Olson and Thomas J. Reynolds, "Understanding Consumers' Cognitive Structures: Implications for Advertising Strategy," in *Advertising and Consumer Psychology*, eds. L. Percy and A. Woodside (Lexington, MA: Lexington Books, 1983), pp. 77–90.

FIGURE 12.2   **A Hypothetical Means-End Chain for Beef**

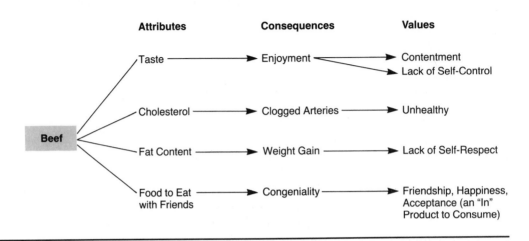

Table 12.1 presents and defines the various levels of the MECCAS model. Note that the components (or levels) include a driving force, a leverage point, executional framework, consumer benefit, the message elements. The *driving force* is the consumer value or end-level that the advertising strategy focuses on. Every other level is geared toward achieving the end-level. Study the definitions carefully in Table 12.1 before moving on to the following examples.

Maytag Appliances.   A long-running advertising campaign for Maytag appliances has concentrated on the "lonely repairman" theme. Maytag has attempted to create an image of reliable, dependable, and trouble-free products. The *driving force,* or end-level, for this campaign would seem to be the value that consumers place on trust, that is, the desire to be able to depend on other people and objects. The *leverage point* in the Maytag commercials is the activation of consumers' desire for trust by emphasizing that Maytag appliances always work and rarely require repairs. The rather pathetic "lonely repairman," who has nothing to do but anxiously await consumers' calls for repairs, represents the *executional framework,* or vehicle, for communicating trust, the key value orientation embodied in the ad. The obvious *consumer benefit* conveyed is the positive consequence of dependable product performance and the associated relief from the inconvenience and expense of product repairs. Finally, the key *message elements,* or product attributes, that convey dependability are the claims that Maytag products are made with great care, precision, and quality.

MECCAS—Means-End Conceptualization of Components for Advertising Strategy   TABLE 12.1

Level	Definition
Driving Force	The value orientation of the strategy; the end-level to be focused on in the advertising.
Leverage Point	The manner by which the advertising will "tap into," reach, or activate the value or end-level of focus; the specific key way in which the value is linked to the specific features in the advertising.
Executional Framework	The overall scenario or action plot, plus the details of the advertising execution. The executional framework provides the "vehicle" by which the value orientation is to be communicated; especially the Gestalt of the advertisement; its overall tone and style.
Consumer Benefit	The major positive consequences for the consumer that are to be explicitly communicated, verbally or visually, in the advertising.
Message Elements	The specific attributes, consequences, or features about the product that are communicated verbally or visually.

Source: *Advertising and Consumer Psychology* edited by Larry Percy and Arch G. Woodside, (Lexington, Mass.: Lexington Books, D. C. Heath and Company, 1983).

Beef Industry Council's 1988–1989 Campaign.   The *driving force* behind this campaign seems to be consumers' need to engage in healthy, acceptable behavior, and to do the "in" thing. The *leverage point* and *executional framework* are both intertwined with the various celebrities shown using and enjoying beef products. In other words, the campaign taps into the end-level of "acceptable behavior" by showing different celebrities using, enjoying, and espousing the merits of beef products. The *consumer benefit* conveyed is actually a class of benefits related to health, enjoyment, and acceptability. *Message elements* used to convey these benefits include shots of mouth-watering beef products and glimpses of celebrities enjoying product usage. The overall impression conveyed is that eating beef is a healthy, enjoyable, and acceptable thing to do. The chosen celebrities apparently represent people who are admired and who appeal to a broad cross section of American society.

Armstrong Magazine Ad.   A magazine advertisement for Armstrong's Trim and Fit® vinyl flooring provides a final illustration of how MECCAS models provide insight into the creative advertising process. As shown in Figure 12.3, this cartoon-like ad is actually a very serious attempt to remove the consumer's fear of making a mistake when installing floor covering. The *driving force* consists of several related values: self-reliance, competency, a sense of accomplishment, and social recognition. That is, a person performing some do-it-yourself home repair accomplishes any or all of these various values. The *leverage point* in the ad for activating these values is the bottom scene,

FIGURE 12.3   **A MECCAS-Model Illustration**

Go on, cut. You'll be brilliant.
Armstrong guarantees it.

Install your new Armstrong sheet vinyl floor with a Trim and Fit ™ kit, and if you goof while cutting or fitting, your Armstrong retailer will replace both the flooring and the kit.

Free. That's the Fail-Safe ™ Guarantee. Just see your local home center or building supply retailer for details.

FREE. For a free Floor Project Planning Pack, call the Armstrong Consumer Line at 1 800 233-3823 and ask for Dept. 69GWD. Or, send this coupon:
Armstrong, Dept. 69GWD, P.O. Box 3001, Lancaster, PA 17604

Name _____
                (please print)
Street _____
City _____
State _____ Zip _____

(A)rmstrong
so nice to come home to ™

Source: Courtesy Armstrong World Industries, Inc.

which shows a man smiling rather smugly as he receives an adoring hug from his wife for a job well done—thereby tapping into his (and, vicariously, the reader's) sense of accomplishment, competency, self-reliance, and recognition. The action plot in the *executional framework* reaches this conclusion by first showing the man in the top scene sweating profusely as he ponders the undesirable consequences of making a bad cut; in the bottom scene, the man is shown receiving the rewards of his endeavors. The major *consumer benefit* is a fail-safe program for installing your own floor covering. *Message elements* point this out in the body copy by stating that "if you goof while cutting or fitting," there is no need for worry: the Armstrong dealer will replace the flooring and the kit.

All-in-all, this "no goof" guarantee is an extremely effective marketing strategy, and the cartoon advertisement is a very creative way to tap into or activate the basic values associated with using this product. How effective do you think this magazine ad would have been if real people had been portrayed instead of cartoon characters? Might not the use of real people poised in this fashion have made the man seem excessively smug and the wife glaringly subservient?

These three examples demonstrate how product attributes are linked with consequences and consumer values to produce a desired end result, namely a clear product or brand meaning (i.e., a personality, so to speak). Effective linkages of attributes, consequences, and values enable advertising to provide psychological benefits to the consumer.[18]

Alternative Creative Strategies

The use of advertising to tap consumer values leaves open the possibility of a variety of different creative approaches. There actually is a continuum of approaches, ranging from *straight product promises and rational appeals* at one extreme to *purely psychological, emotional, or image-oriented ads* at the other extreme. Most actual advertising takes place somewhere between these extremes.

Several relatively distinct creative advertising strategies have evolved over the years. In fact, the bulk of contemporary advertising falls into seven creative categories. These are summarized in Table 12.2 and are described in detail in the following sections.[19]

Generic Strategy

An advertiser employs a **generic strategy** when making a claim that could be made by any company that markets the product. The advertiser makes no attempt to differentiate its brand from competitive offerings or to claim superi-

---

18. Reynolds and Gutman, "Advertising Is Image Management," p. 27.
19. The following discussion is based on Charles F. Frazer, "Creative Strategy: A Management Perspective," *Journal of Advertising,* vol. 12, no. 4 (1983), pp. 36–41.

TABLE 12.2   Summary of Creative Strategy Alternatives

Alternative	Most Suitable Conditions	Competitive Implications
Generic Straight product or benefit claim with no assertion of superiority.	Monopoly or extreme dominance of product category.	Serves to make advertiser's brand synonymous with product category; may be combated through higher-order strategies.
Preemptive Generic claim with assertion of superiority.	Most useful in growing or awakening market where competitive advertising is generic or nonexistent.	May be successful in convincing consumer of superiority of advertiser's product; limited response options for competitors.
Unique Selling Proposition Superiority claims based on unique physical feature or benefit.	Most useful when point of difference cannot be readily matched by competitors.	Advertiser obtains strong persuasive advantage; may force competitors to imitate or choose more aggressive strategy (e.g., "positioning").
Brand Image Claims based on psychological differentiation, usually symbolic association.	Best suited to homogeneous goods where physical differences are difficult to develop or may be quickly matched; requires sufficient understanding of consumers to develop meaningful symbols/associations.	Most often involves prestige claims which rarely challenge competitors directly.
Positioning Attempts to build or occupy mental niche in relation to identified competitor.	Best strategy for attacking a market leader; requires relatively long-term commitment to aggressive advertising efforts and understanding consumers.	Direct comparison severely limits options for named competitor; counterattacks seem to offer little chance of success.
Resonance Attempts to evoke stored experiences of prospects to endow product with relevant meaning or significance.	Best suited to socially visible goods; requires considerable consumer understanding to design message patterns.	Few direct limitations on competitor's options; most likely competitive response is imitation.
Emotional Attempts to provoke involvement or emotion through ambiguity, humor, or the like, without strong selling emphasis.	Best suited to discretionary items; effective use depends upon conventional approach by competitors to maximize difference; greatest commitment is to aesthetics or intuition rather than research.	Competitors may imitate to undermine strategy of difference or pursue other alternatives.

Source: Charles F. Frazer, "Creative Strategy: A Management Perspective," *Journal of Advertising,* Vol. 12, No. 4, 1983, p. 40.

ority. This strategy is particularly appropriate for a company that dominates a product category because the firm will enjoy a large share of any primary demand stimulated by generic advertising.

For example, Campbell's dominates the prepared-soup market in the United States, selling nearly two-thirds of all soup. Any advertising that increases overall soup sales naturally benefits Campbell's. This explains its "Soup is good food" campaign that extolled the virtues of eating soup without arguing why people should buy Campbell's soup. Along similar lines, AT&T's "Reach out and touch someone" campaign is a wise strategy in light of this company's grasp on the long-distance phone market.

Preemptive Strategy

Preemptive strategy is used most often by advertisers in product or service categories where there are few, if any, functional differences among competitive brands. Preemptive advertising by one firm forces competitors into the position of either saying the same thing, and thus being considered copycats, or of finding another advertising alternative.

The maker of Visine eye drops claims that this brand "gets the red out." All eye drops are designed to get the red out, but by making this claim first, Visine made a dramatic statement that the consumer will associate only with Visine. No other company would make this claim now for fear of being labeled a copycat. Likewise, no margarines contain cholesterol, but when one advertiser makes this claim, competitors have to search for something different to say about their brands.

Unique Selling-Proposition Strategy

The **unique selling-proposition (USP) strategy** promotes a product attribute that represents a meaningful, distinctive consumer benefit. A main feature of USP advertising is identifying an important difference that makes a brand unique and then developing an advertising claim that competitors either cannot make or have chosen not to make. The translation of the unique product feature into a relevant consumer benefit provides the unique selling proposition.

The USP strategy is best suited for companies whose products possess relatively lasting competitive advantages, such as makers of technically complex items or providers of sophisticated services.

Hewlett Packard has a USP when claiming that only the HP-28S can do symbolic algebra and calculus and retrieve and combine graphics instantly. Only the Nordic Track cross-country skiing machine can claim that it provides a greater workout than an exercise bike or a rowing machine (see Figure 12.4). Kentucky Fried Chicken has a unique selling proposition when claiming it knows chicken better than the burger places do. Burger King's proposition that

FIGURE 12.4   **Illustration of USP Strategy**

only it (and not McDonald's, Wendy's, or other hamburger chains) broils hamburgers is unique. Webster's *New World Dictionary* can claim uniquely that it is "the world's most up-to-date and authoritative desk dictionary."

In many respects the unique selling-proposition strategy is the optimum creative technique. This is because it gives the consumer a clearly differentiated reason for selecting the advertiser's brand over competitive offerings. The only reason USP advertising is not used more often is because brands in most product categories are pretty much homogeneous. They have no unique physical advantages to advertise and therefore are forced to use strategies favoring the more symbolic, psychological end of the strategy continuum.

Brand-Image Strategy

Whereas the USP strategy is based on promoting physical and functional differences between the advertiser's product and competitive offerings, the **brand-image strategy** involves psychological, rather than physical, differentiation. Advertising attempts to develop an image or identity for a brand by associating the product with symbols and archetypes.

Developing a brand image through advertising amounts to giving a product a *distinct identity or personality*. This is especially important for brands that compete in product categories where there is relatively little physical differentiation and all brands are relatively homogeneous (e.g., beer, soft drinks, cigarettes, blue jeans). Thus Anheuser-Busch has established Michelob beer as the beer that means excitement ("the night belongs to Michelob"); Pepsi is the soft drink for the "new generation"; Marlboro is for cowboys and other rugged individuals (see the *Focus on Promotion*); and Levi's 501 jeans are for "hip" people.

FOCUS ON PROMOTION

Marlboro's Image in Different Countries

What do college students in different countries think when considering Marlboro cigarettes? A researcher at Northwestern University posed this question and put it to the test by researching college students in five countries: Brazil, Japan, Norway, Thailand, and the United States. Small samples of students in each country participated in a word-association test by responding to the statement: "Smoking a Marlboro cigarette. . ."

Responses were sharply mixed. Thai students considered smoking a Marlboro cigarette to be relaxing. Norwegian stu-

Continued

Continued

dents most closely linked smoking Marlboros to disease, and Brazilians associated the brand with pollution. U.S. students responded to "Smoking a Marlboro cigarette. . ." with words like cowboy, horse, and macho—all relating directly to Marlboro's longstanding advertising campaign. The Japanese associated smoking Marlboros with social occasions.

These different images point out that products and brands mean different things around the world because the cultural contexts in which they are interpreted vary greatly. This means that creative advertising needs to be adjusted to accommodate the specific cultural context in which it is placed. For example, because Japanese consumers associate Marlboro cigarettes with being sociable, Marlboro advertisements in Japan could show the cowboy chatting with other cowboys rather than by himself. In Thailand, where consumers perceive cigarettes to be suggestive of relaxation, it may be most effective to show the cowboy in a subdued context rather than chasing wild horses.[20] ■

Positioning Strategy

According to **positioning strategy,** successful advertising must implant in the customer's mind a clear meaning of what the product is and how it compares to competitive offerings. Effective positioning requires that a company be fully aware of its competition and exploit competitive weaknesses. A brand is positioned in the consumer's mind relative to competition. "To be successful today, a company must be 'competitors' oriented. It must look for weak points in the position of its competitors and then launch marketing attacks against those weak points."[21]

Numerous examples are available to illustrate positioning strategies. For example, in the dishwashing-detergent category, Cascade says that it "fights spots," while Sunlight claims that it "cleans dried food from dishes." The automobile industry relies heavily on effective positioning. For example, Pontiac's positioning theme is "We build excitement"; they back this up with exciting stylings and advertising. Volvo positions itself as "a car you can believe in" and supports the claim in advertising by showing how sturdy the product is (see Figure 12.5). Chevrolet uses a patriotic theme in promoting itself as "the

20. The research is by Eduardo Camargo and is summarized in Lenore Skenazy, "How Does Slogan Translate?" *Advertising Age,* October 12, 1987, p. 84.
21. Jack Trout and Al Ries, "The Positioning Era: A View Ten Years Later," *Advertising Age,* July 16, 1979, pp. 39–42.

HOW WELL DOES YOUR CAR STAND UP TO HEAVY TRAFFIC?

What you see here is exactly what you think you see here. A Volvo supporting
the entire weight of a 6¾ ton truck. We sincerely hope you never find yourself in a
predicament like this. But if you do, we also hope you're in a Volvo.

VOLVO
A car you can believe in.

(Dealer Name)

Source: (c) 1987 Volvo North America Corporation. Reprinted with permission.

heartbeat of America." Toyota positions itself as a maker of quality automobiles ("Who could ask for anything more?").

Resonance Strategy

When used in the advertising-strategy sense, the term **resonance** is analogous to the physical notion of resonance, which refers to noise resounding off an object. In similar fashion, an advertisement resonates (or *patterns*) the audience's life experiences. **Resonant advertising strategy** extends from psychographic research and structures an advertising campaign to pattern the prevailing lifestyle orientation of the intended market segment.

Resonant advertising does not focus on product claims or brand images but rather seeks to present circumstances or situations that find counterparts in the real or imagined experiences of the target audience. Advertising based on this strategy attempts to match "patterns" in the commercial or ad with the target audience's stored experiences.[22]

The advertisement for the Pioneer PD-M700 compact disc player illustrates the use of resonance strategy (see Figure 12.6). The ad portrays a situation in which a young father is enjoying the experience of holding his baby and not having to waste time changing discs. Many readers of this ad could easily relate to the benefit of spending less time changing the music and more time enjoying it.

Emotional Strategy[23]

Much contemporary advertising aims to reach the consumer on an emotional level through the use of **emotional strategy.** Many advertising practitioners and scholars recognize that products are bought often on the basis of emotional factors and that appeals to emotion can be very successful if used appropriately and with the right products.

Emotional commercials and ads work especially well for products that naturally are associated with emotions (e.g., foods, jewelry, cosmetics, fashion apparel, soft drinks, and long-distance telephoning). However, emotional strategy can be used when advertising any product.

The Allstate ad in Figure 12.7 typifies the use of emotion in magazine advertising. Many older consumers who grew up in a time when men regularly wore dress hats can easily relate to this ad, which likely evokes strong memories brought back by the thought of their father's or grandfather's favorite spot for hanging his hat.

---

22. Frazer, "Creative Strategy," p. 39.
23. Frazer, ibid., refers to this as "affective strategy," but "emotional strategy" is more descriptive and less subject to alternative interpretations.

Source: Courtesy Pioneer Electronics (USA) Inc.

FIGURE 12.7   **Illustration of Emotional Strategy**

In Sum

Seven general forms of creative strategy have been discussed. These strategic alternatives, although they overlap to some extent, should provide a useful aid to understanding the different approaches available to advertisers and the factors influencing the choice of creative strategy.

It would be incorrect to think of these strategies as "pure" and entirely mutually exclusive. Because there is some unavoidable overlap, it is possible that an advertiser may consciously or unconsciously use two or more strategies simultaneously. For example, positioning strategy can be used in conjunction with any of the other strategies. An advertiser can position a brand against competitors' brands using emotional strategy, image strategy, a unique selling proposition, or other possibilities.

It is also worth noting that some advertising experts contend that advertising is most effective when it reflects both ends of the creative advertising continuum—that is, by addressing both rational product benefits and symbolic/psychological benefits. A New York advertising agency, Lowe Marschalk, provided recent evidence in partial support of the superiority of combined benefits over rational appeals only. The agency tested 168 television commercials, 47 of which contained both rational and psychological appeals and 121 of which contained rational appeals only. Using recall and persuasion measures, the agency found that the ads containing *both* rational and psychological appeals outperformed the rational-only ads by a substantial margin.[24]

Corporate Image and Issue Advertising

The type of advertising discussed to this point is commonly referred to as *product- or brand-oriented advertising.* Such advertising focuses on a product (e.g., beef) or, more typically, a specific brand (e.g., RCA televisions) and attempts ultimately to persuade consumers to purchase the advertiser's product/brand.

An alternative form of advertising, termed **corporate advertising,** focuses not on specific products or brands but on a corporation's overall image or on economic/social issues relevant to the corporation's interests.

There are two rather distinct forms of corporate advertising: image advertising and issue, or advocacy, advertising.[25]

---

24. Kim Foltz, "Psychological Appeal in TV Ads Found Effective," *Adweek,* August 31, 1987, p. 38.
25. This distinction is based on a classification by S. Prakash Sethi, "Institutional/Image Advertising and Idea/Issue Advertising As Marketing Tools: Some Public Policy Issues," *Journal of Marketing,* vol. 43 (January 1979), pp. 68–78. Sethi actually labels these two subsets of corporate advertising as "institutional/image" and "idea/issue." For reading ease they are shortened here to image versus issue advertising.

Corporate Image Advertising

This type of corporate advertising has been defined as follows:

> Corporate image advertising is aimed at creating an image of a specific corporate personality in the minds of the general public and seeking maximum favorable images amongst selected audiences, e.g., stockholders, employees, consumers, suppliers, and potential investors. In essence, this type of advertising treats the company as a product, carefully positioning and clearly differentiating it from other similar companies and basically 'selling' this product to selected audiences. Corporate image advertising is not concerned with a social problem unless it has a preferred solution. It asks no action on the part of the audience beyond a favorable attitude and passive approval conducive to successful operation in the marketplace.[26]

Corporate image advertising attempts to gain name recognition for a company, establish goodwill for it and its products, or identify itself with some meaningful and socially acceptable activity. For example, an ad for Hyundai, a Korean-owned corporation, proudly associates the company with the 1988 summer Olympics in Seoul, Korea (see Figure 12.8). This ad, like other corporate image advertisements, attempts to accomplish two overriding objectives: increase Hyundai's *identifiability* and enhance its *image*.[27]

Corporate advertisements hope to accomplish more than just creating an image. An advertising campaign by the Chevron Corporation provides vivid evidence that corporate ads can influence product sales. Chevron, like other petroleum companies, is often subject to criticism for offshore drilling and other activities that may be environmentally compromising. To overcome negative publicity, Chevron started the "People Do" advertising campaign in 1985 to enhance its image as a company that is interested in protecting and preserving the environment. A storyboard from one commercial in this campaign appears in Figure 12.9.[28]

To test the effectiveness of this campaign, Chevron's periodic tracking studies measure consumers' attitudes and gasoline purchase behavior. Of particular interest is whether the campaign has any impact on consumers who are most sensitive to environmental issues.[29] This is measured by comparing the percentage of environmentally concerned consumers who report Chevron as "the brand last bought."

Results indicate that the percentage jumped from 10 percent in January 1986 (at the beginning of the campaign) to 27 percent in January 1987 (after the

---

26. Ibid.
27. A study of over 200 major U.S. manufacturing and non-manufacturing firms showed that executives regard "image" and "identity" to be the two most important functions of corporate advertising. See Charles H. Patti and John P. McDonald, "Corporate Advertising: Process, Practices, and Perspectives" (1970–1989), *Journal of Advertising*, vol. 14, no. 1 (1985), pp. 42–49.
28. See Lewis C. Winters, "Does It Pay to Advertise to Hostile Audiences with Corporate Advertising?" *Journal of Advertising Research*, vol. 28 (June/July 1988), pp. 11–18.
29. The environmentally sensitive consumers in this research were considered to be the "inner-directeds" based on the VALS lifestyle typology. For further information on VALS, see Arnold Mitchell, *The Nine American Lifestyles* (New York: Macmillan, 1983).

Illustration of Corporate Image Advertising   FIGURE 12.8

Catch The Olympic Spirit

For us at Hyundai, the Olympic Games are something special. Special because they call for the same dedication, commitment, and outstanding performance that we do.

The spirit of achievement is what gives life to the Olympics, and what guides the Hyundai Business Group. It's why we've succeeded in many key industrial sectors, such as automobiles, construction, shipbuilding and steel in the world, and it's why we will continue to set the pace in high-technology fields of electronics, robotics and communications without knowing any limitations.

Hyundai's philosophy of consistent commitment to customer satisfaction has proven itself, making possible Olympic-class achievements time after time and it will surely continue to be our philosophy of business in the future.

Hyundai, Olympians in Business.

140-2 Kye-dong, Chongro-ku, Seoul, Korea.
TEL:741-2111/20, 741-4141/70
TLX:HYUNDAI K23111/5, K23175/7HD CORP.

FIGURE 12.9   **Storyboard from Chevron's "People Do" Campaign**

Radio TV Reports
41 East 42nd Street New York N.Y. 10017
(212) 599-5500

PRODUCT: CHEVRON   A85-19023
PROGRAM: NEWS   8/5/85   30 SEC.
KTTV-TV   (LOS ANGELES)   8:22PM

1. (MUSIC) ANNCR: This eagle could land in trouble.

2. The high point he might decide to rest on

3. could be dangerous.

4. Unaware that 13,000 volts await him,

5. he heads toward it and lands,

6. unharmed.

7. Wooden platforms above power lines now keep him above danger.

8. They were developed and put there by

9. a lot of people whose work brings them

10. to this remote area.

11. Do people really reach that high to protect a natural wonder?

12. People do. (MUSIC OUT)

Source: Courtesy of Chevron U.S.A. Inc.

campaign had run for one full year), a net increase of 17 percent who indicated Chevron as the gasoline brand last purchased. This dramatic finding suggests that it may indeed pay to advertise to hostile audiences with corporate advertising.

In general, corporate image advertising is directed at more than merely trying to make consumers feel good about a company. Companies are increasingly using the image of their firms to enhance sales and financial performance.[30]

Corporate Issue (Advocacy) Advertising

The other form of corporate advertising is **issue, or advocacy, advertising.** When using issue advertising a company takes a position on a controversial social issue of public importance. It does so in a manner that supports the company's position and best interests while expressly or implicitly challenging the opponent's position and denying the accuracy of their facts.[31]

Examples of issue (advocacy) advertising are presented in Figures 12.10 and 12.11. The advertisement in Figure 12.10 is an advocacy position by the Adolph Coors Company in hiring military veterans. In this advertisement, Coors comments on its commendable veteran-hiring practices and encourages other companies to do the same.

It is worth noting that some advertising observers might contend that this ad is not an issue ad at all, but rather a sophisticated, disguised way of enhancing Coors' image to a market segment of relatively heavy beer drinkers. This interpretation may indeed be correct, but on the surface the ad has the appearance of being an advocacy effort. It probably combines features of both image and issue advertising.

A second illustration of issue advertising is presented in Figure 12.11. This is just one of several ads undertaken by Philip Morris in a campaign that describes smokers' economic power. Directed at business executives in wake of the backlash against smokers, the ads apparently are designed to encourage greater tolerance of smokers, tolerance grounded in economic interest— "America's 55.8 million smokers are a powerful economic force."

Issue advertising is a topic of considerable controversy. Business executives are divided on whether this form of advertising represents an effective allocation of corporate resources. What, for example, does the Philip Morris ad hope to accomplish? Will it ultimately increase product sales and profits? How?

---

30. The influx of intense foreign competition and the merger craze of the 1980s have forced companies to reevaluate corporate advertising and to insist that it is a financially prudent investment. Corporate advertising that does not contribute to increased sales and profits is difficult to justify in today's economic climate. For further discussion, see Lori Kesler, "Merger Craze Colors Image," *Advertising Age*, October 5, 1987, pp. S1–S4.
31. Sethi, "Institutional/Image Advertising," p. 70.

FIGURE 12.10   **An Issue Advertisement by Coors**

Source: Courtesy Adolph Coors Company.

An Issue Advertisement Promoting the Economic Power of American Smokers   FIGURE 12.11

$1 trillion is too much financial power to ignore.

America's 55.8 million smokers are a powerful economic force. If their household income of $1 trillion were a Gross National Product, it would be the third largest in the world. The plain truth is that smokers are one of the most economically powerful groups in this country. They help fuel the engine of the largest economy on the globe.

The American Smoker— an economic force.

PHILIP MORRIS MAGAZINE

Presented by Philip Morris Magazine in the interest of America's 55.8 million smokers.
Source: The Roper Organization.

Source: Reprinted by permission of Philip Morris Incorporated.

Critics question the legitimacy of issue advertising and challenge its status as a tax-deductible expenditure. Further discussion of these points is beyond the scope of this chapter. The interested reader is encouraged to review the sources contained in the following footnote.[32]

Summary

The chapter examines creative advertising, advertising-strategy formulation, creative strategies, means-end models, and corporate image and issue advertising. An important initial question is: What are the general characteristics of effective advertising? Discussion points out that effective advertising must: (1) extend from sound marketing strategy, (2) take the consumer's view, (3) be persuasive, (4) break through the competitive clutter, (5) never promise more than can be delivered, and (6) prevent the creative idea from overwhelming the strategy.

Advertising must make some form of impression on consumers to be effective. Research has demonstrated that there is a structured, well-defined hierarchy of impressions. The most likely impression is *retention of the brand name*. This is followed in the hierarchy by the recognition of general characteristics (*generic*) of advertisements such as the characters involved in a television commercial. The *generation of feelings* is the third most likely impression registered by advertising. Retention of *commercial specifics* (e.g., who the spokesperson is, what kind of music was played) is the fourth most frequent form of impression. The *specific sales message* is the fifth and least likely impression accomplished by advertising.

Advertising is executed by formulating advertising strategy. Strategy formulation involves a multi-step process. The strategy is initiated by specifying the *key fact* advertising should convey to the target market. This key fact is translated, in step 2, into the *primary marketing problem*. Extending from this problem statement is the selection of specific *communications objectives*. The guts of advertising strategy consists, in step 4, of designing the *creative message strategy*. This involves selecting the target market, identifying the primary competition, and choosing the primary benefit to emphasize. The last step in the process involves ensuring that the advertisement meets all *corporate/divisional requirements*.

32. Louis Banks, "Taking on the Hostile Media," *Harvard Business Review*, March-April 1978, pp. 123–130; Barbara J. Coe, "The Effectiveness Challenge in Issue Advertising Campaigns," *Journal of Advertising*, vol. 12, no. 4 (1983), pp. 27–35; David Kelley, "Critical Issues for Issue Ads," *Harvard Business Review*, July-August 1982, pp. 80–87; Ward Welty, "Is Issue Advertising Working?" *Public Relations Journal* (November 1981), p. 29. For an especially thorough and insightful treatment of issue advertising, particularly with regard to the measurement of effectiveness, see Karen F. A. Fox, "The Measurement of Issue/Advocacy Advertising," in *Current Issues & Research in Advertising*, vol. 9, eds. James H. Leigh and Claude R. Martin, Jr. (Ann Arbor, MI, Division of Research, Graduate School of Business Administration, University of Michigan, 1986), pp. 61–92.

Advertising Classics

Official ball of the 1988 French Open.

Penn is also the official ball in 1988 for the United States Professional Tennis Association, Nabisco Grand Prix Tournaments, Equitable Family Challenge, Canadian Open, U.S.T.A. Adult League, Domino's Pizza Team Tennis and many other major tournaments. For a poster of this ad, send $3 to Penn, 306 South 45th Avenue, Phoenix, Arizona 85043. ©1988 Penn Athletic Products Division.

1988 Communication Arts Award of Excellence
Source: Courtesy of Penn Athletic Products.
Agency: Fallon McElligott.

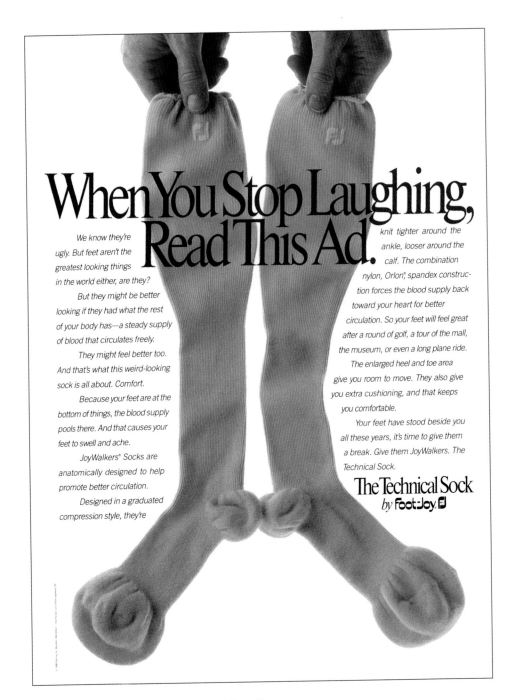

When You Stop Laughing, Read This Ad.

We know they're ugly. But feet aren't the greatest looking things in the world either, are they?

But they might be better looking if they had what the rest of your body has—a steady supply of blood that circulates freely.

They might feel better too. And that's what this weird-looking sock is all about. Comfort.

Because your feet are at the bottom of things, the blood supply pools there. And that causes your feet to swell and ache.

JoyWalkers® Socks are anatomically designed to help promote better circulation.

Designed in a graduated compression style, they're knit tighter around the ankle, looser around the calf. The combination nylon, Orlon®, spandex construction forces the blood supply back toward your heart for better circulation. So your feet will feel great after a round of golf, a tour of the mall, the museum, or even a long plane ride.

The enlarged heel and toe area give you room to move. They also give you extra cushioning, and that keeps you comfortable.

Your feet have stood beside you all these years, it's time to give them a break. Give them JoyWalkers. The Technical Sock.

The Technical Sock
by Foot-Joy ▣

1988 Communication Arts Award of Excellence
Source: Courtesy of Foot-Joy, Inc., Brockton, Massachusetts.

1988 Communication Arts Award of Excellence
Source: Photo courtesy of Nike, Inc.

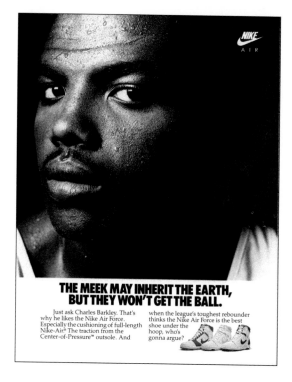

**1988 Communication Arts Award
of Excellence**
Source: Photo courtesy of Nike, Inc.

1988 Communication Arts Award of Excellence; The Show, Merit Award
Source: Courtesy Client, The Lee Company.
Agency: Fallon McElligott.

1988 Communication Arts Award of Excellence
Source: Courtesy Steuben, Client.
Agency: Doyle Graf Mabley; Ann Lemon, Art Director; Sujeong Shin, Copywriter;
Tom Mabley, Creative Director; Craig Cutler, Photographer.

1988 Communication Arts Award of Excellence
Source: Courtesy of The Perrier Group.

Baby Hush Puppies.

These Soft-Puppies from Hush Puppies come with flexible soles, breathable leather uppers and a little stuffed dog in every box. Your customers will go ga-ga.

For more information call (800) 253-2184

©1987 Hush Puppies Shoes is a registered trademark of Wolverine World Wide, Inc., Rockford, MI 49351.

1988 Communication Arts Award of Excellence
Source: Courtesy of Wolverine World Wide, Inc.

Cream good enough for Colombian Coffee
isn't exactly easy to find.

The richest coffee in the world."

**1988 Communication Arts Award of Excellence;
Prints Regional Design Annual, Certificate Award;
Print Casebook, Certificate Award; 1988 DDB
Needham Worldwide, Print, Non-Alcoholic
Beverage, and Agency Pinnacle Awards**
Source: Courtesy National Federation of Coffee
Growers of Colombia.

Colombian coffee is now being served
in the starboard lounge.

The richest coffee in the world."

**1988 Communication Arts Award of Excellence;
CLIO Award; Arts Directors, Merit Award; The
One Show, Merit Award**
Source: Courtesy National Federation of Coffee
Growers of Colombia.

1988 Communication Arts Award of Excellence
Source: Courtesy H. J. Heinz Co. Ltd.
Agency: Carder Gray Advertising Inc.

The next major subject covered in this chapter is the concept of *means-end chains* and the advertising framework extending from the *MECCAS models*. Means-end chains and MECCAS models provide a bridge between product *attributes* (the means), the *consequences* to the consumer of realizing product attributes, and the ability of these consequences to satisfy consumption-related *values* (the end). MECCAS models provide an organizing framework for developing creative ads that simultaneously consider attributes, consequences, and values.

The use of advertising to tap consumer values leaves open the possibility of a variety of different *creative strategies*. Seven specific strategies are described and illustrated with real advertising examples. These strategies are: generic strategy, preemptive strategy, unique selling-proposition strategy, brand-image strategy, positioning strategy, resonance strategy, and emotional strategy.

The final subject covered is *corporate advertising*. A distinction is made between conventional product- and brand-oriented strategy and advertising that focuses on facilitating corporate goodwill, enhancing image, and advocating matters of economic or social significance to a corporation. Two forms of corporate advertising, image and issue (advocacy) advertising, are described.

Discussion Questions

1. Research has shown that television commercials evoke a relatively standard pattern, or hierarchy, of impressions. Describe this hierarchy and explain why brand name is at the top of the hierarchy while specific sales points are at the bottom.

2. One requirement for effective advertising is the ability to break through competitive clutter. Explain what this means and provide several examples of advertising methods that successfully accomplish this.

3. Explain the meaning of the MECCAS model and describe an advertising campaign of your choice in terms of this model. Be specific in terms of the linkages from attributes to consequences to values.

4. Explain the differences between unique selling-proposition and brand-image strategies and indicate the specific conditions under which each is more likely to be used.

5. Positioning strategy is not mutually exclusive of other creative advertising strategies. Explain what this means and discuss how positioning can be achieved using different types of creative strategies.

6. What is a resonant advertising strategy? Explain the similarity between resonant advertising and what some advertising practitioners call "slice of life" advertising.

7. A television commercial for Miller Draft beer starts out by showing scenes of people experiencing a stifling summer day while fantasizing about a cold beer. In a subsequent scene, Miller Draft comes into the picture, and as people open cans of beer, the urban setting miraculously changes from a hot summer day to snow-covered streets. Describe how this television commercial represents a form of preemptive strategy.

8. Explain the preceding commercial in terms of means-end chain components (attributes, consequences, and values).

9. Some critics contend that advocacy, or issue, advertising should not be treated as a legitimate tax-deduction expenditure. Present and justify your opinion on this matter.

Exercises

1. Select two advertising campaigns that have been on television for a while and describe in detail what you think their creative message strategies are.

2. Review magazine advertisements and locate specific examples of the seven creative strategies that were discussed in the chapter. Be sure to justify why each ad is a good illustration of the strategy with which you identify it.

3. Locate two specific illustrations each of corporate image and issue advertising.

4. Along the lines of the Beef Industry Council case described in the chapter, select an advertising campaign and reconstruct in detail your interpretation of all the steps in the campaign's advertising strategy.

5. Present your interpretation of the ''pajama-man'' ad shown in Figure 12.1. Who is he supposed to be? Why is he included in the ad? What effect is his inclusion expected to have on magazine readers? What are the attributes, consequences, and values involved in this ad?

Media Strategy

THE VIDEOCART: A NEW ADVERTISING MEDIUM

he VideOcart was introduced to the advertising scene in 1988. Its developer, Information Resources Inc. (IRI), plans to have 10,000 VideOcarts in U.S. supermarkets by 1991. The VideOcart is potentially a valuable and cost-effective advertising medium as well as a means for increasing consumer shopping pleasure.

The VideOcart is nothing more than a shopping cart with a laptop-type (6-by-8 inch) computer screen on its handle. A computer in each supermarket directs a low-power FM transmitter to send advertisements to each cart's computer memory.

As the shopper moves down an aisle, advertisements for brands on the shelves being passed at that moment are triggered. About two ads per aisle, or approximately 32 ads storewide, will be displayed on the VideOcarts screen during the course of a full shopping trip. Ads are shown at breaks in an information and entertainment program presented on each cart's computer screen. Only about 15 percent of VideOcart's display time will be devoted to advertising.

The VideOcart will tally the amount of time customers spend in each aisle, will send an alarm if carts are taken out of the parking lot, and will allow advertisers the opportunity either to advertise nationally or to individual stores or groups of stores in local areas.

IRI will install the needed equipment in each supermarket, including a satellite dish on the roof (see Figure 13.1), at no cost to the supermarket. Supermarkets will receive a royalty for allowing VideOcart advertisements to be shown. Eventually, VideOcarts will reach 60 percent of all shoppers on a weekly basis at about the same cost per thousand as the cost of a newspaper free-standing insert—$4 to $5 per 1,000 households.[1]■

Creative advertising messages, the subject of the previous chapter, are necessary for advertising success. Outstanding message execution is to no avail, however, unless the messages are delivered to the right customers at the right time and with sufficient frequency. In other words, advertising messages stand a chance of being effective only if the media strategy itself is effective. Good messages and good media go hand in hand; they are inseparable. Improper media selection can doom an otherwise promising advertising campaign.

Creative advertisements are more effective when placed in media whose characteristics enhance the value of the advertising message and reach the advertiser's targeted customers at the right time. For example, the VideOcart is a promising advertising medium because it will deliver messages to shoppers at the time when they are prepared to make a product/brand purchase decision.

In many respects, media strategy is the most complicated of all marketing communications decisions. This is because a variety of decisions must be made when choosing media. In addition to determining which *general media* categories to use (television, radio, magazines, etc.), the media planner must also pick *specific vehicles* within each medium (e.g., choose particular radio stations, select specific magazines) and decide how to *allocate the available budget* among the various media and vehicle alternatives. Additional decisions involve determining *when to advertise*, choosing specific *geographical locations*, and deciding how to *distribute the budget over time and across geographic locations*. The complexity of media selection is made clear in the following commentary:

> An advertiser considering a simple monthly magazine schedule, out of a pool of 30 feasible publications meeting editorial environment and targeting requirements, must essentially consider over one billion schedules when narrowing the possibilities down to the few feasible alternatives that maximize campaign goals within budget constraints. Why over one billion possible schedules? There are two outcomes for each monthly schedule, either to use a particular publication or not to do so. Therefore, the total number of possible schedules equals two raised to the 30th power (i.e., $2^{30} = 1,073,741,800$). If ten *weekly* magazines are involved in a monthly schedule, the choices for each are not to run any advertisement or to run up to 4.3, the average number of weeks in a month. Technically, this presents the planner with over 17 million possible schedules from which to choose (i.e., $(4.3 + 1)^{10}$). Now imagine how the options explode when one is also

---

1. This description is based on "VideOcart Shopping Cart with Computer Screen Creates New Ad Medium That Also Gathers Data," *Marketing News*, vol. 22 (May 9, 1988), pp. 1, 2; and Ira Teinowitz and Judith Graham, "IRI Rolls into Future with VideOcarts," *Advertising Age*, May 2, 1988, p. 6.

FIGURE 13.1

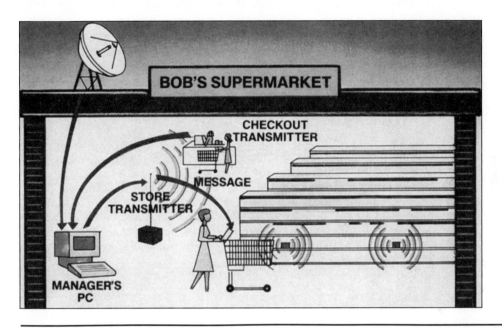

Source: "VideOcart Shopping Cart with Computer Screen Creates New Ad Medium That Also Gathers Data," *Marketing News*, Vol. 22, May 9, 1988, p. 2. Reprinted with permission from *Marketing News*, published by the American Marketing Association.

considering 60 prime time and 25 daytime broadcast television network programs, 12 cable television networks, 16 radio networks, four national newspapers, and three newspaper supplements, with *each vehicle* having between 4.3 and perhaps as many as 30 or more possible insertions per month.[2]

This chapter first reviews the media-planning process and then provides detailed analyses of five major advertising media: television, radio, magazines, newspapers, and outdoor advertising. Discussion of a sixth major medium—direct mail—is delayed until Chapter 15.

The Media-Planning Process

Media planning is "the process of designing a course of action that shows how advertising time and space will be used to contribute to the achievement of marketing objectives."[3] As shown in Figure 13.2, media planning involves co-

2. Kent M. Lancaster, "Optimizing Advertising Media Plans Using ADOPT on the Microcomputer," Working Paper, University of Illinois, December 1987, pp. 2–3.
3. Arnold M. Barban, Steven M. Cristol, and Frank J. Kopec, *Essentials of Media Planning: A Marketing Viewpoint* (Lincolnwood, IL: NTC Business Books, 1987), p.1

FIGURE 13.2   **Overview of the Media-Planning Process**

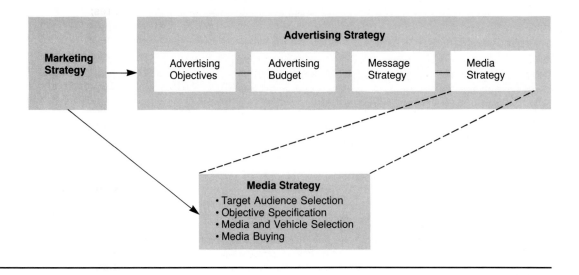

ordination of three levels of strategy formulations: marketing strategy, advertising strategy, and media strategy. The overall *marketing strategy* (consisting of target-market identification and marketing-mix selection) provides the impetus and direction for the choice of both advertising and media strategies. This is to say that the advertising objectives, budget, and message and media strategies extend naturally from the overall marketing strategy. For example, in the previous chapter we discussed General Motors' 1988 introduction of the Buick Reatta. The marketing strategy entailed promoting that this automobile combines the dual features of sportiness and comfort, pricing the car at a mid-price level ($25,000), and aiming it at older baby boomers and affluent elderly consumers.

Media strategy necessarily evolves from the more general *advertising strategy* involving budgeting, objective setting, and message considerations. The Reatta received a $10 million advertising budget in 1988 with the objective to create brand awareness and to convey the idea that the Reatta combines sportiness and comfort. Advertising strategy decisions simultaneously impose constraints on media strategy ($10 million is the maximum amount to be spent on the 1988 Reatta campaign) and provide direction for media selection.

The *media strategy* itself consists of four sets of interrelated activities: (1) selecting the target audience, (2) specifying media objectives, (3) selecting media categories and vehicles, and (4) buying media. The following sections discuss the first three activities in detail. No discussion is devoted to media buying, however, because it is a specialized topic more appropriately treated in texts devoted exclusively to media planning.

Target-Audience Selection

Successful media strategy requires first that the target audience be clearly pin-pointed. Failure to define the audience precisely results in wasted exposures; that is, some nonpurchase candidates are exposed to advertisements, while some prime candidates are missed.

Four major factors are used in segmenting target audiences for media strategy purposes: (1) geographic, (2) demographic, (3) product usage (e.g., heavy, medium, and light product users), and (4) lifestyle/psychographics. Product usage information typically provides the most meaningful basis for segmenting target audiences.[4] Such information is often unavailable, however, and media planners are forced to rely on geographic, demographic, and psychographic data.

Geographic, demographic, and psychographic considerations are typi-cally combined for purposes of target-audience definition. For example, Gen-eral Motors would define the target audience for the Reatta in terms such as the following: managerial and professional men and women between the ages of 45 and 64 (a demographic variable) who have no children younger than 18 years old living at home (demographic), reside predominantly in smaller towns and rural areas (geographic), have incomes exceeding $40,000 (demographic), who are deeply concerned with social acceptability and conformity (psycho-graphic),[5] are avid viewers of televised sporting events (psychographic), and are politically conservative and patriotic (psychographic). A target audience de-fined in such specific terms has obvious implications for both message and media strategy. Magazines appealing to this age group (e.g., *Time*) and televi-sion sports programs would represent two attractive media possibilities.

Media Objectives

A second aspect of media strategy is establishing specific objectives. Four ob-jectives are fundamental to media planning: reach, frequency, continuity, and cost. Media planners seek answers to the following types of questions: (1) What proportion of the target audience do we want to see (or read, or hear) the advertising message? (a *reach* issue); (2) How often should the target audi-ence be exposed to the advertisement? (a *frequency* issue); (3) When is the best time to reach the target audience? (a *continuity* issue); (4) What is the least expensive way to accomplish the other objectives? (a *cost* issue). Each of these objectives is now discussed in detail.

4. Henry Assael and Hugh Cannon, "Do Demographics Help in Media Selection?" *Journal of Ad-vertising Research*, vol. 19 (December 1979), pp. 7–11; Hugh M. Cannon and G. Russell Merz, "A New Role for Psychographics in Media Selection," *Journal of Advertising*, vol. 9, no. 2 (1980), pp. 33–36, 44.
5. Social acceptability and conformity features characterize the "belonger" group in the VALS ty-pology. See Arnold Mitchell, *Consumer Values: A Typology* (Menlo Park, CA: SRI International, 1978).

Reach.   The *percentage of a target audience* that is exposed *at least once* to the advertiser's message during an established time frame (usually four weeks) represents **reach**. In other words, reach represents the number of target customers who see or hear the advertiser's message *one or more times* during the time period. Other terms used by media planners for describing reach are *net coverage, unduplicated audience,* and *cumulative audience* (or *cume*). Later it will become clear why these terms are interchangeable with reach.

A number of factors determine the reach of an advertising campaign. Generally speaking, *the more media used* in a campaign, the more people reached. For example, if the Reatta were advertised only on network television, its advertisements would reach fewer people than if it were advertised in magazines and on radio in addition to television. A second factor influencing reach is the *number and diversity of different media vehicles used*. For example, more of the target audience for the Reatta would be reached by advertising on a number of different television programs compared to advertising exclusively on, say, "60 Minutes." Third, reach can be increased by *diversifying the day parts* used to advertise a program. For example, radio advertising during drive time and television advertising during prime time would reach more people than advertising exclusively during daytime.

Reach by itself is an inadequate objective for media planning because it tells nothing about how often target customers are exposed to the advertiser's message. Frequency of advertising exposures must also be considered.

Average Frequency.   The number of times, on average, within a four-week period that members of the target audience are exposed to (see, read, or hear) the advertiser's message is referred to as **average frequency** (or **frequency**, for short). To better understand the concept of frequency and how it relates to reach, consider the simplified example in Table 13.1. This example provides information about ten hypothetical members of the target audience for the Buick Reatta and their exposure to Reatta advertisements placed in *Time* magazine over four consecutive weeks. Member "A," for example, is exposed to Reatta ads twice, on weeks 2 and 3; "C" is never exposed to a Reatta ad in *Time* magazine; "F" is exposed only once, on week 4; and so on. Notice also in Table 13.1 that for each week, only five of ten households (50 percent) are exposed to the Reatta ad in *Time* magazine. This reflects the dual fact that (1) a single vehicle (*Time* in this case) rarely reaches the full target audience and (2) exposure to a vehicle does not guarantee that consumers will see a particular advertisement.

The frequency distribution and summary reach and frequency statistics are also presented in Table 13.1. The frequency distribution (designated as "f") represents the percentage of audience members (i.e., "% f") exposed 0, 1, 2, 3, or 4 times to the Reatta advertisement. The column labeled "% f+" indicates the percentage of the ten-member audience exposed at a certain level of exposures or greater than that level. For example, 70 percent were exposed two or more times to the *Time* magazine ad for the Reatta.

TABLE 13.1   **Hypothetical Frequency Distribution for Buick Reatta Advertised in *Time* Magazine**

Week	A	B	C	D	E	F	G	H	I	J	Total Exposures
1		x		x	x		x		x		5
2	x	x			x		x		x		5
3	x	x		x				x		x	5
4		x		x		x	x			x	5
Total Exposures	**2**	**4**	**0**	**3**	**2**	**1**	**3**	**1**	**2**	**2**	

Summary Statistics

Frequency Distribution (f)	% f	% f+	Audience Members
0	10%	100%	C
1	20%	90%	F,H
2	40%	70%	A,E,I,J
3	20%	30%	D,G
4	10%	10%	B

Reach (1+ exposures) = 90
Frequency = 2.2
Effective Frequency (3+ exposures) = 30
GRPs = 198 (2.2 × 90)
ERPs = 66 (2.2 × 30)

With this background, we now are in a position to illustrate how reach and frequency are calculated. It can be seen in Table 13.1 that 90 percent of the hypothetical audience for the Reatta have been exposed to one or more ads (i.e., with f = 1, % f+ = 90%). This figure, 90 percent, represents the *reach* for this advertising effort. Ninety percent of the target audience have been exposed to the ad one or more times during the four-week advertising period. When discussing reach statistics, advertising practitioners drop the percent and simply refer to the number. In this case, reach is "ninety."

Frequency is the average of the frequency distribution. In this situation, frequency equals 2.2.

$$\frac{(1 \times 20) + (2 \times 40) + (3 \times 20) + (4 \times 10)}{90} = \frac{200}{90} = 2.2$$

Hence, this hypothetical situation indicates that 90 percent of the Buick Reatta's ten-member target audience are exposed an average of 2.2 times during the four-week advertising schedule in *Time* magazine.

Gross Rating Points (GRPs).   Notice at the bottom of Table 13.1 that this hypothetical schedule yields 198 GRPs. **Gross rating points (GRPs)** are an indicator of the amount of impact, or gross weight, of an advertising schedule. The term *gross* is the key. The number of GRPs indicates the *gross coverage* or *duplicated audience* that is exposed to a particular advertising schedule. Compare these terms with the alternative terms given earlier for reach, that is, *net coverage* or *unduplicated audience.*

Returning to our hypothetical example, the reach (net coverage, unduplicated audience) is 90. The gross rating points (gross coverage, duplicated audience) amount to 198, because audience members on average are exposed multiple times (2.2 times) to the Reatta advertisement during the four-week ad schedule.

It should be apparent from this discussion that GRPs represent the arithmetic product of reach times frequency.

$$
\begin{aligned}
\text{GRPs} &= \text{Reach (r)} \times \text{Frequency (f)} \\
&= 90 \times 2.2 \\
&= 198
\end{aligned}
$$

It also should be apparent that by simple algebraic manipulation the following additional relations are obtained:

$$
r = \frac{\text{GRPs}}{f} \text{ and } f = \frac{\text{GRPs}}{r}
$$

Determining GRPs in Practice.   In actual advertising practice, media planners make media purchases by deciding how many GRPs are needed to accomplish established objectives. However, because the frequency distribution, reach, and frequency statistics are unknown commodities before the fact (i.e., at the time when the media schedule is determined and a media buy is placed), media planners need some other way to determine how many GRPs will result from a particular schedule.

There is, in fact, a simple way to make this determination. GRPs are determined (before the fact!) by simply summing the individual *ratings* obtained from the individual vehicles (television programs, magazine issues, etc.) included in a prospective media schedule. Gross rating points are nothing more than *the sum of individual ratings.* An individual **rating** is simply the proportion of the target audience exposed to a single issue of an advertising vehicle (such as a television program or a particular magazine).

For example, considering the hypothetical target audience specifications for the Buick Reatta given earlier, assume there are 5 million households who satisfy the demographic, geographic, and psychographic specifications that define this product's target audience. Assume further that 1.15 million members of this audience regularly watch "NBC Nightly News" with Tom Brokaw. NBC

News' rating for this target audience would therefore be a 23.0 (1.15/5 = .23, or 23). Finally, assume that one commercial for the Reatta is to be placed in each of the following network television programs. This schedule would yield 112 GRPs.

Program	Hypothetical Rating
"Dear John"	19.7
"NBC Nightly News"	23.0
"Monday Night Football"	22.1
"20/20"	22.5
"Murder, She Wrote"	24.7
	112.0 GRPs

Effective Reach and Effective Rating Points (ERPs). Alternative media schedules are usually compared in terms of the number of GRPs each generates. It is important to realize, however, that more GRPs does not necessarily mean better. Consider, for example, two alternative media plans, X and Z, both of which require the same budget. Plan X generates 90 percent reach and an average frequency of 2, thereby yielding 180 GRPs. (Note again that reach is defined as the proportion of the audience exposed one or more times to the advertising message during the course of the four-week campaign. Reach is referred to in shorthand terms as "1+".) Plan Z provides for 160 GRPs from a reach of 52 percent and a frequency of 3.08. Which plan is better? Plan X is clearly superior in terms of total GRPs and reach, but Plan Z has a higher frequency level. If the product/brand in question requires a greater number of exposures for the advertising to have an impact, then Plan Z may be the superior plan even though it yields fewer GRPs.

It is for the reason suggested in the preceding comparison that many advertisers and media planners have become critical of the GRP concept, contending that "it rests on the very dubious assumption that every exposure is of equal value, that the 50th exposure is the same as the tenth or the first."[6] Media analysts are beginning to think more in terms of effective reach.[7]

Effective reach is based on the idea that an advertising schedule is effective only if it does not reach members of the target audience too few or too many times. In other words, there is a theoretical optimum range of exposures to an advertisement with minimum and maximum limits. But what constitutes too few or too many exposures? This, unfortunately, is one of the most complicated issues in all of advertising. The only statement that can be made with certainty is: "It depends!"

6. A quote from advertising consultant Alvin Achenbaum cited in B. G. Yovovich, "Media's New Exposures," *Advertising Age*, April 13, 1981, p. S–7.
7. As a side note, the term *effective exposure* and *effective frequency* are often used in lieu of *effective reach*. However, the term *effective reach* is preferred here because it creates less confusion when discussing the calculation of *effective rating points (ERPs)*, a concept discussed later.

It depends, in particular, on considerations such as the advertised brand's competitive position, audience loyalty to the brand, message creativity, and what objectives advertising is attempting to accomplish. In fact, high levels of exposure per week may be unproductive for loyal consumers because of a leveling off of ad effectiveness.[8] Specifically, brands with higher market shares and greater customer loyalty probably require fewer advertising exposures to achieve minimal levels of effectiveness. Likewise, it would be expected that fewer exposures would be needed the more creative and distinctive a brand's advertising is. The higher up the hierarchy of effects the advertising is attempting to move the consumer, the greater the number of exposures needed to achieve minimal effectiveness. For example, more exposures probably are needed to successfully convince consumers that the Buick Reatta provides the dual advantages of sportiness and comfort than merely to make them aware of the Reatta's presence on the market.

In the final analysis, the minimum and maximum numbers of effective exposures can be determined only by conducting sophisticated research. Because research of this nature is time consuming and expensive, advertisers and media planners have relied on rules of thumb to indicate minimum and maximum levels of effective advertising exposure. On the low end, *fewer than three exposures* is generally considered ineffective, while *more than ten exposures* is considered excessive.

It cannot be overemphasized that what is effective (or ineffective) for one product/brand may not necessarily be so for another. Although effective reach planning is widely practiced by large consumer-product advertisers, media planners remain divided on the matter of what constitutes effective reach.[9]

The use of effective reach rather than gross rating points as the basis for media planning can have a major effect on overall media strategies. In particular, effective reach planning generally leads to *using multiple media* rather than depending exclusively on television, which is often the strategy when using the gross rating point criterion. Prime-time television is especially effective in terms of generating high levels of reach (1+ exposures), but may be deficient in terms of achieving effective reach (i.e., 3+ exposures). Thus, using effective reach as the decision criterion often involves giving up some of prime-time television's reach to obtain greater frequency (at the same cost) from other media.

This is illustrated in Table 13.2, which compares four alternative media plans involving different combinations of media expenditures from an annual advertising budget of $12 million. Plan A allocates 100 percent of the budget to network television advertising; Plan B allocates 67 percent to television and 33 percent to network radio; Plan C splits the budget between network television and magazines; Plan D allocates 67 percent to television and 33 percent to outdoor advertising.

8. Gerard J. Tellis, "Advertising Exposure, Loyalty, and Brand Purchase: A Two-Stage Model of Choice," *Journal of Marketing Research*, vol. 25 (May 1988), pp. 134–144.
9. Peter B. Turk, "Effective Frequency Report: Its Use and Evaluation by Major Agency Media Department Executives," *Journal of Advertising Research* (April/May, 1988), pp. 55–59.

Alternative Media Plans (Based on a $12 Million Annual Budget and Four-Week Media Analysis)   TABLE 13.2

	Plan A: TV (100%)	Plan B: TV (67%) Radio (33%)	Plan C: TV (50%) Mags. (50%)	Plan D: TV (67%) Outdoor (33%)
Reach[a]	69%	79%	91%	87%
Effective Frequency[b]	29%	48%	53%	61%
Frequency	2.8	5.5	3.2	6.7
GRPs	193	435	291	583
ERPs	81	264	170	409
$ per GRP	$62,176	$27,586	$41,237	$20,583
$ per ERP	$148,148	$45,455	$70,588	$29,340

[a]Based on 1+ exposures.

[b]Based on 3+ exposures.

Source: Adapted from "The Muscle in Multiple Media," *Marketing Communications,* December 1983, p. 25.

Notice first that Plan A (the use of network television only) leads to the lowest levels of reach (defined as 1+ exposures), effective reach (defined as 3+ exposures), frequency, and GRPs. An even split of 50 percent to network television and 50 percent to magazines generates an especially high level of reach (91 percent), while combinations of network television with network radio and network television with outdoor advertising are especially impressive in terms of frequency, GRPs, and the percentage of consumers exposed three or more times.

More specifically to the point, notice that the network television-only plan yields far fewer GRPs (reach × frequency) and considerably fewer **effective rating points, ERPs** (effective reach × frequency) than any of the other plans. Plan D, which combines 67 percent network television and 33 percent outdoor advertising, is especially outstanding in terms of the numbers of GRPs and ERPs generated. This is because outdoor advertising is seen frequently as people travel to and from work.

Should we conclude from this discussion that Plan D is the best and Plan A is the worst? Not necessarily. Clearly, the impact from seeing one billboard advertisement is probably far less than being exposed to a captivating television commercial. This points out a fundamental fact in media planning, namely that subjective factors also must be considered when allocating advertising dollars. The numbers, on the surface, do favor Plan D. However, judgment and past experience may speak in favor of Plan A on the grounds that the only way to effectively advertise this particular product is by presenting dynamic action shots of people consuming and enjoying the product. Only television could satisfy this requirement.

It is useful to return again to a point established in the previous chapter: It is better to be vaguely right than precisely wrong.[10] Reach, frequency, effective reach, GRPs, and ERPs are precise in their appearance, but in application, if used blindly, may be precisely wrong. Intelligent decision makers never become slaves to numbers by relying on numbers to make the decisions for them. Rather, the numbers should be used solely as additional inputs into a decision that ultimately involves insight, wisdom, and judgment.

Continuity.   A third general objective the media planner deals with is the timing of advertising. **Continuity** involves the matter of how advertising is allocated during the course of an advertising campaign. The fundamental issue is this: Should the media budget be *distributed uniformly* throughout the period of the advertising campaign, should it be spent in a *concentrated period* to achieve the most impact, or should some other schedule between these two extremes be used? As always, the determination of what is best depends on the specific product/market situation. In general, however, a uniform advertising schedule suffers from too little advertising weight at any one time. A heavily concentrated schedule, on the other hand, suffers from excessive exposures during the advertising period and a complete absence of advertising at all other times.

Advertisers have three general alternatives related to allocating the budget over the course of the campaign: continuous (and uniform), pulsing, and flighting schedules. To understand the differences among these three scheduling options, consider the advertising decision faced by a hypothetical manufacturer of a product such as hot dogs. Figure 13.3 shows how advertising allocations might differ from month to month depending on the use of continuous, pulsing, or flighting schedules. For illustration, assume the advertising budget for this hypothetical brand of hot dogs is $3 million.

Continuous Schedule.   In a **continuous** advertising schedule, a relatively equal amount of ad dollars are invested in advertising throughout the campaign. The illustration in Panel A of Figure 13.3 shows an extreme case of continuous advertising in which the hypothetical hot dog advertiser allocates the $3 million advertising budget in equal amounts of exactly $250,000 each month.

Such an advertising allocation would make sense only if hot dogs were consumed in essentially equal quantities throughout the year. Although hot dogs are consumed year round, consumption is particularly high during May,

10. Leonard M. Lodish, *The Advertising and Promotion Challenge: Vaguely Right or Precisely Wrong?* (New York: Oxford University Press, 1986).

Continuous, Pulsing, and Flighting Advertising Schedules for a Hypothetical Brand of Hot Dogs   FIGURE 13.3

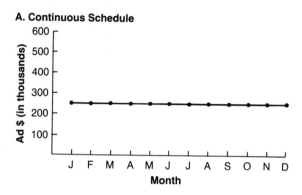

A. Continuous Schedule

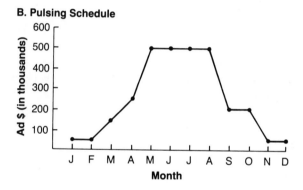

B. Pulsing Schedule

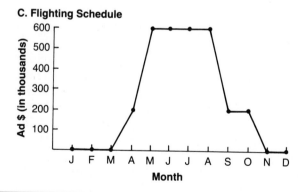

C. Flighting Schedule

June, July, and August. This calls for a discontinuous allocation of advertising dollars throughout the year.

Pulsing. In a **pulsing** advertising schedule, *some advertising* is used during *every period of the campaign,* but the amount of advertising varies considerably from period to period. In Panel B of Figure 13.3 a pulsing schedule for our hypothetical hot dog manufacturer shows the company advertising especially heavy during the high-consumption months of May through August (spending $500,000 each month), but continuing to advertise in every month throughout the year. The minimum advertising expenditure is $50,000 even in the slow months of January, February, November, and December.

Flighting. In a **flighting schedule,** the advertiser varies expenditures throughout the campaign and allocates *zero expenditures in some months.* Thus, pulsing and flighting are similar in that they both involve discontinuous expenditures throughout the advertising campaign, but are different in that some advertising takes place in every period with pulsing but not with flighting.

Panel C in Figure 13.3 illustrates a flighting schedule. The hot dog company allocates $600,000 to each of the four high-consumption months, $200,000 each to moderate-consumption months (April, September, and October), but zero dollars to five low-consumption months (January, February, March, November, and December).

Flighting and pulsing have become matters of necessity because of the tremendous increases in media costs, especially network television (more on this later in the chapter). Few advertisers can afford to advertise heavily throughout the year. They are forced to select periods when advertising stands the greatest chance of accomplishing communication and sales objectives.

Cost Considerations. Cost is a final media objective in addition to reach, frequency, and continuity concerns. Media planners attempt to allocate the advertising budget in a cost-efficient manner subject to satisfying other objectives. One of the most important and universally used indicators of media efficiency is known as cost per thousand. **Cost per thousand** (abbreviated **CPM,** with the "M" being the Roman numeral for 1,000) is the cost of reaching 1,000 people. The measure can be refined to mean the cost of reaching 1,000 members of the *target audience,* excluding those people who fall outside the target market. This refined measure is designated **CPM-TM.**[11]

CPM and CPM-TM are calculated by dividing the cost of an advertisement by a medium's circulation within the total market (CPM) or target market (CPM-TM). By definition, CPM and CPM-TM are:

11. Charles H. Patti and Charles F. Frazer, *Advertising: A Decision-Making Approach* (Hinsdale, IL: The Dryden Press, 1988), p. 369.

$$CPM = \frac{\text{Cost of Ad}}{\text{No. of total "contacts" (in thousands)}}$$

$$CPM\text{-}TM = \frac{\text{Cost of Ad}}{\text{No. of TM "contacts" (in thousands)}}$$

The term "contacts" is used here in a general sense to include any type of advertising audience (television viewers, magazine readers, radio listeners, etc.).

To illustrate how CPM and CPM-TM are calculated, consider the following rough estimates for "The Cosby Show" television series. These include an estimated rating of 25 percent of the approximately 84 million U.S. households, an assumed target market two-thirds the size of the total "Cosby" viewership, and an advertising expenditure of $369,500 for a 30-second commercial.

$$\text{Total viewership} = 21,000,000 \text{ households}$$
$$\text{Target-market viewership} = 14,000,000 \text{ households}$$
$$\text{Cost of :30 commercial} = \$369,500$$

Thus,

$$CPM = \frac{\$369,500}{21,000}$$
$$= \$17.60$$

$$CPM\text{-}TM = \frac{\$369,500}{14,000}$$
$$= \$26.39$$

The CPM and CPM-TM calculations are useful for comparing different advertising schedules. They must be used cautiously, however, for several reasons. First, these are measures of cost efficiency—not of effectiveness. A media schedule may be extremely efficient but totally ineffective because it (1) reaches the wrong audience (if CPM is used rather than CPM-TM) or (2) is inappropriate for the product category advertised. By analogy, CPM is comparable to using miles-per-gallon calculations for comparing automobiles. A Hyundai Excel may be more efficient than a BMW but less effective for one's purposes.[12]

A second limitation with CPM and CPM-TM measures is that it is inappropriate to compare CPMs across different media. CPMs differ across media

12. This analogy is adapted from Patti and Frazer, ibid.

because, as will be elaborated on later, the various media perform different roles and are therefore priced differently. A lower CPM for radio does not mean that buying radio is better than buying a more expensive (CPM-wise) television schedule.

Finally, CPM statistics can be misused unless vehicles within a particular medium are compared on the same basis. For example, the CPM for a daytime-television advertising schedule is less than a prime-time schedule, but this amounts to comparing apples with oranges. The proper comparison is between two daytime schedules or between two prime-time schedules. Similarly, it would be inappropriate to compare the CPM for a black and white magazine ad against a four-color magazine ad.

Tradeoffs, Tradeoffs, Tradeoffs.   The various media-planning objectives (reach, frequency, continuity, and cost) have now been discussed in some detail. Each was discussed without direct reference to the other objectives. It is important to recognize, however, that these objectives are actually somewhat at odds with one another. That is, *given a fixed advertising budget* (e.g., $10 million for the Buick Reatta), the media planner *cannot* simultaneously optimize reach, frequency, and continuity objectives. Tradeoffs must be made.

For example, with a fixed advertising budget, the media planner can choose to maximize reach or frequency, but not both. With increases in reach, frequency is sacrificed, and vice versa—if you want to reach more people, you cannot reach them as often with a fixed advertising budget; if you want to reach them more often, you cannot reach as many.[13] Similarly, with a fixed advertising budget, an advertiser cannot simultaneously increase advertising continuity and also increase reach or frequency.

What is the solution? There is no simple solution. Each media planner must decide what is best given the particular circumstances surrounding the advertising decision. Considering just the tradeoff between reach and frequency, however, there are some general parameters to guide the decision of which to emphasize.[14] In general, a *reach strategy* should be emphasized in the following situations: (1) for *new products* (it is important to create widespread awareness, thus demanding a high level of reach); (2) for products/brands with *undefined markets* (when the market is undefined or diffused, the budget must be spread widely to reach as many people as possible); (3) for brands with *strong brand franchises* (brands with large market shares and loyal customers can expand their markets only by reaching prospective new customers, thus calling for emphasis on reach over frequency); and (4) for product categories charac-

---

13. This discussion may remind you of what you learned in basic statistics about the tradeoff between committing Type I and Type II errors while holding sample size constant. You learned that with a fixed sample size, decisions to decrease a Type I error (say, from alpha = .05 to .01) must inevitably result in an increase in the Type II, or beta, error.

14. This discussion of reach and frequency strategies is based on Don E. Schultz, Dennis Martin, and William P. Brown, *Strategic Advertising Campaigns* (Lincolnwood, IL: NTC Business Books, 1987), chapter 12.

terized by *infrequent purchase cycles* (when products are purchased infrequently, it is unnecessary to reach consumers frequently).

A *frequency strategy* is called for in situations counter to the preceding circumstances. In particular, emphasis on frequency over reach is suggested when: (1) *competitors are strong*, (2) a *complex message* has to be conveyed to the target audience, (3) the product/brand is *purchased frequently*, (4) *brand loyalty is weak*, (5) the *target market is well-defined*, and (6) consumers are *resistant to the product/brand*.

Formal Media Models.

The media planner is faced with the difficult task of trying to accomplish multiple objectives (reach, frequency, etc.) while at the same time having to make intelligent tradeoffs among them. On top of this, there are thousands, if not millions, of possible advertising schedules that could be selected depending on how the various media and media vehicles are combined. Fortunately, this daunting task can be facilitated by computerized mathematical models that assist media planners in making media-selection decisions. These models essentially attempt to optimize some goal, or objective function (e.g., select a schedule such that it yields a lower CPM than any other schedule), subject to satisfying constraints such as the upper or lower limits on the advertising budget. A computerized program then searches through the possible solutions, ultimately selecting a particular media schedule that optimizes the objective function and satisfies all constraints specified.[15]

Though extremely useful, media models are designed for solution on mainframe computers and as such are primarily accessible only to major advertisers and their advertising agencies. A recent model, called ADOPT (which stands for ADvertising OPTimization), has the advantage of being designed for solution with a microcomputer.

ADOPT (pronounced ad-opt) has been described by its developer as "a user-friendly, inexpensive and readily available microcomputer program that allows one to identify optimum advertising media plans. . . . It will easily exceed the requirements of most educators and small to modest size advertisers, agencies and media organizations."[16] ADOPT evaluates media schedules involving up to 30 vehicles in all major media categories (television, newspaper, etc.). It also allows users to evaluate the combined effects of schedules across multiple media.

The user first develops a media database (e.g., provides media vehicle names and costs) and then selects primary and secondary criteria for schedule optimization. The available optimization alternatives include (1) reach (1+), (2) effective reach (3+), (3) average frequency, (4) GRPs, and (5) CPM. The user also specifies the budget constraint (both the minimum and maximum amounts

15. These models go by names such as MEDIAC and ADMOD. For further discussion, see David A. Aaker and John G. Myers, *Advertising Management* (Englewood Cliffs, NJ: Prentice-Hall, 1987), pp. 450–463; and Roland T. Rust, *Advertising Media Models: A Practical Guide* (Lexington Books, Lexington, MA: 1986).

16. Lancaster, "Optimizing Advertising Media Plans Using ADOPT on the Microcomputer."

TABLE 13.3   **Database for the All-Bran Media Scheduling Decision**

Magazine		Rating	Cost	Maximum Insertions
1.	Reader's Digest	26.4%	$104,600	1
2.	TV Guide	25.4	95,900	5
3.	Family Circle	20.8	75,280	1
4.	Good Housekeeping	20.8	80,025	1
5.	Better Homes & Gardens	20.4	95,400	1
6.	Woman's Day	19.4	66,960	1
7.	McCall's	16.8	60,800	1
8.	People	15.2	61,345	5
9.	Ladies Home Journal	14.7	61,300	1
10.	National Geographic	12.9	117,715	1
11.	Time	10.9	114,955	5
12.	Redbook	10.2	55,255	1

Source: Kent M. Lancaster, "Optimizing Advertising Media Plans Using ADOPT on the Microcomputer," Working Paper, University of Illinois, December 1987, p. 12. Ratings data obtained from Simmons Market Research Bureau (Vol. P-20, pp. 38–39, 1985). Cost information obtained from *Leo Burnett 1986 Media Cost and Coverage*, pp. 17–18. Minimum insertions = 0 for each magazine.

to be spent) and the minimum and maximum number of insertions for each vehicle. Once the user has provided this information, ADOPT seeks out the best schedule given the objective function specified and subject to satisfying the budget and insertion constraints.

Illustration.[17]   A media planner for Kellogg's All-Bran cereal is in the process of choosing an optimum schedule from among 12 magazines. She wants to select the best magazine schedule for reaching female homemakers who use cold breakfast cereal. The Simmons Market Research Bureau (SMRB) estimates the market size to be 69,405,000 households. The media planner has prepared a database consisting of 12 magazines suited to reaching the target audience (see Table 13.3). *Reader's Digest,* for example, has a rating of 26.4 percent and charges $104,600 for a one-page advertisement. The media planner wants no more than a single All-Bran advertisement to appear in *Reader's Digest* during the June 1988 planning period, a month with five weeks. Read the remaining entries in similar fashion.

The information in Table 13.3 is inputed into the ADOPT database by specifying each magazine's name, cost, rating, and maximum insertions. The user then inputs the lower and upper budget constraints. In this particular application, the media planner specifies a minimum expenditure of $475,000 and an upper limit of $500,000. Next she inputs the primary and secondary

17. This illustration is adapted from Lancaster, ibid.

optimization criteria, choosing reach (1+) as the primary criterion and CPM as the secondary criterion.

   With this information, ADOPT now seeks a solution that first maximizes reach and secondarily minimizes cost per thousand. Given 12 magazines and different numbers of maximum insertions in each, there are 110,592 total possible schedules! ADOPT seeks from among these thousands of possibilities a single magazine schedule that will maximize reach and minimize CPM. The solution is shown in Table 13.4.

ADOPT Solutions for All-Bran Magazine Decision   TABLE 13.4

Brand = Kellogg's All-Bran
Target = Female homemakers
Target size = 69,405,000
Period = June 1988

Frequency Distribution (f)	% f	% f+
0	30.44%	100.00%
1	30.74	69.56
2	21.10	38.82
3	11.32	17.71
4	4.74	6.40
5	1.43	1.66
6	0.24	0.24

Summary Evaluation

Reach (1+)	69.56%
Effective Reach (3+)	17.71%
Average Frequency	1.93
Gross Rating Points	134.40
Gross Impressions (in thousands)	93,280.34
CPM/Gross Impressions	$5.35
Cost per Rating Point	$3,716.07

Vehicle List	Rating	Ad Cost	CPM	Ads	Total Cost
Reader's Digest	26.4	$104,600	$10.79	1	$104,600
TV Guide	25.4	95,900	10.36	2	191,800
Family Circle	20.8	75,280	9.93	1	75,280
Woman's Day	19.4	66,960	9.47	1	66,960
McCall's	16.8	60,800	9.93	1	60,800
		Totals:	$10.20	6	$499,440

Source: Adapted from Kent M. Lancaster, "Optimizing Advertising Media Plans Using ADOPT on the Microcomputer," Working Paper, University of Illinois, December 1987, Figure 1, p. 15. Adapted with permission.

Table 13.4 shows that the optimum schedule consists of one ad in *Reader's Digest*, two insertions in *TV Guide*, one insertion in *Family Circle*, one ad in *Woman's Day*, and one ad in *McCall's*. The total cost is $499,440, which is just under the specified upper limit of $500,000. This schedule yields a maximum reach (1+) of 69.56 percent of the 69,405,000 female homemakers who are users of cold breakfast cereal. The cost per thousand is also optimized at $10.20. Notice further in the summary evaluation that the effective reach (3+) is only 17.71 percent and that the schedule will generate 134.40 GRPs at a cost of $3,716.07 per rating point.

Is this a good media schedule? In terms of reach and CPM objectives, the schedule is the very best possible out of over 100,000 possibilities. Whether it satisfies other objectives (e.g., effective reach) is a matter that only the media planner and her associates can determine. As noted earlier, a variety of subjective considerations enter into a media choice. Media models such as ADOPT do not make the ultimate media-scheduling decision. All they can do is efficiently perform the millions of calculations needed to determine which single media schedule will optimize some objective function (such as maximizing reach or minimizing CPM). Armed with the answer, it is up to the media planner to determine whether the media schedule satisfies other, nonquantitative objectives such as those described in the following section.

Media and Vehicle Selection

We have reviewed the various objectives (reach, frequency, continuity, and cost considerations) that direct media choice and have described a model for selecting a media schedule that meets an objective function. Ultimately, the media planner must select general media categories (television, radio, magazines, etc.) and then pick specific vehicles (particular television programs, magazines, etc.) within each medium. These decisions are based largely on the previously described objectives (reach, frequency, etc.) but also must take into account less quantitative considerations. Creative considerations are particularly important.

Creative Considerations. Each medium and vehicle has a set of unique characteristics and virtues (see Figure 13.4). This will almost certainly vary with the judgment of the media planner, but advertisers attempt to select those media and vehicles whose characteristics are most compatible with the advertised product and which will enhance the product's image.

If the objective is to demonstrate product features, television is the best medium to use, followed by magazines, newspapers, radio, and outdoor advertising (see Figure 13.4). Television is also particularly strong in terms of its entertainment and excitement value and its ability to have an impact on the viewer. Magazines are strong in terms of elegance, beauty, prestige, and tradition. Newspapers are valuable to advertisers because of their newsworthi-

Which Media Do It Best

	Television	Magazines	Newspapers	Radio	Outdoor
Demonstration					
Elegance					
Features					
Intrusion					
Quality					
Excitement					
Imagination					
Beauty					
Entertainment					
Sex Appeal					
Personal					
One-On-One					
Snob Appeal					
Package I.D.					
Product-In-Use					
Recipe					
Humor					
Tradition					
Leadership					
Information					
Authority					
Intimacy					
Prestige					
Bigger-Than-Life					
News					
Event					
Impact					
Price					

I   II   III   IV   V

Source: Courtesy of Needham Harper Worldwide, Inc.

ness and attractive price. Radio, which is especially personal, allows for the listener's imagination to play a part, while outdoor advertising is particularly good for package identification. Subsequent sections offer detailed descriptions of all five major media: television, radio, magazines, newspapers, and outdoor advertising.

Television

Television is practically an ubiquitous communication medium in the United States as well as in much of the industrialized world. Television sets are present in over 98 percent of all American households. In 1985, 57 percent of American households had two or more sets, and 93 percent had a color set.[18] As an advertising medium, television is uniquely personal and demonstrative, yet it is also expensive and subject to considerable competitive clutter.

Television's specific strengths and weaknesses are elaborated upon in a later section. First it will be instructive to examine two specific aspects of television advertising: (1) the different programming segments, or so-called day parts, and (2) the alternative outlets for television commercials (network, spot, local, and cable).

Television Programming Segments

It would be simplistic to treat all television advertising as if it were equally expensive and effective. Advertising costs, audience characteristics, and programming appropriateness vary greatly at different times of the day and during different days of the week. In television parlance, the times of day are referred to as *day parts*. There are three major day parts: prime time, daytime, and fringe time. Each segment has its own strengths and weaknesses.[19]

Prime Time.   The period between 8:00 p.m. and 11:00 p.m. (eastern time) is known as *prime time*. The best and most expensive programs and actors are scheduled during this period. Audiences are largest during prime time, and the networks naturally charge the highest rates during this time. Advertising rates during prime time have continued to increase year after year because many national advertisers apparently find prime time advertising worthwhile and are willing to pay increasing rates.

Daytime.   The period that begins with the early morning news shows (e.g., "Today Show") and extends to 4:00 p.m. (eastern time) is known as *daytime*. Early daytime appeals first to adults with news programs and then

18. Anthony F. McGann and J. Thomas Russell, *Advertising Media: A Managerial Approach* (Homewood, IL: Irwin, 1988), p. 139.
19. The following discussion is adapted from McGann and Russell, *Advertising Media*, pp. 141–143.

to children with special programs designed for this group. Afternoon programming, with its special emphasis on soap operas, appeals primarily to women working at home and, according to rumor, college students in dormitories.

Fringe Time.   The period preceding and following prime time is known as *fringe time*. Early fringe starts with afternoon reruns and is devoted primarily to children, but it becomes more adult oriented as prime time approaches. Late fringe appeals primarily to young adults.

Network, Spot, Local, and Cable Advertising

Television messages are transmitted by local stations, which are either locally owned cable television systems or are affiliated with the three major commercial networks (ABC, CBS, and NBC) or with an independent cable network (such as WTBS, the Turner Broadcasting System). This arrangement of local stations and networks makes different ways of buying advertising time on television possible.

Network Television Advertising.   Companies that market products nationally often use network television to reach potential customers throughout the country. The advertiser, typically working through an advertising agency, purchases desired time slots from one or more of the major networks and advertises at these times on all local stations that are affiliated with the network.

The cost of such advertising depends on the day part when an ad is aired as well as on the popularity of the television program in which the ad is placed. Figure 13.5 provides prime-time rates charged by the three networks (ABC, CBS, and NBC) for 30-second commercials aired during the 1987–1988 television season. You will note that 30-second rates ranged from a low of $48,120 for "West 57th" to a high of $369,500 for "The Cosby Show."

In spite of these large figures, network television is frequently a cost-efficient means to reach mass audiences. Consider the $79,830 cost for "ABC Thursday Movie" and assume that the average rating during the 1987–1988 season was approximately 20 percent. This means that approximately 17 million households would have tuned in to the movie when it was aired by ABC from 9:00 until 11:00 on Thursday evenings. Thus, an advertiser on this program would have paid approximately only $4.70 to reach every 1,000 households with a 30-second advertising message.

Another point in favor of national advertisers using network television advertising (rather than the alternative, spot television) is that network rates are only 10 to 70 percent of the sum of the individual station (spot) rates, with the actual rate differential depending on time of day and season.[20]

20. John L. Peterman, "Differences between the Levels of Spot and Network Television Advertising Rates," *Journal of Business*, vol. 52, no. 4 (1979), pp. 549–561.

FIGURE 13.5   Prime-Time Network TV Advertising Rates (1987–1988)

Networks' 30-second price list, 1987-88 season

Prices reflect the average advertisers paid for a 30-second prime-time unit in October 1987. NBC's average cost was $150,625; ABC has an average cost of $111,820; CBS' average cost is $103,130. The networks provide these numbers to Broadcast Advertisers Reports and A.C. Nielsen Co. The following reflects the most recent schedule with new-for-fall shows shaded in gray; an asterisk (*) denotes where a time period has a different program since October. Source: BAR and Nielsen.

		7:00 (ET)	7:30	8:00	8:30	9:00	9:30	10:00	10:30
MONDAY	ABC			MacGyver $90,330		Monday Night Football $195,000			
	CBS			Kate & Allie $102,640	Frank's Place* $100,350	Newhart $149,190	Designing Women $124,790	Cagney & Lacey $115,440	
	NBC			ALF $149,500	Valerie's Family $161,000	NBC Monday Night at the Movies $150,000			
TUESDAY	ABC			Who's the Boss? $197,660	Growing Pains $228,350	Moonlighting $249,190		thirtysomething $125,460	
	CBS			Houston Knights $87,850		Jake & the Fatman $91,520		The Law & Harry McGraw $76,060	
	NBC			Matlock $103,000		J. J. Starbuck $82,000		Crime Story $98,000	
WEDNESDAY	ABC			Perfect Strangers $138,110	Head of the Class $159,290	Hooperman $146,780	The "Slap" Maxwell Story $127,090	Dynasty $113,540	
	CBS			The Oldest Rookie $75,360		Magnum, P.I. $140,790		The Equalizer $134,520	
	NBC			Highway to Heaven $109,000		A Year in the Life $134,500		St. Elsewhere $131,000	
THURSDAY	ABC			Sledge Hammer! $38,740	The Charmings $45,860	ABC Thursday Movie $79,830			
	CBS			Tour of Duty $67,590		Simon & Simon* $85,770		Knots Landing $127,050	
	NBC			The Cosby Show $369,500	A Different World $276,000	Cheers $307,000	Night Court $257,500	L.A. Law $205,000	
FRIDAY	ABC			Full House $79,780	I Married Dora $68,660	Mr. Belvedere* $89,960	Pursuit of Happiness* $79,090	20/20 $80,000	
	CBS			Beauty & the Beast $68,900		Dallas $139,470		Falcon Crest $99,700	
	NBC			Rags to Riches $91,500		Miami Vice $171,500		Private Eye $124,000	
SATURDAY	ABC			Ohara* $55,680		Sable* $37,070		Hotel $83,480	
	CBS			CBS Saturday Movie* $57,000-$100,000				West 57th $48,120	
	NBC			Facts of Life $107,000	227 $111,500	Golden Girls $182,500	Amen $135,000	Hunter $121,500	
SUNDAY	ABC	Disney Sunday Movie $78,734		Spenser: For Hire $64,530		The Dolly Parton Show $138,210		Buck James $94,370	
	CBS	60 Minutes $160,300		Murder, She Wrote $140,560		CBS Sunday Night Movie $121,020			
	NBC	Our House $92,500		Family Ties $219,500	My Two Dads $189,000	NBC Sunday Night at the Movies $155,000			

Source: Reprinted with permission from the January 4, 1988 issue of *Advertising Age*, p. 44. Copyright 1988 by Crain Communications, Inc.

Network advertising is inefficient, and in fact infeasible, if the national advertiser chooses to concentrate efforts on selected markets only. Some brands, though marketed nationally, are directed primarily at consumers in certain geographic locales—perhaps either larger cities or small towns and rural areas. In this case, it would be wasteful to invest in network advertising, which would reach many areas where target audiences are *not* located.

Spot Television Advertising   The national advertiser's alternative to network television advertising is spot advertising. As the preceding discussion intimated and as the name suggests, this type of advertising is placed (spotted) only in selected markets.

In some situations network advertising is completely infeasible for the national advertiser, who must then rely on spot television advertising. This may be true when a company rolls out a new brand market by market before it achieves national distribution, or when a company's product distribution is limited to one or a few geographical regions. The trend toward more regional marketing suggests greater use of spot television advertising.

Local Television Advertising.   Historically, television advertising has been dominated by national advertisers, but local advertisers are turning to television in ever greater numbers. Local advertisers often find that the CPM advantages of television, plus the advantage of product demonstration, justify the choice of this advertising medium. Local television advertising is particularly inexpensive during the fringe times preceding and following prime-time programming.

Cable Advertising.   Cable television has been available for a number of years, but only recently have advertisers turned to cable as a potentially valuable advertising medium. Though some national advertisers are still somewhat uncertain about the advertising potential of cable television and regard it as an "experimental buy,"[21] growing numbers of national advertisers are using cable. (For example, Procter & Gamble, Anheuser-Busch, Philip Morris, and General Mills each invested more than $18 million in cable advertising in 1987.)[22] Cable television's household penetration increased from only 22.6 percent in 1980 to 50.5 percent by 1987.[23]

Advertisers' growing dissatisfaction with network television, due to rapidly increasing advertising rates and declining network viewing audiences, has encouraged more and more advertisers to turn to cable television as a viable media alternative. Network advertising costs in 1982, for example, were over three and one-half times higher than they had been in 1967, and they continue

---

21. "Cable: An Experimental Buy," *Marketing Communications*, June 1983, pp. 16, 17.
22. Wayne Walley, "Cable Halfway Home, Picking Up Speed," *Advertising Age*, April 11, 1988, p. S-17.
23. Ibid., p. S-2.

to rise.[24] At the same time, network viewing audiences are continuing to decline. In fact, network television's 24-hour share is only 64 percent of the viewing audience.[25] Thus, the combination of higher rates and smaller audiences has forced advertisers to experiment with new media alternatives.

A third reason for cable advertising's growth is the opportunity for advertisers to be more selective (than with network or spot television) in picking target audiences. There are dozens of national cable systems, each appealing to several million households. For example, these include Black Entertainment Television, Cable Health Network, ESPN (Entertainment and Sports Programming Network), MTV: Music Television, National Jewish Television, and Spanish Universal Network. The names of these systems illustrate the selectivity available to the national advertiser.

A final factor behind cable advertising's rapid growth is the demographic composition of cable audiences. Cable subscribers are more economically upscale, younger, and more likely to be married and to have children than the population as a whole.[26] By comparison, the heaviest viewers of network television tend to be more economically downscale. It is little wonder that the upscale characteristics of cable viewers have great appeal to many national advertisers.[27]

Television Advertising: Strengths and Problems

Each advertising medium possesses relative strengths in comparison with other media. These involve both *quantitative* considerations (the number of target customers a particular medium reaches, its cost, and so on) and *qualitative* matters (e.g., how elegant or personal a medium is). The qualitative factors, though inherently more subjective, often play the determining role in advertisers' media decisions. Figure 13.4, which was introduced earlier, illustrates the types of qualitative considerations that advertising practitioners consider when making media selections and shows the relative strengths of television as well as the other major advertising media.

Television's Strengths.   Beyond any other consideration, television possesses the unique capability to *demonstrate* a product in use. No other medium has the ability to reach consumers simultaneously through both auditory and visual senses. Viewers can see and hear a product being used, identify with the product's users, and imagine themselves using the product.

---

24. Robert J. Coen, "Next Year's Cost Increases May Average Only 6%," *Advertising Age*, November 7, 1983, p. M-20.
25. "Cashing in on Cable," *Marketing Communications*, April 1988, p. 16.
26. Les Luchter, "The Cabling of America," *Marketing Communications*, September 1982, p. 31; and "Cashing in on Cable," ibid.
27. For an informative analysis of different cable networks, see the Special Supplement titled "1989 Advertisers' Guide to Cable," *Advertising Age*, February 20, 1989, pp. Cable–1 to Cable–34.

Television also has *intrusion value* unparalleled by other media. That is, television advertisements engage one's senses and attract attention even when one would prefer not to be exposed to an advertisement. In comparison, it is much easier to avoid a magazine or newspaper ad by merely flipping the page or to avoid a radio ad by changing channels. But it is often easier to sit through a television commercial rather than attempting to avoid it either physically or mentally.

A third relative advantage of television advertising is its combined ability to *provide entertainment and generate excitement*. Advertised products can be brought to life or made to appear even bigger than life. Products advertised on television can be presented dramatically and made to appear more exciting and less mundane than they actually are.

Television also has the unique ability to reach consumers *one on one*, as is the case when a spokesperson or endorser espouses the merits of a particular product. Like a personal sales presentation, the interaction between spokesperson and consumer takes place on a personal level.

More than any other medium, television also has the ability to use *humor* as an effective advertising strategy.

In the final analysis, the greatest relative advantage of television advertising is its ability to achieve *impact*. Impact is that quality of an advertising medium that activates a "special condition of awareness"[28] in the consumer and that "enlivens his mind to receive a sales message."[29]

Problems with Television Advertising.   As an advertising medium, television suffers from three distinct problems. First, and perhaps most serious, is the *rapidly escalating advertising cost*. As noted in a previous section on cable television, the cost of network television advertising has more than tripled over the past two decades. A dramatic illustration of this is the increasing cost of buying advertising time during the Super Bowl. In 1975, the cost was $110,000 for a 30-second commercial. By 1989 the cost had exceeded $650,000.

A second problem is the *erosion of television viewing audiences*. Videocassette recorders, cable television, and other leisure and recreational alternatives have diminished the number of people viewing network television.[30]

Third, even when people are viewing television, cable as well as network, much of their time is spent switching from station to station and *zapping* commercials. The remote control "zapper" has been referred to, (only partially with tongue in cheek) as the greatest threat to capitalism since Karl Marx.[31]

28. Richard C. Anderson, "Eight Ways to Make More Impact," *Advertising Age,* May 17, 1982, p. M-23.
29. Raymond Rubicam quoted in Anderson, ibid.
30. For in-depth discussion, see Dean M. Krugman, "Evaluating the Audiences of the New Media," *Journal of Advertising,* vol. 14, no. 4 (1985), pp. 21–27.
31. "The Toughest Job in TV," *Newsweek,* October 3, 1988, p. 72. For further discussion of zapping, see Dennis Kneale, " 'Zapping' of TV Ads Appears Pervasive," *The Wall Street Journal,* April 25, 1988, p. 21.

Clutter is a fourth serious problem with television advertising. Clutter refers to the growing amount of nonprogram material—commercials, public-service messages, and promotional announcements for stations and programs. Clutter has been created by the network's increased use of promotional announcements to stimulate audience viewing of heavily promoted programs and by advertisers' increased use of shorter commercials. Whereas 60-second commercials once were prevalent, now the vast majority of commercials are 30 seconds or less. Moreover, some advertisers are experimenting with "split-30" commercials, in which two different brands are advertised during a single 30-second commercial. NBC's coverage of the 24th Olympiad from Seoul, Korea, is a classic illustration of advertising clutter. NBC aired 3,500 commercials during the course of its Olympics programming. Possibly because of this massive commercial barrage, NBC's rating throughout the Olympics was only around 18 percent, several percentage points below the projected 21.2.[32]

Regardless of cause, the effectiveness of television advertising has suffered from the clutter problem, which creates a negative impression among consumers about advertising in general and turns viewers away from the television set.[33] One study showed that the percentage of viewers who could correctly recall commercials within five minutes after they aired dropped from 18 percent to 7 percent in a span of 16 years.[34]

A series of experiments aimed at studying the consequences of television clutter revealed that the amount of attention devoted to commercials, the degree of content recall, and the extent of brand-name recognition all suffer from increased levels of clutter. For example, the percentage of subjects who pay full attention to any part of the tested commercials decreases from 56 percent in the least-cluttered experimental condition to 46 percent in the most-cluttered condition. Correct brand-name recognition drops from 22 percent in the least-cluttered version to 10 percent in the most-cluttered version. The extent to which clutter has negative effects on commercial effectiveness depends on a commercial's position in a series or stream of continuous commercial messages. The middle position is worst, the first position is best, and the last position is next best.[35]

Radio

Like television, radio is a nearly ubiquitous medium: 99 percent of all homes in the United States have radios, 77 percent of the homes contain four or more radios, 95 percent of all cars have a radio, and more that 50 million radios are

---

32. "The Toughest Job in TV," p. 72.
33. Verne Gay, "Clutter is Ad Pollution," *Advertising Age*, October 10, 1988, p. 56.
34. Leo Bogart and Charles Lehman, "The Case of the 30-Second Commercial," *Journal of Advertising Research*, vol. 23 (February/March 1983) pp. 11–19.
35. For a review of these studies, see Peter H. Webb and Michael L . Ray, "Effects of TV Clutter," *Journal of Advertising Research*, vol. 19 (June 1979), pp. 7–12.

purchased in the United States each year.[36] These impressive figures indicate radio's strong potential as an advertising medium.

Radio Gets Results

Promotion efforts by the Radio Advertising Bureau, an industry trade association, claim that radio "gets results." The point of this self-promotion is that radio is an effective medium for creating buying action. Trade puffery aside, radio is indeed an effective advertising medium. Although radio has always been a favorite of local advertisers, it is only in recent years that national advertisers have begun to appreciate radio's advantages as an advertising medium. The following section examines these advantages and also explores some of the problems with radio advertising.

Radio Advertising: Strengths and Problems

Like television, radio advertising has its own set of strengths and problems.

Radio's Strengths. Radio is second only to magazines in its *ability to reach segmented audiences*. Radio personifies the notion of **narrowcasting.** Unlike the more shotgun approach with television, radio can be pinpointed to specific groups of consumers: teens, Hispanics, sports nuts, news enthusiasts, and so on. An extensive variety of radio programming enables advertisers to pick specific formats and stations to be optimally compatible with their target audience and creative message strategies. One media director explains radio's narrowcasting versatility this way:

> There's classical music to reach the same kind of educated, high income adults [who] read *Smithsonian* or *Travel and Leisure,* only at less cost. You've got a yen to reach working women? Try an all news station in a.m. drivetime. Blacks? Stations like WBLS in New York reach them more efficiently than TV's "Soul Train" or black magazines such as *Ebony* and *Essence.* You've got teen stations, old lady stations, stations which reach sports nuts, young adults and middle-of-the-roaders. So don't think of radio as a mass medium unless sheer tonnage at the lowest CPM is your game. The radio networks are made up of hundred of stations with different formats, audiences, signal strengths, coverage, etc.[37]

A second major advantage of radio advertising is its ability to reach prospective customers on a *personal and intimate level*. As one illustration of radio advertising's ability to reach the listener at a very personal level, read the award-winning anti-drug radio spot titled "Lanie's Wedding" in the *Focus on Promotion* section.

The CEO of J. Walter Thompson USA, one of the largest advertising agencies in the United States, has metaphorically described radio as a "uni-

---

36. Burt Manning, "Friendly Persuasion," *Advertising Age*, September 13, 1982, p. M-8; Marc Beauchamp, "Radio Days," *Forbes*, November 30, 1987, pp. 200, 204.
37. Cyril C. Penn, "Marketing Tool Underused," *Advertising Age*, September 25, 1978, p. 122.

FOCUS ON PROMOTION

Lanie's Wedding

Joy Golden, president of Joy Radio, New York, had spent most of her professional career writing humorous radio ads until she volunteered her time to write a spot for the anti-drug effort. Her spot, first aired in November 1987, received *Advertising Age's* Best Radio Commercial of 1987 Award and the Hollywood Radio & Television Society's International Broadcasting Award for the World's Best Radio Public Service spot of 1987. As you read "Lanie's Wedding," think of the thousands of people who can personally relate to this situation and who undoubtedly were moved by this commercial.

WOMAN: I'll never forget my best friend Lanie's wedding. It was right before the ceremony and I walked into her bathroom without knocking because like I said she was my best friend and there she was in her gorgeous white lace dress, leaning over the sink with a straw up her nose. I says, hey, what're you doing? She jumps and says shut the door. Then I see the white powder and I froze. She says heh, it's cool. Then she leans over the sink and I say, move it off or I'll blow it off. She said you do and I'll kill you. Then she started to cry. And I started to cry. And we held each other real tight. Then I blew the coke off the sink and bolted outta there. I sent her a silver flower bowl but she never wrote me to thank me. I felt bad so after about 3 months, I broke down and called her. I thought maybe we could bury the hatchet because like I said, she was my best friend. But it was too late. They already buried Lanie.

ANNOUNCER: If you think you can't live without drugs, don't worry. Pretty soon you may not have to. The Partnership for a Drug Free America.[38] ∎

verse of private worlds," and a "communication between two friends."[39] In other words, people select radio stations in much the same way that they select personal friends. People listen to those radio stations with which they closely identify. Because of this, radio advertising is likely to be received when the customer's mental frame is most conducive to persuasive influence.

38. "Print, Radio Winners Honored." Reprinted with permission from the May 2, 1988 issue of *Advertising Age*, p. 56. Copyright 1988 Crain Communications, Inc.
39. Manning, "Friendly Persuasion."

Radio advertising, then, is a personal and intimate form of "friendly persuasion."[40]

Economy is a third advantage of radio advertising. In terms of CPM per target audience, radio advertising is considerably cheaper than other mass media. Since 1967, radio's cost per thousand has increased less than any other advertising medium. The cost of advertising on spot radio and network radio has increased by 158 and 210 percent, respectively. By comparison, the cost of advertising on spot and network television has increased by 238 and 318 percent, respectively.[41]

Flexibility is another relative advantage of radio advertising. Because radio production costs are typically inexpensive and scheduling deadlines are short, copy changes can be made quickly to take advantage of important developments and changes in the marketplace. For example, a sudden weather change may suggest an opportunity to advertise weather-related products. A radio spot can be prepared quickly to accommodate the needs of the situation.

Problems with Radio Advertising. Radio has some of the same weaknesses and problems that television has. Foremost, perhaps, is that both broadcast media are *cluttered with competitive commercials* and other forms of noise, chatter, and interference. Radio listeners frequently switch stations, especially on their car radios, to avoid commercials.[42]

A second limitation is that radio is the only major medium that is *unable to employ visualizations*. Radio advertising is limited in its ability to create vivid images. Although listening to Lanie's friend talk about Lanie's demise from a drug overdose is certainly poignant, it probably would be even more moving to see the same scenario enacted in a television commercial.

Radio advertisers attempt to overcome the medium's visual limitation by using sound effects and choosing concrete words to conjure up images in the listener's "mind's eye." It is important to note that many advertising campaigns use radio as a *supplement* to other media rather than as a stand-alone medium. This reduces radio's task from one of creating visual images to one of reactivating images that already have been created via television or magazines.

A third problem with radio advertising results from the *difficulty of buying radio time*. This problem is particularly acute in the case of the national advertiser who wishes to place spots in different markets throughout the country. With more than 10,000 commercial radio stations operating in the United States, buying time is complicated by unstandardized rate structures that include a number of combinations of fixed and discount rates.

---

40. Ibid.
41. Beauchamp, "Radio Days," p. 204.
42. A thorough study of this behavior was conducted by Avery M. Abernethy, "Determinants of Audience Exposure to Radio Advertising," Unpublished Ph.D. Dissertation, University of South Carolina, 1988.

A Note on Buying Radio Time

Radio advertisers are interested in accomplishing reach, frequency, and GRP requirements while ensuring that the station format is compatible with the advertised product and its creative message strategy. Several considerations influence the choice of station. Station format (classical, progressive, country, top 40, etc.) is a major consideration. Certain formats are obviously inappropriate for particular products and brands.

A second consideration is the choice of geographic areas to cover. National advertisers buy time from stations whose audience coverage matches the advertiser's geographic areas of interest. This typically means locating stations in preferred Standard Metropolitan Statistical Areas (SMSAs) or in so-called Areas of Dominant Influence (ADIs), which are approximately 200 areas in the United States that correspond to the major television markets.

A third consideration in buying radio time is the choice of day part. Most stations offer anywhere from two to five day parts. The following is a typical radio time schedule, with different day parts designated by letter combinations:

AAAA—Monday through Saturday, 5:30 to 10:00 a.m.
AAA—Monday through Saturday, 3:00 to 8:00 p.m.
AA—Monday through Friday, 10:00 a.m. to 3:00 p.m.; Saturday and Sunday, 6:00 a.m. to 8:00 p.m.
A—Monday through Sunday, 8:00 p.m. to midnight.
B—Tuesday through Sunday, midnight to 5:30 a.m.

Rate structures vary depending on the attractiveness of the day part; for example, AAAA is priced higher than B in the preceding schedule. Information about rates and station formats is available in *Spot Radio Rates and Data*, a source published by the Standard Rate and Data Services.

Magazines

Historically, magazines have been considered a mass medium, but this is less true today. Now there are literally hundreds of special-interest magazines, each appealing to audiences that manifest specific interests and lifestyles. In fact, Standard Rate and Data Services, the technical information source for the magazine industry, identifies nearly 1,300 "consumer magazines" and divides these into dozens of specific categories such as "automotive" (e.g., *Motor Trend*), "general editorial" (e.g., *the New Yorker*), "sports" (e.g., *Sports Illustrated*), "women's fashions, beauty, and grooming" (e.g., *Glamour*), and many others. In addition to consumer magazines, there are hundreds of other publications classified as farm magazines or business publications. Advertisers obviously have numerous options when selecting magazines to promote their products.

Buying Magazine Space

A number of factors influence the choice of magazine vehicles in which to advertise. Most important is selecting magazines that reach the type of people who constitute the advertiser's target market. However, because the advertiser typically has several vehicle alternatives that satisfy the target-market objective, cost considerations also play an extremely important role.

The cost-per-thousand (CPM) measure introduced earlier is used by advertisers to compare different magazine buys. Cost-per-thousand information for each magazine is available from two syndicated magazine services: Mediamark Research Inc. (MRI), and Simmons Market Research Bureau (SMRB). These services provide CPM figures for general categories (e.g., "total men") and also break out CPMs for subgroups (e.g., "men aged 18 to 49," "male homeowners"). These more specific subgroupings enable the advertiser to compare different magazine vehicles in terms of cost per thousand for reaching the target audience (i. e., CPM-TM) rather than only in terms of gross CPMs. Cost-per-thousand data are useful in making magazine-vehicle selection decisions, but many other factors must be taken into account. (Are thoughts of vaguely right versus precisely wrong decision making entering you mind?)

Magazine Advertising: Strengths and Problems

As an advertising medium, magazines have strengths and problems that are quite different from those of television and radio.

Magazine's Strengths. Some magazines reach very large audiences. For example, magazines like *TV Guide, Modern Maturity, Reader's Digest,* and *National Geographic* are circulated to over 10 million people.[43]

However, the ability to pinpoint specific audiences (termed *selectivity*) is the feature that most distinguishes magazine advertising from other media. If a potential market exists for a product, there is most likely at least one periodical that reaches that market. Selectivity enables an advertiser to achieve effective, rather than wasted, exposure. This translates into more efficient advertising and lower costs per thousand target customers.

Magazines are also noted for their *long life*. Unlike other media, magazines are often used for reference and kept around the home for several weeks or even longer. Magazine subscribers often pass along their copies to other readers, further extending a magazine's life.

In terms of qualitative considerations (refer again to Figure 13.4), magazines as an advertising medium are exceptional with regard to *elegance, quality, beauty, prestige,* and *snob appeal*. These features result from the high level of

---

43. "Rising above the Crowd," *Advertising Age,* April 18, 1988, p. S-13.

reproduction quality and from the surrounding editorial content that often transfers to the advertised product. For example, food items advertised in *Bon Appetit* always look elegant; furniture items in *Better Homes and Gardens* look tasteful; and clothing items in *Esquire* appear especially fashionable.

Magazines are also a particularly good source for providing *detailed product information* and for conveying this information with a sense of authority.

A final and especially notable feature of magazine advertising is its *creative ability to get consumers involved in ads.* Recent years have witnessed a variety of dramatic and highly successful efforts in magazine advertising to enhance reader involvement. For example, Revlon and Estée Lauder have offered eyeshadow and blusher samples on the pages of fashion magazines. Rolls-Royce included a scent strip in one of its ads that imitated the smell of the leather interior of its cars. Two liquor brands, Canadian Mist whiskey and Absolut vodka, used ads with microchips to play songs when the page opened. (A New York woman reported a case of "Absolut chaos" when she walked into her apartment building to a chorus of noisy mailboxes full of magazine ads gone haywire.[44]) TransAmerican included a pop-up ad in *Time* magazine that featured the insurance company's distinctive pyramidal-shaped building set against the San Francisco skyline.

Perhaps the most creative magazine advertising effort to enhance reader involvement was Toyota's use of three-dimensional viewfinders in 14 million copies of *Time*, *People*, and *Cosmopolitan* magazines. The ads were designed to show off the new look of the redesigned Corolla. Readers looked into the view finder and saw a very realistic three-dimensional portrayal of the Corolla. The ad received exceptionally high recall scores. Recall levels were 83 percent among males and 76 percent among females as compared with average recall rates for a four-page auto ad of 39 percent for males and 31 percent for females.[45]

Problems with Magazine Advertising.   Two distinct limitations are associated with magazine advertising. First, advertisers must often buy *waste circulation* when advertising in magazines. This is because a magazine may reach geographically beyond the advertiser's primary market. For example, a regional food manufacturer whose primary markets are in the two Carolinas and Georgia would experience considerable waste circulation by advertising in a magazine circulated throughout the Southeast. Many magazines have overcome this problem by offering special advertising editions (called regional editions) that enable advertisers to designate specific geographic areas in which to advertise. The regional food manufacturer, for example, might advertise in *Southern Living* and pay for circulation only in the three states that represent the company's primary market.

---

44. "The Escalating Ads Race," *Newsweek*, December 7, 1987, p. 65.
45. "3-D Glasses Double Ad's Impact," *Marketing Communications*, January 1988, p. 10.

A second limitation is *lack of flexibility*. In newspapers and the broadcast media, it is relatively easy to change ad copy on fairly short notice and in specific markets. Magazines, by comparison, have long closing dates that require advertising materials to be on hand many days or weeks in advance of publication. *Reader's Digest*, for example, has a nine-week closing date.[46]

Newspapers

There are over 1,700 daily newspapers in the United States and an additional 7,700 weeklies.[47] Newspapers are by far the leading advertising medium. Advertising expenditures in newspapers exceed $25 billion and represent over 27 percent of total advertising expenditures.[48] These expenditures are mostly in the form of local retail advertising (approximately 50 percent), classified ads (approximately 38 percent), and national ads (approximately 12 percent).[49]

Local advertising is clearly the mainspring of newspapers. However, newspapers have become more active in their efforts to increase national advertising. These efforts have been facilitated by the Newspaper Advertising Bureau (NAB), a nonprofit sales and research organization. The NAB offers a variety of services that assist both newspapers and national advertisers by simplifying the task of buying newspaper space and by offering discounts that make newspapers a more attractive medium. Moreover, the trend toward regional marketing by national companies (e.g., Campbell's Soup) has led to greater use of newspaper advertising by major national corporations.

Buying Newspaper Space

Whereas buying space in magazines is done on the basis of full and fractional pages, space in newspapers is identified in terms of *agate lines* and *column inches*. An agate line is 1/14 inch in depth and one column wide, regardless of the width of the column. The formula for transforming rates charged by different newspapers to a common denominator is called the **milline rate,** which stands for cost per line of advertising space per million circulation.

$$\text{Milline rate} = \frac{\text{Line rate}}{\text{Circulation (in millions)}}$$

---

46. S. Watson Dunn and Arnold M. Barban, *Advertising: Its Role in Modern Marketing*, 6th ed. (Hinsdale, IL: The Dryden Press, 1978), p. 595.
47. McGann and Russell, *Advertising Media*, p. 199.
48. Ibid., p. 200.
49. Tamara Goldman, "Big Spenders Develop Newspaper Strategies," *Marketing Communications*, January 1988, p. 24.

This formula adjusts individual line rates in terms of a newspaper's circulation. Obviously, a higher line rate in one newspaper may well be a better value than a lower line rate in another paper if the circulation in the former newspaper is large enough to offset its higher line rate.

The choice of an advertisement's position must also be considered when buying newspaper space. Agate line rates apply only to advertisements placed *ROP* (run-of-paper), which means that the ad appears in any location, on any page, at the discretion of the newspaper. Premium charges may be assessed if an advertiser has a preferred space positioning, such as at the top of the page in the financial section. Whether premium charges are actually assessed is a matter of negotiation between the advertiser and the newspaper.

Newspaper Advertising: Strengths and Problems

Advertisers must consider newspapers' strengths and problems before placing an ad in this medium.

Newspapers' Strengths. Because people read newspapers for news, they are in the *right mental frame* to process advertisements that present news of store openings, new products, sales, and so forth.

Mass audience coverage is a second strength of newspaper advertising. Newspapers cover as much as 70 percent of all households in some major markets.[50] Coverage is not restricted to specific socioeconomic or demographic groups but rather extends across all strata. However, newspaper readers are on average considerably more *economically upscale* than television viewers. Special-interest newspapers also reach large numbers of potential consumers. For example, it is estimated that 83 percent of all college students read a campus newspaper.[51]

Flexibility is perhaps the greatest strength of newspapers. National advertisers can adjust copy to match the specific buying preferences and peculiarities of localized markets. Local advertisers can vary copy through in-paper inserts targeted to specific zip codes. Short closing times, which permit advertisers to tie in advertising copy with local market developments or newsworthy events are another element of newspaper flexibility. In addition, advertising copy can be placed in a newspaper section that is compatible with the advertised product. Retailers of wedding accessories advertise in the bridal section, sporting-goods stores advertise in the sports section, and so forth.

The ability to use *long copy* is another strength of newspaper advertising. Detailed product information and extensive, editorial passages are used in newspaper advertising to an extent unparalleled by any other medium.

---

50. McGann and Russell, *Advertising Media*, p. 215.
51. "Mediawatch," *Marketing Communications*, February 1983, p. 9.

Problems with Newspaper Advertising. Clutter is a problem in newspapers, as it is in all of the other major media.

A second limitation of newspaper advertising is that newspapers are *not a highly selective medium*. Newspapers are able to reach broad cross sections of people, but, with few exceptions (such as campus newspapers), are unable to reach specific groups of consumers effectively.

Occasional users of newspaper space (such as national advertisers who infrequently advertise in newspapers) *pay higher rates* than do heavy users and *have difficulty in securing preferred, non-ROP positions.*

Newspapers do not offer the same *quality of reproduction* that can be obtained in magazines. For this and other reasons, newspapers are not generally known to enhance a product's perceived quality, elegance, or snob appeal, as do magazines and television.

Buying difficulties is a particularly acute problem in the case of the national advertiser who wishes to secure newspaper space in a variety of different markets. Each newspaper must be dealt with individually, and on top of this, the rates charged to national advertisers are typically higher than those charged to local advertisers.

The Newspaper Advertising Bureau (NAB) is making great strides toward making it easier for national advertisers to buy newspaper space. One program, called Standard Advertising Units (SAUs), has established 25 basic ad sizes that can be used in all broad-sheet newspapers (not tabloids) regardless of their column format or page size. Over 1,400 newspapers have accepted this program.[52] Another NAB program is known by the acronym *CAN DO*, which stands for Computer Analyzed Newspaper Data On-Line System. This program provides national advertisers with pertinent information about newspapers in terms of CPMs and demographic information on age, household income, and household size.[53]

Out-of-Home Advertising

Out-of-home advertising, or *outdoor* for short, is the oldest form of advertising. Although billboard advertising is the major aspect of outdoor, this type of advertising encompasses a variety of other delivery modes: advertising on bus shelters, giant inflatables (e.g., the Goodyear blimp), various forms of transit advertising (e.g., ads painted on the sides of cars and trucks), skywriting, t-shirts emblazoned with a brand logo or company name, and so on. The one commonality among these is that they are seen by consumers outside of their homes (hence the name) in contrast to television, magazines, newspapers, and radio, which are received in the home (or in other indoor locations).

---

52. "Shedding the Local Image," *Marketing Communications*, September 1982, p. 43.
53. Ibid.

Outdoor advertising is regarded as a supplementary, rather than primary, advertising medium. It receives about 2.8 percent of U.S. advertising expenditures, a figure that has been static for many years.[54] Product categories that spend the most on outdoor advertising include cigarettes and other tobacco products ($304.2 million in 1986); beer, wine, and liquor ($100.5 million); travel, hotels, and resorts ($93.5 million); retail establishments ($83.7 million); and automobiles ($81.6 million).[55]

Buying Outdoor Advertising

Outdoor advertising is purchased through individual operators called *plants.* There are approximately 600 plants nationwide that offer outdoor advertising in more than 900 markets.[56] National outdoor buying organizations enable national advertisers to purchase outdoor space at locations throughout the country.

Like television and radio, outdoor advertising space is sold in terms of gross rating points (GRPs). However, the notion of GRP is somewhat different in the case of outdoor advertising. Specifically, one outdoor GRP means reaching 1 percent of the population one time. Outdoor GRPs are based on the daily *duplicated audience* as a percentage of the total potential market. For example, if four billboards in a community of 200,000 population achieve a daily exposure to 80,000 persons, the result is 40 gross rating points. GRPs are sold in units of 25, with 100 and 50 being the two most-purchased levels.[57]

Outdoor Advertising: Strengths and Problems

Outdoor advertising presents the advertiser with several unique strengths and problems.

Outdoor Advertising's Strengths. A major strength of outdoor advertising is its *broad reach and high frequency levels.* Outdoor advertising is effective in reaching virtually all segments of the population. The number of exposures is especially high when signs are strategically located in heavy-traffic areas.

Another advantage is *geographic flexibility.* Outdoor advertising can be strategically positioned to supplement other advertising efforts in select geographic areas where advertising support is most needed.

Low cost per thousand is another advantage. Outdoor advertising is the least expensive advertising medium on a CPM basis.

Because outdoor advertising is "bigger than life," *product identification is substantial.* The ability to use large representations offers marketers excellent opportunities for brand and package identification.

54. Kevin Higgins, "Often Overlooked Outdoor Advertising Offers More Impact and Exposures Than Most Media," *Marketing News,* vol. 17 (July 22, 1983), p. 1.
55. Lisa Philips, "Marketers Look to Local Medium," *Advertising Age,* June 8, 1987, p. S-1.
56. McGann and Russell, *Advertising Media,* p. 272.
57. Ibid., p. 279.

Outdoor advertising also provides an excellent opportunity to reach consumers as a *last reminder before purchasing*. This explains why frequently purchased products (e.g., cigarettes and beer) are the heaviest users of outdoor advertising. Advertisers in these categories hope to have their brands seen just prior to the consumer's brand choice.

Problems with Outdoor Advertising.   One significant problem with outdoor advertising is *nonselectivity*. Outdoor advertising can be geared to general groups of consumers (e.g., inner-city residents) but cannot pinpoint specific market segments (say, professional black men between the ages of 25 and 39).

Short exposure time is another drawback. "Now you see it, now you don't" appropriately characterizes the fashion in which outdoor advertising engages the consumer's attention. For this reason, outdoor messages that have to be read are less effective than predominantly visual ones.

It is also *difficult to measure outdoor advertising's audience*. The lack of verified audience measurement is regarded by some as a significant impediment that must be overcome if outdoor advertising is to become a more widely used advertising medium.

Developments in Outdoor Advertising

A number of technological advancements are enhancing outdoor advertising's attractiveness. *Fiber optics,* the use of light-transmitting glass fibers to give special illumination effects, is one appealing technology. Fiber optics are being used as borders around panels and as tracing around letters in company and brand names. Special applications include using fiber optics in advertisements for beach resorts to emulate the effect of shimmering water. Automobile advertisers use fiber optics to suggest lighted headlights.

Additional innovative developments in outdoor advertising include the use of *reflective discs* that vibrate when the sun hits them. This technology was used to introduce Camel Light cigarettes and to promote a Linda Ronstadt record album. *Backlighting* in billboard advertising involves using an open container on one side that is filled with fluorescent lighting and covering the open side with a sheet of transparent sheeting hand painted with an advertising message. Coca-Cola, Budweiser, and other companies have experimented with this method.

Agency-Client Relations

The subject of agency-client relations is a fitting chapter conclusion because the media strategies and decisions discussed to this point are most often the joint work of advertisers (clients) and their advertising agencies. This section will examine first the advertising-agency role and then the issue of agency compensation.

Advertising-Agency Role

Companies have three alternative ways to perform the advertising function. First, a company can maintain its own, in-house advertising operation. This necessitates employing an advertising staff and absorbing the overhead required to maintain the staff and its operations. Such an arrangement is unprofitable unless a company does a relatively large and continuous amount of advertising.

An alternative arrangement is to contract for advertising services with a *full-service advertising agency*. Full-service agencies perform research, creative, and media-buying services. They are also involved in the advertiser's total marketing process and, for a fee, may perform a variety of other marketing services including sales promotion, publicity, package design, strategic marketing planning, and sales forecasting.

The advantages of using a full-service agency include (1) acquiring the services of specialists with in-depth knowledge of current advertising and marketing techniques, (2) obtaining negotiating muscle with the media, and (3) being able to coordinate advertising and marketing efforts. The major disadvantages are that (1) some control over the advertising function is lost when it is performed by an agency rather than in-house, (2) agencies sometimes cater to larger clients, and (3) agencies sometimes are inefficient in media buying.[58]

A third alternative is to purchase advertising services *a la carte*. That is, rather than depending on a single full-service agency to perform all advertising and related functions, an advertiser may recruit the services of a variety of firms with particular specialties in creative work, media selection, production, advertising research, sales promotion, publicity, new-product development, and so on. The advantages of this arrangement are (1) the ability to contract for services only when they are needed, (2) availability of high-caliber creative talent, and (3) potential cost efficiencies. The disadvantages include (1) a tendency for specialists (so-called "boutiques") to approach client problems in a stereotyped rather than innovative fashion, (2) lack of cost accountability, and (3) the financial instability of many smaller boutiques.[59]

Many advertisers actually employ a combination of the different advertising options rather than using one exclusively. For example, a firm may have its own in-house agency but contract with boutiques for certain needs. Although in-house agencies and boutiques experienced considerable growth during the late 1960s and early 1970s, the trend today is toward full-service agencies and away from in-house agencies—especially among larger advertisers.

58. George Donahue, "Evaluating Advertising Services: Part II," *Marketing Communications*, April 1982, p. 61.
59. Ibid., p. 64.

Agency Compensation

An interesting pricing system for compensating advertising agencies has evolved over the years. This system involves a flat 15 percent commission paid to agencies for all advertising that is placed in behalf of the advertiser in a major commissionable media (newspapers, magazines, radio, and television).[60]

To illustrate, suppose the XYZ Advertising Agency buys $100,000 of space in a certain magazine for its client, ABC Company. When the invoice for this space comes due, XYZ would submit payment of $85,000 to the magazine publisher ($100,000 less the 15 percent discount) and then bill ABC for the full $100,000. The $15,000 in revenue realized by XYZ Advertising Agency historically has been regarded as a fair amount of compensation to the agency for its creative expertise, media-buying insight, and ancillary functions performed in behalf of its client, ABC Company.

The 15 percent compensation system has, as one may suppose, been a matter of some controversy between company marketing executives and managers of advertising agencies.[61] The primary area of disagreement is the matter of whether 15 percent compensation is too much (marketing executives' perspective) or too little (ad agencies' perspective). The disagreement has spurred the growth of an alternative compensation system, called the *fee system*. This system involves price negotiations between advertisers and agencies such that the actual rate of compensation, which may be more or less than 15 percent, is based on mutual agreement concerning the worth of the services rendered by the advertising agency.

A survey by the Association of National Advertisers reveals slippage in the use of the traditional compensation system. Whereas 52 percent of respondents (national advertisers) to a 1983 survey compensated their agencies using the traditional commission system, the percentages for previous surveys were 57 percent in 1979 and 68 percent in 1976.[62] The 1983 survey shows further that 29 percent of respondents reported using a fee arrangement, and 19 percent use some variation of the traditional commission system.[63]

Despite these results, most agency executives believe that the 15 percent commission system will never die. The following quote from an agency executive summarizes well the argument in favor of the traditional commission system:

> The best part about the commission system is that it is easy to understand and operates almost automatically. It can be reviewed periodically. Service can be improved or increased. Or concessions can be made. But the commission system

60. The discount paid to advertising agencies for outdoor advertising is typically 16.67 percent. The extra 1.67 percent is used by outdoor companies (plants) to lure business away from the other major media.
61. For an insightful review of different perspectives on the issue, see Herbert Zeltner, "Sounding Board: Clients, Admen Split on Compensation," *Advertising Age*, May 18, 1981, pp. 63–76.
62. "The 15% Media Commission Plans," *Marketing News*, June 10, 1983, p. 9.
63. Ibid.

actually reduces the chance of friction, which sooner or later can destroy even a productive agency-client relationship.[64]

A counterperspective is offered in the following quote from a marketing executive:

A standard 15% is not always equitable since for some big billing brands it's too much and for other smaller brands [which demand] an inordinate amount of work it's not enough.[65]

In many respects, the matter of agency compensation boils down to an issue of what is fair and workable. Agencies and clients are not in complete harmony on this issue. A survey of 158 members (agency representatives and clients) of an influential group called the Sounding Board offers insight into the perceptions of agencies and advertisers concerning the fairness and work-ability of various compensation systems. Agencies' and advertisers' views are somewhat divergent with regard to the fairness/workability of various compen-sation plans. In general, agencies prefer standard media commissions with ad-ditional fees for extra services rendered, whereas advertisers prefer the stan-dard media commission system with maximum (ceiling) and minimum (floor) percentage adjustments for additional services rendered or not rendered.[66]

Summary

Selection of advertising media and media vehicles is one of the most important and complicated of all marketing communications decisions. Media planning must be coordinated with marketing strategy and with other aspects of adver-tising strategy. The strategic aspects of media planning involve four steps: (1) selecting the target audience toward which all subsequent efforts will be di-rected; (2) specifying media objectives, which typically are stated in terms of reach, frequency, gross rating points (GRPs), or effective rating points (ERPs); (3) selecting general media categories and specific vehicles within each me-dium; and (4) buying media.

Media and vehicle selection are influenced by a variety of factors, the most important being target audience, cost, and creative considerations. Media planners select media vehicles by identifying those that will reach the desig-nated target audience, satisfy budgetary constraints, and be compatible with and enhance the advertiser's creative messages. There are numerous ways to schedule media insertions over time, but media planners are increasingly using some form of pulsed or flighted schedule whereby advertising is on at times, off at others, but never continuous.

Five major media are available to advertising media planners: television, radio, magazines, newspapers, and outdoor advertising. Each medium has its unique qualities and strengths and weaknesses. The chapter provides a de-tailed analysis of each medium.

64. Merle Kingman, "To Fee or Not to Fee," *Advertising Age*, August 29, 1983, p. M-24.
65. Zeltner, "Sounding Board," p. 63.
66. Ibid.

The chapter concludes with a discussion of the role of an advertising agency. Companies basically have three ways to perform the advertising function: set up an in-house advertising operation, use a full-service advertising agency, or buy advertising services on an a la carte basis from specialized advertising services called boutiques.

Discussion Questions

1. Why is target-audience selection the critical first step in formulating a media strategy?

2. Explain the problems associated with using GRPs as a media-selection criterion. In what sense is the concept of ERPs superior?

3. Why is reach also called net coverage or unduplicated audience?

4. As noted in the text and in Figure 13.5, it cost advertisers $369,500 for 30 seconds of advertising on "The Cosby Show" during the 1987–1988 season. This price is over four times more expensive than the $80,000 charge to advertise on "20/20." Does this mean that "The Cosby Show" viewing audience would have to be over four times larger than the "20/20" audience for an advertiser to justify buying time on "The Cosby Show"?

5. What are the advantages and disadvantages of cable television advertising? Why are more national advertisers turning to cable television as a viable advertising medium?

6. Assume you are brand manager for a product line of thermos containers. Your products range from thermos bottles to small ice chests. Assume you have $1 million to invest in a four-week magazine advertising campaign. What magazines would you choose for this campaign? Justify your choices.

7. It was noted in the text that cigarettes and liquor are credited with a very large percentage of all billboard advertising. Why do you think these two product categories dominate the billboard medium?

8. Present your views on whether you think VideOcarts will be an effective advertising medium. Are there any particular product categories with which you expect VideOcarts to be especially effective/ineffective?

9. Assume you are a manufacturer of various jewelry items; graduation rings for high-school and college students are one of the most important items in your product line. Suppose you are in the process of developing a media strategy aimed specifically at high-school students. You have an annual budget of $3 million. What media and vehicles would you use and how would you schedule the advertising over time?

Exercises

1. Examine a copy of the most recent *Spot Radio Rates and Data* available in your library and compare the advertising rates for three or four of the radio stations in your hometown or university community.

2. Select any five magazines and apply the criteria in Figure 13.4 that are especially relevant to magazines (e.g., "elegance"). On the basis of this application, construct a rank ordering from best magazine to worst. Justify your rankings.

3. Pick your favorite clothing store in your university community (or hometown) and justify the choice of one radio station that the clothing store should select for its radio advertising. Do not feel constrained by what the clothing store may already be doing. Focus instead on what you think is most important. Be certain to make explicit all criteria used in making your choice and all radio stations considered.

Assessing Advertising Effectiveness

THE PEOPLE-METER CONTROVERSY

he price that advertisers pay for time on television programs is based on rating statistics. Generally speaking, higher-rated programs command higher prices. The accuracy of rating statistics has substantial implications for advertisers, their agencies, and, of course, the networks.

Historically, the A.C. Nielsen Co. measured television program ratings by combining two data-collection methods. One method involved attaching electronic devices to the television sets of a national sample of households (the "electronic-meter panel"). Information from this panel was used to estimate program ratings. A separate national panel of households (the "diary panel") maintained diaries of their ongoing viewing habits and supplied pertinent demographic information on household size, income, education, race, and so on. When combined, the data from the two panels indicated the program ratings and demographic characteristics of each program's audience. This information was used by networks to set advertising rates and by advertisers to select programs on which to advertise their products.

This method worked well during a simpler time when fewer program options were available to television viewers. It became less suitable as independent stations, cable networks, and VCRs increased the viewer's number of choices. Diary data diminished in accuracy because people became less willing or able to maintain precise accounts of their viewing behavior. Enter the people meter.

The people meter was developed by a British research firm, Audits Great Britain (AGB Television Research). This firm introduced people meters to the United States in late 1984. Nielsen followed with its own people-meter system shortly thereafter.

What is a people meter? The people meter is nothing more than a hand-held device slightly larger than a typical television channel selector. The meter has eight buttons for family members and two additional buttons for visitors. A family member (or visitor) must push his or her designated button each time he or she selects a particular program. The meter automatically records what programs are being watched, how many households are watching, and which family members are watching. Information from each household's people meter is fed daily into a central computer via telephone lines. This viewing information is combined with each household's pertinent demographics profile to provide a single source of data. As of September 1988, Nielsen had people meters installed in a national sample of 4,000 households and AGB had meters in its own sample of 5,000 households.

Why the controversy? Contemporaneous with the transition from diary panels to people meters, a substantial decline in network ratings occurred. From 1986 to 1987, the networks experienced a 9 percent drop in ratings. The networks have placed much of the blame on people meters, claiming that the meters have fundamental faults responsible for erroneous ratings data. Critics have also charged that Saturday-morning television ratings are understated because preschool children refuse to push their people meter buttons.

People meters are here to stay—and probably so is the controversy surrounding their use.[1] ■

Massive amounts, well over $100 billion, are spent annually on advertising in the United States. For this reason, much effort and investment are made to test advertising effectiveness. The people meter is just one of many techniques used in the advertising-research business. This chapter introduces you to advertising research by describing many of the research techniques used and explaining when and why they are used as well as the problems and issues involved in their use.

---

1. Many articles have been written about people meters. Two recent articles are Verne Gay, "Vindication?" *Advertising Age,* May 30, 1988, p. 66, and Ira Teinowitz, "People Meters Miss Kids: JWT," *Advertising Age,* July 18, 1988, p. 35. For a technical analysis, see Roland Soong, "The Statistical Reliability of People Meter Ratings," *Journal of Advertising Research,* vol. 28 (February/March 1988), pp. 50–56.

Overview of Advertising Research

Measuring advertising effectiveness is a difficult and often expensive task. Nonetheless, the value gained from undertaking the effort typically outweighs the expense and difficulty. In the absence of formal research, most advertisers would not know whether their advertising is doing a good job, nor could they know what should be changed so that their future advertising could do an even better job. Advertising research enables management to increase advertising's contribution toward achieving marketing and corporate goals.

What Does Advertising Research Research?

Advertising research involves a wide variety of purposes, methods, measures, and techniques. Effectiveness is measured in terms of achieving awareness, conveying copy points, influencing attitudes, creating emotional responses, and affecting purchase choice.

Sometimes research is done under natural advertising processing conditions and other times in simulated or laboratory situations. Measures of effectiveness range from paper-and-pencil instruments (e.g., attitude scales) to physiological devices (e.g., pupillometers).

It should be clear that there is no such thing as a single form of advertising research. Rather, the measurement of advertising effectiveness is exceptionally diverse because the questions asked are themselves diverse.

Advertising research in all its various forms is needed for determining the effectiveness of two general aspects of an advertising program. First, **message research,** also called **copytesting,** is needed to test the effectiveness of creative messages. Copytesting involves both *pretesting* a message during its development and prior to its actually being placed in a medium and *posttesting* after the message has been aired and printed. Pretesting is performed to eliminate ineffective ads before they are ever run, while posttesting is conducted to determine whether the message achieved the objectives established for it.

Media research is a second general category of advertising research. Whereas copytesting asks questions about the message per se, media research attempts to determine whether the chosen advertising medium was effective. Questions about vehicle distribution are prominent in media research. AGB's and Nielsen's people meters represent one form of media research to measure program ratings.

Idealism Meets Reality in Advertising Research

The role, importance, and difficulty of assessing advertising effectiveness can perhaps best be appreciated by first examining what an ideal system of advertising measurement would entail and then comparing this against the reality of advertising research.

First, an ideal measure would provide an *early warning signal*, that is, a "reading" of ad effectiveness at the earliest possible stage in the advertisement development process. The sooner an advertisement is found to be ineffective, the less time, effort, and financial resources will be wasted. Early detection of effective advertisements, on the other hand, enables marketers to hasten the developmental process so that the ads can generate return on investment as quickly as possible.

Second, an ideal measurement system would evaluate advertising effectiveness in terms of *sales response*, the ultimate advertising objective. A measure of advertising effectiveness becomes less valuable the further removed it is from the advertisement's potential for generating sales volume. Thus, a measure of awareness is less valuable than an attitude measure, which itself is less useful than a measure of actual purchase behavior resulting from advertising impact.

Third, an ideal measurement system would satisfy the standard research requirements of *reliability and validity*. Advertising measures are reliable when the same results are obtained on repeated occasions, that is, the results are replicable. Measures are valid when they predict actual marketplace performance.

Finally, an ideal system would permit *quick and inexpensive measurement*. The longer it takes to assess advertising effectiveness and the more it costs, the less valuable is the measuring system.

The ideal conditions just discussed are rarely satisfied. In fact, several are inconsistent. For example, a measurement system capable of predicting sales potential is likely to be expensive. Similarly, one that provides an early warning signal is less likely to be reliable and valid. Advertising research must necessarily deviate from the ideal circumstances described previously. However, the gap between idealism and reality in advertising research is narrowing with advances in technology and greater ingenuity in developing testing procedures.

Advertising Research Methods

Dozens of methods have evolved over the years for measuring advertising effectiveness. The following sections discuss some of the most frequently used procedures in advertising copytesting and media research. First, however, it is important to establish why and when different methods are used. It will become clear that the various methods serve different purposes and are not substitutable for one another.

Table 14.1 organizes the methods to be discussed. The table displays four general categories of advertising-research methods. The first category, *exposure*, involves media research. Exposure studies are performed in all of the major advertising media to determine the number of people exposed to the various advertising vehicles available within a medium. The purpose of these studies is to determine ratings for different television programs, magazines,

Categories of Advertising Research and Illustrative Methods   TABLE 14.1

   I.   *Exposure*
         Simmons Media Studies
         Mediamark Research Studies
         Local Arbitron Radio
         Nielsen and AGB People Meters

  II.   *Awareness*
         Starch Readership Studies
         Burke Day-After Recall

 III.   *Persuasion*
         Consumer Information Processing Model Methods
            Measures of Cognition
                Belief Formation or Change
            Measures of Affect
                ASI Theater Testing
                AHF Competitive Environment Testing
            Measures of Conations
                Purchase Intentions
         Hedonic, Experiential Model Methods
            Measures of Emotions
                The Warmth Monitor
                TRACE
            Physiological Arousal Measures
                Psychogalvanometer
                Pupillometer
                Voice-Pitch Analysis

  IV.   *Action*
         Split-Cable Tests

and other advertising vehicles. Obviously, an advertisement stands no chance of achieving its objectives unless members of the target audience are exposed to the vehicle that carries the ad.

The remaining three categories of research methods include various copy-testing procedures. *Awareness* studies examine consumers' ability to recognize or recall advertisements that they may have been exposed to on television, in a magazine, or in another advertising medium. The assumption underlying awareness measurement is that an advertisement cannot possibly influence subsequent purchase behavior unless consumers have at least registered the advertisement's presence.

The third category, *persuasion*, encompasses a number of different methods for assessing advertising effectiveness. Persuasion research is used here in a generic sense to mean measurement of (1) consumers' brand-specific beliefs, attitudes, and purchase intentions formed or altered as a function of processing advertisements promoting a particular brand, or (2) consumers' feelings or emotions as they relate to the advertisement itself.

Appropriate research methods to measure persuasion depend upon the nature of the product advertised, the type of creative strategy employed (recall discussion in Chapter 12), and the researcher's underlying model of consumer behavior. Table 14.1 shows that different methods are more or less appropriate depending on whether consumer response behavior to the advertisement in question is better characterized in terms of the consumer information processing model (CIP) or the hedonic, experiential model (HEM).[2]

Research methods to measure beliefs, attitudes, and purchase intentions are appropriate given that the consumer information processing model correctly captures consumer response to the advertised product. On the other hand, if the product in question and the advertising execution involve efforts to activate emotions, fantasies, and feelings, the hedonic, experiential model is more appropriate, and measures of emotional reactions are especially justified. These points are elaborated upon later.

Methods to measure sales response, or *action*, represent the ultimate way of assessing advertising effectiveness. Such measurement has been spurred on with the development of optical-scanner equipment and the use of split-cable television facilities. Specifics underlying these technologies and the procedures involved in measuring action-oriented ad effectiveness are described thoroughly after the pre-action methods have been discussed.

Finally, it is important to realize that advertising effectiveness measures are *not* generally interchangeable with one another. In other words, the choice of method is tied inextricably to the advertising objective that precipitated the ad campaign in the first place. If the ad objective is primarily one of creating awareness, then different methods are required in comparison to when, for example, attitude enhancement is the objective.

Measurement of Exposure

The initial task an advertiser faces is to ensure that sufficient numbers of potential customers are actually exposed to its advertisements. This requires that (1) media vehicles (television programs, magazine issues, etc.) be distributed, (2) customers be exposed to these vehicles (by watching the television program, reading a specific magazine issue, etc.), and (3) customers be exposed to the advertiser's specific advertisement(s) carried in these vehicles.

It is common practice in advertising research to infer ad exposure from vehicle exposure. It is assumed that consumers who are exposed to a particular media vehicle are also exposed to advertisements within that vehicle. This assumption is made of necessity, due to the difficulty of determining the actual advertisements to which consumers have been exposed.

---

2. The CIP and HEM models were previously detailed in Chapter 4.

Various companies specialize in measuring vehicle exposure. Simmons Market Research Bureau (SMRB) and Mediamark Research Inc. (MRI) specialize in measuring magazine readership. Arbitron is well known for its measurement of local radio-station audiences. And as described in the chapter's opening vignette, Audits Great Britain (AGB) and Nielsen use people meters to measure television-audience size and composition.

Magazine-Audience Measurement. It may seem at first that determining the size of a particular magazine's readership would be an easy task. All that is needed is to count the number of people who subscribe to the magazine, right? Wrong!

Several complicating factors make subscription counting an inadequate way of determining a magazine's readership: (1) magazine subscriptions are collected through a variety of middlemen, making it difficult to obtain accurate lists of which people subscribe to which magazines; (2) magazine purchases are often made from newsstands, in supermarkets, and from other retail outlets rather than through subscriptions, thus completely eliminating knowledge of who purchases which magazines; (3) a single magazine issue at a public location (e.g., doctors' offices, barber shops) is read by numerous people; and (4) people often share magazines with one another.

For all of these reasons, the number of subscribers to a magazine and the number of people who actually read the magazine may be very different. Companies began specializing in magazine readership analysis in order to determine audience size. Simmons Market Research Bureau (SMRB) and Mediamark Research Inc. (MRI) are the dominant firms in this area of media research.

SMRB assesses magazine vehicle exposure for over 100 consumer magazines. A national probability sample of approximately 20,000 individuals are interviewed, and their magazine-reading habits are examined. Here is how SMRB's research is performed. SMRB's research staff goes into the field and shows interviewees representations of the logos of more than 100 magazines. Interviewees are asked to identify those magazines (as identified by their logos) they may have read or looked through during the last six months. This recognition-assisted method is called the *through-the-book-technique,* or TTB for short. For each magazine logo correctly identified, respondents then are asked to look through a stripped-down version of a recent magazine issue. Through a series of questions, SMRB's interviewers attempt to determine whether respondents have truly been exposed to the particular magazine issue. Statistical inference procedures are used to generalize total vehicle exposure from the sample results. Advertisers and media planners use the readership information along with detailed demographic and product-usage data to evaluate the absolute and relative value of different magazines.

Critics have challenged the TTB methodology, claiming the technique tends to understate audience size and fails to yield consistent results from year to year. Mediamark Research Inc. (MRI) came into being to provide advertisers and agencies with an alternative magazine-readership source. MRI interviews 20,000 adults per year and, like SMRB, obtains readership statistics for over

100 magazines. However, MRI's measurement technique differs from SMRB's approach. MRI gives each participant a deck of cards, with each card containing a magazine logo. The participant then sorts the cards into three piles based on whether she or he has read the magazine, has not read it, or is not sure. The advantage of MRI's procedure is that the participant can control the pace of evaluating whether he or she has read a particular magazine.

Because these two readership services use different research methods, their results are often discrepant. Media planners are faced with the task of determining which service is right or whether both are wrong in their estimates of magazine audience size.[3]

Much useful information is obtained from these services in addition to information on magazine-audience size. Each service also acquires detailed information on a magazine audience's product-usage patterns and demographic characteristics. Advertisers use this information for selecting particular magazines that best match their intended target markets.

An example will illustrate the valuable information that these readership services provide. The illustration is potato-chip usage as reported by "female homemakers" in response to the following questions posed by Simmons Market Research Bureau: "Do you or other members of your household use potato chips?" "About how many bags, boxes or cannisters of potato chips were used by your entire household in the last 30 days?"[4]

Responses to the first question, when extrapolated from the sample to the total population, reveal that of the 82,369,000 American households with a female homemaker present, 76.1 percent (nearly 63 million households) reported that potato chips are a product they consume at least occasionally. Slightly over 19 percent of all the households are "heavy users" (buying four or more bags, boxes, or cannisters of potato chips in the last 30 days), approximately 35 percent are "moderate users" (buying two or three units of potato chips during this same period), 22 percent are "light users" (having bought none or one unit in the last 30 days), and the remainder never buy potato chips.

Useful information is provided media decision makers when product-usage information is combined with demographic characteristics and with media consumption habits. We learn from the SMRB report that potato-chip usage is disproportionately higher among white than black families, in the midwest and south compared to the northeast and west, and in middle-income compared to low-income households. Also, readers of different magazines are disproportionately heavy or light users of potato chips. For example, readers of the following magazines tend to be disproportionately heavy potato-chip users:

3. For additional information on magazine audience measurement, see Thomas C. Kinnear, David A. Horne, and Theresa A. Zingery, "Valid Magazine Audience Measurement: Issues and Perspectives," in *Current Issues and Research in Advertising*, eds. James H. Leigh and Claude R. Martin, Jr. (Ann Arbor, MI: Division of Research, Graduate School of Business, University of Michigan, 1986), pp. 251–270. See also Joanne Lipman, "Readership Figures for Periodicals Stir Debate in Publishing Industry," *The Wall Street Journal*, September 2, 1987, p. 21.
4. This and all following statistics are from Simmons Market Research Bureau, Inc., vol. P-22, 1986, pp. 0631–0649.

Esquire, Essence, Field & Stream, Gentlemen's Quarterly, Hot Rod, Jet, Playboy, Sports Afield, and *Sports Illustrated.* In comparison, readers of magazines such as *The New Yorker, Scientific American, Smithsonian,* and *The Wall Street Journal* tend to be disproportionately light users or nonusers of potato chips.[5]

This information has obvious implications for potato-chip advertisers when choosing magazines in which to insert their advertisements. SMRB also provides data showing the relationship of product usage with television-program viewing, radio-program listening, and newspaper reading. Thus, vehicle-selection information is provided for these media as well as magazines.

Radio-Audience Measurement. Arbitron measures radio listening patterns in over 250 local markets based on data from 250 to 13,000 individuals age 12 or over who are randomly selected in each market. Respondents maintain diaries of their listening behavior. Subscribers to the Arbitron service (over 5,000 radio stations, advertisers, and agencies) receive detailed reports involving listening patterns, station preferences, and demographic breakdowns. This information is invaluable for selecting stations whose listener composition matches the advertiser's target market.

Measurement of Awareness

Several levels of awareness may occur after a consumer is exposed to an advertisement. At the most basic level, the consumer may simply notice an ad without noticing specific executional elements. However, the advertiser hopes that the consumer will become aware of specific parts, elements, or features of an ad and associate these with the specific product, brand, or service being advertised.[6]

The advertiser's task is to ensure that consumers become aware of specific parts of the advertisement, recognize the specific product/brand advertised, and associate the key advertising elements with the advertised item. Accomplishing these tasks is critical to advertising success. Research by the Strategic Planning Institute, which operates the prestigious Profit Impact of Marketing Strategy program (PIMS), has established a clear link between consumer brand awareness and a company's market share, which itself has a strong influence on profitability.[7] Figure 14.1 shows the relationships between awareness and market share and between market share and pretax return on investment.

---

5. Statements about "disproportionately" heavy or light usage are based on *index numbers* presented in SMRB's reports. For example, of the total 82,369,000 households with a female home-maker, 62,701,000 (or 76.1 percent) of these households consume potato chips. This percentage, 76.1 percent, is called *base 100*. Of the 1,497,000 households that SMRB reports read *Field & Stream* magazine, 1,242,000 (or 83.0 percent) consume potato chips. *Field & Stream's* index is thus 109 (83.0 ÷ 76.1), which indicates that readers of this magazine are disproportionately more likely (by 9 percent) than the population at large to consume potato chips.
6. Ivan L. Preston, "The Association Model of the Advertising Communication Process," *Journal of Advertising,* vol. 11, no. 2 (1982), pp. 3–15.
7. "Brand Awareness Increases Market Share, Profits: Study," *Marketing News,* November 28, 1980, p. 5.

FIGURE 14.1   **Awareness-Market Share and Market Share-ROI Relations**

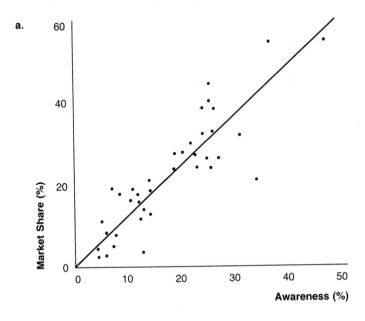

a.

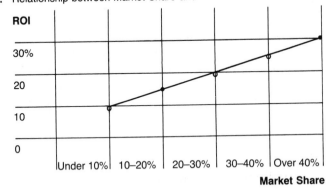

b. Relationship between Market Share and Pretax ROI

Source: "Brand Awareness Increases Market Share, Profits: Study," *Marketing News,* November 28, 1980, p. 5. Reprinted with permission from *Marketing News,* published by the American Marketing Association.

Several commercial research firms provide advertisers with information on how well their ads perform in terms of generating awareness, which typically is measured in terms of *recognition* or *recall*. Communicus Inc., Gallup & Robinson, Inc., McCollum/Spielman, Starch Message Report Service, and Burke Day-After Recall Tests are some of the well-known commercial research services that have testing programs for measuring the awareness-generating ability of advertisements.[8] The research services performed by Starch and Burke are described in the following sections.

Magazine-Readership Measurement. The Starch Message Report Service reports on reader awareness of advertisements in consumer magazines and business publications. Over 75,000 advertisements are studied annually based on interviews with more than 100,000 people involving over 140 publications. Sample sizes range from 100 to 150 individuals of each sex per issue, with most interviews conducted in respondents' homes or, in the case of business publications, in offices or places of business. Interviews are conducted during the early life of a publication. Following a suitable waiting period after the appearance of a publication to give readers an opportunity to read or look through their issue, interviewing continues one week for a weekly publication, two weeks for a bi-weekly, and three weeks for a monthly publication.

Starch interviewers locate eligible readers of each magazine issue studied. An eligible reader is one who has glanced through or read some part of the issue prior to the interviewer's visit and who meets the age, sex, and occupation requirements set for the particular magazine. Once eligibility is established interviewers turn the pages of the magazine, inquiring about each advertisement being studied. Respondents are first asked, "Did you see or read any part of this advertisement?" If a respondent answers "Yes," a prescribed questioning procedure is followed to determine the respondent's awareness of various parts of the ad (illustrations, headline, etc.). Respondents are then classified as follows:

- *Nonreader*—A person who did not remember having previously seen the advertisement in the issue.
- *Noted Reader*—A person who remembered having previously seen the advertisement in the issue.
- *Associated Reader*—A person who not only "noted" but also saw or read some part of the advertisement that clearly indicates the brand or advertiser.
- *Read-Most Reader*—A person who read half or more of the written material in the ad.

8. For details, see David W. Stewart, David H. Furse, and Randall P. Kozak, "A Guide to Commercial Copytesting Services," in *Current Issues and Research in Advertising* eds. James H. Leigh and Claude R. Martin, Jr., (Ann Arbor, MI: Division of Research, Graduate School of Business, University of Michigan, 1983), pp. 1–44.

Figure 14.2 illustrates a Starch-rated advertisement with actual scores for a Sure ad that ran in *Sports Illustrated*. It can be seen that 46 percent of the respondents remembered having previously seen the ad (i.e., noted it), 33 percent associated it, 7 percent read most of it, 22 percent read the headline, and so on.

A basic assumption of the Starch procedure is that respondents in fact do remember whether they saw a particular ad in a particular magazine. The Starch technique has sometimes been criticized because in so-called "bogus ad" studies that use pre-publication or altered issues, respondents report having seen ads that actually never ran. The Starch organization does not consider such studies valid because of the failure of researchers to follow proper procedures for qualifying issue readers and questioning respondents. Research by the Starch organization demonstrates that when properly interviewed, most respondents are able to identify the ads they have seen or read in a specific issue with a high degree of accuracy; false reporting of ad noting is at a minimum.[9]

Another study suggests that the Starch procedure identifies qualities in ads that respondents believe they have noticed. This study also suggests that actual recognition of previously seen advertisements is not precisely measured.[10]

Nonetheless, any misreporting that occurs represents a form of systematic (nonrandom) error that applies to all magazine issues studied. The relative scores among different magazine issues and advertisements are what is important. Because Starch has been performing these studies for well over 50 years and has compiled a wealth of baseline data, advertisers and media planners can make informed decisions concerning the relative merits of different magazines.

Television-Commercial Recall. Various companies copytest new television commercials to determine whether viewers have been sufficiently influenced to recall having seen the copytested commercial. One well-known research service is Burke's day-after recall (DAR) procedure. Test commercials are embedded within normal daytime television programming. The following day Burke's telephone staff conducts interviews with a sample of 150 consumers. Contacted individuals are first qualified as having watched the program in which the test commercial was placed and as having been physically present at the time the commercial was aired. Once qualified, individuals receive a product or brand cue, are asked whether they saw the test commercial in question, and then are asked to recall all they can about it.

Findings are reported as (1) *claimed-recall scores*, which indicate the percentage of respondents who recall seeing the ad, and (2) *related-recall scores*,

9. D.M. Neu, "Measuring Advertising Recognition," *Journal of Advertising Research*, vol. 1 (1961), pp. 17–22.
10. George M. Zinkhan and Betsy D. Gelb, "What Starch Scores Predict," *Journal of Advertising Research*, vol. 26 (August/September 1986), pp. 45–50.

Source: Courtesy Starch INRA Hooper, Inc.

which indicate the percentage of respondents who accurately describe specific advertising elements.

Advertisers and agencies use this information, along with verbatim statements from respondents, to assess the effectiveness of test commercials and to identify commercials' strengths and weaknesses. On the basis of this information, a decision is made to advertise the commercial nationally, to revise it first, or possibly even to drop it.

The Recall-Measurement Controversy. Many national advertisers pretest new commercials using day-after recall procedures. However, considerable controversy has surrounded the use of DAR testing in recent years. David Ogilvy, a famous advertising practitioner, contends that recall testing "is for the birds."[11] Coca-Cola executives reject recall as a valid measure of advertising effectiveness because, in their opinion, recall simply measures whether an ad is received but not whether the message is accepted.[12]

The strongest challenge to day-after recall testing comes from a study performed by Foote, Cone & Belding, a major advertising agency. The FCB agency claims that DAR copy tests significantly understate the memorability of commercials that employ emotional or feeling-oriented themes.[13] This is because the test procedures emphasize respondents' ability to verbalize key copy points, thereby biasing the results in favor of rational or thought-oriented commercials and against emotional or feeling-oriented commercials, which rarely make explicit selling points.

Foote, Cone & Belding conducted a study comparing three thinking and three feeling commercials. The six commercials were copytested with two methods: the standard DAR measurement described previously and a *masked-recognition test*. The latter test involves showing a commercial to respondents on one day, telephoning them the next, requesting that they turn on their television sets to a given station where the commercial is shown once again (but this time masked, i.e., without any brand identification), and then asking them to identify the brand. FCB defines correct brand-name identification by this masked-recognition procedure as "proven recognition" or "true remembering."[14]

The research results, as shown in Table 14.2, demonstrate clearly the bias in day-after recall procedures against emotional, feeling commercials. For example, Commercial B's DAR score is only 21 percent, but its masked-recognition score of 37 percent is considerably higher. Overall, the masked-recognition method reveals that proven recognition for the three feeling commercials is 68 percent higher than the day-after recall scores (see ratio of 168 in Table 14.2).

11. David Ogilvy, *Ogilvy on Advertising* (New York: Crown Publishers, 1983).
12. "Recall Not Communication: Coke," *Advertising Age*, December 26, 1983, p. 6.
13. Jack Honomichl, "FCB: Day-After-Recall Cheats Emotion," *Advertising Age*, May 11, 1981, p. 2; David Berger, "A Retrospective: FCB Recall Study," *Advertising Age*, October 26, 1981, pp. S-36, 38.
14. Honomichl, "FCB," p. 82.

Day-After Recall versus Masked-Recognition Research Findings   TABLE 14.2

"Thinking" Commercials	Day-After Recall	Masked Recognition	Ratio of Masked Recognition to Recall
A	49%	56%	114
D	24	32	133
E	21	24	114
Average	31	37	119
"Feeling" Commericals			
B	21%	37%	176
C	25	36	144
F	10	23	230
Average	19	32	168

Source: "FCB Says Masked-Recognition Test Yields Truer Remembering Measures Than Day-After Recall Test," *Marketing News*, June 12, 1981, p. 1.

The implication is clear: Day-after recall tests *are* biased against feeling commercials. A different research method, such as masked recognition, is needed when testing whether this type of commercial accomplishes suitable levels of awareness.[15]

Measurement of Persuasion

As noted earlier, persuasion research deals with advertising efforts to influence consumer beliefs, attitudes, purchase intentions, feelings, and emotions. Proper research methods for measuring persuasive effects depend on whether the creative strategy and advertising objective are better characterized as adhering to a consumer information processing model (CIP) or to a hedonic, experiential model (HEM).

       CIP-Oriented Methods. The CIP model assumes that advertising "transports" consumer from an initial state of unawareness toward a product or brand, to awareness, positive attitude, favorable purchase intention, and ultimately purchase. The model assumes that advertising works on consumers in a progressive, hierarchical fashion. With this assumption, appropriate research methods involve measures of belief formation or change, attitudes, attitude change, preference formation, and purchase intentions.

15. Ibid.

These methods, it will be noted, break down along the lines of the three-level hierarchy-of-effects framework covered back in Chapter 11: *cognition* (beliefs), *affect* (attitude, attitude change, and preference), and *conation* (purchase intentions). Various research methods are available for testing each of these hierarchy levels.

Measures of Cognition.   In their periodic tracking studies, advertising researchers routinely measure consumer beliefs with respect to important product attributes. Advertising effectiveness can be assessed by comparing preadvertising beliefs (i.e., those measured before an advertising campaign begins) against postadvertising beliefs. Advertising is successful to the extent that consumers' brand-specific beliefs become more positive over time.

Measures of Affect.   As intended in the present context, affect represents consumers' attitudes toward advertised brands and brand preferences. Advertising effectiveness can be assessed using this criterion by measuring attitudes/preferences both before and after an advertising campaign and noting whether attitudes have become more favorable or preference has shifted toward the advertised brand.

A number of commercial-advertising research firms have procedures for copytesting an advertisement's effect on attitudes and brand preferences. These procedures generally involve (1) recruiting a sample of representative consumers and having them meet at a central location (e.g., a movie theater, a room in a shopping mall, a conference room), (2) initially measuring their attitudes/preferences for a "target" brand (i.e., the brand paying for the research), (3) possibly measuring attitudes/preferences toward one or more competitive brands, (4) exposing consumers to a new television commercial for the target brand in context of a television pilot program or some other realistic viewing context, and (5) again measuring attitudes/preferences toward the target and competitive brands following the program and advertising exposure. Commercial effectiveness is assessed by determining the amount of attitude change or preference shift for the target brand.

Commercial research firms doing this type of research include AHF Marketing Research's competitive-environment testing, ASI Market Research, Inc., Gallup & Robinson, Inc., McCollum/Spielman, and Mapes and Ross.[16] ASI's theater testing and AHF's competitive-environment testing are described to illustrate the type of attitude/preference testing provided by commercial research firms.

ASI performs *theater testing* of new television commercials. A total of 250 consumers are recruited and invited to attend a preview of new television programs. Once they are in the ASI theater, consumers are told that prizes from various product categories will be awarded in a drawing, and they are asked to identify for each product the specific brand they would prefer receiving if their name should happen to be drawn. They are then exposed to a pilot tele-

---

16. For details, see Stewart, Furse, and Kozak, "A Guide to Commercial Copytesting Services."

vision program followed by test commercials for each of the product categories mentioned in the drawing. After being exposed to a second pilot television program, the participants are led to believe that one product was inadvertently omitted from the list of products for which the drawing will be held and that they will have to complete a new brand-preference sheet that includes the omitted product as well as the others.

Commercial effectiveness is determined by comparing the two sets of brand preferences. A commercial is considered effective to the extent that more consumers indicate a higher preference for the test product on the second preference sheet (i.e., after they have been exposed to a commercial for the brand) than on the first sheet (before they were exposed to the test commercial). Based on numerous past studies, ASI has been able to develop norms indicating the actual magnitude of shifting in brand preferences that advertisers in particular product categories should expect. In addition to the brand-preference measurement, ASI theaters are equipped with electronic "Instantaneous Reaction Profile Recorder" dials, which permit respondents to register continuously their likes and dislikes regarding the pilot programs and the test commercials. These specific likes and dislikes concerning commercial elements are used to explain the brand-preference shifts.

AHF's *competitive-environment test* represents an adaptation of the ASI methodology. Between 150 and 250 respondents are recruited from shopping centers and directed to an adjacent research test site (such as a specially equipped mobile trailer). Once they are at the test location, respondents are asked to allocate ten hypothetical purchases among competitive brands in the test-product category. They then are exposed to a test commercial for one of the brands (which, unbeknown to respondents, is the one being tested) and to commercials for two or three competitive brands. (The ASI method, by comparison, does not expose respondents to competitive commercials.) Following the commercial exposure, respondents are again asked to allocate ten hypothetical purchases among the competing brands in the product category.

Advertising effectiveness is determined by the shift in brand preference, just as it was in the ASI test. However, the difference here is that the competitive-environment test portrays reality more accurately by exposing respondents to several commercials within a product category rather than to a single commercial.

Measures of Conation.
Though no commercial-advertising research firm offers services to measure purchase intentions alone, several research organizations conduct tests to measure intentions along with attitudes and preferences. Advertising is judged more effective to the extent that purchase intentions are more positive following exposure to a test commercial than before.

HEM-Oriented Methods.
As discussed back in Chapter 4 and alluded to earlier in this chapter, the hedonic, experiential model employs different assumptions about consumer behavior than does the consumer infor-

mation processing (CIP) perspective. The HEM looks upon consumer behavior using concepts such as fantasies, feelings, emotions, and symbolism. The consumer is *not* seen strictly as an information gatherer motivated by desires to achieve economic goals, but rather as someone who uses products and brands as means of creating meaning out of life in the pursuit of fun, fantasies, and feelings.[17]

But what does this have to do with advertising research? Everything! A different research agenda is called for by the HEM perspective in comparison to the CIP view.[18] The HEM agenda emphasizes measuring *emotions* evoked by advertisements rather than counting the number of copy points correctly recognized; it emphasizes measuring *symbolic meaning* of products rather than perceptions of product attributes; and its uses *qualitative research methods* (e.g., open-ended questioning, role playing, and other methods often used by anthropologists) over the quantitative methods typically used by psychometricians (e.g., attitude scales and multivariate statistical techniques).

Measurement of warmth in advertising reflects the HEM research agenda. **Warmth** is one of various emotional responses that consumers have to advertisements. Warmth from viewing a television commercial occurs when the viewer experiences a positive emotional reaction, albeit one which is mild and short-lived. This emotion involves physiological arousal and is precipitated by experiencing a sense of love, family, or friendship.[19]

You no doubt can think of several television commercials that have evoked warmth in you. A commercial that had this effect on me was aired during the 1988 Summer Olympics. It showed a dejected athlete returning home by train after failing to qualify for the Olympics. Much to his surprise and delight, he receives a hero's welcome from his family and friends at the train station. The commercial warmly conveys the message that success comes from trying—not just from achieving. The commercial was presented in a touching but not syrupy fashion.

Research has shown that warmth in advertising increases physiological arousal in response to an advertisement, increases how much consumers like the ad, and is correlated with the likelihood of purchasing the advertised product.[20] A technique called the "warmth monitor" is used to measure emotional warmth in television commercials. It is described in the *Focus on Promotion* section.

A more technologically sophisticated measure of consumers' feelings toward advertisements is a technique called TRACE that is used by the research

---

17. It would be useful to return briefly to the discussion in Chapter 4 to familiarize yourself with more specific aspects of the distinction between the CIP and HEM models of consumer behavior.
18. Judie Lannon, "New Techniques for Understanding Consumer Reactions to Advertising," *Journal of Advertising Research*, vol. 26 (August/September 1986), pp. RC6–RC9.
19. David A. Aaker, Douglas M. Stayman, and Michael R. Hagerty, "Warmth in Advertising: Measurement, Impact, and Sequence Effects," *Journal of Consumer Research*, vol. 12 (March 1986), p. 366.
20. Ibid. See Studies 2 and 3, pp. 371–377.

FOCUS ON PROMOTION

The Warmth Monitor

The warmth monitor is nothing more than a sheet of paper containing four vertical lines running from top to bottom. From left to right these lines are labeled "absence of warmth," "neutral," "warmhearted/tender," and "emotional (moist eyes)." While viewing a test commercial, respondents move a pencil down the paper, moving it to the left and right to continuously reflect their feelings about the commercial. Respondents are instructed to chart how warm they feel and how warm or good they think the commercial is. They are directed to maintain a constant rate of speed in moving their pencils down the page while keeping their eyes fixed on the commercial and not on the page. Most respondents do not need to look down at all and others do so only rarely.[21] ∎

firm Market Facts, Inc. TRACE enables consumers to reveal their feelings toward what they are seeing in a television commercial by pressing a series of buttons on a hand-held microcomputer. Responses are synchonized with commercial content, and the microcomputer then plays back the consumer's feelings, expressed as a TRACEline across the television screen. The TRACEline moves up when the consumer feels good about what he or she sees and down when he or she feels bad about it. At points of critical change in the TRACEline, consumers are asked to discuss why their feelings changed at that point. In light of these vivid changes, consumers seem willing to talk about their feelings.[22]

Advertising researchers have also turned to a variety of *physiological testing devices* to measure consumers' emotional reactions to advertisements. These include such techniques as the psychogalvanometer (which measures minute levels of perspiration in response to emotional arousal), pupillometric tests (pupil dilation), and voice-pitch analysis. Psychologists have concluded that these physiological functions are indeed sensitive to psychological processes of concern in advertising.[23]

All of the bodily functions cited are controlled by the *autonomic nervous system*. Because individuals have little voluntary control over the autonomic nervous system, changes in bodily functions can be used by advertising researchers to indicate the actual, unbiased amount of emotional arousal resulting from advertisements.

21. This description is based on ibid., p. 368.
22. "New Technology 'TRACES' Reaction to TV Ads," *Marketing News*, May 25, 1984, p. 3.
23. Paul J. Watson and Robert J. Gatchel, "Autonomic Measures of Advertising," *Journal of Advertising Research*, vol. 19 (June 1979), pp. 15–26.

In order to appreciate the potential value of such physiological measurement, consider the case of a (sexist) advertisement intended for a male audience that portrays a product in association with a scantily clad female model. In pretesting this ad, some men, when asked what they think about it, may feign disgust or aggravation in order to make a favorable impression on the interviewer. These men may actually enjoy the ad, and their true emotional reactions could not be hidden when measured by sensitive physiological devices.

The **psychogalvanometer** is a device for measuring galvanic skin response. When the consumer's autonomic nervous system is activated by some element in an advertisement, one bodily function affected is the activation of *sweat glands* in the palms and fingers, which open in varying degrees depending on the intensity of the arousal. Skin resistance drops when the sweat glands open. By sending a very fine electric current through one finger, out the other, and completing the circuit through the galvanometer, the instrument measures both the degree and frequency with which an advertisement activates emotional responses.[24] Simply, the psychogalvanometer assesses the degree of emotional response to an advertisement by indirectly measuring minute amounts of perspiration.

Pupillometric tests in advertising are conducted by measuring respondents' *pupil dilation* as they view a television commercial or focus on a printed advertisement. Respondents' heads are in a fixed position to permit continuous electronic measurement of changes in pupillary responses. Responses to specific elements in an advertisement are used to indicate positive reaction (in the case of greater dilation) or negative reaction (smaller relative dilation). Although not unchallenged, there has been scientific evidence since the late 1960s to suggest that pupillary responses are correlated with people's arousal to stimuli and perhaps even with their likes and dislikes.[25]

A complaint leveled against the psychogalvanometer, pupillometric tests, and other physiological measurement devices is that they are capable of indicating the amount of emotional arousal but not the direction of arousal. One advertising commentator stated it this way: "The problem. . .is that once you have the data, you don't know what to do with it. All you have is a reading of physiological changes in a person. You have to get from there to whether that is good or bad."[26]

24. "Psychogalvanometer Testing 'Most Predictive'," *Marketing News*, June 17, 1978, p. 11.
25. For detailed discussion of pupil dilation and other physiological measures, see Joanne M. Klebba, "Physiological Measures of Research: A Review of Brain Activity, Electrodermal Response, Pupil Dilation, and Voice Analysis Methods and Studies," in *Current Issues and Research in Advertising*, eds. James H. Leigh and Claude R. Martin, Jr. (Ann Arbor MI: Division of Research, Graduate School of Business, University of Michigan, 1985), pp. 53–76.
26. Comment by William Wells as quoted in Mark Liff, "Cataloging Some Tools," *Advertising Age*, October 31, 1983, p. M-54.

Voice-pitch analysis (VOPAN) is one physiological measurement device that purportedly overcomes the preceding criticism.[27] A specially programmed computer analyzes a person's voice pitch in response to a question about a test commercial to see whether the pitch differs in relation to the individual's normal or baseline pitch levels. When an individual has emotional commitment, the vocal chord, which is regulated by the autonomic nervous system, becomes abnormally taut, and the pitch is higher than normal. Thus, the voice-pitch reading indicates the amount of emotional involvement, and the person's response (yes or no) to a question about an advertisement is used to identify whether the emotion is positive or negative.

Truthfulness of responses is established by comparing changes in voice pitch over the respondent's preinterview levels. Changes in voice pitch greater than a certain range indicate conscious or unconscious lies or confused responses.[28]

Voice-pitch analysis is potentially a valuable research technique; unfortunately, research purporting its virtues and validity is without scientific merit. Thus, it is not yet known whether VOPAN is a valuable addition to the advertising researcher's repertoire or a case of commercial hype.[29]

Measurement of Action

The ultimate issue in measuring advertising effectiveness is whether advertising leads to increased sales activity. Measuring anything other than sales response is considered by some to represent another case of substituting precisely wrong for vaguely right action. Awareness measures, for example, have the appearance of being precisely right (e.g., research shows that 75 percent of the target market knows of our new brand), but in certain situations might be precisely wrong because mere awareness does not translate into product sales.

Determining the sales impact of advertising is, as explained in Chapter 11, a most difficult task. However, substantial efforts have been made in recent years toward developing research procedures that are able to assess the sales-generating ability of advertising.

The most fascinating of the new techniques are procedures that combine *split-cable television with optical scanning equipment.* Companies that offer these services (e.g., AdTel and BehaviorScan) measure the sales impact of advertising by the ingenious combination of household panels with checkout scanning equipment and split-cable television facilities.

27. The following discussion is based on material from several sources: Glen A Brickman, "Voice Analysis," *Journal of Advertising Research,* vol. 16 (June 1976), pp. 43–48; Ronald G. Nelson and David Schwartz, "Voice Pitch Gives Marketer Access to Consumer's Unaware Body Responses," *Marketing News,* January 28, 1977, p. 21; Ronald G. Nelson and David Schwartz, "Voice-Pitch Analysis," *Journal of Advertising Research,* vol. 19 (October 1979), pp. 55–59.
28. Nelson and Schwartz, "Voice-Pitch Analysis," p. 55.
29. For further discussion, see Klebba, "Physiological Measures of Research," pp. 70–73.

The pioneer in this field, Information Resource's BehaviorScan, can be used to illustrate how advertising's impact on sales can be measured. BehaviorScan operates test markets in 12 communities around the United States. The cities are relatively small, because all grocery stores have to be equipped with automatic scanning devices that read UPC symbols from grocery packages. In each community there is a panel of 2,500 households. Each household receives a coded identification card that must be used each time the shopper visits the supermarket. Panel members are eligible for prize drawings as remuneration for their participation.

Suppose a company is interested in testing a new television commercial. BehaviorScan would do the following: (1) stock the company's product in supermarkets in two or three test-market communities, (2) selectively broadcast the new commercial using special split-cable television so that the commercial is received by only a portion of the panel members in each market, (3) record electronically (via optical scanners) grocery purchases made by all panel members, and (4) compare the purchase behavior of those panel members who were potentially exposed to the new commercial with those who were not exposed.

If the advertising is effective, a greater proportion of the panel members exposed to the test commercial should buy the promoted item in comparison to those members not exposed to any advertising.

This type of research is not restricted to testing the effects of advertising. It can be used to examine other marketing-mix variables such as price, sales promotions, and in-store merchandising activity. The technology also permits forecasts of product success. For example, when G. D. Searle introduced a low-calorie sweetener *Equal*, BehaviorScan predicted annual initial sales after a national rollout of $50 million. According to Searle executives, this prediction proved to be 100 percent correct.[30] Without question, this technology will facilitate a more sophisticated understanding of how marketing communications and other marketing variables interact to affect consumer choice behavior.

Copytesting Principles

We have covered a variety of copytesting methods. It is instructive, though a bit sobering, to note that much advertising research is not of the highest caliber. Sometimes it is unclear exactly what research is attempting to measure; measures often fail to satisfy basic reliability and validity requirements; and results have little to say about whether copytested ads stand a good chance of being effective.

30. Grace Conlon, "Closing in on Consumer Behavior," *Marketing Communications*, November 1986, p. 56.

The PACT Document

Members of the advertising-research community have been mindful of these problems and have sought a higher standard of performance from advertising researchers. A major statement prepared jointly by 21 leading U.S. advertising agencies typifies the concern and offers steps toward remedying the problem of mediocre or flawed advertising research. This document, called **Positioning Advertising Copytesting (PACT),** represents a consensus of the advertising community on fundamental copytesting principles. The PACT document is directed primarily at television advertising but is relevant to the testing of advertising in all media.

PACT consists of nine copytesting principles.[31] These principles are more than mere pronouncements; they are useful guides to how copytesting research should be conducted or supervised.

Principle 1. A good copytesting system needs to provide *measurements that are relevant to the advertising objectives.* The specific objective(s) that an advertising campaign is intended to accomplish (creating brand awareness, influencing brand image, creating warmth) should be the first consideration in determining the copytesting methods to assess advertising effectiveness. For example, if the objective for a particular campaign is to evoke strong emotional reactions, a measure of day-after recall would be inappropriate.

Principle 2. A good copytesting system is one that requires agreement about how the results will be used in advance of each specific test. Specifying how research results will be used *before* data are collected ensures that all parties involved (e.g., advertiser, agency, and research firm) agree on the research goals and reduces the chance of conflicting interpretations of test results. This principle's intent is to encourage the use of decision rules or *action standards* that, in advance of actual testing, establish the test results that must be achieved for the test advertisement to receive full media distribution. Consider the following illustrative action standard: Commercial X must receive a minimum Burke-rated day-after recall score of 40, or the commercial will not be run.[32]

Principle 3. A good copytesting system provides *multiple measurements* because single measurements are generally inadequate to assess the performance of an advertisement. Because the process by which advertising influences customers is complex, multiple measures are more likely to capture the various advertising effects and are therefore preferred over single measures.

---

31. Material for this section is extracted from the PACT document, which is published in its entirety in the *Journal of Advertising*, vol. 11, no. 4 (1982), pp. 4–29.
32. A score of 40 would indicate that 40 percent of the queried respondents correctly recalled the test commercial the day after it was aired on television.

Principle 4. A good copytesting system is based on a *model of human response to communications*—the reception of a stimulus, the comprehension of the stimulus, and the response to the stimulus. Because advertisements vary in the impact they are intended to achieve, a good copytesting system is capable of answering a number of questions. The earlier discussion of the CIP versus HEM perspectives of consumer behavior identify how different models of advertising response call for different measures of advertising effectiveness.

Principle 5. A good copytesting system allows for consideration of whether the advertising stimulus should be *exposed more than once*. This principle addresses the issue of whether a single test exposure (i.e., showing an ad or commercial to consumers only once) provides a sufficient test of potential impact. Because multiple exposure is often required for advertisements to accomplish their full effect, copytesting procedures should expose a test ad to respondents on two or more occasions when the communication situation calls for such a procedure.[33] For example, a single-exposure test is probably insufficient to test whether an advertisement successfully conveys a complex benefit. On the other hand, a single exposure may be adequate if an advertisement is designed solely to create name awareness for a new brand.

Principle 6. A good copytesting system recognizes that the more finished a piece of copy is, the more soundly it can be evaluated; therefore, a good system requires, at minimum, that *alternative executions be tested in the same degree of finish*. Test results can often vary depending on the degree of finish of the test executions. Sometimes the amount of information lost from testing a less-than-finished ad may be inconsequential; sometimes it may be critical.

Principle 7. A good copytesting system provides *controls to avoid the bias normally found in the exposure context*. The context in which an advertisement is contained (e.g., the clutter or lack of clutter in a magazine) will have a substantial impact on how the ad is received, processed, and accepted. For this reason, copytesting procedures should attempt to duplicate the actual context that an advertisement or commercial may eventually have. This is why the competitive-environment test, discussed previously under affect measures of persuasion, is superior to other tests that fail to incorporate competitive commercials into the testing program.

Principle 8. A good copytesting system is one that takes into account *basic considerations of sample definition*. Any good research requires that the sample be representative of the target audience to which test results are to be generalized and that the sample size be sufficiently large to permit reliable statistical conclusions.

---

33. Herbert E. Krugman, "Why Three Exposures May be Enough," *Journal of Advertising Research*, vol. 12 (December 1972), pp. 11–14.

Summary of the Nine PACT Principles   TABLE 14.3

Principle 1: A good copytesting system needs to provide *measurements that are relevant to the advertising objectives.*
Principle 2: A good copytesting system sets *action standards* before data are collected.
Principle 3: A good copytesting system provides *multiple measurements.*
Principle 4: A good copytesting system is based on a *model of human response to communications.*
Principle 5: A good copytesting system considers the need for *multiple exposures* rather than a single exposure of the tested advertisement.
Principle 6: A good copytesting system tests alternative ads *in the same degree of finish.*
Principle 7: A good copytesting system provides *controls to avoid bias created by the exposure context.*
Principle 8: A good copytesting system attempts to use *representative samples.*
Principle 9: A good copytesting system demonstrates *reliable and valid measurement.*

Principle 9.   A good copytesting system is one that can demonstrate *reliability and validity.* Reliability and validity are basic requirements of any research endeavor. As applied to copytesting, a reliable test is one that yields consistent results each time an advertisement is tested, and a valid test is one that is predictive of marketplace performance.

The foregoing principles establish a high set of standards for the advertising-research community. Yet, they should not be regarded in the same sense that the earlier discussion of research ideals were. Rather, these principles should be viewed as mandatory if advertising effectiveness is to be tested in a meaningful way. Table 14.3 summarizes the nine PACT principles.

Summary

Though difficult and often expensive, measuring advertising effectiveness is essential so that advertisers can better understand how well their ads are performing and what changes need to be made to improve performance. The actual conduct of advertising copytesting should adhere to strict measurement procedures. A group of representatives from leading U.S. advertising agencies recently proposed a set of nine principles (PACT) to guide copytesting efforts. One principle, for example, makes the critical point that the choice of copytesting techniques for assessing the effectiveness of advertising campaigns depends first and foremost on the specific objective an advertising campaign is intended to accomplish.

Dozens of copytesting techniques for measuring advertising effectiveness have evolved over the years. The reason for this diversity is that advertisements perform a variety of functions, and multiple methods are needed to test different indicators of advertising effectiveness.

The Nielsen and Audits Great Britain (AGB) people meters, Simmons Market Research Bureau, Mediamark, and Arbitron are well-known, widely used commercial services that measure advertising exposure in television, magazines, and local radio, respectively. Starch Message Report Service and Burke Day-After Recall Tests are techniques for measuring various aspects of awareness.

Persuasion measures vary widely depending both on the model directing the research (either CIP or HEM) and the specific issue at hand. Theater testing is performed to measure attitudinal responses and preference shifts to advertising, while techniques such as the warmth monitor and TRACE are used to measure emotional reactions to advertising. Various physiological measures (e.g., galvanic skin response, pupil dilation, and voice pitch) are used to assess physiological arousal activated by advertisements. The impact of advertising on actual purchase behavior (action) is assessed by integrating the use of controlled consumer panels with supermarket optical scanning equipment and split-cable television.

No single copytesting technique is ideal, nor is any particular technique appropriate for all occasions. The choice of technique should depend on the specific objective an advertising campaign is intended to accomplish. Moreover, it is typically preferable to use multiple measurement methods rather than any single technique in order to answer the diversity of questions that are typically involved in attempts to assess advertising effectiveness.

Discussion Questions

1. It is desirable that the measurement of advertising effectiveness focus on sales response rather than on some precursor to sales, yet measuring sales response to advertising is typically difficult. What complicates the measurement of sales response to advertising?

2. PACT principle 2 states that a good copytesting system should establish how results will be used in advance of each copy test. Explain the specific meaning and importance of this copytesting principle. Construct illustrations of an anticipated result lacking a sufficient action standard and one with a suitable standard.

3. In reference to PACT principle 9, explain in your own words what "valid" measurement means. Suppose a research firm offers television advertisers an inexpensive method of testing commercials in which consumers merely evaluate photographed pictures of key commercial scenes. Comment about the probable validity of this approach.

4. Advertising research often measures vehicle exposure to indicate advertising exposure. What is the difference between these two types of exposure, and why do researchers measure the former when advertising decision makers are really interested in the latter?

5. If you were an account executive in an advertising agency, what would you tell clients to convince them to use (or not to use) the Starch Message Report Service?

6. An advertising agency is in the process of arranging research services to assess advertising effectiveness for two clients: one advertising campaign is for a unique financial service that is advertised with a number of specific selling points; the other campaign involves a very touching family scene used to advertise another client's food product. The agency proposes that day-after recall tests be conducted for both clients. Comment.

7. As advertising manager for a brand of toothpaste, you are considering using a physiological measurement technique to assess consumers' evaluative reactions to your new advertisements. Present an argument in favor of using VOPAN rather than pupil dilation testing or galvanic skin-response measurement.

8. Present an argument in favor of using the AHF's competitive-environment test rather than the ASI's theater testing procedure.

9. A scanner-cable test performed by BehaviorScan will cost you, as brand manager of a new brand of cereal, approximately $150,000. Why might this be a prudent investment in comparison to spending $50,000 to perform an awareness study?

10. The chapter's opening vignette noted that network representatives claim people meters are flawed. What are some of the reasons why people meters may not yield precise information about the number of households tuned into a specific television program?

Exercises

1. Visit your library and examine the most recent Arbitron local radio ratings for the various stations that are located in your university town or city. Before the visit, construct a demographic profile for each station, and then compare the correspondence between your subjective profile and Arbitron's objective, measured profile.

2. Arrange a meeting at a local advertising agency with an account executive for purposes of getting his or her views toward the following research services: Burke day-after recall measurement, Starch magazine readership studies, and Arbitron local radio ratings.

3. Select two or three national television commercials, identify the objective(s) each appears to be attempting to accomplish, and then propose a procedure for how you would go about testing the effectiveness of each commercial. Be specific.

4. Locate a recent Simmons Market Research Bureau in your library. Select a product that is consumed by large numbers of consumers (e.g., soft drinks, cereal, candy bars). Pick out the index numbers for the 18 to 24, 25 to 34, 35 to 44, 45 to 54, 55 to 64, and 65 and older age categories based on "All Users" columns. Show how the index numbers in column "D" were calculated. Also, identify some magazines that would be especially suitable for advertising to the "Heavy Users" of your selected product category.

PART 5

Direct Marketing, Point-of-Purchase Communications, and Public Relations

Part 5 covers three topics that are growing in importance in today's promotion management and marketing communications programs. Direct-marketing communications, point-of-purchase communications, and public relations and sponsorship marketing combine many features of media advertising; however, their distinct features and individual importance deserve separate coverage.

Chapter 15 describes the phenomenal growth that direct selling and direct-response advertising—the two major aspects of direct-marketing communications—have experienced in recent years. In addition, the chapter discusses direct-mail advertising and telephone marketing in particular detail.

Chapter 16 describes the ever-growing marketing practice of point-of-purchase communications. The growth is explained in terms of the valuable functions that P-O-P performs for consumers, manufacturers, and retailers. Specific topics include unplanned purchasing and electronic retailing.

Chapter 17 covers the related topics of public relations and sponsorship marketing. The section on public relations includes treatment of the historically entrenched practice of reactive public relations as well as coverage of the more recent practice of proactive public relations. A special section is devoted to negative publicity, including a discussion of rumors and how to handle them. The final major section covers both cause and event marketing—the two specific aspects of sponsorship marketing.

Direct Marketing Communications

WHAT KINDS OF PRODUCTS CAN BE DIRECT MARKETED?

ll kinds of firms are beginning to market products directly to consumers. Following are several illustrations.

K-Pauls Louisiana Kitchen, the famous New Orleans restaurant that specializes in cajun cooking, ships dinners to customers around the country. K-Pauls sends the ingredients, and all the consumer needs to do is combine them. The average cost is $85 for an eight-person meal. K-Pauls has a mailing list of over 100,000 customers, consisting mainly of professionals and managers who travel and like to eat well.[1]

Edgar B Furniture markets top-line furniture directly to consumers, who select furniture pieces from a catalog and place orders by telephoning a toll-free number. Delivery takes about 10 to 12 weeks, and customers pay shipping charges amounting to about 5 to 12 percent of the total order cost. Typical customers are from time-pressured, economically upscale households with incomes of approximately $70,000. The company claims average sales of $2,500, with even larger orders from repeat purchasers.[2]

1. Cyndee Miller, "New Meaning for 'Box Lunch'," *Marketing News*, August 15, 1988, p. 10.
2. Cyndee Miller, "Edgar B's Customers Buy Their Sofas through the Mail," *Marketing News*, October 9, 1987, p. 6.

Prison Industries, an arm of the South Carolina Department of Corrections, has plants in several correctional facilities where inmates manufacture office furniture, refurbish used furniture, a*d restore vehicles. These products and services are sold to state or local governments and nonprofit organizations. Annual sales were running around $6 million until the state governor ordered a task force to come up with a plan to increase sales in three years to $25 million and to expand the number of inmates involved from 900 to 2,500.

An advertising agency was awarded a $19,000 contract to develop a direct-mail campaign for achieving these objectives. The agency formulated a humorous campaign directed at purchasing agents, directors of state agencies, and other potential customers. In one direct mailing, a stern-looking man with arms folded is pictured next to the headline "Reverend Marvin Wood has information that will send you to prison." The reader soon learns that Reverend Wood's church has used Prison Industries' vehicle-restoration program and wants to send you to prison for "top notch work at rock bottom prices." The program is an innovative way to keep inmates gainfully and meaningfully occupied and to raise revenue for supporting the cost of state correctional facilities.[3]■

Preceding chapters introduced various aspects of advertising management with emphasis on the major advertising media: television, magazines, newspapers, radio, and outdoor advertising. Advertising in these media is designed primarily to create brand awareness, convey product information, and to build or reinforce a brand's image.

These conventional media are *not* particularly effective, however, for the purpose of creating immediate response. Moreover, although they permit varying degrees of selectivity in audience reach, they do not permit marketers to aim specifically at carefully defined and narrow market segments. For these and other reasons, marketers have turned increasingly to direct marketing. The 1980s, in fact, has been characterized as the decade of direct marketing.[4] Marketers are using techniques such as those described in the opening vignette to fine tune their customer selection, better serve customer needs, and better serve their own needs by creating immediate and measurable results.

This chapter focuses on various aspects of direct marketing. The three major topics covered are direct selling, direct-response advertising, and telemarketing. An overview of direct marketing is provided before turning to each of these specific topics.

3. Thom Fladung, "Cook Ruef Campaign Urges Consumers to Go Directly to Jail," *The State*, Columbia, SC, January 18, 1988, p. 9.
4. Stan Rapp and Thomas L. Collins, *MaxiMarketing* (New York: McGraw-Hill, 1987).

Direct Marketing

The Direct Marketing Association, a trade group whose members practice various forms of direct marketing, offers the following definition:

> **Direct marketing** is an *interactive system* of marketing which uses *one or more advertising media* to effect a *measurable response* and/or transaction *at any location.*[5]

Note the special features in this definition. First, direct marketing involves interactive marketing in that it entails one-on-one communication between marketer and prospect. Second, direct marketing is not restricted to a single medium such as direct mail, but rather involves *one or more media* (e.g., direct mail with telephone marketing). Third, marketing via media such as direct mail allows for relatively greater *measurability of response* in comparison to indirect media such as television advertising. Greater measurability is possible because purchase responses to direct marketing are typically more immediate than responses to mass-media advertising. Finally, direct marketing takes place *at a variety of locations*—by phone, at a kiosk, by mail, or by personal visit.

A Semantic Jungle

At this point you have a general understanding of direct marketing. You probably remain a little confused, however, as to just exactly what it is. This confusion is understandable because the terminology of direct marketing is somewhat of a semantic jungle due to the word "direct" being used in several different ways: "direct marketing," "direct selling," "direct-response advertising," and "direct mail."

Figure 15.1 provides a framework to help clarify the distinctions among these various "D words." The figure depicts the total marketing process as consisting of indirect and direct marketing. Direct marketing involves both direct selling and direct-response advertising, the latter of which breaks out into direct mail and other media.

Indirect marketing includes the use of middlemen in the channel of distribution; examples include distributors or dealers in industrial-goods marketing and retailers in consumer-goods marketing. Indirect marketing is what typically comes to mind when one thinks of marketing.

In *direct marketing* the marketer solicits orders from customers who order directly from the seller, and the seller ships the product directly to the buyer (as in the case of Edgar B. Furniture in the opening vignette).[6] (By comparison, in *indirect marketing a manufacturer's sales force sells to middlemen.) The

---

5. *1982 Fact Book on Direct Response Marketing* (New York: Direct Marketing Association, Inc., 1982), p. xxiii. Italics not in original.
6. Chaman L. Jain and Al Migliaro, *An Introduction to Direct Marketing* (New York: Amacom, 1978), p. 7.

FIGURE 15.1   **Distinctions among Various "Direct" Concepts**

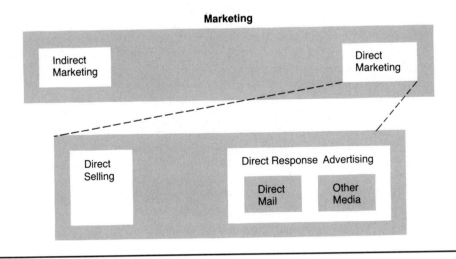

direct marketer's purpose is to establish a direct relationship with a customer in order to initiate immediate and measurable responses. Direct marketing is accomplished using direct selling and/or direct-response advertising.

Direct selling is the use of salespeople (e.g., Avon or Tupperware salespeople) who sell directly to the final consumer. *Direct-response advertising* involves the use of any of several media to transmit messages that encourage buyers to purchase directly from the advertiser. *Direct mail* is the most important direct-advertising medium, but certainly not the only one. Direct-response advertising also uses television, magazines, and other media with the intent of creating immediate action from customers. In comparison, general advertising (i.e., nondirect response) more often intends to build consumer awareness and company and brand images rather than to create immediate sales.

Direct Marketing's Phenomenal Growth

Historically, direct marketing represented a relatively small part of most companies' marketing efforts. However, by the mid-1980s American consumers were estimated to have spent over $200 billion annually through mail- and telephone-order sales. Experts place the annual growth rate between 10 and 16 percent.[7] Direct mail is the leading medium used by national advertisers, accounting for over 29 percent of all advertising expenditures.[8] Mail-order buying is growing 50 percent faster than store retailing in the United States.[9] In fact, mail order is the fastest growing form of product distribution in the United States.

A variety of factors help to explain direct marketing's growth. Fundamental *societal changes* (including more women in the work force, greater time pressures, greater use of credit cards, and more discretionary income) have created a need and opportunity for the convenience of direct-marketed products and services. Direct marketing provides shoppers with an easy, convenient, and relatively hassle-free way to buy. This is particularly important to working women and other time-pressured consumers.[10]

Major advances in *computer technology* and *database management* have made it possible for companies to maintain huge databases containing millions of prospects/customers. *Niche marketing* can be fully realized by targeting promotional efforts to a company's "best" prospects (based on past product-category purchasing behavior), and who can be identified in terms of specific geographic, demographic, and psychographic characteristics.

Business-to-Business Direct-Marketing Growth

In addition to the growth of consumer-oriented direct marketing, there has been a tremendous increase in applications of direct marketing for businesses that market to other businesses. Nearly one-third of all money invested in business-to-business marketing and advertising goes to direct marketing, especially telemarketing.[11]

A major reason for this trend is the cost of a personal industrial-sales call, which is estimated to exceed $250 per call.[12] Direct marketing through telemarketing and direct mail actually replaces the sales force in some companies, whereas in other cases it is used to supplement the sales force's efforts by building goodwill, generating leads, and opening doors for salespeople.

7. William A. Cohen, "The Future of Direct Marketing," *Retailing Issues Letter*, vol. 1, published by Arthur Andersen & Co. in conjunction with the Center for Retailing Studies, Texas A&M University, November 1987.
8. Jerrold Ballinger, "Direct Mail Is Now Number One in Ad Expenditures, DDB Reports," *DM News*, vol. 8 (May 1, 1986).
9. "Sroge Lists Leading Mail Order Firms," *Marketing News*, June 12, 1981, p. 3.
10. Larry J. Rosenberg and Elizabeth C. Hirschman, "Retailing Without Stores," *Harvard Business Review*, July-August 1980, pp. 103–112.
11. Kevin Brown, "Mail, Phone Sell Business-to-Business," *Advertising Age*, May 18, 1987, p. S-1.
12. Ernan Roman, "The Newest Member of the Media Mix," *Marketing Communications*, June 1987, p. 72; and "Average Business-to-Business Sales Call Increases by 9.5%," *Marketing News*, September 12, 1988, p. 5.

A direct-marketing program developed by an Atlanta advertising agency illustrates how a creative direct-marketing program can accomplish various business-to-business marketing objectives. The agency developed a direct-mail promotion to attract interest in a series of data-processing seminars conducted by its client, the Merlyn Corporation. These seminars are presented to data-processing professionals and involve detailed information for various data-processing products. Videotaped sales presentations sponsored by companies selling data-processing products are used as teaching tools. Merlyn Corporation funds the seminars by finding companies to sponsor the videotape presentations. However, because the product category is so narrow, only 12 prospects could be identified. A direct-mail program was designed to reach and elicit interest from these 12 prospects.

Here is how it was done. A shoebox was delivered by Federal Air Express to each prospect. Inside the box was a man's new shoe with a microcassette recorder attached. The recorded message read: "Good morning, Mr. (recipient's surname), my name is Vaughn Merlyn, and I'd like to point out that I just got my foot in your door for under $100, and, if my calculations are correct, that's about one-tenth of what it costs you every time one of your salespeople makes a call on a qualified prospect." The tape, which was over three minutes long, went on to explain how sponsorship of a videotaped segment could enable the sponsor to reach up to 300 qualified buyers (i.e., the data-processing professionals who would be seminar attendees) at a cost of only $35 per person.

One hundred percent of the shoebox recipients responded when follow-up sales calls were made, and six of the 12 prospects bought the idea. This program was a success because it found a unique and meaningful way to gain the attention and interest of busy executives.[13]

Business-to-business direct marketing can reduce marketing costs substantially and provide firms with larger potential markets. Consider the case of General Binding Corporation (GBC), a marketer of printing-related machines and other printing products. GBC's sales force consisted of more than 300 salespersons who sold to tens of thousands of small, medium, and large businesses throughout the country. Escalating sales costs forced the company to find ways other than direct sales contact to do business with its many smaller customers. GBC found that mail order provided it with an efficient distribution method for serving the many customers that make small purchases individually but represent huge sales potential collectively.[14]

General Binding's experience is similar to that of many other businesses. Mail-order selling and other forms of direct marketing provide attractive options for firms who either prefer to avoid the tremendous expense of a sales

13. This case is described in Kevin Higgins, "Ad Agency's 'Talking Shoe' Promotion Effectively Reaches Seminar Prospects," *Marketing News*, February 19, 1982, p. 15.
14. Jack Miller, "Several Factors Converge to Spawn Mail Order's Business-to-Business Sales Growth," *Marketing News*, July 8, 1983, p. 8.

force or desire to supplement sales-force effort with supportive marketing communications.

Direct Selling

An important though relatively minor aspect of direct marketing is direct selling. **Direct selling** involves the personal explanation and demonstration of products and services to consumers in their homes or at their jobs. Avon, Tupperware, and Mary Kay Cosmetics are just a few of the hundreds of companies that market directly to consumers.

Total direct sales in the United States were approximately $8.62 billion in 1987.[15] Japan, where annual direct sales exceed $16 billion, is the only country where direct-selling activity is greater than in the United States. Nearly everything is sold direct in Japan—including products ranging from condoms to automobiles. Over 75 percent of all automobiles sold in Japan are sold by direct salespeople!

Returning to the United States, it is estimated that approximately 4.5 million people work in direct sales. The vast majority work part-time. For the most part, direct salespeople are *independent contractors* and not employees of the firms whose products they represent. In fact, ninety-eight percent of all direct salespeople work as independent contractors. The rate of salesperson turnover is very high, over 100 percent annually.

Three primary types of direct-selling programs are practiced: (1) *repetitive person-to-person selling* occurs when salespeople visit homes or job sites to sell frequently purchased products/services (e.g., Avon cosmetics); (2) *nonrepetitive person-to-person selling* is used for infrequently purchased products/services (e.g., encyclopedias); and (3) *party plans* are used in which salespeople offer products to groups of people at homes or job sites (e.g., Tupperware parties).

Direct Selling Moves to the Office

In past years, when fewer women worked outside the home, door-to-door direct selling was effective. Now that the number of women in the work force is approaching 60 percent, in-home selling has diminished due to both fewer customers *and* fewer salespeople. Tupperware alone lost over 10,000 salespeople during the early-to-mid 1980s. As a result, more and more direct selling is taking place in the workplace. Avon, for example, now gets 25 percent of its sales from buyers at businesses.[16] Many of the direct-selling industry's current

15. This statistic is from Neil H. Offen, president of the Direct Selling Association, in *Proceedings of the Education Foundation Academic Seminar* (Washington, DC: Direct Selling Education Foundation, 1987), p. 7. All statistics and details that follow are from this source unless otherwise noted.
16. Kate Ballen, "Get Ready for Shopping at Work," *Fortune*, February 15, 1988, pp. 95, 98.

sales representatives are themselves in the work force, and their customers are work associates.

On-the-job direct selling is not restricted to cosmetics and food containers. For example, the clothier Alfred Dunhill of London sends tailors with fabric swatches to fit executives on the job. The average Dunhill sale is $4,000. (Top-of-the-line Dunhill suits are priced at about $3,000!)[17]

Whether door-to-door or office-to-office, direct selling has a promising future in the United States and elsewhere. The industry has begun to adapt to social changes and is showing signs of growing sophistication. One remaining negative that needs to be overcome is the presence of a relatively small number of shysters such as those who operate pyramid schemes.[18]

However, most direct-selling operations are legitimate businesses. The day of the quick-talking, high-pressure salesman ended in the 1970s with the enactment of *cooling-off laws*. Consumers were given three business days to back out of a purchase (i.e., to "cool off") and obtain a full refund.

Direct-Response Advertising

Three distinct features characterize direct-response advertising: (1) it makes a definite offer, (2) it contains all the information necessary to make a decision, and (3) it contains a response device (coupon, phone number, or both) to facilitate immediate action.[19]

An illustration of direct-response advertising is the RADARMASTER™ ad shown in Figure 15.2. This ad satisfies the requirements of a direct-response advertisement in its appeal to readers of *Psychology Today* and other magazines in which it was placed. Note the detailed information and the conspicuous toll-free number. The ad provides prospective customers with solid reasons to buy a RADARMASTER™ and with convenient mechanisms—the toll-free number and ability to purchase by credit—to actualize their purchase desires. In addition, the ad promises a five-year factory warranty, a 30-day free trial and permission to return the device within 30 days if the purchase is not fully satisfied, and a free bonus value at $39.50. The consumer has little to lose when responding to this offer, which is essential for successful direct marketing.

The direct marketer's objective is to select a medium (or multiple media) that provides maximum ability to segment the market at a reasonable cost. Effective direct-response media selection demands that the marketer have a clearly defined target market in mind. For example, the target market for the

17. Ibid.
18. The Direct Selling Association defines pyramid schemes as "illegal scams in which large numbers of people at the bottom of the pyramid pay money to a few people at the top. Each new participant pays for the chance to advance to the top and profit from payments of others who might join later." DSA distinguishes between illegitimate pyramid schemes and legitimate multi-level marketing involving different levels of product distributorships.
19. Bob Stone, "For Effective Direct Results," *Advertising Age*, March 28, 1983, p. M-32.

Illustration of Direct-Response Advertising   FIGURE 15.2

*THE NATIONAL RADAR
DETECTOR SURVEY:*
"Some are good...
Some are better...
RADARMASTER is the best!!"

RADARMASTER™
*The Most Technologically
Advanced Radar Detector Made*

$295 Value. Now, Yours For Only $159
Faster Warnings...Greater Reliability...

Now, own **RADARMASTER**™ the world's most advanced Radar Detector and save a whopping $136.00.

State of The Art Technology
Designed with "breakthrough" receiving circuitry, **RADARMASTER**™ gives you the best protection, fastest warnings and greatest reliability at a price well below that of other leading detectors.

RADARMASTER™ is built with a computer brain that gives *you* the edge. Its superior capabilities sniff out police radar faster than more expensive detectors, interpret the signals with remarkable efficiency, tell you when they are present and how strong they are.

Easiest Detector To Use
Just plug **RADARMASTER's**™ power cord into your cigarette lighter and its computer brain is activated. Its as easy as that. **RADARMASTER**™ will do all the work by alerting you to stationary, moving, trigger *and* pulsed radar. If there's police radar around a curve, on the straightaway or in a tunnel, you can depend on **RADARMASTER**™ to warn you in plenty of time. **RADARMASTER**™ comes complete with a visor attachment bracket, dashboard mount fastener, power cord and an easy to follow owners manual. **RADARMASTER**™ is covered by an unprecedented five year factory warranty.

RADARMASTER™
Is A Superior
American Made Product

BUY AMERICAN

SYMBOL OF QUALITY

World's Leading Manufacturer
RADARMASTER™ is made by B.E.L-Tronics, one of the world's most highly regarded and experienced manufacturers of Radar Detectors. B.E.L-Tronics produces more radar detectors than any other company and is widely known for its leading edge discoveries in radar detection technology as well as its high grade precision manufacturing.

RADARMASTER™
*fits easily in your
shirt pocket.*

Handsome Carrying Case
A Plushly-lined Deluxe case is included with each **RADARMASTER**™ shipped.

Act Now.
Receive a Valuable Free Bonus
For a limited time only, we'll send you a free **Driver Safety Companion**™ for test driving **RADARMASTER**.™ This revolutionary Life-Saving alarm, valued at $39.50 fits comfortably behind your ear and transmits a signal to keep you awake if

you nod off to sleep as you drive. This reliable safety device will be shipped while supplies last. Reserve yours by ordering today!

Try RADARMASTER™
Without Obligation
On A 30 Day Free Trial
Test drive **RADARMASTER**™ for 30 days without obligation. If you're not completely satisfied, for any reason, with the world's most advanced radar detector, return it and you owe nothing. Keep the Special **Driver Safety Companion**™ Bonus. You have everything to gain when you test drive **RADARMASTER**™.

RADARMASTER™
Only $159
Shipping, Handling, & Insurance FREE

CALL TOLL-FREE
1-800-845-6000

[MasterCard] [VISA]

or write:
The Travel Connection™
Special Products Offer Center
4931 South 900 East, Dept. TC-16
Salt Lake City, UT 84117

Copyright 1988 by The Travel Connection.

RADARMASTER® probably consists of people with the following general profile: (1) they are salespeople and other businesspeople whose jobs require frequent travel; (2) they are high achievers who work hard, feel a strong sense of time pressure, and occasionally break the speed limit when rushing from one obligation to the next; and (3) they want quality products but are price conscious. The marketer no doubt felt that the audience for *Psychology Today* (the magazine in which the RADARMASTER® ad was placed) was a good match to this general profile.

Direct-response advertisers use various media. Direct mail is by far the most important direct-response medium, but advertisers also use magazines (such as the ad for RADARMASTER®), television, newspapers, and radio to reach targeted audiences and generate measurable results.

Direct Mail

Direct mail advertising is any advertising matter sent through the mail directly to the person whom the marketer wishes to influence; these advertisements can take the form of letters, postcards, programs, calendars, folders, catalogs, blotters, order blanks, price lists, or menus. Direct mail's primary advantages are that it enables companies to pinpoint messages to specific market segments and to measure success immediately by knowing how many customers actually respond.

Additional positive features of direct mail are that it permits greater personalization than does mass media advertising; it can gain the prospect's undivided attention because it is not subject to competing adjacent ads (as is the case with advertising in other printed and broadcast media); it has no constraints in terms of form, color, or size (other than those imposed by cost and practical considerations); and it is relatively simple and inexpensive to change direct-mail ads.[20]

An alleged disadvantage of direct mail is that it is more expensive than other media. On a cost-per-thousand (CPM) basis, direct mail *is* more expensive. For example, the CPM for a particular direct mailing may be as high as $250, whereas a magazine's CPM might be as low as $4. However, compared with other media, direct mail is much less wasteful and will usually produce the highest percentage of responses. Thus, on a *cost per order* basis, direct mail is often less expensive and a better bargain.

Consumer Responsiveness to Direct Mail. American consumers are much more likely than consumers anywhere else in the world to buy through the mail. On a dollars-per-capita basis, U.S. consumers spent $642 in 1984–1985 buying by mail, whereas the next largest expenditure was in West Ger-

20. Richard Hodgson, *Direct Mail and Mail Order Handbook* (Chicago: Dartnell Publishing Corporation, 1974).

Factor	Percent Rating Factor: Very Important or Important[a]
1. Products are from companies I can trust	81.9%
2. Money-back guarantee	77.5
3. Better quality	75.2
4. Products were from well-known companies	71.0
5. Can't find product anywhere else	70.9
6. Speedy delivery	66.4
7. More adequate buying information	65.5
8. Convenience	62.6
9. Greater variety of choices	61.5
10. Mail-order prices are lower	61.2
11. Free trial period to examine merchandise	54.7
12. Free telephone ordering service	53.6
13. Major credit cards acceptable	45.1
14. Coupons for order information	43.0
15. Fun of anticipating arrival of merchandise	23.2
16. Enjoy buying by mail	20.9

[a]Percentages based on 1,120 responses.

Source: A.R. Pironti, Morton M. Vitriol, and Andrew Thurm, "Consumer Interest in Mail Order Purchasing," *Journal of Advertising Research*, June 1981, p. 36. Reprinted with permission from the *Journal of Advertising Research.* © Copyright 1981 by the Advertising Research Foundation.

many, with expenditures of $124 per capita. Other per-capita expenditures include $67 in the United Kingdom, $53 in France, $33 in the Netherlands, and $4 in Spain.[21]

Why do American consumers buy by mail? A survey examined this question and also queried which items consumers are most willing to buy.[22] Table 15.1 lists 16 major factors that are important to consumers in deciding to purchase by mail. Nearly 82 percent of the 1,120 survey respondents indicated that it is important or very important that merchandise be from trustworthy companies. Other major reasons for purchasing by mail are the availability of money-back guarantees, better product quality than what is available from retail stores, product unavailability in retail outlets, speedy delivery, and more adequate buying information than can be obtained from retail stores.

The same survey also identified the specific items that consumers are most interested in purchasing through the mail. The top two categories are

21. Lori Kesler, "U.S. Agencies Stake Claims around the Globe," *Advertising Age*, January 12, 1987, p. S-1.
22. A. R. Pironti, Morton M. Vitriol, and Andrew Thurm, "Consumer Interest in Mail Order Purchasing," *Journal of Advertising Research* (June 1981), pp. 35–38.

books and magazines; over 40 percent of the respondents indicated that they are interested or very interested in buying books and magazines by mail. Garden supplies, hobby and craft items, and gift merchandise are other products for which over one-third of the respondents indicated mail-order purchase interest. More than one-fourth of the respondents also indicated interest in purchasing clothing and housewares by mail.

Database Management.   Success with direct mail depends greatly upon the quality of *mailing lists*. Mailing lists, which contain past customers and prospects, enable direct marketers to pinpoint the best candidates for future purchases. One observer has aptly dubbed mailing lists "windows to our pocketbooks."[23]

As mentioned in the chapter introduction, the success of modern direct marketing is largely due to the availability of huge computer databases. **Database management** is the construction and maintenance of data lists containing customer and/or prospect names and detailed information for each listing. There are two broad categories of lists: internal (house lists) and external (public lists).[24]

House Lists.   A company's own internal records are used to generate **house lists.** Because these lists contain the names of customers who previously responded to a company's offering, they are generally more valuable than external lists. Useful house lists are segregated by the *recency* (R) of a customer's purchase, the *frequency* (F) of purchases, the *monetary value* (M) of each purchase, and the *type* of products purchased. Companies typically assign point values to accounts based on the recency, frequency, and monetary value of the consumers' purchases. Each company has its own customized procedure for point assignment (i.e., its own *R-F-M formula*), but in every case more points are assigned to more recent, more frequent, and larger monetary purchases. The R-F-M system offers tremendous opportunities for database manipulation and direct-mail targeting. For example, a company might choose to send out free catalogs only to those accounts whose point totals exceed a certain amount. In addition to R-F-M information, house lists often categorize customers by geographic, demographic, or psychographic characteristics.

Maintaining a database of current customers is advantageous for several reasons.[25] It provides a company with an opportunity to practice *relationship marketing*—that is, working toward building long-term relations with existing customers rather than focusing solely on cultivating new customers. It enables a firm to build *customer loyalty and encourage repeat purchasing* by directing promotions to known customers of its products or services. (Airline frequent-flyer programs typify this application.) An additional advantage of maintaining cus-

23. Robert J. Samuelson, "Computer Communities," *Newsweek*, December 15, 1986, p. 66.
24. Bob Stone, *Successful Direct Marketing Methods* (Lincolnwood, IL: NTC Business Books, 1988), p. 164
25. Rapp and Collins, *MaxiMarketing*, p. 216ff.

tomer lists is the *possibility for cross promotions.* Cross promotions encourage customers of one product to purchase other products marketed by the same company.

External Lists.   There are two types of **external lists.** The first type—**house lists of other companies**—is bought by a firm to promote its own products. These lists are effective because they comprise the names of people who have responded to another company's direct-response offer. The greater the similarity of the products offered by both the buyer and the seller of the list, the greater the likelihood that the purchased list will be effective.

For example, imagine a company that markets coverings that protect automobile exteriors from exposure to the elements. New automobile purchasers who do not have a garage are the best market for this company's products. The coverings marketer could purchase mailing lists from automobile manufacturers and specify names of only those buyers who have purchased an automobile within the last, say, six months *and* who rent an apartment rather than own their own home.

Compiled lists, the second type of external list, include lists compiled by a company for its own purposes or lists purchased from another company that specializes in list compilation. The first type of compiled list is illustrated by a direct-marketing effort at Kimberly-Clark, makers of Huggies disposable diapers. Each year, Kimberly-Clark's database identifies by name 75 percent of the 3.5 million new mothers in the United States. (The names are obtained from hospitals and doctors.) Kimberly-Clark sends the new mothers personalized letters, educational literature about caring for a new baby, and cents-off coupons for Huggies. The program has been extremely effective.[26]

The other type of compiled list comes from businesses that specialize in compiling lists and selling them to other companies. List compilers are typically involved in businesses that give them access to millions of consumer names and vital statistics. For example, *The Lifestyle Selector,* a service of National Demographics and Lifestyles Inc., is a data-list service provided by a company that originally handled processing of warranty cards for dozens of manufacturers. For each of the millions of names on file, the database contains 10 demographic characteristics (e.g., age, sex, education) and 50 lifestyle characteristics (sports participation, travel activities, etc.).

The Lifestyle Selector enables a direct-mail marketer to order a list containing names and addresses that have been identified based on any combination of lifestyle and demographic characteristics. A manufacturer of men's sporting goods, for example, would be able to request a list matching its desired target market. A possible description of the target market could be the following: males between the ages of 25 and 44 who play golf and enjoy fashion clothing, who are business executives, professionals, or technicians earning $40,000 or more annually, and who possess an American Express credit card.

26. Ibid.

Donnelly's Share Force program compiles names by including a questionnaire in its coupon mailings (under the name "Carol Wright") that go out twice a year to 45 million households. Recipients are households with above-average incomes and greater-than-average numbers of children. Identified as the Carol Wright Super Saver Gift, the mailing offers free gifts, coupons, and product samples to consumers who answer approximately 50 questions related to usage in select product categories and brand preferences. The information is then used to target users of competing brands with coupons and/or samples.[27]

Compiled lists play an important role for marketers of packaged-good products, because these companies are obviously much less able than business-to-business marketers to maintain customer lists. Compiled lists are not as desirable as house lists, however, because they do not contain information about the willingness of a person to purchase by mail. The characteristics of the members of compiled lists may also be too diversified to serve the purposes of the direct mailer. However, some compiled lists are put together with considerable care and may serve the direct mailer's specific needs.

Effective Direct-Mail Advertising Copy.   Effective copy is the other critical element in direct-mail advertising. As with all forms of advertising, it is essential that direct mailers pattern their communications to match the backgrounds and interests of target customers. Certain generalizations apply, however, regardless of the audience. These include striving for clarity, insisting on brevity, being courteous and polite, and writing believable copy.[28] The following principles underlie successful direct-mail advertising.[29]

1. *Get attention.* This is usually done by stating (in a few words) a believable promise or by showing a picture of the reward that the advertised product offers. For example, the ad for the RADARMASTER™ (refer back to Figure 15.2) states in its headline "$295 Value. Now, Yours for Only $159. Faster Warnings . . . Greater Reliability . . ."

2. *Hold attention.* Subheads, subillustrations, or the first paragraph are used to hold the consumer's attention. The RADARMASTER™ advertisement accomplishes this by stating: "Now, own RADARMASTER™ the world's most advanced Radar Detector and save a whopping $136."

3. *Create desire.* Benefits stated in the copy should create desire. RADARMASTER™ claims it is "designed with 'breakthrough' receiving circuitry," and is "built with a computer brain."

---

27. This description is based on "Donnelley Seems To Be Asking All the Right Questions," *Advertising Age*, May 16, 1988, p. S-5.
28. Bodo Von Der Wense, "Planning, List Selection, Copy, Layout, Timing, Testing Can Make or Break Direct Mail Pieces," *Marketing News*, November 14, 1980, p. 7.
29. These principles are those of John Caples, who has been characterized as representing to direct-response advertising what Abner Doubleday was to baseball. Bob Stone, "Long Narrative Copy: A Marketer's Views," *Advertising Age*, August 25, 1980, p. 48. (By the way, Abner Doubleday invented baseball.)

4. *Make it believable.* Facts, figures, testimonials, and guarantees are just some of the methods used to establish believability. The ad for the RA-DARMASTER™ attempts to establish believability by stating that it is made by B.E.L-Tronics, "one of the world's most highly regarded and experienced manufacturers of radar detectors."

5. *Prove it's a bargain.* Price reductions and advertising copy that build up the value of the selling proposition serve to prove that the offer is a bargain. The RADARMASTER™ ad says: "Now Yours for Only $159."

6. *Make it easy to buy.* This is done by telling potential customers how to order and by making it easy for them to order. RADARMASTER™ has a toll-free number for placing orders and allows credit-card purchasing.

7. *Give a reason to buy now.* Rewards for promptness and special offers are used to promote quick ordering. RADARMASTER™ offers as a free bonus the Driver Safety Companion™, a "life-saving alarm" valued at $39.50, but "for a limited time only."

Catalog Marketing

Though a form of direct mail, catalog marketing deserves a separate section due to its distinctiveness and tremendous growth in recent years.[30] For clarity, it should be noted that there are actually four types of catalogs: (1) *retail catalogs* designed by retailers to increase store traffic; (2) *full-line merchandise catalogs* (e.g., Sears, J. C. Penney); (3) *consumer specialty catalogs* (e.g., the L. L. Bean sporting goods and ready-to-wear catalog); and (4) *industrial specialty catalogs,* which are used by business-to-business marketers to reach smaller customers while freeing up the sales force's time to devote to larger, more promising accounts.

The greatest growth in cataloging is consumer specialty catalogs. Name the product, and at least one company is probably marketing that item via catalog—food items (cheese, candy, pastry, steaks), clothing, furniture. . . the list goes on and on.

Catalog sales in the United States exceeded $38 billion in 1988, an increase of nearly 15 percent over 1987 and well above the 3 percent growth rate for retailers.[31] Various factors account for this tremendous growth. From the *marketer's perspective,* catalog selling provides an efficient and effective way to reach prime prospects. From the *consumer's perspective* (1) catalogs save time because people do not have to find parking spaces and deal with in-store crowds; (2) catalog buying appeals to consumers who are fearful of shopping due to rising crime rates; (3) catalogs allow people the convenience of making purchase decisions at their leisure and away from the pressure of a retail store; (4) the availability of toll-free 800 numbers and credit-card purchasing has

30. The growth in catalog marketing is typified by the number of catalogs distributed. The average American household is estimated to receive 50 catalogs per year!

31. Ed Fitch, "Election Year Frenzy Bane of Catalogers," *Advertising Age,* August 1, 1988, p. S-2.

FOCUS ON PROMOTION

Catalog Marketing in the Maturity Stage

You learned in a principles of marketing course that all products and services go through a life cycle—from introduction, to growth, maturity, and eventually decline. The same can be said for catalog marketing. The early through mid–1980s represented a period of rapid growth for catalog marketing, a period characterized by tremendous increases in sales and profits. Now catalog marketing has arrived at the maturity stage in its life cycle. A variety of factors point to this fact.

First, according to industry observers, consumers are spending less time looking at catalogs because they are overwhelmed with the large numbers of catalogs they receive (an estimated 12 billion catalogs were received by consumers in 1988, up from fewer than five billion in 1980). The novelty of catalog scanning apparently has worn off for many consumers.

Continued

made it easy for people to order from catalogs; and (5) people are confident in purchasing from catalogs because merchandise quality is often excellent, prices are fair, and guarantees are incomparable.[32]

As examples of this last point, consider the policies of two very successful catalog marketers, Lands' End and L. L. Bean. Lands' End's "Fair Pricing Policy" states:

> We price our products fairly and honestly. We do not, have not, and will not participate in the common retailing practice of inflating markups to set up a future phony "sale."

L. L. Bean's guarantee claims:

> All of our products are guaranteed to give 100% satisfaction in every way. Return anything purchased from us at any time if it proves otherwise. We will replace it, refund your purchase price or credit your credit card, as you wish. We do not want you to have anything from L. L. Bean that is not completely satisfactory.

Although catalog marketing is pervasive, signs are appearing that it now is in the maturity stage of its life cycle. The *Focus on Promotion* section elaborates on this point.

Videologs. A recent development in catalog marketing is the distribution of catalogs via videocassettes—*videologs*. Over 50 million American households have VCRs. A California company, Home Video Marketplace (HVM), developed a 38-minute videolog that showed 29 products priced from $25 to $6,500. HVM placed its videolog in 3,000 video-rental stores. The rental

---

N 32. Bob Stone, "Factors in the Growth of Catalog Sales," *Advertising Age*, March 26, 1979, p. 61.

Second, as is typically the case when a product or service reaches the maturity stage, the costs of catalog marketing have increased dramatically. A primary reason is that firms have incurred the expenses of developing more attractive catalogs and compiling better mailing lists in the effort to out perform their competitors. Costs have been further strained by third-class postal rate increases of 25 percent in recent years and sharp increases in paper prices.

Some catalog companies have responded to the slow down by sending out even more catalogs than they mailed in the past. Other companies are scaling back their efforts. Many marginal companies are beginning to drop out, which invariably is the case when an industry arrives at the maturity stage of its life cycle.

In sum, the best days in catalog marketing are history for most catalog companies. Some companies will continue to flourish, but many others will find it unprofitable to remain in the catalog business.[33] ∎

is free, but viewers are asked to return the videolog the following day. Sears distributed 10,000 videos to customers who bought both toys and VCRs. Sears was pleased with the response to the videolog, which promoted high-tech toys. Murjani International tested a videolog to promote its Coca-Cola clothing line for direct orders, but was disappointed with the results due to the high cost per order.[34]

It is too early to tell how successful videologs might become in consumer-goods direct marketing. Cost is a potential problem. Also, it is unknown at this writing whether consumers will enjoy viewing products from start to finish on a videotape as compared to the freedom that comes with paging back and forth through a catalog.

Other Media for Direct Marketing

Direct marketing is not limited to mail and catalog vehicles. Magazines, newspapers, and television, though minor vehicles of direct marketing in comparison with direct mail, provide direct marketers with alternative means to achieve specific objectives.

Magazines are useful to direct marketers because this medium offers a tremendous diversity of vehicles that appeal to specialized consumer groups. Ef-

---

33. Adapted from Francine Schwadel, "Catalog Overload Turns Off Consumers," *The Wall Street Journal*, October 28, 1988, p. B-1.
34. Information on videologs is from Anita M. Busch, "Emerging Technologies on Horizon," *Advertising Age*, January 18, 1988, p. S-1; and Janice Steinberg, '"Retailers Page through Videolog Possibilities," *Advertising Age*, January 18, 1988, pp. S-13–S-15.

fective direct marketing demands an ability to pinpoint audiences. Magazines, in addition to providing selectivity, also offer good color reproduction, relatively low cost, and the capability of testing different creative approaches by running one ad version in one magazine edition and a different version in another.

Newspapers, another useful direct-marketing medium, offer the advantages of geographic selectivity, a variety of formats and reproduction methods, and the ability to position an ad in a section (financial, fashion, sports, etc.) that matches the interests of the designated market segment. Direct-response advertising is often placed in special locations including syndicated newspaper supplements, mail-order shopping sections, inserts or preprints, and comic sections.

Television represents a relatively minor medium for direct-response advertising and accounts for a little over 1 percent of total direct-advertising expenditures. However, developments in cable television and two-way interactive systems portend considerable growth for direct marketing on television.[35] One noteworthy trend is *home-shopping shows*. Home-shopping services such as Home Shopping Network, Cable Value Network, Quality Value Network, and America's Value Network sell jewelry, electronics, toys, clothing, and other merchandise. Home-shopping revenues were estimated to be approximately $2.5 billion in 1988.[36]

Summary

The tremendous growth in direct marketing promises to continue. Analysts expect nonstore sources to obtain as much as one-third of retail sales in the United States by 1990; retailers are being warned to prepare for the challenge.[37] Conventional marketers realize direct marketing's potential. Many companies have responded to the rapid growth in direct marketing by establishing their own direct-marketing departments.[38]

Telemarketing

Telephone marketing, (or **telemarketing**) is *the* dominant form of direct marketing. It is estimated to account for 46 percent of all direct-marketing purchases.[39] What exactly is telemarketing?

35. Mary McCabe English, "Videotech Brightens Marketers' Screens," *Advertising Age*, January 19, 1981, pp. S-14–S-17.
36. Joanne Cleaver, "Consumers At Home With Shopping," *Advertising Age*, January 18, 1988, p. S-16.
37. Mike Slosberg, "Direct Marketing and Retailing in the 80's," *Direct Marketing*, October 1980, pp. 100–110.
38. Cecilia Lautini, "A Basic Part of the Plan," *Advertising Age*, July 19, 1981, pp. S-1, S-39.
39. Ernan Roman, "The Newest Member of the Marketing Mix," *Marketing Communications*, June 1987, p. 72.

Telemarketing is a low cost, highly efficient method of conducting business. Applied properly, telemarketing can increase sales, open new accounts, qualify advertising leads, establish new markets and efficiently service existing business, i.e., reorders and customer service. Telemarketing can be used in conjunction with advertising, direct mail, catalogue sales, face-to-face selling, plus other communication modes. When used properly, telemarketing enables a business or individual to target market his message, at low cost, to customers and prospects. It enables a salesman to carry on a two-way conversation, thus allowing him to answer any questions, and eventually close a sale without leaving his office.[40]

As the preceding description indicates, telemarketing can accomplish a variety of tasks. Telemarketing's versatility applies to both consumer-oriented products and business-to-business marketing.

Two forms of telemarketing are practiced extensively. One involves *outbound calls* from telephone salespersons to customers and prospects; the other involves handling *inbound orders, inquiries, or complaints.* The distinction between outbound and inbound telemarketing is somewhat analogous to the personal-selling distinction between order getting and order taking. Outbound telemarketers solicit orders and service accounts. Inbound telemarketers take orders that have been generated by other media. However, a later discussion will point out that inbound telemarketing is not limited to order taking.

Outbound Telemarketing

Consider these facts: The average personal sales contact costs more than $250; a telephone sales call, by comparison, costs between $7 and $15.[41] For this reason, many companies are using the telephone to support or even replace their conventional sales forces.

A survey of over 500 industrial salespeople found that 88 percent use a combination of telephone and in-person selling; 6 percent use in-person selling exclusively; and 6 percent rely entirely on the telephone. The survey revealed further that telephone applications include generating or qualifying leads, arranging face-to-face sales calls, upgrading orders or cross-selling (i.e., encouraging a customer who has purchased one product to buy another item), prospecting for new accounts, reactivating old accounts, and full account management.[42]

IBM, for example, uses telemarketing to cover its small- to medium-size accounts, generate incremental sales, enhance the productivity of traditional sales representatives via the leads and information that it provides, and ensure customer satisfaction and buying convenience. IBM has a fully integrated system of mail, catalog, and inbound and outbound telephone activity for its

40. This description is contained in the undated promotional literature of *Telemarketing* magazine, which charaterizes itself as "the magazine of electronic marketing and communication." *Telemarketing* is a publication of the Technology Marketing Corporation, Norwalk, CT.
41. Roman, "The Newest Member of the Marketing Mix."
42. Hubert D. Hennessey, "Matters to Consider Before Plunging into Telemarketing," *Marketing News*, July 8, 1983, p. 2.

hardware, software, supplies, and services. The strategy is to transform a prospect or a dormant account into an active account, then to service the account with as little in-person sales contact as possible. Junior and senior college students are used as telephone salespersons. They work a maximum of 20 hours a week and are paid on an hourly basis supplemented with incentive rewards.[43]

Who Should Use Outbound Telemarketing?

Telemarketing is not appropriate for all sales organizations. The following eight factors should be considered when evaluating the suitability of introducing a telephone sales force.[44]

1. An initial consideration is an evaluation of *how essential face-to-face contact is*; the more essential it is, the less appropriate is telemarketing.

2. A second consideration is *geographical concentration*. Telephone selling may represent an attractive alternative to in-person selling if customers are highly dispersed; if however, customers are heavily concentrated (e.g., apparel makers in Manhattan, automobile manufacturers in Detroit), minimal travel time is required and personal selling is probably preferable.

3. *Economic considerations* involving average order size and total potential should be estimated to determine whether in-person sales is cost-effective. In cases of small and marginal accounts, customers may be served more economically by telephone.

4. A fourth area for evaluation is *customer decision criteria*. Telephone sales may be sufficient if price, delivery, and other quantitative criteria are paramount, but in-person sales may be essential in instances where product quality, dealer reputation, and service are uppermost in importance.

5. A fifth factor is *the number of decision makers typically involved* in purchasing a company's product. Face-to-face contact is typically necessary when several decision makers are involved—for example, when an industrial engineer, a purchasing agent, and financial representative all have input into a purchase decision.

6. Another consideration is the *nature of the purchase*. Routine purchases (e.g., office supplies) can be handled easily by phone.

7. The *status of the major decision maker* is a seventh consideration. The telephone is acceptable for buyers, purchase agents, and engineers, but probably not for owners, presidents, and vice-presidents.

43. This description is an adaptation of remarks from Peter DiSalvo in "3 Telemarketers Tell How to Hire, Train, Organize for This Profitable Direct Medium," *Marketing News*, July 8, 1983, p. 4.
44. Hennessey, "Matters to Consider."

8.   A final consideration is *an evaluation of the specific selling tasks* that telephone sales is or is not capable of performing. For example, telephone
representatives may be particularly effective for prospecting and postsale
follow-ups, whereas in-person sales effort is needed for the intervening
sales task—preapproach, approach, presentation, objection handling,
and closing.

These eight factors make it apparent that telephone selling is appropriate
and effective in certain situations but not others. Systematic application of this
eight-step process should enable a company to determine whether and to what
extent telemarketing is appropriate for serving its customers.

Inbound Telemarketing

There are two general forms of inbound telemarketing. One involves the nearly
ubiquitous toll-free, or 800, number. The other is the Dial-It, or 900, number
service, which is not a free call for the user.

Toll-Free (800 Number) Telemarketing.   800 numbers are virtually everywhere. Every time you open a magazine, turn on the television, or pick up
a newspaper, you hear, "Call 1-800-XXX-XXXX." For example, General Electric
urges readers to call its toll-free number for product information and the name
of the nearest dealer. Bryant, a company that sells gas furnaces, encourages
consumers to call 1-800-HOT-SALE for the name of the nearest Bryant dealer.
Trident asks consumers to call its 800 number to receive information on how
chewing gum reduces the threat of tooth decay.

An 800-number telecommunication program uses an incoming WATS
(wide area telecommunication service) telephone system to encourage potential
customers to phone a publicized number (an 800 number) in response to media
advertising or other marketing communications. This 800 number, correctly
inserted in advertisements, can be used by motivated, self-qualified consumers
to request product or service information, place direct orders, express complaints or grievances, request coupons or other sales-promotion materials, and
inquire about the nearest dealers or outlets.

Customer-service representatives who receive 800 calls can provide immediate responses to requests for merchandise and product information and
can handle complaints. Additionally, representatives can record callers' names
and addresses to initiate immediate follow-ups by sending promotional materials. Also, the effectiveness of an advertising campaign can be measured
quickly.

Toll-free numbers are widely used and will be used increasingly because
they are valuable adjuncts to marketing communications programs. Although
there are distinct benefits with 800 numbers, there also are potential problems.
One problem is that 800 service communicators are sometimes improperly

trained or unskilled. A second potential problem is that there may be an insufficient number of lines to handle incoming calls. Third, failure to integrate the 800 number carefully into a company's marketing program can be extremely wasteful. Advertising, sales promotions, and 800 numbers need to be coordinated carefully to achieve their maximum, synergistic effects.

Dial-It (900 Number) Telemarketing.   The Dial-It, or 900 number, service was introduced by AT&T to permit callers, who pay a fee, to phone a central number and register an opinion on a particular issue. The 900 service is the only national communication medium that can accept simultaneous calls by large numbers of people at a flat rate (50¢ for the first minute and 35¢ for each additional minute) from anywhere in the United States.[45] The first major use of the Dial-It service was during the Carter-Reagan debate on October 28, 1980, when over 700,000 people spent 50 cents each to call a 900 number and register their opinions about who won the debate.[46]

The 900-number technology offers various marketing-communications possibilities. One possible use would be to update customers about services that are subject to frequent changes. For example, the American Bankers Association sponsors a 900-number service to inform callers of the most recent interest rates on various financial instruments.[47]

Dial-It numbers can also be used by advertisers to test the effectiveness of their media buys. The calls (paid for by the advertiser) generated by an ad tagged with a 900 number can be delineated by geographical area to determine where the ad had its greatest impact. By cutting in and talking live with callers, advertisers can acquire additional useful information, such as demographic data, product-usage characteristics, and advertising-recall measures for recent television commercials.[48]

A 900 number can also be used during corporate emergencies. Johnson & Johnson immediately instituted a Dial-It service when its product, Extra-Strength Tylenol, was linked to seven deaths in the Chicago area. J & J developed a recorded message that informed callers about the problem and encouraged them to call a toll-free (800) number if they had further questions.[49]

Quaker Oats Company targeted parents of preschool-age children to call a 900 number placed on advertising inserts for instant oatmeal. Nearly 300,000 parents and children called to hear a message from the talking teddy bear, Teddy Ruxpin.[50]

Although the use of 900 numbers is in its infancy, this technology is another potentially valuable tool for marketing communicators. The whole field

45. Richard Edel, "900 Numbers Add Up for Telemarketers," *Advertising Age*, January 18, 1988, p. S-7.
46. Theodore J. Gage, "900 Is Batting 1,000," *Advertising Age*, January 19, 1981, pp. S-33, 34.
47. Bernie Whalen, "Marketers Expand Applications of Dial-It 900 Technology," *Marketing News*, November 26, 1982, p. 23.
48. Ibid.
49. Ibid.
50. Edel, "900 Numbers Add Up for Telemarketers."

of telemarketing is developing rapidly, and many exciting and effective applications are available to companies willing to diverge from conventional business conduct.

Telemarketing under Attack

The dramatic increase in the use of telemarketing has inevitably included some untoward practices. Consumers are besieged by calls from telemarketers at undesirable times, particularly during the dinner hour. More extreme are telemarketing scams that deceive credulous individuals into thinking they are dealing with legitimate businesspeople. Vitamin-pill ripoffs, travel scams, fake AIDS cures, and phony art reproductions are just some of the fraudulent telemarketing practices used in recent years.[51]

In response to consumer complaints, two companion bills titled "The Telemarketing Fraud Prevention Act of 1988" are working their way through the House and Senate at the time of this writing. The act specifies that products must be delivered within 30 days and that consumers must be notified of a cooling-off period; it also warns against harassment of consumers by telemarketers. In addition, this act would authorize the Federal Trade Commission to serve as a clearinghouse for information on telemarketing operations.[52]

Summary

Direct marketing is the most rapidly growing aspect of marketing activity in the United States. Direct mail is the dominant direct-marketing advertising medium. The outstanding advantages of this medium are that marketers can target messages to specific market segments and determine success (or failure) virtually immediately. Direct mail also permits greater personalization than does mass media advertising and is not subject to the "clutter" of competing ads such as those that appear in other print and broadcast media. On a cost-per-order basis, direct mail is often less expensive and more efficient than alternative media.

Magazines, newspapers, and television are additional media used by direct marketers. Catalog marketing is a form of direct marketing that has enjoyed spectacular success but is now abating. Factors that account for this growth include consumer time savings, buying freedom, greater disposable income, and increased confidence in mail-order buying. Video catalogs—videologs—represent an emerging technology with considerable potential.

Telemarketing is a special form of direct marketing in which the telephone is the major direct-marketing medium. Two forms of telemarketing are practiced. One involves outbound calls from telephone salespersons to custom-

51. "Dial M for Marketing Fraud," *Newsweek*, May 16, 1988, p. 56.
52. "Telemarketing Scams Come Under Fire," *The 4A's Washington Newsletter*, June 1988, p. 6.

ers and prospects; the other involves handling inbound calls for orders, inquiries, and complaints. The growth of outbound telemarketing is attributable in large part to the enormous expense of in-person sales contacts, which exceed $250 on average. A telephone call, by comparison, costs between $7 and $15. Telemarketing can be used to support or even replace a conventional sales force.

Inbound telemarketing includes the well-known toll-free, or 800 number, programs and the lesser known Dial-It, or 900 number, service. Toll-free programs have experienced tremendous growth, with the market growing at an annual rate of 25 percent. Dial-It (900 number) telemarketing was introduced initially by AT&T to permit callers to pay a fee for a phone call to register an opinion on a particular issue. Beyond this, Dial-It service offers marketing communicators additional possibilities, such as encouraging customers to call a designated 900 number and request product information.

Discussion Questions

1. Explain the differences among direct marketing, direct sales, direct-response advertising, and direct mail.

2. Why has direct marketing enjoyed such rapid growth in recent years?

3. Direct selling plays a much bigger role in Japan than elsewhere in the world. Salespeople go door-to-door and office-to-office to make sales. What is it about Japanese society compared to U.S. society that explains the greater importance of direct selling in Japan?

4. As noted in the chapter, direct marketing constitutes around 75 percent of the automobile sales in Japan. Could direct selling be used in the United States for selling automobiles? Justify your response.

5. Your company, Computer Supplies Inc., sells computer supplies (paper, ribbons, diskettes, etc.) to thousands of business and nonbusiness organizations. Because most orders are relatively small, selling costs are extremely high relative to revenues. The vice-president of sales is evaluating the implementation of a telemarketing program directed at all accounts whose annual purchases are less than $10,000. What factors should the V.P. consider? Be specific.

6. Figure 15.2 in the text was an ad for the RADARMASTER™. Assume the manufacturer of this product chose to use direct mail to market the RADARMASTER™ in addition to advertising it in magazines. Explain how you, as vice-president of marketing for this company, would acquire a mailing list. What demographic and lifestyle factors would you select in generating the list?

7. Jewelry, clothing, electronics, toys, and exercise equipment are some of the products frequently featured on televised home-shopping programs. Why are these particular products suitable for this form of direct marketing? Profile the "typical" consumer who buys products via home-shopping programs.

8. John Deere, a major company in the lawn-tractor business, includes an 800 number at the bottom of its advertisement. A relatively unknown competitor, Kubota, includes this statement at the bottom of its ads: "To learn more about our tractors

and other power products, please write Kubota Tractor Corporation [address followed]." How responsive do you think consumers would be in writing for more information? How could a company like Kubota justify not installing an 800-number service?

9.　Compare and contrast 800- and 900-number telemarketing programs.

Exercises

1.　Gather two illustrations of direct-mail advertisements and critique each using the seven direct-mail-advertising principles discussed in the chapter.

2.　Clip two or three direct-response advertisements from magazines and apply the seven principles to these ads.

3.　Assume you are a direct marketer of a line of merchandise imprinted with major-university logos. These items are targeted to the fans and supporters of the universities' athletic programs. Detail how you would compile a mailing list. Use your college/university for illustration.

4.　Conduct interviews with five to ten consumers and investigate their attitudes toward catalog usage. Why, specifically, do these people use (or not use) catalogs? What products are they most likely to purchase by catalog? How satisfied have they been with their past catalog purchases?

5.　Along the same lines, conduct five to ten interviews with nonstudent adults regarding their attitudes toward telemarketing. Are they hassled often? Do they mind having telephone salespeople call them? What specific complaints do they have?

6.　Go through a recent magazine and list every advertiser that employs a toll-free 800 number. Describe the specific function that the 800 number is apparently intended to serve for each advertiser.

Point-of-Purchase Communications

BUYING A COLLEGE CLASS RING

Y ou have probably considered buying a college class ring. You have probably wondered how much they cost and what styles are available. You have probably seen them displayed in your local bookstore. You probably have not bought one yet.

Balfour, a company that markets high school and college class rings, realizes how difficult it is to buy a class ring. Selling class rings is no easy task either. For many years Balfour sent sales representatives to campuses for several days, hoping that the reps would meet prospective customers and take as many orders as possible.

This selling system worked, but its hit-or-miss nature left considerable room for improvement. When the Balfour rep was on campus, the student may not have been in a buying mood. Or when the student was in a buying mood, the rep may not have been there. There had to be a better way.

Balfour has indeed devised a better way, called the "Balfour Collegiate Express." The Collegiate Express, located in college bookstores, is a video merchandising center that performs both informational and transactional functions. It combines still and motion photography, computer graphics, stereo sound, and an interactive touchscreen to make it possible for students to obtain information and transact orders. A student interested in purchasing a class ring can obtain information about styles, sizes, and prices by simply touching the computer screen in response to computer prompts. Orders are placed directly through the Collegiate Express system by entering one's name and address on an attached keyboard.

The Balfour Collegiate Express supplements Balfour's personal selling effort rather than replacing it. These video merchandising centers were initially installed at Penn State, Marquette, Oregon State, Florida State, University of Mississippi, University of Texas, University of Denver, University of Virginia, University of South Carolina, and Louisiana State University. Maybe the Collegiate Express is available in your bookstore—a nice thing to know the next time *you're* in the mood to buy![1]■

Overview of P-O-P Communications

The Balfour Collegiate Express epitomizes the modern, sophisticated use of point-of-purchase communications and merchandising. In general, the **point of purchase (P-O-P)** in a retail store represents the time at which the consumer makes product and brand choices. The point of purchase is a time when the marketer can have a major influence on the choices made; it is the time and place at which all elements of the sale (consumer, money, and product) come together.[2]

Marketers attempt to influence consumers' buying decisions at the point of purchase by using various communication vehicles—displays, packaging graphics, sales promotions (samples, price-off deals, etc.), salespeople, and so on. This chapter focuses exclusively on displays and other point-of-purchase materials.

Spectrum of P-O-P Materials

Marketers use a variety of items in point-of-purchase communications. These include various types of signs, mobiles, plaques, banners, shelf tapes, mechanical mannequins, lighted units, mirror units, plastic reproductions of products, checkout units, full-line merchandisers, wall posters, and numerous other materials.

Many of these materials are temporary items, with useful life spans of only weeks or months. Others are permanent fixtures that can be used for many months or years. Whereas temporary displays are particularly effective for promoting impulse purchasing, permanent P-O-P units compartmentalize

---

1. This description is an adaptation of Mark Paul, "The Electronic Salesman," *Marketing Communications*, December 1986, pp. 27–32.
2. John A. Quelch and Kristina Cannon-Bonventre, "Better Marketing at the Point-of-Purchase," *Harvard Business Review*, November-December 1983, pp. 162–169.

and departmentalize a store area to achieve high product visibility, facilitate customer self-service, prevent stock-outs, and help control inventory.[3]

An award-winning *temporary display* for Coca-Cola is shown in Figure 16.1. This floor stand, shaped like a Christmas tree, is perfectly suited to the Christmas season. It attracts consumer attention and stimulates purchases of the two-liter bottles especially popular at this time of year. It also satisfies the retailer's needs by permitting a large quantity of product to be merchandised in a relatively small selling space.

The display for Clarion cosmetics shown in Figure 16.2 illustrates an exceptionally effective *permanent display*. This in-store merchandising unit includes the Clarion Personalized Color Computer, which queries women on their coloring and skin types. Women enter their responses on a membrane key pad (as shown in the figure). The liquid crystal display (LCD) then presents recommended shades and formulas. Products specified on the LCD are available at the display. This display is appealing and useful to consumers, effective for retailers, and extremely successful for Noxell Corporation, the makers of Clarion.

How to Fight Your Way into a Paper Bag[4]

In a phrase, this is what point-of-purchase communication is ultimately designed to do—to enable marketers (manufacturers and retailers) to fight the competition in getting their products into the customers shopping bag.

In general, P-O-P performs four important marketing functions. *Informing* consumers is P-O-P's most basic communications function. Signs, posters, displays, and other P-O-P materials alert consumers to specific items and provide information. A second communications function is *reminding* consumers of brands they previously have been informed about via broadcast, print, or other advertising media. This reminder role serves to complement the job already performed by advertising prior to the consumer's entering a store. *Persuading* consumers to buy a specific item or brand is P-O-P's third communications function. Encourage may be a more appropriate term than persuade, since the latter suggests greater influence than P-O-P items generally have; regardless of the term, it is undeniable that effective P-O-P materials influence product and brand choices at the point of purchase. The actual presentation of the product itself to facilitate customer inspection and to enable retailers to utilize floor space effectively is the *merchandising* function of point of purchase.

---

3. "Merchandising Power: Maximizing Consumer Potential at Retail," *Marketing Communications*, January 1983, p. 12P.
4. This catchy title served as the theme line for the Point-of-Purchase Advertising Institute's (POPAI) 1988 trade show called Marketplace '88.

FIGURE 16.1   **Illustration of a Temporary P-O-P Display**

Source: Courtesy Point-of-Purchase Advertising Institute.

Illustration of a Permanent P-O-P Display　　　　　　　　　FIGURE 16.2

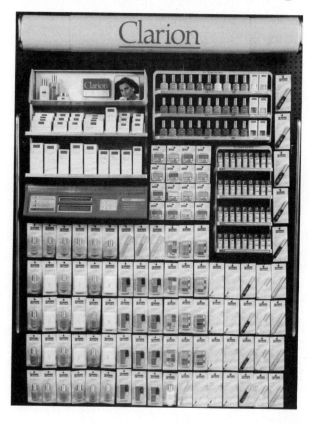

Successful Applications of P-O-P

It will be useful to examine a few success stories to illustrate the kind of impact point-of-purchase materials can have when used effectively.

The ALIGN Singles Server II. The Seven-Up Company decided to develop a modular device in an effort to facilitate the stocking and displaying of single soft-drink cans in convenience stores. Research indicated that 60 percent of soft drinks sold in convenience outlets are single-can sales; as a consequence, six packs are broken, coolers are disorganized, and sales are reduced. The research further indicated that convenience-store executives desire a total soft-drink system that will help them achieve better cooler management. The ALIGN Singles Server II (shown in Figure 16.3) was the solution.

Seven-Up's objectives in developing the ALIGN system were to increase consumers' purchase convenience and to improve retailers' inventory control and eliminate dead space on soft-drink shelves. As shown, the ALIGN system provides retailers with individual injection-molded dispensers. Each row holds eight cans, or 24 cans per dispenser, and up to five full 24-can cases when five dispensers are snap-locked together. The system is intended not only to stock

FIGURE 16.3   Seven-Up's ALIGN Singles Server II System

Source: POPAI News, Vol. 6, No. 2, 1982, p. 3. Reprinted with permission.

Seven-Up but to provide space for various other brands, with allocations ideally proportional to each brand's past sales performance in local markets.

Market-test results clearly demonstrated the system's effectiveness. Consumer purchases in Singles Server II stores outperformed control stores by an average of 23.5 percent, and gross profits in the Singles stores exceeded the control stores' profits by an average of nearly 22.7 percent.[5]

Clairol's Haircoloring Information Center. Clairol developed its information center for women who are uninformed about hair-coloring products or who have been dissatisfied with these products. Clairol designed the information center to answer women's major questions concerning hair-coloring products. This information appears on large, colorful header signs above the actual products on gondola shelves. The information center also makes product selection easy: Color-coded labels identify product subcategories, and shelf dividers separate the various products. Moreover, the center invites customers to call Clairol's hair-coloring consultants on a toll-free 800 number for additional assistance.

Clairol sales increased an average of 32 percent in retail outlets that installed the information center, and shelf space devoted to Clairol products averaged 15 percent more linear feet in those retail accounts. Furthermore, the 800 telephone number received more than 400,000 calls in the first year of operation from consumers seeking additional information about hair coloring and Clairol products.[6]

The Thomas Flexible Paint Accessories System. Paint brushes and other painting accessories are often poorly displayed and merchandised in a confusing cluttered fashion. The Thomas Paint Accessories System was created to remove clutter and confusion, promote a positive brand image, and reduce out-of-stock problems. The eight-foot-wide unit separates different product areas to display a full line of painting accessories. Retailers can adjust the shelves and partitions to meet their own specific merchandising needs. The Thomas display system boosted sales by an impressive 30 percent.[7]

Role of Motion in P-O-P Displays

Point-of-purchase displays come in two general forms: static displays and motion displays. Motion displays, though typically more expensive, represent a sound business investment because they attract significantly higher levels of

5. Adapted from "Marketing Textbook: Seven-Up Company's ALIGN Singles Server II," *POPAI News*, vol. 6, no. 2 (1982), p. 3.
6. Adapted from "Marketing Textbook: Clairol's Haircoloring Information Center," *POPAI News*, vol. 7, no.1 (1983), p. 3.
7. Adapted from "Case Histories: Analyzing What Makes this Display Work," *POPAI News*, vol. 8, no. 3 (1984), p. 6.

shopper attention and therefore move more merchandise. Research evidence from three studies shows that motion displays are often worth the extra expense.[8]

Olympia Beer. Researchers tested the relative effectiveness of motion and static displays for Olympia beer by placing the two types of displays in a test sample of liquor stores and supermarkets in California. Each of the sampled stores was stocked either with static or motion displays. Another sample of stores, serving as the control group, received no displays. Over 62,000 purchases of Olympia beer were recorded during the four-week test period.

Static displays in liquor stores increased Olympia sales by 56 percent over stores with no displays (the control group). In supermarkets, static displays improved Olympia sales by a considerably smaller, though nonetheless substantial, amount (18 percent). More dramatic, however, was the finding that motion displays increased Olympia sales by 107 percent in liquor stores and by 49 percent in supermarkets.

S. B. Thomas English Muffins. Two groups of 40 stores each were matched by store volume and customer demographics. One group was equipped with an S. B. Thomas English muffin post sign that moved from side to side. The other 40 stores used regular floor displays with no motion. Follow-up interviews indicated that motion displays aided shoppers in recalling what they had seen and heard in an accompanying media advertising campaign. Records of product movement revealed that sales in the stores stocked with motion displays increased by 473 percent! Part of this increase was due to the concurrent advertising effort; yet the sales increase in stores using static displays was only 370 percent, a full 103 percent below that of the sales generated by motion displays.

Eveready Batteries. A study of motion displays for Eveready batteries was conducted in Atlanta and San Diego. In each city, six drugstores, six supermarkets, and six mass merchandisers were studied. The stores were divided into two groups, as in the English muffin study. Some newspaper advertising appeared during the test period, but special pricing was the primary promotional element. For mass merchandisers, the static display increased sales during the test period by 2.7 percent over the base period, but surprisingly, sales in the drug and food outlets utilizing the static displays were slightly less (each 1.6 percent less) than those not using the static displays. By comparison, the motion displays uniformly increased sales by 3.7

8. "The Effect of Motion Displays on the Sales of Beer"; "The Effect of Motion Displays on Sales of Baked Goods"; "The Effect of Motion Displays on Sales of Batteries." All from the Point-of-Purchase Advertising Institute, New York, undated.

percent, 9.1 percent, and 15.7 percent in the drug outlets, supermarkets, and mass merchandisers, respectively.

Results from the preceding studies convincingly demonstrate the effectiveness of motion displays. The consumer information-processing rationale (see Chapter 4) is straightforward: Motion displays attract attention. Attention, once attracted, is directed toward salient product features, including recognition of the displayed brand's name. Brand name information activates consumers' memories pertaining to brand attributes previously processed from media advertising. Information on brand attributes, when recalled, supplies a reason for the consumer to purchase the displayed brand.

Hence, a moving display performs the critical in-store function of bringing a brand's name to active memory. The probability of purchasing the brand increases, perhaps substantially (as in the case of S. B. Thomas' English muffins), if the consumer is favorably disposed toward the brand. The Eveready display was less effective apparently because the selling burden was placed almost exclusively on the display. Without prior stimulation of demand through advertising, the static display was ineffective and the motion display was not as effective as it might have been.

P-O-P's Dramatic Growth

U.S. companies spend heavily on point-of-purchase materials. In 1987 P-O-P expenditures reached $11.8 billion, representing a 10 percent increase over 1986. P-O-P has experienced a 12 percent annual increase since 1983.[9]

This impressive growth is because point-of-purchase materials provide a useful service for all participants in the marketing process. For a manufacturer, P-O-P keeps the company's name and the brand name before the consumer and reinforces a brand image that has been previously established through advertising. Discussion back in Chapter 10 pointed this out in the case of Du Pont's Stainmaster[cm] carpet. P-O-P calls attention to special offers such as sales promotions and helps stimulate impulse purchasing. It also helps to enhance the manufacturer's position with retailers.

P-O-P serves retailers by attracting the consumer's attention, increasing his or her interest in shopping, and extending the amount of time spent in the store—all of which mean increased sales. P-O-P helps retailers utilize available space to the best advantage by displaying several manufacturers' products in the same unit (e.g., many varieties of vitamins and other medicinal items all in one well-organized unit). It enables retailers to better organize shelf space and to improve inventory control, volume, stock turnover, and profitability.

Consumers are served by point-of-purchase units that deliver useful information and simplify the shopping process by setting products apart from similar items.

9. "P-O-P Spending Hits $11.8 Billion," *POPAI News*, vol. 12 (September 1988), p. 19.

In addition to benefiting all participants in the marketing process, point-of-purchase plays another important role: It serves as the *capstone for an integrated promotional program*. P-O-P by itself may have limited impact, but when used in conjunction with other marketing communications (advertisements, sales promotions, and sales clerks), P-O-P can create a synergistic effect. In fact, point-of-purchase techniques have been so effective that manufacturers are using media advertising to focus consumer attention on in-store promotional and display vehicles.[10]

In short, point-of-purchase performs useful functions for all participants in the marketing communications process. Let us examine these functions from each participant's perspective.

Manufacturer's Perspective

Point-of-purchase materials perform several beneficial functions for the manufacturers who supply P-O-P items.

Hierarchy-of-Effects Functions. P-O-P accomplishes tasks relevant to all levels of the hierarchy. It can generate awareness for the manufacturer's brand, provide product information (as in the case of the Clarion interactive display in Figure 16.2), possibly influence the consumer's attitude (either negatively or positively, depending on the quality and suitability of the P-O-P material), and encourage trial-purchase behavior.

Merchandising Functions. A well-designed temporary or permanent display enables a manufacturer to present products attractively, to organize items in a convenient fashion, and to maintain stock at the point of purchase rather than in the retailer's storeroom.

Targetability. Point-of-purchase items can be designed for special target groups to meet current marketing needs. For example, if a brand is not selling well in a certain geographical region or in a particular demographic group, say with Hispanics, P-O-P displays can be designed specifically for that region or group.

Cost. On a cost-per-thousand (CPM) basis, point-of-purchase materials are extremely cost efficient. CPMs range from $.04 to $.15, depending on the expense of the materials used.[11]

10. "Merchandising Triangle: Retailers, Advertisers, and Manufacturers Make P-O-P a Promotional Powerhouse," *Marketing Communications*, July 1983, p. 8P.
11. Kristina Cannon-Bonventre, "Point-of-Purchase Advertising: A Marketer's In-Store Arsenal," Point-of-Purchase Advertising Institute Brochure, undated (circa 1987).

Retailer's Perspective

Retailers benefit in various ways by using P-O-P materials.

Decline in Personal Service + Consumer Need for Information = Opportunity for P-O-P.[12]   Many retailers have difficulty attracting and holding qualified salespeople. Point-of-purchase materials help compensate for the decline in service by performing both informational and transactional functions (e.g., the Balfour Collegiate Express described in the opening vignette).

Merchandising Function.   Displays perform merchandising functions for retailers as well as for manufacturers. For retailers, displays provide a way to maintain stock levels on the sales floor in an eye-catching and convenient fashion.

Image Function.   Displays and other point-of-purchase materials can enhance or diminish a store's image. They can help project a positive image of shopping excitement, convey a leading-edge image, and suggest the availability of bargains. If used inappropriately, they might portray a store as dirty, out-of-date (due to ragged-looking displays), and cluttered.

Consumer's Perspective

An example will help illustrate how point-of-purchase materials perform useful functions for consumers. Consider the situation faced by the consumer when purchasing a product such as exterior paint. Price, quality, and ease of application are important purchase considerations, but especially important to the consumer is accurate color information presented in an easy-to-process manner.

The Sherwin-Williams display shown in Figure 16.4 illustrates the solution that this manufacturer came up with to satisfy consumers' dual needs for product information and convenience. The display presents samples of hundreds of paint combinations in one small space, thereby making it easy for the consumer to select colors and evaluate different color combinations.

The Result of P-O-P: Increased Unplanned Purchasing

Studies of consumer shopping behavior have shown that a high proportion of all purchases in supermarkets, drug stores, and other retail outlets are un-

---

12. This equation is from Kristina Cannon-Bonventre and Robert J. Kopp, "New Opportunities for P-O-P: A Consumer Perspective," *Comments to POPAI Marketplace*, New York, November 19, 1987.

FIGURE 16.4   **Illustration of an Informative and Convenient P-O-P Display**

Source: Courtesy of The Sherwin-Williams Company.

planned. In a general sense, this means that many product- and brand-choice decisions are made while the consumer is in the store rather than before he or she arrives at the store. Point-of-purchase materials play a role, perhaps the major role, in influencing unplanned purchasing. The remainder of this section explains unplanned purchasing and describes the research revealing the high incidence of this type of purchase behavior.

The 1986 Supermarket Consumer Buying Habits Study, conducted by the Point-of-Purchase Advertising Institute (POPAI), determined that approximately two-thirds of all grocery purchase decisions are made while the consumer is in the supermarket aisle. The study measured the behavior of 4,000 shoppers nationwide who made over 65,000 purchases.

Figure 16.5 compares the 1986 study findings with comparable results obtained in 1977. The last column shows that in 1977 64.8 percent of purchases

Supermarket Buying Habits Study Results, 1977 and 1986

FIGURE 16.5

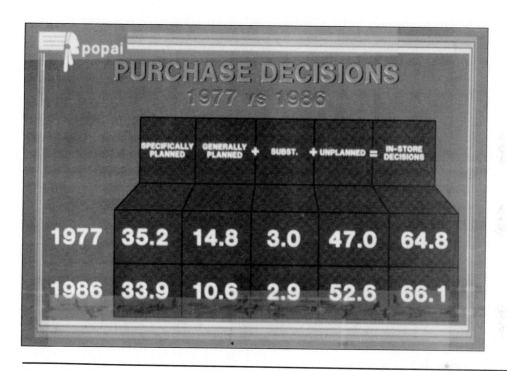

	SPECIFICALLY PLANNED	GENERALLY PLANNED +	SUBST. +	UNPLANNED =	IN-STORE DECISIONS
1977	35.2	14.8	3.0	47.0	64.8
1986	33.9	10.6	2.9	52.6	66.1

Source: Courtesy Point-of-Purchase Advertising Institute.

involved "in-store decisions," whereas in 1986 the percentage increased to 66.1 percent. Explanations of study procedures and terminology are needed to fully appreciate these results.

POPAI's ongoing research is conducted in the following manner. Upon entering a supermarket, a shopper is queried about his or her purchase plans. This initial questioning is used to identify which specific product and brand purchases are planned. Then, actual purchases are compared against planned purchases. This comparison leads to the classification of four types of purchase behaviors:

1. *Specifically planned.* This category represents purchases where the consumer indicates an intent to purchase a specific brand and in fact proceeds to buy that brand. For example, the purchase of Diet Pepsi would be considered a **specifically planned purchase** if a consumer mentioned her intention to purchase that brand and in fact bought Diet Pepsi.

2. *Generally planned.* This classification applies to purchases for which the shopper indicates an intent to buy a particular product (say, a soft drink)

but has no specific brand in mind. The purchase of Diet Pepsi in this case would be classified as a **generally planned purchase** rather than a specifically planned purchase.

3. *Substitute purchases.* Purchases where the shopper does not buy the product or brand he or she indicates constitute **substitute purchases.** For example, if a consumer says she will buy Diet Pepsi but actually purchases Tab, or no diet soft drinks at all, her behavior would be classified as a substitute purchase.

4. *Unplanned purchases.* Under this heading are purchases for which the consumer had no prior purchase intent. If, for example, she buys Diet Pepsi without having informed the interviewer of this intent, the behavior would be recorded as an **unplanned purchase.**

A technical point needs to be addressed at this time. Specifically, it is important to recognize that not all purchases recorded as unplanned by POPAI interviewers are truly unplanned. Rather, some purchases are recorded as such simply because shoppers are unable or unwilling to inform interviewers of their exact purchase plans.

This is not to imply that the POPAI research is seriously flawed, but rather that the measurement of unplanned purchases probably is somewhat overstated due to the unavoidable bias just described. Other categories may be biased also. For example, by the same logic, the percentage of specifically planned purchases is probably somewhat understated. In any event, POPAI's findings are important even if they are not precisely correct.

Notice in Figure 16.5 that the "generally planned," "substitute," and "unplanned" purchases are summed to form total "in-store decisions." In other words, the three categories representing purchases that are not specifically planned all represent decisions influenced by in-store factors.

The percentage of in-store decisions was 66.1 percent in 1986. To the extent that the figure is accurate, this indicates that nearly two out of every three supermarket decisions are influenced by in-store factors. It is apparent that P-O-P materials represent a very important determinant of consumers' product- and brand-choice behaviors.

Retailers' Use of P-O-P Materials

Various reasons explain why retailers would want to use the point-of-purchase materials supplied by manufacturers. Figure 16.6 highlights the advantages that P-O-P materials hold for retailers. Advantages notwithstanding, the fact remains that a large percentage of all signs, posters, wall units, racks, displays, and other P-O-P materials supplied by manufacturers are never used.

Advantages for Retailers of P-O-P Materials

FIGURE 16.6

Why should the retailer use P-O-P materials? The following points highlight its advantages:

1. P-O-P creates consumer excitement.
2. P-O-P creates a "buying" atmosphere.
3. P-O-P creates impulse sales.
4. P-O-P creates extra selling space. (Prepacks; dump bins.)
5. P-O-P creates cross merchandising opportunities.
6. P-O-P makes it easy for a customer to locate the product.
7. P-O-P makes it easy for a customer to select the product.

8. P-O-P acts as a silent salesman.
9. P-O-P gives a customer product information.
10. P-O-P demonstrates product features.
11. P-O-P reinforces the advertising campaign at the retail level.
12. P-O-P serves as a vehicle to dramatize consumer offers such as cents off, premiums, etc.

Source: POPAI News 3, October 15, 1987.

Why P-O-P Materials Go Unused

Three major reasons explain why retailers choose not to use P-O-P materials.[13] First, there is no incentive for the retailer to use certain P-O-P materials because they are not designed with the retailer's needs in mind. Second, some displays take up too much space for the amount of sales they generate. Third, some materials are too unwieldly, too difficult to set up, too flimsy, or have other construction defects.

Ways to Get Retailers to Use P-O-P Materials

Getting retailers to use P-O-P materials is a matter of basic marketing. Persuading the retailer to enthusiastically use a display or other P-O-P device means that the manufacturer must view the material from the retailer's perspective. First and foremost, P-O-P materials must satisfy the retailer's needs and the needs of the retailer's customer, the consumer, rather than just the manufacturer's needs. This is the essence of marketing, and it applies to getting P-O-P materials used just as much as it applies to getting products accepted.

P-O-P materials must be designed so that:

1. they are the right size and format;

---

13. Don E. Schultz and William A. Robinson, *Sales Promotion Management* (Lincolnwood, IL: NTC Business Books, 1982), p. 279.

2.   they fit the store decor;

3.   they are "user friendly"—that is, easy for the retailer to attach, erect, or otherwise use;

4.   they are sent to stores when they are needed (e.g., at the right selling season);

5.   they are properly coordinated with other aspects of the marketing communications program (e.g., they should tie-in to a current advertising or sales-promotion program); and

6.   they are attractive, convenient, and useful for consumers.[14]

Electronic Retailing

Balfour's Collegiate Express system described in the chapter's opening vignette is one of many examples of electronic retailing. In general, electronic retailing employs in-store **video merchandising centers (VMCs)** to display and sell entire product lines through audio and video presentations.

VMCs perform both *informational* and *transactional* functions.[15] That is, they inform and educate consumers about product features and process orders for delivery. A report by the accounting firm Touche Ross & Company predicts that by 1990 more than 100,000 informational and transactional VMCs will generate annual sales of as much as $5 billion.[16]

The heralded explosion of video merchandising centers is understandable, for this technology offers important benefits to all participants in the marketing process. A major advantage for manufacturers is the ability to broaden product lines at the point of purchase without requiring retailers to increase inventory. For example, the Florsheim Shoe Company's video center "Express Shops" enable Florsheim dealers to carry limited assortments of styles and sizes while using the video center to supplement in-store offerings.

For retailers, VMCs broaden product lines without increasing inventories, turn shoppers into buyers, increase sales per square foot, supplement the selling-floor staff, create on-line inventory replenishment systems, and provide a leading-edge image.[17]

14. Adapted from Schultz and Robinson, *Sales Promotion Management*, pp. 278–279.
15. In their role as transactional centers, VMCs are actually a form of direct marketing and, for this reason, could have been covered in the previous chapter on direct marketing. However, as information centers, VMCs are point-of-purchase devices rather than direct marketing units, which justifies their coverage in the present chapter.
16. "Electronic Retailing: The Marriage of All Media," *POPAI News*, vol. 12 (September 1988), p. 25.
17. "Interactive Videodiscs Combine Technology with Simplicity to be Consumer Friendly," *POPAI News*, vol. 11 (October 15, 1987), p. 15.

FOCUS ON PROMOTION

The World's Smallest Shoe Stores

ByVideo Inc., the developers of the Florsheim Express Shops, describes them as "the world's smallest shoe stores with the world's largest selection of shoes." Over 17,000 combinations of styles, sizes, and widths are available through the Express Shop. This helps retailers avoid losing sales due to a store not having a particular style, size, or color in stock. The customer merely touches the screen, explores different styles and sizes, makes a selection, and slides a credit card through a reader or pays at the cash register. Orders are transmitted electronically to a central warehouse, and the shoes are delivered to the customer's home within a week.[18] ■

Additional Illustrations of Electronic Retailing

The following vignettes identify creative applications of electronic retailing.

AMC's Video Catalog and Interactive Kiosk. American Motors Corporation's interactive kiosks were designed to increase product visibility and generate sales leads. Located in shopping malls, a video monitor attracts viewers with an action-packed sequence showing AMC products. A touchscreen permits prospects to peruse automobile styles from a video catalog of standard features, options, and prices. Viewers enter their responses simply by touching the screen. The system then delivers a printout of the user's preferred model, selected options, and prices. A map of the United States invites viewers to enter the regions where they live and their names, addresses, and phone numbers. This information provides dealers with lists of prospective customers.[19]

Pantene Hair Care Consultant. Richardson-Vicks had experienced weak distribution and poor in-store visibility for its Pantene line of hair care products. Sales were being lost due to these problems and because retail sales personnel were not always well-informed about Pantene's advantages. The video merchandising center was developed to improve Pantene's performance (see Figure 16.7). This VMC includes a video monitor that continuously shows animated graphics to attract customer traffic. After being instructed to touch the screen, customers are guided through a series of multiple-choice questions

18. "Florsheim's Pushbutton Sales Force," *Sales and Marketing Management*, June 1987, p. 23.
19. This description is based on trade literature from Intermark Corporation, the developers of AMC's video kiosk (1985).

FIGURE 16.7   **Illustration of a Video Merchandising Center**

High-Tech Marketing Builds Distribution and Sales

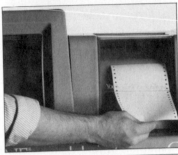

The Client

Pantene, a Brand of
The Procter & Gamble Company

The Product

Established line of upscale hair-care products with special formulas for individual hair conditions.

The Need

Create a self-service merchandiser.

The company sought to achieve a marketing turn-around in department stores.

Distribution was weak and in-store visibility poor. Both distribution and sales hinged on the display. Without prominent display space, the brand could never be perceived as top of the line and sales volume would stay well below its potential.

In addition, continuous staff turn-over meant "line girls" were not always well-informed. This, in turn, meant sales were being lost because customers could not figure out which products were right for their hair.

Source: Courtesy of The Procter & Gamble Company. Used with permission.

to find out what products have been designed for their particular hair condition. A printout of Pantene's hair-care prescription is automatically provided; the customer can then select the recommended product directly from the display below the monitor. Initial testing in two markets revealed sales increases in excess of 400 percent.[20]

Levi's Video Merchandising Center. Video merchandising centers for Levi's enable customers to view and purchase jeans in a variety of sizes and styles that are not available in every store. By touching the center's video screen, customers view audio and video presentations of different products. After a purchase selection is made, the VMC generates a printout of the item's description, price, and order and stock numbers. The customer completes the transaction with the assistance of a salesperson and receives home delivery of the jeans within two weeks.[21]

Electronic Gift Shops

In addition to in-store merchandising centers, electronic retailing has moved into the realm of gift giving. Sears has placed electronic "Shop-A-Gift" kiosks at downtown Chicago locations. They use video disc technology to offer consumers about 100 products ranging from flowers to clothing. Kiosk functions are controlled by a touch-sensitive screen. A keyboard allows the name and address of the gift recipient to be typed in along with a personalized message.[22]

Origin Technologies has installed an electronic retailing kiosk, called the PS Personal Shopper, in a Memphis office building and plans to install kiosks in Chicago and New York offices as well. Customers are able to order flowers, food, gift baskets, jewelry, watches, apparel, and accessories. The 12.5 square-foot kiosk is linked by computer directly to distributors who mail the merchandise. Origin Technologies receives a percentage of each sale.[23]

Electronic Shopping in the Future

Incredible developments in computer technology portend an exciting future for electronic shopping. One prospect is the possibility of an electronic dressing room. Based on audio/video technology called digital video interaction (DVI), it will be possible for a consumer to "try on" multiple outfits in a matter of

20. This description is based on trade literature from Intermark Corporation, the developers of Procter & Gamble's Pantene merchandising center (1985).
21. This description is based on a public relations release for ByVideo Incorporated, the developers of Levi's VMC (May 21, 1987).
22. "Sears, F. W. Woolworth Implement Interactive Video Kiosks," *POPAI News,* vol. 12 (September 1988), p. 27.
23. "Kiosk Set Up as Retail Outlet," *Advertising Age,* October 31, 1988, p. 31.

seconds or minutes because the outfits will be modeled by the consumer's video body image on a television monitor. A video camera will scan the shopper's body and place the image on a compact video disc similar to the CDs used for music. The body image will then have the image of different outfits reprogrammed over it. The shopper views the television monitor to see how he or she looks in each outfit.[24]

Electronic shopping can move beyond the clothing department to other areas as well. A video camera can scan a shopper's face and allow her to "try on" different shades of lipstick or eye shadow. Different hair styles could be modeled electronically. Taking an image of a customer's wrist would enable him or her to see how different watches or bracelets would look. Foot imaging would allow a customer to see how different shoe styles would look on his or her foot.

This same technology could be used in a variety of other applications, such as for home decorating purposes. Different furniture styles, colors, and arrangements could be superimposed over a room's image to visualize what the finished product would look like. The possibilities are endless.

Summary

Point-of-purchase performs both communications and merchandising functions. A variety of P-O-P materials are used. These are distinguished broadly as either temporary (e.g., signs) or permanent (e.g., integrated merchandising systems). Permanent displays are becoming more common for two principal reasons: They offer the manufacturer substantial savings, and they enable the retailer to merchandise the product more effectively.

Research has documented the high incidence of consumers' in-store purchase decision making and the corresponding importance of P-O-P materials in these purchase decisions. The POPAI Supermarket Consumer Buying Habits Study classified all consumer purchases into four categories: specifically planned, generally planned, substitutes, and unplanned decisions. The last three categories combined represent in-store decisions that are influenced by P-O-P displays and other store cues. In-store decisions represent nearly two out of every three purchase decisions (66.1 percent in 1986).

One of the most exciting developments in P-O-P is the growth of electronic retailing involving in-store video merchandising centers (VMCs). These units offer important benefits to all participants in the marketing process. It is estimated that by 1990 more than 100,000 units will be in use, accounting for over $5 billion in sales.

Discussion Questions

1. What functions can point-of-purchase materials accomplish that mass-media advertising cannot?

24. Lenore Skenazy, "Intel Brings Computers to Life," *Advertising Age*, October 31, 1988, p. 54.

2. In consumer information processing terms (see Chapter 4), explain the synergistic effect between advertising and P-O-P.

3. Explain why the POPAI Supermarket Consumer Buying Habits Study probably overestimates the percentage of unplanned purchases and underestimates the percentage of specifically planned and generally planned purchases.

4. Suggest an alternative measurement procedure (i.e., different methods and different measurements) that would answer the same question addressed by the POPAI study yet would avoid the biases you identified in response to the previous question.

5. The percentage of in-store decisions for pet foods and supplies was 55.7 percent in 1977. The comparable percentage for herbs and spices was 81.5 percent. What accounts for the 26 percent difference in in-store decision making for these two products? Go beyond these two product categories and offer a generalization as to what product categories likely have high and low proportions of in-store decision making.

6. What role does point-of-purchase perform for retailers? For consumers?

7. The discussion of the S. B. Thomas English muffin study pointed out that in stores using motion displays, sales increased by 473 percent. By comparison, sales of Eveready batteries, when promoted with motion displays, increased anywhere from 3.7 percent to 15.7 percent, depending on the type of store in which the display was placed. How would you account for the tremendous disparity in sales impact of motion displays for English muffins compared to batteries?

8. Why were motion and static displays considerably more effective in increasing Olympia beer sales in liquor stores than in supermarkets?

9. What types of product categories do you think are most appropriate for the use of video merchandising centers? Provide a rationale for your response.

Exercises

1. The best way to appreciate P-O-P is to systematically examine its use. Visit a supermarket and provide an accounting of the types and number of point-of-purchase materials used for five different product categories. Select three particular displays and evaluate their effectiveness. Be explicit in identifying the criteria used in performing your evaluations.

2. Use the same accounting approach that is described in Exercise 1 in a drugstore or general merchandise store (e.g., K-Mart).

3. Interview two or three proprietors/managers of small retail stores (e.g., a camera shop, a sporting goods store) and investigate their experiences with point-of-purchase materials provided by manufacturers. (Develop a specific list of four or five questions before you go on your interviews. Try to determine what they most like and dislike about P-O-P materials.)

4. Go to a location where there is an interactive video merchandising center. Interview store personnel, if possible, to determine their experience with the VMC.

CHAPTER SEVENTEEN

Public Relations and Sponsorship Marketing

NEGATIVE PUBLICITY AND THE SUZUKI SAMURAI

American Suzuki Motor Corporation, marketers of the Samurai, achieved tremendous success after introducing the Samurai to the United States in 1985. Over 160,000 Samurais were sold in just three years. The Samurai appealed primarily to youthful consumers who identified with the product's inexpensive and fun-oriented positioning. For example, one television spot featured two young couples leaving an ice-cream shop singing "Born To Be Wild" as they approached their Samurais.

Samurai's future looked positive, to say the least. But the situation changed dramatically in March 1988 when NBC-TV aired a report that revealed the Samurai's high propensity to tip over. Then in June, Consumers Union, publishers of *Consumer Reports*, announced it had found the Samurai "not acceptable." No vehicle had received that rating in nearly 10 years. Consumers Union's testing revealed that the Samurai toppled repeatedly when making sharp turns at about 40 miles per hour. The U.S. Government's Office of Defects Investigation had identified 67 rollover accidents involving the Samurai. As of late June 1988, those accidents had resulted in 20 deaths and 87 injuries.[1]

1. "Follow-Up: Some Suzuki Rollovers," *Consumer Reports*, August 1988, p. 487.

Consumers Union felt that the product was so unsafe that Suzuki should buy back every one of the Samurais sold in the United States since 1985.

A Suzuki spokesman defended the Samurai record, claiming "We have absolute confidence that we are selling a safe and stable vehicle."[2] The company also conducted a news conference in which it challenged Consumers Union's report. Although Suzuki stopped airing the "Born To Be Wild" commercial, it continued to advertise by aggressively promoting the Samurai's positive features.

Nonetheless, sales immediately fell following Consumers Union's report—to 2,199 units in June 1988 from 6,074 in May.[3] Sales in July rebounded to 6,327 units, but this was due in great part to strong dealer and consumer incentives.[4] One Ohio dealer, for example, offered Samurai buyers free insurance. Other dealers cut prices by more than 10 percent.

In March 1989, Suzuki settled law suits with seven states (California, Massachusetts, Minnesota, Missouri, New York, Texas, and Washington). Suzuki agreed to announce in future advertising that the Samurai may roll over if turned too sharply.■

The opening vignette points out a potential problem that all companies may face—the possibility of negative publicity and the disastrous consequences that may follow. Handling negative publicity is one of the roles relegated to public relations. Public relations involves much more than crisis management, however. In this chapter we will explore the multiple roles performed by the public-relations function.

The chapter also treats the related topics of event and cause marketing as part of the more general practice known as sponsorship marketing. These growing aspects of the promotion mix are conceptually aligned with public relations and in some organizations are administratively part of the public-relations department.

Public Relations

Public relations, or **PR** as it is typically shortened, is that aspect of promotion management uniquely suited to fostering *goodwill* between a company and its various publics. PR efforts are aimed at various publics, primarily the following: consumers, employees, suppliers, stockholders, governments, the general public, labor groups, and citizen action groups (see Figure 17.1).

When effectively integrated with advertising, personal selling, and sales promotion, public relations is capable of accomplishing objectives other than goodwill. It also is able to increase brand awareness, build favorable attitudes toward a company and its products, and encourage purchase behavior.[5]

2. "A Tough Turn for the Suzuki Samurai," *Newsweek,* June 13, 1988, p. 49.
3. Janice Steinberg, "Suzuki Acts to Right Slipping Samurai Sales," *Advertising Age,* July 25, 1988, p. S-10.
4. Jack Bernstein, "Crisis Communications L.A.-Style," *Advertising Age,* September 5, 1988, p. 29.
5. "PR's Value Enhanced As Marketers Turn to Integrated Communications," *Marketing News,* April 25, 1988, p. 5.

The Various Publics with Which Public Relations Interacts   FIGURE 17.1

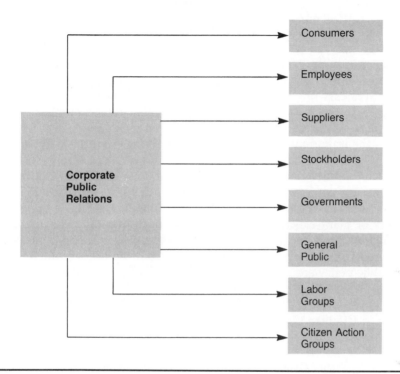

Public Relations Activities and Functions

Public relations entails a variety of specific functions and activities, of which the following are most important.[6]

Advice and Counsel.   Public-relations input is required in any decision that has significant implications for any of an organization's publics. For example, a decision to construct a new manufacturing facility in a geographic area where wildlife may be disturbed would require PR advice and counsel to determine how best to deal with environmentalists and other concerned citizens groups.

Publications.   Public-relations personnel prepare a variety of publications: newsletters for employees, pamphlets and brochures for stock-

6. Raymond Simon, *Public Relations: Concepts and Practices* (Columbus, OH: Grid Publishing, 1980), pp. 86, 87.

holders, reports for governmental agencies on matters involving corporate interests, and so on.

Publicity.   The public-relations department serves as the prime source of an organization's contact with the news media. News releases and press conferences are two of the most important avenues for corporate publicity. Publicity activities take two extreme forms: (1) disseminating *positive publicity* (e.g., news about product innovations, announcements of corporate philanthropic activities), or (2) dealing with *negative publicity* during periods of corporate crisis (such as the situation with the Suzuki Samurai and Exxon's handling of the massive oil spill in Valdez, Alaska, in early 1989). More information on the important topic of publicity will be offered in a later section.

Relations with Publics.   Public-relations personnel deal with various publics in matters involving any company decisions, policies, or impending actions that have ramifications for these publics. Dealing with employees in matters of plant closings, with stockholders during times of financial exigency (such as a takeover crisis), with environmentalists during periods of ecological conflict (Exxon's oil spill, for example), and with governments in matters of public policy are some of the major forms of public relations.

Corporate Image Advertising.   This form of advertising, which was discussed in Chapter 12, is often the work of the public-relations department in coordination with the organization's advertising department.

Public Opinion.   Public-relations departments work closely with marketing-research departments or perform the research themselves on matters involving public opinion. Because public opinion is often volatile, it is important that PR departments spot emerging trends that have relevance for corporate policies and actions.

Miscellaneous.   Public-relations departments are sometimes responsible for handling speaker's bureaus, corporate donations, scholarships and awards programs, and other specialized programs.

Specific Forms of Public Relations

The preceding discussion provides an overview of public relations. It is important now to make some finer distinctions so that the promotion management and marketing communications aspects of public relations are brought into sharper focus and distinguished from the more general management aspects of public relations.

As just described, PR involves relations with all of an organizations' relevant publics—employees, stockholders, governments, etc. Most PR activities do *not* involve marketing per se, but rather deal with general management concerns. This more encompassing aspect of public relations can be called *general PR*. Interactions with employees, stockholders, labor groups, citizen action groups, and suppliers are typically part of a company's general, nonmarketing public relations.

Our concern is only with the more narrow aspect of public relations involving an organization's interactions with consumers or with other publics (e.g., governments) regarding marketing matters (e.g., product safety). We will call this aspect of public relations marketing-oriented PR, or *marketing PR* for short.[7]

Marketing PR can be further delineated as involving either proactive or reactive public relations. **Proactive marketing PR** is *dictated by a company's marketing objectives*. It is offensively rather than defensively oriented and opportunity-seeking rather than problem-solving.[8] Proactive PR is another tool in addition to advertising, sales promotion, and personal selling for promoting a company's products and services.

Reactive marketing PR, by comparison, is the conduct of public relations *in response to outside influences*. It is undertaken as a result of external pressures and challenges brought by competitive actions, changes in consumer attitudes, changes in government policy, or other external influences. Reactive PR typically deals with changes that have *negative consequences* for the organization. "Unlike proactive PR, which tries to enhance the company's image and increase it revenues, reactive PR tries to restore the company to the status quo— by repairing its reputation, preventing market erosion, and regaining lost sales."[9]

Proactive and reactive PR will now be examined in greater detail.

Proactive Marketing PR

The major role of proactive marketing PR is in the area of new-product introductions or product revisions. Proactive PR is integrated with other promotional devices to give a product additional exposure, newsworthiness, and credibility. This last factor, *credibility*, largely accounts for the effectiveness of proactive marketing-oriented PR. Whereas advertising and personal selling claims are sometimes suspect, product announcements by a newspaper editor or television broadcaster are notably more believable. Consumers are less likely to question the motivation underlying an editorial-type endorsement. In comparison, we often question salespeople's and advertisers' motives, because we know they personally stand to gain when we engage in behaviors they encourage us to undertake.

---

7. The distinction between general and marketing-oriented PR appears also in Jordan Goldman, *Public Relations in the Marketing Mix* (Lincolnwood, IL: NTC Business Books, 1984).
8. Ibid., p. xi.
9. Ibid., p. xii.

Publicity is the major tool of proactive marketing PR. Like advertising and personal selling, the fundamental purposes of marketing-oriented publicity are to engender brand awareness, enhance attitudes toward a company and its brands, and possibly influence purchase behavior.

Some Tools of Proactive Marketing PR.   Companies obtain publicity using various forms of news releases, press conferences, and other types of information dissemination. News releases concerning new products, modifications in old products, and other newsworthy topics are mailed or hand carried to editors of newspapers, magazines, and other media. Press conferences announce major news events of interest to the public. Photographs, tapes, and films are useful for illustrating product improvements, new products, advanced production techniques, and so forth. Of course, all forms of publicity are subject to the control and whims of the media. However, by disseminating a large volume of publicity materials and by preparing materials that fit the media's needs, a company increases its chances of obtaining beneficial publicity.

Several widely used forms of publicity in marketing-oriented PR are product releases, executive-statement releases, and feature articles. The **product release** announces a new product, provides relevant information about product features and benefits, and tells how additional information can be obtained. A product release is typically published in a product section of trade magazines and business publications such as *Business Week, Forbes,* and *Fortune* or in the business section of consumer magazines such as *Time* or *Newsweek.*

The **executive-statement release** is a news release quoting a corporate executive such as the CEO. Unlike a product release, which is restricted to describing a new product or product improvement, an executive-statement release may deal with a wide variety of possible issues relevant to a corporation's publics. Topics covered may include:[10]

- Views on pricing.
- Statements about long-run industry trends.
- Company sales forecasts.
- Views on the economy.
- Comments on new markets or on old markets that are drying up.
- Comments on recent market-research findings.
- Announcements of new marketing programs launched by the company.
- Views on foreign competition or on foreign-market opportunities.
- Comments on environmental issues.

The value of the executive statement is that it comes across to readers and viewers as a significant piece of news. Whereas product releases are typically published in the business or product section of a publication, executive-state-

10. Goldman, *Public Relations in the Marketing Mix,* pp. 36–37.

ment releases are published in the *news section*. This location carries with it a significant degree of credibility. Note that any product release can be converted into an executive-statement release by changing the way it is written.

A **feature article** may be submitted to the media in finished form, that is, suitable for publication. At other times, the PR department may provide background information that can be used as input to a staff-written article. A feature article for Le Crystal Naturel, a deodorant imported from France and marketed in the United States by French Transit Ltd., is shown in Figure 17.2. Prepared by Edelman Public Relations, an international public relations firm, this article was mailed to approximately 400 newspapers with circulations exceeding 45,000 and to top beauty magazines such as *Glamour* and *Cosmopolitan*. Materials such as this are inexpensive to prepare, yet, they can provide companies with tremendous access to many potential customers.

Effective Proactive PR: Some Case Histories.   The following cases illustrate the effective use of proactive marketing-oriented public relations.

Cabbage Patch Kids.   Cabbage Patch Kids dolls, marketed by Coleco Industries, were the selling sensation of the 1983 and 1984 Christmas seasons. Retailers could not keep the dolls in stock, and some consumers traveled long distances to purchase the doll. There were even newspaper reports of people fighting over the last-available doll. What accounted for this phenomenal success? While the product itself was largely responsible, marketing PR also played a very important role in creating consumer interest and demand for the Cabbage Patch Kids.

Here are some of the things that Coleco's public-relations agency did to promote the dolls: (1) the agency sent a doll to Jane Pauley of the "Today" television program, who spent five minutes of program time discussing Cabbage Patch Kids; (2) a number of women's magazines were encouraged to mention the dolls as good Christmas gift ideas in their November magazine issues; (3) the dolls were featured several times on Johnny Carson's "Tonight" show; (4) a number of newspapers and radio stations were encouraged to use the dolls as prizes for their readers and listeners; (5) children's hospitals were given free dolls to give to their young patients, which generated favorable media coverage for Coleco.

These and other programs generated an enormous amount of publicity. All of this was accomplished with a PR budget of less than $500,000, a virtual pittance compared to what it would have cost to generate the same amount of product interest and demand via media advertising.[11]

Raid Bug Killer.   Johnson Wax undertook a publicity campaign directed at making consumers more aware of a nasty household problem— roaches. Raid Bug Killer, manufactured by Johnson Wax, was the product that

---

11. "Behind Scenes Look At Cabbage Patch PR," *Advertising Age*, December 26, 1983, pp. 2, 18.

ᒪᓐ

FIGURE 17.2   **An Illustrative Feature Article**

Only the Best—Today There's An Upscale Deodorant For Health-Conscious Consumers

Every year, Americans spend almost two billion dollars to prevent body odor. We spritz, spray and roll and, although we have more than 100 brands of deodorants and antiperspirants to choose from, there is little to distinguish one from the next. Most brands look alike, work alike and contain the same hard to pronounce ingredients—aluminum chlorohydrate, isopropyl palmitate, and cyclomethicone. The latest product to enter this hotly contested category, however, contains only mineral salt.

As the newest personal hygiene product to enter the market since the 1970s, Le Crystal Naturel is a palm-sized stone of 100 percent natural mineral salts. The sparkling crystalline stone looks different, feels different and goes on differently than any other brand. What makes Le Crystal Naturel so unique, aside from its dramatic appearance, is that it actually kills odor-causing bacteria while allowing the body to perform naturally.

Cool It

Body odor occurs when the wetness from perspiration comes into contact with bacteria on the skin's surface. In order to eliminate this odor, either the wetness or the bacteria must be eliminated.

Currently, personal hygiene products fall into two categories: antiperspirants and deodorants. Antiperspirants work by shrinking the opening of the sweat glands, reducing the flow of perspiration and eliminating wetness. Although antiperspirants are extremely effective, they interrupt the body's natural cooling process and make it difficult (if not impossible) for the body to excrete toxic substances. In addition, inert oils that are used to bind antiperspirants to the skin often clog pores, causing rashes and infections.

Deodorants, on the other hand, allow the body to perspire and cool, but not eliminate odor. Rather, they mask the odor with a stronger, and hopefully more pleasant, scent.

The Difference Is Crystal Clear

Le Crystal Naturel is the only deodorant available that allows the body to perspire and cool while *eliminating* odor. When moistened and smoothed over the skin, Le Crystal Naturel creates an invisible, non-sticky layer of mineral salts that effectively eliminates odor-causing bacteria. Pores remain open, minimizing the risk of infection, and allowing the body to cool itself naturally.

"Le Crystal Natural is the only product on the market that destroys odor by getting rid of the bacteria," said Jerry Rosenblatt, president of French Transit, Ltd., sole U.S. importer of the crystal. "Both hypoallergenic and noncomedogenic, it's one of the healthiest products on the market. And, since the protection is invisible, it won't stain clothing."

In addition to its unique odor-eliminating abilities, Le Crystal Naturel contains no chemical, dyes or perfumes, making it ideal for sensitive or allergy-prone skin.

From Bendels to Broadway

French Transit, Ltd. began importing Le Crystal Naturel in 1985. Immediately, the prestigious Henri Bendel department store in New York City stocked the product and introduced it to consumers through the store's cooperative advertising programs.

"Henri Bendel opened up sales for us and started a kind of snowball effect," said Rosenblatt. "Other department stores wanted what other stores had and soon we had stores coming to us."

Rosenblatt said that since introduction in the United States four years ago, product sales have increased a minimum of fifty percent per year.

Because the crystal is 100 percent natural and doesn't produce ozone, health food stores were also eager to snap up the product. Today, Le Crystal Naturel is sold in over 2,000 retail outlets, as well as through mail order catalogues.

For the Person Who Has Everything

Although the health benefits of Le Crystal Naturel outweigh those of traditional deodorants, Rosenblatt believes consumers buy the crystal in great part because it's so unique. The only deodorant on the market imported from France, Le Crystal Naturel possesses spa-like quality that people find ideal, even for gift giving.

"Because the crystal is so different, many people buy it as a novelty gift," said Rosenblatt. "That's something you definitely couldn't do with any other deodorant."

# # #

Source: Courtesy Daniel J. Edelman, Inc. and French Transit, Ltd.

stood to gain from heightened consumer awareness. The campaign's major objective was to remove the guilt feelings associated with having roaches in one's house and to remove the misconception that poor cleaning practices and household filth breed roaches.

Johnson Wax's PR agency devised an award-winning campaign. Public-service announcements (PSAs) were distributed through the National Home-owners Association to 650 television stations and 2,400 cable television outlets. Pamphlets, brochures, and consumer-education booklets concerning roach problems were developed and delivered to media representatives by Johnson Wax's home economists. Efforts to gain broadcast time and newspaper space were facilitated by using a 250-pound actor dressed as a humanoid cockroach.

During a three-month period the PSAs reached 115 million households, and numerous newspapers carried roach-related articles. The advantages of obtaining media support for a PR campaign such as this were detailed vividly by an account executive for Johnson Wax's PR agency: "Getting the media to disseminate PR information creates the added allure of a third party endorse-ment. When a magazine or newspaper runs an article on how to get rid of bugs and attributes it to Raid, it's almost like them saying 'go out and buy Raid.' You can't beat that kind of endorsement."[12]

This example supports the earlier point that consumers tend to view pub-licity as a form of news. The result is that information received via publicity gives consumers the impression that the transmitting medium supports the information. This provides a level of credibility that is missing from adver-tising.

Shakespeare Corporation.   Business-to-business marketers also are active users of proactive marketing PR. The Shakespeare Corporation, a large maker of fiberglass light poles, aimed a publicity campaign at electrical utilities, architects, and electrical contractors. The objective of Shakespeare's campaign was to reach influential decision makers and to enhance the credibility of fiber-glass light poles by comparing the relative advantages of fiberglass with the more dominant metal poles.

Shakespeare's strategy was to inform engineers, architects, and other tar-get markets by having product releases published in leading engineering and building-trade journals. Shakespeare's sales representatives distributed article reprints to potential buyers as hard evidence that fiberglass poles work. This program was responsible for accomplishing impressive gains in the number of prospective customers who were willing to consider fiberglass as an alternative to metal poles.[13]

12. Theodore J. Gage, "PR Ripens Role in Marketing," *Advertising Age,* January 5, 1981, p. S-11.
13. Arch G. Woodside, "Industrial Marketers Can Gain Credibility and Impact from Public Rela-tions by Following These 10 Guidelines," *Marketing News,* December 10, 1982, p. 7.

Favored Media for Publicity. *Advertising Age* conducts an annual survey of senior public-relations executives to determine which media are considered most desirable for placing an important, favorable business story. Results from the 1988 survey are shown in Table 17.1. The left column contains responses from corporate PR personnel, while reactions from PR agency personnel are in the right column. Corporate PR executives regard the *newspaper* as the single most important medium for an important news story, whereas PR agency personnel prefer *business publications.* Preferences within each specific medium also are shown in the table.

How PR Executives Rank the Media

TABLE 17.1

Asked how they rank the media if they have a very important and favorable corporate story to place, public relations executives responded as follows:

Corporate PR	PR agency
Most important medium:	
1. Newspaper	1. Business publications
Assuming the story could only be placed in newspapers:	
1. Wall Street Journal	1. New York Times
2. New York Times	2. Wall Street Journal
3. USA Today	3. USA Today
Assuming only general news magazines could be used:	
1. Time	1. Time
2. Newsweek	2. Newsweek
3. U.S. News & World Report	3. U.S. News & World Report
Assuming only business publications:	
1. Business Week	1. Business Week
2. Fortune	2. Fortune
3. Forbes	3. Forbes
Which TV news shows:	
1. NBC Nightly News	1. NBC Nightly News
2. CBS Evening News	2. CBS Evening News
3. ABC World News Tonight	3. ABC World News Tonight
Any other TV show:	
1. Today[a]	1. Today
Good Morning America[a]	2. Good Morning America

[a]Indicates a tie.

Source: Jack Bernstein, "PR Execs Pick Favored Media," *Advertising Age,* October 31, 1988, p. 12.

Reactive Marketing PR

As noted earlier, a variety of marketplace developments can place an organization in a vulnerable position that demands reactive marketing PR. The Suzuki Samurai episode presented in the opening vignette is a vivid example. In general, *product defects and failures* are the most dramatic factors underlying the need for reactive PR, but other forces are also at play. *Changes in consumers' tastes* can place a business or entire industry in a vulnerable position requiring reactive PR.[14]

For example, as noted several times throughout the text, American eating habits have moved away from red meats and toward "light" meats, that is, poultry and seafood. Sales of beef and pork have declined measurably. The "Beef Is Good Food" campaign (discussed in Chapter 12) and the pork industry's "The Other White Meat" campaign (see Figure 17.3) are advertising efforts designed to slow or reverse the decline in red-meat consumption. Supplementing these ad campaigns have been active PR efforts directed at the major media. Media kits mailed to nutrition editors of newspapers, magazines, and television stations place these products in a favorable light and provide recipes showing alternative ways to prepare beef and pork dishes. The PR campaigns for beef and pork have garnered favorable commentary in many newspaper and magazine pages as well as air time.

The Specter of Negative Publicity.   A number of celebrated negative-publicity cases have received widespread media attention in recent years.

Some Celebrated Cases.   Audi of America had realized record sales in 1985 and was moving toward recognition alongside Mercedes-Benz and BMW as one of the "Big 3" manufacturers of German luxury performance cars. Then consumers started complaining and the media (e.g., CBS's "60 Minutes") started reporting that the *Audi 5000-S* sometimes lunged out of control when shifted into drive or reverse gears. Sales plummeted from approximately 74,000 units in 1985 to projected sales of approximately only 26 to 28 thousand units in 1988.[15]

Seven people in the Chicago area died in 1982 from cyanide poisoning after ingesting *Tylenol capsules*. Many analysts predicted that Tylenol would never regain its previously sizable market share. Some observers even questioned whether Johnson & Johnson ever would be able to market anything under the Tylenol name.

14. For a detailed discussion of common vulnerabilities that demand reactive PR, see Goldman, *Public Relations in the Marketing Mix.*
15. These statistics are extrapolated from two sources: Fannie Weinstein, "One Foot in the Junkyard," *Advertising Age,* October 19, 1987, p. 92; and Raymond Serafin and Cleveland Horton, "Crucial Drive for Audi, Peugeot," *Advertising Age,* August 8, 1988, p. 40. The massive decline in Audi sales is also partially explained by exchange rate adjustments during this period that were unfavorable to exports to the United States.

A Campaign in Response to Changes in Consumers' Tastes   FIGURE 17.3

Have you tried the other white meat?

If you think you have to serve fish or fowl to get the light, wholesome nutrition and easy convenience that today's life-styles demand, take a fresh look at pork — the *other* white meat.

Pork gives you the lighter meals and versatility you associate with white meat. Plus, it provides you and your family the great taste you want, and the nutrition and protein you need.

And of course the mouth-watering taste and savory flavor of pork blend deliciously with all kinds of sauces, spices, stuffings and side dishes.

Pork can easily be substituted for any other white meat in many recipes — in fact, in most meal preparation.

With a variety of new, leaner boneless cuts of pork to choose from, your menu plans have more flexibility than ever.

What's the best way to cook pork?

Often.

For a free recipe book containing light, easy, nutritious and creative ways to serve new meals with pork, just send a stamped self-addressed envelope to Pork Recipes, Box 10383-B, Des Moines, Iowa 50306.

pork

The Other White Meat.

This message is brought to you by America's pork producers.

° 1987 National Pork Producers Council in cooperation with National Pork Board.

Pork Kiev

Pork Primavera

Pork à la King

Pork Divan

Pork Marsala

Pork Au Vin

Between July 1985 and October 1986 thousands of *Chrysler automobiles* were test driven by company personnel after the odometers had been disconnected. Unbeknownst to buyers, the cars were later sold as new—that is, until the media learned of Chrysler's practice.

Post-Mortem Analyses.   How did PR personnel at Audi, Johnson & Johnson, and Chrysler handle the negative publicity affecting their firms, and what were the consequences?

Audi represents a classic illustration of how *not* to respond to negative publicity. Audi's response was to deny any product problems and instead to blame drivers. As one auto industry analyst put it: "[For Audi to announce] to the world that the reason people are accelerating through their garages is because they're hitting the accelerator instead of the brake is not exactly going to make you a lot of friends."[16]

In contrast, Johnson & Johnson's handling of the Tylenol tragedy was near brilliant. Rather than denying that a problem existed, Johnson & Johnson acted swiftly by removing Tylenol from retail shelves. Spokespersons appeared on television and cautioned consumers not to ingest Tylenol capsules. A tamper-proof package was designed, setting a standard for other companies. As a final good-faith gesture, Johnson & Johnson offered consumers free replacements for products they had disposed of in the aftermath of the Chicago tragedy. Figure 17.4 shows a Tylenol advertisement that offered consumers a $2.50 certificate for obtaining a free bottle of Tylenol. Tylenol regained its market share shortly after this campaign began, even though its major competitor, Datril, had launched an intensive advertising campaign and cents-off deal to steal Tylenol consumers.

And what about Chrysler's odometer fraud? Chrysler's Chairman, Lee Iacocca, responded with a television commercial. After asking rhetorically, "Did we screw up?" he responded "You bet we did." This response conveyed to consumers that Iacocca and the Chrysler Corporation realized a mistake had been made. The public acknowledgement and apology basically put the issue to rest. It seems that consumers are willing to accept imperfections in companies and products so long as they know efforts are being made to correct the problem.

Negative publicity can hit any company at any time. The extent of the damage depends on how a company responds to the publicity. Audi may never regain its 1985 market position. Chrysler Corporation was virtually unscathed by its untoward behavior. The Tylenol tragedy cost Johnson & Johnson millions of dollars, but the actual cost was a fraction of what it could have been had Johnson & Johnson not handled the problem the way it did. It is too soon to know, but it will be interesting to learn what impact the oil spill in Valdez, Alaska will have on Exxon's sales and market share.

16. Weinstein, "One Foot in the Junkyard."

Johnson & Johnson's Effort to Retain Customers   FIGURE 17.4

The makers of TYLENOL® want to say

"Thank You America"

for your continuing confidence and support.

Since the recent tragic criminal tampering incident in Chicago involving Extra-Strength TYLENOL Capsules, we've talked with many people all over the country.

The attitude toward TYLENOL is overwhelmingly positive. People tell us they have trusted the TYLENOL name for many, many years, that they still have the highest regard for TYLENOL, and that they will continue to use TYLENOL. We are delighted by this response, because for over 20 years we have worked hard to earn your trust. We are now working even harder to keep it.

Following the Chicago tragedy, we know that many of you disposed of your TYLENOL product. We want to help you replace that product—*at our expense*. Just tear out the attached $2.50 certificate and redeem it at your local store.

You have made TYLENOL a trusted part of your health care program for over 20 years. This offer is a token of our appreciation for your loyalty, understanding, and continued trust.

Free!

A $2.50 certificate to purchase a free bottle of Regular Strength or Extra-Strength TYLENOL (24's/30's size) or to apply against the purchase of any other TYLENOL product. Just tear it out and take it to your local store.

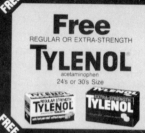

Free
REGULAR OR EXTRA-STRENGTH
TYLENOL®
acetaminophen
24's or 30's Size

Take this coupon to your local store for ONE free package of either Regular Strength tablet/capsule 24's or Extra-Strength TYLENOL® tablet 30's/capsule 24's size up to a retail price of $2.50. If your store does not carry this size, you may redeem this coupon for credit up to $2.50 toward the purchase of a larger size of Regular or Extra-Strength TYLENOL® tablets or capsules. You may also redeem this coupon for up to $2.50 toward the purchase of any Children's TYLENOL®, Children's or Adult COTYLENOL®, or Maximum-Strength TYLENOL® sinus medication product. You must pay any applicable sales tax.

Dealer: See reverse side for redemption

The lesson to be learned is that quick and positive responses to negative publicity are imperative. Negative publicity is something to be dealt with head-on, not denied. When done effectively, reactive PR can virtually save a product or a company.

"Did You Hear About. . .?".   You have heard them and probably helped spread them since you were a small child in elementary school. They are often vicious and malicious. Sometimes they are just comical. Most always they are false. We are talking about *rumors*.

Commercial rumors are widely circulated but unverified propositions about a product, brand, company, store, or other commercial target.[17] Rumors are probably the most difficult problem public-relations personnel deal with. What makes rumors so troublesome is that they spread like wildfire and most always state or imply something very undesirable, and possibly repulsive, about the target of the rumor.

Following are various rumors you have probably heard at one time or another. None are true, but all have been widely circulated.

- The McDonald's Corporation makes sizable donations to the Church of Satan.
- The Procter & Gamble logo is associated with witchcraft and Satan. (See Figure 17.5.)
- Wendy's hamburgers contain something other than beef, namely red worms. (Other versions of this rumor have substituted McDonald's or Burger King as the target.)
- "Pop Rocks" (a carbonated candy-type product made by General Foods) explode in your stomach when mixed with soda.
- "Bubble Yum" chewing gum contains spider eggs.
- A woman was bitten by a poisonous snake in a K-Mart store when trying on a coat imported from Taiwan.
- A boy and his date stopped at a Kentucky Fried Chicken restaurant on their way to a movie. Later the girl became violently ill and the boy rushed her to the hospital. The examining physician said the girl appeared to have been poisoned. The boy went to the car and retrieved an oddly shaped half-eaten piece from the KFC bucket. The physician recognized it to be the remains of a rat. It was determined that the girl died from consuming a fatal amount of strychnine from the rat's body.[18]

The preceding examples illustrate the two basic types of commercial rumors: conspiracy and contamination.[19] *Conspiracy rumors* involve supposed

---

17. This definition is adapted from Fredrick Koenig, *Rumor in the Marketplace: The Social Psychology of Commercial Hearsay* (Dover, MA: Auburn House Publishing Company, 1985), p. 2.
18. These rumors, all of which are false, have been in circulation at one time or another since the 1970s. All are thoroughly documented and analyzed in the fascinating book by Koenig, ibid.
19. Ibid., p. 19.

Rumored Symbolism and P&G's Explanation   FIGURE 17.5

Rumored symbolism

Connected to one another, the stars form the number 666, a symbol of the Antichrist. Curls in the "sorcerer's" beard also form 666 when the logo is held up to a mirror.

P&G's explanation

The man-in-the-moon was "a popular decorative fancy" adopted in an early version of the logo in 1859. The 13 stars represent the original United States colonies.

Source: Reprinted with permission from the August 9, 1982 issue of *Advertising Age.* Copyright 1982 Crain Communications, Inc.

FOCUS ON PROMOTION

Examples of Conspiracy and Contamination Rumors

The AIDS Conspiracy

Leo's Restaurant in Kankakee, Illinois, did a brisk lunch business until the rumor spread that one of its employees had AIDS. Leo's lunch traffic fell to a trickle. Determined to squelch the rumor, Leo's owner aired a 60-second radio spot that featured two women talking about Leo's. "Haven't you heard the rumor?" one woman asked. The other woman, though never mentioning AIDS by name, responded by saying that the rumor wasn't true. The spot ended with the women agreeing to meet at Leo's for lunch.[20]

Beer Contaminated with Urine

In 1987 a rumor started in Reno, Nevada, that Mexican-import beer, Corona, was contaminated with urine. The rumor was started by a beer distributor in Reno who handled Heineken, a competitive brand. Corona sales fell by 80 percent in some markets. The rumor was hushed when an out-of-court settlement against the Reno distributor required a public statement declaring that Corona is not contaminated.

company policies or practices that are threatening or ideologically undesirable to consumers. *Contamination rumors* deal with undesirable or harmful product or store features. The McDonald's Church of Satan and P&G logo rumors are of the conspiracy genre, whereas the remainder of the examples are contamination rumors. The *Focus on Promotion* section contains recent examples of conspiracy and contamination rumors.

What Is the Best Way to Handle a Rumor?   When confronted with a rumor, some companies believe that the best way to handle it is to do nothing. This cautious approach is apparently based on the fear that an anti-rumor campaign will call attention to the rumor itself.[21]

---

20. "Eatery Ads Hit Gossip," *Advertising Age*, August 3, 1987, p. 6.
21. Koenig, *Rumor in the Marketplace*, p. 163.

An expert on rumors claims that rumors are like fires, and like fires, time is the worst enemy. His advice is to not merely hope that a rumor will simmer down but rather to combat it swiftly and decisively to PUT IT OUT![22] Recommended steps for rumor control are presented in Table 17.2.

Sponsorship Marketing

A rapidly growing aspect of U.S. marketing is the practice of corporate sponsorships. Sponsorships range from supporting athletic events (e.g., Volvo's support of tennis tournaments) to underwriting rock concerts (e.g., Reebok spent $10 million as the sole sponsor for "Human Rights Now!" a 20-city tour organized by Amnesty International).

Sponsorships involve investments in *events* or *causes* for the purpose of achieving various corporate objectives: increasing sales volume, enhancing a company's reputation or brand's image, increasing brand awareness, and so on.[23]

At least four factors account for the growth in sponsorships.[24] First, by attaching their names to special events and causes, companies are able to *avoid the clutter* inherent when advertising in traditional advertising media. Second, sponsorships help companies *respond to consumers' changing media habits.* For example, with the decline in network television viewing, sponsorships offer a potentially effective and cost-efficient way to reach consumers. Third, sponsorships help companies to *gain the approval of various constituencies,* including stockholders, employees, and society at large. Finally, the sponsorship of special events and causes enables marketers to *target their communication and promotional efforts* to specific geographic regions and/or to specific lifestyle groups. For example, General Foods Corporation (GFC) sponsored "March Across America" to benefit Mothers Against Drunk Driving (MADD). In sponsoring this cause, GFC was able to reach a relatively narrow segment of people who identify with MADD's laudable efforts. GFC raised $100,000 for MADD and in so doing experienced a 13 percent increase in the sales of Tang drink mix.[25]

Cause-Related Marketing

As mentioned, sponsorships involve both events and causes. *Cause-related marketing (CRM)* is a relatively narrow aspect of overall sponsorship. CRM involves an amalgam of public relations, sales promotion, and corporate philanthropy;

22. Ibid., p. 167.
23. Meryl Paula Gardner and Phillip Joel Shuman, "Sponsorship: An Important Component of the Promotions Mix," *Journal of Advertising*, vol. 16, no. 1 (1987), pp. 11–17.
24. The first three are adapted from Ibid., p. 12.
25. Laurie Freeman and Wayne Walley, "Marketing with a Cause Takes Hold," *Advertising Age*, May 16, 1988, p. 34.

TABLE 17.2   **Recommended Steps for Rumor Control**

A.   Alert Procedure
1.   On first hearing a rumor, note the location and wording of the allegation and target.
2.   Keep alert for any other rumors to see if the original report was spurious.
3.   If rumors increase to ten or more, send requests to distributors, franchise managers, and whoever else meets the public to find out who told the rumor to the person reporting it. It is important to specify the regional boundaries of the problem and the characteristics of the participating population. Distribute forms that can be filled out for the above information, as well as fact sheets rebutting the rumor.
4.   Check with competitors to see if they share the problem. Try to find out if the target has moved from your company to them or from them to yours, or if it has spread throughout the industry.

B.   Evaluation
1.   Check for a drop in sales or a slowdown in sales increase.
2.   Monitor person-hours required to answer phone calls and mail.
3.   Keep tabs on the morale of the company personnel meeting people in the corporation. Do they feel harassed? Do they feel that management is doing enough to help them?
4.   Design a marketing survey to find out what percentage of the public believes any part of the rumor.
5.   Make an assessment of the threat or potential threat the rumor poses to profits. Is the corporation in danger of appearing to be an inept, impotent, and passive victim of the rumor problem? How much is management's image affected by the way things are going? The next move is a judgment call. If it seems that something more should be done, then it is time to move to the next square.

C.   Launch a Media Campaign
1.   Assemble all facts about the extent of the problem to present to co-workers and superiors. Be prepared for resistance from people who support the myth that "pussyfooting is the best policy."
2.   Based on information gathered in the previous phases, decide on the geographical regions for implementing the campaign. If it is a local rumor, treat it locally; if it is a national rumor, treat it nationally.
3.   Based on information gathered in the previous phases, decide on the demographic features of the carrying population.
4.   Select appropriate media outlets and construct appropriate messages.
5.   Decide on what points to refute. (Don't deny *more* than is in the allegation.) If the allegation is of the contamination variety, be careful not to bring up any offensive association or to trigger potential "residuals" in the refutation.
6.   Two important points to make in any campaign are that the allegations are *untrue* and *unjust*. It should be implied that the company's business is not suffering, but that "what's right is right" and that people who pass on the rumor are "going against the American sense of fair play!"
7.   Line up spokespeople such as scientists, civic and/or religious leaders, rumor experts—whoever you think appropriate—to make statements on the company's behalf.

If all of the above is done properly, the problem is well on the way to being solved.

Source: From Fredrick Koenig, *Rumor in the Marketplace: The Social Psychology of Commercial Hearsay* (Dover, MA: Auburn House Publishing Company, 1985), pp. 171–173. Reprinted with permission.

however, the distinctive feature of CRM is that a company's contribution to a designated cause *is linked to customers' engaging in revenue-producing exchanges with the firm.*[26] Cause-related marketing, in other words, is based on the idea that a company will contribute to a cause every time the customer undertakes some action. The contribution is *contingent* on the customer performing a behavior (e.g., buying a product, redeeming a coupon) that benefits the firm.

The following examples illustrate how cause-related marketing operates. For each Heinz baby-food label mailed in by consumers, H. J. Heinz Company contributes six cents to a hospital near the consumer's home. In 1983, American Express donated a penny to the Statue of Liberty renovation for each use of its charge card and one dollar for each new card issued during the last quarter of that year. In 1988, Nabisco Brands donated one dollar to the Juvenile Diabetes Foundation for each one dollar donation certificate that was redeemed with a Ritz brand proof of purchase. Ocean Spray made a donation to the Cystic Fibrosis Foundation for every bottle of cranberry drink purchased (see Figure 17.6).

Cause-related marketing is corporate philanthropy based on profit-motivated giving.[27] Corporate interests are served while helping worthy causes. Some of the numerous causes supported by corporations include (1) Procter & Gamble's support of the Special Olympics, (2) Lever Brothers' cause-related support for the Cystic Fibrosis Foundation, (3) Johnson & Johnson's help in funding a toll-free hotline staffed by the National Coalition Against Domestic Violence, and (4) Scott Paper Company's help in raising money to support Ronald McDonald Houses.[28]

In addition to helping these and other worthy causes, corporations satisfy their own tactical and strategic objectives when undertaking cause-related efforts. By supporting a deserving cause, a company can (1) enhance its corporate or brand image, (2) thwart negative publicity, (3) generate incremental sales, (4) increase brand awareness, (5) broaden its customer base, (6) reach new market segments, and (7) increase a brand's level of merchandising activity at the retail level.[29]

Event Marketing

Though relatively small compared to the major components of the promotions mix, event sponsorship totaled $1.35 billion in 1987.[30] Approximately 2,700 companies invest in some form of event sponsorship.[31] Definitionally, **event**

26. P. Rajan Varadarajan and Anil Menon, "Cause-Related Marketing: A Coalignment of Marketing Strategy and Corporate Philanthropy," *Journal of Marketing*, vol. 52 (July 1988), pp. 58–74.
27. Ibid., p. 58.
28. Freeman and Walley, "Marketing with a Cause Takes Hold."
29. Varadarajan and Menon, "Cause-Related Marketing."
30. Laurie Freeman, "Sponsors Flock to Local Fetes," *Advertising Age*, January 25, 1988, p. 48-S.
31. Robert Selwitz, "Special Impact with Special Events," *Marketing Communications*, May 1987, p. 58.

FIGURE 17.6   **Cause-Related Marketing for Ocean Spray Cranberry Drink**

marketing is a form of brand promotion that ties a brand to a meaningful cultural, social, athletic, or other type of high-interest public activity. Event marketing is separate from advertising, sales promotion, point-of-purchase merchandising, or public relations, but it generally incorporates elements from all of these promotional tools.

Event marketing is growing rapidly because it provides companies alternatives to the cluttered mass media, an ability to segment on a local or regional basis, and opportunities for reaching narrow lifestyle groups whose consumption behavior can be tied in to the local event. For example, Volvo sponsors the Grand Prix tennis tour because the audience for tennis events contains large numbers of economically upscale people who are potential Volvo purchasers. Procter & Gamble sponsors racing cars emblazoned with P&G's Tide, Crisco, and Folgers brands because auto-racing audiences in the Southeast and Midwest are heavy consumers of these brands. Mercedes-Benz co-sponsors the Los Angeles Marathon because that market is its largest in the United States. Frito-Lay sponsors events such as the Three Rivers Regatta in Pittsburgh and the All-American Soap Box Derby in Akron because these events and their spectators have natural tie-ins with Frito-Lay's snack food products.[32]

Using Event Marketing Effectively.   As with every other marketing and promotion-management decision, the starting point for effective event sponsorship is to clearly *specify the objectives* that an event is designed to accomplish. Event marketing has no value unless it accomplishes these objectives. Two examples of effective event marketing follow.

Procter & Gamble sponsored the Mexican Festival weekend of Cinco de Mayo, the May 5th anniversary of Mexico's victory in its war against France. The objective was to strengthen P&G's relations with Hispanic retailers and consumers in the Los Angeles and Santa Ana areas of California. Over 100 festivals in supermarket parking lots were conducted during and after the official Cinco de Mayo celebration. The result: More than 4 million Hispanic consumers were reached through various Spanish-language media, and nearly 85 percent of the retailers participated in the promotion. By supporting an important community event P&G was able to increase its standing with Hispanic consumers and community leaders.[33]

General Food's Crystal Light Drink Mix was the beneficiary of another successful application of event marketing. General Food's objective was to sponsor an event compatible with Crystal Light's image and appropriate for its target market, women aged 18 to 34 who are concerned with health and fitness. The event selected was an aerobic dance competition. The Crystal Light National Aerobic Championship consists of regional aerobic dance competitions in nine malls around the country, topped off by a national championship

32. Freeman, "Sponsors Flock to Local Fetes."
33. Adapted from William A. Robinson, "Adweek's First Annual Achievements in Event Marketing," Promote section of *Adweek*, November 16, 1987, p. 12.

from among the regional winners. Crystal Light backs up each regional aerobic dance competition with point-of-purchase merchandising support and product sampling. Extensive media exposure for Crystal Light is obtained by having touring aerobic experts give interviews about the event on local television, radio, and in newspapers and magazines. Crystal Light also makes available a videotape of the national championship as a self-liquidating premium item.[34] This event sponsorship has provided General Foods with an effective way to reach prime consumers and to enhance the brand's image.[35]

Summary

This chapter covers two major topics: public reactions and sponsorship marketing. *Public relations (PR)* involves a variety of functions and activities directed at fostering harmonious interactions with an organization's publics (customers, employees, stockholders, governments, etc.). An important distinction is between general public relations (*general PR*), which deals with overall managerial issues and problems (e.g., relations with stockholders and employees), and marketing-oriented public relations (*marketing PR*). The chapter focuses on marketing PR.

Marketing PR consists of proactive PR and reactive PR. *Proactive PR* is another tool, in addition to advertising, personal selling, and sales promotion, for promoting a company's products and brands. Proactive PR is dictated by a company's marketing objectives. It seeks opportunities rather than solving problems. *Reactive PR* responds to external pressures and typically deals with changes that have negative consequences for an organization. Handling negative publicity and rumors are two areas in which reactive PR is most needed.

The other major topic covered in this chapter is *sponsorship marketing*. Sponsorships involve investments in events or causes in order to achieve various corporate objectives. *Cause-related marketing (CRM)* is a narrow aspect of overall sponsorship. The distinctive feature of CRM is that a company's contribution to a designated cause is linked to customers' engaging in revenue-producing exchanges with the firm. Cause-related marketing serves corporate interests while helping worthy causes.

Event marketing is a rapidly growing aspect of the promotional mix. Though small in comparison to advertising and other major promotional elements, expenditures on event promotions exceed $1 billion. Event marketing is a form of brand promotion that ties a brand to a meaningful cultural, social, athletic, or other type of high-interest public activity. Event marketing is growing because it provides companies with alternatives to the cluttered mass me-

---

34. A self-liquidating premium is one in which the consumer buys the item at a price much lower than what it would cost at retail. The manufacturer recovers its cost but earns no direct profit from the premium item. More will be said about self-liquidators in Chapter 20.
35. "Special Events as a Growing Marketing Tool," *DFS Promotion Report*, a publication of the Dancer Fitzgerald Sample, Inc., vol. 7, July 1986, pp. C,D.

dia, an ability to segment on a local or regional basis, and opportunities for reaching narrow lifestyle groups whose consumption behavior can be tied in to the local event.

Discussion Questions

1. What role might sponsorship marketing perform for a nationally distributed consumer-goods product such as a brand of soft drink?

2. Explain how a local business in your area (a bank, manufacturer, etc.) might use event marketing to its advantage. Be specific in describing the objectives that event marketing would satisfy and the type of event that would be compatible with these objectives.

3. It is said that public relations is to publicity what marketing is to salesmanship. Explain.

4. Explain the similarities and differences among public relations, marketing PR, and publicity.

5. What are the advantages of publicity in comparison with advertising? What are some of the objectives that both of these marketing communications techniques fulfill?

6. Some marketing practitioners consider publicity to be too difficult to control and measure. What is meant by these criticisms?

7. As the brand manager of Planter's Peanuts, an old and mature brand, how might you use proactive PR to create some inexpensive brand exposure and incremental sales?

8. Assume you are the athletic director of your college or university's athletic department. A major story hits the news claiming that a high proportion of the school's athletes use steroids. How would you handle this negative publicity? Describe the specific steps you would follow.

9. With reference to the negative publicity about the Suzuki Samurai (as described in the chapter's opening vignette), what would you have done if you had been the CEO of this firm?

10. Faced with the rumor about Corona beer being contaminated with urine (as described in the *Focus on Promotion* section), what course of action would you have taken *if* the Heineken distributor in Reno had not been identified as starting the rumor? In other words, if the source of the rumor were unknown, what steps would you have taken?

Exercises

1. Identify three examples of event marketing *other* than ones mentioned in the text. For each example, explain what the sponsoring company, or brand, would have hoped to accomplish. Also, specify the characteristics of the people who participate or spectate in each event and compare these characteristics with your interpretation of the characteristics of the sponsor's primary market.

2. Describe two or three commercial rumors other than those mentioned in the chapter. Identify each as either a conspiracy or contamination rumor. Describe how you think this rumor started and why people apparently consider it newsworthy enough to pass along. (Note: Local rumors originating in your hometown or local area are fine. You have probably heard more of these than rumors about national companies and brands.)

3. Review the pages of a major (noncollege) newspaper (preferably on a heavy news day, like Thursday or Sunday). Identify two or three instances of editorial content that, in your opinion, are probably based on news releases from companies or trade associations. Explain why you think each of these publicity releases is effective or ineffective.

PART 6

Sales Promotion

Part 6 covers the increasingly important practice of sales promotion. Chapter 18 overviews sales promotion by explaining the types of sales promotions used, the targets of sales promotion, the reasons for its growth, and the tasks sales promotion is and is not capable of performing. The chapter also explains the conditions under which sales promotion is and is not profitable and describes a process for planning sales promotions.

Chapter 19 focuses on trade-oriented sales promotion. The chapter describes the most important and widely used forms of trade promotions: contests and incentives, trade-oriented point-of-purchase materials, retailer-training programs, trade shows, trade allowances, cooperative advertising and vendor support programs, and specialty advertising programs.

Consumer-oriented sales promotion is the subject of Chapter 20. Primary focus is placed on the major forms of sales promotions that are directed at consumers. These include sampling, couponing, premiums, price-offs, bonus packs, refunds and rebates, contests and sweepstakes, and overlay and tie-in promotions. The chapter concludes with a three-step procedure for evaluating sales promotion ideas.

Overview of Sales Promotion

RING AROUND THE COMPETITION

ever Brothers, makers of Wisk liquid detergent, needed an exciting sales promotion in 1987 to maintain Wisk's sales in face of intensified competitive pressures. The "Wisk Bright Nights '87" campaign was designed as an integrated sales-promotion and event-marketing effort. The campaign's objectives were to help Wisk keep its number-one position with consumers, to obtain a high-level of retailer support for the brand, and to develop local market goodwill.

Wisk's sales-promotion program was tied in to the first national fireworks tour ever held in the United States. Each show consisted of a 24-minute fireworks display with a special ring-in-the-sky segment symbolizing Wisk's famous "ring around the collar" advertising theme. In addition to the fireworks shows, extensive advertising was undertaken, high-value coupons were distributed via free-standing newspaper inserts, and a sweepstake offered consumers the chance to win a trip to the International Fireworks Competition in Monte Carlo.

Special sales promotions were directed at retailers, who were offered handsome display allowances for devoting special display space to Wisk. Also, Lever Brothers held parties for supermarket buyers and their families at the site of each fireworks show.

The Wisk Bright Nights '87 campaign was the most successful program in Lever Brothers's history. Wisk set new sales records while maintaining its category leadership. Wisk's sales volume went up 5 percent in comparison to the product-category average increase of only 1.5 percent.[1] ∎

An Introduction to Sales Promotion

The opening vignette illustrates the effective use of sales promotion when integrated with other elements of the promotional mix such as event sponsorship and media advertising. The vignette also introduces some terminology you have not previously been exposed to in this text (e.g., free-standing inserts and display allowances). The objective of this chapter and the two chapters that follow is to provide a thorough introduction to the sales-promotion function. You will see how sales promotion complements other elements of the promotion mix along with performing its own unique functions. Sales promotion's role in influencing wholesaler and retailer behavior, on the one hand, and its role in influencing consumer behavior, on the other, are covered in detail in separate chapters.

What Exactly Is Sales Promotion?

From your introductory marketing course and possibly from other courses, you no doubt have at least a general understanding of sales promotion. You probably are a bit uncertain, however, as to *exactly* what it is. Join the crowd! The fact is that sales promotion is a term often used rather indiscriminately to encompass all promotional activities other than advertising, personal selling, or public relations. Evidence of this type of general usage is shown in Table 18.1, which was prepared by *Marketing Communications*, a publication widely read by marketing practitioners.

Table 18.1 contains a list of advertising and so-called sales promotion expenditures by U.S. companies for the years 1985, 1986, and 1987. Note in 1987 that more than $60 billion was invested in various forms of advertising (accounting for 35 percent of total expenditures), whereas purported sales-promotion expenditures amounted to over $111 billion (65 percent of the total). Note further the specific types of expenditures included under sales promotion. Three of the spending categories have been treated as separate chapters in the text—direct mail (11 percent of total expenditures), P-O-P display (6 percent), and telemarketing (11 percent). Also included as a sales-promotion expenditure is "meetings & conventions" (14 percent of total), a category that includes the cost of *sales* meetings and conventions.

These four categories combined represent 42 percent of all advertising and sales promotion, or approximately two-thirds of the 65 percent that supposedly is sales promotion's portion of total expenditures. What is the point of

---

∎ 1. Russ Bowman, "The Envelope, Please," *Marketing & Media Decisions*, April 1988, pp. 130, 132.

Advertising and Promotion Spending, 1985–1987 (in millions)   TABLE 18.1

Advertising	1985	1986	1987	1987% of Grand Total
Television	19,520	21,737	22,709	13%
Radio	6,170	6,602	6,846	4%
Business Publications	2,375	2,382	2,458	a
Consumer Magazines	4,639	4,785	5,046	3%
Newspapers	20,126	20,587	22,059	13%
Farm Publications	186	192	196	a
Outdoor	945	985	1,025	a
Total	**53,961**	**57,270**	**60,339**	**35%**
Sales Promotion				
Direct Mail	15,500	17,145	19,111	11%
P-O-P Display	9,500	10,800	11,800	6%
Premiums & Incentives[b]	12,770	13,140	13,968	8%
Meetings & Conventions	28,400	26,506	24,612	14%
Trade Shows/Exhibits	6,200	6,708	7,258	4%
Prom. Adv. Space	7,403	8,412	9,469	6%
A/V[c]	2,700	2,200	2,500	a
Coupon Redemption	3,588	4,225	4,436	3%
Telemarketing[d]	15,180	16,700	18,370	11%
Total	**101,241**	**105,836**	**111,524**	**65%**
Grand Total: ADV & SP	**155,202**	**163,106**	**171,863**	

[a]Less than 2%

[b]Premiums & Incentives Magazine

[c]T. Hope, The Hope Report

[d]A. Fishman, Marketing Logistics

Source: Nathaniel Frey, "Ninth Annual Advertising & Sales Promotion Report," *Marketing Communications,* August 1988, p. 11. Reprinted with permission.

this? The point is that *these four categories of marketing activities are not sales-promotion elements.* They represent elements of the overall promotion mix, but they are *not* sales-promotion tools.

Sales promotion, unfortunately, means exactly what each user intends it to mean, sometimes more and sometimes less than what others have in mind. The result of this crude usage is that communication suffers. Moreover, statistics concerning sales-promotion expenditures are meaningless when non-sales promotion activities are included. For example, removing the four categories just mentioned from the total assigned to sales promotion in Table 18.1 reveals that sales promotion expenditures in 1987 actually amounted to approximately $38 billion rather than the $111 billion shown in the table.

Sales promotion is undeniably an extremely important component of modern marketing and promotion management. Yet, it is crucial that we know exactly what we are talking about when using the term. The following discussion offers this specification.

In this text, **sales promotion** will be understood to mean the use of any *incentive* by a manufacturer to induce the *trade* (wholesalers and retailers) and/ or *consumers* to buy a product or service; the incentive is *additional to the basic benefits provided* by the product or service and *temporarily changes* the *perceived price or value* of that product or service.[2] *Trade shows* also will be treated as a form of sales promotion, although they are not an incentive in the same sense as other sales promotion tools.

The italicized features require comment. First, by definition, sales promotions involve incentives—that is, a bonus or reward for purchasing one product or brand rather than another. Second, these incentives (e.g., coupons, premiums, display allowances) are additions to, not substitutes for, the basic benefits a purchaser typically acquires when buying a particular product or service. For example, getting 50 cents off the price of a new brand of shampoo would be little consolation if the shampoo failed to work properly. Third, the target of the incentive is the trade, consumers, or both. Finally, the incentive changes a product's or a service's perceived price/value, but only temporarily. This is to say that a sales-promotion incentive for a particular brand applies to a single purchase or perhaps several purchases during a period, but not to every purchase a consumer would make over an extended period.

The Targets of Sales Promotion

To more fully appreciate the role of sales promotion, consider the *promotional imperatives* faced by the brand management for a consumer packaged good— for example, Wisk liquid detergent that was highlighted in the opening vignette. For this brand to meet its marketing objectives (sales volume, market share, etc.), several things must happen (see Figure 18.1): First, Lever Brothers' *sales force* has to enthusiastically and aggressively sell the product to the trade. Second, *retailers* have to be encouraged to allocate sufficient shelf space to the product and provide merchandising support to enable Wisk to stand out from competitive brands. Third, *consumers* need reasons for selecting Wisk rather than competitive brands.

All three groups are targets of sales-promotion efforts. Allowances and advertising-support programs encourage retailers to stock and promote a particular brand. Coupons, samples, premiums, cents-off deals, and other incentives encourage consumers to purchase a brand on a trial or repeat basis. Trade- and consumer-oriented sales promotions also provide salespeople with

---

2. This definition combines thoughts from two sources: Roger A. Strang, "Sales Promotion Research: Contributions and Issues," unpublished paper presented at the AMA/MSI/PMAA Sales Promotion Workshop, Babson College, May 1983; and James H. Naber in his James Webb Young address at the University of Illinois, Urbana-Champaign, IL, October 21, 1986.

the necessary tools for aggressively and enthusiastically selling to wholesale and retail buyers.

The Shift from Pull to Push Marketing and from Advertising to Sales Promotion

Advertising spending as a percentage of total promotional expenditures has declined in recent years, while sales promotion, direct marketing, telemarketing, and other forms of promotion have increased. This can be seen vividly in Figure 18.2, which shows promotion/advertising splits of 58 percent/42 percent, 62 percent/38 percent, and 65 percent/35 percent for 1977, 1982, and 1987.[3]

Reasons for the Shift

A variety of factors account for the shift in the allocation of advertising budgets away from advertising toward sales promotion and other nonadvertising promotions. To understand the underlying reasons, it will be beneficial to review briefly the concepts of push and pull marketing strategies.

Push and Pull Strategies.   As noted back in Chapter 8, the concepts of push and pull are physical metaphors that characterize the promotional activities manufacturers undertake to encourage channel members (the trade) to handle products. **Push** implies a forward thrust of effort whereby a

3. These figures are based on Nathaniel Frey, "Ninth Annual Advertising & Sales Promotion Report," *Marketing Communications*, August 1988, p. 11. As discussed previously, the nonadvertising portion includes expenditures from four categories of promotional activities (e.g., direct mail) that are not considered sales promotion per se.

FIGURE 18.2   **Split of Advertising vs. Promotion Budgets**

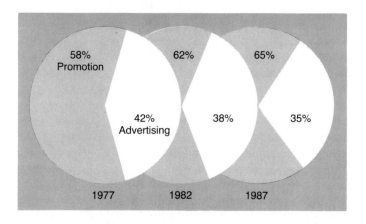

Source: Nathaniel Frey, "Ninth Annual Advertising & Sales Promotion Report," *Marketing Communications,* August 1988, p. 11. Reprinted with permission.

manufacturer directs personal selling, trade advertising, and trade-oriented sales promotion to wholesalers and retailers. **Pull** suggests a backward tug from consumers to retailers. This tug, or pull, is the result of a manufacturer's successful advertising and sales-promotion efforts directed at the consumer. Successful marketing involves a combination of forces: exerting push to the trade and creating pull from consumers.

Table 18.2 illustrates the differences between push-and pull-oriented promotional strategies based on two companies' allocations of $20 million among different promotional activities. Company A emphasizes a *push strategy* by allocating most of its promotional budget to personal selling and sales promo-

TABLE 18.2   **Push versus Pull Promotional Strategies**

	Company A (Push)	Company B (Pull)
Advertising to Consumers	$1,200,000	$13,700,000
Advertising to Retailers	1,600,000	200,000
Personal Selling to Retailers	9,000,000	4,000,000
Sales Promotion to Consumers	200,000	2,000,000
Sales Promotion to Retailers	8,000,000	100,000
Total	$20,000,000	$20,000,000

Source: Arnold M. Barban, Steven M. Cristol, and Frank J. Kopec, *Essentials of Media Planning: A Marketing Viewpoint* (Lincolnwood, IL: NTC Business Books, 1987), p. 15.

tions that are aimed at retail customers. Company B, on the other hand, utilizes a *pulling strategy* by investing the vast majority of its budget in advertising to ultimate consumers.

It should be clear that pushing and pulling are *not* mutually exclusive. Both efforts occur simultaneously. Manufacturers promote both to consumers (creating pull) and to trade members (accomplishing push). The issue is not which strategy to use, but rather, which to emphasize. Historically, at least through the early 1970s, the emphasis in consumer packaged-goods marketing was on promotional *pull* (such as Company B's budget). Manufacturers advertised heavily, especially on network television, and literally forced retailers to handle their products by virtue of the fact that consumers demanded heavily advertised brands. However, over the past 15 years or so, pull-oriented marketing has become less effective. Along with this reduced effectiveness has come an increase in the use of push-oriented sales promotion practices (such as company A's budget).[4]

Increased investment in sales promotion, *especially trade-oriented sales promotion*, has gone hand-in-hand with the growth in push marketing. Major developments that have given rise to sales promotion follow.

Balance of Power Transfer. Until recently, national manufacturers of consumer packaged goods generally were more powerful and influential than the supermarket and drug store retailers that merchandised their offerings. The reason was twofold. First, manufacturers were able to create consumer pull by virtue of heavy network-television advertising, thus effectively requiring retailers to handle their brands whether retailers wanted to or not. Second, retailers did little research of their own and, accordingly, were dependent on manufacturers for information such as whether a new product would be successful. A manufacturer's sales representative could convince a buyer to carry a new product using test-market results suggesting a successful product introduction.

The balance of power began shifting when *network television dipped in power* as an advertising medium and, especially, with the advent of *optical scanning equipment.* Armed with a steady flow of data from optical scanners, retailers now know immediately which products are selling, which advertising and sales promotion programs are working, and so on. Retailers no longer need to depend on manufacturers for "facts." Retailers possess the facts. They demand terms of sale rather than merely accepting manufacturers' terms. The consequence for manufacturers is that for every promotional dollar used to support retailers' advertising or merchandising programs, one less dollar is available for the manufacturer's own advertising.

---

4. Alvin A. Achenbaum and F. Kent Mitchel, "Pulling Away from Push Marketing," *Harvard Business Review*, vol. 65, May-June 1987, pp. 38–40; Robert J. Kopp and Stephen A. Greyser, "Packaged Goods Marketing—'Pull' Companies Look to Improved 'Push'," *The Journal of Consumer Marketing*, vol. 4 (Spring 1987), pp. 13–22; F. Kent Mitchel, "Strategic Use of A&P," *Marketing Communications*, April 1986, pp. 34–36.

Increased Brand Parity and Price Sensitivity.   In earlier years when truly new products were being offered to the marketplace, manufacturers could effectively advertise unique advantages over competitive offerings. As product categories have matured, however, there are now more similarities between brands than there are differences. With fewer distinct product differences, consumers have grown more reliant on price and price incentives (coupons, cents-off deals, refunds, etc.) as a way of differentiating alternative parity brands.[5] Because real, concrete advantages are often difficult to obtain, more firms have turned to sales promotion to achieve at least temporary advantages over competitors.

Reduced Brand Loyalty.   Consumers are not as brand loyal as they once were, possibly because brands have grown increasingly similar. A consequence is that many consumers are willing to switch from brand to brand; sales promotion is an effective way to induce switching.

Splintering of the Mass Market and Reduced Media Effectiveness.   Advertising efficiency is directly related to the degree of market homogeneity. The more homogeneous consumers' consumption needs and media habits are, the less costly it is for mass advertising to reach them. As consumer lifestyles have become more diverse and advertising media have become more narrow in their appeal, mass-media advertising is no longer as efficient as it once was. On top of this, advertising effectiveness has declined with increases in ad clutter. These combined forces have influenced many brand managers to turn to sales promotion. Moreover, rapidly escalating media costs, particularly for network television, have led many executives to reduce advertising expenditures and to devote proportionately larger budgets to sales promotions, which often are more cost effective.

Short-Term Orientation and Corporate Reward Structures.   Although several large companies have recently turned to regionalized organizational structures and category-management systems (see Chapter 8), the brand-management structure remains dominant in U.S. packaged-goods firms. The brand-management system and sales promotion are perfect partners. The reward structure in firms organized along brand-manager lines emphasizes short-term sales response rather than slow, long-term growth. Sales promotion is incomparable when it comes to generating quick sales response.

Consumer Responsiveness.   A final force that explains the shift toward sales promotion at the expense of advertising is that consumers respond favorably to money-saving opportunities. A recent national survey of more than 7,500 households revealed that over 90 percent of consumers had taken

---

5. Bud Frankel and J. W. Phillips, "Escaping the Parity Trap," *Marketing Communications*, November 1986, pp. 93–100.

advantage of some form of promotion in the past month. Coupons in particular have nearly universal acceptance with 83 percent of respondents acknowledging that coupons increase shopping value.[6]

Allocating the Promotion Budget between Advertising and Sales Promotion

In all likelihood, sales promotion will continue to grow. However, excessive promotional activity may damage a product's image, diminish brand loyalty, and possibly even reduce consumption.[7] The important point, stressed throughout the text, is that no single promotional tool is a cure-all; rather, the various promotional tools must be blended together intelligently without inordinate emphasis on any one.

Advertising and sales promotion both play important roles in most companies' promotional mixes. What determines which receives greater budgetary support? A study based on interviews with marketing executives who represent a variety of grocery, personal care, toiletry, and household products determined that:

1. Advertising plays a dominant role in the promotional mixes of *more profitable brands*.

2. *Premium-priced brands* place greater reliance on advertising.

3. *Low-growth brands* place greater emphasis on sales promotion.

These findings taken together suggest that managers of successful brands support success with advertising, while managers who desire greater success (i.e., faster growth, larger market shares, etc.) attempt to achieve it with relatively greater emphasis on sales promotion.[8]

In addition to the preceding results, several environmental factors also influence the sales promotion versus advertising allocation decision (see Table 18.3). The executives interviewed consider *product life-cycle stage* to be the single most important consideration in their allocation decisions. Advertising is more critical in the introductory and growth stages (in order to create consumer awareness and establish a brand's image), whereas sales promotion dominates the promotional mix in later stages (to ensure repeat purchasing). In addition, sales promotion is considered more important (1) for *regional brands* that cannot afford to compete in advertising against dominant national brands, (2) when *competitors emphasize sales promotion* over advertising, and (3) when a brand is especially *vulnerable to losing retail distribution*. In comparison, advertising receives a larger share of the promotional budget for (1) *highly differentiated prod-*

6. Scott Hume, "Coupons Score with Consumers," *Advertising Age*, February 15, 1988, p. 40.
7. Roger A. Strang, *The Promotional Planning Process* (New York: Praeger Publishers, 1980), p. 7.
8. Strang, *The Promotional Planning Process*.

TABLE 18.3   **Major Environmental Determinants of the Advertising versus Sales-Promotion Allocation Decision**

	Impact on Allocation	
Factor	Increase Advertising	Increase Sales Promotion
Stage in brand life cycle		
Introduction	X	
Growth	X	
Maturity		X
Decline		X
Regional brand		X
Market dominance	X	
Promotion-oriented competitor		X
Advertising-oriented competitor	X	
High differentiation	X	
High purchase frequency	X	
Distribution vulnerability		X

Source: Roger A. Strang, *The Promotional Planning Process* (New York: Praeger Publishers, 1980), p. 94.

ucts, (2) products with *high purchase frequencies,* and (3) in situations where *competitors emphasize advertising.*[9]

It should be apparent that the allocation of the promotional mix between advertising and sales promotion varies from situation to situation; there is no best solution in general. Rather, the best allocation depends on the specific conditions a brand encounters in the marketplace. Generally speaking, *sales promotion takes on added importance for more mature product categories where competition is intense and both the trade and consumers have various suitable options from which to choose.*

What Sales Promotion Can and Cannot Do

As established throughout the text, every promotion-mix element is capable of accomplishing certain objectives and not others. Sales promotion is well suited for accomplishing certain tasks but incapable of achieving others.[10] It is instructive to examine first the tasks that sales promotion cannot accomplish.

9. Ibid.
10. The discussion is guided by Charles Fredericks, Jr., "What Ogilvy & Mather Has Learned About Sales Promotion," *The Tools of Promotion* (New York: Association of National Advertisers, 1975), and Don E. Schultz and William A. Robinson, *Sales Promotion Management* (Lincolnwood, IL: NTC Business Books, 1986), Chapter 3.

Tasks Sales Promotion Cannot Accomplish

Sales promotion *cannot* . . .

Compensate for a Poorly Trained Sales Force or for a Lack of Advertising.
When suffering from poor sales performance or inadequate growth, some companies consider sales promotion to be the solution. However, sales promotion will provide at best a temporary "fix" if the underlying problem is due to a poor sales force, a lack of brand awareness, a weak brand image, or other maladies that only proper sales management and advertising efforts can overcome.

Give the Trade or Consumers any Compelling Long-Term Reason to Continue Purchasing a Brand.
The trade's decision to continue stocking a brand and consumers' decision to repeat purchase are based on continued satisfaction with the brand. Satisfaction results from the brand's meeting profit objectives (for the trade) and fulfilling benefits (for consumers). Sales promotion cannot compensate for a fundamentally flawed or mediocre product.

Permanently Stop an Established Product's Declining Sales Trend or Change the Basic Nonacceptance of an Undesired Product.
Declining sales over an extended period indicate poor product performance or the availability of a superior alternative. Sales promotion cannot reverse the basic nonacceptance of an undesired product. A declining sales trend can be reversed only through product improvements or perhaps an advertising campaign that breathes new life into an aging product. Sales promotion used *in combination* with advertising effort or product improvements may reverse the trend, but sales promotion by itself is a waste.

Tasks Sales Promotion Can Accomplish

Sales promotion cannot work wonders, but it is ideally suited to accomplishing various tasks. Specifically, sales promotion *can* . . .

Stimulate Sales-Force Enthusiasm for a New, Improved, or Mature Product.
There are many exciting and challenging aspects of personal selling; there also are times when the job can become dull, monotonous, and unrewarding. For example, imagine what it would be like to repeatedly call on a customer if you never had anything new or different to say about your products or the marketing efforts supporting your products. Maintaining enthusiasm would be difficult, to say the least. Exciting sales promotions give salespeople extra ammunition to use when interacting with buyers; they revive enthusiasm and make the salesperson's job easier and more enjoyable.

FOCUS ON PROMOTION

A Shot in the Arm for Cap'n Crunch

Cap'n Crunch—Quaker Oats's leading cereal—is the number two presweetened cereal behind Kellogg's Frosted Flakes. After nearly a quarter of a century on the market, Cap'n Crunch dropped from a 3.2 percent market share to a 2.8 percent share in less than two years—a loss of over $16 million in annual sales in the $4.1 billion ready-to-eat-cereal business.

A major promotional effort was needed to invigorate sales. The promotional objective was to increase brand interest among children between the ages of 6 and 12 and encourage repeat purchasing. The "Find the Cap'n" sales promotion game was developed. Cap'n Horatio Crunch's picture was temporarily dropped from the cereal package; in his place appeared the question "Where's the Cap'n?" Package directions informed children (and also parents, no doubt) that they could share in a $1 million reward for finding the Cap'n. Consumers had to buy three boxes of Cap'n Crunch to get clues to Horatio Crunch's whereabouts. At the game's end, ten thousand children's names were drawn from the pool of thousands of correct answers, and each child received $100.

The "Find the Cap'n" promotion involved heavy television and magazine advertising along with the sales-promotion effort. In addition to the cash giveaway, coupons and cents-off deals were used to stimulate consumer purchasing.

The result: an incredible 50 percent increase in sales during the promotion.[11] ∎

Invigorate Sales of a Mature Product. As mentioned earlier, sales promotion cannot reverse the sales decline for an undesirable product. However, sales promotion can invigorate sales of a mature product that remains desirable but needs a boost. A case in point is Quaker Oats's efforts with Cap'n Crunch as described in the *Focus on Promotion* section.

Facilitate the Introduction of New Products to the Trade. Sales promotions to wholesalers and retailers are often necessary to encourage the trade to handle new products. In fact, many retailers refuse to carry new products unless they receive extra compensation. One such practice is the use of *slotting allowances*, which require a manufacturer to pay a retailer simply for the privi-

---

11. "Quaker Oats Finds Cap'n Crunch Loot with Hide-and-Seek," *Advertising Age*, May 26, 1986, p. 53.

lege of opening a new slot in the retailer's warehouse. The following chapter discusses slotting allowances in detail.

Increase On- and Off-Shelf Merchandising Space.   Trade-oriented sales promotions (such as the display allowance for Wisk liquid detergent described in the chapter's opening vignette) enable a manufacturer to obtain extra shelf space for a temporary period. This space may be in the form of extra *facings* on the shelf or off-shelf space in a gondola or end-aisle display.[12]

Reinforce Advertising.   An advertising campaign can be strengthened greatly by a well-coordinated sales promotion effort. The Cap'n Crunch example illustrates this feature of sales promotion. Quaker Oats would not have been nearly as successful at increasing sales had the company used only advertising to enhance consumer interest in the Cap'n Crunch name.

Neutralize Competitive Advertising and Sales Promotion.   Sales promotions are used to offset competitors' advertising and sales-promotion efforts. For example, one company's 25 cents-off coupon loses much of its appeal when a competitor comes out simultaneously with a 40 cents-off coupon.

Obtain Trial Purchases from Consumers.   Manufacturers use samples, coupons, and other sales promotions to encourage *trial purchases* of new products. Many consumers would never try new products without these promotional inducements.

Hold Current Users by Encouraging Repeat Purchases.   Brand switching is a fact of life faced by all brand managers. The strategic use of certain forms of sales promotion can encourage at least short-run repetitive purchasing. Cap'n Crunch's program is a case in point. More generally, premium programs, refunds, and various other devices (discussed in Chapter 20) are used to encourage repeat purchasing.

Increase Product Usage by Loading Consumers.   Consumers tend to use more of certain products (e.g., snack foods and soft drinks) the more they have available in their homes. Thus, sales-promotion efforts that *load* consumers generate greater product usage temporarily. Bonus packs and two-for-the-price-of-one deals are particularly effective loading devices.

Preempt Competition by Loading Consumers.   When consumers are loaded with one company's brand, they are temporarily out of the marketplace

12. In retailer terminology, a facing is a row of shelf space. Brands within a product category are typically allocated facings proportionate to their profit potential to the retailer. Manufacturers must pay for extra facings by offering display allowances or other inducements that increase the retailer's profit.

for competitive brands. Hence, one brand's sales promotion serves to preempt sales of competitive brands.

The can-do capabilities of trade- and consumer-oriented sales promotions have been described briefly. The next two chapters will elaborate on these objectives as well as on the specific sales-promotion methods that accomplish them.

When Is Sales Promotion Profitable?

A brand's *sales volume* is almost always increased during the period of a sales promotion. However, not all sales promotions are profitable. Whether or not a particular sales promotion is profitable depends on the composition of consumers in the product category. For example, if all consumers are *insensitive* to promotional deals, sales promotions are necessarily unprofitable. This is because per-unit profit margin is reduced during a sales promotion and no additional sales volume is realized to offset the reduction in profit margin.[13] In general, whether a sales-promotion deal is profitable depends on the types of consumers that comprise a product's market. The ensuing discussion describes various types of consumers based on their responsiveness to deals and explains the profit implications associated with each.

Consumer Responsiveness to Sales-Promotion Deals

The market for any product category is made up of consumers who differ in their responsiveness to *deals*.[14] Some consumers are loyal to a single brand in a category and buy only that brand. Other consumers have absolutely no brand loyalty and will purchase any brand so long as it is on deal. Most consumers lie somewhere between these extremes. Figure 18.3 presents a framework showing various segments of consumers in terms of their deal proneness. Each segment will be described and then the matter of when sales promotion is profitable will be addressed.[15]

As shown in Figure 18.3, a brand's market can be segmented into eight groups based on their responsiveness to deals. The most general distinction is between consumers who purchase *only when a brand is on deal* (Segment 8) and consumers who do *not* restrict their purchasing to times when a product is on

---

13. You probably recall the accounting concept of *contribution margin,* or simply *margin,* which is a brand's per-unit selling price minus its variable cost. When a brand is on a promotional deal, its price typically remains constant but its variable cost increases due to the promotional expense. The result, of course, is a reduction in margin.
14. The term **deal** refers to any form of sales promotion that delivers a *price reduction* to consumers. *Coupons* and *cents-off offers* are the most frequent forms of deals.
15. The following discussion is based on the work of Leigh McAlister, "Continued Research into Sales Promotion: Product Line Management Issues," a research report and proposal prepared for the Marketing Science Institute and other sponsors (circa 1986); also, Leigh McAlister, "A Model of Consumer Behavior," *Marketing Communications,* April 1987, pp. 27–30.

A Segmentation Model of Consumer Response to Sales-Promotion Deals

FIGURE 18.3

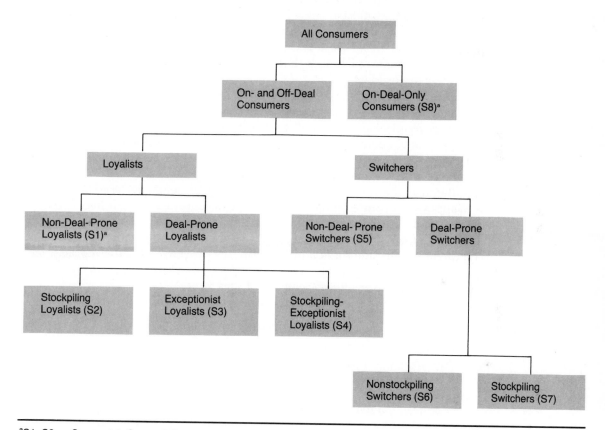

[a]S1–S8 = Segment 1–Segment 8.

Source: Adapted from Leigh McAlister, "Continued Research into Sales Promotion: Product Line Management Issues," A Research Report and Proposal Prepared for the Marketing Science Institute and Other Sponsors (circa 1986). Adapted with permission.

deal. This latter general category can be delineated into seven specific segments. *Loyalists* are consumers who buy only a single brand when no deal is offered (i.e., when the category is off promotion). *Switchers* buy any of several brands when all brands are off promotion. Loyalists and switchers are further classified based on how they respond to sales promotions.

Loyalist consumers are either non-deal prone or deal prone. *Non-deal-prone loyalists* (Segment 1) are consumers who buy a single brand and are not influenced by deals. Most brands today have relatively few consumers who are non-deal-prone loyalists. On the other hand, *deal-prone loyalists* come in three varieties: *Stockpiling loyalists* (Segment 2) purchase only the single brand to which they are loyal but take advantage of savings by stockpiling when that brand is on deal (e.g., buying three instead of the customary one box of their favored cereal when a 35 cents-off deal is offered). *Exceptionist loyalists* (Segment 3), though loyal to a single brand when all brands in the category are *off deal*, will make an exception and purchase a nonprefered brand when it is on deal. *Stockpiling-exceptionist loyalists* (Segment 4) not only make exceptions by choosing nonpreferred brands but also stockpile quantities of other brands when they are on deal.

Switcher consumers, like loyalists, also can be delineated as *non-deal-prone* (Segment 5) or deal-prone switchers. *Deal-prone switchers* break into two groups: *Nonstockpiling switchers* (Segment 6) are responsive to deals but do not purchase extra quantities when any of their acceptable brands are on deal. *Stockpiling switchers* (Segment 7) exploit deal opportunities by purchasing multiple units when any acceptable brand is on deal.

Because several of the loyalist and switcher segments are conceptually overlapping, we can eliminate any further need to distinguish between Segments 1 and 5, Segments 3 and 6, and Segments 4 and 7. The remaining five categories of consumers are based on how they respond to sales promotions. The categories include the following:

1. Promotion Insensitives (Segments 1 and 5)
2. Stockpiling Loyalists (Segment 2)
3. Nonstockpiling Promotion Sensitives (Segments 3 and 6)
4. Stockpiling Promotion Sensitives (Segments 4 and 7)
5. On-Deal-Only Consumers (Segment 8)

Profit Implications for Each Consumer Category

You now have some intuitive idea as to why profitability from promotional deals varies across each of the five groups. The following sections offer specific explanations. All explanations are in reference to a hypothetical brand of shampoo called, disingenuously, "HairRelief." (For the moment, return to Figure 18.3 and identify which segment of the shampoo market you belong to on the basis of your responsiveness, or lack of responsiveness, to deals in this category.)

Promotion Insensitives.   For shampoo consumers who are insensitive to promotional deals, HairRelief would find the use of deals *unprofitable*. The reason for this is depicted in Figure 18.4, which portrays the sales pattern that would result from a market made up entirely of promotion insensitives. Because, by definition, these consumers will not alter their purchase behavior in response to HairRelief's promotional deal, the result would be the same

Promotion Insensitives' Deal Responsiveness   FIGURE 18.4

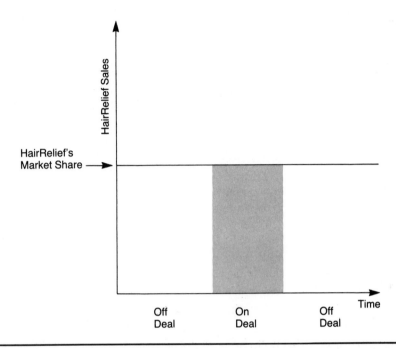

Source: Adapted from Leigh McAlister, "Continued Research into Sales Promotion: Product Line Management Issues," A Research Report and Proposal Prepared for the Marketing Science Institute and Other Sponsors (circa 1986), p. 7. Adapted with permission.

number of units sold that would have been sold without the promotion *but at a lower profit margin.* The total amount of loss from the sales promotion would equal the number of units sold when HairRelief is on deal times the cost per unit of running the deal.

Stockpiling Loyalists.   A subsegment of shampoo purchasers are loyal to a single brand and will stockpile quantities of that brand when it is on deal. It would be *unprofitable* for HairRelief to use a deal if the shampoo market were made up entirely of stockpiling loyalists. The reason is shown in Figure 18.5. Note first that *sales depression* results from HairRelief's own sales promotions when the brand is off deal. In other words, during off-deal periods sales are below the brand's regular market share because consumers who stockpiled in response to past promotions have no need to now purchase HairRelief at its regular, non-deal price. When HairRelief *is* on deal, sales bump up considerably because stockpiling loyalists avail themselves of the deal (see Figure 18.5).

▰▰

FIGURE 18.5   **Stockpiling Loyalists' Deal Responsiveness**

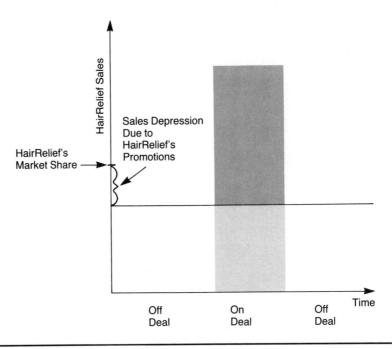

Source: Adapted from Leigh McAlister, "Continued Research into Sales Promotion: Product Line Management Issues," A Research Report and Proposal Prepared for the Marketing Science Institute and Other Sponsors (circa 1986), p. 7. Adapted with permission.

As a result, when HairRelief is on deal it is simply *borrowing from future sales*. The promotion results in a sales bump, but it is unprofitable for two reasons: (1) sales made when HairRelief is on deal are made at a lower profit margin, and (2) when HairRelief is off deal, fewer sales are made at the full margin.

Nonstockpiling Promotion Sensitives.   This segment consists of loyalists and switchers who *take advantage of promotional deals but do not stockpile*. In terms of shampoo purchasing, these consumers will *switch* among several brands of acceptable shampoos depending on which brand is on deal on any particular shopping occasion. They do not choose to stockpile, however. This segment represents a large percentage of consumers in many product categories. For example, one study determined that increases in coffee sales from promotions were due almost entirely to brand switching (84 percent) rather than from accelerated purchasing (14 percent) or stockpiling (2 percent).[16]

16. Sumil Gupta, "Impact of Sales Promotion on When, What, and How Much to Buy," *Journal of Marketing Research*, vol. 25 (November 1988) pp. 342–355.

How profitable would a promotional offering by HairRelief be if the market for shampoo consisted entirely of consumers who switch among shampooo brands but do not stockpile? Figure 18.6 displays this situation. As in the case of stockpiling loyalists, a sales depression exists between HairRelief's market share and its non-deal, or baseline, sales level. However, in the present case the depression is *due entirely to competitive promotions*. When HairRelief is on deal its sales are bumped up measurably over the baseline level. This, of course, is due to capturing purchases from consumers who have switched from competitive shampoo brands.

HairRelief's sales during the promotional period are made at a margin M_P, which stands for the profit margin per unit during the promotion period. If HairRelief did *not* promote, its sales volume would remain at a level equal to the light gray portion in Figure 18.6 (labeled S_N). These sales would have been made at a margin M_N. (HairRelief's profit margin is, of course, greater when it is *not* on promotion compared to when it is; i.e., $M_N > M_P$.) Total sales due to the deal are shown in Figure 18.6 by S_P, which includes incremental sales from the promotion (darker gray area) plus regular nonpromotional sales (S_N).

Nonstockpiling Promotion Sensitives' Deal Responsiveness   FIGURE 18.6

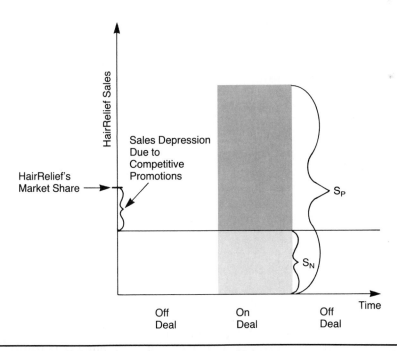

Source: Adapted from Leigh McAlister, "Continued Research into Sales Promotion: Product Line Management Issues," A Research Report and Proposal Prepared for the Marketing Science Institute and Other Sponsors (circa 1986), p. 7. Adapted with permission.

Let us define R as the ratio of sales volume when HairRelief is on deal to when it is not on deal (i.e., R equals the ratio of S_P to S_N). We conclude that it will be *profitable* to put HairRelief on deal only if $(R \times M_P) > M_N$. An example will clarify the point. Assume HairRelief's sales volume (S_N) is 2,000,000 units when it is *off deal* and its profit margin (M_N) is 25 cents. *On deal* assume that HairRelief's sales volume (S_P) increases to 4,200,000 units at a reduced profit margin (M_P) of 15 cents. In this case, R equals 2.1 (i.e., 4,200,000/2,000,000). Hence, it would be profitable to promote HairRelief because $R \times M_P$ is greater than M_N; that is, $2.1 \times 15 = 31.5 > 25$.

Stockpiling Promotion Sensitives.   This segment switches among brands depending on which is on deal and stockpiles extra quantities when an attractive deal is located. In this case, HairRelief's baseline sales are depressed both by its own dealing activity *and* by competitive dealing. If HairRelief's dealing activity is profitable when consumers do not stockpile (i.e., the situation in the previous case), then stockpiling behavior will lead to even greater profitability. This is because HairRelief will profit both by taking consumers away from competitors during the period HairRelief is on deal *and* by preempting competitors' sales in subsequent off-deal periods when consumers are "working off" their stockpiles of HairRelief.

On-Deal-Only Consumers.   Because, by definition, HairRelief makes no sales to these consumers *unless it is on deal*, it follows that promotions to a market made up exclusively of on-deal-only consumers will be *profitable*. The total amount of profit would equal the number of units sold (Q) times the profit margin when the brand is on deal (M_P).

In Conclusion

The discussion to this point has provided several guidelines regarding sales promotion.

1.   Putting a brand on deal is *unprofitable* if the market is composed of either promotion-insensitive consumers or stockpiling loyalists.
2.   Putting a brand on deal *may or may not be profitable* if the market consists of nonstockpiling or stockpiling promotion-sensitive consumers.
3.   Putting a brand on deal is *profitable* if the market contains on-deal-only consumers.

The preceding statements are based on the assumption that a brand's market consists exclusively of one or another type of consumer—for example, promotion insensitives or stockpiling loyalists. This obviously is an untenable assumption. The market for any product (such as our illustrative shampoo brand, HairRelief) contains consumers from all segments. The matter of whether promotion is profitable or not thus depends on the *relative composition* of customer types.

Fortunately, the availability of scanner data makes it possible for researchers to identify the percentage of consumers who fall into each of the categories that were just described.[17] Armed with this information, brand managers can determine whether dealing activity is profitable or whether it merely results in a revenue-increasing but profit-losing endeavor.

Sales-Promotion Planning

Business practice requires that systematic planning precede decision making. In the past, sales promotion often suffered from informal, seat-of-the-pants decision making. Significant changes are taking place, however, and a notable trend toward professional planning is occurring.[18] Planning is essential for successful sales-promotion campaigns. Figure 18.7 depicts the fundamental elements of a formal sales-promotion planning process.[19] The following discussion describes the elements in the planning process and illustrates their application with HairRelief.

The first step, *environmental analysis,* includes the dual activities of performing a situation analysis and, from the information generated, identifying the problems and opportunities facing the target brand (HairRelief in this case). The output of such an analysis is a determination of the possibilities of using sales promotion in view of the identified problems and opportunities confronting the brand. For example, the brand manager of HairRelief might determine that brand sales are declining because two competitors have launched major advertising and sales-promotion campaigns. This may suggest an opportunity for creative sales-promotion activity (perhaps an attractive coupon offer along with an exciting sweepstakes) to neutralize competitive efforts.

The next step, *internal analysis,* involves an assessment of the firm's promotional philosophy and an evaluation of sales promotion's role in the brand's marketing mix. Management may decide that sales promotion's proper role is to complement advertising effort but not attempt to replace advertising. Regardless of the specific determination, a formal evaluation of the specific role that sales promotion should have in the overall marketing mix is a valuable exercise.

17. If you are wondering how this is possible, spend a little time reviewing the discussion back in Chapter 14 on the role of services such as Adtel and BehaviorScan (see pp. 427–428). Basically, these research services make it possible to trace panel households' purchase patterns over an extended time period. Hence, users of each product category can be classified as loyalists, switchers, stockpilers, and so on.
18. William A. Robinson, "Plan to Avoid Wheel-Spinning," *Advertising Age,* November 8, 1982, p. M-50.
19. This figure combines ideas from Bud Frankel, "Sales Promotion Is Marketing Giant, But It's Misunderstood, Underestimated, and Mishandled," *Marketing News,* October 7, 1977, p. 6; Robinson, ibid.; and Tony Spaeth, "Planning Matrix Gives Boost to Today's Promotion," *Advertising Age,* October 3, 1977, pp. P-2–P-4.

FIGURE 18.7   **Sales-Promotion Planning Process**

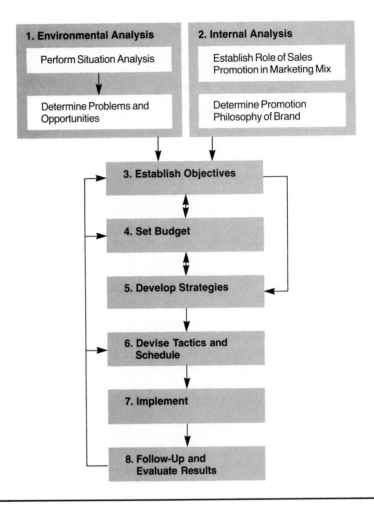

The two background analyses, environmental and internal analyses, lead to the all-important third step, the *establishment of objectives*, or motives, for the contemplated sales-promotion campaign. Both trade- and consumer-oriented objectives need to be established for HairRelief's anticipated promotional activities. At the trade level, the objective may be to encourage greater shelf space or advertising activity by retailers. At the consumer level, the objective may be to generate trial purchases, establish repeat purchase behavior, preempt competition, or something else. It is critical that the specific objective(s) be established at the early stages of the planning process. The choice of objective(s) will determine the specific form of sales promotion that is ultimately implemented.

The fourth step involves *setting the budget*, or means, for the proposed campaign. The budget and objectives are interdependent, as indicated by the two-headed arrow in Figure 18.7. That is, program objectives determine how much money will be needed to accomplish desired goals in promoting Hair-Relief, yet budgetary restrictions impose limits as to how grandiose the objectives can be.

The *development of strategies*, step five, follows from the budgetary and objective-setting activities. At this point, the planner must determine which sales promotion technique or combination of techniques will accomplish the designated objectives. Suppose the objective is to neutralize competitive promotional efforts and to encourage consumers of competitive brands to try HairRelief. Strategic opinions include coupons, price-offs, refunds, and samples. The strategist must decide which of these is best suited to the task at hand in light of budgetary restrictions. Once the strategy is formulated, management often must reevaluate and perhaps revise the proposed budget (as indicated by the double-headed arrow in Figure 18.7).

Steps six and seven represent the detailed, operational aspects of promotion planning: *devising tactics, setting the time schedule,* and *implementing* the campaign. Here, creativity is essential. It is also important to time the program to coordinate with advertising campaigns, to tie in with sales force incentive compensation, and to be compatible with retailers' requirements. The challenge is to devise delivery instruments (for instance, coupons or samples) that can break through the tremendous competitive clutter, attract consumer attention, and produce the desired response.

The final activity in formal sales-promotion planning, *follow-up and evaluation of results,* is a continuing process that involves comparing results with objectives, evaluating whether or not the program was accomplished within budget, and determining whether the schedule was followed as closely as possible. This information provides a measure of performance, which is useful in the evaluation of personnel responsible for the execution of the program.

Because the purpose of sales promotion is to provide a short-term incentive to buy, the only valid basis for evaluating the success or failure of a promotional undertaking is sales.[20] Evaluation can be accomplished by comparing sales volume during the promotion to sales from a comparable previous period or comparing sales after the promotion to before-promotion sales.

Summary

The topic of sales promotion is introduced in this first of three chapters devoted to the topic. The precise nature of sales promotion is described, and specific forms of trade- and consumer-oriented sales promotion are discussed. Sales promotion is explained as having three targets: the trade (wholesalers and retailers), consumers, and a company's own sales force.

20. Schultz and Robinson, *Sales Promotion Management.*

The chapter proceeds to explain the reasons underlying a significant trend in U.S. marketing toward greater sales promotion in comparison with advertising. This shift is part of the movement from pull- to push-oriented strategies. Underlying factors include a balance-of-power transfer from manufacturers to retailers, increased brand parity and growing price sensitivity, reduced brand loyalty, splintering of the mass market and reduced media effectiveness, a growing short-term orientation, and favorable consumer responsiveness to sales promotions.

The specific tasks that sales promotion can and cannot accomplish are discussed. For example, sales promotion cannot give the trade or consumers compelling long-term reasons to purchase. However, it is ideally suited to generating trial-purchase behavior, facilitating the introduction of new products, gaining shelf space for a brand, encouraging repeat purchasing, and performing a variety of other tasks.

Detailed discussion is devoted to the conditions under which sales promotion is profitable. Various segments of consumers based on their responsiveness to promotional deals are described. It is concluded that sales promotion is unprofitable if a brand's market is composed of promotion insensitive or brand-loyal stockpilers; sales promotion is always profitable if the market contains consumers who buy only on deal; and sales promotion may be profitable if the market consists primarily of consumers who switch from brand to brand depending on which brand is on deal.

The chapter concludes with a discussion of an eight-step, formalized sales-promotion process. The following chapter picks up with a detailed treatment of sales promotion's role in influencing trade behavior, while Chapter 20 examines its role in influencing the behavior of ultimate consumers.

Discussion Questions

1. The term *promotional inducement* has been suggested as an alternative to sales promotion. Explain why this new term is more descriptive than the established term.

2. Describe the factors that have accounted for sales promotion's rapid growth. Do you expect sales promotion to continue to grow over the next ten years?

3. Explain in your own words the meaning of push- versus pull-oriented promotional strategies. Using a well-known supermarket brand of your choice for illustration, explain which elements of this brand's promotion mix embody push and which embody pull.

4. Assume you are the vice-president of marketing for a large, well-known manufacturer of consumer packaged goods (e.g., Procter & Gamble, Lever Brothers, Johnson & Johnson). What steps might you take to restore a balance of power favoring your company in its relations with retailers?

5. Are sales promotions able to reverse a brand's temporary sales decline and/or a permanent sales decline? Be specific.

6.   The allocation of promotional dollars to advertising and sales promotion is influenced by a variety of factors, including life-cycle stage, the degree of brand differentiation, and the degree of brand dominance. Explain how these factors influence the allocation decision.

7.   How can sales-promotion techniques generate enthusiasm and stimulate improved performance from the sales force?

8.   Offer a specific explanation of why you think the "Find the Cap'n" promotional campaign for Cap'n Crunch cereal was so successful (refer to the *Focus on Promotion* section).

9.   If a market for a brand were composed entirely of brand-loyal stockpilers, why would promotional deals for this brand necessarily be unprofitable? Why are promotional deals profitable when a market consists of on-deal-only consumers?

10. Why is it critical that objectives be clearly specified when formulating a sales-promotion program?

Exercises

1.   Interview two or three salespeople who represent manufacturers' lines of grocery, drug, or general merchandise products and determine what sales-promotion techniques their firms use. Get their opinions of the effectiveness of these sales-promotion efforts. Try to get a sense of whether these techniques increase their selling enthusiasm.

2.   Conduct interviews with two or three retail managers or buyers and question them about trade allowances and display programs currently in effect in their stores. Determine what they like and dislike and what they consider effective and ineffective. Get their impressions of which consumer-oriented sales promotions are most successful in moving products off the shelves.

Trade-Oriented Sales Promotion

STREET MONEY

magine you are the marketing and sales manager for a regional manufacturer of canned goods headquartered in Massachusetts. Your company has a fine reputation for high-quality seafood products such as clam chowder. Your market includes grocery stores throughout New England. Unfortunately, sales growth has been minimal in recent years, averaging only two percent annually. A marketing-research study performed by a professor at a nearby university shows that many consumers are not purchasing your products because they perceive them to be too fattening, canned as they are in creamy sauces. The professor recommends a new line of low-calorie items. This should pose quite a challenge for the company, since you have not introduced a single new product for over ten years.

After months of planning and testing, you are prepared to introduce the new line of low-calorie canned goods. Knowing that retailer support is absolutely critical for product success, you decide to personally call several major grocery chains to sell them on the new product idea.

The first person you see, a buyer for a 250-store regional chain, is excited about the new product and considers the price reasonable. She agrees to carry your new low-calorie canned seafood in all 250 stores, subject to one condition: Your company will have to pay a fee of $100 for each store in the chain, for a total of $25,000. The buyer explains that this is a typical charge necessary to compensate her company for the extra expenses it incurs when taking on new products.

You leave the buyer's office in a state of disbelief. You've never heard of such an arrangement—$25,000 just to get one of the numerous chains to handle your new product line. You learn several days later that arrangements such as this have become widespread in grocery marketing. They go by different names, but practitioners often refer to them as "slotting allowances," "stocking allowances," or just plain "street money."

You feel that you are between a rock and a hard place. If you don't go along with the offer, you won't be able to get your new product distributed. If you do go along with the offer, you'll go broke because your budget can't afford this amount of trade support.■

An Introduction to Trade Promotion

The growth of slotting allowances is just one of the various reasons, as discussed in the previous chapter, why sales-promotion spending has increased in recent years while advertising spending has declined as a percentage of the total promotion budget. A major survey of packaged-goods marketers reveals that in 1987 allocations of promotion dollars among consumer promotion, trade promotion, and media advertising were 25.5 percent, 39.3 percent, and 35.2 percent respectively.[1] In other words, trade promotions represent nearly $40 out of every $100 invested to promote new and existing products. Dramatic increases in the number of new products and growth in retailer power are two of the major factors that have fostered heavy trade-promotion spending. Allowances in the form of slotting fees are just one of the consequences of this shift toward increased trade promotion.

The General Nature and Objectives of Trade Promotion

As discussed in the previous chapter, manufacturers use some combination of push and pull strategies to accomplish both retail distribution and consumer purchasing. Trade promotions, which are directed at wholesalers, retailers, and other marketing intermediaries, represent the first step in any promotional effort. Consumer promotions are likely to fail unless trade-promotion efforts have succeeded in getting wholesalers to distribute the product and retailers to stock adequate quantities.

A manufacturer has various *objectives* for using trade-oriented sales promotions: (1) to introduce new or revised products, (2) to increase distribution of new packages or sizes, (3) to build retail inventories, (4) to increase the manufacturer's share of shelf space, (5) to obtain displays outside normal shelf

1. Nathaniel Frey, "Ninth Annual Advertising & Sales Promotion Report," *Marketing Communications*, August 1988, pp. 9–12.

locations, (6) to reduce excess inventories and increase turnover, (7) to achieve product features in retailers' advertisements, (8) to counter competitive activity, and, ultimately, (9) to sell as much as possible to final consumers.[2]

To accomplish these myriad objectives, several ingredients are critical to building a successful trade-promotion program.[3]

Financial Incentive. The trade promotion must offer retailers increased profit margins and/or increased sales volume.

Correct Timing. Sales promotions to the trade are appropriately timed when they are (1) tied in with a seasonal event during a time of growing sales (e.g., candy sales during Halloween), (2) paired with a consumer sales-promotion effort, or (3) used strategically to offset competitive promotional activity.

Minimize the Retailer's Effort and Cost. The more effort and expense required, the less likely it is that retailers will cooperate in a program they see as benefiting the manufacturer but not themselves.

Quick Results. The most effective trade promotions are those that generate immediate sales or increases in store traffic.

Improve Retailer Performance. Promotions are effective when they help the retailer do a better selling job in the store or improve merchandising methods (e.g., superior display devices).[4]

Types of Trade Promotions

Manufacturers employ various trade-oriented promotional inducements. The following are the most important and widely used: trade contests and incentives, point-of-purchase materials, training programs, trade shows, trade allowances, cooperative advertising/vendor support programs, and specialty advertising. The sections that follow discuss each of these practices.

Trade Contests and Incentives

Contests and incentive programs are developed by manufacturers to encourage better performance from retail-management personnel and store salespersons. A **trade contest** typically is directed at store-level or department managers and

2. These objectives are adapted from a consumer-promotion seminar conducted by Ennis Associates, Inc., and sponsored by the Association of National Advertisers, Inc., New York, undated.
3. Don E. Schultz and William A. Robinson, *Sales Promotion Management* (Lincolnwood, IL: NTC Business Books, 1986), pp. 265–266.
4. For further reading see Kenneth G. Hardy, "Key Success Factors for Manufacturers' Sales Promotions in Package Goods, *Journal of Marketing*, vol. 50 (July 1986), pp. 13–23.

generally is based on managers *meeting a sales goal* established by the manufacturer. For example, a manufacturer of electronic equipment may offer a new digital audio tape player to store managers if sales of compact disc players during the Christmas season exceed last year's sales by, say, 25 percent.

Whereas contests are typically related to meeting sales goals, **trade incentives** are given to retail managers and salespeople for *performing certain tasks*. For example, when running sweepstakes or contests directed to final consumers (discussed fully in the following chapter), manufacturers often encourage retailers to display the object of merchandise that is being offered to consumers (e.g., a soccer ball). As an incentive to encourage retailer participation, the manufacturer gives the item to the store manager when the sales promotion is completed. Bigger prizes in the form of vacations and other high-ticket items are sometimes used as incentives.

Another form of incentive is directed at retail salespeople. Called *push money*, or "spiffs," the manufacturer provides cash to salespeople to encourage them to "push" certain products in the manufacturer's line. For example, a manufacturer may pay retail salespeople $10 for every unit of a particular compact disc player that they sell. Of course, the purpose of the push money is to encourage salespeople to favor the manufacturer's model over competitors' offerings.

When structured properly, trade contests and incentives can serve the manufacturer's interests very well. These programs may not serve the retailer's or the consumer's interests however. For example, push money can cause retail salespeople to be overly aggressive in pushing products on consumers. For this reason, many stores have policies that prevent their managers and salespeople from accepting any form of incentives from manufacturers.

Point-of-Purchase Materials

When point-of-purchase (P-O-P) materials were discussed in Chapter 16, the discussion focused primarily on how these materials serve the manufacturer's interests in activating consumer responses. The present emphasis is on how these materials enable manufacturers to obtain better retail distribution for their products while simultaneously serving the retailer's needs.

Anything a manufacturer can do to assist the retailer in using store space more efficiently, in expanding product-category sales volume, or in increasing store traffic will likely meet with retailer acceptance. A variety of P-O-P materials are used to achieve these objectives: dump bins, motion pieces, stand-up racks, end-of-counter displays, posters, shelf cards, and a variety of other materials. All of these items are designed to attract consumer attention by enhancing either the conspicuousness or attractiveness of the displayed merchandise.

Manufacturers generally must use a price discount (called a *display allowance*) to obtain trade support for displays, especially elaborate ones such as the center-of-aisle or end-of-aisle displays seen in grocery stores and other outlets. For example, assume a manufacturer's regular price to the retailer is $18 per 12-item case. This price is reduced to $15.75, a 12.5 percent display allowance, if the retailer constructs and merchandises the manufacturer's products from a special display. Display allowances are particularly effective for brands that the trade accepts as good display brands, namely, those with strong consumer franchises. Display promotions are relatively ineffective for small-volume brands.

Because point-of-purchase materials are frequently developed by manufacturers without considering the retailer's needs, the materials (especially posters, shelf cards, and other smaller items) often go unused. They are delivered to retailers but are never brought out of storage areas or, worse yet, immediately end up in retailers' trash bins. It has been estimated that only 25 percent of all point-of-purchase materials sent by manufacturers are eventually used in retail stores. The reasons are that (1) display materials often are poorly planned by manufacturers and are unsuitable for retailers, (2) the materials take up too much space for the amount of sales generated, and (3) they are too difficult to set up.[5]

Training Programs

Many products at the retail level are sold on a self-service basis due to their simplicity and because they have been presold by manufacturers' advertising efforts. Numerous other products require sophisticated selling assistance in the retail outlet. Cosmetics, machinery, appliances, jewelry, and other (typically high-ticket) items require knowledgeable salespeople who can present consumers with relevant information about a product's performance and its relative advantages compared with competitive offerings. Lamentably, retail salespeople often are not adequately trained in how to properly sell a particular product or brand. Hence, it is in both the manufacturer's and retailer's best interest to provide this training.

Manufacturer's sales representatives typically perform this function as part of their routine sales calls on retail accounts. Training is time well spent, because the more knowledge retail salespeople have about a particular product, the greater their confidence and the more effort they will devote to that item compared to competitive offerings.

In addition to face-to-face training conducted by the manufacturer's own sales representatives, training can also be accomplished through literature mailed to retail clerks and, increasingly, through videocassettes. Videocassettes provide the manufacturer with an ideal medium for supplying retail salespeople with detailed product information, product-use demonstrations, and selling tips.

5. Schultz and Robinson, *Sales Promotion Management*, pp. 278–279.

Merely making videocassettes or other forms of training materials available is no assurance that they will be reviewed or will have any effect. A fundamental requirement for successful training materials is that they be readily understandable and interesting. As with any form of promotion, this requires the creative development of persuasive and interesting messages.

Trade Shows

A **trade show** is a temporary forum (typically lasting several days) where sellers of a product category (small appliances, toys, clothing, furniture, industrial tools, etc.) exhibit and demonstrate their wares to present and prospective buyers. It is expected that by 1991 over 145,000 U.S. companies will participate in trade shows each year.[6]

Trade-show attendees include most of an industry's important manufacturers and major customers. This encapsulated marketplace enables the trade-show exhibitor to accomplish both selling and nonselling functions. Specific functions include (1) servicing present customers, (2) identifying prospects, (3) introducing new or modified products, (4) gathering information about competitors' new products, (5) taking product orders, and (6) enhancing the company's image.[7]

Trade shows are an excellent forum for introducing new products. Products can be demonstrated and customer inquiries can be addressed at a time when customers are actively soliciting information. This allows companies to gather both positive and negative feedback about the product. Positive information can be used in subsequent sales presentations and advertising efforts, while negative information can guide product improvements or changes in the marketing program. Trade shows also provide an ideal occasion to recruit dealers, distributors, and sales personnel.[8]

Trade Allowances

Trade allowances, or trade deals, are offered to retailers for performing activities in support of the manufacturer's brand. These allowances/deals are needed to encourage retailers to stock the manufacturer's brand, discount the brand's price to consumers, feature it in advertising, or provide special display or other point-of-purchase support.[9]

6. Edward M. Mazze, *Trade Shows in Black and White: A Guide for Marketers* (New Canaan, CT: Trade Show Bureau, 1986), p. 3.
7. Roger A. Kerin and William L. Cron, "Assessing Trade Show Functions and Performance," *Journal of Marketing*, vol. 51 (July 1987), p. 88.
8. "The Trade Show Comes of Age," *Marketing Communications*, April 1986, pp. 97–102.
9. Ronald C. Curhan and Robert J. Kopp, "Obtaining Retailer Support for Trade Deals: Key Success Factors," *Journal of Advertising Research*, vol. 27 (December 1987/January 1988), pp. 51–60.

Buying Allowances

Buying allowances provide deals to the trade in the form of *free goods or price reductions* in return for the purchase of specific quantities of goods. For example, Shell offered retailers of its Fire & Ice Motor Oil 5 free cases (120 free quarts) with every purchase of 45 cases. The makers of ACTIFED, a nasal decongestant/antihistamine, provided a trade allowance of 16⅔ percent off the retail invoice price for all purchases during the deal period.

By using buying allowances, manufacturers hope to accomplish two interrelated objectives: (1) increase retailers' purchasing of the manufacturer's brand, and (2) increase consumers' purchasing from retailers. This latter objective is based on the expectation that consumers are receptive to price reductions, and that retailers will in fact pass along to consumers the discounts they receive from manufacturers.

Manufacturers find allowance promotions attractive because they are easy to implement, can successfully stimulate initial distribution, are well accepted by the trade, and can increase trade purchases during the allowance period. However, a major disadvantage is that buying allowances may induce the trade to stockpile a product in order to take advantage of the temporary price reduction. This merely shifts business from the future to the present. Two prevalent practices in current business are forward buying and diverting.

Forward Buying.   To take advantage of trade allowances, retailers buy larger quantities than needed for normal inventory and warehouse the excess quantity, thereby avoiding purchasing the product at list price. Retailers often purchase enough product on one deal to carry them over until the manufacturer's next regularly scheduled deal. For this reason, **forward buying** also is called "bridge buying."

When a manufacturer marks down a product's price by, say, 10 percent, wholesalers and retailers commonly stock up with a 10 to 12 week supply. [10] A conservative estimate would place the amount of forward buying by wholesalers and retailers at about one-quarter of their inventories.[11] A number of manufacturers sell 80 to 90 percent of their volume on deal.[12]

The practice of forward buying has given rise to computer models that enable wholesale and retail buyers to estimate the profit potential from a forward buy and the optimum weeks of inventory to purchase. The models take into consideration the amount of savings from a deal and then incorporate into their calculations the various added costs from forward buying: warehouse storage expenses, shipping costs, and the cost of money.

10. Ronald Alsop, "Retailers Buy Far in Advance to Exploit Trade Promotions," *The Wall Street Journal*, October 9, 1986, p. 37.
11. Monci Jo Williams, "The No-Win Game of Price Promotion," *Fortune*, July 11, 1983, pp. 92–102.
12. Willard R. Bishop, Jr., "Trade Buying Squeezes Marketers," *Marketing Communications*, May 1988, pp. 50–54.

FOCUS ON PROMOTION

Forward Buying of Campbell's Chicken Noodle Soup

The Campbell Soup Company is one of the most respected packaged-goods marketers in the United States, but like many other companies, it suffers from forward-buying practices. Campbell's chicken noodle soup, a staple item in many homes and in most supermarkets, provides a telling example of this problem. Sometimes the company sells as much as 40 percent of its annual chicken noodle soup production to wholesalers and retailers in just six weeks!

When wholesalers and retailers forward buy chicken noodle soup in large quantities, Campbell must schedule extra work shifts and pay overtime to keep up with the accelerated production and shipping schedules. Later, layoffs result when demand for chicken noodle soup falls off.

These problems can be partially avoided with the use of a "bill and hold" program. In other words, the manufacturer invoices (bills) the retailer as soon as the order is placed but delays shipping (holds) the order until desired quantities are requested by the retailer. Such programs smooth out production and shipping schedules by allowing retailers to purchase large amounts at deal prices but delay receiving shipments until inventory is needed.[13] ■

It may appear that forward buying benefits all parties to the marketing process, but this is not the case. First, retailers' savings from forward buying often are not passed on to consumers. Second, forward buying leads to increases in distribution costs since wholesalers and retailers pay greater carrying charges in inventorying larger quantities. Third, manufacturers experience reduced margins because of the price discounts that they offer as well as the increased costs that result from factors illustrated in the *Focus on Promotion* section. It is estimated that forward buying costs manufacturers between 1 and 1.3 percent of the selling price.[14]

Diverting.   Another growing buying practice, **diverting,** occurs when a manufacturer restricts a deal to a limited geographical area rather than making it available nationally. The manufacturer's intent is that only wholesal-

---

13. Adapted from Alsop, "Retailers Buy Far in Advance to Exploit Trade Promotions."
14. Walter Salmon, "Trade Promotion and Food Distribution Costs," cited in Bishop, "Trade Buying Squeezed Marketers," p. 52.

ers and retailers in that area will benefit from the deal. However, what happens with diverting is that wholesalers and retailers buy abnormally large quantities at the deal price and then transship the excess quantities to other geographical areas.

Diverting has been practiced for a number of years, but until recently diverting operations were run in "bookie-joint" fashion. That is, shady characters working in small offices wheeled and dealed in lining up sellers of diverted products in one geographical area with buyers in another. Recently, diverting has taken on the appearance of a high-tech business. There now are sophisticated electronic diverting networks in the United States doing millions of dollars of diverting business.[15]

The practice of diverting probably is no less unethical than it ever was, but now it is more out in the open than before. Many retailers contend it is the manufacturers' fault for offering irresistible deals; the retailers argue that they must take advantage of the deals in any way legally possible in order to remain competitive with other retailers. Manufacturers could avoid the problem by placing brands on national deal only. This solution is more ideal than practical, however, since regional marketing efforts are expanding (as discussed in Chapter 8), and local deals and regional marketing go hand in hand.

Slotting Allowances

Slotting allowances are a special form of buying allowance that apply specifically to *new products*. As noted in the chapter's opening vignette, slotting allowances are also called stocking allowances or just plain "street money." Definitionally, a **slotting allowance** is the fee a manufacturer pays a supermarket chain or other retailer to get that retailer to handle the manufacturer's new product. The allowance is called "slotting" in reference to the slot, or location, that the retailer must make available in its warehouse to accommodate the manufacturer's product. A slotting allowance is a business variant of the vernacular expression "If you can't pay, you can't play."

You probably are thinking "This sounds like bribery." You also may be wondering "Why do manufacturers tolerate slotting allowances?" Let's examine each issue.

First, slotting allowances are indeed a form of bribery. The retailer who demands slotting allowances denies the manufacturer shelf space unless the manufacturer is willing to pay the upfront fee, the slotting allowance, to acquire that space for its new product. Second, manufacturers "tolerate" slotting allowances because they are confronted with a classic dilemma: Either they pay the fee and eventually recoup the cost through increased sales volume, or they refuse to pay the fee and in so doing accept a fate of not being able to successfully introduce new products. The expression "between a rock and a hard place" is as appropriate here as it was in the opening vignette.

15. Bishop, "Trade Buying Squeezes Marketers," pp. 52–53.

In certain respects, slotting allowances are a legitimate cost of doing business. When a retailer such as a large multi-store supermarket chain takes on a new product, it incurs several added expenses. These expenses arise because the retailer must make space for that product in its distribution center, create a new entry in its computerized inventory system, redesign store shelves, and notify individual stores about the new product.[16] In addition to these expenses, a retailer takes the risk that the new product will fail. This is a likely result in the grocery industry, where at least half of the 10,000 products introduced annually fail. Hence, the slotting allowance serves as a form of insurance policy against product failure.

It is doubtful, however, that the actual expenses incurred by retailers are anywhere near the slotting allowances they charge. Actual charges are highly variable. Some supermarkets charge as little as $5 per store to stock a new item, while others charge as much as $50 or $100 per store. Some Northeastern grocery chains charge as much as $15,000 to $40,000 for a single new product.

Large companies can afford to pay slotting allowances, because their volume is sufficient to recoup the expense. However, brands with small consumer franchises are frequently unable to afford these fees. For example, one grocery chain demanded $1,000 per store to introduce Frookie cookies in its 100 stores. To have paid this fee would have required the retail price for a package of Frookie cookies to jump by 50¢ from $1.79 to $2.29. The makers of Frookie cookies were forced to turn down the opportunity to sell their product in this chain.[17]

How Can They Get Away With It? This question has probably entered your mind. How, in fact, are retailers able to charge such huge fees? The reason is straightforward: As noted in the previous chapter, the balance of power has shifted away from manufacturers and toward retailers. Power means being able to call the shots, and increasing numbers of retailers are doing this. Also, manufacturers have hurt their own cause by introducing thousands of new products each year, most of which are trivial variants of existing products rather than distinct new offerings with meaningful profit opportunities for the retailer. As such, every manufacturer competes against every other manufacturer for limited shelf space, and slotting allowances are simply a mechanism used by retailers to exploit the competition among manufacturers. Furthermore, many grocery retailers find it easy to rationalize slotting allowances on the grounds that their net-profit margins in selling groceries are miniscule (typically 1 to 1.5 percent) and that slotting allowances enable them to earn returns comparable to what manufacturers earn.

---

16. Laurie Freeman and Janet Meyers, "Grocer 'Fee' Hampers New-Product Launches," *Advertising Age*, August 3, 1987, p. 1.
17. Richard Gibson, "Supermarkets Demand Food Firms' Payments Just to Get on the Shelf," *The Wall Street Journal*, November 1, 1988, pp. A1, A19.

Further understanding of the rationale and dynamics underlying slotting allowances is possible by drawing an analogy with prices for apartments in any college community. When units are abundant, different apartment complexes compete aggressively with one another and force prices down. On the other hand, when apartments are scarce (which typically is the case on most college campuses), prices are often inflated. The result: You may be forced to pay an arm and a leg to live in a conveniently located apartment.

Such is very much the case in today's marketing environment. Retailers are confronted with thousands of new products (renters) each year. The amount of shelf space (the number of apartments) is limited because relatively few new stores are being built. Hence, retailers are able to command slotting allowances (higher rent), and manufacturers are willing to pay the higher rent to "live" in desirable locations.

Avoiding Slotting Allowances.   What can a manufacturer do to avoid paying slotting allowances? Sometimes nothing, but powerful manufacturers like Procter & Gamble and Kraft, for example, are less likely to pay slotting fees than are weaker national and regional manufacturers. Retailers know that P&G's and Kraft's new products probably *will* be successful. This is because P&G and Kraft invest heavily in research in order to develop meaningful new products, they spend heavily on advertising to create consumer demand for these products, and they use extensive sales promotions (e.g., couponing) that serve to create strong consumer pull.

Seller Beware!

Trade allowances are effective in gaining retail distribution and sometimes in encouraging retailers to devote more or better shelf space and displays to the manufacturer's brand. Trade promotion is fraught with problems, however, mainly because some retailers take advantage of allowances without performing the services for which they receive credit. In fact, it has been estimated that perhaps as much as two-thirds of trade-promotion dollars are wasted.[18]

One study determined that large chain retailers are particularly likely to take advantage of manufacturers' trade allowances *without passing the savings along to consumers*. Table 19.1 shows that large chains account for 29 percent of all retail sales but only 17 percent of sales for items featured in advertisements at below-normal prices. In other words, large chains sell *disproportionately less* than their share of products at reduced prices (as indicated by the "trade-performance index" of 59 in Table 19.1). This is another way of saying that large chains often keep the manufacturer's trade allowance without passing the savings along to consumers. By comparison, medium-sized chains' sales of fea-

18. *Insights: Issues 1–13, 1979–1982* (New York: NPD Research, 1983), p. 8.

TABLE 19.1   **Deal versus Nondeal Sales by Store Size**

Store Size	Nondeal Sales (1)	Feature Sales (2)	Trade Performance Index (2 ÷ 1)
Large chains	29%	17%	59
Medium chains	7	7	100
Small chains and independents	64	76	119
	100%	100%	

Source: Adapted from *Insights: Issues 1–13, 1979–1982* (New York: NPD Research, 1983), p. 9.

tured merchandise is exactly proportionate to their nondeal sales (providing a trade performance index of 100), and small chains and independent retailers sell proportionately more than their share at reduced prices.[19]

One major reason large chains are disproportionately less likely to pass price reductions from manufacturers along to consumers is that, unlike smaller chains and independents, they are able to promote and sell their own *private brands*. Because private brands can be sold at lower prices than manufacturers' comparable brands, large chains are able to use private brands to satisfy the needs of price-sensitive consumers while selling manufacturers' brands at their normal price and pocketing the trade allowance as extra profit. This certainly is not meant to imply that all large chains exploit manufacturers and consumers. It does point out, however, a serious problem that manufacturers must deal with when offering trade deals. In fact, many manufacturers have responded to this problem by tightening performance requirements and requiring retailers to do more to earn their allowances.

Cooperative Advertising and Vendor Support Programs

Another form of trade promotion occurs when manufacturers of branded merchandise pay for part of the expense that retailers incur when they advertise manufacturers' brands. Both cooperative advertising and vendor support programs deal with the advertising relation between manufacturers and retailers. A fundamental distinction between the two is that cooperative advertising programs are initiated by the manufacturer, whereas vendor support programs are retailer initiated. The significance of this distinction will become clear in the discussion that follows.

19. Ibid.

Cooperative Advertising

As the name suggests, **cooperative (co-op) advertising** is a cooperative arrangement between a manufacturer and retailer. Co-op programs, which are initiated by manufacturers, permit retailers to place ads in an advertising medium that promotes the manufacturer's product and its availability at the retailer's place of business. (For example, see the ad for Sperry Top-Sider® in Figure 19.1.) The cost of the ad placement is shared by the manufacturer and retailer according to the terms that follow.

Though cooperative advertising programs vary, five elements are common to all. These elements are illustrated with the 1988 co-op advertising program from La-Z-Boy®, a well-known manufacturer of reclining chairs and sofas.

1. *Specified Time Period.* Co-op funds typically apply to a specified time period. La-Z-Boy®'s program applies to funds accrued between January 1 and December 31. These funds can only be applied to advertising that is run during the same period.

2. *Accrual.* The retailer receives from the manufacturer an advertising fund, called an *accrual account*, against which advertising costs are charged. The accrual typically is based either on a fixed amount or a percentage of a retailer's net purchases from the manufacturer during the term of the co-op contract. In the case of La-Z-Boy®, which applies a *fixed accrual*, the retailer accrues $3 on each chair purchased from La-Z-Boy® and $6 on each sofa.

   To illustrate a *percentage accrual*, suppose a certain appliance retailer purchases $200,000 from a manufacturer in one year. Suppose further that the manufacturer's cooperative program allows 3 percent of purchases to accrue to the retailer's cooperative advertising account. Thus, the retailer would have accrued $6,000 worth of cooperative advertising dollars.

3. *Payment Share.* This is the amount of advertising reimbursement the manufacturer pays the retailer. Manufacturers generally agree to pay a set percentage ranging from 50 to 100 percent of the cost for each advertisement placed by the retailer. La-Z-Boy® pays 50 percent of each advertisement.

   Continuing the preceding example for the appliance manufacturer, now suppose the manufacturer's co-op program pays 50 percent of individual advertising charges and that the retailer places a $1,000 newspaper ad featuring the manufacturer's brand of appliances. The manufacturer would pay 50 percent of this amount, that is, $500; the retailer would pay the remaining $500 and would have $5,500 remaining in its accrual account for future advertising.

FIGURE 19.1   **Cooperative Advertisement for Sperry Top-Sider®**

Source: Courtesy Wallace Associates, 1331 Palmetto Ave., Winter Park, Florida 32789.

4. **Performance Guidelines.** These are the manufacturer's requirements that the retailer must satisfy in order to qualify for advertising reimbursement. Guidelines typically deal with suitable media, size and type of logos, the use of trademarks, copy and art directions, and product content. For example, La-Z-Boy® requires the following (1) The name La-Z-Boy® must never be used a as noun (e.g., a retailer could not say "Looking for a La-Z-Boy®? We have it!"); the purpose of this requirement is to prevent the name La-Z-Boy® from becoming generic, that is, being used synonymously with the product category. (2) A trademark symbol (i.e., ®) must follow the name La-Z-Boy at least once in the advertising copy, preferably the first time the name appears. (3) Competitive products cannot appear or be mentioned in the retailer's advertising.

5. **Billing for Reimbursement.** This prescribes how the retailer is to be reimbursed. To receive reimbursement from La-Z-Boy®, the retailer must present a copy of the invoice from the newspaper or other medium where the ad was placed along with evidence of the actual advertising copy.

Why Is Cooperative Advertising Used? There are several reasons.[20] First, manufacturers know that potential consumers of infrequently purchased goods (e.g., appliances, expensive wearing apparel, chairs and sofas) are responsive to retailer advertisements, especially preceding a major buying decision. Co-op advertising is thus a stimulant to immediate consumer purchases.

Second, manufacturers have found that cooperative advertising stimulates greater retailer buying and merchandising support. Retailers, knowing they have accrued co-op dollars, are more likely to aggressively promote and merchandise a specific manufacturer's products. From the manufacturer's perspective, this amounts to greater stocking and more display space for its brands as well as more retail advertising support.

A third advantage of co-op advertising is that it enables manufactures to have access to local media at an advertising rate lower than would be paid if the manufacturer advertised directly rather than through retailers. This cost premium reflects the fact that local media, particularly newspapers, charge lower advertising rates to local advertisers than to national advertisers. For example, in 1987 average national rates for advertising in major U.S. newspapers were over 66 percent higher than the average local rates.[21] Hence, by using cooperative advertising, a manufacturer gets exposure in local markets at a reduced rate.

From the retailer's perspective, cooperative advertising, is a relatively inexpensive form of advertising. The advertising is not truly free, however, because the manufacturer's cooperative advertising costs are built into the price

20. Stephen A. Greyser and Robert F. Young, "Follow 11 Guidelines to Strategically Manage Co-op Advertising Program," *Marketing News*, September 16, 1983, p. 5.
21. *Newspaper Rate Differentials 1987* (New York: American Association of Advertising Agencies, 1988).

of the merchandise. Failure to take advantage of accrued co-op dollars means that the retailer is effectively paying more for the same merchandise than retailers who do utilize co-op funds.

Much cooperative advertising accruals are never spent by retailers. Over $11 billion is available annually in co-op funds and fully one-third of that amount goes unspent each year.[22] Research by the Newspaper Advertising Bureau shows that only about 40 percent of all retailers take advantage of co-op accruals.[23] For this reason manufacturers are developing new cooperative advertising programs to make it easier and more lucrative for retailers to utilize co-op funds. The objective is to make the program instructions simpler to read and easier to implement. Advertising media are also offering new programs to attract more co-op dollars. For example, the Newspaper Advertising Bureau has developed a program whereby salespeople who sell newspaper space are able to identify all the products in a retailer's store that carry co-op, determine how much the retailer has accrued for each product, and then run an ad for the retailer that will use the accrued co-op funds.[24]

Open-Ended Co-op Advertising. The cooperative advertising programs discussed to this point relate the amount of co-op funds to the amount of product purchased by a retailer from a particular manufacturer. The more product purchased, the more co-op funds available. *Open-ended co-op advertising* involves paying for part of the retailer's advertising cost *without relating the reimbursement to the amount of product purchased from the manufacturer.*[25]

Open-ended programs make considerable sense when the manufacturer (1) wants to encourage the use of co-op funds by *smaller retailers* or (2) when the manufacturer *sells through intermediaries* and does not have access to retailers' purchase figures. Major advantages of open-ended programs involve simplifying the record-keeping task and, more importantly, making it possible to use advertising for generating sales rather than relying on sales to generate advertising.

Vendor Support Programs

In contrast to cooperative advertising, **vendor support programs (VSPs)** are initiated by retailers.[26] A retailer, such as a supermarket chain, develops an advertising program in consultation with local advertising media and then in-

22. Martin Everett, "Co-op Advertising and Computers," *Sales and Marketing Management,* May 1987, p. 56.
23. Renee Blakkan, "Savory Deals Tempt Hungry Retailers," *Advertising Age,* March 7, 1983, p. M-11.
24. Ibid.
25. Ed Crimmins, "Why Open-Ended Co-op Is on the Rise," *Sales and Marketing Management,* December 1986, pp. 64, 67.
26. The following is based on John Killough and Terence A. Shimp, "Vendor Support Programs: Accomplishing Trade Push Or Being Pushed Around?" in *1987 Educators' Proceedings* (Chicago: American Marketing Association, 1987).

vites its suppliers to pay for a specific percentage of the media cost for the proposed campaign. In other words, the retailer creates advertising dollars by exerting its power over a manufacturer, or vendor, who depends on the retailer for its marketplace success.

To illustrate, consider a hypothetical 250-store grocery chain called BuyRight. BuyRight's advertising agency recommends that the chain undertake a heavy advertising campaign in April. The objective is to have enough newspaper insertions and television placements to yield an average of 150 gross rating points for each of four weeks. The campaign will cost BuyRight $250,000. Where is the money to come from? Solution: Get 25 vendors (manufacturers) to contribute $10,000 each to BuyRight's April campaign. In return for their participation, manufacturers will receive feature time and space in BuyRight's advertisements as well as extra display space. Extra sales volume, BuyRight assures the manufacturers, will more than compensate for their advertising support funds.

VSPs have clear advantages for the retailer. Indeed, these programs seem to benefit everyone (retailers, ad agencies, media), except perhaps the manufacturers who provide the financial support.[27] Often a manufacturer pays a large sum to support a retailer's advertising efforts but receives very little actual promotion of its own brands to end users. The manufacturer's products may be lost amid the clutter of the other brands featured in, say, a supermarket chain's newspaper advertisement.

Why Do Manufacturers Participate in VSPs?   Vendor support programs are most likely used when the retailer's channel power is greater than that of manufacturers who compete against one another for the retailer's limited shelf space. This is particularly true in the case of smaller, regional manufacturers who have not created strong consumer franchises for their brands. These weaker manufacturers cannot afford to invest in consumer-pull programs, because their promotion funds are almost fully consumed by retailers' vendor support programs. As such, it becomes an irrevocable cycle: The less powerful a manufacturer is, the more susceptible it is to retailers' demands for advertising support funds. In turn, the more the manufacturer invests in the retailers' advertising programs, the less funds there are available for building demand for the manufacturer's own brands.

Specialty Advertising

Specialty advertising is a hybrid form of marketing communications. On the one hand, it is very much like direct-mail advertising in that both pinpoint their communication efforts toward specifically defined audiences. On the

27. Ed Crimmins, "Dispelling the Hype of 'Vendor Support'," *Sales and Marketing Management*, December 9, 1985, pp. 54–57.

other hand, specialty advertising is like public relations in that both engender goodwill. In another respect, specialty advertising is like sales promotion in that both involve the use of incentives given to recipients to encourage certain forms of behavior.

In more specific terms, **specialty advertising** is "that advertising/sales promotion medium which utilizes useful articles to carry the advertiser's identification and advertising message to its target audience."[28] Specialty advertising complements other forms of promotion by providing another way to keep a company's name before customers and prospects.[29] Specialty-advertising expenditures are small in comparison with other forms of trade promotion, yet $3.6 billion was spent in the United Sates in 1987 on specialty merchandise.[30]

This form of promotion can help companies achieve a variety of marketing communications objectives: (1) promoting new store openings, (2) introducing new products, (3) motivating salespeople, (4) establishing new accounts, (5) developing trade-show traffic, (6) improving customer relations, and (7) activating inactive accounts.[31]

Specialty advertising generally takes two forms. One is the random distribution of items to prospects and customers as a type of *reminder advertising*. Typical specialty items in this category include matchbooks, calendars, ballpoint pens, and T-shirts—all of which are inscribed with a company or brand name and other relevant information. A second form of specialty advertising is the *structured promotion*, which calls for planning and analyzing promotion objectives, identifying target audiences, creating promotional themes, budgeting, and developing systems for distributing specialty items.[32] It is this latter, more sophisticated use of specialty advertising that is pertinent to the present discussion. It can be considered a form of trade promotion when the target audience is a company's wholesaler, distributor, retailer, or other intermediate customer. The following case illustrates how specialty advertising works as a form of structured trade promotion.

Xerox undertook a specialty-advertising program to generate sales leads for its printing systems. The designated target audience was 3,800 information-services and data-processing managers. Based on research showing this audience to be composed largely of upscale individuals with sophisticated tastes, the creative appeal centered around a music theme. A promotion was assembled showing how Xerox could orchestrate a system to meet corporate requirements. The first of five music-theme mailings consisted of a record-album package with an imprinted pencil housed in blueprint graphics with copy stat-

28. *Success Stories: 25 Award-Winning Specialty Advertising Promotions* (Irving, TX: Specialty Advertising Association International, 1988), p. 1.
29. George L. Herpel and Richard A. Collins, *Specialty Advertising in Marketing* (Homewood, IL: Dow Jones-Irwin, 1972).
30. "Ad Specialty Sales Hit 3.6 Billion," *Marketing Communications*, February 1988, p. 14.
31. "The Case for Specialty Advertising," Specialty Advertising Association International, Irving, TX, undated.
32. Richard G. Ebel, "Specialties: Gifts of Motivation," *Marketing Communications*, April 1986, pp. 75–80.

ing: "For a perfect arrangement, Xerox presents products that work in perfect harmony with your system." A second mailing depicted an orchestra conductor and included a conductor's baton and a response card promising a free gift (a recording of Vivaldi's "The Four Seasons") to those who replied. Later mailings tied the music theme into the idea that Xerox could orchestrate a system meeting the buyer's needs. The promotion generated a very high response rate: over one-third of all recipients responded. Salespersons found the promotion to be a helpful "door opener" in acquiring appointments.[33]

Summary

This chapter presents the topic of trade-oriented sales promotions and describes the various forms widely in use. As of 1987, trade-oriented sales promotion represented nearly 40 percent of consumer packaged-good companies' promotional budgets. These programs perform a variety of objectives.

Trade contests and incentives encourage retailer performance by offering gifts for meeting sales goals or for performing certain tasks deemed important for the success of the sponsoring manufacturer's products. Push money is one form of trade incentive used to encourage special selling effort from retail salespeople.

Point-of-purchase materials are another form of trade promotion that serve both the manufacturer's and retailer's economic interests. Display allowances are provided by manufacturers to obtain trade support for center-of-aisle or end-of-aisle displays.

Training programs are undertaken by manufacturers to facilitate distributors' and retail salespersons' efforts in selling the manufacturer's products. Training is typically performed by the manufacturer's own sales force, but written literature and videocassettes are additional training media.

Trade shows are another important element of manufacturers' sales-promotion programs. It is estimated that by 1991 over 145,000 U.S. companies will participate in trade shows each year. Specific functions of trade shows include (1) servicing present customers, (2) identifying prospects, (3) introducing new or modified products, (4) gathering information about competitors' new products, (5) taking product orders, and (6) enhancing the company's image.

Trade allowances, or trade deals, are offered to retailers for performing activities in support of the manufacturer's brand. Manufacturers find allowance promotions attractive for several reasons: The are easy to implement, can successfully stimulate initial distribution, are well accepted by the trade, and can increase trade purchases during the allowance period. However, a major disadvantage is that buying allowances may induce the trade to stockpile a product in order to take advantage of the temporary price reduction. This merely

---

33. *Success Stories: 25 Award-Winning Specialty Advertising Promotions*, p. 15.

shifts business from the future to the present. Two prevalent practices in current business are forward buying and diverting. Another form of trade deal, called a slotting allowance, applies to new-product introductions. Manufacturers of grocery products typically are required to pay retailers a slotting fee for the right to have their product carried by the retailer.

Cooperative advertising and vendor support programs are trade promotions in which manufacturers and retailers jointly pay for the retailer's advertising that features the manufacturer's product. Co-op advertising is initiated by the manufacturer, whereas vendor support programs are initiated by retailers.

A final trade-oriented sales-promotion practice is *specialty advertising*. This hybrid form of marketing communications uses articles of merchandise to carry a company's message to its target audience. Specialty advertising is a form of trade-oriented sales promotion when the audience consists of the manufacturer's distributors or other intermediate customers.

Discussion Questions

1. A number of retailers have explicit policies that prevent their managers or salespeople from receiving any form of incentives from manufacturers. Are these policies wise? Under what conditions might manufacturer-sponsored incentives benefit the retail firm above and beyond the obvious benefit that they hold for individual managers or salespeople?

2. You are the marketing manager of a company that manufacturers a line of paper products (tissues, napkins, etc.). Your market share is 7 percent in a market where you are considering offering retailers an attractive allowance for giving your brand special display space. Comment on this promotion's chances for success.

3. Identify concepts in Chapter 6 ("Message and Source Factors") that would be relevant to a furniture company in its efforts to develop an effective exhibition at a trade show attended by major furniture retailers from around the country.

4. In your own words, explain the practices of forward buying and diverting. Also, describe the advantages *and* disadvantages of "bill and hold" programs.

5. Assume you are a buyer for a large supermarket chain and that you have been asked to speak to a group of marketing students at a nearby university. During the question-and-answer session following your comments, one student remarks: "My father works for a grocery-product manufacturer, and he says that slotting allowances are nothing more than a form of larceny!" How would you respond to this student's comment in defense of your company's practice?

6. Explain why selling private brands often enables large retail chains to pocket trade deals instead of passing their reduced costs along to consumers in the form of lower product prices.

7. It is estimated that at least one-third of the billions of co-op advertising dollars offered by manufacturers go unspent. Why? What could a manufacturer do to encourage greater numbers of retailers to spend co-op dollars? Do you think some manufacturers may not want their retail customers to spend co-op funds?

8. In discussing open-ended co-op programs, the text stated that this type of cooperative advertising makes it possible to use advertising for generating sales rather than relying on sales to generate advertising. Explain precisely what this means.

9. You are the Midwest sales manager for a product line marketed by a large, highly respected national manufacturer. Most of your products hold market shares of 30 percent or higher. The promotion manager for a large Midwestern grocery chain approaches you about a vendor support program his company is in the process of putting together. It will cost you $50,000 to participate. What would be the reasons for and against your participation? On balance, would it be in your company's long-term interest to participate in this or other VSPs?

Exercises

1. Interview a department or store manager. Have him or her identify two recent trade deals manufacturers have offered his or her store. Determine the specific conditions of the deals. What are the stated requirements that the retailer must satisfy in order to receive the allowance, and what amount of discount is involved?

2. Locate and summarize recent articles from business periodical literature on each of the following topics: slotting allowances, forward buying, and diverting. The articles should be less than one year old.

3. Go to any retailer in your hometown or college community and ask for several outdated copies of cooperative advertising programs. Analyze each program in terms of the five essential features identified in the text. Also, ask the retailer why his or her store does or does not use cooperative advertising funds.

Consumer-Oriented Sales Promotion

A SELF-TEST OF COUPON USAGE

What follows is a short survey on your coupon-usage behavior. Answer the questions yourself if you are a regular grocery shopper (i.e., you shop in a grocery store or supermarket at least once every two weeks). If you are not a regular grocery shopper, answer the questions from the vantage of your spouse, parent, or other close relative/friend. (Note: The response headings are to be read as follows: N = never, AN = almost never, S = sometimes, AA = almost always, A = always.)

		N	AN	S	AA	A
1.	Do you use coupons for brands normally bought?	—	—	—	—	—
2.	Do you use coupons to try new brands or products?	—	—	—	—	—
3.	Do you use coupons that you get in groceries?	—	—	—	—	—
4.	Do you use coupons that enter you in sweepstakes?	—	—	—	—	—
5.	Do you send in labels or proofs of purchase for refunds or rebates?	—	—	—	—	—

A national sample of households responded to these questions in 1988. The percentage of respondents answering "always" or "almost always" to each question was as follows:

Q.#1—84%
Q.#2—32%
Q.#3—29%
Q.#4—21%
Q.#5—54%

The study found that fully 97 percent of all households had used coupons in the past 30 days. Over 80 percent of all grocery shoppers regularly take coupons when going grocery shopping.[1]■

An Introduction to Consumer-Oriented Sales Promotion

The opening vignette highlights the important role of coupons in consumers' grocery-shopping routines. Of course, marketers use a variety of other sales-promotion techniques (e.g., samples, premiums, cents-off deals) to encourage desired behaviors from consumers. This chapter builds on the base developed in Chapter 18 and focuses exclusively on consumer-oriented sales promotions. The unique character of each sales-promotion technique is described and specific objectives that each technique is intended to accomplish are explained.

Consumer Rewards and Manufacturer Objectives

Why do consumers respond to coupons and other sales-promotion techniques? What objectives do manufacturers hope to accomplish by using these techniques? Answers to these interrelated questions are the core of this chapter's purpose.

Consumer Rewards. Consumers would not be responsive to sales promotions unless there was something in it for them—and, in fact, there is. All sales-promotion techniques provide consumers with *rewards* (i.e., incentives or inducements) that encourage certain forms of behavior desired by marketers. Rewards are typically in the form of cash savings or free gifts. Sometimes rewards are immediate, while other times they are delayed.

An *immediate* reward is one that delivers the savings or gift as soon as the consumer performs a marketer-specified behavior. For example, you receive

---

1. The survey was conducted by Frankel & Co., a marketing services firm, and is reported in Ira Teinowitz, "Coupons Gain Favor with U.S. Shoppers," *Advertising Age*, Novemeber 14, 1988, p. 64.

cash savings at the time that you redeem a coupon; pleasure is obtained immediately when you try a free candy bar. *Delayed* rewards are those that follow the behavior by a period of days, weeks, or even longer. For example, you may have to wait weeks before a free-in-the-mail premium object can be enjoyed. Generally speaking, *consumers are more responsive to immediate rather than delayed rewards.* Of course, this is in line with the natural human tendency to seek immediate rather than delayed gratification.

Manufacturer Objectives.   As discussed in Chapter 18, manufacturers use sales promotions to accomplish various objectives. There are three general categories of objectives: trial impact, franchise holding/loading, and image reinforcement.

Some sales promotions (e.g., samples, coupons) are used primarily to have *trial impact.* A manufacturer uses these techniques to induce nonusers to try a brand for the first time or to encourage retrial for consumers who have not purchased the brand for an extended period. At other times, manufacturers use sales promotions to hold on to their franchise of current users by rewarding them for continuing to purchase the promoted brand or to load them so they have no need to switch to another brand. This objective is referred to as *franchise holding/loading.* Sales promotions also can be used for *image-reinforcement* purposes. For example, the careful selection of the right premium object or appropriate sweepstake prize can serve to reinforce a brand's high-quality, luxury image.

Classification of Sales-Promotion Methods

It is insightful to consider each consumer-oriented sales-promotion technique in terms of the type of reward provided and the nature of objective accomplished. Table 20.1 presents a six-cell typology.

Cell 1 includes two sales-promotion techniques—sampling and P-O-P coupons—that are used to induce trial purchase behavior by providing consumers with an immediate reward. The reward is either monetary savings, in the case of instant coupons, or a free product, in the case of sampling. Media- and mail-delivered coupons and free-in-the-mail premiums, found in Cell 2, are techniques that produce trial impact yet delay the reward to consumers.

Cells 3 and 4 contain franchise holding/loading tools. Marketing communicators design these techniques to keep existing customers (a brand's franchise) from switching to competitive brands, to reward present customers, and to encourage repeat purchasing in general. Immediate reward/franchise holding methods (Cell 3) are price-offs, bonus packs, and in-, on-, and near-pack premiums. Delayed reward/franchise holding techniques, found in Cell 4, are in- and on-pack coupons and refund and rebate offers.

Building a brand's image is primarily the task of advertising; however, sales-promotion tools may support advertising efforts by reinforcing a brand's

▬ ▬

T A B L E 20 . 1   **Major Consumer-Oriented Forms of Sales Promotions**

Consumer Reward	**Manufacturer's Objective**		
	Trial Impact	**Franchise Holding/Loading**	**Image Reinforcement**
Immediate	(1) Sampling P-O-P coupons	(3) Price-offs Bonus packs In-, on-, and near-pack premiums	(5)
Delayed	(2) Media- and mail- delivered coupons Free-in-the-mail premiums	(4) In- and on-pack coupons Refunds and rebates	(6) Self-liquidating premiums Contests and sweepstakes

image. By nature, these techniques are incapable of providing consumers with an immediate reward; therefore, Cell 5 is empty. Cell 6 contains self-liquidating premiums and contests/sweepstakes; in addition to performing other tasks, these techniques serve to strengthen a brand's image.

Several concluding observations concerning Table 20.1 are needed before proceeding. A first important point is that each technique is classified under the specific objective that it is *primarily* responsible for accomplishing. This should not be interpreted to mean a technique is capable of performing only a single objective. For example, refunds and rebates are classified as franchise holding/loading techniques, but on some occasions they may also encourage trial purchasing. Second, note that two techniques, coupons and premiums, have multiple entries. This is because these techniques achieve different objectives depending on the specific form of *delivery vehicle*. Coupons delivered through the media (e.g., newspapers) or in the mail offer a form of delayed reward, whereas coupons that can be peeled from a package at the point of purchase offer an immediate reward. Similarly, premium objects that are delivered in, on, or near a product's package provide an immediate reward, while those requiring mail delivery yield a reward only after some delay.

The remainder of the chapter will discuss each of these techniques in some detail.

Sampling

The baby-food division of Heinz foods developed a rather revolutionary product idea—a powdered instant baby food. Although Heinz's management was optimistic about instant baby food, they knew consumers would resist trying the product because of the natural inertia consumers have in making any dramatic product shift and for fear of treating their new babies as guinea pigs. A further complication was the difficulty of communicating the product's benefits by advertising alone.

Heinz needed a way to get mothers to try instant baby food. The solution was to employ the services of Giftpax, a company that annually delivers over 3.5 million product samples to mothers of newborn infants. This form of sampling avoided waste distribution and gave mothers firsthand experience with preparing and feeding their babies instant food. Many sample users became loyal users.[2]

This case illustrates the power of sampling as a promotional technique. Most practitioners agree that sampling is the premier sales-promotion device for generating trial product or brand usage. In fact, some observers believe that sample distribution is almost a necessity when introducing new or improved products or when seeking new markets for established products.

By definition, **sampling** includes any method used to deliver an actual- or trial-size product to the consumer. Marketers deliver samples in a variety of ways: (1) by direct mail, either alone or in cooperation with other brands; (2) through flat samples included in print media; (3) door to door by special distribution crews; (4) in or on the package of another product that serves as the sample carrier; (5) at high-traffic locations, such as shopping centers or special events; and (6) in store, where demonstrator samples are available for trial.

When the objective is to reach a broad cross section of consumers, door-to-door and mail delivery are the most effective means. The other sampling methods cost substantially less but do not reach nearly as many consumers. Promotion practitioners recommend using those other techniques only when funds are limited.[3]

Sampling Problems

There are several problems with using sampling. First, sampling is *expensive.* Second, mass mailings of samples can be *mishandled* by the postal service. Third, samples distributed door to door or in high-traffic locations may suffer from *wasted distribution* and not reach the hands of the best potential customers. Fourth, in- or on-package sampling *excludes consumers* who do not buy the carrying brand. Finally, in-store sampling often *fails to reach sufficient numbers of consumers* to justify the expense.

Due to its expense and because of waste and other problems, the use of sampling decreased in the early 1970s as many marketers turned to coupons

2. "Products on Trial," *Marketing Communications,* October 1987, pp. 73–74.
3. *ANA Consumer Promotion Seminar Fact Book* (New York: Association of National Advertisers, undated).

as a cheaper alternative.[4] However, with the development of creative solutions and innovations in sampling, promotion managers have again become enthusiastic about sampling. Sampling has become more efficient in reaching specific target groups, results are readily measurable, and the rising costs of media advertising have increased the relative attractiveness of sampling.

Sampling Trends

Two major trends have evolved in conjunction with the renewed use of sampling.[5]

Increased Selectivity.   Sampling services that specialize in *precision distribution* (targeting) have emerged in recent years. Giftpax's distribution of Heinz baby food to mothers of newborns is one example. Another is John Blair Marketing, which offers the "JBM Sample Pack," a service that pinpoints and selectively delivers samples to consumers who are either product nonusers or users of competitive brands. Sample recipients are surveyed initially by questionnaire and identified by demographic and product/brand-usage characteristics. Individual sample packs are then assembled specifically for each person: he or she receives only products that match his or her product and brand consumption patterns. Sampled products are delivered directly by mail to recipients' homes.

The MarketSource Corporation is another selective sampling service. It offers the Bonus Pak, a hand-delivered package of product samples and coupons, to blue-collar employees at workplace sites.[6]

New Techniques and Ideas.   Numerous creative ideas are being applied in an effort to get sample merchandise into the hands of targeted consumers. Any college student who has traveled to Florida over spring break is familiar with the product sampling techniques used by brewers and other companies.

An especially creative product distribution took place recently in Brazil. In trying to grab market share from Coca-Cola, Pepsi-Cola hired male students to walk the beaches of Rio de Janeiro and distribute free Pepsi samples from refrigerated containers carried on their backs. The objective was to reach the prime market of consumers under the age of 20, who represent 50 percent of Brazil's population.[7]

4. George Donahue, "Sampling Update, Part I: Direct Response Offers, New Distribution Methods, and Co-op Promotions Help Improve Sampling Efficiency," *Marketing Communications*, September 1980, pp. 61–63.
5. George Donahue, "Sampling Update, Part II: A Guide to Distribution Methods and Services," *Marketing Communications*, October 1980, pp. 82–87.
6. "Targeting the Blue Collar Market," *Marketing Communications*, May 1987, p. 10.
7. Tania Anderson, "Pepsi Rescues Parched Beachgoers," *Advertising Age*, May 2, 1988, p. S-9.

How Effective Is Sampling?

How effective is sampling in influencing trial purchase behavior? What influence does it have on stimulating repeat purchase behavior? NPD Research, Inc., a firm that collects data from a panel of over 30,000 households who maintain continuous diaries of their packaged goods purchases, has shed light on these questions. Their composite results for eight brands show that of the households who did *not* receive free samples (the control group), an average of 11.4 percent made trial purchases of the eight brands. By comparison, 16 percent of the recipients of free samples made trial purchases. Moreover, 35.7 percent of the families who made purchases after receiving a sample repurchased the brand, whereas only 31.8 percent of the control-group triers repurchased.[8]

These results are particularly interesting because they run somewhat contrary to more theoretically based research, which has detected a tendency for sampling to diminish repeat purchasing.[9] According to *attribution theory*, sampling should diminish repeat purchasing because the sample users should infer that the only reason they consumed the sampled product was because it was free. The users are said to make an *external attribution*, that is, to discount their personal liking for a sampled item in favor of the alternative explanation that they tried it only because it was free. Comparatively, those who try a product without first receiving a sample are more likely to attribute their trial to a personal liking for the item (an *internal attribution*). This internal attribution fosters a positive attitude and is hypothesized to enhance the probability of repeat purchasing.[10]

When Should Sampling Be Used?

Promotion managers use sampling to induce consumers to try either a brand that is new or one that is moving into a different market. While it is important to encourage trial usage for new brands, sampling is not appropriate for all new or improved products. Ideal circumstances include the following:[11]

8. *Insights: Issues 1–13, 1979–1982* (New York: NPD Research, 1983), pp. 6–7.
9. Carol Scott, "Effects of Trial and Incentives on Repeat Purchase Behavior," *Journal of Marketing Research*, vol. 13 (August 1976), pp. 263–269. See also Joe A. Dodson, Alice M. Tybout, and Brian Sternthal, "Impact of Deals and Deal Retraction on Brand Switching," *Journal of Marketing Research*, vol. 15 (February 1978), pp. 72–81.
10. For more discussion of applications of attribution theory in marketing and consumer behavior, see Richard W. Mizerski, Linda L. Golden, and Jerome B. Kernan, "The Attribution Process in Consumer Decision Making," *Journal of Consumer Research*, vol. 6 (September 1979), pp. 123–140; Valerie S. Folkes, "Recent Attribution Research in Consumer Behavior: A Review and New Directions, *Journal of Consumer Research*, vol. 14 (March 1988), pp. 548–565.
11. Charles Fredericks, Jr., "What Ogilvy & Mather Has Learned about Sales Promotion," in *The Tools of Promotion* (New York: Association of National Advertisers, 1975).

1. Sampling should be used when a new or improved brand is either *demonstrably superior* to other brands or when it has *distinct relative advantages* over products that it is intended to replace.

2. Sampling should be used when the product concept is so innovative that it is *difficult to communicate by advertising alone.* The earlier example of Heinz instant baby food illustrates this point.

3. Sampling should be used when promotional *budgets can afford to generate consumer trial quickly.* Broad-scale sampling is extremely expensive. Imagine the expense incurred by Lever Brothers when it distributed samples of Sun Light dishwashing liquid to over 50 million households. (See Figure 20.1 for additional information about the sampling of this product.)

4. Sampling should be used when the *product class has almost universal usage.* Broader product usage makes sampling easier because selectivity is not as critical, and waste is not a problem. With the advent of selective-sampling services, this factor is not as important as it was in years past.

Couponing

Coupons provide cents-off savings to consumers when the coupon is redeemed. The major delivery modes are at the point-of-purchase, via direct mail, in the mass media, and in or on packages. Not all delivery methods have the same objective. Coupons distributed at the point of purchase provide immediate rewards to consumers and encourage trial purchases. Mail- and media-delivered coupons delay the reward, although they also generate trial purchase behavior. In comparison, package-delivered coupons are used to accomplish franchise holding rather than product trial. This section will discuss all of the coupon delivery modes in detail. Before discussing any specific delivery mode, it will be instructive to examine the growth of couponing, its economic impact, and consumer redemption patterns.

FIGURE 20.1   **Murphy's Law in Sampling**

As with all forms of marketing communications, things sometimes do not work in sampling the way they are designed. Take the previously mentioned case of Sun Light dishwashing liquid, a product of Lever Brothers. This product, which smells like lemons and contains 10 percent lemon juice, was extensively sampled to more than 50 million households. However, for some odd reason in Maryland, nearly 80 adults and children became ill after consuming the product, having mistaken the dishwashing liquid for lemon juice! According to a Lever Brothers' marketing research director, there is always a potential problem of misuse when a product is sent to homes rather than purchased with prior product knowledge at a supermarket.

Source: Lynn G. Reiling, "Consumers Misuse Mass Sampling for Sun Light Dishwashing Liquid," *Marketing News,* September 3, 1982, pp. 1, 2.

Growth and Trends in Coupons

In 1970 U.S. marketers distributed fewer than 17 billion coupons.[12] By 1983, they distributed nearly 143 billion, and in 1987 over 215 billion coupons were distributed.[13] This means approximately 900 coupons were distributed in 1987 to every man, woman, and child in the United States! As noted in the chapter's opening vignette, 97 percent of consumers use coupons for shopping.

This massive increase in the number of coupons distributed in the United States reflects the growing importance of couponing to marketers, especially packaged-good companies, and the growing number of marketers using coupons as an integral part of their promotional activities. Fully 96 percent of packaged-goods marketers used coupons in 1987.[14] While packaged-goods manufacturers are major users of coupons, coupon use has spread to producers of appliances and other durables, apparel, and numerous other products. Perhaps the most innovative of all couponing applications in recent years was by United Airlines following a devastating 55-day labor strike. By offering passengers half-fare coupons, United regained its prestrike market share in only 11 days rather than the seven months company financial executives feared it would take for recovery.[15]

Concurrent with the rising trend in the use of coupons, significant developments have taken place regarding the manner in which coupons are distributed. Changes have been instigated primarily because of *the need to avoid competitive clutter.* Coupons must stand out so that they will be clipped and ultimately redeemed by consumers.

Table 20.2 compares total coupon distribution across the major distribution vehicles for the years 1985 through 1988. Two major developments are apparent. First, the percentages of coupons delivered as part of the regular newspaper pages and via magazines have fallen considerably during this brief period. These statistics are even more dramatic in light of the fact that in 1979 nearly 75 percent of all coupons were distributed via newspapers and magazines as non-freestanding inserts.[16] A related development is that the percentage of coupons distributed via freestanding inserts (FSIs) increased from 59.9 percent in 1985 to 77.3 percent in 1988. This compares with approximately only 15 percent of coupons distributed by FSI in 1979. The reason for these changes

12. Roger A. Strang, "The Economic Impact of Cents-off Coupons," *Marketing Communications,* March 1981, pp. 35–44.
13. Nathaniel Frey, "Sales Promotion Analysis," *Marketing Communications,* August 1988, pp. 14–20.
14. Len Strazewski, "Promotion 'Carnival' Gets Serious," *Advertising Age,* May 2, 1988, p. S-2.
15. "The Toothpaste Tube That Saved United," *Advertising Age,* October 29, 1979, p. 14. This article's interesting title provides a clue as to the reason United decided on its couponing campaign. It seems that corporate executives were having difficulty coming up with a major promotional program to regain market share until one employee entered a meeting with a tube of toothpaste in his hand and claimed that just that morning he had gone to the store to get toothpaste and rather than buying the regular brand he switched to another brand that offered a 50 cents-off coupon. Why couldn't United do the same to get customers to switch back to it?
16. "Couponing Distribution Trends and Patterns," *PMAA Promotion Update '82* (New York: Promotion Management Association of America, Inc., 1983).

TABLE 20.2   **Coupon Distribution by Vehicle, 1985–1988 (Percent of Total Distribution)**

	1985	1986	1987	1988
FSI[a]	59.9	68.0	72.7	77.3
Newspaper ROP/Solo[b]	12.2	7.4	5.9	5.4
Newspaper Co-op	8.0	7.1	4.6	2.4
Direct Mail	4.4	4.0	5.3	5.0
In/On Pack	4.8	5.8	5.3	5.2
Magazines	8.6	6.5	3.7	2.4
Other	2.1	1.2	2.5	2.3

[a]Freestanding inserts. [b]ROP = Run of paper.
Source: Manufacturer's Coupon Control Center.

should be obvious: Freestanding inserts capture the consumer's attention more readily and therefore are superior in overcoming competitive clutter.

Another major trend in coupon distribution has been the establishment of *cooperative coupon programs.* These are programs in which a couponing distribution service distributes coupons for a single company's multiple brands or brands from multiple companies. Cooperative programs enable companies to expand coupon reach and gain the economies of scale resulting from shared distribution costs. Some illustrative cooperative programs are "Newspaper Co-op Couponing" by the Marketing Corporation of America (a daily newspaper distribution program), "Blair Inserts" by John Blair Marketing (a Sunday insert program), "Thermatics" by Synergistic Marketing (a magazine insert program), "Intercept" by Stratmar Systems (store handouts), and "Carol Wright" by Donnelley Marketing (direct mail).

Donnelley Marketing's "Carol Wright" service provides a good illustration of how cooperative couponing services operate. Donnelley Marketing mails questionnaires to millions of households and collects information on product and brand usage. Figure 20.2 shows one page from a three-page questionnaire mailed to consumers in 1988. Note that respondents are asked about general product usage and specific brand usage. Donnelley enters returned surveys into a huge data base containing names and addresses on more than 80 million unduplicated households. Coupons and samples are then mailed to product/brand *nonusers* and *competitive brand users.* For example, with regard to question 3 (brands of pain relievers used), the makers of Advil, say, would find it advantageous to mail coupons to people who are heavy users of other brands.

Economic Impact

The growth in coupon offers (over 215 billion coupons are now distributed annually) has not occurred without criticism. On average, slightly more than three percent of all distributed coupons are redeemed. Some critics contend

Questionnaire from Donnelley Marketing's "Carol Wright" Cooperative Service

FIGURE 20.2

Even if you've answered before, please help with this NEW SURVEY

Plus FREE!!! Carol Wright's All New Coupon Wallet

America's leading manufacturers want to know what smart shoppers like you are looking for when they go to the store. So, when you send us your answers to this survey, they'll say "Thanks" with a pack of discount coupons, special offers, FREE samples plus your FREE Carol Wright COUPON WALLET. Thanks.

Carol Wright

Please help us to read your survey by answering within the squares.

1. Which brand(s) of toothpaste was used most often by your household in the past three months?
1. ☐ Aim   3. ☐ Close-Up   5. ☐ Crest
2. ☐ Aqua-Fresh   4. ☐ Colgate   6. ☐ Other

1A. Which form of toothpaste do you use most often?
7. ☐ Paste   8. ☐ Gel

1B. Do you have a child twelve years or younger living in your household?   09. ☐ Yes   10. ☐ No

2. Do you use milk additive products to make cold chocolate milk?   1. ☐ Yes   2. ☐ No

2A. If yes, which of the following milk additive products do you use most often to make cold chocolate milk?
3. ☐ Hershey's Syrup   5. ☐ Nestle Powder
4. ☐ Nestle's Syrup   6. ☐ Other

3. Which brand(s) of pain relievers are used in your home regularly?
01. ☐ Advil   07. ☐ Datril   12. ☐ Nuprin
02. ☐ Anacin   08. ☐ Excedrin   13. ☐ Panadol
03. ☐ Anacin-3   09. ☐ Tylenol   14. ☐ Store Brand
04. ☐ Bayer   10. ☐ E.S. Tylenol   15. ☐ Other
05. ☐ Max. Bayer   11. ☐ Medipren   16. ☐ None
06. ☐ Bufferin

3A. How many tablets of pain relievers are used in your household each month?
17. ☐ 1-4   18. ☐ 5-10   19. ☐ 11-20   20. ☐ 21+

3B. Did you ever use non-prescription pain relievers in capsule form?   21. ☐ Yes   22. ☐ No

4. How many times did you or any member of your household purchase eye drops in the past 6 months?
1. ☐ 1   2. ☐ 2 to 4   3. ☐ 5 or more   4. ☐ None

4A. Which of the following brands of eye drops have you or any member of your household purchased in the past 6 months?
05. ☐ Clear Eyes   08. ☐ OcuClear   10. ☐ Visine A.C.
06. ☐ Murine   09. ☐ Visine   11. ☐ Other
07. ☐ Murine Plus

5. Do you use an air freshener or carpet deodorizer?
1. ☐ Yes   2. ☐ No

5A. If yes, how often do you make a purchase?
3. ☐ Once a month   5. ☐ Less than every
4. ☐ Once every three months   three months

6. Do you own an automatic dishwasher?
1. ☐ Yes   2. ☐ No

6A. If yes, about how many loads of dishes do you do in your automatic dishwasher in an average week?
3. ☐ 7+   4. ☐ 3-6   5. ☐ 1-2   6. ☐ Less than 1

6B. Which brands of automatic dishwasher detergents have you used in the past year? (Check all that apply.) Which brand do you buy most often? (Check only one.)

	Have Used	Use Most Often (Check only one)
Cascade Powder Regular	07. ☐	17. ☐
Lemon	08. ☐	18. ☐
Liquid Cascade	09. ☐	19. ☐
Electrasol Powder	10. ☐	20. ☐
Liquid Electrasol	11. ☐	21. ☐
Liquid Palmolive Automatic Regular	12. ☐	22. ☐
Lemon	13. ☐	23. ☐
Sunlight Powder	14. ☐	24. ☐
Liquid Sunlight	15. ☐	25. ☐
Other	16. ☐	26. ☐

7. Over the past 2 years which of the following all purpose spray cleaners have you purchased?
1. ☐ Formula 409   6. ☐ Pine Sol
2. ☐ Fantastik   7. ☐ Lysol Direct
3. ☐ Lemon Fantastik   8. ☐ Pine Magic
4. ☐ Scrub Free Kitchen   9. ☐ Other
5. ☐ Scrub Free Pine

8. Do you or does anyone in your household have thinning hair, that is, hair that is now not as full and dense as it once was when you were younger?
1. ☐ Yes   2. ☐ No

8A. Which one of the following statements best describes the feelings you or another household member have about his or her own thinning hair?
3. ☐ Not at all concerned about thinning hair
4. ☐ Somewhat concerned about thinning hair
5. ☐ Very concerned about thinning hair
6. ☐ Extremely concerned about thinning hair

8B. Would you or the person in your household who has thinning hair use a scientifically formulated shampoo to gently, but effectively clean thinning hair?
7. ☐ Yes   8. ☐ No

9. Which best describes your dress size?
1. ☐ Petite   3. ☐ Misses   5. ☐ Women   7. ☐ Tall
2. ☐ Junior   4. ☐ Maternity   6. ☐ Half-size

10. Which of these pads and/or tampons is your usual brand?
TAMPONS   09. ☐ Playtex Super
(check one)   10. ☐ Playtex Super Plus
01. ☐ Tampax Slender   11. ☐ Other _____
02. ☐ Tampax Regular   **PADS**
03. ☐ Tampax Super   **(check one)**
04. ☐ Tampax Super Plus   12. ☐ Always Plus Super
05. ☐ Kotex Security Regular   13. ☐ Kotex Overnites
06. ☐ Kotex Security Super   14. ☐ Stayfree Super Maxi
07. ☐ Playtex Slender   15. ☐ Stayfree Maxi
08. ☐ Playtex Regular   16. ☐ Other _____

11. Do you, or anyone in your household use a laxative?
1. ☐ Yes   2. ☐ No

11A. If yes, which brand is used most often? (Check One)
03. ☐ Citrucel   07. ☐ Dulcolax   16. ☐ Naturacil
04. ☐ Correctol Powdered Fiber   08. ☐ Effer-Syllium   17. ☐ Nature's Remedy
   09. ☐ Ex-Lax   18. ☐ Perdiem
   10. ☐ Feen-A-Mint   19. ☐ Phillips' Milk of Magnesia
05. ☐ Correctol Tablets or Liquid   11. ☐ Fiberall
   12. ☐ Fibercon
   13. ☐ Fiberway   20. ☐ Prompt
   14. ☐ Haley's M-O   21. ☐ Serutan
06. ☐ Doxidan   15. ☐ Metamucil   22. ☐ Other

11B. When a laxative is used, how many days during a one-month period is it taken? (Check One)
23. ☐ Less than one day per month   26. ☐ One day per week
24. ☐ One day per month   27. ☐ 2-3 days per week
25. ☐ 2-3 days per month   28. ☐ 4 or more days per week

11C. On those days when this product is used, how many times a day do you use it? (Check One)
29. ☐ More than once a day   30. ☐ Once a day

12. How many times have you shopped by mail in the last six months? In total, what did you spend?
1. ☐ Once or twice   3. ☐ Under $50
2. ☐ 3 or more times   4. ☐ Over $50

Please answer questions on inside. ►

Source: Courtesy Donnelley Marketing.

that coupons are wasteful and may actually increase prices of consumer goods.

Whether or not coupons are wasteful and inefficient remains problematic. However, it is undeniable that coupons are an expensive proposition. To get a better feel for coupon costs, consider the case of a hypothetical cake-mix marketer that offers a 25 cents-off coupon to consumers. The coupon's actual cost to the manufacturer is considerably more than 25 cents. Table 20.3 details the actual full cost per coupon. The actual cost of nearly 56 cents per coupon indicates that coupon activity requires substantial investment to accomplish desired objectives. Obviously, programs that aid in reducing costs, such as cooperative delivery programs, or in enhancing redemption rates, as in the case of freestanding inserts, are eagerly sought. Creative and innovative couponing programs are constantly being developed.

Coupons are indeed costly, some are clearly wasteful, and other promotional devices may be better. However, the extensive use of coupons either suggests that there are a large number of incompetent marketing executives or that better promotional tools are not available or are economically infeasible. The latter explanation is the more reasonable when considering how the marketplace operates. If a business practice is uneconomical, it will not continue to be used for long. When a better business practice is available, it will replace the previous solution. Conclusion: It appears that coupons are extensively used because marketers have been unable to devise more effective and economical methods for accomplishing the objectives achieved with couponing.

TABLE 20.3   **Full Coupon Cost per Redeemed Coupon[a]**

1.	Distribution cost: 10,000,000 coupons circulated at $5 per thousand	$ 50,000
2.	Redemption rate = 3.5%	350,000 redeemed coupons
3.	Redemption cost: 350,000 redemptions at 25¢ face value	$ 87,500
4.	Handling cost: 350,000 redemptions at 8¢ each[b]	$ 28,000
5.	Total program cost: 1 + 3 + 4	$165,500
6.	Cost per redeemed coupon: $165,500/350,000	47.3¢
7.	Actual product sold on redemption: With misredemption estimated at 15%, product sold by redemption = 350,000 × 85%	297,500 coupons
8.	Actual cost per redeemed coupon: Total program cost ($165,500)/actual number of redeemed coupons (297,500)	55.6¢

[a]Adapted from Louis J. Haugh, "How Consumers Measure Up," *Advertising Age*, June 1981, p. 58.

[b]A handling charge is the amount paid by manufacturers to retailers to compensate them for their costs incurred while handling coupons.

Coupon Redemption

The cost and ultimate profitability of couponing depends both on the number of consumers who redeem coupons and the characteristics of those who redeem. For example, as described in Chapter 18, if the only consumers who redeem are those who would have bought the brand anyway, then the couponing has increased costs while reducing the per-unit profit margin.

What types of consumers are most likely to redeem coupons? Of course this varies from product to product and brand to brand, but evidence shows that households most likely to redeem are those that were the most likely to buy the brand in the first place. It has been estimated that as much as 70 to 80 percent of coupons are redeemed by a brand's current users.[17] Moreover, most consumers revert to their precoupon brand choice immediately after making a coupon redemption.[18]

The implication is that much couponing activity is unprofitable because it fails to build a brand's franchise. Promotion managers continuously seek ways to increase couponing profitability and to target coupons to those consumers who may otherwise not purchase their brands. The following sections describe the major forms of couponing activity, the objectives each is intended to accomplish, and the innovations designed to increase couponing profitability.

Point-of-Purchase Couponing

The presentation of couponing delivery methods is ordered along the lines of the framework presented earlier in Table 20.1 **Point-of-purchase coupons** are those that are simultaneously distributed and redeemable at the point of purchase. As such, these coupons are used primarily to generate *trial purchase behavior*. They accomplish this by providing consumers with an *immediate reward*. Point-of-purchase couponing comes in two forms: instant and in-store.

Instant Coupons. Most coupon-distribution methods have delayed impact on consumers because the coupon is received in the consumer's home and held for a period of time before it is redeemed. Instant coupons, which are *peelable from the package* at the point of purchase, represent an immediate reward that can spur the consumer to undertake a trial purchase of the promoted brand. Wheaties cereal provides an illustration of instant couponing. General Mills, the maker of Wheaties, wanted a promotional program that would provide a significant price reduction and an immediate point-of-purchase incentive for consumers. Rather than use a price-off deal, which often creates problems for retailers, General Mills offered a 15 cents *peel-off coupon*

17. Nathaniel Frey, "Targeted Couponing: New Wrinkles Cut Waste," *Marketing Communications,* January 1988, p. 40.
18. Kapil Bawa and Robert W. Shoemaker, "The Effects of a Direct Mail Coupon on Brand Choice Behavior," *Journal of Marketing Research,* vol. 24 (November 1987), pp. 370–376.

attached to the front of the Wheaties package. The coupons were designed to be removed by the consumer and redeemed when checking out. The program gained strong retailer acceptance and high coupon-redemption levels.[19]

Although the instant coupon is a minor form of couponing, it has emerged in recent years as an alternative to price-off deals (in which every package must be reduced in price). Moreover, the redemption level of around 25 percent is considerably higher than the level for other couponing techniques.[20]

In-Store Coupons.   Several electronic systems for dispensing coupons at the point of purchase have been introduced in recent years. Most have failed due to poor technology and costs to the manufacturer that are much higher than FSIs—$75 per thousand electronic coupons versus $10 per thousand FSI coupons.[21]

One system that appears to be a success is the "Coupon Solution" from Catalina Marketing Corporation. As of 1988 the Coupon Solution was available in over 1,000 supermarkets nationwide. Major companies such as Campbell Soup, Kellogg, Procter & Gamble, and Quaker Oats pay Catalina to put coupons in all the supermarkets it serves. The Coupon Solution system is connected electronically by a personal computer to a supermarket optical scanner. Once the scanner records the shopper has purchased a *competitor's brand*, a coupon from the participating manufacturer is dispensed. For example, a consumer who has just purchased Heinz ketchup receives a coupon for Hunt's ketchup. By targeting competitors' customers, the Coupon Solution ensures the manufacturer of reaching people who buy the product category but are not currently purchasing the manufacturer's brand.[22] Redemption rates for the Coupon Solution coupons are said to be 14.4 percent, which far exceeds the 4.5 percent rate for FSIs.[23]

Mail- and Media-Delivered Coupons

These coupon delivery modes initiate *trial purchase behavior* by offering consumers *delayed rewards*. As previously shown in Table 20.2, direct-mail-delivered coupons represented only 5 percent of the manufacturer-distributed coupons in 1988. Mass-media modes (newspapers and magazines) are clearly dominant, carrying about 87 percent of all coupons distributed in 1988; the bulk of this was in the form of freestanding inserts (FSIs). While there are advantages and disadvantages to employing either mode, each performs a different function.

19. Adapted from Richard H. Aycrigg, *Promotion Update '82*, a publication of the Promotion Marketing Association of America, Inc., New York, 1982.
20. Ed Meyer, "It's on the Package," *Advertising Age*, May 17, 1982, p. M-27.
21. Liz Murphy, "Redemption Isn't Always Salvation in Couponing," *Sales and Marketing Management*, January 13, 1986, pp. 45–47.
22. Lori Kesler, "Catalina Cuts Couponing Clutter," *Advertising Age*, May 9, 1988, p. S-30.
23. Murphy, "Redemption Isn't Always Salvation in Couponing," p. 46.

Mail-Delivered Coupons. Marketers typically use mail-delivered coupons to introduce new or improved products. Mailings can be directed either at a broad cross section of the market or targeted to specific demographic segments. Mailed coupons achieve the highest household penetration. Whereas coupon distribution via magazines rarely reaches more than 60 percent of all homes, mail can reach as high as 95 percent. Moreover, when consumers receive coupon offers in the mail, they are able to make a purchase decision at home, away from the competitive influences of the supermarket. Furthermore, direct mail achieves the highest redemption rate of all mass-delivered coupon techniques. A. C. Nielsen estimates the direct-mail redemption rate to be 11.6 percent. Comparatively, the estimated redemption rates for ROP solo newspaper, Sunday freestanding inserts, and ROP magazine were 3.1, 5.1, and 2.6 percent, respectively.[24]

The major disadvantage of direct-mailed coupons is that they are relatively expensive compared with other coupon-distribution methods. Another disadvantage is that direct mailing is especially inefficient and expensive for brands that enjoy a high market share. This is because a large proportion of the coupon recipients may already be regular users of the coupon brand, thereby defeating the primary purpose of generating trial purchasing.

Media-Delivered Coupons. Most coupon distribution is achieved through various newspaper delivery modes (ROP solo, co-op, Sunday paper, and freestanding inserts) and magazines (see Table 20.2). The major advantage of media coupons is their broad exposure; they are limited only by media circulation. Media coupons also can be directed to specific market segments. While magazines and newspapers both permit geographical selectivity, magazines also permit demographic and psychographic pinpointing. Moreover, while freestanding inserts cost only 50 to 60 percent of the cost of direct-mail coupons, their redemption rate is close to 80 percent of that of direct mail.

The disadvantages of media-delivered coupons are that they generate relatively low levels of redemption; they do not, with the exception of freestanding inserts, generate much trade interest; and they suffer from considerable misredemption. The latter problem is so significant to all parties involved in couponing that it deserves a special section later in the chapter.

In- and On-Pack Coupons

In- and on-pack coupons are distributed by inclusion either inside a product's package or as a part of a package's exterior. This form of couponing should not be confused with the previously discussed instant, or peelable, coupon. Whereas the latter is removable at the point of purchase and redeemable *for*

24. Louis J. Haugh, "How Coupons Measure Up," *Advertising Age*, June 8, 1981, p. 58. Note: ROP stands for run of paper, or run of press, which means that the ad carrying a coupon is part of the regular newspaper/magazine pages and not a separate section or insert.

that particular purchase, an in- or on-pack coupon cannot be removed until it is in the shopper's home and cannot be redeemed *until a subsequent purchase.*

Frequently, a coupon for one brand is promoted by another brand. For example, General Mills promoted its brand of granola bars by placing cents-off coupons in cereal boxes. Practitioners call this practice *crossruffing,* a term borrowed from bridge and bridge-type card games where partners alternate trumping one another when they are unable to follow suit.

Though marketers use crossruffing to create trial purchases or to stimulate purchase of products such as granola bars that are not staple items, in- and on-pack coupons carried by the same brand are generally intended to stimulate *repeat purchasing.* That is, once consumers have exhausted the contents of a particular package, they are more likely to repurchase that brand of product if an attractive inducement, such as a cents-off coupon, is available immediately. In other words, the coupon has *bounce back* value. An initial purchase, the "bounce," may stimulate another purchase, the "bounce back," when a hard-to-avoid inducement such as an in-package coupon is made available.

A major advantage of in- and on-pack coupons is that there are virtually no distribution costs. Moreover, redemption rates are much higher because most of the package-delivered coupons are received by brand users. The major limitations of these coupons are that they offer *delayed value* to consumers, they do not reach nonusers of the carrying brand, and trade interest is relatively low due to the delayed nature of the offer.

Coupon Misredemption

As alluded to earlier, misredemption is a major problem, especially in the use of media-delivered coupons. The best way to understand how misredemption occurs is to examine the *redemption process.*

The process begins with a shopper presenting the checkout clerk with coupons that are then subtracted from the total bill. Certain conditions and restrictions must be met: The consumer must buy the merchandise specified on the coupon in the size, brand, and quantity directed; only one coupon can be redeemed per item; cash may not be given for the coupon; and the coupon must be redeemed before the expiration date.

Retailers, in turn, redeem the coupons they have received in order to obtain reimbursement from the manufacturers that sponsored the coupons. Retailers typically hire another company, called a *clearinghouse,* to sort and redeem the coupons in return for a fee. Clearinghouses, acting on behalf of a number of retail clients, consolidate coupons by redemption address before forwarding them. Legitimate clearinghouses maintain controls by ensuring that their clients are legitimate retailers who are likely to sell the products in the amounts they are submitting for redemption. Clearinghouses forward the coupons to *redemption centers,* which serve as agents of the manufacturers that issue the coupons. The redemption center pays off on all properly redeemed coupons. If a center questions the validity of certain coupons, it may go to its client, a manufacturer, for approval on redeeming suspected coupons.[25]

The system is not quite as clear-cut as it may appear from this description. Some large retailers act as their own clearinghouses, some manufacturers serve as their own redemption centers, and some independent firms, e.g., the A. C. Nielsen Co. offer both clearinghouse and redemption-center services. However, regardless of the specific mechanism by which a coupon is ultimately redeemed (or misredeemed), the retailer is reimbursed for the amount of the face value paid to the consumer and for payment of a handling charge, which currently is 8 cents per coupon. Herein rests the potential for misredemption: A single coupon with, say, a face value of 40 cents pays the unscrupulous person 48 cents. One thousand such misredeemed coupons are worth $480!

Now that the reader has a grasp of the redemption mechanism, the discussion of how misredemption occurs and who participates in it can be continued. Misredemption is a major problem, but it is difficult to accurately measure its magnitude. Estimates of the misredemption rate range from a low of 15 percent to a high of 40 percent. Many product managers estimate a 20 to 25 percent rate of misredemption when budgeting for coupon events.[26] A. C. Nielsen estimates the amount of coupon misredemption at $250 million per year—if not higher.[27]

Misredemption occurs at every level of the redemption process. Sometimes *consumers* at the checkout counter present coupons that have expired, coupons for items not purchased, or coupons for a smaller-sized product than that specified by the coupon. Some *clerks* take coupons to the store and exchange them for cash without making a purchase. At the *store management* level, retailers may boost profits by submitting extra coupons in addition to those redeemed legitimately. A dishonest retailer can buy coupons on the black market, age them in a clothes dryer, mix them with legitimate coupons, and then mail in the batch for redemption.[28] Shady *clearinghouses* engage in misredemption by combining illegally purchased coupons with real ones and certifying the batch as legitimate.

The major source of coupon misredemption is *large-scale professional misredeemers* who either (1) recruit the services of actual retailers to serve as conduits through which coupons are misredeemed, or (2) operate phony businesses that exist solely for the purpose of redeeming huge quantities of illegal coupons.[29] Illegal coupons typically are obtained from *gang cutting or tearing*

25. "The Route to Redemption," *Advertising Age*, May 30, 1983, p. 57.
26. Louis J. Haugh, "What Are the Added Costs of Coupon Misredemption?" *Advertising Age*, February 6, 1978, p. 42.
27. "Computers Help Foil Coupon Fraud," *Marketing News*, August 15, 1986, p. 1.
28. Vincent Coppola and David Friendly, "Coupon Caper," *Newsweek*, November 27, 1978, pp. 89–90.
29. Ibid.

mint-condition coupons from numerous copies of the same issue of a newspaper or magazine.

The following examples reveal how professional misredeemers operate. "Jimmy's Coupon Redemption Center" was the front for a six-man misredemption ring. Jimmy's acquired bulk coupons from sources such as scrap dealers, newspapers, and charity groups, and then designated fictitious stores as payees for redeemed coupons. The gang managed to acquire $750,000 from nearly 200 manufacturers before they were caught.[30]

Another case involving coupon fraud was discovered by employees of Colgate-Palmolive's coupon redemption center in Kentucky. The redemption center received coupons that had been printed but had never been used in a promotion. The discovery of these stolen coupons led investigators to uncover a large-scale fraud scheme run by four supermarket operators, who during an 11-month period defrauded companies of about $500,000.[31]

A Los Angeles accountant recruited coupon clippers from California charities and paid them $5 for each pound of coupons they collected. Needless to say, he accumulated huge quantities of coupons and was able to redeem millions of dollars before the scheme was detected.[32]

The Sting.   Due to the pervasiveness of the coupon-misredemption problem and especially because of the role played by organized crime, postal authorities and local governments have been forced to take action. Two celebrated *sting operations* were undertaken in an attempt to identify fraudulent coupon redemption schemes. In both cases, coupons for *fictitious products* were advertised heavily in newspapers. The first undercover operation was undertaken by the Brooklyn district attorney's office and involved a fictitious detergent brand, "Breen," that was advertised with 25 cents-off coupons. Of course, because Breen was a fictitious brand, any redemption of the coupons amounted to misredemption. Twenty-six retailers, who collected more than $122,000 from a variety of coupon refunds including over $100,000 paid out by A. C. Nielsen, were indicted on various charges of larceny and fraud.[33]

A second sting operation took place in Florida. U.S. Postal Service (USPS) inspectors finally busted a well-organized misredemption ring, but not before the ring had bilked manufacturers out of an astounding $186 million. The ring had organized between 700 and 800 otherwise legitimate grocery retailers through which they redeemed gang-clipped coupons.

In order to catch the ring in action, the USPS used a coupon for a nonexistent bug killer named "Broach." Broach ads carrying 25 cents-off coupons

30. Louis J. Haugh, "Feds Smash Profitable Coupon Fraud Operation," *Advertising Age*, June 9, 1975, p. 27.
31. Coppola and Friendly, "Coupon Caper," pp. 89–90.
32. Ibid.
33. "Coupon Fraud Indictments Termed 'Only Tip of Iceberg', " *Advertising Age*, December 18, 1978, pp. 1, 77.

The Bait: Coupon for Fictitious "Broach"   FIGURE 20.3

Source: "Coupon Fraud Indictments Termed 'Only Tip of Iceberg,'" *Advertising Age,* December 18, 1978, pp. 1, 77.

(see Figure 20.3) were run in three Florida newspapers as part of a cooperative freestanding-insert package. Coupon misredemptions for this fictitious product led to the arrest of dozens of retailers and four independent newspaper distributors, who sold freestanding-coupon inserts in bulk to the misredemption ring.

Foiling Coupon Fraud. In addition to government-sponsored sting operations, individual companies can take steps to reduce the loss from coupon misredemption. Quaker Oats, for example, maintains a computerized database of the coupon-redemption histories of over 100,000 retail grocers. The data file for each retailer contains information on whether the retailer has a history of misredemption along with data on normal redemption patterns. Hence, an abnormally large coupon submission from a particular retailer signals the possibility of a misredemption attempt.[34]

Another method of reducing coupon misredemption is the use of *actual bank checks* instead of traditional coupons. With this method, the customer receives a check from a manufacturer through the mail. The check permits the customer to receive a cash discount when purchasing the manufacturer's product. The retailer deposits redeemed checks into its bank account and does not have to go through a clearinghouse, with the accompanying delay, to get reimbursed—reimbursement is immediate with the deposit. While it is too early to know how extensively bank checks will be used in lieu of conventional coupons, preliminary evidence indicates that the misredemption rate is reduced from upwards of 20 percent for coupons to 4 percent or less with checks.[35]

34. "Computers Help Foil Coupon Fraud."
35. Len Strazewski, "Checks May Replace Some Coupons," *Advertising Age,* October 12, 1987, p. 30.

Premiums

Broadly defined, **premiums** are articles of merchandise or services (e.g., travel) offered by manufacturers to induce action on the part of the sales force, trade representatives, or consumers. This section focuses on consumer motivation. Many types of premium offers are used to motivate consumers; these include free-in-the-mail premiums; in-, on-, and near-pack premiums; and self-liquidating premiums. All three forms serve fundamentally different purposes. Free-in-the-mail premiums are useful primarily for generating initial brand trial or retrial; in-, on-, and near-pack premiums serve franchise-holding purposes; and self-liquidators perform image-reinforcement functions.

Free-in-the-Mail Premiums

By definition, a free-in-the-mail premium is a promotion in which consumers receive a premium item from the sponsoring manufacturer in return for submitting a required number of proofs of purchase. For example, with two Skippy peanut butter proofs of purchase, consumers receive a free Anchor Hocking pop-top container. With one proof of purchase for Woolite, consumers obtain free Sheer & Silky pantyhose (see Figure 20.4).

In addition to stimulating consumer trial, free-in-the-mail premiums can achieve other objectives. When directed at adult audiences, these premiums can accomplish *franchise-holding* objectives by rewarding consumers' brand loyalties and encouraging repeat-purchase behavior.

Relatively few consumers who are exposed to free mail-in offers actually avail themselves of the opportunity. The national average redemption rate is estimated to be between 2 and 4 percent.[36] However, these premiums can be extremely effective if the premium item is appealing to the target market, as is probably the case with Woolite's offer of free pantyhose.

In-, On-, and Near-Pack Premiums

In- and on-pack premiums offer a premium item inside a package, attached to a package, or the package itself is reusable. For example, in a delightful promotional program for Cap'n Crunch cereal, the box was labeled "Christmas Crunch" and Captain Horatio was shown on the package dressed like Santa Claus. The package advertised a free Christmas tree ornament inside the box— a premium offer with much appeal to small children. In general, in- and on-package premiums offer consumers *immediate value* and thereby encourage increased product consumption.

36. William R. Dean, "Irresistible But Not Free of Problems," *Advertising Age,* October 6, 1980, pp. S-1, S-12.

Illustration of a Free-in-the-Mail Premium Offer   FIGURE 20.4

MAIL-IN CERTIFICATE/NOT REDEEMABLE IN STORES

FREE SHEER & SILKY PANTYHOSE

with proof of purchase* from WOOLITE® Cold Water Wash plus $1.00 for postage and handling

Complete the following to select your
No nonsense® style and shade:
☐ SHEER & SILKY
    Style (choose one) ☐ Regular ☐ Control Top
    Shade (choose one) ☐ Nude ☐ Tan
☐ DRESS SHEER & SILKY (style: Sheer to Waist)
    Shade (choose one) ☐ Nude ☐ Tan ☐ Black
Indicate your size:
☐ Petite to Medium ☐ Medium to Tall ☐ Queen
Ht. 4'11" to 5'7"   Ht. 5'0" to 6'0"   Ht. 5'2" to 6'0"
Wt. 95-150 lbs   Wt. 110-175 lbs   Wt. 136-200 lbs
To receive your free pair of pantyhose, send $1.00 (for postage and handling) plus one proof of purchase from any size Woolite® Cold Water Wash.

* For the proof of purchase, submit register-tape with purchase price circled AND write-in the UPC Code # on this form.

Mail to:
Woolite and SHEER & SILKY Offer
Suite 68
1512 Cross Bean Drive
Charlotte, NC 28217

Woolite UPC Code # _____

Name: _____

Address: _____

City/State/Zip: _____

Phone _____

Offer expires 5/31/89. Void where prohibited, taxed or restricted by law. Offer good while supplies last. Only one pair per name and address. Mechanical duplicates of this form are not permitted. Please allow 6-8 weeks for delivery.

WO-PTY-11888

MANUFACTURER'S COUPON/EXPIRES 5/31/89   **15¢**

SAVE 15¢

When you buy any size

Woolite®
COLD WATER WASH

Consumer: Only one coupon is redeemable per purchase. Retailer: We will redeem this coupon for face value plus 8¢ handling provided you have redeemed it with the purchase of product specified. Void if taxed, restricted or prohibited by law. Cash value 1/100¢. Limit — one coupon per purchase. Mail coupon to Boyle-Midway Household Products, Inc., P.O. Box 700027, El Paso, TX 88570-0027.

03

5 62338 13015 1

Contrary to what you probably think, this form of premium is not restricted to children. For example, Ralston Purina offered tiny sports-car models in about 11 million boxes of six cereal brands. Ten of these boxes contained scale-model red Corvettes. Lucky consumers turned in the models for real Corvettes, each valued at about $29,000.[37]

Near-pack premiums provide the retail trade with specially displayed premium pieces that retailers then give to consumers who purchase the promoted product. Near-pack premiums have the added advantage of being less expensive than on-pack premiums because additional packaging is not required. Furthermore, near-pack premiums can effectively build sales volume in stores that put up displays and participate fully.

Disadvantages of these techniques are (1) a lead time of 12 to 18 months is often required to develop and implement these types of promotions, (2) extra manufacturing and packaging effort is required in the case of in- and on- pack premiums, and (3) both on- and near-pack premiums are susceptible to mutilation and pilferage.[38] Another major problem with in- and on-pack premiums is that a poor premium can actually reduce sales by preventing regular purchasers from rebuying a brand.

Self-Liquidating Premiums

The *self-liquidating premium* gets its name from the fact that the consumer mails in a stipulated number of proofs of purchase *along with sufficient money to cover the manufacturer's purchasing, handling, and mailing costs of the premium item.* In other words, the actual cost of the premium is paid for by consumers; from the manufacturer's perspective the item is cost free, or, in other words, self-liquidating.

The premium object is generally a product other than the brand that promotes the deal. However, the premium may be related to the sponsoring brand (e.g., a cooking utensil as a premium for a processed food product) but it need not be. For example, for $1.99 and several proofs of purchase, consumers of Huggies disposable diapers were able to obtain an "I Love Huggies" knit hat for their infants.

In addition to reinforcing and strengthening a brand's image by associating it with an attractive premium object, self-liquidating premiums are a very effective means of obtaining store displays and encouraging trade support for the brand. Another positive feature is that this type of promotion does not require extensive packaging changes and, therefore, can be executed relatively simply at the factory level.

37. "Ralston-Purina Offers Adult Incentive in Kids' Cereal Boxes," *Marketing News*, April 25, 1988, p. 1.
38. "Premiums and Incentives in the Strategic Plan," *Marketing Communications*, June 1983, pp. 8, 9.

The limitations of self-liquidators are that they do not generate trial usage, and fewer than 10 percent of all households have ever sent for a premium.[39] Companies generally expect only 0.1 percent of self-liquidators to be redeemed. A circulation of 20,000,000, for example, would be expected to produce only about 20,000 redemptions.[40]

Industry specialists generally agree that the most important consideration in developing a self-liquidator program is that the premium be appealing to the target audience and represent a value. Most sources agree that consumers look for a savings of at least 50 percent of the suggested retail price.[41]

Price-Offs

Price-off promotions entail a reduction in a brand's regular price. A price-off is clearly labeled as such on the package. Price-offs typically range from 10 to 25 percent. This type of promotion is effective when the marketer's objective is any of the following: (1) to reward present brand users; (2) to get consumers to purchase larger quantities of a brand than they normally would (i.e., to "load" them), thereby effectively preempting the competition; (3) to establish a repeat purchase pattern after an initial trial; (4) to ensure that promotional dollars do, in fact, reach consumers (no such assurance is possible with trade allowances); (5) to obtain off-shelf display space provided that display allowances are offered to retailers; and (6) to provide the sales force with an incentive to obtain retailer support.[42]

Price-offs cannot reverse a downward sales trend, produce a significant number of new users, or attract as many trial users as sampling, coupons, or premium packs. Furthermore, retailers often dislike price-offs because they create inventory and pricing problems, particularly when a store has a brand in inventory at both the price-off and regular prices. Despite trade problems, price-offs have strong consumer appeal.

FTC Price-Off Regulations

Manufacturers cannot indiscriminately promote their products with continuous or near-continuous price-off labeling. To do so would deceive consumers into thinking the product is "on sale" when in fact the pronounced sale price is actually the regular price.

39. William A. Robinson, "What Are Promos' Weak and Strong Points?" *Advertising Age*, April 7, 1980, p. 54.
40. Francine Schore, "Inflation Hurts Cheaper Items," *Advertising Age*, October 6, 1980, pp. S-19, S-20.
41. Ibid.
42. Fredericks, "What Ogilvy & Mather Has Learned about Sales Promotion."

The Federal Trade Commission controls price-off labeling with the following regulations: (1) price-off labels may only be used on brands already in distribution with established retail prices; (2) there is a limit of three price-off label promotions per year per brand size; (3) there must be a hiatus period of at least 30 days between price-off label promotions on any given brand size; (4) no more than 50 percent of a brand's volume over a 12-month period may be generated from price-off label promotions; (5) the manufacturer must provide display materials to announce the price-off label offer; and (6) the dealer is required to show the regular shelf price in addition to the new price reflecting the price-off label savings.[43]

Bonus Packs

Bonus packs are extra quantities of a product that a company gives to consumers at the regular price (e.g., a sleeve of four Tourney golf balls for the price of three; 20 percent more Planter's peanuts at the regular price). Bonus packs are sometimes used as an alternative to price-off deals when the latter are either overused or resisted by the trade. The extra value offered to the consumer is readily apparent and for that reason can be effective in *loading* current users and thereby removing them from the market—a defensive tactic that is used against aggressive competitors. Perhaps the biggest drawback of bonus packs is that a large proportion of the bonus-packed merchandise will be purchased by regular customers who would have purchased the brand anyway.

Refunds and Rebates

The terms *refund* and *rebate* both refer to the practice in which manufacturers give a *cash discount or reimbursement* to consumers who submit proofs of purchase. Though often used interchangeably, a **refund** typically refers to cash reimbursement for *packaged goods*, whereas a **rebate** more often refers to reimbursements for *durable goods* (especially small appliances). Both offer consumers *delayed* rather than immediate value since the consumer has to wait to receive the reimbursement. Although the reward is delayed, consumers nevertheless are generally very responsive to attractive refund/rebate offers. The number of households using refunds/rebates increased from 27 percent in 1977 to 51 percent by 1987.[44]

In using these programs, manufacturers achieve *franchise holding* objectives by encouraging consumers to make multiple purchases or large-quantity purchases (refund programs) or by rewarding previous users with an attractive cash discount for again purchasing the manufacturer's brand (rebate pro-

43. *ANA Consumer Promotion Seminar Fact Book*, p. 7.
44. "Cashing in on the Power of Refunds," *Marketing Communications*, January 1988, p. 39.

grams). Packaged-good marketers are fond of refund offers because they stimulate purchase behavior and provide an alternative to the more costly and wasteful use of coupons.[45] Numerous manufacturers use refunds to appeal to savings-conscious consumers. For example, in 1988 Tropicana offered a $3 refund for 10 proofs of purchase from 32 or 64 ounce cartons of Tropicana juices (see Figure 20.5); BVD underwear offered a $3 refund for the purchase of six men's or boys' underwear garments; and Coors offered a $2 refund for buying one case of Coors beer. On the rebate side, Polaroid offered a $30 rebate with the purchase of the Spectra System instant camera; Nikon promoted a $55 rebate of the N2020 Autofocus System; and Lincoln-Mercury offered a $3,000 cash-back rebate from the $19,284 suggested retail price for the XR4Ti.

Refund offers sometimes provide consumers with the choice between receiving a cash refund or coupons. For example, the makers of Pampers disposable diapers offered consumers the choice of a $1.00 cash refund or $2.00 in Pampers coupons. The refund offer was doubled—to $2 cash or $4 in coupons—if the consumer also included a tear-off "refund doubler" certificate obtained from a Pampers display at a grocery store. When manufacturers promote products in this manner, retailers are more likely to provide display support, which increases the likelihood that consumers will come into contact with the promoted brand.

Overall, refunds represent a useful technique: They reinforce brand loyalty, provide the sales force with something to talk about, and enable the manufacturer to flag the package with a potentially attractive deal. However, because of the delayed reward, interest is limited among many consumers and much of the retail trade. Many consumers consider using refunds/rebates to be too much of a hassle, and some even think that manufacturers only use these programs when their products are not selling well.[46] In order to overcome the delay problem and provide consumers with instant gratification, some companies are starting to mail check-like forms to households. Consumers receive an immediate refund when purchasing the product and submitting the "check" to the salesclerk.

Contests and Sweepstakes

Both contests and sweepstakes offer consumers the opportunity to win cash, merchandise, or travel prizes. In a **sweepstakes,** winners are determined *purely on the basis of chance.* Accordingly, proofs of purchase cannot be required as a condition for entry. In a **contest,** the consumer must *solve the specified contest problem* (e.g., a puzzle) and may be required to submit proofs of purchase.

45. Ronnie Telzer, "Rebates Challenge Coupons' Redeeming Values," *Advertising Age,* March 23, 1987, p. S-18.
46. Peter Tat, William A. Cunningham III, and Emin Babakus, "Consumer Perceptions of Rebates," *Journal of Advertising Research,* vol. 28 (August/September 1988), pp. 45–50.

FIGURE 20.5   **Illustration of a Refund Offer**

Source: Courtesy Tropicana Products, Inc.

FOCUS ON PROMOTION

A Contest Gone Awry

Beatrice Company, the makers of many consumer packaged goods, initiated a contest involving "Monday Night Football." Contestants scratched silver-coated footballs off of cards and hoped the numbers on the cards matched the number of touchdowns and field goals scored in the weekly Monday night NFL game. Contest planners intended the chances of getting a match to be infinitesimal. However, to Beatrice's great surprise, a salesman for rival Procter & Gamble put in a claim for a great deal more money than they had planned on paying out.

A computer buff, the salesman cracked the contest code and determined that 320 patterns showed up repeatedly in the cards. By scratching off just one line, he could determine which numbers were underneath the rest. With knowledge of the actual numbers of TDs and field goals scored on a particular Monday night, he would start scratching cards until winning numbers were located. He enlisted friends to assist in collecting and scratching the cards. Thousands of cards were collected, mostly from Beatrice salespeople. The P&G salesman and friends identified 4,000 winning cards worth $21 million in prize money! Beatrice discontinued the game and refused to pay up.[47] ∎

Because they require less effort from consumers and generate greater response, sweepstakes are much preferred to contests. The *Focus on Promotion* section illustrates one reason why contests are less desirable than sweepstakes.

Beatrice is not the only company that has been burned with a contest gone awry. For example, PepsiCo ran a spell-your-surname contest with letters printed on bottle caps. Because very few caps bore vowels, PepsiCo assumed that only a small number of people would win the contest. What the contest planners failed to realize, however, was that many Asian names contain only consonants (e.g., Ng).[48]

These and other problems lead many companies to shy away from contests. Sweepstakes, on the other hand, have experienced a tremendous increase in popularity. The apparent reason is that compared with many other sales-promotion techniques, sweepstakes are relatively inexpensive and simple to execute and are able to accomplish a variety of marketing objectives.[49] In

47. Laurie Baum, "How Beatrice Lost At Its Own Game," *Business Week*, March 2, 1987, p. 66.
48. Ibid.
49. Thomas J. Conlon, "Sweepstakes Rank As Tops," *Advertising Age*, October 6, 1980, pp. S-6, S-7; Don Jagoda, "It's Not What You Give But What You Get," *Marketing Communications*, April 1984, pp. 27–31.

addition to *reinforcing a brand's image and attracting attention to advertisements,* well-designed sweepstakes can promote distribution and retailer stocking, increase sales-force enthusiasm, and reach specific groups, such as ethnic markets, through a prize structure that is particularly appealing to those groups.[50]

The majority of sweepstakes offer a prize or group of prizes to entrants, who mail an entry blank along with a proof of purchase (or a facsimile, since purchase cannot legally be required) to the manufacturer's judging agency. For example, Procter & Gamble offered five trips for two to both the 1989 Super Bowl in Miami and the Pro Bowl in Honolulu (see Figure 20.6).

The effectiveness and appeal of a sweepstakes is generally limited if the sweepstakes is used alone. However, when tied in with advertising, point-of-purchase displays, and other promotional tools (such as Procter & Gamble's use in Figure 20.6), sweepstakes can work effectively to produce significant results.

Overlay and Tie-In Promotions

Discussion to this point has concentrated on individual sales promotions. In practice, sales-promotion techniques are often used in combination to accomplish a number of objectives that any one tool could not accomplish alone. Furthermore, these techniques, individually or in conjunction with one another, are frequently used to promote simultaneously two or more brands either from the same company or from different firms.

The use of two or more sales-promotion techniques in combination with one another is called an **overlay,** or combination, program. The simultaneous promotion of multiple brands in a single promotional effort is called a **tie-in,** or group, promotion. In other words, overlay refers to the use of multiple sales promotion *tools,* whereas tie-in refers to the promotion of multiple *brands.* Overlay and tie-ins often are used together, as the following sections illustrate.

Overlay Programs

Media clutter, as noted repeatedly in past chapters, is an ever-growing problem facing marketers. When used individually, sales-promotion tools, particularly coupons, may never be noticed by consumers. A combination of tools, such as Procter & Gamble's overlay of a coupon offer and a sweepstakes (Figure 20.6), increases the likelihood that consumers will attend the advertisement and process the sales-promotion offer. In addition, the joint use of several techniques in a well-coordinated promotional program equips the sales force with a strong sales program. Overlays are more attractive to the trade and, as a result, can induce higher levels of purchasing and increase display activity. In short, overlay programs are *synergistic.*

50. Stanley N. Arnold, "Consumer Sweepstakes and Contests," in *The Tools of Promotion* (New York: Association of National Advertisers, 1975), pp. 4, 5.

Illustration of a Sweepstakes

FIGURE 20.6

A campaign by Welch's Jam & Jelly illustrates the use of overlay and tie-in promotions in conjunction with one another. Welch's primary objectives were to load existing customers and to induce users of competitive brands to make a trial pruchase. Their strategy consisted of overlaying coupons with a self-liquidating premium. At the same time, the promotion was tied in with two natural partners, the Quality Bakers of America and the American Dairy Association.

Welch's selected a family-oriented vehicle, the Sunday comics, for delivering the coupon and announcing a free milk offer. Consumers would receive a free half-gallon of milk for submitting the net weight statements from any three jars of Welch's grape jelly or strawberry jam and from any Quality Bakers of America brand bread. In addition, display materials in stores offered consumers a soccer ball (with a retail value of $27) in return for only $11.95 and the UPC codes from any two jars of Welch's jam or jelly. Moreover, a trade-oriented contest was run in an effort to stimulate retailer support. Prizes included a Nassau vacation for two people and 500 soccer balls for store managers to give to their children.

As a result of this creative and well-coordinated program, initial sales exceeded levels forecasted to the trade by 30 percent, the increase in in-store display activity was double that originally estimated, and Welch brands experienced a 3.9 percent increase in market share over the eight weeks following the promotion.[51]

Tie-In Promotions

A growing number of companies are using tie-ins (group promotions) to generate increased sales, to stimulate trade and consumer interest, and to gain optimal use of their promotional budgets. Figure 20.7, which contains a coupon offer for five healthcare products, is an example of a tie-in promotion. By encouraging consumers to purchase each of the participating brands, a group promotion can lead to *greater total sales volume*. In addition, the *cost of a group promotion is less* than the cost would have been had each brand been promoted separately. This is because the cost of running a coupon-carrying advertisement, such as the freestanding insert in Figure 20.7, is shared among five brands.

Types of Tie-In Promotions. By definition, a tie-in promotion involves the *pooling of resources* between two or more products, brands, or services. The exact nature of the pooling can take on various forms.[52] Two major

51. Adapted from Joseph S. Maier, *Promotion Update '82*, a publication of the Promotion Marketing Association of America, Inc., New York, 1982.
52. Melvin Scales, "What Tie-in Promotions Can Do for You," *Outlook*, a publication of the Promotion Marketing Association of America, vol. 12, Fall 1988, pp. 10–11; P. "Rajan" Varadarajan, "Horizontal Cooperative Sales Promotion: A Framework for Classification and Additional Perspectives," *Journal of Marketing*, vol. 50 (April 1986), pp. 61–73.

A Tie-In Promotion for Five Brands   FIGURE 20.7

forms are intra- and inter-company tie-ins. *Intra-company* pooling involves a joint sales promotion for two or more distinct brands from a single company. For example, the H. J. Heinz Company offered a free 10 oz. jar of Heinz relish with the purchase of two 40 oz. bottles of Heinz ketchup. General Foods gave consumers a free container of its French's mustard when they purchased a canister of its Country Time lemonade-flavor mix.

Inter-company tie-ins involve coordinated activities between products from *distinct companies* that are not in direct competition with one another. For example, Thomas J. Lipton Inc. wanted a promotion that would attract consumer attention to its Lipton tea, Wish-Bone salad dressings, and other Lipton products and would generate retail display space in the competitive pre-summer holiday period. A tie-in was arranged with Walt Disney Productions, which was looking for a way to build awareness for the 50th anniversary re-release of the motion picture *Snow White*. Lipton distributed freestanding inserts to 21 million households. The FSI overlayed coupons with a special premium item for children—a personalized birthday tale from Snow White that imprinted the child's name, age, and hometown. The promotion was supported by heavy advertising to retailers and an incentive program for the sales force that offered all-expense trips to Disney World for successful sales performance. The promotion was extremely appealing to retailers and consumers and satisfied both Lipton's and Walt Disney Production's objectives.[53]

Another inter-company tie-in is shown in Figure 20.8. Ralston's Chex Snack Mix, a product consumers often eat while watching television, is tied-in with the natural partners shown in the ad. This promotion overlays a coupon offer with a premium (the Casio portable television) and ties in Chex with a $10 subscription rebate for HBO® or Cinemax. This creative promotion stands to stimulate increased consumption of Chex Snack Mix and to increase subscriptions to HBO® and Cinemax, thereby benefiting all parties.

Objectives Accomplished with Tie-In Promotions.   Companies attempt to accomplish diverse objectives with tie-in promotions. Some major objectives are:[54]

1. *To increase sales* by taking advantage of opportunities for joint sales between complementary products or brands.

2. *To promote new product uses* in combination with other products (e.g., a promotion between Reach toothbrush and Aqua-Fresh toothpaste).

3. *To promote new use occasions* (e.g., a promotion between Tylenol cold tablets and Kleenex facial tissue).

4. *To broaden the product user base* by tying in with products that have a high level of household penetration.

53. Adapted from Ronnie Telzer, "Dickering Done, Tie-ins Prove Worth," *Advertising Age*, May 2, 1988, p. S-4.
54. Varadarajan, "Horizontal Cooperative Sales Promotion," pp. 66–68.

An Inter-Company Tie-In Promotion

FIGURE 20.8

5. *To promote trial use among new customer groups.*

6. *To neutralize competitors' sales-promotion efforts.*

7. *To increase sales by capitalizing on the strength or reputation of another product or brand.*

8. *To increase retail display space* (as was accomplished by Lipton's promotion with *Snow White*).

Implementation Problems and Considerations.   Tie-in promotions are capable of accomplishing useful objectives, but not without potential problems.[55] Promotion *lead time* is lengthened because two or more entities have to coordinate their separate promotional schedules. *Creative conflicts* and *convoluted messages* may result from each partner trying to receive primary attention for its product/service.

To reduce problems as much as possible and to accomplish objectives, it is important that (1) the *profiles of each partner's customers be similar* with regard to pertinent demographic or other consumption-influencing characteristics; (2) the partners' images should *reinforce one another* (e.g., Lipton iced tea and *Snow White* both have wholesome images); and (3) partners must be *willing to cooperate* rather than imposing their own interests to the detriment of the other partner's welfare.[56]

An Unsuccessful Tie-In Promotion.   As with all aspects of promotion management, a tie-in promotion can go awry if it is not thought out fully prior to its implementation. A classic illustration of an unsuccessful promotion is the 1984 tie-in between Trans World Airlines Inc. and Polaroid Corporation.[57] These two companies entered into an arrangement whereby purchasers of Polaroid cameras would receive a coupon worth 25 percent off the price of a TWA ticket. The tie-in was intended to increase sales of Polaroid's camera and film during the Christmas season and to sell TWA airline tickets during the slow, postholiday period. Anyone buying specified cameras or film during the period between October 1, 1984, and January 31, 1985, was eligible to receive the TWA discount. The discounts applied to all coach fares, including international flights.

This tie-in promotion held promise of being an excellent promotion for both companies; unfortunately, from TWA's perspective, there was one major oversight—TWA neglected to put a "one per customer" limit on the offer. Consequently, commercial customers (corporate travel departments and travel agencies) purchased Polaroid cameras by the hundreds to take advantage of the attractive coupon offer. For example, a St. Louis travel agency bought 10,000 cameras so that it would offer attractive flight discounts to its commer-

55. Scales, "What Tie-in Promotions Can Do for You," p. 11.
56. "Creating Synergy through Tie-in Promotions," *Marketing Communications*, April 1988, p. 45.
57. "How Polaroid and TWA Created a Monster," *Business Week*, January 21, 1985, p. 39.

cial customers. Even Polaroid's own travel department purchased 2,000 of the company's cameras to obtain discounted TWA tickets!

Polaroid obviously benefited from this poorly executed promotion, but TWA did not. More than 150,000 coupons were redeemed for a 25 percent discount from the airline's normal rates. Moreover, customers used the discount for international flights when, in fact, the promotion was intended primarily to increase domestic activity. The moral is clear: Be extremely careful in designing sales promotions so that there are no loopholes for customers to exploit.

Evaluating Sales-Promotion Ideas

Numerous alternatives are available to sales-promotion planners. There also are a variety of objectives that effective sales-promotion programs are able to achieve. The combination of numerous alternatives and diverse objectives leads to a staggering array of possibilities. A straightforward three-step procedure has been recommended by promotion experts as an aid in determining which sales promotion ideas and approaches have the best chance of succeeding.[58]

Step 1: Identify the Objectives

The most basic yet important step toward successful sales promotions is the clear identification of the specific objective(s) that is(are) to be accomplished. Objectives should be specified as they relate both to the trade and to ultimate consumers; for example, the objectives may be to generate trial, to load consumers, to preempt competition, to increase display space, and so on. In this first step, the promotional planner must commit the objectives to writing and state them specifically and in measurable terms. For example, the objective "to increase sales" is too general. In comparison, the objective "to increase display space by 25 percent over the comparable period last year" is specific and measurable.

Step 2: Achieve Agreement

Everyone involved in the marketing of a product category or brand must agree with the objectives developed. Failure to achieve agreement on objectives results in different decision makers (e.g., the advertising, sales, and sales-promotion managers) pushing for different programs because they have different

---

58. Don E. Schultz and William A. Robinson, *Sales Promotion Management* (Lincolnwood, IL: NTC Business Books, 1986), pp. 436–445.

objectives in mind. Also, a specific sales-promotion program can more easily be evaluated in terms of a specific objective than in terms of some vague generalization.

Step 3: Evaluation System

With specific objectives established and agreement achieved, the following five-point evaluation system should be used to rate any sales-promotion program or idea:

1. **How good is the general idea?** Every idea should be evaluated against the promotion's objectives. For example, if the objective is to increase product trial, a sample or a coupon would be rated favorably, while a sweepstake would flunk this initial evaluation.

2. **Will the sales-promotion idea appeal to the target market?** A contest, for example, might have great appeal to children, but for certain adult groups it would have disastrous results. In general, remember that the target market represents the bedrock against which all proposals should be judged.

3. **Is the idea unique or is the competition doing something similar?** The prospects of receiving both trade and consumer attention depend on developing promotions that are not ordinary. Creativity is every bit as important to sales-promotion success as it is with advertising.

4. **Is the promotion presented clearly so that the intended market will notice, comprehend, and respond to the deal?** Sales-promotion planners should start with one fundamental premise: Most consumers are not willing to spend much time and effort figuring out how a promotion works. It is critical to a promotion's success that instructions be user friendly. Let consumers know quickly and clearly what the offer is and how to respond to it.

5. **How cost-effective is the proposed idea?** This requires an evaluation of whether or not the proposed promotion will achieve the intended objectives at an affordable cost. Sophisticated promotion planners cost out alternative programs and know in advance the likely bottom-line payoff from a promotion.

Summary

This chapter focuses on consumer-oriented sales promotions. The various sales-promotion tools available to marketers are classified in terms of whether the reward offered consumers is immediate or delayed and in terms of whether the manufacturer's objective is to achieve trial impact, franchise holding/loading, or image reinforcement. Specific sales-promotion techniques fall into one of five general categories: immediate reward/trial impact (e.g., sampling), delayed reward/trial impact (e.g., media- and mail-delivered coupons), immediate reward/franchise holding (e.g., price-off deals), delayed reward/franchise holding (e.g., refunds and rebates), and delayed reward/image reinforcement (e.g., self-liquidating premiums). Eleven specific techniques are discussed in detail.

Specific topics addressed in the chapter include the following: sampling effectiveness; conditions when sampling should be used; coupon usage and growth; couponing costs; coupon misredemption; reasons for using in- and on-pack premiums and self-liquidators; FTC price-off regulations; differences between refunds and rebates and when each is used; the role of contests and sweepstakes; the nature of overlay and tie-in promotions and various other topics.

The first and most critical requirement for a successful sales promotion is that it be based on clearly defined objectives. Second, the program must be designed with a specific target market in mind. It should also be realized that many consumers, perhaps most, desire to maximize the rewards gained from participating in a sales promotion while minimizing the amount of time and effort invested. Consequently, an effective sales promotion, from a consumer-response perspective, must make it relatively easy for consumers to obtain their reward, and the size of the reward must be sufficient to justify the consumer's efforts. A third essential ingredient for effective sales promotions is that programs must be developed with the interests of retailers in mind—not just the manufacturer's interests.

Discussion Questions

1. Sales promotions offer consumers immediate or delayed rewards. The former is more effective in inducing behaviors desired by the marketer. Explain why and back it up with a specific, concrete illustration from your own experience.

2. Explain in your own terms the meaning of franchise holding and loading objectives.

3. One of the major trends in product sampling is selective sampling of targeted groups. Assume your company has just developed a new candy bar substitute that tastes almost as good as a regular candy bar but is much lower in calories. Marketing research has identified the target market as economically upscale consumers, aged 34 to 55, who reside in urban areas. Explain specifically how you might selectively sample over 5 million such consumers.

4. Compare and contrast sampling and media-delivered coupons in terms of objectives, consumer impact, and overall roles in marketing-communications strategies.

5. A packaged-goods company plans to introduce a new bathroom soap that differs from competitive soaps by virtue of a distinct new fragrance. Should sampling be used to introduce the product?

6. Present your personal views concerning the number of coupons distributed annually in the United States. Is widespread couponing in the best interest of consumers? Could marketers use other promotional methods to more effectively and economically achieve the objectives accomplished with coupons?

7. Compare instant coupons, freestanding inserts, and in-package coupons in terms of purpose and consumer impact.

8. Explain the rationale for cooperative couponing programs.

9. Your company markets hot dogs, bologna, and other processed meats. You wish to offer a self-liquidating premium that would cost consumers approximately $25, would require 10 proofs of purchase, and would be appropriately themed to your product category during the summer months. Your primary market segment is families with school-aged children crossing all socio-economic strata. Suggest two premium items and justify your choice.

10. What is the purpose of the FTC price-off regulations?

11. Compare bonus packs and price-off deals in terms of consumer impact.

12. What is crossruffing in sales promotion, and why is it used?

13. How can sales promotion reinforce a brand's image? Is this a major objective of sales promotion?

14. Compare contests and sweepstakes in terms of how they function and in terms of relative effectiveness.

15. Your company markets antifreeze. Sales to consumers take place in a very short period, September through December. You want to tie in a promotion between your product and the product of another company that would bring more visibility to your brand and encourage retailers to provide more shelf space. Recommend a partner for this tie-in promotion and justify the choice.

Exercises

1. Conduct interviews with two store managers to get their views on the causes and magnitude of coupon misredemption in their stores. Determine what actions their stores take to minimize misredemption.

2. Go through old copies of major magazines and Sunday newspaper FSIs and clip examples of ten different sales promotions. For each example, analyze what you think the objectives are. Give your opinion of whether the promotion is another run-of-the-mill promotion or potentially much more effective than the average sales promotion.

3. Browse the shelves of a major supermarket or drug store and identify two specific examples of each of these forms of sales promotions: bonus packs; price-offs; in-, on-, or near-pack premiums; and saleable samples.

4. Conduct interviews with three or four nonstudent adults and investigate whether or not they have participated in any sweepstakes, contests, refund offers, or mail-in premium deals within the past year or so. Also, evaluate their personal attitudes toward each of these sales-promotion methods.

5. Find two examples of tie-in promotions and for each evaluate why you think the different brands are involved in a joint promotion.

PART 7

Personal Selling
and Sales
Management

The two chapters in Part 7 examine the face-to-face communication, or personal selling, aspect of the promotion mix. Chapter 21 introduces students to the job of the salesperson and its unique characteristics. The chapter covers a broad array of ideas about the nature of personal selling, including personal selling's role in the promotion mix, attractive features of a personal selling job, and the kinds of activities performed by a salesperson. The chapter also discusses the seven basic steps involved in personal selling, factors that determine salesperson performance, requirements for becoming an outstanding salesperson and the types of available selling jobs.

Chapter 22 overviews the managerial aspects of personal selling. The practice of sales management involves planning, organizing, staffing, directing, and controlling an organization's selling function. Each of these sales-management activities is explored. Students will acquire a general understanding of the tasks involved in sales management and learn that organizational success greatly depends on how well the sales-management function is performed.

CHAPTER TWENTY-ONE

Personal Selling

WHAT QUALITIES ARE LIKED AND DISLIKED IN A SALESPERSON?

recent survey of purchasing agents determined what buyers value most and least in a salesperson.[1] Based on the ratings of 206 purchasing agents, the most- and least-valued qualities in salespeople are:

Most Valued

Reliability/credibility	98.6%
Professionalism/integrity	93.7
Product knowledge	90.7
Innovativeness in problem solving	80.5
Presentation/preparation	69.7

Least Valued

Supplies market data	25.8%
Appropriate frequency of calls	27.3
Knowledge of competitor's products	31.2
Knowledge of buyer's business and negotiation skills (tie)	45.8

1. "PAs Examine the People Who Sell to Them," *Sales and Marketing Management*, November 11, 1985, pp. 38–41.

In purchasing agents' own words, here are some of the specific qualities and behaviors in salespeople that are most liked, disliked, and despised—the good, the bad, and the ugly.

The Good	The Bad	And the Ugly
"Honesty"	"No follow-up"	"Wise-ass attitude"
"Lose a sale graciously"	"Walking in without an appointment"	"Calls me 'dear' or 'sweetheart' (I am a female)"
"Admits mistakes"	"Begins call by talking sports"	"Gets personal"
"Problem-solving capabilities"	"Puts down competitor's products"	"Doesn't give purchasing people credit for any brains"
"Friendly but professional"	"Poor listening skills"	"Whiners"
"Dependable"	"Too many phone calls"	"Bullshitters"
"Adaptability"	"Lousy presentation"	"Wines and dines me"
"Knows my business"	"Fails to ask about needs"	"Plays one company against another"
"Well prepared"	"Lacks product knowledge"	"Pushy"
"Patience"	"Wastes my time"	"Smokes in my office"■

A good sales force that embodies the positive qualities identified in the opening vignette is crucial to corporate success. Personal selling is the last promotion-mix element covered in the text, but it certainly is not the least important. Indeed, popular business wisdom holds that everything starts with selling. Personal selling provides the push (as in *push strategy*) needed to get customers to carry new products, increase their amount of purchasing, and devote more effort in merchandising a product or brand. At the retail level, personal selling can determine whether a purchase is made or not and how often a consumer shops at a particular store.

This chapter's objective is to present the reader with a broad array of ideas about the nature of personal selling, perhaps resulting in a greater appreciation of the opportunities and challenges for career success in this field. Toward this end, the chapter explores several dimensions of personal selling. First, in an overview section, the chapter discusses the role of personal selling in the promotional mix, its advantages and disadvantages, society's attitudes toward this activity, and the attractive characteristics of personal selling and opportunities in this field. A second section examines selling activities, duties, and types of selling jobs. Specific phases of the selling job are examined in the third section. Determinants of salesperson performance and effectiveness are covered in the fourth section. A final section examines characteristics of excellence in selling.

Personal Selling: An Overview

Personal selling is a form of person-to-person communication in which a salesperson works with prospective buyers and attempts to influence their purchase needs in the direction of his or her company's products or services. The most important feature of this definition is the idea that personal selling involves *person-to-person interaction*. This contrasts with other forms of marketing communications in which the audience typically consists of multiple people, sometimes millions (as in the case of mass-media advertising).

Importance of Personal Selling

To place the importance of the personal-selling function into perspective, consider the following facts. First, in the United States alone over six million people (approximately 1 out of every 16 workers) are responsible for selling billions of dollars worth of goods and services. Second, employers annually spend thousands of dollars per new employee in training, travel, and various other expense accounts. The average cost of training one industrial salesperson, for example, is in excess of $25,000.[2] Third, the average cost of an industrial-sales call in 1988 was $217.92.[3] Fourth, the typical field salesperson earned a median income of $41,000 in 1987.[4]

Overall, selling benefits the U.S. economy in several ways. Personal selling influences *product innovation* through continual salesperson feedback to company management concerning customer questions, needs, and problems. Personal selling promotes a *higher standard of living* by changing and improving dissatisfied consumers' consumption patterns. Personal selling *enhances economic growth* by encouraging consumption of improved products, which brings about increased mass production, more jobs, and greater capital investment.[5]

Personal Selling's Role in the Promotion Mix

As explained at various points throughout the text, all elements of the promotion mix work together to achieve overall organizational objectives. Each promotional element has its own unique characteristics, purposes, and advantages. Personal selling's primary purposes include educating customers, providing product usage and marketing assistance, and providing after-sale service and support to buyers. Personal selling, in comparison to other promotional elements, is uniquely capable of performing these functions as a

---

2. "Section IV: Sales Meetings and Sales Training," *Sales and Marketing Management*, February 16, 1987, p. 62.
3. "1989 Survey of Selling Costs," *Sales and Marketing Management*, February 20, 1989, p. 15.
4. "The Cost of Putting a Person in the Field," *Sales and Marketing Management*, October 1988, p. 43.
5. Charles A. Kirkpatrick and Frederick A. Russ, *Effective Selling* (Cincinnati: South-Western Publishing Co., 1981), pp. 4–7.

result of the person-to-person interaction mode that characterizes this form of marketing communications. Consequently, various advantages accrue to personal selling compared to other promotional tools.[6]

1. Personal selling contributes to a *relatively high level of customer attention*, since in face-to-face situations it is difficult for a potential buyer to avoid a salesperson's message.

2. It enables the salesperson to *customize the message to the customer's specific interests and needs*.

3. The two-way communication characteristic of personal selling yields *immediate feedback*, enabling an alert salesperson to know whether or not his or her sales presentation is working.

4. Personal selling enables a salesperson to *communicate a larger amount of technical and complex information* than could be communicated using other promotional methods.

5. In personal selling there is *a greater ability to demonstrate a product's functioning and performance characteristics*.

6. Frequent interactions with a customer permit the *opportunity for developing long-term relations* and effectively merging selling and buying organizations into a coordinated unit where both sets of interests are served.

The primary disadvantage of personal selling is that it is *more costly* than other forms of promotion because sales representatives typically interact with only one customer at a time. Hence, when considering only the outcomes or results accomplished with the personal-selling effort (an effectiveness consideration), personal selling is generally more *effective* than other promotion elements. However, when considering the ratio of inputs to outputs (e.g., cost to results), personal selling is typically less *efficient* than other promotion tools. In practice, allocating resources to personal selling and the other promotion elements amounts to an effort at balancing effectiveness and efficiency considerations.

Attitudes toward Selling

Unfortunately, even with its contributions to individual firms and to the economy in general, personal selling has historically been held in low esteem. This reputation dates back at least to the time of the ancient Greek philosophers and continues to be perpetrated today by movie and television directors and playwrights. For example, Arthur Miller's classic *Death of a Salesman* and David Mamet's more recent *Glengarry Glen Ross* both depict salesmen as rather pathetic characters who struggle for an existence and earn their living through ingratiation, deceit, and other unethical and immoral practices.

6. Gilbert A. Churchill, Jr., Neil M. Ford, and Orville C. Walker, Jr., *Sales Force Management: Planning, Implementation, and Control* (Homewood, IL: Richard D. Irwin, 1985), p. 67.

In real life, there are indeed con men and women who rely on deception, false promises, trickery, and misrepresentation to persuade people to buy products and services they do not need or items that do not work. Although this still happens today, it represents a very small percentage of the personal-selling business. Nevertheless, some people continue to hold negative attitudes toward selling in general. For example, a study of college students' views toward selling as a personal career uncovered these attitudes:

- Selling is a job, not a profession or a career.
- Salespeople must lie and be deceitful in order to succeed.
- Salesmanship brings out the worst in people.
- To be a good salesperson, you have to be psychologically maladjusted.
- A person must be arrogant and overbearing to succeed in selling.
- Salespeople lead a degrading and disgusting life because they must pretend all the time.
- The personal relations involved in selling are repulsive.
- Selling benefits only the seller.
- Salespeople are prostitutes because they sell all their values for money.
- Selling is not the job for a person with talent or brains.[7]

You may hold some of these views. This type of attitude is unfortunate, however, because it discourages many students from pursuing excellent job opportunities in the selling field.

Attractive Features of Personal Selling

Although personal selling receives much criticism, numerous challenging and exciting job opportunities are available in this field. The attractive features of a sales job include freedom of action, variety and challenge, opportunities for advancement, and desirable financial and nonfinancial rewards.[8]

Job Freedom.   In sales positions outside of retail settings (i.e., field sales), the individual is primarily responsible for most of his or her day-to-day activities. Many sales positions involve little direct supervision. Salespeople may go days or even weeks without seeing their bosses. Of course, with freedom comes responsibility. The unsupervised salesperson is expected to conduct his or her business professionally and to achieve the sales objectives established by the sales supervisor.

Variety and Challenge.   Managing one's own time presents a challenge that professional salespeople enjoy. Much like the person who operates his or her own business, a salesperson can invest as much time and energy

7. Study cited in Ronald B. Marks, *Personal Selling: An Interactive Approach* (Boston: Allyn and Bacon, 1988), p. 39.
8. Churchill, Ford, and Walker, *Sales Force Management: Planning, Implementation, and Control.*

into the job as desired and can generate as many rewards as he or she is willing to work for.

Opportunities for Advancement.   More and more companies expect their middle- and upper-level managers to have had sales experience because they believe it helps an individual understand a business from the ground-level up. More corporate presidents come from the sales ranks than from any other position; sales experience provides them with a knowledge of the customers, the trade, the competition, and their own company.

Attractive Compensation and Nonfinancial Rewards.   Personal selling is potentially both lucrative and rewarding. As noted earlier, the median income for field salespeople was $41,000 in 1987. Nonfinancial rewards include feelings of self-worth for a job well done and the satisfaction that comes from providing a customer with a solution to a problem or with a product or service that best meets his or her needs.

Modern Selling Wisdom

As this section's heading implies, before "modern" selling wisdom there must have been an earlier variety. Let us label this earlier version "antiquated" and place the two in stark contrast, realizing of course that any such comparison is necessarily simplified.

In a word, *antiquated selling wisdom* is *seller-oriented.* Selling practices and purposes in this older view are undertaken with the seller's interests paramount. Manifestations of this approach include high-pressure selling tactics, little effort to understand the customer's business, and little post-sale follow through and attention to customer satisfaction. Are these antiquated practices truly antiquated in the sense that they are no longer practiced? Certainly not. Some firms are still "antiquated," but although they remain in business, they no longer thrive. Their selling practices lag behind contemporary forces that have imposed a higher standard on sales performance than ever before. These forces include intense competition, narrow profit margins, sophisticated buying practices, and expectations of reliable and dependable service from vendors.

In most prospering firms, *modern selling wisdom* has supplanted this seller-oriented approach. A *partner-oriented* selling mind-set exists in most successful firms. These firms realize that their success rests with their customers' successes. Hence, modern partner-oriented wisdom makes *customer satisfaction* its highest priority. Modern selling practice is based on the following principles.[9]

9. These points are adapted from two excellent practitioner-oriented books: Anthony Alessandra, James Cathcart, and Phillip Wexler, *Selling by Objectives* (Englewood Cliffs, NJ: Prentice-Hall, 1988); and Paul Hersey, *Selling: A Behavioral Science Approach* (Englewood Cliffs, NJ: Prentice-Hall, 1988).

1. *The sales process must be built on a foundation of trust and mutual agreement.* Selling should not be viewed as something someone "does to" another; rather, it should be looked upon as something two parties agree to do for their mutual benefit. In fact, it is easy to argue that modern salespeople do not sell, but rather, they *facilitate buying.* This difference is not merely semantics—it is at the root of what is being described as the move from the antiquated to modern selling philosophies.

2. *A customer-driven atmosphere is essential to long-term growth.* This point is a corollary to the preceding principle. Modern selling requires that the customer's welfare, interests, and needs be treated as equal to the seller's in the partnership between seller and buyer. A customer-oriented approach means avoiding high-pressure tactics and focusing on customer satisfaction. Salespeople have to be trained to know the customer and to speak in a language that the customer understands. Perhaps the preceding points are best summed up in these terms: "Be product-centered, and you will make a few sales; be prospect-centered, and you will gain many customers."[10]

3. *Sales representatives should act as if they were on the customer's payroll.* The ultimate compliment a salesperson can receive is a comment from a customer to the sales supervisor along these lines: "I'm not sure whether your sales rep works for me or for you."[11] The closer salespeople are to the customer, the better they will be at providing solutions to the customer's problems.

4. *Getting the order is only the first step; after-sales service is what counts.* No problem a customer has should be too small to do something about. Modern selling wisdom calls for doing whatever is necessary to please the customer in order to ensure a satisfying *long-term relationship.*

5. In selling, as in medicine, *prescription before diagnosis is malpractice.* This principle holds that no one solution is appropriate for all customers any more than any single diagnosis is appropriate for all patients. Customers' problems have to be analyzed by the modern salesperson and solutions customized to each problem. The days of "one solution fits all" are gone. Moreover, because most people like to make their own decisions or at least be involved in making them, a salesperson should treat the customer as a partner in the solution.

6. *Salesperson professionalism and integrity are essential.* Customers expect high standards of conduct from their salespeople and dislike unprofessional, untrustworthy, and dishonest behavior. (As evidence of this, reexamine "the bad" and "the ugly" in the chapter's opening vignette.)

10. C. Conrad Elnes, *Inside Secrets of Outstanding Salespeople* (Englewood Cliffs, NJ: Prentice-Hall, 1988), p. 6.
11. Hersey, *Selling: A Behavioral Science Approach*, p. xi.

Selling Activities and Types of Personal-Selling Jobs

Up to this point in the chapter, personal selling has been treated rather generally; different types of selling jobs have not been distinguished. This section first describes the various kinds of activities that salespeople perform and then identifies six types of personal-sales jobs.

Selling Activities

What exactly does a salesperson do? In actuality there are dozens of different selling activities. The exact activities performed and the extent to which they are performed vary greatly from sales job to sales job. In general, however, selling activities fall into ten categories.[12]

Selling Function.   Selling-function activities include planning the sales presentation, making the presentation, overcoming objections, trying to close the sale, and so on.

Working with Orders.   Much of a salesperson's time is spent writing up orders, working with lost orders, handling shipment problems, expediting orders, and handling back orders.

Servicing the Product.   These activities include testing a newly sold product (e.g., a new industrial machine) to ensure that it is working properly, training customers to use the product, and teaching safety procedures. These activities are performed primarily by people who sell technical products.

Information Management.   These activities involve receiving feedback from customers and then relaying the information to management. Much of this is done in the course of day-to-day selling, but some information-management work requires the salesperson to serve in the capacity of a field marketing researcher.

Servicing the Account.   These activities include inventory control, stocking shelves, handling local advertising, and setting up and working with point-of-purchase displays. These activities are primarily performed by salespeople who call on retail customers such as grocery and drug stores.

Conference/Meetings.   Attending conferences, working at trade shows, and attending sales meetings are activities most all salespeople participate in to some extent.

---

12. William C. Moncrief III, "Selling Activity and Sales Position Taxonomies for Industrial Selling," *Journal of Marketing Research*, vol. 23 (August 1986), pp. 261–270.

Training/Recruiting. Salespeople who are in more advanced stages of their careers often become involved in training new salespeople, traveling with trainees, and similar duties.[13]

Entertaining. Some sales positions involve entertaining customers through activities such as dining and playing golf. Parenthetically, the antiquated view of selling would hold that you can "buy" customers by "wining and dining" them. Modern selling wisdom includes a role for customer entertainment, but recognizes that customers are "earned" (through loyal, efficient, dependable service) rather than bought.

Out-of-Town Travel. Although sales jobs involve some traveling, the amount of time spent out of town is highly variable, ranging from virtually no travel to journeying thousands of miles each month.

Working with Distributors. A final category of selling activity is selling to or establishing relations with distributors and collecting past-due accounts.

Types of Sales Jobs

There are many different kinds of sales jobs. Nonetheless, it is possible to classify the diverse sales positions into a few general categories. The following six categories encompass the major types of sales jobs.[14]

Trade Selling. A sales representative for a food manufacturer who sells to the grocery and drug industries typifies trade selling. The primary task of trade salespeople is to build sales volume by providing customers with promotional assistance in the form of advertising and sales promotion. Trade selling requires limited prospecting and places greater emphasis on *servicing accounts*. Trade salespeople, who typically are hired out of college, may work for companies such as Noxell, Beecham Products, Johnson & Johnson, Campbell's Soup, Procter & Gamble, and many other consumer packaged-goods companies.

Missionary Selling. Like trade salespeople, missionary salespeople typically are employees of manufacturers. However, the difference is that trade salespeople sell *through* their direct customers, whereas a missionary sales force sells *for* its direct customers.[15]

---

13. For a discussion of different stages of sales careers, see William L. Cron, Alan J. Dubinsky, and Ronald E. Michaels, "The Influence of Career Stages on Components of Salesperson Motivation," *Journal of Marketing*, vol. 52 (January 1988), pp. 78–92.
14. Marks, *Personal Selling: An Interactive Approach*.
15. Ibid., p. 45.

The pharmaceutical industry typifies missionary selling. Nearly two-thirds of all pharmaceutical sales to retailers are through wholesalers. In other words, manufacturers of pharmaceuticals typically market their products to wholesalers, who in turn market to pharmacies and other retailers. Thus, the wholesaler is the pharmaceutical manufacturer's direct customer. Sales representatives for pharmaceutical manufacturers (called "detail reps") nonetheless call on physicians and pharmacies to detail (explain) the advantages of the manufacturer's brands compared to competitive offerings. Detail reps are *not* selling directly to physicians (i.e., selling in the sense that a physician will place an order with the salesperson's company), rather, they are trying to get physicians to prescribe their brands. In so doing, they benefit both themselves (via increased sales volume) and their direct customers (wholesalers).

Technical Selling.   Technical salespeople are present in industries such as chemicals, machinery, mainframe computers, and sophisticated services (e.g., complicated insurance and other financial programs). They are typically trained in technical fields such as chemistry, engineering, computer science, and accounting. For example, in the chemical division of Du Pont, 95 percent of the company's salespeople start out in a technical field and then are recruited into sales.[16] Later, many sales technicians attain advanced training in business administration. *Selling functions* and *servicing the product* are the two categories of activities that most distinguish technical selling from other selling jobs. Good technical salespeople must be especially knowledgeable of their company's product lines and they must be able to communicate complicated features to prospective customers.

New-Business Selling.   This type of selling is prevalent with products such as office copiers, data-processing equipment, personal computers, business forms, and personal insurance. Practitioners use terms such as "bird-dogging," "cold calling," and "canvassing" to characterize this type of selling. These terms capture the idea that new-business salespeople must call on new accounts continuously. Salespeople involved in any of the previous categories of sales jobs do some prospecting for new customers, but most of their time is spent working with and servicing existing accounts. New-business salespeople continually work to open new accounts, because sales to most customers are infrequent.

Retail Selling.   The distinguishing characteristic of retail selling is that the customer comes to the salesperson. Many retail sales jobs require limited training and sophistication, but others demand salespeople who have considerable product knowledge, strong interpersonal skills, and an ability to work with a diversity of customers.

---

16. "Du Pont Turns Scientists into Salespeople," *Sales and Marketing Management*, June 1987, p. 57.

Telemarketing. Telemarketing was discussed in detail in Chapter 15. Suffice it to repeat that telemarketing is a rapidly growing form of selling activity. Telephone salespeople perform essentially the same types of selling activities as do salespeople who meet customers face to face.

The Basic Steps in Personal Selling

Regardless of the specific type of job, all forms of personal selling can be represented by a common set of steps, or phases, that must be performed in the process of making a sale (or, as stated earlier, facilitating buying).

The Seven Basic Steps

There are seven basic steps involved in personal selling:[17]

1.   Locating and prospecting for customers.
2.   The preapproach.
3.   The approach.
4.   The sales presentation.
5.   Handling objections/sales resistance.
6.   The close.
7.   The postsale follow-up.

Step 1: Locating and Prospecting for Customers. This first step involves identifying potential buyers (prospects) who have the need, willingness, ability, and authority to buy. That is, the salesperson looks for names, addresses, telephone numbers, and other general facts about prospective customers. This involves using *internal sources* of information (e.g., company records, membership lists, and other written documents) and *external sources* of information (e.g., referrals from existing customers, sales leads from organizations, friends, noncompeting salespeople, and so on). As noted earlier, prospecting is especially critical for *new-business selling jobs.*

Step 2: The Preapproach. This requires the salesperson to arrange a meeting with the prospective customer and to acquire, prior to the meeting, more specific information about him or her and his or her business. The initial sales meeting is arranged in a variety of ways: by asking mutual friends to set

---

17. Alan J. Dubinsky, "A Factor Analytic Study of the Personal Selling Process," *The Journal of Personal Selling & Sales Management*, vol. 1, issue 1 (Fall–Winter, 1980–81), pp. 26–33. The following discussion borrows freely from Dubinsky's excellent review and analysis of the steps in the selling process.

up the meeting, by sending personal letters to prospects, or by having a present customer send a letter that introduces the salesperson and requests a sales interview.

Acquiring meaningful information about prospective customers and their businesses is an essential aspect of the preapproach. For example, the salesperson may learn that the prospect's business is expanding rapidly; therefore, the salesperson's product could be needed to accommodate the growing business. Salespeople use a variety of information sources for learning about prospective customers: current customers, newspapers and other media, observing the prospect's business facilities while waiting to meet with the prospect, and so on.

Step 3: The Approach.

This third step is the prelude to the actual sales presentation. The first few moments a salesperson spends with a prospect and the initial impressions that the prospect forms are critical to the salesperson's chances of eventually making a sale. A sale is unlikely to result if the salesperson has failed to do his or her homework in the preapproach stage.

Salespeople use a variety of approach techniques, often in combination with one another, to gain the prospect's attention and interest. A few of the more widely used approaches are (1) using a present customer's name as a reference to the prospect, (2) giving the prospect a token gift, (3) offering a benefit that has appeal to the prospect's curiosity, (4) opening the sales interview with a question to get the prospect's attention and interest, and (5) handing the product to the prospect for him or her to inspect.

Step 4: The Sales Presentation.

This fourth step, the actual sales presentation, is the fundamental part of the selling activity. The salesperson presents the product, explains what it will do for the prospective customer, demonstrates its strengths, and so forth. Efforts are made to arouse the prospect's interest and desire for the product.

Successful sales presentations result from the salesperson having *impact* on the customer. *Having impact* can be defined as the salesperson's ability to get prospective customers to tune out the distractions, listen to what the salesperson is saying, and eventually follow his or her lead in a buying decision.[18] To repeatedly have high impact on prospects, a salesperson must appreciate four fundamental features of the buying process. These features represent the four tenets of *high-impact selling:*

First, *prospects pay attention only to salespeople that they believe have something important to say.* This fundamental characteristic of all communication exchanges means that a salesperson must develop an interesting and informative sales presentation that gives the prospect a reason to pay attention.

---

18. The notion of "high impact" selling and the principles that follow are based on William T. Brooks, *High Impact Selling: Power Strategies for Successful Selling* (Englewood Cliffs, NJ: Prentice-Hall, 1988).

Related to the idea of having something interesting and important to say is the need for *credibility*. Source credibility, which was examined in Chapter 6, suggests that a source is generally more persuasive when he or she is perceived as being high in credibility. Recall also that credibility is a multifaceted concept, which may be established by the source's perceived prestige, expertise, or trustworthiness. However, a salesperson's persuasiveness is reduced if he or she is perceived by the customer to be motivated primarily by personal gain. Prospective customers recognize a sales representative's intentions to manipulate and are aware of the gains he or she will derive from a sale. Therefore, a sales representative must fight an uphill battle to establish some degree of credibility in the eyes of a customer. A sales representative who can project confidence in what he or she says and who can demonstrate a high level of expertise for the product enhances his or her chances of being perceived as a credible source.

A second fundamental requirement for high-impact selling is the recognition that *people buy for their own reasons; not for the salesperson's reasons*. One author claims that all people have an inner-radio that is pretuned to pick up only one station: WII-FM, which stands for <u>W</u>hat's <u>I</u>n <u>I</u>t <u>F</u>or <u>M</u>e? "Nothing can give you as much customer impact as knowing how to make your every appeal to the prospect's self-interests."[19]

A third tenet of high-impact selling is that *people do not want to be sold; they want to buy*. This principle is an extension of the earlier point that salespeople do not really sell; what they really do is facilitate buying. When a salesperson accepts this fact, the selling orientation becomes one of understanding and satisfying the buyer's interests and needs rather than focusing exclusively on the seller's own interests.

A final tenet of high-impact selling is that *buying is basically an emotional response*. This point does not deny the fact that logic and analysis are involved; instead, it emphasizes that all buying eventually gets down to feelings, emotions, fears, hopes, fantasies, and so forth. These emotions play a prominent role in consumer buying, and they also are involved in buying decisions made by professional buyers. For example, a corporation that purchases a major new telephone system undoubtedly uses objective considerations such as cost, efficiency, clarity of voice transmission, and so forth. However, emotional considerations also come in to play; examples include fears that the new system may not be as reliable as the old standby, hopes that the buyer will receive praise from superiors for making a prudent decision, and concerns that the transition from the old to new system will wreak havoc with day-to-day telephone activities.

Step 5: Handling Objections. In many, if not most, selling situations, prospects feel they have reasons not to buy the product or service offered by the salesperson. The salesperson must be prepared to *handle objections*

---

19. Ibid., p. 15.

and sales resistance. At this point the salesperson must reiterate how the product meets the customer's needs and problems, what benefits the product offers, and how the prospect can most easily make the decision (credit terms, for example). Also, the salesperson should make statements that help the customer reduce any perceived risk in making the buying decision.

Different methods are used for handling objections and reducing buying resistance. For example, the salesperson may stall the objection by telling the prospect that the question will be handled later in the presentation. The salesperson may also dispute the objection and provide solid reasons for the disputation. On the other hand, the salesperson may concede to parts of the objection and then dispute other parts of the objection in an inoffensive manner. Also, salespeople sometimes use humor to relieve the pressure associated with an objectionable part of a sales presentation or simply dismiss the objection with a smile or other nonverbal gesture.

Step 6: The Close.   In step six, the close, the salesperson attempts to gain a commitment from the customer to purchase the product or service. In other words, the salesperson asks for the order. Salespeople use different techniques in closing a sale to make it easier for the prospect to commit to a purchase. For example, the salesperson may (1) tell the prospect about a previous customer whose needs were similar to the prospect's and who benefited from the salesperson's product, (2) present the prospect with two or more product versions and ask which he or she prefers, (3) assume the prospect is ready to buy and focus on purchase details such as the delivery date and credit terms, (4) ask for the order in a straightforward fashion, or (5) offer some incentive to get the prospect to buy now.

Step 7: Postsale Follow-Up.   Finally, in step seven, postsale follow-up, the salesperson attempts to reduce the consumer's postpurchase doubt (especially for products requiring a high level of effort, time, or money), suggests additional products and accessories, determines problems the customer may be having with the product, and develops a firmer relationship with the customer in the hope of creating future sales.

Effective follow-up is critical for establishing long-term *relationships* with customers. Successful salespeople do not discontinue contact once they have made a sale. They make sure that the product truly fits the customer's needs, that it is being used properly, that customer complaints are remedied expeditiously, and so on. Follow-up includes sending letters of appreciation to customers, training the customer's exployees in the proper use of the product, addressing the customer's complaints or product-related problems, and making adjustments if the product does not meet the customer's expectations.

In Summary.   It would be erroneous to think that the preceding step-by-step presentation means that all selling efforts progress in such an orderly fashion and that each preceding step must be completed before the next one follows. Nothing could be further from the truth. The point, instead, is that the seven steps are involved to one degree or another in all selling jobs and that all must be performed at one time or another. However, rather than occurring in some linear, lockstep fashion, the steps actually mingle and often occur over an extended time period with iterations. For example, a salesperson may try to close a sale early in the presentation but find her effort rebuffed. Unable to handle the buyer's objection at that time, she courteously asks for an opportunity to do some more research (preapproach activity) and to return at a later date. Her additional study of the buyer's needs and objections leads her to employ a different presentation, to delay attempting to close the transaction, and to use a different tactic in handling the buyer's objections. Her persistence eventually pays off when the buyer is convinced that her offering is the best for his company.

Salesperson Performance and Effectiveness

People in all facets of life are ultimately judged in terms of their performance and effectiveness. Typically these evaluations are based on quantitative assessments: number of arrests by a police officer, number of indictments by a prosecuting attorney, number of hits by a baseball player, number of units produced by a factory worker, number of articles published by a professor, and so on. Likewise, salespeople are typically judged in terms of the number of units sold or dollar volume. For many years academic and business researchers have posed a fundamental question: What determines how well a salesperson performs? Before reading on, you should think about your own ideas on this. Jot down what you think are the most important considerations.

Before talking specifics about the determinants of salesperson performance and effectiveness, two general points require careful attention. The first point is that *no single factor is able to adequately explain salesperson performance*. In a very thorough and insightful analysis of sales research conducted during the past 40 years, researchers examined over 100 separate studies and over 1,500 correlations in these studies relating salesperson performance with a wide variety of potential predictors. A dramatic finding from this research is that no single predictor on average explained more than *four percent* of the variability in salesperson performance![20] The conclusion is apparent: Sales performance is based on various considerations; to expect any single factor (or even several factors) to adequately explain a complex behavior is expecting too much.

A second general point is that salesperson performance and effectiveness are contingent on a host of factors that reside both within and outside the salesperson. *Selling performance and effectiveness depend on the total situation in*

---

20. Gilbert A. Churchill, Jr., Neil M. Ford, Steven W. Hartley, and Orville C. Walker, Jr., "The Determinants of Salesperson Performance: A Meta Analysis," *Journal of Marketing Research*, vol. 22 (May 1985), pp. 103–118.

FIGURE 21.1   **Contingency Model of Salesperson Effectiveness**

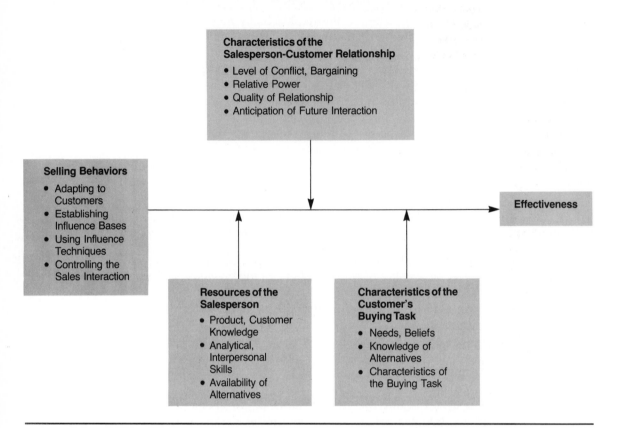

Source: Barton A. Weitz, "Effectiveness in Sales Interactions: A Contingency Framework," *Journal of Marketing*, vol. 45, Winter 1981, p. 90. Reprinted with permission from *Journal of Marketing*, published by the American Marketing Association.

which sales transactions take place. Specifically, salesperson performance is contingent upon (1) the salesperson's own resources (e.g., product knowledge, analytical skills), (2) the nature of the customer's buying task (e.g., whether it is a first-time or repeat decision), (3) the customer-salesperson relationship (e.g., relative power, level of conflict), and interactions among all three of these general sets of factors.[21] Figure 21.1 displays the relations among these various contingency factors.

In this model, effectiveness is defined in terms of the salesperson. That is, salesperson effectiveness is measured by long-term sales of the company's

21. Barton A. Weitz, "Effectiveness in Sales Interactions: A Contingency Framework," *Journal of Marketing*, vol. 45 (Winter 1981), pp. 85–103.

products and services. Customer satisfaction is implicit in this measurement because short-term strategies would not meet long-term sales goals.

As Figure 21.1 demonstrates, *selling behaviors* are an important set of factors influencing the outcome of a potential sale. Some of these include (1) adapting to customers, (2) establishing influence bases, (3) using influence techniques, and (4) controlling the sales interaction. *Characteristics of the customer's buying task* include (1) an examination of how people buy according to their needs and beliefs, (2) their knowledge of the alternatives, and (3) the characteristics of the buying task (e.g., whether the decision is made by a single person or involves group influence). The *salesperson's resources* include his or her personal resources and company resources. Together, these resources include (1) product and customer knowledge, (2) analytical and interpersonal skills, and (3) the availability of alternatives (e.g., different products for solving the customer's specific problem).

Finally, the *characteristics of the salesperson-customer relationship* also moderate the salesperson's effectiveness. This set of variables includes (1) the level of conflict and bargaining, (2) relative power, (3) quality of the relationship, and (4) the anticipation of future interactions. The salesperson must know how to handle such conflicts as policy differences, hostility, stress, anxiety, and customer aggression in any and all kinds of sales situations.

In summary, the contingency approach strongly advocates that a salesperson must be flexible and adaptable to a wide array of selling situations. However, simply engaging in adaptive behavior does not guarantee high sales performance. Salespeople must also have skills that help them make appropriate adaptations. These skills will be elaborated on in a subsequent section on salesperson excellence.

Specific Determinants of Salesperson Performance

It now has been established that salesperson performance and effectiveness are contingent on various factors. Going into detail on all of these factors would take us beyond the scope of this overview. In the remainder of this section we will examine in greater detail just the salesperson-characteristics aspect of the contingency model. Scholars have hypothesized that salesperson performance depends on five sets of individual factors: (1) aptitude, (2) skill level, (3) motivational level, (4) role perceptions, and (5) personal characteristics.[22]

Aptitude. An individual's ability to perform certain tasks depends greatly on his or her interests, intelligence, and personality characteristics. Because different salespeople have different tasks and activities to perform, some people are better suited to one type of sales job than another.

22. Gilbert A. Churchill, Jr., Neil M. Ford, and Orville C. Walker, Jr., *Sales Force Management: Planning, Implementation, and Control* (Homewood, IL: Richard D. Irwin, 1985). The following discussion is based on views presented in this text.

Technical sales positions require individuals with the strong analytical aptitude and technical knowledge needed for explaining complex product features to customers. Trade selling requires individuals who have good interpersonal skills and are highly adaptive, because they meet with many different types of customers. Regardless of the specific type of sales position, however, all professional salespeople must be customer oriented and empathetic. They must be able to view the world from the outside in and not just in terms of their own limited perspective.

Skill Level.   Whereas aptitude is a matter of native ability, skill level refers to an individual's *learned proficiency* at performing necessary selling tasks. These skills include salesmanship skills (such as how to close a sale), interpersonal skills (such as how to cope with and resolve conflict), and technical skills (such as knowledge about the product's features, performance, and benefits). These skills are partially brought to a sales job, as a function of an individual's educational preparation, but are also learned and fostered on the job.

Companies with effective sales programs instill in their sales force the skills needed for success. In fact, many sales organizations prefer to recruit salespeople directly out of college rather than from other sales positions so that they do not have to retrain sales candidates and overcome bad habits and conflicting skills learned elsewhere. For example, Armstrong World Industries, a maker of carpeting and other products, is legendary for hiring salespeople directly from college and sending them through the same basic training program that all Armstrong salespeople have undergone for over 60 years. In explaining the company's attitude toward sales training, Armstrong's director of human resources explains: "We prefer to hire people without any biases, conflicting opinions, or bad traits—and then we train them ourselves. We've had great success doing things our way, and if we're doing it that way and other companies aren't, well, then they're doing it wrong."[23] This may sound arrogant, but it merely represents the belief that it is often easier to train than it is to retrain.

Motivational Level.   Motivational level refers to the amount of time and energy a person is willing to expend performing tasks and activities associated with a job. These tasks typically include filling out reports, calling on new accounts, creating new sales presentations, following up on sales, and so forth. An interesting thing about motivation is that it is *reciprocally related with performance*. That is, motivation is a determinant *of* performance and also is determined *by* performance—we often become even more motivated after we have enjoyed some success.

---

23. "Armstrong Salespeople Are to the Manor Born," *Sales and Marketing Management*, June 1987, p. 46.

Another important characteristic of salesperson motivation is the *distinction between working hard and working smart*. Motivation is not simply amount of effort but also how the effort is directed. Salespeople who work smart are typically more effective than those who just work hard.[24] Of course, a truly dynamite combination for a salesperson is to work both smart and hard.

Role Perceptions.   In order to perform their jobs well, salespeople must know what is expected of them and have accurate perceptions of their role. Their jobs are defined by people both within and outside the organization, including family, sales managers, company executives, and customers. Thus, how well people perform in sales jobs depends on the accuracy of their perceptions of management's stated goals, demands, policies, procedures, and organizational lines of authority and responsibilities.

Very often salespeople face role conflicts that inhibit their sales performance. For example, a customer may want special price or advertising concessions that the company has policies against. Salespeople have been trained to meet customers' needs; however, they have also learned to follow company policies. They are put in the role of customer satisfier but also of company satisfier. What do sales representatives do? If a salesperson can negotiate differences between the two parties he or she may be able to resolve the conflict and make the sale. In general, accurate role perceptions are a very important determinant of sales performance and effectiveness. Accurate perceptions are instilled during initial sales training and over time during periodic sales meetings and through periodic interactions with sales supervisors.

Personal Characteristics.   A final determinant of salesperson effectiveness is the individual's characteristics. Factors such as age, physical size and appearance, race, and sex are some of the personal characteristics expected to affect sales performance. Research has shown that these personal factors may be even more important than the other factors in determining sales performance.[25] It would be misleading to interpret this finding to mean that, say, one's physical characteristics ensure sales success or prevent success. To the contrary, personal characteristics may make it more or less difficult to succeed in sales, but performance by any single individual depends ultimately on his or her ability, skill, and motivation. One can either misuse personal advantages or overcome disadvantages. There are enough different types of selling positions available to accommodate anyone who is willing to work hard. Even physically handicapped individuals who are unable to perform field sales duties can thrive in the area of telemarketing. The number of sales opportunities

24. Harish Sujan, "Smarter Versus Harder: An Exploratory Attributional Analysis of Salespeople's Motivation," *Journal of Marketing Research,* vol. 23 (February 1986), pp. 41–50.
25. Churchill, Ford, Hartley, and Walker, "The Determinants of Salesperson Performance: A Meta Analysis."

for women and blacks have increased dramatically, partly because both groups have overcome what used to be perceived as sales-related disadvantages.[26]

Excellence in Selling

What does it take to be a truly outstanding salesperson, to be a high performer, to excel in sales? As is always the case, there are no simple answers. Moreover, achieving excellence in one type of sales endeavor, say selling personal insurance, undoubtedly requires somewhat different aptitude and skills than achieving excellence when selling sophisticated information systems to corporate buyers. However, although there are differences from sales job to sales job, there also are similarities.

High-performing salespeople generally differ from other salespeople in terms of some general attitudes they have about the job and the manner in which they conduct their business. High-performing salespeople do the following:

- Represent the interests of their companies and their clients simultaneously to achieve *two-way advocacy*.
- Exemplify *professionalism* in the way they perform the sales job.
- Are *committed to selling* and the sales process, because they believe the sales process is in the customer's best interest.
- Actively *plan and develop strategies* that will lead to programs benefiting the customer.[27]

Specific Characteristics of High-Performers

In addition to these general practices, excellence in selling is associated with a variety of specific characteristics that are reflected in the salesperson's personal features and job behavior. These include the first impression a salesperson makes, his or her depth of knowledge, breadth of knowledge, flexibility, sensitivity, enthusiasm, self-esteem, extended focus, sense of humor, creativity, risk taking, and sense of honesty and ethics.[28]

---

26. See, for example, Michelle Block Morse, "Rich Rewards: For Ambitious Blacks, Selling Can Mean Pride, Power, and High Pay," *Success*, vol. 35, March 1988, pp. 50–61.

27. Thayer C. Taylor, "Anatomy of a Star Salesperson," *Sales and Marketing Management*, May 1986, pp. 49–51.

28. These characteristics and the following discussion are based on Alessandra, Cathcart, and Wexler, *Selling by Objectives*, pp. 59–76. A related perspective is provided by Lawrence W. Lamont and William J. Lundstrom, "Identifying Successful Industrial Salesmen by Personality and Personal Characteristics," *Journal of Marketing Research*, vol. 14 (November 1977), pp. 517–529.

The First Impression.   The outcome of a sales call is greatly influenced by the first impression that a salesperson makes on the customer. The likelihood that a salesperson's ideas will be accepted depends largely on the initial impression made. Determinants of the first impression include personal looks, dress, body language, eye contact, handshake, punctuality, and courtesy.

Depth of Knowledge.   A salesperson's depth of knowledge reflects how well he or she understands the business, products, company, competitors, and general economic climate related to the sales job. Depth of knowledge is obtained in part through an individual's *self-study* efforts. Knowledgeable salespeople stay alert to what is going on by listening carefully to customers, reading general business publications (e.g., *The Wall Street Journal*, *Business Week*), and getting the most out of company sales meetings and conferences. Another source of company knowledge is the initial *training* a salesperson receives. The *Focus on Promotion* section highlights one company's outstanding training program.

FOCUS ON PROMOTION

Sales Training at Merck Sharp & Dohme

Merck Sharp & Dohme is a pharmaceutical company that is known for its outstanding sales-training programs. Merck's philosophy is that a well-trained salesperson is the absolute key to building a relationship of trust with the customer. The vice-president of sales proclaims: "We have an obsession about it. Training drives the whole sales force and it separates us from everybody else."

Merck's training program involves three phases of instruction. The first phase is a primer on medicine basics such as anatomy and physiology. Phase two lasts from one-half to one full year and consists of an in-depth program on the presentation of products in the field. The third phase concentrates on providing Merck's sales reps with knowledge of the diseases and maladies that the company's products treat.

Merck's training goes beyond this initial in-depth program. Once every two years each salesperson is sent to medical school for detailed instruction concerning the latest developments in diseases and in medicine in general. In addition, each representative works with a physician/mentor in a hospital setting and learns practical aspects of medicine and the effects of

Continued

Continued

pharmaceutical products. Beyond this, every two months district meetings are held that focus on specific topics dealing with state-of-the-art developments in the treatment of diseases and maladies.

It comes as little surprise that Merck's salespeople are among the best trained in any industry. Customers are extremely pleased, and the turnover rate of top salespeople is much lower at Merck than at other companies.[29] ■

Breadth of Knowledge.   This third characteristic of selling excellence is based on one's *scope of knowledge*. Salespeople who have a wide breadth of knowledge are conversant on a broad spectrum of subjects and, therefore, are able to interact effectively with a variety of customers. Salespeople who possess a broad scope of knowledge make customers feel relaxed and are able to share common interests (via comments or discussions concerning world events, athletics, cultural affairs, or whatever the customer's interests may be). One acquires this facet of excellence via expansive reading, taking a variety of courses while in college, continuous studying, and good listening skills. In general, breadth of knowledge is a matter of being alert, attentive, and interested in different people and events.

At a minimum, any college graduate who expects to be conversant and effective in a selling position should read a daily newspaper and a weekly magazine such as *Newsweek* or *Time*.

Flexibility.   This fourth characteristic of excellence is the willingness and ability to adapt your interactional style to match the other person's. Because salespeople interact with a wide variety of customers, those who are more flexible tend to be more effective. Flexibility in this sense is *not* to be misinterpreted as suggesting that a salesperson should alter his or her presentation to accommodate what each prospect might want to hear, regardless of the truth. Rather, the point is that people differ in terms of how open, sociable, and communicative they are, and a salesperson must adjust his or her interactional style to the customer's preferred style.

Sensitivity.   The essence of this fifth characteristic of excellence is *empathy*, or the ability to place oneself in the other person's position. That is, the successful sales representative shows a genuine interest in the prospect's needs, problems, and concerns. Also, the salesperson demonstrates respect for customers and does not talk down to them. Most people are quick to notice a sales representative's positive attitude toward them, and they react favorably to it.

29. Based on "Merck's Grand Obsession," *Sales and Marketing Management*, June 1987, p. 65.

Good *listening skills* are another facet of sensitivity. Listening enables the salesperson to understand the needs of the customer and to adjust the sales message accordingly. Listening is a rare skill. But why? One reason is that people are usually absorbed in their own lives and activities and listening to someone else becomes boring for them. Most of us enjoy a conversation only when the other person is finished talking and we can start talking. The fact that so many people look upon listening as something irksome reflects the scarcity of good listeners.

Enthusiasm.   Enthusiasm, the fifth characteristic of excellence, reflects a salesperson's deep-seated commitment to his or her company's products and to customers' needs. Enthusiastic salespeople tend to be more motivated than less enthusiastic people, and customers are responsive to the salesperson's enthusiastic efforts.

Self-Esteem.   This involves feelings of self-worth and personal confidence. A salesperson is more successful if he or she has a positive self-concept, likes his or her product and company, and looks forward to meeting prospects. A salesperson who does not have self-confidence will seldom be successful in selling. Furthermore, a salesperson must have a positive attitude toward the product, company, and sales message. A person who does not fully believe in what he or she sells will be seen as insincere. After all, if the salesperson does not believe in the product, how can the customer?

Extended Focus.   Excellent people in any endeavor have specific goals and purpose, that is, a sense of focus. "Most people aim at nothing in life and hit it with amazing accuracy."[30] The term "extended focus" means the ability to simultaneously focus on the specific and look at the big picture. This eighth characteristic of excellence is based on the idea that salespeople must focus their efforts into achieving specific goals that they have established; they must not permit themselves to be distracted.

Sense of Humor.   This ninth characteristic of excellence stresses the ability to laugh with others as well as to laugh at yourself. Humor helps customers relax. It also helps customers remember you. There is a difference, however, between having a sense of humor and being a clown or buffoon.

Creativity.   Salespeople who exhibit this tenth characteristic have an ability to connect seemingly unrelated ideas and to arrive at unique solutions to problems. This ability is critical in many selling positions, such as trade selling and technical selling, where the salesperson is often selling a total system rather than a single product. Often competing companies' basic products and nonproduct offerings (e.g., promotional programs) are very similar;

---

30. Alessandra, Cathcart, and Wexler, *Selling by Objectives*, p. 73.

hence, what distinguishes one company from the next are the creative solutions that salespeople devise for addressing customers' needs or solving problems. Creativity does not stop with merely coming up with an idea; rather, "Creativity is not the quality of the idea; it is the quality of the action that puts the idea into being."[31]

Taking Risks.　Closely related to creativity is the eleventh characteristic of excellence, the willingness to take risks. To be creative you must be willing to take risks, to recommend solutions that might backfire or be ridiculed, to risk change rather than sameness, to offer new solutions. Excellent salespeople are always looking for new ideas, new methods, and new solutions that will benefit their customers, themselves, and their companies.

Sense of Honesty and Ethics.　This twelfth characteristic is last but certainly not least. Contrary to widespread myths about personal selling, excellence in personal selling requires as high a degree of honesty and ethical behavior as in any of life's lasting relationships. The key word is *relationship*. There are some sales jobs where a single transaction between buyer and seller takes place; however, most personal-selling interactions involve building long-term relationships with customers. This is not accomplished with deceit, misrepresentation, and undependable behavior. The excellent salesperson is seen by the customer as trustworthy and dependable. We expect these same qualities in our friends, and the same expectations carry over on a professional level to the marketplace. You may recall the opening vignette identifying the qualities most and least valued by purchasing agents in salespeople. The two most valued qualities are reliability/credibility and professionalism/integrity.

Summary

This chapter presents a broad array of ideas about the nature of personal selling. Personal selling's role in the promotion mix includes educating customers, providing product usage and marketing assistance, and providing after-sale service and support to the buyer. As a personal career, sales includes the attractive features of freedom of action, variety and challenge, opportunities for advancement, and desirable financial and nonfinancial rewards.

　　A *partner-oriented* selling mind-set is in operation in most successful firms today. These firms realize that their success rests with their customers' successes. Hence, modern partner-oriented wisdom makes *customer satisfaction* its highest priority. Modern selling practice is based on principles such as the following: trust and mutual agreement must exist between buyer and seller; getting the order is only the first step, after-sales service is what counts; salesperson professionalism and integrity are essential.

---

31. Ibid., p. 75.

Personal selling is a broad field consisting of a variety of different types of sales jobs and entailing different activities, including: making sales presentations, working with orders, servicing the product and the account, managing information, participating in conferences and meetings, training, entertaining, traveling, and working with distributors. Sales jobs include trade selling, missionary selling, technical selling, new-business selling, retail selling, and telemarketing.

The basic steps in the selling process are (1) locating and prospecting for customers, (2) the preapproach, (3) the approach, (4) the sales presentation, (5) handling objections, (6) the close, and (7) the postsale follow-up.

A contingency model of the selling process is presented to explain that salesperson performance and effectiveness are dependent on a variety of factors. Specific determinants of salesperson performance include (1) aptitude, (2) skill level, (3) motivational level, (4) role perceptions, and (5) personal characteristics.

A final section examines excellence in selling. Twelve basic characteristics of excellence include the first impression a salesperson makes, his or her depth of knowledge, breadth of knowledge, flexibility, sensitivity, enthusiasm, self-esteem, extended focus, sense of humor, creativity, risk taking, and sense of honesty and ethics.

Discussion Questions

1. Personal selling is more effective than advertising but less efficient. Explain.

2. Many people hold personal selling in low esteem. Many students rebel at the idea of taking a sales job out of college. Why do you think these attitudes persist?

3. Comment on the following statement: Salespeople must lie and be deceitful in order to succeed.

4. Contrast "antiquated" and "modern" selling practices. In rethinking your response to question 2, what additional insight can you offer by taking into consideration the antiquated-modern distinction?

5. One form of sales presentation is called a "canned presentation." This means that a salesperson uses the identical presentation time after time. How would you evaluate the canned sales presentation? What are the advantages and disadvantages of this form of presentation?

6. "Sales representatives should act as if they were on the customer's payroll." Evaluate this statement by explaining in your own words what it means and by describing the advantages *and* disadvantages that may result when a salesperson acts in this manner.

7. In view of the different types of sales jobs described in the chapter (e.g., trade selling, technical selling), identify the job types you would or would not be willing to take as a first job out of college. Provide your rationale for each decision.

8. No single factor is able to adequately explain salesperson performance. Comment.

9. Clearly distinguish among aptitude, skill, and personal characteristics as unique determinants of salesperson performance. Considering only aptitude and per-

sonal characteristics, provide an assessment of whether you possess the aptitude and personal features for a successful career in (1) computer sales for a company like IBM, and (2) trade sales for a company such as Procter & Gamble. Offer reasons for why or why not.

10. Distinguish between working hard and working smart. As a student, which behavior better characterizes your own performance? What behaviors would a salesperson manifest in demonstrating an ability to work smart rather than simply hard? Be specific.

11. Based on the 12 characteristics of personal excellence described in the text, which of these do you think most salespeople with whom you have come in contact lack? Do you possess the potential for excellence in selling? Why or why not?

Exercises

1. Interview three sales representatives and describe the differences in their philosophies and approaches to personal selling. Compare your findings with the ideas presented in the text.

2. A study of college students' views toward personal selling was mentioned in the chapter. Ten negative attitudes toward selling were listed. Interview five students and ask them to rate each of the statements on a five-point scale labeled "strongly agree," "agree," "neither agree nor disagree," "disagree," and "strongly disagree." Summarize the results from your small survey and draw implications based on the assumption that the five students you queried hold representative views.

3. Write a two- to three-page essay on why you would or would not be a good salesperson.

Sales Management

SELECTING TOP-PERFORMING SALESPEOPLE[1]

Q: Sales managers know they've hired the best when a salesperson sells the most, but how do they know how to find this kind of person again?

A: You identify what you've learned that can apply the next time you hire a salesperson. That is, you need a system that keeps track of what it is about a person's background, experience, and abilities that is relevant to picking another like that. For example, what qualities does a person have before joining your organization that lead to success? You will not be able to find duplicate people, but you can find persons with approximately the same characteristics. In short, we're talking about the ability to identify specific qualities that contribute to success and to apply this information to your next selection decision. Obviously everyone can't be the best. But you can expect the average performance per salesperson to get better if you have a system that tracks performance and constantly identifies success characteristics—and you use this information when hiring in the future. This approach translates into increased productivity and sales revenues.

1. These questions were posed by interviewers for *Sales and Marketing Management* and were answered by Dr. David W. Merrill, chairman of Tracom Corp., a psychological consulting firm located in Denver. Source: "New England Life Takes Steps to Insure Its Future," *Sales and Marketing Management*, August 12, 1985, p. 77. Copyright 1985; reprinted by permission of Sales & Marketing Management.

Q: Can't psychologists simply provide a test that predicts sales success?

A: There is no single psychological test or set of characteristics that assures that you will get the best person for a position. And even if you could find one, it would not work across all companies or industries; there is no way to determine a single generic standard to pick what is best for all companies. Top performance in one company can't assure success in another. There is no single golden person who will perform best everyplace. Each organization must develop its own model of what is best based upon everything in its recruiting and selection process.

Q: Why can't sales success be defined generically?

A: It is vital for you to know what is best for your company, rather than in a generic sense because sales success is much more dependent upon an individual's background and experience relevant to a company's products and services than it is upon personality types. It is true that some generalized characteristics are needed for all sales jobs. You need to find people who are willing to talk to prospects, and to answer questions about the commodity they sell.■

The opening vignette deals with one of the most important yet most difficult tasks confronting sales managers—selecting salespeople who have the potential to become top performers. But sales management is by no means limited to this staffing function. In general, **sales management** is the process of planning, organizing, staffing, directing, and controlling an organization's selling function within the context of environmental limitations and corporate and marketing constraints. The purpose of sales management is to acquire, direct, and stimulate competent salespeople to perform tasks that move the organization toward its objectives and mission. Sales management provides a significant link between an organization's corporate and marketing strategies and the salespeople who actuate the marketing transaction. A sales manager is:

> the tactician who translates plans into action. He or she implements the various programs for market analysis, direction of sales effort, training, performance appraisal and compensation. . .[and] also has a longer-term responsibility for planning market development and account coverage in his/her area. He or she provides management with information on the organization's effectiveness and conditions in the marketplace as inputs to management's analysis, planning and control activities.[2]

In an overall sense, sales management involves the performance of five basic functions: (1) planning, (2) organizing, (3) staffing, (4) directing, and (5) controlling sales-force efforts. Each function is discussed in the following sections.

---

2. John P. Steinbrink, "Field Sales Management," in *Marketing Manager's Handbook,* eds. Steuart Henderson Britt and Norman F. Guess (Chicago: Dartnell Corporation, 1983), p. 984.

Planning the Sales Function

Planning is the process of establishing a broad set of goals, policies, and procedures for achieving sales and marketing objectives. Three of the most important planning activities undertaken by sales managers are (1) developing sales budgets, (2) designing sales territories, and (3) setting sales-force quotas.

Developing Sales Budgets

"The sales force budget is the amount of money available or assigned for a definite period of time, usually a year. It is based on estimates of expenditures during that period of time. . .[and] depends on the sales forecast and the amount of revenue expected to be generated for the organization during that period."[3] The first step in developing a budget is to analyze market opportunity and forecast sales potential. Then management must estimate the amount of money required to accomplish the tasks necessary to achieve its forecasted sales. Two basic procedures for allotting funds are (1) the line-item budget and (2) the program-budget method.

In **line-item budgeting,** management allocates funds in meticulous detail to each identifiable cost center. For example, the sales department may budget funds for areas such as office supplies, wages, research, and travel.[4] This budgeting procedure requires management to forecast and account for each item in great detail. **Program budgeting** avoids many of the problems of line-item budgeting. With this approach, management provides each administrative unit with a lump sum of money that each administrative head can use as he or she sees fit to accomplish the stated objectives. This method provides considerable flexibility by allowing each administrative head to shift funds as deemed necessary. For example, funds for travel and/or entertainment can be shifted to recruitment in the event that one or more salespersons change jobs, retire early, or die.

Designing Sales Territories

A **sales territory** consists of present and prospective customers assigned to a salesperson, sales branch, or distributor for a specified period.[5] The ideal situation is to create sales territories of *equal potential and equal workload.* In this way, the sales manager can more easily evaluate and control each salesperson's performance. Also, having equal workloads among the sales representatives leads

3. Charles M. Futrell, *Fundamentals of Selling* (Homewood, IL: Richard D. Irwin, 1984), p. 465.
4. William J. Stanton and Richard H. Buskirk, *Management of the Sales Force* (Homewood, IL: Richard D. Irwin, 1983), p. 431.
5. Gilbert A. Churchill, Jr., Neil M. Ford, and Orville C. Walker, Jr., *Sales Force Management: Planning, Implementation and Control* (Homewood, IL: Richard D. Irwin, Inc., 1985), p. 175.

FIGURE 22.1   **Stages in Territory Design**

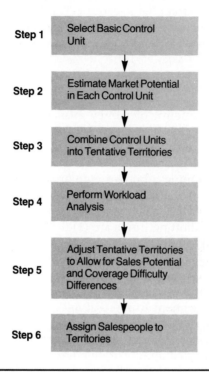

Step 1 — Select Basic Control Unit

Step 2 — Estimate Market Potential in Each Control Unit

Step 3 — Combine Control Units into Tentative Territories

Step 4 — Perform Workload Analysis

Step 5 — Adjust Tentative Territories to Allow for Sales Potential and Coverage Difficulty Differences

Step 6 — Assign Salespeople to Territories

Source: Gilbert A. Churchill, Jr., Neil M. Ford and Orville C. Walker, Jr., *Sales Force Management,* (Homewood, IL: Richard D. Irwin, 1985), p. 188. Copyright 1985 by Richard D. Irwin, Inc. Reprinted with permission.

to greater sales force motivation and morale. Unfortunately, achieving this ideal situation is rare, if not impossible.

Although each company has its own unique procedures for designing sales territories, the following steps are generally adhered to in the design process: (1) select a basic control unit, (2) estimate the market potential in each control unit, (3) combine control units into tentative territories, (4) perform a workload analysis, (5) adjust tentative territories to allow for differences in potential sales and workload across territories, and (6) assign salespeople to territories (see Figure 22.1).[6] Each of these steps will now be discussed in detail.

Select a Basic Control Unit.   Sales managers design territories along lines of elemental geographical areas: geographical regions, states, re-

6. These steps and related discussion are based on ibid., pp. 187–204.

gions within states, counties, cities, parts of cities, and so on. The basic control unit selected depends on the size of the company, the products the company sells, and the nature of the customers called on. For example, larger geographical units (e.g., states rather than counties) could serve as the basic unit for an industrial-goods company whose salespeople each call on relatively few large accounts. Comparatively, individual counties, or even zip-code areas, might represent a superior control unit for a company selling personal insurance.

Estimate Market Potential. The second step is to estimate the market potential of each basic control unit. Previous sales records, emerging sales opportunities, and competitive concentration help the sales manager in making these estimates.

Form Tentative Territories. In step three, the sales manager combines contiguous control units (e.g., five adjoining counties) into a tentative territory. Again, the objective is to develop sales territories of equal potential.

Perform a Workload Analysis. In step four, the sales manager must consider the amount of work that is necessary to attain the territory's potential. Although two salespeople may have equal sales potential in their respective territories, the workloads necessary to reach those potentials could be unequal. For example, one salesperson may have to travel longer distances, endure more severe weather conditions, and have many small accounts to call on.

Adjust Tentative Territories. In step five, the sales manager attempts to equalize sales potentials and workloads across all territories. In this stage the sales manager often must rely on a combination of quantitative tools, subjectivity, and trial and error.

Assign Salespeople to Territories. Finally, the sales manager must assign salespeople to the various sales territories. If we assume that all territories have the same workload and have the same sales potential, and we further assume that all salespeople have the same selling skills, product knowledge, and so on, then the territorial assignment task would be simple. However, all salespeople are not the same; the sales manager must devise a method that is fair to all and that optimizes the firm's profits.

Setting Sales-Force Quotas

Sales quotas are specific performance goals that management sets for territories, branch offices, and individual sales representatives. The primary functions of quotas are to establish goals and incentives for the sales force and to give management yardsticks by which to evaluate each salesperson's performance on the job, thus providing a basis for job promotion and/or salary raises.[7]

Sales managers most frequently base quotas on (1) sales volume, (2) profit, (3) activities performed, or (4) some combination of the preceding methods.[8]

The most typical method for developing quotas is by the use of **sales-volume quotas.** These quotas are based on geographical areas, product lines, individual customers, time periods, or a combination of these factors. For example, a quota for a particular sales representative might be to sell at least 20 units of product X in region Z during the next quarter. The major advantage of basing quotas on sales volume is these quotas are easy to understand and simple to use. A disadvantage, however, is that sales-volume quotas, if used alone, can encourage selling behaviors that disregard expenses and neglect nonselling activities. In other words, in attempting to meet and exceed sales-volume quotas, sales might be made that are not profitable because expenses are excessive, accounts are not adequately serviced, and so on.

Profit quotas are based on the profits (sales minus expenses) generated rather than amount of sales per se. Since sales representatives often prefer to sell low-profit, fast-moving items rather than harder-to-sell products that often contribute greater amounts to company profits, profit quotas offer an obvious advantage over sales volume quotas for sales management. However, whereas measurement of sales-volume-quota achievement is a straightforward matter of simply tabulating the number of units or dollars sold by a salesperson, measurement of profit-quota achievement also requires calculating the expenses incurred in generating the sales volume. Two potential problems result: (1) calculating profit quotas can require inordinate amounts of clerical and administrative efforts; and (2) sales representatives may have problems with profit-based quotas since some of the expenses that go into their calculation are perceived to be beyond the salesperson's direct control.

Activity quotas are used to encourage sales representatives to perform specific activities such as calling on new accounts, making product demonstrations, building displays, and so forth. Although in principle these types of quotas stimulate a balanced approach to sales representatives' jobs, in actuality they may encourage little more than perfunctory effort to satisfy the activity quota without any effort to do it well or effectively.

In summary, sales quotas are an extremely important aspect of the sales-management function. If set fairly and realistically, they can encourage highly motivated salesperson performance and reward quota achievers for their efforts. On the downside, quotas may be set too low and fail to provide sufficient challenge or incentive for the sales force; or quotas may be set too high and serve as a disincentive because salespeople feel they cannot possibly meet what

7. Stanton and Buskirk, *Management of the Sales Force*, pp. 474–476.
8. Ibid., pp. 476–479.

is expected of them. Setting challenging yet realistic quotas is truly an art that only the most effective sales managers ever accomplish.

Organizing the Sales Function

Most companies organize or specialize their sales departments in one of four ways: (1) geographically, (2) by product types, (3) by customer classes, or (4) in some combination of these ways.

Geographical Organization

Specialization by **geographical territories** is probably the most common form of sales management organization. As discussed back in Chapter 8, the trend toward *regional marketing* has encouraged many firms to reorganize their sales departments along geographical lines (see the *Focus on Promotion* section on Campbell Soup). Figure 22.2 provides an illustrative organizational chart that is based on geographical specialization. Depending on the size of the business,

Illustration of a Geographically Based Sales Organization   FIGURE 22.2

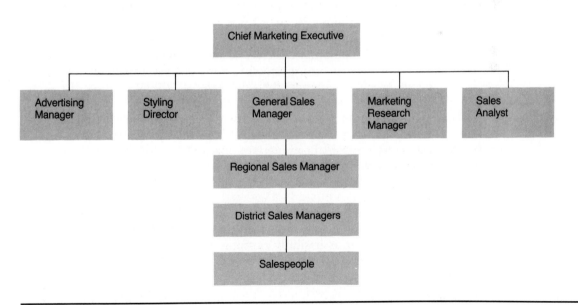

Source: William J. Stanton and Richard H. Buskirk, *Management of the Sales Force,* Sixth Edition (Homewood, IL: Richard D. Irwin, 1983), p. 61. Copyright 1983 by Richard D. Irwin, Inc. Reprinted with permission.

F O C U S   O N   P R O M O T I O N

Sales Department Reorganization at Campbell Soup

For many years, the sales function at Campbell Soup was organized along product lines. Each of four product lines (canned foods, frozen foods, special products, and fresh foods) had its own vice-president of sales. Reporting to each vice-president was a chain of sales managers and sales representatives. This arrangement created a major problem: up to four different Campbell sales representatives, one from each product line, called on a single retail account. Duplicated efforts made the selling costs excessive, and the rigid sales structure was unable to accommodate new product introductions. These factors along with the growing power of supermarket chains and the increased sophistication in their buying practices necessitated sales reorganization at Campbell in the mid-1980s.

Campbell reorganized along geographical lines. *General sales managers* head up sales departments in each of four U.S. regions: west, central, south, and east. Reporting to these four general managers are 22 *regional managers*. *Directors of retail operations* report to each regional manager. The director of retail operations is responsible for the field sales force. Sales representatives now sell *all* Campbell products rather than only a single product line as they did in the past.

Another fundamental change involves the manner in which sales-promotion decisions are made. Under the product-organization structure, promotion decisions were made at corporate headquarters and then delegated to the sales force. In effect, this meant that all areas of the country were told to use the same promotions. Now, local sales forces in each region have their own promotion budgets, develop promotion ideas, get approval from headquarters, execute the promotion, and are held accountable for the results.[9] ■

the manager who runs a geographical sales unit is called a regional, divisional, or district sales manager. In many cases the sales manager, regardless of the title he or she is given, is basically running his or her own business within a business. That is, he or she is like the president of his or her own firm.

---

9. Adapted from Rayna Skolnik, "Campbell Stirs Up Its Sales Force," *Sales and Marketing Management*, April 1986, pp. 56–58.

Product-Line Organization

Although a company's sales organization can be very effective for one product line, the same type of organizational structure may not be effective for a company that carries *highly diverse product offerings*. That is, a company that offers a set of unrelated or heterogeneous products should consider organizing or reorganizing by **product types or groups.** Figure 22.3 shows a basic example of a sales organizational structure used in product specialization.

Management's idea is that sales representatives should use their particular knowledge about specific products to increase company profits. That is, sales representatives may have a good understanding of, say, the company's electrical equipment but not the chemical operations. This organizational structure works well if the customers the sales representatives call on *do not overlap*, which was the problem with Campbell Soup's old product-based sales structure.

Customer-Based Organization

This structure emphasizes customer groups rather than products. A customer-based sales structure is needed when a company sells to multiple customers whose buying needs and procedures differ greatly. For example, a manufac-

---

Sales Organization with Product Specialization　　　　　　FIGURE 22.3

Source: William J. Stanton and Richard H. Buskirk, *Management of the Sales Force*, Sixth Edition (Homewood, IL: Richard D. Irwin, 1983), p. 63. Copyright 1983 by Richard D. Irwin, Inc. Reprinted with permission.

FIGURE 22.4   **Sales Organization Specialized by Type of Customer**

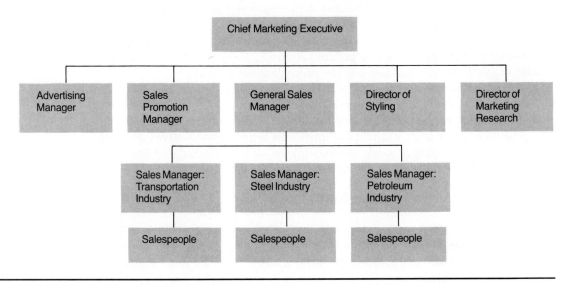

Source: William J. Stanton and Richard H. Buskirk, *Management of the Sales Force*, Sixth Edition (Homewood, IL: Richard D. Irwin, Inc., 1983), p. 67. Copyright 1983 by Richard D. Irwin, Inc. Reprinted with permission.

turer of processed meats, when organized along customer lines, would have one sales organization selling to large supermarket chains, another organization selling to small, independent grocery stores, and another selling to hospitals, restaurants, and other institutional accounts. Figure 22.4 illustrates an organization based on customer type.

Companies may find that specialization by customer type is to their advantage when their customer groups' needs differ significantly, when the customer groups are geographically concentrated, and/or when the company uses different channels of distribution and therefore wants to minimize friction among them.[10]

We can understand why an automobile manufacturer, for example, may want to have different sales forces (and in fact, a different marketing plan) when selling to the government market (post office, military, etc.), to the industrial market, and to the ultimate consumer (through dealers). Each market's buying behavior is different and therefore requires a different approach and a different sales organization.

10. Stanton and Buskirk, *Management of the Sales Force*, pp. 67–68.

Staffing the Sales Function

To staff any organization properly, the manager must understand fundamental principles in the recruiting and selection process. Several steps should be followed in creating or reorganizing a sales staff.[11]

First, the sales manager must perform a job analysis. A **job analysis** identifies the activities, duties, responsibilities, knowledge, selling skills, and personal attributes a sale representative should have in order to function effectively in the organization.

Next, the sales manager needs to write a job description. This document is a written statement of the job analysis described in step 1. The **job description** includes a job title, the specific duties and responsibilities of the sales representative, the authoritative relationships with other immediate members of the organization, and the opportunities for advancement. Good job descriptions include the following:

1. A description of the products or services the sales representative will sell.

2. The types of customers the sales representative must call on, the desired frequency of sales calls, and the specific personnel the sales representative should contact.

3. The specific tasks and responsibilities the sales representative must carry out, including customer service, clerical work, reports, information collection, and promotional activities.

4. The authoritative relationships between the sales representative and other positions within the company. This statement provides information regarding who the sales representative reports to and under what circumstances he or she interacts with other departmental personnel.

Table 22.1 provides a typical job description for a field sales representative.

Finally, the sales manager should develop a statement of job qualifications. Whereas the job description provides information on the salesperson's activities, responsibilities, assignments, and authorities, the **job-qualifications document** describes the personal features, characteristics, and abilities that management believes a salesperson needs in order to perform the job effectively and efficiently. These qualifications may include educational background, business experience, personality, perceived attitude toward the work ethic, ability to get along with others, personal appearance, and so forth.

11. Adapted from Churchill, Ford, and Walker, *Sales Force Management: Planning, Implementation, and Control*, pp. 362–364.

TABLE 22.1   **Job Description for a Sales Representative**

I.   Basic Function

The sales representative is charged with building profitable volume, broadening distribution, and maintaining a professional image with assigned accounts.

II.   Specific Duties

A.   Sells sufficient profitable products to customers to reach assigned objectives.

B.   Calls on selected commercial consumers in order to convert them to the use of our products.

C.   Organizes and plans territory coverage for the most effective use of time.

D.   Gains commitment from assigned accounts for our promotions.

E.   Conducts effective organized product knowledge and promotional sales meetings with assigned accounts.

F.   Prospects for new business at the distributor and consumer levels.

G.   Maintains an awareness of competitive activity and opportunities.

H.   Submits concise and accurate reports on time; maintains records and responds to assignments.

I.   Transmits marketing and sales intelligence relating to competition and changes in the marketplace.

J.   Works within assigned expense budget.

III.   Relationships

A.   Reports to and is accountable solely to regional/district sales manager.

B.   Has a close working relationship with other members of the region and district.

C.   Develops effective relationships with decision makers in assigned accounts.

Developing a Recruiting System

The purpose of a recruiting system is to match people who have the specific and desired qualifications with management's written job descriptions in order to meet the sales, marketing, and company goals and objectives. Figure 22.5 provides a model of the recruiting system.

To locate potentially qualified applicants for a sales job, recruiters use advertising, employment agencies, employee referrals, internal training programs, educational institutions, internal transfers, unsolicited applications, competitors' employees, and those people with whom management deals— from suppliers of products or information (such as an account executive from an advertising agency) to customer salespeople (someone in a wholesale or retailing business, for example).

Interviewing, Testing, and Hiring

In the final stage of the staffing function, the manager must determine whether applicants match the company's job specifications and which applicant(s) will do the best job. Several methods for accomplishing this objective are available

Simple Model of the Recruiting System

FIGURE 22.5

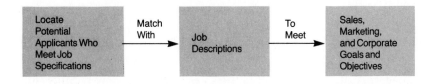

to the sales manager, including interviews, telephone checks, and various types of intelligence, aptitude, and personality tests.

The initial source of information typically available to a sales manager is an applicant's *résumé*. Applicants who pass the initial "résumé inspection" are *personally interviewed*. The interview allows sales management to verify the information in the prospect's application form and gives the interviewer the opportunity to evaluate the prospect in person. The recruiter can evaluate the applicant's verbal skills—vocabulary, grammar, and general conversational ability—and can observe the prospect's mannerisms, physical appearance, voice quality, and eye contact to gain insights into the candidate's personal and persuasive skills.

Sales managers often use *references* as an additional source of information in the evaluation of prospective sales representatives. However, it must be noted that the references suggested by the candidate are often highly biased in his or her favor because they are typically friends and relatives. For this reason, sales managers or their staffs often check with sources that are probably more impartial, such as the prospect's present and former employers and professors. The best way for an interviewer to obtain solid references is through face-to-face contact or voice-to-voice contact on the telephone with each referent. More open dialogue occurs in these ways rather than by letter.

Psychological tests are another valuable input to a sales manager's selection decision. The four most common tests are (1) personality tests, (2) sales-aptitude tests, (3) interest tests, and (4) intelligence tests. **Personality tests** attempt to measure a person's affability, confidence, poise, aggressiveness, and other job-related attributes. **Sales-aptitude tests** are designed to measure a person's verbal ability, tactfulness, persuasiveness, tenacity, memory, and social extroversion/introversion, among many other traits. **Interest tests** are designed to identify a person's vocational and avocational inclinations. **Intelligence tests** attempt to measure memory ability, critical-reasoning ability, and ability to draw inferences.

Sales managers should consider these tests as useful inputs to their decisions, but not as final hiring decisions. The sales manager's *judgment* is the final test of which prospective candidates to hire. A good sales manager tempers the results of measurement tools with his or her judgment and intuition. This is absolutely essential, because as noted in the opening vignette, there is no such thing as an all-purpose test that will ensure the selection of a top-performing salesperson.

Directing the Sales Force

This sales-management function involves the sales training of new recruits, the continuing education of existing personnel, and motivational and incentive plans for all sales personnel. This section describes briefly the elements of sales-force direction.

Sales Training

Training programs vary considerably from company to company, but all successful sales organizations have excellent training programs for new members of the sales force as well as refresher courses that current sales people undergo periodically. Merck's sales-training program, which was described in the previous chapter, embodies all of the elements of an outstanding training program.

Objectives of Training. The general objectives of sales training should be to (1) provide new salespeople with product, customer, and competitor knowledge; (2) improve salesperson morale and reduce turnover; (3) establish expected salesperson behavior (and, therefore, control); (4) improve customer relations; (5) lower selling costs; and (6) show salespeople how to use time efficiently. These broad sales-management objectives for a sales-training program should then be broken down into specific objectives for the sales representatives. These objectives may include training sales representatives to fill out reports, demonstrating how management uses reports, providing salespeople with methods for keeping records, training salespeople how to allocate their selling time with and among customers, suggesting ways to improve prospecting, and explaining how to handle objections.[12]

Content of Training. The content of the sales training program varies from company to company depending on the level of sophistication among the firm's sales personnel. Also, the content varies according to whether new sales personnel or veteran sales personnel are the audience. However, the content generally focuses on corporate policies, selling techniques, product knowledge, and self-management skills.

12. Stanton and Buskirk, *Management of the Sales Force*, pp. 186–188.

Training Personnel.   There are three basic sources of trainers: *line personnel* (e.g., district sales manager), *staff trainers* (either people already within the existing structure of the company or people hired for the exclusive purpose of training sales personnel), and *outside training specialists* (hired consultants who either provide general training programs or specialize in particular aspects of sales techniques).

Location of Training.   Some initial training is conducted in the classroom, and additional training is done in the field. The classroom setting is usually in the home or district office.

Timing of Training.   Companies vary in their philosophies regarding when training should take place. Some companies feel that extensive training in basic product knowledge, sales techniques, company policies, and so on should be concentrated in the first several weeks after a person is hired. After this period of training, the person is qualified to go out and sell. Other companies prefer to give new hires a quick, basic course, have the applicants go into the field and gain some practical experience, and then provide them with an intensive period of training. Some companies schedule several one- to two-day training seminars per year, whereas others schedule several intensive one- to two-week training programs per year.

Training Techniques.   The training techniques a company uses depend on the objectives that sales managers want to accomplish and on the amount of time that the trainer has to achieve these objectives. Lectures, discussion, demonstration, role playing, and on-the-job training are the basic training techniques.

The *lecture method* is the most efficient way to present company policies, procedures, and selling concepts and principles. Lectures provide the new salesperson with an introduction to the company and the subject of selling. The *discussion method* provides salespeople with the opportunity to state their ideas and opinions on a variety of subjects related to personal selling and company policies. These thoughts are most often expressed through pedagogical devices such as cases, round-table discussions, and panels. By using the discussion method, the group leader can often draw out experiences from the new sales representatives that are informative and useful to other members who have had or are having similar problems in the field.

Demonstration involves showing rather than explaining the best way to sell a product. Sales representatives can see how their job should be performed instead of merely hearing an explanation. *Role playing* places sales trainees closer to the actual sales situation by having them sell a product in a hypothetical situation. If the situation and the prospect are presented realistically, the trainee learns how to translate lectured concepts and principles into real-life presentations. Sales trainers often videotape the sales trainees as they role play, because seeing and reviewing one's nonverbal behavior in a selling situation and listening to one's voice and presentation mode can be very enlightening. Finally, in *on-the-job training*, the sales trainer accompanies the sales trainee in actual selling situations. Feedback, either positive or negative, is provided immediately after the fledgling salesperson has performed admirably or made mistakes.

Motivating the Sales Force

In motivating the sales force, sales management can use both financial and nonfinancial incentives. As the following sections explain, financial rewards are usually not enough.

Financial Incentives.   Sales managers use three basic compensation plans: salary plan, commission plan, and a combination plan (e.g., salary plus commission). Within the three basic plans, there are many possible combinations involving base earnings and incentive pay. Six of the most common methods of paying the sales force are

- Straight salary
- Straight commission
- Draw against commission
- Salary plus commission
- Salary plus bonus
- Salary plus bonus plus commission

Figure 22.6 presents statistics on the frequency that each form of sales force compensation is used in different industry groups. For example, 28 percent of manufacturers use the salary plus commission method. Although administratively complex, combination plans (e.g., salary plus commission) are most commonly used by sales managers because they provide sales representatives with a broader range of earnings opportunities. Regardless of the plan that management selects, the plan should meet the following three criteria: (1) be competitive within the industry, (2) be equitable within the company, and (3) be fair among members of the sales force.[13]

Straight salary is often called a *base salary*. It provides sales representatives with a fixed amount of income regardless of sales productivity. This method of compensation gives management maximum control over the sales force's activities because management can dictate the activities salespeople must perform in servicing current customers, creating new merchandise displays, and filling out reports for the home or district office. Thus, this plan is best for companies who have a large amount of work devoted to *nonselling*

---

13. Steinbrink, "Field Sales Management," p. 992.

Frequency of Sales Force Compensation

FIGURE 22.6

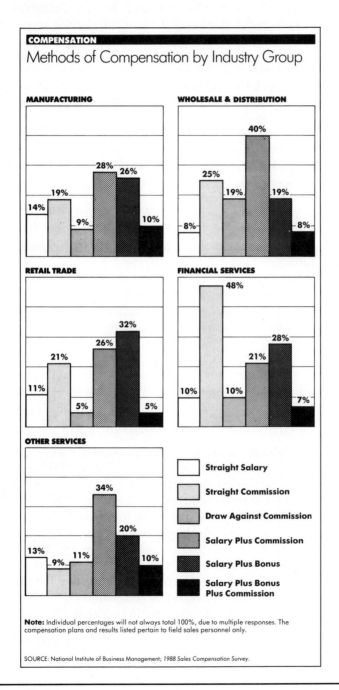

COMPENSATION

Methods of Compensation by Industry Group

MANUFACTURING

14%   19%   9%   28%   26%   10%

WHOLESALE & DISTRIBUTION

8%   25%   19%   40%   19%   8%

RETAIL TRADE

11%   21%   5%   26%   32%   5%

FINANCIAL SERVICES

10%   48%   10%   21%   28%   7%

OTHER SERVICES

13%   9%   11%   34%   20%   10%

☐ Straight Salary

☐ Straight Commission

☐ Draw Against Commission

☐ Salary Plus Commission

☐ Salary Plus Bonus

☐ Salary Plus Bonus Plus Commission

Note: Individual percentages will not always total 100%, due to multiple responses. The compensation plans and results listed pertain to field sales personnel only.

SOURCE: National Institute of Business Management; *1988 Sales Compensation Survey.*

Source: Sales & Marketing Management, February 20, 1989, p. 20. Copyright 1989 Survey of Selling Costs. Reprinted by permission of Sales & Marketing Management.

activities and routine selling tasks. Such selling jobs are found in the grocery and pharmaceutical industries.

A straight salary provides little incentive for sales representatives to increase sales. However, it is a good plan for new salespeople who are still learning the ropes.

A **commission** plan is payment based directly on performance. There are two basic commission plans: straight commission or draw against commission. *Straight commissions* can be based on a fixed percentage of a sales representative's dollar sales or product units sold or can be based on a multiple percentage rate that increases as dollar sales volume or some other performance measure increases. The *draw against commission* method is based on draw accounts, which are accounts from which the sales representative receives (or draws) a fixed sum of money on a regular time basis. The money in a draw account comes from either earned or unearned commissions. A salesperson, for example, may draw $1,000 per pay period but may have earned $800 or $1,200 during the same period. In the case of an underage ($800), the salesperson owes the company money. In the case of an overage ($1,200), the salesperson may take the extra commission, apply it against past underages, or defer the amount to the future.

A **bonus** is usually a lump-sum payment that the company makes to sales representatives who have exceeded a set sales quota. However, management may use bases other than sales, such as number of new accounts opened, reduction in expenses, and divisional profits, to set the requirements for a bonus.

In sum, straight salary provides sales managers with maximum control over the sales representative's routine duties, whereas the straight-commission plan provides the sales representatives with maximum financial incentive to sell the company's line of products. Most companies use some combination of salary plus commission (or bonus).

Nonfinancial Incentives. Job satisfaction and motivation rest strongly on nonfinancial rewards. *Achievement or recognition awards* are commonly presented to sales representatives at sales meetings and award banquets as a means of giving sales representatives psychological rewards. Companies also frequently use newsletters, publicity in local media, published sales results, personal letters of commendation, and other psychological rewards to encourage sales performance. Sales managers also motivate sales-force members with face-to-face encouragement, telephone calls of commendation, and by providing assistance when the salesperson requires help in closing a sale or performing other job responsibilities. Some companies also award honorary job titles to outstanding sales representatives, induct them into honor societies, and present distinguished sales awards, often in the form of plaques or certificates.[14]

14. Ibid.

Sales managers frequently conduct annual sales meetings in attractive vacation sites as another incentive to the sales force. A company may take its sales representatives to a beach retreat and schedule sales meetings in the morning and recreation in the afternoon. During the morning meetings, the sales managers generate enthusiasm for new product lines and marketing/selling programs. Generally, the sales representatives remain extremely enthusiastic for weeks following these meetings.

Overall, sales managers must find ways to meet not only the immediate financial needs of their sales representatives but also (and perhaps more important) their employees' security needs, opportunities for advancement, personal ego and status needs, personal power needs, desires for a meaningful job, beliefs in self-determination, and requirements for pleasant working conditions. These sales-management considerations both attract and maintain a sales force.

Controlling Sales Performance

Given the overall view of the company's environment, its marketing strategy, and the interaction between sales-management functions and salesperson potential, certain outcomes (performances) can be measured to determine the entire system's effectiveness. This management function (control) requires the sales manager to monitor actual salesperson and sales-force performance against planned performance standards. Performance standards include the sales representative's sales volume, percentage of quota met, selling expenses, profit contributions, and customer services rendered. Through sales analysis, cost analysis, and personal evaluations, sales managers can often determine key differences in the performances of good salespeople and poor salespeople.

When the actual and planned performances of a salesperson differ significantly, the sales manager must determine the underlying reasons and take appropriate corrective actions. For example, a union strike in a particular territory may have affected sales; a salesperson may have suffered from an extended illness; he or she may be experiencing marital difficulties; or the sales quota may be unattainable. These and other factors should be taken into consideration by the sales manager in evaluating a sales representative's performance and in determining what measures are necessary to control behavior.

Summary

Sales management involves the process of planning, organizing, staffing, directing, and controlling a company's sales force. A sales manager determines sales opportunities, analyzes his or her resources, sets goals and objectives, develops good recruiting and selection procedures, sets up clear lines of authority and responsibilities, creates sales training programs, utilizes sound motivational approaches, and thoroughly analyzes sales and costs, among many other activities. All of these functions must be performed within the context of both external and internal environments of the firm. Furthermore, these functions must be coordinated with the other elements of the firm's overall marketing strategy.

A good sales manager must have a clear understanding of what determines a salesperson's performance. These determinants include the salesperson's view of his or her job requirements as well as his or her aptitude, skill level, and motivational level.

Finally, the sales manager must evaluate the performance of the sales force by examining the outcomes of their efforts. This stage of the sales-management process includes an analysis of sales volume, selling expenses, customer-service reports, and overall profitability. These and other performance evaluations help the sales manager to control and therefore direct (or redirect) the sales force. Needless to say, the sales-management process is truly a complex and time-consuming job.

Discussion Questions

1. Explain why a management-science model (e.g., linear programming) is unsuitable by itself for establishing sales-force territories.

2. Although sales quotas are most often based on sales volume, they can also be based on profit or activities performed. Explain why you as a salesperson would probably prefer to have a quota established in terms of sales volume, whereas you as a sales manager would prefer to establish quotas for your sales force in terms of nonsales criteria.

3. Explain the rationale favoring customer- , product- , and geographically-based selling organizations. Assume you are the vice-president of sales for a sporting-goods firm that markets several product lines (apparel, shoes, equipment) to large and small retail stores and to schools and other institutions. How might you organize your sales force?

4. What are the shortcomings of evaluating sales representatives' performance solely in terms of unit sales?

5. Discuss the relationship between sales-territory design and sales-force morale.

6. Business students are sometimes told that their résumé should never exceed one page in length. What are your views on this matter?

7. Sometimes salespeople are placed in conflicts that result from customers having expectations that are counter to a sales manager's expectations. How can sales training help to reduce this conflict?

8. What are the possible drawbacks to using sales contests to motivate salespeople?

9. As a salesperson, would you prefer to work on a straight-salary or straight-commission basis? Why? As a sales manager, would you prefer to pay your salespeople on a straight-salary or straight-commission basis? Why?

Exercises

1. Call, write, or personally interview a sales manager and describe his or her methods of managing a sales force.

2. Interview someone such as a local football coach, basketball coach, tennis coach, baseball coach, or band director and find out the methods they use in their "sales management" efforts. That is, how do they recruit personnel, motivate team members, evaluate performance, and so on. Compare their methods with those of a sales manager for a profit-oriented business.

Glossary

Active-synthesis The second stage of perceptual encoding, active-synthesis involves a more refined perception of a stimulus than simply an examination of its basic features. The context of the situation in which information is received plays a major role in determining what is perceived and interpreted.

Activity quotas Salesperson performance goals that emphasize such tasks as (1) daily calls, (2) new customers called on, (3) orders from new accounts, (4) product demonstrations made, and (5) displays built. This type of quota stimulates a balanced approach to sales representatives' jobs; however, it fails to show whether the activity was actually performed or whether it was done effectively.

Adoption process The mental stages through which an individual passes in accepting and becoming a repeat purchaser of an innovation.

ADSPLIT An advertising budgeting model that seeks to optimize overall corporate profit from advertising by determining the advertising budgets for multiple brands rather than setting budgets for each brand independently of other brands' budgets.

Advertising A form of either mass communication or direct-to-consumer communication that is nonpersonal and is paid for by various business firms, nonprofit organizations, and individuals who are in some way identified in the advertising message and who hope to inform or persuade members of a particular audience.

Advertising objectives Motives or goals that advertising efforts attempt to achieve. Examples include the following: to increase sales volume, consumer brand awareness, or favorability of attitudes.

Advertising plans Provide the framework for the actual execution of advertising strategies.

Advertising strategy A plan of action that is guided by corporate and marketing strategies. Corporate and marketing strategies determine how much can be invested in advertising, at what markets advertising efforts need to be directed, how advertising must be coordinated with other marketing elements, and, to some degree, how advertising is to be executed.

Affect referral A choice strategy in which the customer retrieves from memory his or her attitudes (i.e., affect) toward relevant alternatives and picks the alternative with the most positive affect. This type of choice strategy is evident in frequently purchased items where risk is minimal (i.e., low-involvement items).

Affective component of attitude The emotional component of an attitude.

Affordability method An advertising budgeting method that sets the budget by spending on advertising those funds that remain after budgeting for everything else.

Allegory A form of figurative language that equates the objects in a particular narrative (such as an advertised brand in a television commercial) with meanings lying outside of the narrative itself.

Anticlimax order A form of message structure in which the most important points are presented at the beginning of the message. See **Climax order** and **Pyramidal order.**

Attitude A general and enduring positive or negative feeling about some person, object, or issue.

Attributes In the means-end conceptualization of advertising strategy, attributes are features or aspects of the advertised product or brand.

Awareness class The first step in product adoption. Four marketing-mix variables influence the awareness class: samples, coupons, advertising, and product distribution.

Baby boom Demographers refer to the 74 million Americans born between 1947 and 1964 as the baby-boom generation.

Basic offer Mode 1 of the three modes of marketing. Consists of the product itself and associated terms of sale. In general, the basic offer consists of the benefits the marketer offers to the target market as a solution to some problem.

Bonus Usually a lump-sum payment that a company makes to sales representatives who have exceeded a set sales quota.

Brand-concept management The planning, implementation, and control of a brand concept throughout the life of the brand.

Brand-image strategy A creative advertising strategy that involves psychological rather than physical differentiation. The advertiser attempts to develop an image for a brand by associating it with symbols.

Brand-name impression The name of the brand that was advertised is the most likely aspect of a commercial that viewers retain in memory.

Central route The message-processing strategy, or pathway, in the elaboration likelihood model that occurs when consumers are involved in a communication topic and diligently process message arguments contained in the communications. If the message arguments are sound, consumers' attitudes will be influenced. See **Peripheral route.**

Climax order A form of message structure in which a communicator presents the strongest arguments at the end of the message. See **Anticlimax order** and **Pyramidal order.**

Cognitive component of attitude The intellectual component of attitude. In marketing, it is the consumer's knowledge, thoughts, and beliefs about an object or issue.

Cognitive response A self-generated thought that consumers produce in response to persuasive efforts. Includes counter arguments, support arguments, and source derogation.

Commercial rumors Widely circulated but unverified propositions about a product, brand, company, store, or other commercial topic. Rumors pose a difficult public-relations problem.

Commercial specifics The fourth most frequent form of advertising impression. Commercial specifics involve elements in the execution of the advertisement such as the spokesperson, the music, and the overall advertising situation.

Commission Payments to salespeople based directly on performance. Commissions take the form of either straight commissions or a draw against commission.

Communications Process whereby individuals share meaning and establish a commonness of thought.

Comparative message A form of message structure in which marketing communicators directly compare their products or brands with competitive offerings, typically claiming that the advertised item is superior in one or more important purchase considerations. Comparative advertising may be either one- or two-sided.

Compatibility The degree to which an innovation is perceived to fit into a person's ways of doing things. The more compatible an innovation is with a person's need structure, personal values and beliefs, and past experiences, the more rapid the rate of adoption.

Compensatory heuristic A choice strategy in which the customer ranks each of the criteria he or she would like to be met, decides how well each alternative will satisfy these criteria, and integrates this information to arrive at a "score" for each alternative. Theoretically the consumer selects the alternative with the highest overall score. This procedure is likely to be used in risky (high-involvement) circumstances; that is, when a decision involves considerable financial, performance, or psychological risk.

Compiled list   A compiled direct-mail list contains prospect names that are gathered from a variety of data sources such as census reports, telephone directories, and car registrations.

Complexity   The degree of perceived difficulty of an innovation. The more difficult an innovation is to understand or use, the slower the rate of adoption.

Compliance   The source attribute of power influences message receivers via a process of compliance; that is, a receiver complies with the persuasive efforts of the source because the source has the power to administer rewards or punishments.

Conative component of attitude   The action component of an attitude; a person's behavioral tendency toward an object. In marketing, it is the consumer's intention to purchase a specific item. Also called *behavioral component*.

Confirmation stage   The stage in the new-product adoption process after a decision has been made in which postdecisional dissonance, regret, and dissonance reduction occur.

Conjunctive heuristic   One of three noncompensatory choice strategies in which the consumer establishes cutoffs, or minima, on all pertinent criteria; an alternative is retained for further consideration only if it meets or exceeds all minima.

Consequences   In the means-end conceptualization of advertising strategy, consequences represent the desirable or undesirable results from consuming a particular product or brand.

Consumer information processing (CIP) perspective   A model of consumer choice behavior in which marketers view the consumer as a logical, highly cognitive, and systematic decision maker. See **Hedonic-experiential model (HEM).**

Contest   A form of consumer-oriented sales promotion in which consumers have an opportunity to win cash, merchandise, or travel prizes. Winners become eligible by solving the specified contest problem.

Continuity   A media planning consideration that involves the matter of how advertising should be allocated during the course of an advertising campaign.

Continuous advertising schedule   In a continuous schedule, a relatively equal amount of ad dollars are invested in advertising throughout the campaign.

Continuous innovation   A new product or product change that represents a minor alteration from existing products and has limited impact on customers' consumption patterns. See **Discontinuous innovation.**

Cooperative (co-op) advertising   Co-op programs are initiated by manufacturers and permit retailers to place ads promoting the manufacturer's product and receive partial or full reimbursement from the manufacturer.

Copytesting   Advertising research undertaken to test the effectiveness of creative messages. Also called *message research*.

Corporate advertising   This form of advertising focuses not on specific products or brands but on a corporation's overall image or on economic/social issues relevant to the corporation's interests.

Corporate image advertising   A specific form of corporate advertising that attempts to gain name recognition for a company, establish goodwill for it and its products, or identify itself with some meaningful and socially acceptable activity. See **Issue advertising.**

Corporate strategy A plan of action set by top management that represents the long-range (typically three to five years) objectives, plans, and budgets for all corporate units and departments. Corporate strategy (1) is based on situation analyses of economic, competitive, social, and other pertinent factors that represent opportunities and threats for a business enterprise and (2) is formulated in view of the enterprise's inherent strengths and weaknesses.

Cost per thousand (CPM) A measure of advertising efficiency based on the cost of reaching 1,000 people.

Counter argument A form of cognitive response that occurs when the receiver challenges message claims. See **Source derogation** and **Supportive argument.**

CPM-TM A refinement of CPM that measures the cost of reaching 1,000 members of the target market, excluding those people who fall outside of the target market.

Database management Used in direct marketing, database management is the construction and maintenance of data lists containing customer and prospect names and detailed information for each listing.

Deceptive advertising Advertising is considered deceptive by the Federal Trade Commission if there is a representation that misleads reasonable consumers by influencing their product preferences and choices.

Decision stage The stage of new-product adoption that represents the period during which a person mentally chooses either to adopt or reject an innovation.

Decoding The mental process of transforming message symbols into thought; consumers' interpretations of marketing messages. See **Encoding.**

Demographic variables Measurable characteristics of populations, including characteristics such as age, income, minority population patterns, and regional population statistics.

Diffusion In a marketing communications sense, diffusion means that a product or idea is adopted by more and more customers as time passes. In other words, a new product "spreads out" through the marketplace.

Direct advertising objectives Objectives that seek an overt behavioral response (e.g., product purchase) from the audience. See **Indirect advertising objectives.**

Direct mail The use of mail deliveries sent to current or prospective customers. Examples include letters, postcards, programs, calendars, folders, catalogs, order blanks, and price lists.

Direct marketing Activities by which products and services are offered to market segments in one or more media for informational purposes or to solicit responses from present or prospective customers or contributors by mail, telephone, or other access.

Direct-response advertising The use of any medium (direct mail, television, etc.) with the intent of creating immediate action from customers. Three distinct characteristics of direct-response advertising are (1) it makes a definite offer, (2) it contains all of the information necessary to make a decision, and (3) it contains a response device (coupon, phone number, or both) to facilitate immediate action.

Direct selling Involves the personal explanation and demonstration of products and services to consumers in their homes or at their jobs.

Discontinuous innovation A new product or product change that requires substantial relearning and fundamental alterations in basic consumption patterns. See **Continuous innovation.**

Disjunctive heuristic One of three noncompensatory choice strategies in which the consumer accepts an alternative if it meets any one of his or her minimum standards; that is, an alternative is acceptable if it meets or exceeds choice criterion 1, choice criterion 2, or choice criterion *n*.

Diverting   This practice takes place when a manufacturer offers a trade deal that is restricted to a limited geographical area. Wholesalers and retailers often buy abnormally large quantities at the deal price and then transship the excess quantities to other geographical areas.

Dual-coding theory   A theory of memory that states that pictures are stored in an individual's memory in both verbal and visual form, whereas words are less likely to have visual representations.

Dynamically continuous innovation   A new product or product change that requires some disruption in established consumer behavior patterns rather than fundamental alterations.

Effective rating points (ERPs)   A statistical measure of an advertising campaign based on the idea that each exposure to an advertisement is not of equal value. ERPs are used in media planning to achieve the maximum impact for a product; what is effective (or ineffective) for one product may not necessarily be so for another. Hence, ERPs represent an alternative media selection criterion to gross rating points (GRPs).

Effective reach   Based on the idea that an advertising schedule is effective only if it does not reach members of the target audience too few or too many times. What exactly is too few or too many depends on the specific advertising situation, but many media planners consider fewer than three exposures as too few and more than ten as too many.

Elaboration likelihood model (ELM)   A theory of persuasion and attitude change that predicts two forms of message processing and attitude change: central and peripheral routes. The former occurs under high involvement and leads to a more

permanent attitude change than does the latter.

Emotional strategy   A creative advertising strategy that uses appeals to the consumer's emotions.

Encoding   The process of putting thoughts into symbolic form. See **Decoding.**

Environmental management   The idea that through its promotional efforts and other marketing activities, a firm can attempt to modify existing environmental conditions.

Event marketing   A form of brand promotion that ties a brand to a meaningful cultural, social, athletic, or other type of high-interest public activity.

Executive-statement release   A tool of proactive marketing PR that quotes a corporate executive in a news release on matters of interest to prospective customers and other interested parties such as stockholders.

Experiential needs   Represent desires for products that provide sensory pleasure, variety, and stimulation.

Exposure   The consumer information processing stage in which consumers come in contact with the marketer's message.

External lists   Mailing lists bought from other companies rather than being based on a company's own internal list of customers.

Feature analysis   The initial stage of perceptual encoding whereby a receiver examines the basic features of a stimulus (brightness, depth, angles, etc.) and from this makes a preliminary classification.

Feature article   A form of proactive marketing PR that consists of a full-length article about a company and its products that is suitable for publication in a newspaper or other media.

Federal Trade Commission (FTC)   The U.S. governmental agency that has primary responsibility for regulating unfair and deceptive promotion.

Feedback Affords the source of marketing communications with a way of monitoring how accurately the intended message is being received and offers some measure of control in the communications process.

Feelings Represent the third most frequent impression made by television commercials after the brand name and selling claims. Feelings include reactions such as pride, excitement, warmth, boredom, and disgust.

Figurative language Includes simile, metaphor, and allegory.

Flighting A form of discontinuous advertising schedule in which some periods in the campaign receive zero expenditures. See **Pulsing.**

Forward buying The practice whereby retailers take advantage of manufacturers' trade deals by buying larger quantities than needed for normal inventory. Retailers often buy enough product on one deal to carry them over until the manufacturer's next scheduled deal; hence, forward buying also is called *bridge buying*.

Frequency The number of times, on average, within a four-week period that members of the target audience are exposed to the advertiser's message. Also called *average frequency*.

Functional needs Those needs involving current consumption-related problems, potential problems, or conflicts.

Generally planned purchase A form of purchase behavior based on POPAI's supermarket buying-habits study in which a shopper indicates an intent to buy a particular product but has no specific brand in mind.

Generic strategy A creative advertising strategy in which the advertiser makes a claim about its brand that could be made by any company that markets the product.

Generics The second most typical impression made by advertising, generics represent major selling claims that are associated with the advertised brand.

Geographical territories The most common form of sales-management organization.

Gross rating points (GRPs) A statistic that represents the mathematical product of reach multiplied by frequency. The number of GRPs indicates the total weight of advertising during a time frame, such as a four-week period. The number of GRPs indicates the gross coverage or duplicated audience that is exposed to a particular advertising schedule.

Hedonic-experiential model (HEM) This perspective of consumer behavior views consumers as driven not by rational and purely logical considerations but, rather, by emotions in pursuit of fun, fantasies, and feelings. See **Consumer information processing (CIP) perspective.**

Hedonistic consumption The consumer's multisensory images, fantasies, and emotional arousal elicited when purchasing and using products.

Hierarchy-of-effects models There are numerous hierarchy-of-effects models, all of which are predicated on the idea that advertising moves people from an initial state of unawareness about a product/ brand to a final stage of purchasing that product/brand.

House list Names of customers that are generated from a company's own internal records. Customers' names are often grouped into active, recently active, long-since-active customers, or inquiry categories. A list may be subdivided by the recency of a customer's purchase, the frequency of a customer's purchase, the monetary value of each purchase, or the type of products purchased. Customers may be categorized by geographic, demographic, or psychographic characteristics.

Identification The source attribute of attractiveness influences message receivers via a process of identification, that is, receivers perceive a source to be attractive and therefore identify with the source and adopt the attitudes, behaviors, interests, or preferences of the source.

Implementation stage The stage in the new-product adoption process in which a person puts the new product or idea to use.

Indirect advertising objectives Those objectives aimed at communication tasks (e.g., awareness, knowledge) that need to be accomplished before overt behavioral responses can be achieved. See **Direct advertising objectives.**

Innovation An idea, practice, product, or service that an individual perceives to be new. The consumers' view of the product is the critical factor.

Integrated information-response model This model takes its name from the idea that consumers integrate information from two sources—advertising and direct product-usage experience—in forming attitudes and purchase intentions toward products and brands.

Internalization The source attribute of credibility influences message receivers via a process of internalization; that is, receivers perceive a source to be credible and therefore accept the source's position or attitude as their own. Internalized attitudes tend to be maintained even when the source of the message is forgotten and even when the source switches to a new position.

Involuntary attention One of three forms of attention that requires little or no effort on the part of the message receiver; the stimulus intrudes upon a person's consciousness even though he or she does not want it to. See **Nonvoluntary attention** and **Voluntary attention.**

Issue advertising A form of corporate advertising that takes a position on a controversial social issue of public importance. It does so in a manner that supports the company's position and best interests. Also called *advocacy advertising.* See **Corporate image advertising.**

Job analysis Identifies the activities, duties, responsibilities, knowledge, selling skills, and personal attributes a sales representative should have in order to function effectively in an organization.

Job description Includes a job title, the specific duties and responsibilities of the sales representative, the authoritative relationships with other company personnel, and other pertinent information about the sales job.

Lexicographic heuristic One of three noncompensatory consumer strategies in which the consumer ranks his or her criteria according to relative importance. Alternatives are then evaluated on each criterion, starting with the most important. An alternative is selected if it is judged superior on the most important criterion. If two or more alternatives are judged equal on the most important criterion, the consumer examines these alternatives on the next most important criterion, then on the next most important, and so on until a tie is broken.

Line-item budgeting With this form of budgeting, management allocates funds in meticulous detail to each identifiable cost center. See **Program budgeting.**

Market maven An individual who has information about many kinds of products and places to shop and shares this information with fellow consumers.

Marketing Process whereby businesses and other organizations facilitate exchanges, or transfers of value, between themselves and their customers and clients.

Marketing communications The collection of all elements in an organization's marketing mix that facilitates exchanges by establishing shared meaning with the organization's customers or clients.

Marketing concept Philosophy in which the marketer adapts to the customers' needs and wants. This is usually accomplished by satisfying the customers' needs and by offering superior value. See **Promotion concept.**

Marketing mix Consists of four sets of decision spheres: product, pricing, distribution, and promotion decisions.

Marketing objectives Objectives for marketing actions include setting overall sales levels, establishing marketing cost requirements, and setting performance requirements for specific market segments and geographical locales.

Marketing strategy A plan of action that is an extension of corporate strategy and involves plans, budgets, and controls needed to direct a firm's product, promotion, distribution, and pricing activities.

Marketing structure The organizational arrangement employed in a company to achieve its overall marketing and promotional objectives.

Match-competitors method An advertising budgeting method that sets the ad budget by basically following what competitors are doing.

Mature market Although there is disagreement about what age group constitutes this market, this text adopts the U.S. Bureau of the Census' designation, which classifies mature people as those who are 55 and older.

Meaning The set of internal responses and resulting predispositions evoked within a person when presented with a sign or stimulus object.

Means An organization's wherewithal or resources represent its means for accomplishing the motives it has established for its various promotional tools.

Media research Advertising research undertaken to test the effectiveness of creative media.

Message A symbolic expression of a sender's thoughts; the instrument (e.g., advertisement) used to share thought with a receiver. More practically, the term *message* refers to the verbal and nonverbal persuasive techniques that are used in all forms of marketing communications.

Message channel The path through which the message moves from source to receiver; for example, from a marketer via a magazine to consumers.

Message content Includes the types of appeals used in marketing-communications messages. Examples include the use of humor, fear appeals, sex appeals, and subliminal techniques.

Message structure The organization of elements in a message. Three structural issues have particular relevance to marketing communicators: (1) message-sidedness, (2) order of presentation, and (3) conclusion drawing.

Metaphor A form of figurative language that applies a word or a phrase to a concept or object, such as a brand, that it does not literally denote in order to suggest a comparison with the brand (e.g., Budweiser is "the king of beers").

Milline rate Used for comparing the cost of advertising in different newspapers, the milline rate is the cost per line of advertising space per million circulation.

Morals The set of principles and standards that individual managers bring to the job and that the corporate culture encourages.

Motives The underlying objectives or goals on which promotion managers base their general and specific choices.

Narrowcasting The pinpointing of advertising exposures to specific groups of consumers such as teens, Hispanics, and news enthusiasts.

National Advertising Review Board (NARB) Part of the National Advertising Division (NAD) of the Council of Better Business Bureaus, NARB is a court of appeals in the self-regulation of deceptive advertising cases.

National Association of Attorneys General (NAAG) Includes attorneys general from all 50 states. In recent years this group has played an increasingly active role in regulating advertising deception and other business practices.

Noise Extraneous and distracting stimuli that interfere with reception of a message in its pure and original form. Noise occurs at all stages of the communications process.

Noncompensatory heuristics Choice behavior based on strategies such as conjunctive, disjunctive, or lexicographic heuristics. Contrasts with the compensatory heuristic to choice.

Nonvoluntary attention One of three forms of attention that occurs when a person is attracted to a stimulus and continues to pay attention because it holds interest for him or her. A person in this situation neither resists the stimulus nor willingly attends to it initially; however, once his or her attention is attracted, the individual continues to give attention because the stimulus has some benefit or relevance. Also called *spontaneous attention.* See **Involuntary attention** and **Voluntary attention.**

Normative influence Represents the influence that important others, or referent groups, have on us. See **Theory of reasoned action.**

Objective-and-task method This budgeting method establishes the advertising budget by determining the communication tasks that need to be established. See **Percentage-of-sales method.**

Observability The degree to which other people can observe one's ownership and use of a new product. The more a consumption behavior can be sensed by other people, the more observable it is and typically the more rapid is its rate of adoption.

One-sided message In this type of message, the entire orientation is toward the communicator's position. The weaknesses in the communicator's position or the strengths of opposing views are never mentioned. See **Two-sided message.**

Opinion leader A person who frequently influences other individuals' attitudes or overt behavior.

Overlay The use of two or more sales-promotion techniques in combination with one another.

Percentage-of-sales method This budgeting method involves setting the budget as a fixed percentage of past or anticipated (typically the latter) sales volume. See **Objective-and-task method.**

Perceptual encoding The process of interpreting stimuli, which includes two stages: feature analysis and active-synthesis.

Peripheral route In the peripheral route of the elaboration likelihood model, persuasion occurs not as a result of a consumer's processing salient message arguments but by virtue of his or her attending to relevant (though peripheral to the main message argument) persuasion cues. See **Central route.**

Personal selling A form of person-to-person communication in which seller attempts to persuade prospective buyers to purchase his or her company's (organization's) product or service.

Personality test A psychological test that attempts to measure a prospective salesperson's affability, confidence, poise, aggressiveness, and so on.

Persuasion In marketing, persuasion is an effort by a marketing communicator to influence the consumer's attitude and behavior in some manner.

Persuasive communications Mode 2 of the three modes of marketing. Consists of various forms of marketing-communications messages designed to enhance customers' impressions of the basic offer.

Phased strategies Procedure in which consumers use a combination of choice heuristics in sequence or in phase with one another to make decisions.

Planning The process of establishing a broad set of goals, policies, and procedures for achieving sales and marketing objectives.

Point-of-purchase (P-O-P) communications Promotional elements, including displays, posters, signs, and a variety of other in-store materials, that are designed to influence the customer's choice at the time of purchase.

Point-of-purchase coupons Coupons that are simultaneously distributed and redeemable at the point of purchase.

Positioning advertising copytesting (PACT) A set of nine copytesting principles developed by leading U.S. advertising agencies.

Positioning strategy A creative advertising strategy in which an advertiser implants in the consumer's mind a clear understanding of what the brand is and how it compares to competitive offerings.

Preemptive strategy A creative advertising strategy in which the advertiser that makes a particular claim effectively prevents competitors from making the same claim for fear of being labeled a copycat.

Premiums Articles of merchandise or services offered by manufacturers to induce action on the part of the sales force, trade representatives, or consumers.

Proactive marketing PR A form of PR that is offensively rather than defensively oriented and opportunity-seeking rather than problem-solving. See **Reactive marketing PR.**

Product release A tool of proactive marketing PR that announces a new product, provides relevant information, and tells how additional information can be obtained.

Product types or groups Companies that offer a set of unrelated or heterogeneous products should consider organizing by product type or group.

Profit quotas Performance goals based on the total amount of revenue generated by a salesperson for the organization rather than on the number of items sold.

Program budgeting A procedure that provides each administrative unit with a lump sum of money that each administrative head can use as he or she sees fit in order to accomplish the stated objectives. See **Line-item budgeting.**

Promotion The aspect of general marketing that promotion management deals with explicitly. Promotion includes the practices of advertising, personal selling, sales promotion, publicity, and point-of-purchase communications.

Promotion concept Marketing practices that attempt to adapt the customer to the marketer's needs and wants. See **Marketing concept.**

Promotion management The practice of coordinating the various promotional-mix elements, setting objectives for what the elements are intended to accomplish, establishing budgets that are sufficient to support the objectives, designing specific programs to accomplish objectives, evaluating performance, and taking corrective action when results are not in accordance with objectives.

Promotional inducements Mode 3 of the three modes of marketing. More commonly referred to as *sales promotion,* promotional inducements comprise extra benefits beyond the basic offer that are intended to motivate particular customer actions.

Promotional mix An organization's blend of advertising, personal selling, sales promotion, publicity, and point-of-purchase communications elements.

Psychogalvanometer A device for measuring galvanic skin response that is used as an indicator of advertising effectiveness, specifically by determining whether the consumer's autonomic nervous system is activated by some element in an advertisement.

Public relations (PR) A practice that includes all nonadvertising and nonselling activities that are designed explicitly to engender a desired corporate image. This corporate-image engineering is directed at promoting harmonious relations with various publics: consumers, employees, suppliers, stockholders, governments, the general public, labor groups, and citizen-action groups.

Publicity Nonpersonal communication to a mass audience that is not paid for by an organization. Examples include news items or editorial comments about an organization's products or services.

Pull strategy Marketing efforts directed to ultimate consumers with the intent of influencing their acceptance of the manufacturer's brand. Manufacturers hope that the consumers will then encourage retailers to handle the brand. Typically used in conjunction with *push strategy.*

Pulsing A form of discontinuous advertising-schedule in which some advertising is used in every period of the campaign, but the amount of advertising varies considerably from period to period. See **Flighting.**

Pupillometric tests A measure of advertising effectiveness that records a consumer's pupil dilation, an autonomic response, as the consumer views a television commercial or printed advertisement. Greater pupil dilation is thought to indicate greater arousal from attending the advertisement.

Push strategy A manufacturer's selling and other promotional efforts directed at gaining trade support from wholesalers and retailers for the manufacturer's product.

Pyramidal order A message-structure component in which the most important points appear in the middle of the message. This is the least effective order of message presentation. See **Anticlimax order** and **Climax order.**

Rating The proportion of the target audience exposed to a single issue of an advertising vehicle such as a television program or a particular magazine.

Reach The percentage of an advertiser's target audience that is exposed to at least one advertisement over an established time frame (a four-week period represents the typical time frame for most advertisers). Reach represents the number of target customers who see or hear the advertiser's message one or more times during the time period. Also called *net coverage, unduplicated audience,* or *cumulative audience (cume).*

Reactive marketing PR Undertaken as a result of external pressures and challenges brought by competitive actions, changes in consumer attitudes, or other external influences. It typically deals with changes that have negative consequences for the organization. See **Proactive marketing PR.**

Rebate A cash reimbursement to consumers from the manufacturer whose product the consumer has purchased. Typically refers to cash reimbursement for durable goods. See **Refund.**

Receiver The person or group of people with whom the sender of a communication shares thoughts. In marketing, the receivers are the prospective and present customers of an organization's product or service.

Refund A cash reimbursement to the consumer by the manufacturer whose product the consumer has purchased. Typically refers to cash reimbursement for packaged goods. See **Rebate.**

Relative advantage The degree to which an innovation is perceived as better than an existing idea or object in terms of increasing comfort, saving time or effort, and increasing the immediacy of reward.

Repeater class This third stage in the adoption process is influenced by four marketing-mix variables: advertising, price, distribution, and product satisfaction.

Resonance strategy A creative advertising strategy that structures an advertising campaign to pattern the prevailing lifestyle orientation of the intended market segment.

Sales-aptitude test A psychological test that is designed to measure a person's verbal ability, tactfulness, persuasiveness, tenacity, memory, and social extroversion/introversion, among other traits.

Sales management The process of planning, organizing, staffing, directing, and controlling an organization's selling function within the context of environmental limitations and corporate and marketing constraints. The purpose is to acquire, direct, and stimulate competent salespeople to perform tasks that move the company or organization toward its objective and mission.

Sales promotion Marketing activities intended to stimulate quick buyer action by offering extra benefits to customers. Examples include coupons, premiums, free samples, and sweepstakes. Also called *promotional inducements*.

Sales quotas Specific performance goals that management sets for sales representatives, sales territories, organizational branches, middlemen, and other marketing units.

Sales territory Consists of present and prospective customers assigned to a salesperson, sales branch, or distributor for a specified period.

Sales-volume quotas Performance goals that are based on geographical areas, product lines, individual customers, time periods, or a combination of these factors.

Sales-volume quotas do not, however, measure or control expenses, profits, nonselling activities, and so on.

Sampling The use of various distribution methods to deliver actual- or trial-size products to consumers. The purpose is to initiate trial-usage behavior.

Semiotics The study of meaning and the analysis of meaning-producing events.

Sensation transference The consumer's tendency to equate a brand with an information cue such as the package; that is, the consumer imputes characteristics to the product from the package.

Sign Something physical and perceivable by our senses that represents or signifies something (the referent) to somebody (the interpreter) in some context.

Signal A product or specific brand is a signal of something if it is causally related to it either as the cause of something or the effect of something.

Simile A form of figurative language that uses a comparative term such as *like* or *as* to join items from different classes of experience (e.g., "love is like a rose").

Slotting allowance The fee a manufacturer pays a supermarket or other retailer to get that retailer to handle the manufacturer's new product. The allowance is called *slotting* in reference to the slot, or location, that the retailer must make available in its warehouse to accommodate the manufacturer's product.

Source In marketing communications, a source is a person, group, organization, or label that delivers a message. Marketing communications sources influence receivers by possessing one or more of three basic attributes: power, attractiveness, and credibility.

Source derogation A form of cognitive response that occurs when the receiver disputes the source's ability to make certain message claims. See **Counter argument** and **Supportive argument**.

Specialty advertising A hybrid form of marketing communications that combines elements of advertising and, at times, trade-oriented sales promotion. Specialty advertisers imprint merchandise with an advertiser's message and distribute the merchandise without obligation to designated recipients. Specialty advertising complements other forms of advertising by providing another way to keep a company's name before customers and prospects.

Specific sales message The last impression viewers typically retain from a television commercial.

Specifically planned purchase A form of purchase behavior based on POPAI's supermarket buying-habits study in which the consumer indicates an intent to purchase a specific brand and in fact proceeds to buy that brand.

Sponsorship A form of marketing whereby a company invests in special events or causes for the purpose of achieving various promotional and corporate objectives.

Straight commission Payment based directly on sales performance. Straight commission can be based on a fixed percentage of a sales representative's dollar sales, product units sold, type of product sold, season sales, dollars of profit, and so on, or can be based on a multiple percentage rate that increases as dollar sales volume or some other performance measure increases.

Straight salary Payment that provides a sales representative with a fixed amount of income regardless of sales productivity. Also called *base salary.*

Substitute purchases A form of purchase behavior based on POPAI's supermarket buying-habits study in which the shopper does not buy the product or brand he or she indicates will be purchased.

Supportive argument A form of cognitive response that occurs when a receiver agrees with a message's arguments. See **Counter argument** and **Source derogation.**

Sweepstake A form of consumer-oriented sales promotion in which winners receive cash, merchandise, or travel prizes. Winners are determined purely on the basis of chance.

Symbolic needs Those involving internal consumer needs such as the desire for self enhancement, role position, or group membership.

Telemarketing The use of the telephone for direct-marketing purposes. Telemarketing represents nearly one-half of all direct marketing.

Theory of reasoned action A theory that predicts behavior based on the idea that normative influences and attitudes influence behavior indirectly by directly influencing people's behavioral intentions.

Three modes of marketing Consists of the basic offer (Mode 1), persuasive communications (Mode 2), and promotional inducements (Mode 3).

Tie-in The simultaneous promotion of multiple brands in a single sales-promotion effort.

Trade allowances Also called *trade deals,* trade allowances are offered to retailers for performing activities in support of the manufacturer's brand.

Trade contest A form of trade-oriented sales promotion that is directed at store-level or department managers and generally is based on managers meeting a sales goal established by the manufacturer.

Trade incentives In contrast to trade contests, trade incentives are given to retail managers and salespeople for performing tasks such as displaying merchandise or selling certain lines of merchandise.

Trade show A temporary forum where sellers of a product category exhibit and demonstrate their wares to present and prospective buyers.

Trialability The extent to which an innovation can be used on a limited basis. Trialability is tied closely to the concept of perceived risk. In general, products that lend themselves to trialability are adopted at a more rapid rate.

Trier class The group of consumers who actually try a new product; the second step in which an individual becomes a new brand consumer. Coupons, distribution, and price are the variables that influence consumers to become triers.

12-M model This is an integrative framework of the promotion-management process in which each element begins with the letter M.

Two-sided message In an attempt to establish credibility, a two-sided message presents the product in a positive fashion on the basis of attributes that are important to brand choice, but disclaims or limits product or brand performance claims on product attributes that are of relatively minor significance to the consumer. See **One-sided message.**

Unfair advertising The Federal Trade Commission regards advertising as unfair if it is immoral, unethical, oppressive, or unscrupulous and causes substantial injury to consumers, competitors, or other businesses.

Unique-selling proposition strategy A creative advertising strategy that promotes a product attribute that represents a meaningful, distinctive consumer benefit.

Unplanned purchase A form of purchase behavior based on POPAI's supermarket buying-habits study in which the consumer purchases a product or brand for which he or she had no prior purchase intent.

Values In the means-end conceptualization of advertising strategy, values represent important beliefs that people hold about themselves and that determine the relative desirability of consequences.

Vendor support programs (VSPs) A form of cooperative advertising program initiated by retailers whereby the retailer features one or several manufacturers' products in local advertising media and has the manufacturer(s) pay for the advertising.

Vicarious modeling A type of behavior modification in which advertisers attempt to influence consumers' perceptions and behaviors by having them observe the actions of others and the resulting consequences.

Video merchandising centers (VMCs) Electronic devices that display and sell entire product lines through audio and video presentations. VMCs perform both informational and transactional functions.

Visibility The degree to which other people can observe one's ownership and use of a new product. The more a consumption behavior can be sensed by other people, the more visible it is and typically the more rapid is its rate of adoption.

Voice-pitch analysis (VOPAN) A physiological measurement device that assesses the consumer's physiological reaction to an advertisement by using a specially programmed computer to analyze a person's voice pitch in response to questions about a test advertisement.

Voluntary attention One of three forms of attention that occurs when a person willfully notices a stimulus. See **Involuntary attention** and **Nonvoluntary attention.**

Warmth One of the various emotional responses that consumers have to advertisements. This emotion involves physiological arousal and is precipitated by experiencing a sense of love, family, or friendship.

N A M E I N D E X

SUBJECT INDEX